and Sectional Alignment in the Civil War

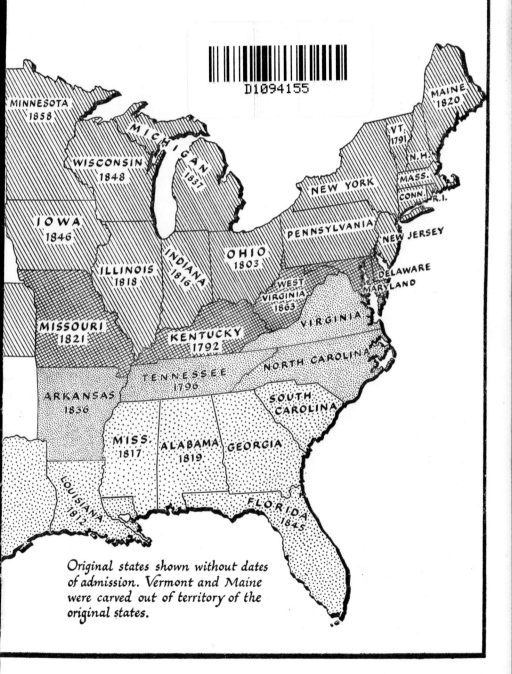

D1094155

Original states shown without dates of admission. Vermont and Maine were carved out of territory of the original states.

THE PRICE OF
UNION

BY HERBERT AGAR

The People's Choice
Land of the Free
Pursuit of Happiness
A Time for Greatness
The Price of Union

THE PRICE OF
UNION

BY HERBERT AGAR

The Riverside Press Cambridge

HOUGHTON MIFFLIN COMPANY
BOSTON

E
178
.A3
1950a

The Riverside Press

CAMBRIDGE • MASSACHUSETTS

PRINTED IN THE U.S.A.

IN MEMORY OF JOHNNY WALLACE

*who asked many of the questions which this book tries
to answer, but who died before he could read it.*

Preface

THE HUNDRED AND SIXTY YEARS of American history since George Washington first took the oath as President comprise a tale of adventure which has been told from many points of view, to support many theories. Here it is used to illustrate the birth and growth of a unique political system. The system can be understood only by studying the men who built it and the forces which impelled them. It is a flexible system, which will continue to change from President to President, from crisis to crisis, and from Supreme Court to Supreme Court. Yet if we know what it is today, and how it came to be, we can follow its shifting pattern in the future and perhaps direct it nearer to the heart's desire. This book, however, does not discuss or suggest improvements. It describes "what men do, and not what they ought to do."

The detailed history is carried to 1909. Thereafter, the political passions of today confuse the issue, and much of the evidence is not yet sifted. Two chapters of modern instances apply the findings from the past to scenes from recent politics.

Footnotes which enlarge or comment upon the text will be found at the bottom of the page. Those which merely give references are numbered by chapters and are at the back of the book.

The following friends have been good enough to read large parts of this work in manuscript, and to help immeasurably on matters of fact, judgment, and proportion: Henry Steele Commager, R. J. Cruikshank, Harold Guinzburg, Allan Nevins, Joseph Links, Robert E. Sherwood, and Milton Waldman. My publishers in England and America have criticized the text with minute care, to my great advantage. And I am deeply in debt to Mr. Harold Epstein, who has helped me throughout in finding material and in raising well-informed objections to some of my use of it. All the chapters, and most of the pages, have been improved by his help.

The good will and assistance of my friends, however, will not have sufficed to prevent errors. For them I claim sole responsibility.

HERBERT AGAR
Beechwood, Petworth, Sussex

June, 1949

vii

Contents

CONCLUSION

List of Maps

List of Maps

Introduction

IN 1788, when Alexander Hamilton, James Madison, and John Jay were struggling to persuade the New York convention to ratify the Constitution of the United States, young De Witt Clinton composed a prayer for the Opposition: "From the insolence of great men—from the tyranny of the rich—from the unfeeling rapacity of the excise-men and tax-gatherers—from the misery of despotism—from the expense of supporting standing armies, navies, placemen, sinecures, federal cities, senators, presidents, and a long train of etceteras, Good Lord deliver us." There speaks the deep American distaste for government, the belief that it is evil and that it must be kept weak.

The proposed constitution seemed weak enough to its friends—too weak for safety in the opinion of Hamilton. The thirteen states were left with all the powers which would normally concern "the lives, liberties and properties of the people," while the delegated powers of the Union were divided among the Executive, the Legislature, and the Judiciary in the belief that they would check each other and prevent rash or oppressive deeds. Yet behind this modest proposal Clinton saw threats of insolence, rapacity, misery, needless expense, and all the corruptions of history. There is little doubt that he spoke for the majority in New York; and many citizens would still agree with him. A constant factor in American history is the fear of Leviathan, of the encroaching state.

We can trace this fear from prerevolutionary days, and we can trace the forces which have nevertheless caused Leviathan to grow steadily more ponderous. War and industrial revolution promote strong government. Foreign dangers, business depressions, sectional or class strife—whenever these are acute the people look to central power for help. Yet they have not abandoned hope that life might sometime be peaceful and that government might become frugal and unassuming, as Jefferson promised. And they have not abandoned the constitution which seemed to many of those who wrote it to err on the side of weakness, to put the liberties of the citizen before the safety of the commonwealth. Yet by unwritten means, out of simple self-protection, that constitution has been given strength and flexibility to meet the threats and disasters of a hundred and sixty years. The result is one of the most interesting forms of government the world has seen, and in the light of its problems one of the most successful.

2

The special problems of the American Government derive from geography, national character, and the nature both of a written constitution and of a federal empire. The government is cramped and confined by a seemingly rigid bond; yet it must adapt itself to a rate of change in economics, technology, and foreign relations which would have made all previous ages dizzy. In good times the government must abide by the theory that its limited sovereignty has been divided between the Union and the several states; yet when the bombs fall or the banks close or the breadlines grow by millions it must recapture the distributed sovereignty and act like a strong centralized nation. The government must regard the separation of its own powers, especially those of the Executive and the Legislature, as an essential and indeed a sacred part of the system; yet when the separation threatens deadlock and danger it must reassemble those powers informally and weld them into a working team. Finally, the government must accept the fact that in a country so huge, containing such diverse climates and economic interests and social habits and racial and religious backgrounds, most politics will be parochial, most politicians will have small horizons, seeking the good of the state or the district rather than of the Union; yet by diplomacy and compromise, never by force, the government must water down the selfish demands of regions, races, classes, business associations, into a national policy which will alienate no major group and which will contain at least a small plum for everybody. This is the price of unity in a continent-wide federation. Decisions will therefore be slow, methods will be cumbersome, political parties will be illogical and inconsistent; but the people remain free, reasonably united, and as lightly burdened by the state as is consistent with safety.

It may be asked, if the inevitable problems are so acute and so contradictory why not change the form of government? The answer is that the American political system with all its absurdities is one of the few successes in a calamitous age. Step by step, it has learned to avoid many of the worst mistakes of empire, in a nation which would stretch from London to the Ural Mountains and from Sweden to the Sahara; it has learned to circumvent threats of secession (the mortal illness of federalism) before they appear; it has learned to evade class warfare (the mortal illness of liberty), and to the dismay of its critics it shows no sign of moving toward class parties. Once, in the midst of the long period of learning, the political system failed totally. The result was civil war. The system must always fail partially, since politics cannot rise above the mixed nature of man. "Government is a very rough business," said Sir George Cornewall Lewis to the young Gladstone; "you must be content with very unsatisfactory results." In a world condemned to such results the American political system deserves attention—especially that part of the system which combines compromise with energy, minority rights with government by a majority which may live thousands of miles away. This is the special province of the unwritten constitution.

3

The written constitution has been unofficially revised, without the change of a word or a comma, in several ways. First, the government which had been planned as a very loose federation grew steadily more centralized. Not even the most power-fearing statesmen could prevent this drift.

Second, the office of the presidency was captured by the emerging democracy—much to the surprise of the Fathers, who thought they had put it beyond the clutches of what they called the "mob." The President, thereafter, was the one man elected by all the voters,* so when the country became a thorough democracy the President became the voice of the people. For the most part the members of the Senate and of the House must represent their own states and districts. It is not waywardness which makes them do this; it is the nature of the federal system. The representatives from Delaware do not and should not spend their time serving the interests of Idaho. Yet there may be occasions when the welfare of the national majority conflicts with that of Idaho. It then becomes the duty of the congressmen from Idaho to argue for their own region and to ask for compromise. But the President talks for the nation.

Third, when the President became the voice of the people it was important that his voice carry weight. Under the written constitution, as interpreted from the days of Madison (who came to the White House in 1809) to those of J. Q. Adams (who left it in 1829), not even the most popular President could impose a national policy. The Congress was "a scuffle of local interests," and could make only desultory policy. So the nation drifted: in and out of war, in and out of depression, in and out of sectional strife. Thus came the demand for the third unwritten change, which stabilized the others and saved the system from stagnation: the modern political parties.

These parties are unique. They cannot be compared to the parties of other nations. They serve a new purpose in a new way. Unforeseen and

*Except for the Vice-President, who does not matter unless the President dies.

unwanted by the Fathers, they form the heart of the unwritten constitution and help the written one to work.

It is through the parties that the clashing interests of a continent find grounds for compromise; it is through the parties that majority rule is softened and minorities gain a suspensive veto; it is through the parties that the separation of powers within the federal government is diminished and the President is given strength (when he dares use it) to act as tribune of the people; it is through the parties that the dignity of the states is maintained, and the tendency for central power to grow from its own strength is to some extent resisted. It is through the parties, also, that many corruptions and vulgarities enter the national life, and many dubious habits—like that of ignoring issues which are too grave for compromise.

The parties are never static. They are as responsive to shifting conditions as the Constitution of Great Britain. Above all, they are not addicted to fixed ideas, to rigid principles. It is not their duty to be Left, or Right, or Center—but to be all three. It is not their function to defend political or economic doctrines, but to administer the doctrines chosen by the majority, with due regard to special interests and to the habits of the regions.

Third parties may preach causes and adhere to creeds. They may educate the public and thus mold history. But the two major parties have a more absorbing, a more subtle, and a more difficult task. The task is peculiar to a federal state covering so much land and containing so many people that its economic and cultural life cannot and should not be merged. Over such an area, where there is no unity of race, no immemorial tradition, no throne to revere, no ancient roots in the land, no single religion to color all minds alike—where there is only language in common, and faith, and the pride of the rights of man—the American party system helps to build freedom and union: the blessings of liberty, and the strength that comes from letting men, money, goods, and ideas move without hindrance.

4

Although the major parties do not stand for opposed philosophies and do not represent opposed classes, there are traditional differences which divide them. On the whole, it is roughly true that the ancestors of the Democratic Party are Thomas Jefferson and his friends, who made a political alliance in the seventeen-nineties and who came to power in 1801. And it is roughly true that the ancestors of the Republican Party are Alexander Hamilton and his friends, who formed the dominant group in the Cabinets of the first two Presidents (1789–1801).

Broadly speaking, and subject to many qualifications, the Jeffersonians drew their strength from the landed interests (the small farmers and in some cases the great plantation owners) and from the mechanics and manual workers of the towns, whereas the Hamiltonians drew their strength from the business and banking and commercial communities, from the middle-class workers who associated their interests with these communities, and from some of the richest owners of plantations. There are so many exceptions to the above statements that it would be misleading to take them literally; yet in a very general sense they tend to be true. Some such alignment existed in most sections of the country, not only in the days of Jefferson and Hamilton, but in the days of Andrew Jackson and Henry Clay and Daniel Webster (1820–1850), and in the days of Bryan and McKinley, and in the days when Woodrow Wilson ran against Theodore Roosevelt and Taft, and again in the days of Franklin Roosevelt. Yet the alignment is insignificant compared to the fundamental forces which make the party system.

Another tendency toward strict party alignment stems from the Civil War—a tendency which cuts across and confuses the alignment which has just been described. The Republican Party was the party of Union during the Civil War, the party of Northern victory. As a result the farmers of the Middle West and of New England, for whom the Union was a sacred cause, long tended to vote the Republican ticket. So did the Negroes, for whom Northern victory meant release from slavery. And so did the veterans of the Union armies, for whom the Republican Party meant generous pensions. And on the other side the states of the Confederacy formed the "solid South" wherein only the Democratic Party was respectable. It is the remnants of such wartime passions which explain the Georgia judge who said, "I shall die a penitent Christian, but meet my Maker as an impenitent Democrat."

Yet in recent years Franklin Roosevelt won the whole of the Middle West for the Democrats, and the whole of New England with the exception of Maine and Vermont. And in two elections he received most of the Negro votes. And in 1928 (under very exceptional circumstances, to be sure) Herbert Hoover, the Republican candidate, received the votes of Virginia, Tennessee, Texas, North Carolina, and Florida—all parts of the "solid South."

The meaning and the purpose of the national parties cannot be sought in traditional alignments or old animosities, and still less in economic or political creeds. They can only be understood in the light of the regional problem created by America's size, and of the constitutional problem created by the separation of powers.

5

The American political system sometimes fails lamentably. Although on the whole it promotes freedom and union, too many citizens have a sham freedom, and too often the Union is used to press colonial servitude upon entire regions. Yet we must remember, as Dennis Brogan says, that when the Constitution went into effect in 1789 "there was still a King of France and Navarre, a King of Spain and the Indies, a Venetian and a Dutch Republic, an Emperor in Pekin; a Pope-King ruled in Bologna, a Tsarina in Petersburg and a Shogun in Yedo, not yet Tokio and not yet the residence of the Divine Mikado."

The form of government which has weathered the wars, revolutions, and economic collapses ravaging the world during this century and a half must satisfy some deep need of man. And it must have resilience and adaptability. The unwritten constitution supplies the latter qualities.

PART ONE
1763–1850

I

The Nature of the Revolution
1763–1788

THE AMERICAN REVOLUTION divides conveniently into three periods. During the first, the colonists were slowly pushed by circumstances into claiming autonomy within the Empire. This led them into war with the mother country, and incidentally into stating their claims on grounds which called for social revolution at home. During the second period the war was fought, the state constitutions were created, and the social revolution begun. During the third period a conservative revolt took effect, the loose confederation of the war-days was attacked on the ground that it made for anarchy, and the present Constitution of the United States was framed.*

The years preceding the formal break with England, from 1763 to 1776, were a time when man's will did not control his fate, a time when he was pushed by implacable forces into deeds which he had not chosen or foreseen. At the beginning of this period there were very few in America, and none in Britain, who wished to see the Empire broken; yet the defeat of France in the Seven Years War, and her expulsion from Canada at the peace of 1763, had brought a revolutionary change in the North American balance of power, and the revolutionary change produced a revolution.

The balance was upset domestically as well as internationally. The mechanics in the towns and the back-country farmers had long resented the rule of the colonial oligarchy—a rule based on property qualifications for voting and officeholding, and on a refusal to give the citizens of the newly settled western counties representation according to their numbers. In every colony the seaboard aristocrats were distrusted by the artisans and by the men of the frontier; and in every colony the privileges of the rich were supported by the distant power of Britain. Yet when that power was no longer needed as a guard against France, the merchants and planters felt free to protest against the mother country's interference

* The first period was from 1763 to 1775. The second period was from 1775 to 1783. The third period ended in 1788, when the required number of states had accepted the Constitution. In 1789 the federal government, which forms the subject of this book, was installed.

with their business profits, and the poor felt free to protest against the
political inequalities contrived by the merchants and planters and bol-
stered by the government in London. Professor Merrill Jensen writes:

> Colonial radicalism did not become effective until after the French
> and Indian War.* Then, fostered by economic depression and aided
> by the bungling policy of Great Britain and the desire of the local gov-
> erning classes for independence within the empire, it became united
> in an effort to throw off its local and international bonds. The discon-
> tented were given an opportunity to express their discontent when
> the British Government began to enforce restrictions upon the colonies
> after 1763. The colonial merchants used popular demonstrations to give
> point to their more orderly protests . . . and it was only a step from
> such riots, incited and controlled by the merchants, to the organization
> of radical parties bent on the redress of local grievances which were of
> far more concern to the masses than the more remote and less obvious
> effects of British policy. . . . Used as tools at first, the masses were
> soon united under capable leadership in what became as much a war
> against the colonial aristocracy as a war for independence.[1]

It is amusing to notice how the leaders were driven step by step to
justify the democratic aspirations of the colonial poor. The oligarchy
could not find a good reason for pressing their case against England without giving the disfranchised and underrepresented colonists a good reason
for pressing their case against the oligarchy; for if the Revolution concerned the rights of man, those rights must prevail between the western
and eastern counties as truly as between Boston and London. We shall
trace the results of the people's revolt later; but first we must follow the
revolt of the well-to-do and the educated against British trade laws and
taxation. This revolt was the prime mover in all the ferment, and it was
stimulated by British success in the Seven Years War. Behind the long
transatlantic argument about prerogative, about the powers of Parliament, about internal versus external taxation, there stands the fact that
when France was driven from Canada, and her Indian allies were thus
rendered comparatively harmless, the colonists no longer had a reason
to accept vexing interference from a faraway power. There might still
have been room for America within a twentieth-century Commonwealth
of Nations, but there was no room within an eighteenth-century mercantile empire—even an enlightened, and on the whole benevolent, empire such as the British. No one need be blamed for the fact that the
eighteenth century was not the twentieth; George III should be forgiven
for finding it impossible to be George VI.

It was inherent in the theory of eighteenth-century imperialism that

* This was the colonial name for the North American branch of the Seven
Years War.

colonies should be used for the good of the mother country, producing raw materials, absorbing finished products, trading only with such ports and in such bottoms as the central power decreed. Although the theory was tempered for the American colonies because they were partly self-governing and inhabited by Englishmen, it was inherent in human nature that such a faraway people, feeling themselves potentially rich and finding themselves suddenly safe, should object to all restraint from the day when the mother country could produce no compensating service. The service ended with the Seven Years War; the restraints continued.

In fact the restraints increased, just when the motive for bearing them diminished. England felt poor in 1763; she wanted the colonists, who had received much benefit from the recent war, to pay some of the costs. She decided on a stern enforcement of the trade restrictions, which in the past had been mitigated by smuggling. And she undertook to raise extra money from the colonists by means of a stamp tax, imposing heavy duties on legal papers, liquor licenses, pamphlets, newspapers, etc. In London, this seemed a mild way of insuring a contribution to the common cause. As George Grenville pointed out, the stamp tax was only expected to raise about £60,000 a year, whereas the annual cost of maintaining a British army in North America was about £350,000. But the colonists no longer felt they needed a British army.

The stamp tax was a burden on the three most vocal classes in the community, the clergy, the lawyers, and the journalists; and the decision to enforce the trade laws was a burden on the New England merchants and shippers, a group of men who had developed to an unusual extent the Puritan ability to identify good business with the will of God. Yet the decision was not tyrannous,* and the stamp tax did not in fact go counter to the laws of nature. It was merely inexpedient, in that the Americans did not have reason to accept it and the Parliament did not have power to enforce it. Benjamin Franklin, the wisest of Americans, was in London at the time, and although he had opposed the Stamp Act he failed to foresee the explosion which would follow at home. In fact, he procured for several of his closest friends the appointment as local "stamp master," a job which he thought both pleasing and profitable since it meant little work and carried three hundred pounds a year. Within a few months his friends were lucky to escape with their lives from angry American mobs.

Even more important than the resistance to the Stamp Act was the excuse given for resisting. As early as 1761 James Otis of Massachusetts had opposed writs of assistance, or search warrants, on the ground that

---

* It was, however, foolish; for the illicit trade with the French and Spanish Indies provided the colonies with the necessary cash to maintain the unfavorable balance of trade with Britain.

they were unconstitutional. Parliament itself, said Otis, did not have the right to disregard the traditional privileges of Englishmen or to violate the principles of the British Constitution. "As to Acts of Parliament," he said,[2] "an act against the Constitution is void. . . . The executive courts must pass such acts into disuse." And he referred to an opinion of Coke, in which that famous jurist asserted, "In many cases the common law will control Acts of Parliament and adjudge them to be utterly void; for where an Act of Parliament is against common right and reason or repugnant or impossible to be performed, the common law will control it and adjudge it to be void."

Whether it was good law or bad, it was already a basic American belief that man's rights are independent of government and that laws contradicting such rights are void. The same point was raised against the Stamp Act. Thomas Hutchinson, Royal Governor of Massachusetts, reported home that "the prevailing reason at this time is, that the Act of Parliament is against Magna Charta, and the natural rights of Englishmen, and therefore, according to Lord Coke, null and void." John Adams argued that the Act "is . . . of no binding force upon us; for it is against our rights as men and our privileges as Englishmen. An act made in defiance of the first principles of justice. . . . There are certain principles fixed unalterably in nature." Otis of course took the same view, and in 1766 a county court in Virginia declared the Stamp Act unconstitutional and said that it need not be obeyed.[3]

The doctrine that men have rights which are not the gift of government, and which government may not override, was rooted in the religious as well as the political history of New England. The colonists, in other words, did not invent the theory that unjust government is illegal government in order to excuse their disobedience. The theory was an old one; it was "the common sense of the matter," as Jefferson put it, to many eighteenth-century minds; and in the case of the New England colonists it had been taught by their ministers for over a century. The theory might not have been called upon in the case of the stamp tax, which was surely a mild evil, if there had not been many minor and sometimes unconscious reasons for wishing to be quit of the British connection, or at least to loosen the bonds.

Each section of the community had a reason of its own. The merchant-lawyer-journalist group was annoyed by the stamp tax and the suppression of smuggling. The Southern planters were deep in debt to their London agents, who paid poor prices for tobacco and overcharged for the goods they shipped in return; yet the mercantile system bound the planters to their agents and seemingly doomed them to eternal debt. And the frontier farmers had three grievances. The first was the quitrent, a feudal due payable by freeholders to the crown and to the proprietor. The second was the Proclamation of 1763 (reaffirmed in 1774 by the Quebec Act), which forbade settlers from crossing the Appalachian Mountains into the Indian country beyond. In London this doubtless seemed a reasonable way of preserving the fur trade, controlling the Indians, and avoiding border warfare. On the frontier it seemed madness, for the American pioneer regarded the Indian as someone whose land tenure expired automatically the moment the white man was ready to inherit it.

The third agrarian grievance was that the British prohibited the printing of paper money. Since it is natural for a debtor to have faith in the wealth-making powers of the printing press, this prohibition was resented not only by the small farmers but by the artisans and laborers in the cities, many of whom were out of work because of the post-war business depression and who felt that the rule against paper money was part of a conspiracy between Britain and the colonial rich to oppress the colonial poor.

Behind all this lay a still greater trouble, intangible, seldom expressed, but widely felt.

It is impossible [writes F. S. Oliver] to conduct successfully the infinitely complex affairs of an ordinary business from a center separated by great distances from its branches, unless the manager be given so free a hand that he becomes in fact the predominant partner within his own sphere. The British king and people failed to realize this essential limitation of their sovereignty. It was no wonder, for no country in the world had ever realized it before them. The essence of the difficulty was never clearly stated by either side, so little was it grasped by reason, so much was it a matter of mere instinct. Americans felt that a free hand was a necessity, and that under existing circumstances they would never obtain it. It seemed to them that they were not understood, which was true, and that they could never hope to be understood, which was probable.[4]

Even in a unified and efficient modern state, even with cables and wireless and world-wide telephones, every government mission abroad becomes irked and oppressed by the feeling that it is too little consulted from home and that its wise suggestions are given too little heed. How much more burdensome must the feeling have been in a sprawling ill-administered empire, in days when the fastest communication might be three months at sea. Only danger could impose unity under such conditions, and after 1763 the danger was gone.

There was also a creative side to the revolt against far-off control; British interference not only caused financial loss to the colonists, it frustrated their sense of destiny. Without knowing it, they were beginning to think of themselves as Americans, as members of a new type of nation. Franklin used the word "American" in this sense in the seventeen-fifties, Washington not long after; John Adams in the seventies; and

Jefferson, who had lived on the frontier, apparently never thought in other terms. In his *Autobiography* he writes: "I took the ground which, from the beginning, I had thought the only one orthodox or tenable, which was that the relation between Great Britain and these colonies was exactly the same as that of England and Scotland after the accession of James and until the union, and the same as her present relations with Hanover, having the same executive chief but no other necessary political connection." He added that many others "stopped at the half-way house of John Dickinson, who admitted that England had a right to regulate our commerce and to lay duties on it for the purposes of regulation but not of raising revenue."[5]

The halfway house was untenable. One by one the other leaders were driven to Jefferson's position, not because Jefferson was right in law or in his appeal to history, but because it was the only consistent position, and because it expressed the sense of independence which climate, geography, natural resources, and a reassuring absence of Frenchmen to the north, had created in the American mind. By 1763, England had served her purpose in the thirteen colonies. She had made possible the birth of a nation, and it was too late to undo the work. Had King George been as wise as Plato, and Lord North as just as Aristides, the nation would still have insisted on being born. The British might have postponed the birthday; but nothing short of a modern federalist system could have prevented it. Lord North, in fact, came closer than most of the contestants to seeing the real point; he said that the dispute was not about taxation but about whether Great Britain possessed any authority whatever over the "haughty American Republicans." The answer was "No."

2

The famous tea party at Boston shows the ignorance and misunderstanding, caused by great distance and slow communications, which helped to promote the break. The East India Company had been on the verge of bankruptcy, and Parliament came to the rescue with the Tea Act of 1773, designed to help the company sell its surplus tea. The act allowed the company to send tea to the American colonies in its own ships, and to sell it through its own agents. Instead of paying the English tax of a shilling, such tea had only a duty of threepence at the American ports. The result was a drop of ninepence in the price of tea. American merchants who had bought their stocks legally in London (and even the more enterprising merchants who had smuggled their stocks from Holland) could now be undersold by the East India Company, while shipowners and sailors who lived on the tea trade would be out of a job.

Parliament, seeking to help the East India Company, had acted without knowledge of the American mind. It may have been thought in London that the cheapness of the new tea would more than compensate for the ill treatment of the tea merchants; but it was not the loss of the tea trade which stirred the merchant class in America; it was the fear of monopoly. If Parliament favored other English trading houses in the same fashion, it might end by ruining all the American merchants as well as all the smugglers. Doubtless it would never have occurred to Parliament to do anything of the sort; but if the members of that body had not been three thousand miles away from the people for whom they were legislating they would have known that Burke was right when he said the Americans "anticipate the evil, and judge of the pressure of the grievance by the badness of the principle. They augur misgovernment at a distance, and snuff the approach of tyranny in every tainted breeze."

Calm and sensible men in America seriously believed that the Tea Act was the beginning of a plan to drain the colonies of their wealth. In some ports, therefore, the tea was landed but not sold. In others it was returned to England. And in Boston, on the night of December 16, 1773, a group of men disguised as Indians flung the cargoes from three of the East India Company's ships into the sea.

In London the deed must have seemed wanton and anarchic, because London did not know enough about Boston to see a connection between tyranny and cheap tea. That was the wrong which could not be repaired: London and Boston were too far apart, and it would be many decades before man's inventiveness could bring them closer. In reply to the tea party, London could think of nothing to do but assert its authority and "restore law and order"—a phrase that runs like a note of warning throughout the history of empires. The steps taken to assert authority united all the colonies with Massachusetts, and united the conservative merchant class with the more aggressive rebels.

If it had not been tea it would have been something else. The world had not then evolved a type of international society in which the colonies could continue an unsuspicious collaboration with the mother country. Seventy years later, when discontent arose in Canada, the British Government sent a commission to study the problem in the light of the American revolt. As a result of the commission's report, the Empire began to move toward the modern Commonwealth of Nations. But it was too soon for such ideas in London, in 1773. The wisest of the colonists—Franklin, Jefferson, James Wilson, John Adams—all had dreamed of a federal empire as the basis for unity. It was easy to have such dreams in America, where the need for home rule was clear. It was still impossible in London, where the power resided, and the habits of authority.

Only adversity can bring new ideas to men who have been long steeped in power. After the battle of Saratoga, in October, 1777, Lord North wished to recognize American independence at once. The king forbade it. Lord North then introduced a bill which might have changed history. The bill authorized a treaty with the colonies granting complete home rule if they would acknowledge the sovereignty of the king. This, in effect, is modern dominion status. It is independence without disunity. It would perhaps have been accepted in November; but Parliament took a long Christmas holiday and the bill was not passed until February, 1778. By that time France, fearing that such concessions might be made, and might bring peace, had signed a treaty of alliance with America. The war had to continue to the end; but at least the new British Empire would one day profit from the mistakes of the old.

3

Needless to say, the men who made the Revolution did not think they were merely, and inevitably, sloughing off an imperial bond which was no longer useful and which could no longer be enforced. They saw their drive for independence as a drive for justice and for the blessings of liberty, a conflict between good and evil. "Britain," wrote John Adams to his wife on July 3, 1776, "has been filled with folly, and America with wisdom." This complacent view of the problem had two results: it led the colonists to invent a theory of the British Empire which, though unhistoric, gave them ethical grounds for revolution, and it led them to state their case before the world in terms of good and evil—of natural law, the rights of man, and the compact-theory of the state. The effort to embody these moral doctrines in political institutions led to a new form of government, a new and distinctively American effort to solve the old problem of power versus individual liberty.

It was hard to picture the Empire in terms which would permit the colonists, while flouting authority, to persuade themselves that they were merely defending the right. When they called the Stamp Act unconstitutional, for example, they did so on the ground that nobody with the rights of a British citizen could be legally taxed except with the consent of his representatives. Since the Americans were not represented in Parliament, they could not be taxed by Parliament. Yet this was awkward ground, for the colonists had frequently been taxed by Parliament without complaint. The argument was therefore narrowed, and the claim made that Parliament could not impose *internal* taxes, such as the stamp tax, although it could impose *external* taxes such as customs duties.

It soon became clear that this too was shaky doctrine. The Stamp

Act was repealed in 1766, and in the following year Parliament passed the Townshend Acts. Townshend had declared that the difference between internal and external taxes was "perfect nonsense"; yet if it amused the Americans to make the distinction he was prepared to humor them. So the Townshend Acts laid duties, to be collected in American ports, on glass, lead, paper, tea, etc. Customs Commissioners were appointed for the collection of these duties, and were sent to Boston. Unlike the Stamp Collectors, they did not run away when the mob opposed them; they called British troops to their support.

The colonists began to feel that Townshend had been right in calling the distinction between internal and external taxes "perfect nonsense." A tax was a tax, it seemed, and the only good tax was a tax which was not collected. Yet no one could claim this doctrine was part of the British Constitution. Neither could anyone deny that Parliament for a hundred years had imposed customs duties (that is, external taxes) for the regulation of trade, and that some of these duties had brought revenue to the Exchequer. Yet if the Townshend Acts were also to be flouted, a reasonable excuse was required; so the next step was to draw a distinction between customs duties laid for the regulation of trade and customs duties laid for the purpose of bringing in a revenue. The former, said John Dickinson[6] and his many followers, were constitutional; the latter were not. How was the distinction to be drawn, since any customs duties were likely to raise some revenue? The distinction must rest upon the "intention" of the framers of the law. But might not Parliament profess the intention of regulating trade when it really intended to raise revenue? In that case, said Dickinson, the intention must be inferred from the nature of the law.

Professor Becker comments:

> To derive the nature of an act from the intention of its framers, and the intention of its framers from the nature of the act, was no doubt what logicians would call reasoning in a circle; but whatever the technical defects of the argument might be, the colonists could, and did, lay firm hold of the general conclusion that Americans have "the same right that all states have, of judging when their privileges are invaded."[7]

Here, of course, was the point. The colonists did not choose to pay taxes or to suffer restrictions for the sake of an empire they no longer needed. It was not in their interest to do so, and it was not to be supposed that they, alone among mankind, would sacrifice interest to sentiment. But neither did they choose to make such a blunt, ungrateful statement. They were breaking the law because they did not like the law, and because they felt strong enough to break it. They meant to continue breaking it, and they wanted a clear and flattering excuse. The logic-chopping of John Dickinson would not suffice, so at this time they began to talk less about their constitutional rights as British subjects and more about their natural rights as members of the human race. The ground was safer; the statutes were less precise and the precedents less discouraging. Also, the doctrine of natural rights was at home in the American mind.

In 1768 Benjamin Franklin, with his refreshing realism, wrote:

The more I have thought and read on the subject, the more I find myself confirmed in opinion, that no middle ground can be well maintained, I mean not clearly with intelligible arguments. Something might be made of either of the extremes: that Parliament has a power to make *all laws* for us, or that it has a power to make *no laws* for us. . . . Supposing [the latter] doctrine established, the colonies would then be so many separate states, only subject to the same king, as England and Scotland were before the union.

How was the doctrine to be "established," since Parliament had been legislating for the colonies ever since 1645? Franklin did the best he could on purely historical grounds; but the result was frustrating.

That the colonies were originally constituted distinct states [he wrote in 1770], and intended to be continued such, is clear to me from a thorough consideration of their original Charters, and the whole conduct of the Crown and nation towards them until the Restoration. Since that period, the Parliament here has usurped an authority of making laws for them, which before it had not. We have for some time submitted to that usurpation.

This was a mild way of putting it, since the phrase "for some time" covered a hundred and ten years.* Clearly the argument from history was disappointing; yet the statement that Parliament "has a power to make *no laws* for us" must somehow be supported. All attempts to find a middle ground had proved illogical and confusing; yet the colonists were unwilling to appeal to naked force, resting their argument on power alone. They still wished a constitutional and moral reason for opposing authority. In the end they found it where the English Whigs had found it before them: in natural law.

James Wilson of Pennsylvania published in 1774 his *Considerations on the Nature and Extent of the Legislative Authority of the British Parliament.*** He agreed with Franklin that Parliament must have all power

* Franklin was mistaken in his dates. Between 1645 and 1651 the Long Parliament laid down many regulations which controlled colonial commerce in the interest of English shipping and manufactures.
** This was probably written in 1770.

or none. "There can be no medium," he said, "between acknowledging and denying that power in all cases." So in order to deny it effectively he appealed to "the principles of liberty," to "the ultimate end of all government," and to "the happiness of the colonies." In words that forecast the great Declaration of 1776, he wrote: "All men are, by nature, free and equal: no one has a right to any authority over another without his consent: all lawful government is founded in the consent of those who are subject to it. . . . The happiness of the society is the first law of every government." And again: "Will it ensure and increase the happiness of the American colonies, that the British Parliament should possess a supreme, irresistible, uncontrolled authority over them?"

At last the days of tortured legal quibbles were ending. At last the argument was moving to high ground, where men could differ sensibly and in the fresh air. At last the right questions were being asked, questions which could only be answered by statesmen or by war, not by lawyers or by textbooks. It was no longer a puny question of what was legal; it was becoming a question of what was reasonable and right. Step by step the Americans were driven to this position, and when they finally occupied it they found it was a place which a man could defend. In the process of defending it they were led to invent a wholly new model of British Empire, a better model, which London was to accept one day. Meanwhile, London was irked at hearing that the new Empire of American fantasy was really the old Empire, and that it was only the British, who had made it, who were too stupid or too wicked to know what it was.

The difficulty of abandoning the low ground of legalism and Parliamentary precedent for the high ground of natural law is shown by the First Continental Congress, which met in the year when Wilson published his pamphlet, and when John Adams and Jefferson were publishing similar views. The Congress was called to unite the colonies in their opposition to British "usurpations"; but there were yet no plans for independence. The members were almost evenly divided between the legalistic position of Dickinson and the moralistic position of Wilson and Jefferson and Adams; so their Declaration of Rights took both grounds. It appealed to "The immutable laws of nature"; but it also stated, "*We cheerfully consent* to the operation of such acts of the British Parliament as are *bona fide* restrained to the regulation of our external commerce . . . excluding every idea of taxation internal or external, for raising a revenue on the subjects, in America, without their consent." The members, and the colonies for which they were delegates, could stand with Wilson and the rights of man (not to be governed without his consent), or with Dickinson and the rights of British subjects (not to be taxed without representation).

Two years later, when events had forced independence upon a largely reluctant people, the Declaration of Independence made no mention of Parliament and no mention of the rights of British subjects.* The appeal was to natural law, and the assumption was that the British Empire had always been a federation of independent states and that Parliament had no power outside the United Kingdom. Yet for ten years most of the colonists had founded their case on "the rights of British subjects," and had admitted the authority of Parliament in certain fields. Suddenly the wicked Parliament was replaced by the wicked king, and the rights of man became supreme.

Professor Becker explains the change in tone between the Declaration of Rights (1774) and the Declaration of Independence (1776), as follows:

> The primary purpose of the Declaration [of Independence] was to convince a candid world that the colonies had a moral and legal right to separate from Great Britain. . . . Accordingly, the idea around which Jefferson built the Declaration was that the colonies were not rebels against established political authority, but a free people maintaining long-established and imprescriptible rights against a usurping king. . . . The king is represented as exclusively aggressive, the colonists are represented as essentially submissive. In this drama the king alone acts—he conspires, incites, plunders; the colonists have the passive part, never lifting a hand to burn stamps or destroy tea; they suffer while evils are sufferable. It is a high literary merit of the Declaration that by subtle contrasts Jefferson contrives to conjure up for us the virtuous and long-suffering colonists standing like martyrs to receive on their defenseless heads the ceaseless blows of the tyrant's hand.[8]

Five generations of Americans have absorbed this impression from Jefferson's masterly work, so it is interesting to recall the difficulties of the revolutionary leaders in deciding which "rights" they were defending, British or universal, and against whom, Parliament or King. Events decided for them; the necessities of the occasion were well met by the Declaration of Independence, and could not have been met by a text from John Dickinson. Yet it was a fateful decision, as we shall see, to base the new nation's life on natural law.

---

* The existence of Parliament and of British rights had sometimes to be implied; but this was done in the most delicate and distant manner. For example: "He [the king] has combined with others to subject us to a jurisdiction foreign to our Constitution, and unacknowledged by our laws; giving his assent to their acts of pretended legislation." And among the enumerated "acts of pretended legislation" were those "for abolishing the free system of English laws in a neighboring province" (Quebec). It would be difficult to treat Parliament more disdainfully than by referring to it vaguely as "others," or to pass over British rights more lightly than by citing them only in connection with Canada.

4

The plain people in the colonies, in 1776, were delighted to learn they had so many and such indefeasible rights. They had thought so for a long time, but nobody seemed to agree with them. Now they were prepared to insist that when freed from what they were told was a hideous British tyranny they should enjoy these rights and find life more friendly and more prosperous. They read Thomas Paine's pamphlet, *Common Sense,* which closed with these words:

> O! ye that love mankind! Ye that dare oppose not only tyranny but the tyrant, stand forth! Every spot of the old world is overrun with oppression. Freedom hath been hunted round the Globe. Asia and Africa have long expelled her. Europe regards her as a stranger and England hath given her warning to depart. O! receive the fugitive and prepare in time an asylum for mankind.

This seems a long way from a quarrel about extra taxes. Who can blame the people for believing that a war fought in such a cause should bring, not only freedom from England, but equity and equality into their lives?

A number of the leaders (such as Patrick Henry, Samuel Adams,* Jefferson, and Paine) agreed with the people on this point. They believed that American society must be reorganized in all its relations, and that the work should begin at once, in the midst of the war, while the new state governments were being formed. They saw themselves as founding, not merely an independent nation, but one based squarely on the concept of natural law, a concept which to many was almost a religious faith in the late eighteenth century. Whence did the faith arise?

Aristotle had proclaimed that there were two sorts of law,

> the particular and the universal. *Particular* law is the law defined and declared by each community for its own members. . . . Universal law is the law of nature. . . . There really exists, as all of us in some measure divine, a natural form of the just and unjust which is common to all men, even when there is no community or covenant to bind them to one another. It is this form which the Antigone of Sophocles' play evidently has in her mind, when she says that it was a just act to bury her brother Polynices in spite of Creon's decree to the contrary—just, she means, in the sense of being *naturally* just.

> Not of today or yesterday its force:
> It springs eternal: no man knows its birth.

* The radical second cousin of the conservative John Adams.

Aristotle also quotes Alcidimas, justifying the Thebans for freeing the Messenian serfs of Sparta: "God has left all men free, and nature has made no man a slave."

Thomas Aquinas, in the thirteenth century, said there were four types of law: Eternal Law, which was the mind of God; Divine Law, which was that part of the mind of God revealed in the Bible or through the Church; Natural Law, which was that part of the mind of God which man could discover through the use of his reason; and Human Law, which was Aristotle's *particular* law, "the law defined and declared by each community." Natural law thus took precedence over human law; it was a method of learning the mind or law of God, whereas human law might bear no relation to the mind of God. Human law was what the state declared it to be, so long as the state had the power to compel obedience. But, said Aquinas, "every human law has just so much of the nature of law, as it is derived from the law of nature. But if in any point it deflects from the law of nature it is no longer a law; it is but a perversion of law."

From the time of the Renaissance until the eighteenth century, a new and daring hope began to grow in men's minds. The Protestant Reformation with its emphasis on personal interpretation of the Bible, the startling discoveries of science from Copernicus to Newton, both suggested that man by the use of his reason might be able to understand the whole of God's universe, and thus the whole of His mind. If man were diligent the final secrets of nature might some day be revealed; the mind of God would at last be understood; Natural law would then be the same as Eternal law. It was a stimulating but complacent idea; it assumed that common sense and reasonableness were the road to God and to fulfillment; it found expression in the poetry of Alexander Pope, and in the politics of John Locke, which became the politics of Jefferson and the Declaration of Independence.

Locke taught that since the will of God was revealed in nature, we could learn what God intended the government of man to be by studying the nature of man. What political forms would man accept, what political compact would he make, if he acted according to his true nature? Locke answers that it is natural for men to be "free, equal, and independent," that it is natural for them "to order their actions and dispose of their possessions and persons as they think fit, within the bounds of the law of nature," and he adds that the law of nature is nothing but reason, which "teaches all mankind, who will but consult it, that being all equal and independent, no one ought to harm another in his life, health, liberty, or possessions." It sounds very simple. Law and government, according to this theory, are not based on expediency and force; they are based on morals, on an objective right and wrong that binds all men.

A just government does not confer rights upon the citizen; it proclaims and protects the rights which are inherent in the nature of man.

Since men are reasonable, they will voluntarily join with their neighbors to promote safety, comfort, peace, and the enjoyment of property. They may enter into this social compact themselves (as in the case of the Americans who made the new state governments during the Revolution), or they may inherit it from their forebears; but no compact can give away their inalienable rights; no government which conforms to natural law can be omnipotent. Authority must always be limited; an act of authority beyond the assigned limits is neither just nor legal. Such was the eighteenth-century faith. Such is the central dogma of the American constitutional system.

Clearly, this eighteenth-century version of natural law was a blessing for the makers of the Revolution. It was moral, since it was based on a faith in God and in the perfection of His creation; it was effective, since it denied the authority of any government which did not rest on consent; and it was "in the air": it did not have to be argued or justified. It was easily accepted by the eighteenth-century mind, and could be stated as a set of self-evident truths. Yet it is doubtful whether some of the more conservative men who signed the Declaration foresaw the fatefulness of their act. Modern criticism may have made nonsense of the "universal and eternal laws" which the eighteenth century thought it was uncovering; modern nationalism and industrialism may have made nonsense of the religion of Humanity which the eighteenth century thought it was erecting; but the Declaration of Independence remains the first American deed. The life of the nation is based upon it and the children of the nation memorize it, and it leaves upon their minds a mark which is not always approved by authority. The children never quite forget that law, as defined at the birth of their country, should be Reason backed by Justice, not Will backed by Force. When the world which surrounds them does not seem to live up to the statement, they tend to remember that there is a higher law than the law of man, that there is a higher court than the Supreme Court at Washington, and that the people may "alter or abolish" a government which infringes their inalienable rights. This is what an American means when he talks of "the ideas of 1776." The ideas do not make for docility, or for reverence toward the police; but when felt with the fervor which inspired the first Americans, they do make for hope.

In later and darker days, Americans had to return to the sad task of reconciling belief in an absolute standard of justice with knowledge of the perennial injustice of life, or they had to fail in the reconciliation and abandon the initial American faith; but in the happy dawn of the Revolution men truly thought that reason and good sense were about to make a better world. For a moment, man's powers of self-improvement seemed limitless. In the Virginia Bill of Rights,* George Mason stated: "That no free government, or the blessings of liberty, can be preserved to any people, but by a firm adherence to justice, moderation, temperance, frugality and virtue, and by frequent recurrence to fundamental principles." And the somber John Adams, writing to Mercy Warren in that same year of 1776, said: "There must be a positive passion for the public good, the public interest, honor, power, and glory, established in the minds of the people, or there can be no republican government, nor any real liberty; and this public passion must be superior to all private passions. . . . The only reputable principle and doctrine must be that all things must give way to the public."** A few weeks later he wrote to his wife: "The new governments we are assuming in every part will require a purification from our vices, and an augmentation of our virtues, or they will be no blessings."

This is the view of Milton, and of Plato, and of most of the poets and philosophers who have dealt with government: liberty is impossible without the sternest self-discipline on the part of the free citizens. In our disenchanted world, the statement sounds like an elaborate way of saying "liberty is impossible." To our forefathers, for a few rosy years, it sounded like a bracing challenge. John Adams, later to become famous for his gloomy view of man's nature, wrote to the venerable George Wythe, in 1776, in terms that suggest the young Wordsworth: "You and I, my dear friend, have been sent into life at a time when the greatest lawgivers of antiquity would have wished to live. How few of the human race have ever enjoyed an opportunity of making an election of government, more than of air, soil, or climate, for themselves or their children!"

In such a mood, and by such men, America was committed to the doctrine of natural law. The mood passed but the doctrine remained, to become at times a moral strength for the country, and at times a source of contention and of physical weakness. When a powerful minority feels itself oppressed, especially if it be a regional minority, the cry goes up that the "just powers" of government have been exceeded, and that in obedience to the law of heaven the law of man must be disregarded. Jefferson himself was the author of the first and most famous of such cries. In 1798, he recommended that a federal law be declared void by the states composing the Union, and he stated that "it would be a dangerous delusion were a confidence in the men of our choice to silence our fears for the safety of

---

* Adopted June 12, 1776.

** Twelve years later, in volume III of his *Defence of the Constitutions of Government of the United States of America,* Adams wrote: "Very few in any nation are enlightened by philosophy or religion enough to be at all times convinced that it is a duty to prefer the public to a private interest, and fewer still are moral, honorable, or religious enough to practise such self-denial."

our rights: that confidence is everywhere the parent of despotism; free government is founded in jealousy and not in confidence; it is jealousy and not confidence which prescribes limited Constitutions to bind down those whom we are obliged to trust with power."⁹

When this jealousy of government is combined with a written constitution, the opportunities for obstruction are many. The whole of American history is colored by the struggle, on the one hand to confer upon government sufficient power so that the public business may go forward, and on the other hand to withhold from government the power to override the self-defined "natural rights" of minorities.

5

The leaders of the Revolution agreed on the Declaration of Independence as an indictment of George III; but they did not even pretend to agree on the deductions which might be made from that document. Jefferson and his friends thought it meant a new and radically democratic social order in America. This was not the view of John Adams or of most New England leaders; it was not the view of Alexander Hamilton, or of George Washington.

During the war, however, and for a few years thereafter, the radicals were influential in most of the states and in the Congress of the Confederation.* They rode to power on the arguments which the conservatives were forced to use against the British. As early as 1774 one of the wisest of the colonial oligarchs wrote: "Farewell aristocracy. I see, and I see with fear and trembling that if disputes with Great Britain continue, we shall be under the worst of all possible dominions; we shall be under the domination of a riotous mob. It is to the interest of all men, therefore, to seek for reunion with the parent state."**

During their time in power the radicals laid the foundation for a more egalitarian life. They annulled the Proclamation of 1763 and disregarded the Quebec Act, thus opening the western lands for settlement. They confiscated the Crown domains and the estates of most of the men who had remained loyal to England, redistributing the land in part at least to farmers and war veterans. They abolished entails in every state but two. They disestablished the Church in five states. They suppressed the feudal

---

* The Confederation was the loose central government which sought to run the country from 1781, the year of its adoption, until the acceptance of the present constitution in 1788. Between 1775 and 1781 the Second Continental Congress, a self-constituted central committee with undefined powers, had given the thirteen colonies such unified guidance as they possessed.

** Gouverneur Morris, quoted in Jensen, *The Articles of Confederation,* pp. 34–35. It is interesting that when the break came Morris was on the side of the rebels.

quitrents, and primogeniture, and titles of nobility. They of course did away with the old vexatious curbs on American industry, whereby Britain had interfered with the wool trade, the hat trade, the making of iron and steel. In all but four states they liberalized colonial laws on the franchise, so that in most states every taxpayer was allowed to vote.* And they wrote bills of rights into the new state constitutions, guarding the citizen from arbitrary power and proving that the compact-theory of government had become the faith of the people.

The Virginia constitution declared "That all men are by nature equally free and independent, and have certain inherent rights, of which, when they enter into a state of society, they cannot, by any compact, deprive or divest their posterity; namely, the enjoyment of life and liberty, with the means of acquiring and possessing property, and pursuing and obtaining happiness and safety." And the Massachusetts Constitution of 1780 said: "The body politic is formed by a voluntary association of individuals: it is a social compact, by which the whole people covenants with each citizen, and each citizen with the whole people, that all shall be governed by certain laws for the common good." It might have amused the men who made these governments to read certain modern writers on the absurdity of the compact theory and its lack of historic truth. What had been stated by Locke as little more than a parable was carried out literally in the colonies. "The people of Massachusetts," said an orator in 1781, "have reduced to practice the wonderful theory. A numerous people have convened in a state of nature, and, like *our ideas* of the patriarchs, have deputed a few fathers of the land to draw up for them a glorious covenant."[10]

This making of governments in the midst of war and social upheaval was an impressive achievement. Massachusetts took the lead in the spring of 1775 by asking the Continental Congress for "explicit advice respecting the taking up and exercising the powers of civil government, which we think absolutely necessary for the salvation of our country." The following year the Congress recommended all the colonies to form governments, and the mood in which the great task was attempted is shown in John Adams's *Autobiography.*

> With a view to this subject [he wrote], I had looked into the ancient and modern confederacies for examples, but they all appeared to me to have been huddled up in a hurry, by a few chiefs. But we had a people of more intelligence, curiosity, and enterprise, who must be all consulted, and we must realize the theories of the wisest writers, and

* " 'We the people of the United States,' " writes J. Franklin Jameson in *The American Revolution Considered as a Social Movement* (p. 62), "who gave consent to the establishment of the Constitution was a much larger and more democratic body than 'We the people of the United States' who acquiesced in the Declaration of Independence, though universal suffrage was yet a long way off."

invite the people to erect the whole building with their own hands, upon the broadest foundation. . . . This could be done only by conventions of representatives chosen by the people in the several colonies, in the most exact proportions. . . . These were new, strange, and terrible doctrines to the greatest part of the members [of the Congress], but not a very small number heard them with apparent pleasure.

New, strange, and terrible the doctrines might be; but they were carried out with a sobriety and a political tact which do honor to the American people. When the fighting was over the future of the states was not in the hands of revolutionary committees, violent and extreme, but of popular governments whose powers were derived from a voluntary social contract. Perhaps this is why no revolution has ever been less revolutionary.

Moderate as they seem in the light of history, the radicals in charge of the war-born state governments were naturally inclined to experiment, and were naturally inexperienced. They issued paper money at a disastrous rate. And they indulged their local, rural isolationism, their fear that any centralized power must mean oppression, to such an extent that the war was hampered; the Congress was unable to pay its bills; foreign nations, contemptuous of the talkative but paralyzed confederation, withheld credits and trade agreements. By the middle eighties the country felt a serious depression.

The alarm of the conservative classes over this libertarian ferment was expressed by General Knox in a letter to Washington in October, 1786:

> Their creed [that is, the creed of those calling for paper money to reduce the burden of debt] is, that the property of the United States has been protected from the confiscation of Britain by the joint exertions of all, and therefore ought to be the common property of all. . . . This dreadful situation, for which our government have made no adequate provision, has alarmed every man of principle and property in New England. They start as from a dream, and ask what can have been the cause of this delusion? What is to give us security against the violence of lawless men? Our government must be braced, changed, and altered to secure our lives and property.

General Knox had reason for his worry. Yet within two and a half years of the writing of that letter the government had in fact been "braced, changed, and altered"; a new constitution had been contrived by the well-to-do and accepted by the people; General Knox's property was as safe as could be expected in this shaky world. Such a conservative reformation by consent is unusual. It was possible for two reasons. First, because many of the leaders in the fight for independence were men of a strong conservative bent. Heroes of the war but also contemners of the radical movement, they gave prestige and wise leadership to the trend toward stronger government from 1785–1788. And the second reason was George Washington. His character and influence did much to help the people to accept that markedly conservative document, the Constitution of the United States, and to trust the central government with powers of coercion which the radicals deeply feared.

Needless to say, Washington did not escape criticism. He was accused of betraying his cause when he became head of the new federal government. While he was President of the United States Thomas Paine addressed him as follows in an open letter: "As to you, sir, treacherous in private friendship . . . and a hypocrite in public life, the world will be puzzled to decide whether you are an apostate or an imposter; whether you have abandoned good principles or whether you ever had any." The extreme American radicals abused Washington with similar violence, calling him "crocodile," "hyena," "traitor." Yet Washington had not changed sides; he was fighting for the same cause still, though some of his former admirers were just beginning to discover what that cause was. Washington did not believe in democracy. "Mankind," he wrote to Henry Lee, "when left to themselves, are unfit for their own government." He wanted an independent American republic, strong, free, proud, able to take possession of its immense heritage, yet restrained by law from usurping the rights of man. He thought, for reasons which will become clear, that such a republic should be governed by men of property. This was the prevailing view among the constitution-makers—a view which found ready acceptance because most Americans could own property in those days.

6

There was a third group in the colonies, in addition to the radical and the conservative revolutionists. This was composed of the loyalists, or Tories. Some of the Tories had taken part in the early protests against the Stamp Act, but had withdrawn when they saw that they were raising a whirlwind and that the plain people would not be content with safeguarding the profits of the well-to-do from British interference but would expect large dividends for themselves. The rest of the Tories were men who on principle remained loyal to the Empire, who could not break an old tie because it had become a new burden. They were important in number as well as in quality.

Professor C. H. Van Tyne, in his *Loyalists in the American Revolution,* writes:

> After the revolution passed the bounds of peaceful resistance, it was [except in Virginia] distinctly a movement of the middle and lower

classes. A new set of leaders came forward, hitherto unknown, less educated, and eager for change. The very public documents became more illiterate. To the aristocratic and cultured class it seemed that the unlettered monster was unchained, and while they waited for British power to restore the old order they withdrew for the most part from what seemed an undignified contest.

One possible reason why Virginia was an exception has already been mentioned: the debts of the great landowners to their London agents. Another reason may be that there were no cities in Virginia, and therefore no riotous mechanics, organized as "Sons of Liberty," to give warning that the question of home rule for the colonies could not be separated from the question of which class was to do the ruling at home. It was fortunate for the Revolution that a majority of the Virginia gentry supported it, and that in New England the merchants were fairly evenly divided, for in New York,* New Jersey, and Georgia the loyalists were perhaps in a majority, and they were strong in Pennsylvania and the Carolinas.

When the British had contrived (against all predictions and probabilities) to lose the war, the loyalists suffered the usual fate of the defeated in fraternal strife: exile and confiscation, aggravated by the wholly unjust assertion that they had acted from the lowest motives.

7

In spite of the fate of the loyalists, the American Revolution was clearly more political than social. No class was expropriated, but merely a group of people who had taken the losing side. Few serious economic changes were made, though certain bulwarks of aristocracy, such as entails and primogeniture, were abolished. Property was held as before, even if there had been a shift of names on the property lists; and it conferred most of its old privileges, including the privilege of the franchise. Its power was briefly threatened in a few states; but by 1789 it was re-established.

Politically, however, the Revolution brought immense changes: first, independence; second, the establishment of state constitutions based on a belief in limited powers and in natural law, and some of them embodying all the fashionable devices for popular rule; third, the invention of a federal government similarly based and similarly limited, but without the more alarming novelties of the state constitutions; and fourth, the first tentative steps toward true democracy, as in the enthusiasm of the masses for the Declaration of Independence (an enthusiasm which has never been downed), and in the constitution of the state of Vermont which

* New York supplied 15,000 regulars and 8500 militia to the British armies.

abolished slavery and accepted universal male suffrage.* In 1788, when
the conservatives had persuaded the country to accept the new constitution, the movement toward democracy may have seemed very slight. The
legal and social barriers against it may have seemed strong. Yet the new
idea was spreading through the Western world, and in America it could
not be restrained. By 1800 the democrats had achieved a symbolic triumph
in the election of Jefferson to the presidency; by the eighteen-thirties they
had conquered and their creed was enthroned.

* Vermont was not officially admitted as a state in the Union until 1791; but it
considered itself a state, and a highly independent one, from the time of the
adoption of its constitution in 1777.

II

War and Peace: Prelude to a Federation

THE THIRTEEN COLONIES might have lost the war with England and postponed their independence, if it had not been for George Washington. And the subsequent effort to unite them in a stable federal government might have failed, except for Washington. It was no exaggeration to call him "first in war, first in peace, and first in the hearts of his country-men";* yet the nature of his pre-eminence is baffling. It is easy to feel but hard to portray. Character, strength, good sense, the ability to apply simple ideas to complex problems and to find answers which if not subtle are strong and enduring—these rare but undramatic traits appear throughout Washington's life. They gave him a mastery which was never successfully challenged, and which was never used except to support the Commonwealth. The founding of the nation cannot be explained without this influence.

Washington's relatives in Virginia were neither conspicuous nor rich until his half-brother, Lawrence, married into a family which owned six million acres of land beyond the Blue Ridge Mountains. In 1748, at the age of sixteen, George was given the job of surveying this tract, thus gaining his first view of the western country which was to play so large a part in his plans and hopes. Learning through experience that the illimitable West was too vast to be developed either from London or from weak and separate states, he began to think in terms of a common and splendid destiny for all the colonies—within the Empire if possible, but a common destiny in any case. He became one of the first Americans to plan and act nationally. He lacked formal learning, having pieced out his education chiefly from the local clergyman and from the libraries in the houses of his kinsmen; but his grasp of the West, and of what it might mean in the future, was decisive in his own life and in that of his country.

When Washington was twenty his fortunes were changed by the death of Lawrence, and of Lawrence's daughter. George inherited the pleasant property of Mount Vernon, becoming a moderately wealthy landowner. As a sign of his new estate he was appointed Adjutant General of the Vir-

---

* The words of General Henry Lee, incorporated in John Marshall's resolutions in Congress on the death of Washington, and repeated in Lee's memorial oration, December 26, 1799.

ginia militia with the rank of major, and in the same year he had his first taste of war.

The French and the British both claimed the Indian lands across the mountains, between the Great Lakes and the Ohio River. It was a huge region to which neither nation had any rights except on the assumption that the Indian was a wild animal whose claims to proprietorship were as negligible as those of a wolf to his lair. The Governor of Virginia sent Washington into this disputed country to order a French commander to leave. Since the order was ignored Washington was sent back the next year with a hundred and fifty men, to seize the fork of the Monongahela and Allegheny Rivers. At first successful, he was later compelled to surrender to a superior French force. In this tiny battle on the remote frontier, fought for the riverfork which is the seat of modern Pittsburgh, Washington witnessed the start of the Seven Years War. It was to rage across the world, from the rivers of the Red Indian to the rivers of the Hindu, and in America it was to lead not only to the expulsion of the French but to a new mood of independence among the thirteen colonies.

In 1755 General Braddock arrived from England with two regiments to lead a joint English and colonial attack against the French in the Ohio Valley. Washington had an unofficial position on Braddock's staff, and was thus present at the ambush on the Monongahela where the French and Indians routed the British force. Out of Braddock's 1300 men, 456 were killed and 421 wounded. The French commander, who had under him 250 of his own troops and 600 Indians, lost 30 men. Washington, one of the few officers to be unhurt, sent his Virginians into the woods where they could at least fight instead of huddling as defenseless targets. After the rout he arranged for the removal of the wounded Braddock, who soon died, and he guarded the rear of the fleeing regiments with the only soldiers who had kept their discipline. The incident gave him a reputation in the colonies which was to be useful when it came to choosing a leader for the rebel armies.

In 1759 Washington married a rich widow, and thereafter took no part in the French and Indian War. For the next sixteen years he lived at Mount Vernon, improving his estates, buying new farms, speculating in western lands, and taking a seat in the colonial legislature. He was twice defeated for the Virginia House of Burgesses; but with customary matter-of-factness he studied his electioneering mistakes. As a result he was successful the third time by 310 votes to 45. In view of the number of voters it is interesting to note that Washington supplied about forty gallons of rum punch, twenty-eight gallons of wine, twenty-six gallons of rum, forty-six gallons of beer, six gallons of madeira, and three and a half pints of brandy. Having learned the secret of success, he remained in the House of Burgesses until he left Virginia to head the Army of the Revolution.

Washington's energy could not be satisfied with caring for his estates and sitting in a provincial legislature, especially since his practical brain preferred not to bother with politics until forced to do so by events. Unlike Patrick Henry and the Adamses, he did not scent the coming dangers from afar. His mind held a few clear political principles as in a vice, and when forced to deal with public affairs he applied these principles lucidly and without doubts; but so far as possible he left the alien world of government to other men. Meanwhile he turned to western land development. As early as 1770 he was planning a canal to connect the Ohio and Potomac Rivers—the great central valley of the continent and the Atlantic coast. He saw that when this was done, and the Indians were suppressed, settlement across the mountains would become easy and profitable.

As soon as Washington began to push his project for a canal he came hard against British interference. This boded ill for the Empire. It was a mistake for the rulers in London to teach this calm, stubborn Virginia farmer that his plans for the new world could not be made real so long as America was tied to the old. At first he had not taken the mother country's obstruction in the West too seriously. In 1763—the year of the proclamation which forbade settlement across the mountains—he sent his land agent into the Ohio country to buy "some of the most valuable lands in the King's part, which I think may be accomplished after a while, notwithstanding the proclamation which restrains it at present, and prohibits the settling of them at all; for I can never look upon that proclamation in any other light (but this I say between ourselves) than as a temporary expedient to quiet the minds of the Indians." But in 1774 Parliament passed the Quebec Act, closing the great triangle between the Ohio, the Lakes, and the Mississippi to all further expansion from the seaboard. The new English policy was clearly no "temporary expedient."

2

Late in 1774 Washington attended the First Continental Congress as a member of the Virginia deputation. The Congress, which met in Philadelphia, was a revolutionary body—at least, it was extra-legal, chosen and instructed by local congresses or popular conventions. It was expected to assert colonial rights and to work for liberty (in the sense of freedom from Parliamentary control), but not for independence. As we have seen, it drafted a Declaration of Rights. The following spring the Second Continental Congress, which chose Washington for Commander-in-Chief, met at Philadelphia on May 10, three weeks after the fighting had begun in Massachusetts. Almost fourteen months were still to pass before the Congress adopted the Declaration of Independence.

Washington was forty-three when he became Commander-in-Chief. He was six feet three inches tall, lean, muscular, with a square jaw and strong hands. He had large features, gray-blue eyes, and his lips closed hard, giving his face a stern expression. Since he was not interested in political maneuvers, he may not have foreseen the calculations that led John Adams to back him for the chief military post. He may have thought the job should go to the man of most experience; but Adams knew better. The Revolution up to this point had been largely the work of New Englanders, and Adams knew there would never be strong Southern support for a war waged under a New England general. Massachusetts would accept a Virginian because Massachusetts was already committed to fighting; but Virginia was not. Also, the Commander-in-Chief ought to be a rich man. New York had quaintly instructed her delegates that the general must be a man of fortune in order that "he may rather communicate luster to his dignities than receive it, and that his country, in his property, his kindred and connections, may have some pledge that he will faithfully perform the duties of his office." There were few rich Southerners who had had even as much fighting experience as Washington, and there was no one else in all the colonies with his quiet massive capacity to create confidence and to add dignity to a cause. In managing the appointment of Washington, Adams did the first of his many great deeds for America.

The question of Washington's military capacities may never be settled, for his was not a strictly military task. It may be true that he neglected his cavalry and made inadequate use of artillery support; but he seldom had an army with which he could oppose the enemy in decisive battle, and he never had a united country behind him. His job was to keep an army of some sort in the field and wait for the English to lose the war. This the English did, though at times it seemed impossible.

The active rebels in the colonies were probably not more than a third of the white population of two and a half millions. There were seven hundred thousand men between the ages of eighteen and sixty, yet Washington seldom had more than twelve thousand regular troops under his command. Even counting the state militia there were only 90,000 troops in 1776, and 45,000 in 1779.* Washington's regard for the militia was never warm. "The militia," he wrote, "come in you cannot tell how, go out you cannot tell when; consume your provisions, exhaust your stores, and leave you at last in a critical moment." He seems to have agreed with Dryden:

> The country rings around with loud alarms,
> And raw in fields the rude militia swarms;

* In the course of the war another 90,000 men found service at sea, mostly in privateers. Cp. Jameson, *The American Revolution Considered as a Social Movement*, p. 103.

> Mouths without hands; maintained at vast expense,
> In peace a charge, in war a weak defence;
> Stout once a month they march, a blust'ring band,
> And ever, but in times of need, at hand.

The shortage of arms, ammunition, clothes, food, medicine, further reduced the effectiveness of the little army. In the summer of 1776 nearly a quarter of the troops had no arms. "If we should fail at last," wrote the hot-tempered Timothy Pickering in 1778, "the Americans can blame only their own negligence, avarice, and want of almost every public virtue." This seemed a reasonable comment on the military conduct of the rebels; yet in civil affairs they were planning soberly for the future, showing a restraint and a faith in constitutional law which is unusual in the midst of revolution.

Throughout the war the loyalists were overconfident, feeling that they need not exert themselves unduly since the British Army and Navy could be trusted to put down this rioting. Yet Professor Van Tyne estimates that fifty thousand loyalists served at one time or another with the British forces. Under such conditions, even if his military knowledge was faulty, Washington was the one man who could conquer the political chaos. Without his character and example the American Army would have dwindled into a mob and the English could have found no way of failing.

One reason they did manage to fail was Lord George Germaine, the Secretary of State for War. Having disgraced himself at the battle of Minden under the name of Lord George Sackville, he had been tried and dismissed from the army as "unfit to serve his Majesty in any military capacity whatsoever." An English historian describes him as follows:

> Two figures in this war occupy a unique position: Washington, because it has never been possible to praise him beyond his merits; Germaine, for the reason that no blame has ever done justice to his incompetency. A nation can only expect humiliation when, regardless of its interest and its honor, it entrusts its War Office to a soldier of battered reputation, incapable of transacting the simplest business with industry and despatch.[1]

A second reason for failure was that the brothers Howe (one an admiral and one a general) were put in charge of operations. There was a small but active group in England, to which the Howes belonged, which saw the war as part of a struggle against ministerial autocracy which affected both countries.* This was a reasonable view; but it was scarcely reasonable

---

* Ironically, these friends of America may have contributed to the difficulty of raising troops in England, and thus to the decision to hire Hessian mercenaries—a decision which did more to embitter American opinion than any other episode in the war.

to ask men holding such opinions to take charge of the fighting. When the loyalists in America wished to fit out privateers to attack the privateers of the rebels, Admiral Howe indignantly asked, "Will you never have done oppressing these poor people?" And when General Howe, in 1776, had Washington's whole army at his mercy in New York, he allowed it to escape with its wounded, its stores, and its artillery—apparently from a family distaste for "oppressing these poor people." The American General Putnam, who was present, wrote to the Governor of Connecticut: "General Howe is either our friend or no general." After the subsequent retreat across New Jersey Washington commented, "Nothing was more easy to them, with a little enterprise and energy, than to dissipate the remaining force which still kept alive our expiring opposition."

It seems fair to assume that the British strategy of unco-ordinated nibbling was based on the belief that the rebel armies must sooner or later collapse from weariness, or from hunger, or from general discouragement over the increasing chaos and the pro-British behavior of the loyalists. Washington's character alone prevented the collapse. So again we come back to Washington. No amount of sloth or bad planning could have lost the war unless there had been an American army by whom, from time to time, the British could get themselves beaten. And Washington alone was responsible for this army—that is, for the nucleus of regular troops without which nothing could have been accomplished. How he kept his troops in the field is one of the puzzles of history. They were unpaid, except for almost worthless paper and promises of distant land in a distant future. They were never properly clothed and were at times shoeless. They were badly fed, and often they were faced with the discouraging knowledge that the farmers in the country where they camped resented selling them food in exchange for their paper money, preferring to sell it to the English for real cash.

Washington's proud self-confidence must have helped him to maintain the war almost single-handed. Although he painted conditions in dark colors to Congress (since the facts admitted of no other colors), he seems to have found it incredible that the cause he represented could fail. During the fierce winter of 1777–78, when the remnant of his army was at Valley Forge and it looked as if the rebellion was being starved and frozen into defeat, Washington wrote to his stepson: "Lands are permanent—rising fast in value—and will be very dear when our independency is established."

3

In 1777 Congress approved a plan for a confederacy, known as the Articles of Confederation. The plan had to be ratified by all the states before it could take effect, and this was not done until 1781. Since the Articles of Confederation said that "each state retains its sovereignty, freedom and independence, and every power, jurisdiction, and right which is not by this confederation expressly delegated to the united states in Congress assembled," the new government seemed to proclaim itself a league of nations. Yet the Articles provided for a court of justice with the right to settle disputes between the states; so if the Union was in fact a mere league the court was a form of international tribunal.

The sole agency of government, under the articles, was Congress. Each state was to appoint from two to seven delegates annually; but each state, regardless of size or population, was to have one vote, as in a conference of ambassadors, and unanimous consent was needed for an amendment. The Congress had no direct authority over the citizens of the states, and could only petition the states for money, could only request them to carry out the provisions of the treaties it might make with foreign powers. On the other hand, Congress had authority to make war and peace, borrow money on the credit of the United States, establish a post office, and raise and equip an army and navy. It is little wonder that foreign nations did not know whether they were dealing with a government or with a wartime alliance. Madison himself defined the Confederation as "nothing more than a treaty of amity of commerce and of alliance, between independent and sovereign states."

The Confederation of 1781, however, is the first chapter in the history of the United States Government, and a vital chapter if that history is to be understood. The Articles, which were debated and drafted by Congress during 1776 and 1777, were the work of the radical democrats. They were a part of the people's revolution, of the egalitarian movement which accompanied the break with England. The men who wrote the Articles believed that the democracy of their desire was impossible under a strong government ruling a large area. They thought that only local government could be democratic. They disliked the Empire because they disliked far-off control. They were fighting for home rule, and they were not prepared to grant to a central power within America the authority which they were in the act of snatching from Parliament.

They were confident that weak local governments, with state sovereignty, would breed a simple agrarian democracy. Most of the people in the colonies were farmers, who could control their local governments, but who would be lost and helpless at the seat of a national government with its elaborate financial machinery and its executive organization wherein business or legal training are an asset. Centralization, thought the radicals, meant the rule of the rich, decentralization the rule of the plain people.

In all this they may have been right. They were certainly in agreement with Jefferson, the author of the Declaration of Independence. They were steadily opposed by the conservatives, who wanted a government which would create a stable money and pay its debts, which would enforce contracts and treaties, and which would operate directly upon the citizens and not merely upon the states. As the conservatives well knew, a citizen can be arrested, tried, and made to obey; but nothing can be done to a state, short of war. Yet the conservatives were voted down and the radicals won the constitution of their hopes. As they foresaw, it led to the creation of agrarian democracies; but the agrarian democracies, loosely united in an ambassadorial congress, did not prove capable of governing the country, or even of preserving its freedom. As a result, the conservatives in 1787 were able to remake the form of government.

Two main questions were raised during the writing of the Articles. The first was the question of sovereignty: Should it reside in Congress or in the states? As we have seen, the radicals had their way and sovereignty was reserved to the states. The Articles were so positive on this point that Professor Jensen can write: "According to the constitution which united the thirteen states from 1781 to 1789, the several states were *de facto* and *de jure* sovereign. No partisan treatises were able to eliminate that fact."[2] Yet as early as 1785 James Wilson, the conservative Scot who had settled in America and become a leader in politics and law, was arguing that the Continental Congress had powers before there was a Confederation and that the states were therefore never sovereign. The states, according to this view, did not evolve out of the colonial governments until the Continental Congress had first suggested a procedure and then declared independence.* This was the view of Abraham Lincoln, who said in a special message to Congress in 1861, "The Union is older than the states, and in fact created them as states." If the Union is older than the states, then the oft-repeated arguments for secession are illogical; but if the states are older than the Union, and created the Union by a compact among themselves, then it would seem that the states have a right to secede. Unhappily, it was not a question which could be settled by reason, so in the end it was settled by war.

The second main question raised during the writing of the Articles has not been settled at all. Even if the states were sovereign, it was admitted

---

* Yet New Hampshire, South Carolina, Virginia, and New Jersey had drawn up state constitutions before the Declaration of Independence.

that some central authority was needed, with delegated powers. But what powers should be delegated? What powers are properly "national," and what are "local"? The radicals triumphed in the Confederation, and the Congress was given the minimum of powers. Yet from that day to this, and seemingly inevitably, there has been a movement toward centralization. The first and perhaps the longest step was taken in 1787. "The Articles of Confederation were designed to prevent the central government from infringing upon the rights of the states, whereas the Constitution of 1787 was designed as a check upon the power of the states and the democracy that found expression within their bounds."[3] Yet the change could not have been avoided if America was to remain free. Thirteen weak little democracies would have been reabsorbed by Europe.

The same sense of inevitability accompanies all the moves toward centralization which we shall review in this book. Always the centralization is resisted, in the name of freedom, by some of the wisest men of the time. Always it is unpopular with many of the citizens, perhaps with a majority. And always it seems to be unavoidable, if the nation's business is to be done and the nation's interest served. The decentralizing democrats had their chance under the Articles of Confederation. They had written the constitution they wanted, and it was a good constitution for their purposes; but their purposes were not adequate in a world of power and cruelty and greed.

4

The Confederation was by no means a total failure. It could not govern but it could think, and during its brief years of life it developed a policy for the Western lands which has been a boon to America and which determined the political development of large parts of the country.

Before the war seven of the colonies had western land claims, many of which overlapped.* By 1786 a number of the claims had been ceded to the Confederation, and it seemed obvious that in the end they would all be ceded. How was this empire of land to be governed? How was it to be settled? What was to be its political future? The answer to these questions would decide whether America must repeat the pattern of all previous empires, or whether she could devise a colonial system which would satisfy the colonists. In 1787 the Congress of the Confederation passed "An Ordinance for the government of the Territory of the United States northwest of the River Ohio." The territory was organized as a district and ruled by a governor appointed by Congress. When the territory should contain five thousand free male inhabitants of voting age it

* Between them they claimed all the British lands from the Allegheny Mountains to the Mississippi River.

could elect a legislature and send a non-voting delegate to Congress. In the course of time, no more than five or less than three new states were to be formed from the territory, and whenever one of these states had sixty thousand free inhabitants it was to be admitted to the Union "on an equal footing with the original states in all respects whatever." This momentous law established the colonial policy which made it possible for America to expand to the Pacific, and to forty-eight states, as a national community rather than as a mother country plus a set of dependencies.* It meant that the thirteen original states would soon be a minority, and that the time would come when the new members of the Union could make national policy.

Meanwhile the weakness of the Confederation, combined with a postwar depression and a devalued paper currency, led to a state of near anarchy in parts of the country. Where debtors gained control of the state legislature, as in Rhode Island, they passed laws insisting that creditors accept worthless paper at its face value. Where commercial interests were in control, as in Massachusetts, the desperate farmers banded together to prevent the county courts from sitting, since the only alternative they could see was debtors' prison and the loss of their lands. Men of property, and men with a feeling for order and authority in government, were either longing vainly for the good old days or planning for a reformation before the country foundered and proved itself unworthy of independence. It was in these circumstances that Washington was induced to emerge from the retirement into which he had gone so thankfully in 1783, and to become the guarantor of a moderate counter-revolution.

It was, significantly, an interference with his plans for western land development that caused Washington to take action in support of the Federalists (as the proposers of a strong central government came to be called). In 1784, a year after resigning his commission as Commander-in-Chief, Washington set out on a trip through the Ohio and Kanawha river country to look into the condition of his own lands and to find the best trade routes from the Ohio basin to the East. He went no farther than to George's Creek, near the mouth of the Cheat River in western Pennsylvania; but the trip convinced him of what he had long believed, that the whole country west of Virginia, between the mountains and the Mississippi, would be open to development the moment the Ohio River was connected by canal with the Potomac and the James. If some such connection were not made the western country would soon attract settlers

---

* The statement applies to the political development of the nation, not to the economic. As will be seen below, many of the economic mistakes of earlier empires were repeated in the United States. The economic colonialism later imposed upon the South and West by the money power of the East is reminiscent of eighteenth-century mercantilism. It forms one of the chief problems of American history from the eighteen-thirties to the present.

CANADA

(In dispute with Great Britain)

Quebec

Montreal

SHB

Lake Ontario

NORTHWEST

Claimed by Virginia to 1784
By Mass. to 1785

Claimed by Va. to 1784
" " Conn. to 1786

Lake Erie
Western Reserve

Mass. N.Y. claims adjusted 1786

Claimed by Mass. and N.Y. (Adjusted 1791)

V.T. 1791

(MASS.)

N.H

N.Y.

MASS.

CONN.

R.I.

TERRITORY
Organized in 1787
Claimed by Va. to 1784

Claimed by New York to 1781

PENNSYLVANIA

N.J.

MD.

Ohio R.

DISTRICT
OF KENTUCKY
Claimed by Virginia until
admitted as state 1792

VIRGINIA

LOUISIANA
(Ceded by Spain to France 1800)

TERRITORY SOUTH
OF THE OHIO
N. Carolina claims ceded 1790

NORTH CAROLINA

S. Carolina claims ceded 1787

Claimed by Georgia
until 1802, added to
MISSISSIPPI TERR.
1804

SOUTH
CAROLINA

Claimed by Spain to 1795
Organized as MISSISSIPPI
TERRITORY 1798

GEORGIA

West Florida

EAST

FLORIDA

Atlantic Ocean

Claims of the States to Western Lands
1783 — 1802

anyway (indeed, it was already doing so); but with no outlet to the east the settlers would be compelled to use the Mississippi for their trade route. The mouth of the Mississippi, as well as the whole right bank, was in the hands of Spain. Washington foresaw the menace to his national hopes if the time came, as it soon might, when Spain could offer the Westerners trade and prosperity whereas the young United States could not.

The first step toward Washington's cherished canal scheme was to secure the co-operation of Virginia and Maryland. The Potomac River was the boundary between these "sovereign" states, and trade on the river and in Chesapeake Bay could never run freely until the states agreed on duty-charges and other commercial regulations. In 1785, delegates from the two states met at Mount Vernon and an agreement was reached. This meeting led to an effort (at the Annapolis convention of 1786) to establish similar agreements between all the states of the Confederation, many of which had proved their sovereignty by erecting trade barriers against their neighbors. Only five states were represented at Annapolis, so the delegates took no action except to recommend that a larger convention be held the following year. The suggestion was endorsed by the Congress of the Confederation, and in May, 1787, there assembled at Philadelphia the convention which devised the present Constitution of the United States. Sixty-five delegates had been chosen by the legislatures of twelve states, and fifty-five attended. George Washington was made presiding officer. The convention soon agreed to ignore its instructions, which were to revise the Articles of Confederation, and to produce a wholly new document. This was a revolutionary act, done in the name of conservatism.

The question then arose, How would the document be ratified? Whence would it derive authority? Some wished to refer it to the legislatures of the states; but George Mason of Virginia convinced the delegates that the people alone, through state conventions, had the authority to accept or reject such momentous proposals. The legislatures, he said, "are the mere creatures of their state Constitutions, and cannot be greater than their creators. . . . Whither then must we resort? To the people with whom all power remains that has not been given up in the Constitutions derived from them." Chief Justice John Marshall of the Supreme Court was later to make telling use of this "resort to the people."

"There is nothing more common," said Dr. Benjamin Rush of Philadelphia* in January, 1787,

> than to confound the terms of the American revolution with those of the late American war. The American war is over: but that is far from

* Physician, philosopher, signer of the Declaration of Independence, friend of John Adams and other leading conservatives.

being the case with the American revolution. On the contrary, nothing but the first act of the great drama is closed. It remains yet to establish and perfect our new forms of government; and to prepare the principles, morals, and manners of our citizens, for these forms of government, after they are established and brought to perfection.

This was the mood in which the Convention met. The early course of the American Revolution had been displeasing to most of the delegates, and they meant to redirect it, to "establish and perfect" a new government, and to induce the people to consent. Their success is one of the marvels of history. It was strange enough that they should come to agree with one another; but that they should bring the nation to accept the results of their arguments and their compromises was a masterpiece of persuasion.

As Bryce points out,

the Convention met at the most fortunate moment of American history. . . . Had it been attempted four years earlier or four years later . . . it must have failed. In 1783 the people, flushed with their victory over England, were full of confidence in themselves and in liberty, persuaded that the world was at their feet, disposed to think all authority tyranny. In 1791 their fervid sympathy with the Revolution in France had not yet been damped by the excesses of the Terror nor alienated by the insolence of the French government and its diplomatic agents in America. But in 1787 the first reaction from the War of Independence had set in. Wise men had come to discern the weak side of popular government; and the people themselves were in a comparatively humble and teachable mind. Before the next wave of democratic enthusiasm swept over the country the organization of a national government under the Constitution was in all its main features complete.[4]

5

It was inevitable that Washington, having presided over the Convention, should be asked to take the chief part in the new government. It was inevitable that he should fear the call to active politics, and be filled with misgivings, but that his sense of duty should force him to accept.

Ever since the close of the war with England Washington had wanted a stronger Union. In 1783 he wrote to Hamilton, "It is clearly my opinion, unless Congress have powers competent to all general purposes, that the distresses we have encountered, the expense we have incurred, and the blood we have spilt, will avail us nothing." And shortly before the Convention met in 1787 he said, "I do not conceive we can exist long as a nation without having lodged somewhere a power, which will pervade the whole Union in as energetic a manner as the authority of the state governments extends over the several states." This puts both the convention's problem, and the answer, as succinctly as possible. Washington could not refuse to serve the Constitution he had done so much to bring into being. He had insisted that the Articles of Confederation give way to a stronger government; the people had a right to insist that the stronger government be headed by Washington.

Yet we may feel sure that on the April morning of 1789 when he took the oath of office as President of the United States, on a balcony overlooking Wall Street in New York City, he regretted that he had once more been compelled to leave his agricultural experiments at Mount Vernon and to become the leader of his country.

III

The Constitution: Written and Unwritten

Washington would not have found it easy to describe the duties of the office he had accepted. While presiding over the Constitutional Convention at Philadelphia he had listened with his usual care to many long debates on the subject; but the debaters themselves were uncertain. The wisest of them admitted that the nature of the new government would be largely determined by the men who took part in it and by the spirit of the country. In this they were more right than they suspected; for even when they thought they knew exactly what type of government they were building, time was often to prove that they were building the opposite.*

They thought they were creating a government which would save the country from further excesses of democracy; they were really creating a government which would transform itself, with hardly a change in the written constitution, into a democracy more thorough than anything they foresaw in their gloomiest visions. They thought they were creating a government which would save the country from faction and from political parties; they were really creating a government which would soon prove that it could not perform its duties without the help of political parties. They thought they were creating a government which adapted to the uses of a republic the main features of the British Constitution; they were really creating a government which made forever impossible the constitutional development at that moment taking place in England.

The mood in which the constitution-makers assembled at Philadelphia is described in the fifteenth number of *The Federalist*.** Discussing the state of the Union under the Articles of Confederation, Hamilton wrote:

> We may indeed with propriety be said to have reached almost the last stage of national humiliation. There is scarcely anything that can wound the pride or degrade the character of an independent nation which we do not experience. Are there engagements to the performance of which we are held by every tie respectable among men? These are

* The Constitution of the United States, a model of brevity, is printed in full in the Appendix.

** The best contemporary gloss on the Constitution, and one of the wisest of political commentaries. Eighty-five essays by Alexander Hamilton, James Madison, and John Jay, defending the new plan of government. The essays appeared serially in 1787 and 1788, during the struggle for ratification.

the subjects of constant and unblushing violation. Do we owe debts to foreigners and to our own citizens contracted in a time of imminent peril for the preservation of our political existence? These remain without any proper or satisfactory provision for their discharge. Have we valuable territories and important posts in the possession of a foreign power which, by express stipulations, ought long since to have been surrendered? These are still retained, to the prejudice of our interests, not less than of our rights. . . . What indication is there of national disorder, poverty, and insignificance that could befall a community so peculiarly blessed with natural advantages as we are, which does not form a part of the dark catalogue of our public misfortunes?

Few of the radical leaders were present at the Philadelphia Convention. Jefferson was in Paris, as American Minister; Patrick Henry refused to attend; Samuel Adams was not chosen. The Convention consisted mostly of the friends of property and business. These men attributed much of Hamilton's "dark catalogue of public misfortunes" to the fact that democracy had been making headway among the new state governments. Professor Henry Jones Ford writes:

> That which they had feared all along, which had made them so reluc-
> tant to carry their resistance to parliamentary oppression to the point
> of declaring their independence of the British crown—the outbreak of
> democratic licentiousness—had come to pass, and they were aghast
> at the evil look of the times. They met behind closed doors and could
> talk freely. Roger Sherman, a signer of the Declaration of Independ-
> ence, and a man of the humblest origin, solemnly laid down the rule that
> "the people should have as little to do as may be with the government."
> George Mason thought "it would be as unnatural to refer the choice of
> a proper character for chief magistrate to the people, as it would be to
> refer a trial of colors to a blind man."[1]

John Adams, who was abroad during the Convention, went even further, describing democracy as "the most ignoble, unjust and detestable
form of government." Even in 1815, long after the country's drift toward
this "detestable form" had become clear, Adams was unreconciled. He
wrote to John Taylor:

> Democracy has never been and never can be so desirable as aristoc-
> racy or monarchy, but while it lasts, is more bloody than either. Re-
> member, democracy never lasts long. It soon wastes, exhausts and
> murders itself. There never was a democracy that did not commit
> suicide.*

* At times the Federalist fathers, especially John Adams, seemed to be attacking
"pure" democracy, in which all the citizens assemble together to vote and debate
as in a Greek city-state, rather than representative democracy in the modern Ameri-

This was the prevailing view of the gentry throughout the Union. Gouverneur Morris,* New York's most distinguished cynic, predicted: "give the votes to the people who have no property and they will sell them to the rich." Fisher Ames** of Massachusetts wrote: "Our country is too big for union, too sordid for patriotism, too democratic for liberty. . . . Its vice will govern it by practising upon its folly. This is ordained for democracies." And once, feeling more than usually mournful, Ames remarked that democracy, like death, is "only the dismal passport to a more dismal hereafter." Another disgruntled New England worthy, George Cabot,*** said, "I hold democracy in its natural operation to be the government of the worst." And again, "If no man in New England could vote for legislators who was not possessed in his own right of $2,000 value in land, we could do something better." Pinckney of South Carolina advocated a property qualification of $100,000 for the president, of $50,000 for justices of the Supreme Court, and of a proportionate sum for mem-

can sense. Their worst animadversions, nevertheless, and their gloomiest predictions, were called forth by the election of Jefferson in 1800, so it seems fair to say that they feared democracy in any form. When it was pointed out to Fisher Ames that Jefferson was behaving mildly in the White House, he refused to take comfort—on the ground that if Jefferson continued to behave well he would be displaced by men more terrible than himself. "Brissot," said Ames, "will fall by the hand of Danton, and he will be supplanted by Robespierre." Yet for all their anti-democratic talk these men made and administered a government which gave the people wide power.

* The charming and talented Morris was lord of the great manor at Morrisania. He had more to say than any other delegate at the Philadelphia Convention, and took the most conservative view of all. He served as Minister to France for a time under President Washington, and then briefly as senator from New York. Like many conservatives, he became embittered against his country during the long rule of the Jeffersonians after 1801.

** Son of the famous almanac-maker, innkeeper, and physician of Dedham, Massachusetts. Educated at Harvard, he became one of the most widely read and interesting men in public life. He went to Congress in 1789, defeating Samuel Adams. He was an ardent Hamiltonian, and a strong anti-democrat; he was also the greatest orator of his day. When Washington retired from the presidency, Ames refused re-election and left public life. He later refused the presidency of Harvard College. After the election of Jefferson, he became another victim of the anti-democratic rage, convinced that his country was doomed: first to anarchy, and then to despotism. "Our days," he wrote, "are made heavy with the pressure of anxiety, and our nights restless with visions of horror."

*** "George Cabot," wrote John C. Hamilton, "was one of those rare men, who, without ambition, without effort, almost without the consciousness of admitted superiority, control, and become the oracles of communities." (*History of the Republic,* quoted by Samuel Eliot Morison in his article on Cabot in the *Dictionary of American Biography.*) At the age of eighteen, having left Harvard to escape admonition for "idle behavior," Cabot was skipper of a schooner carrying codfish from Beverley, Massachusetts, to Bilbao. Fifteen years later, in 1785, he was a rich man, ready to retire from business and to devote his life to idle behavior and to politics. In 1791 he became Senator from Massachusetts; but his important role in public affairs was as the elder statesman of the Essex Junto: the group which might have started a secession movement in New England if it had not been for the lethargy and caution of George Cabot.

bers of the Congress. And he said that the election of Representatives by popular vote was theoretical nonsense that would bring the councils of the United States into contempt. While discussing the subject of suffrage in the Convention, Madison stated:

> The Freeholders of the country would be the safest depositories of Republican liberty. In future times a great majority of the people will be not only without land, but any other sort of property. These will either combine under the influence of their common situation; in which case, the rights of property and the public liberty will not be secure in their hands, or, which is more probable, they will become the tools of opulence and ambition; in which case there will be equal danger on another side.

It was this relation between property and political power which filled the minds of the delegates. "Power follows property," said John Adams, and there was no one at the Convention to disagree with him.[2] It seemed clear that unless all men could have property all men should not have the vote, for the propertyless (if they one day became a majority) must either combine to oppress the minority or, in Madison's words, they must "become the tools of opulence and ambition." As we shall see, there were many who felt that America could still choose to remain an agrarian community of small farmers, turning its back upon industrialism, and could thus move safely toward a democracy of widespread ownership. It was this half-conscious assumption in many of their minds which gave them hope, in spite of their acceptance of Madison's gloomy views on the relation between property and free government.

> Those who hold and those who are without property [wrote Madison in *The Federalist*] have ever formed distinct interests in society. Those who are creditors, and those who are debtors, fall under a like discrimination. A landed interest, a manufacturing interest, a mercantile interest, a moneyed interest, with many lesser interests, grow up of necessity in civilized nations, and divide them into different classes, actuated by different sentiments and views. . . . Is a law proposed concerning private debts? It is a question to which the creditors are parties on the one side and the debtors on the other. Justice ought to hold the balance between them. Yet the parties are, and must be, themselves the judges; and the most numerous party, or, in other words, the most powerful faction must be expected to prevail. . . .
>
> It is vain to say that enlightened statesmen will be able to adjust these clashing interests, and render them all subservient to the public good. Enlightened statesmen will not always be at the helm.[3]

A selfish minority, Madison continues, may be held in check in a republic; but a selfish majority can "sacrifice to its ruling passion or interest both the public good and the rights of other citizens." How can we hope to protect "the public good and private rights" from such oppression? Not, said Madison, by moral or religious means, for these have small effect on individuals and no effect on large and greedy groups.

It will be seen that the men who made the Constitution were neither misled by optimism nor cheered by ignorance of the past. They had never heard or read of a government which worked satisfactorily, and they were not so rash as to assume they could create one. The brief bright hours of revolutionary enthusiasm were over, and men had reverted to the normal mood of the eighteenth century, which was not addicted to Songs Before Sunrise, but rather to prayers lest the sun should irrevocably set.*

2

The Convention's answer to Madison's question was twofold. The majority must be kept from oppressing the minority, first, by excluding the propertyless from any direct share in politics;** second, by distributing authority, and balancing the powers of government, so that no selfish or self-righteous party could impose its will unchecked. This was a negative plan, based on the deep American jealousy of power. It sought to avoid corruption, injustice, and the tyranny of numbers by ensuring that power must always be limited, rather than by accepting the fact of power and ensuring that it be used responsibly. In this we see the influence of America's colonial history, and of her experience with the constitutions of the several states.

By 1777 all the ex-colonies had adopted constitutions. Three had merely reaffirmed their old charters, but the rest had devised new documents. In general, the state governments preserved the outlines of the colonial governments. They were, as Professor Nevins says, "the fruit of

* Benjamin Franklin, the oldest and perhaps the wisest of the delegates, expressed the prevailing mood on the last day of the Convention: "I agree to this Constitution with all its faults, if they are such; because I think a general government necessary for us, and there is no form of government but what may be a blessing to the people if well administered; and believe farther that this is likely to be well administered for a course of years and can only end in despotism, as other forms have done before it, when the people shall become so corrupt as to need despotic government, being incapable of any other. . . . When you assemble a number of men to have the advantage of their joint wisdom, you inevitably assemble with those men all their prejudices, their passions, their errors of opinion, their local interests, and their selfish views. From such an assembly can a perfect production be expected? . . . Thus I consent, Sir, to this Constitution because I expect no better, and because I am not sure that it is not the best. The opinions I have had of its errors, I sacrifice to the public good."

** The President was to be elected indirectly; the Senators were to be chosen by the state legislatures; and the members of the House of Representatives were to be "chosen every second year by the people of the several states." In 1789, however, "the several states" allowed only a restricted group of their people to vote.

a growth which had begun when, under the King's charter, the Governor, Council, and Burgesses of Virginia met in the little Jamestown church in 1619 to hold the first representative legislature on American soil."[4] The growth, however, was distinctively American, and did not follow the constitutional change taking place in England. In America the steady struggle against the authority of the colonial governors, and the strife between the governors and the elected legislatures, seemed to confirm everything which had been written by Locke and Montesquieu about the need for the separation of powers. While England moved toward her modern Parliamentary system, which in effect annuls the separation of powers, Americans were convincing themselves that only by keeping the Executive, the Legislature, and the Judiciary in tight compartments could they hope to preserve their freedom.

The state constitutions were not written by specially elected conventions,* but by the revolutionary legislatures which were mostly in the hands of radicals. These were the men who, drafting the Articles of Confederation, had insisted that state sovereignty was the friend of freedom. Similarly, when they drafted the state constitutions, they insisted that a weak local government would benefit the masses, a strong one the aristocracy. They thought the governor should have the least possible powers and a short term, that the legislature should be elected annually, that the judges should be removable with ease. They wanted an extension of the suffrage, and fair representation for the western counties. The conservatives, on the other hand, wanted a stronger governor and a more accurate balance of powers, an independent judiciary, high property qualifications for voting and office-holding, and underrepresentation for the radical West. The conservatives were usually successful in maintaining an undemocratic suffrage and unequal electoral districts; but for the rest, half of the early constitutions were written by the radicals.

In North Carolina, for example, the governor was a shadow. He was surrounded, and hampered, by an executive council. He had no veto, could make few appointments, and could not even call the legislature in special session. And in Pennsylvania there was an executive council instead of a governor, a unicameral legislature, annual elections, and no property qualification for voting or office-holding. This headless monster of a constitution was abandoned in 1790 for one of marked conservatism.

These extremely radical constitutions fortified the delegates to the Convention at Philadelphia both in their conservatism and in their theory of divided powers. North Carolina and Pennsylvania, they believed, had shown that the legislature could not govern; yet the people, after their long jealousy of royal governors, would not accept an executive who

---

* Until Massachusetts abandoned her charter and wrote a new constitution in 1780.

could control policy; thus it seemed sensible to check and balance the departments of government according to the plans of Locke and Montesquieu. And it was agreed that the popular branch of the legislature must be checked with special care.

Edmund Randolph of Virginia told the Convention, "our chief danger rises from the democratic parts of our constitutions. It is a maxim which I hold incontrovertible, that the powers of government exercised by the people swallow up the other branches. None of the [state] constitutions have provided sufficient checks against the democracy." He added that Maryland had tried to provide a check, and that New York and Massachusetts had done still better; "but they all seem insufficient."[5]

The conservative state constitutions were carefully studied by the delegates. The brevity and clarity of New York's document were taken as a model; Maryland supplied the elaborate but vain device of an electoral college; and Massachusetts, when she abandoned her charter and accepted a new constitution in 1780, insisted on a special drafting convention and on ratification by all adult freemen—an important precedent for Philadelphia. "The American Constitution," says Bryce, "is no exception to the rule that everything which has power to win the obedience and respect of men must have its roots deep in the past, and that the more slowly every institution has grown, so much the more enduring is it likely to prove. There is little in this Constitution that is absolutely new. There is much that is as old as Magna Charta."[6]

Not only did the delegates have the British Constitution to build on, and colonial experience, and the century and a half of keen political thinking since the days of Harrington and Milton, and the Articles of Confederation, and the state constitutions, good and bad, but as a result of the argument with England between 1763 and 1775 they had seized "one principle of the English common law whose importance deserves special mention, the principle that an act done by any official person or lawmaking body in excess of his or its legal competence is simply void. Here lay the key to the difficulties which the establishment of a variety of authorities not subordinate to one another, but each supreme in its own defined sphere, necessarily involved."[7] Here lay the key to federation, to the distribution between state and central governments of an indivisible sovereignty.

The central government of the United States was not superior to the state governments; the state and the federal governments each had their share of sovereignty; each operated directly upon its citizens; each was supreme in its own field. Like many successful devices in politics, this was unreasonable. The great question which preceded the Revolution was whether federalism within an empire was possible. Great Britain said that it was not, that sovereignty cannot be divided. In logic she won the argument; but in fact she lost the empire. And the illogical American federation still rests on the faith that governments may be limited by law, that a constitution which has been accepted as "the supreme law of the land" automatically renders void any act which contravenes it. If the Constitution decrees that in certain areas the states are sovereign and in other areas the federal government, and if any act contrary to the Constitution is self-destructive, then the distribution of powers is self-preserving—so long as the Constitution is accepted. Until the people choose to exercise their right of revolution under the Declaration of Independence, or of revision under the Constitution, that document not only divides power among the three main branches of the federal government, but shares sovereignty between the central power and the states. The fact that in strict logic this is impossible may explain some of the complications of federal politics.

The Constitution-makers had their full share of the American fear that governments capable of swift, decisive action will usually act unjustly. "The less government we have the better," said Ralph Waldo Emerson, echoing Jefferson, and there has never been a time when a majority of his fellow citizens would not sign the statement. Government and oppression, government and waste, government and cumbersome folly: these are synonymous in the average American mind. Thus everything was done at Philadelphia to make government action slow, cautious, and easily checked. The delegates believed that they were sacrificing efficiency for liberty. They believed, in the words of Madison, that they were "so contriving the interior structure of the government as that its several constituent parts may, by their mutual relations, be the means of keeping each other in their proper places." Yet in fact they were contriving a government with a perilously weak legislature and therefore with an executive which circumstances would compel to become the agent of the democratic will. Time and the demands of democracy, and the repeated mortal dangers of the world, were to force the presidency in the direction of the oldest of political institutions: an elective kingship.*

3

The latter development would have surprised the delegates more than anything else which has happened to their handiwork; for they were

---

* George Mason of Virginia told the delegates: "We are not indeed constituting a British government, but a more dangerous monarchy, an elective one." And in the eighteen-sixties Lincoln's secretary of state said to a correspondent of *The Times* of London: "We elect a king for four years, and give him absolute power within certain limits, which after all he can interpret for himself."

confident that they had protected the executive from democratic control. Their Constitution provided that each state should appoint, in such manner as the legislature might direct, a number of electors equal to the number of Senators and Representatives to which the state was entitled in Congress. These electors were to meet in their respective states and vote by ballot for the two men they thought most suitable, "one of whom at least shall not be an inhabitant of the same state as themselves." The ballots were to be sent to the President of the Senate, opened in the presence of the two Houses, and counted. "The person having the greatest number of votes shall be President," says the Constitution, "if such number be a majority of the whole number of electors appointed." If no one had such a majority the House of Representatives, casting one vote for each state, would choose a President from the five highest on the list. If two people had a majority, and an equal number of votes, the House of Representatives would choose one of them for President.* And the Constitution adds: "After the choice of the President, the person having the greatest number of votes of the Electors shall be the Vice President. But if there should remain two or more who have equal votes, the Senate shall choose from them by ballot the Vice President."

It seemed a safe way to keep the "turbulent mob," as the people were then described, from seizing the presidency. Yet it proved a frail defense, for reasons which are easy to understand as we study the history of the next forty years, but which were unforeseen.

It was the House of Representatives which was intended to be the voice of the people, so far as the people were to have a voice. Members of the House were the only federal officers for whom the people were to vote, the Constitution providing that whoever voted for "the most numerous branch of the state legislature" might also vote for a federal Representative. In 1790, all but three states had property qualifications for the franchise, and those three states had taxpaying qualifications.** It was foreseen with dismay that these qualifications might in time be lowered and that the "mob" might one day elect the members of the House. Such a House, it was thought, would have an immense vitality and might grow

---

* It was assumed that in most cases the electors, voting blindly in their several states, would fail to give a majority to any candidate. The large states, with their numerous electoral votes, would thus have the advantage in nominating the candidates among whom the House must later choose; but the small states would come into their own in the House of Representatives, which would elect the president on the basis of one vote to each state. This was another plan which went wrong because of the rise of the party system.

** Vermont had universal suffrage; but Vermont had not yet been formally admitted as a state. Connecticut's requirements were the most original: "Maturity in years, quiet and peaceable behavior, a civil conversation, and 40 shillings freehold or £40 personal estate."

too strong; so the delegates undertook to check the legislature by a careful description of its powers. Section 8 of Article I of the Constitution contains eighteen paragraphs in which the powers assigned to Congress are defined and therefore limited. This reassured the delegates who feared too strong a House, and also the delegates who feared too strong a central government. It was, according to Professor McLaughlin,

> the most satisfying answer to the critical problem of granting adequate authority to the central government without destroying the states. . . . The states, as part of the federal system, were given substantial security by the enumeration of the powers. Combined with the principle that the Constitution is law, the designation of powers granted to the central government marks out the essentials of federalism established on a legal foundation.[8]

That was all very well as a solution to the problem of balance between the central and the state governments; but it tended to upset the balance within the federal government, tipping it in favor of the President. The delegates, with the example of the radical state constitutions before them, were afraid of a weak Executive; so Executive power was conferred in blanket form. The President was made Commander-in-Chief of the Army and Navy; he was given control of the patronage of the government;* he was required "from time to time to give to the Congress information of the state of the Union, and recommend to their consideration such measures as he shall judge necessary and expedient"; and he was given power to make treaties "by and with the advice and consent of the Senate . . . provided two thirds of the Senators present concur." Most important of all, the President was given the power to veto acts of Congress, with the provision that his veto can be overridden by a two-thirds majority of both Houses. Since the President, if impeached, can only be convicted by a majority of two thirds of the Senators present, he cannot be punished by Congress for his use of the veto. A Congress which could not override the veto could not secure a conviction. Finally, the President's oath is made to read that he will "faithfully execute the office of President of the United States." There can be little doubt that the accurate authors of the Constitution saw the difference between "executing an office" and merely "enforcing the law." Within a few years Hamilton was arguing that the Executive had plenary powers under the Constitution, except as to the few enumerated prohibitions. The President could do anything he was

* The Constitution vested the appointing power in the President, subject in many cases to the advice and consent of the Senate; but the First Congress decided that the Senate held no check on the President's power of removal. Many years later, as we shall see, this became the subject of fierce controversy; yet on the whole the decision has stood. It was inevitable, therefore, that the President should become the main source of patronage.

not forbidden; but the Congress could do nothing that was not authorized in the eighteen paragraphs.

The presidency was thus made an office of great power and independence; in the hands of strong men it has become an office of the greatest power ever exercised in a free country; but one thing it was not—an office of clearly defined relations. Nobody could tell, when Washington was inaugurated, and nobody has decided to this day, exactly what are the intended relations between the President and the Congress. As we shall see, Washington and Hamilton and John Marshall had their own theory of what the relation should be. It was probably the theory of most of the delegates, and it had the virtue of being workable; but they failed to establish it in practice. Jefferson and his friends proposed an alternative theory, which they did for a time establish. Unfortunately, it was a theory which could only work when the President was a political genius. It broke down when Jefferson retired. Finally, in the eighteen-thirties under Andrew Jackson, an entirely new type of presidency was established, unknown to the Constitution, unimagined by the Fathers, buttressed by a massive party system equally unforeseen but without which the new presidency could not function. It, too, had the defect that while it worked reasonably well in the hands of a strong man it scarcely worked at all when the president was weak. And as Madison pointed out, "enlightened statesmen will not always be at the helm."

4

The delegates at Philadelphia felt they could safely leave a number of important questions unanswered in the written document because they themselves would be members of the new government, and because Washington would be the first President. According to Charles A. Beard, "four fifths of the active, forceful leaders of the Convention helped to realize as a process of government the paper constitution they had drafted."[9]

It is fortunate, in view of their experience, wisdom and freedom from illusions, that so many of the men of Philadelphia were on hand at New York when the government was born. Their presence, however, made inevitable the destruction of one of their major hopes: that America would be governed without political parties. For there was another group at New York, a pressing and articulate group which had been virtually unrepresented at Philadelphia, and which took a different view of the Constitution from that of the men who had written it. This is the group of which Jefferson was to become the leader. It was largely composed of the men who had backed the Articles of Confederation, and who were sorry to see them abandoned.

Henry Adams has summarized the views of this dissenting group as follows:

> At the bottom of its theories lay, as a foundation, the historical fact that political power had, in all experience, tended to grow at the expense of human liberty. Every government tended towards despotism; contained somewhere a supreme, irresponsible, self-defined power called sovereignty, which held human rights, if human rights there were, at its mercy. Americans believed that the liberties of this continent depended on fixing a barrier against this supreme central power called national sovereignty, which, if left to grow unresisted, would repeat here all the miserable experiences of Europe, and, falling into the grasp of some group of men, would be the center of a military tyranny; that, to resist the growth of this power, it was necessary to withhold authority from the government, and to administer it with the utmost economy, because extravagance generates corruption, and corruption generates despotism; that the Executive must be held in check; the popular branch of the Legislature strengthened, the Judiciary curbed, and the general powers of government strictly construed; but, above all, the States must be supported in exercising all their reserved rights, because, in the last resort, the States alone could make head against a central sovereign at Washington. These principles implied a policy of peace abroad and of loose ties at home, leaned rather toward a confederation than toward a consolidated union, and placed the good of the human race before the glory of a mere nationality.[10]

This was the philosophy of government of the men who wrote the "radical" state constitutions and who lamented the passing of the old Confederation. It would be difficult to find a theory more sharply opposed to that of George Washington, John Marshall, Alexander Hamilton, and the majority of the delegates at Philadelphia. Yet it was consistent with the words of the Constitution, and it made such an appeal to the American heart that it was soon to be given a trial at the demand of the people. Indeed, it has never been relinquished as an ideal and a hope. It was perhaps unfortunate for the theory, with its emphasis on "loose ties" and "a policy of peace," that it was first tested during the Napoleonic wars; but it might not have survived at any time in this stormy world, for a government which insists that its duty is to be weak is likely to find itself incapable of governing. It was not Jefferson's fault that he was obliged as President either to abandon the national interest, which he would not do, or to use powers more autocratic than any which he had decried in his predecessors.

The other theory, the theory of most of the delegates and of *The Federalist*, was that man can be protected from despotism and the suppression of his rights, not by denying power to government but by enforcing constitutional controls.

In the twenty-eighth number of *The Federalist* Hamilton dealt as follows with the question whether government should be allowed to maintain an army in time of peace:

> Independent of all other reasonings upon the subject, it is a full answer to those who require a more peremptory provision against military establishments in time of peace, to say that the whole powers of the proposed government is to be in the hands of the representatives of the people. This is the essential, and, after all, only efficacious security for the rights and privileges of the people, which is attainable in civil society.

The Jeffersonians did not feel it was an "efficacious security." They wanted to have the "whole powers" of government in the hands of the representatives of the people; but they also wanted to have the "whole powers" so unpowerful that they could not be distorted into tyranny even if the representatives were willing.

Government, replied Hamilton, must be strong, and the people must be protected against government by due process of law rather than by a denial of necessary powers. In the fifty-first number of *The Federalist* either Hamilton or Madison* wrote: "In framing a government which is to be administered by men over men, the great difficulty lies in this: you must first enable the government to control the governed, and in the next place, oblige it to control itself." Hamilton and his friends, who were soon to become a political party, put the emphasis on the first part of the difficulty: enabling the government to control the governed. They believed that the quickest route to tyranny was a government incompetent to forward the public business.** Jefferson and his friends, who were soon to become the opposition party, put the emphasis on the need to compel government to control itself. They were so impressed by the tendency of power to breed corruption that they were prepared to risk inefficiency, and even disunion, rather than to permit a concentration of power in the hands of the rulers.

The form of corruption they most feared was the unjust use of the powers of government to help commerce and industry and finance at the expense of agriculture. For the most part, the interests of the Jeffersonians lay in the land, of the Hamiltonians in the cities. An economy of factories and shipping lines and commercial paper needs the support of government more than an economy of land and horses and crossroads blacksmith shops. The former wants a strong government to enforce contracts; the latter prefers a weak government which will let it alone.

The American people have usually followed Jefferson in their hearts,

* This is one of several numbers of *The Federalist* whose authorship is in dispute.
** "The public business must, in some way or other, go forward." (*The Federalist*, no. 22.)

but they have often followed Hamilton in their deeds; for the hard fact
remains that "the public business must go forward." The tendency of all
governments is to grow stronger, because in each new crisis new powers
seem needed for the emergency. They are more easily given than withdrawn.

5

Jefferson and Hamilton: each a luminous representative of his own view
of life; each essential for the health of the republic; and each forever
opposed to the other. It is doubtful if in all their lives they could have
found one point of agreement, except the need for American independence. They were such perfect opposites that to this day most Americans
make a cult of the one or the other; few are able to do justice to both.

The fact that Washington put these two men into his Cabinet shows the
strength of feeling against political parties. It was thought to be the duty
of every man to serve the government and to refrain from faction. Hamilton and Jefferson might as well have been asked to refrain from breathing.
Each thought that the other would destroy the Constitution and drag
down the country; in honor, each was compelled to say so and to act
accordingly.

Jefferson was the first great American to apply the optimism of the
natural-rights philosophy: optimism as to man's nature, as to his future,
as to the inevitability of progress, and therefore as to the help man would
need from the institutions of society. He might have subscribed without a
qualm to the hopefulness of Shelley:

> The world's great age begins anew,
> The golden years return,
> The earth doth like a snake renew
> Her winter weeds outworn:
> Heaven smiles, and faiths and empires gleam
> Like wrecks of a dissolving dream.

It is no censure of Jefferson to say that he held these views. For a hundred
years his faith seemed to be justified, and it was fortunate for America
that in her youth she had a leader to give wings of words to the faith. It
was also fortunate that she had another leader who took a more somber
position. Hamilton wrote: "Have we not already seen enough of the
fallacy and extravagance of those idle theories which have amused us
with promises of an exemption from the imperfections, weaknesses, and
evils incident to society in every shape?" And in the same essay he warned
that it would be dangerous "to forget that men are ambitious, vindictive,

and rapacious."[11] If Hamilton had wished to give thanks in verse for the death of the old age, and to salute the new, he would have chosen the careful language of the seventeenth century:

> All, all of a piece throughout:
> Thy Chase had a Beast in View;
> Thy Wars brought nothing about;
> Thy Lovers were all untrue.
> 'Tis well an Old Age is out,
> And time to begin a New.

He would have added that the new age would soon be as disheartening as the old unless man built strong institutions to curb his ambition, vindictiveness, and rapacity.

There could be no compromise between those who felt that man need only be freed from restraint in order to move toward perfection, and those who felt that the wisest and most unchallengeable restraints could barely save man from wasting all that the painful ages had built. Looking into the future, the Jeffersonians feared the corruption of power; the Hamiltonians feared the corruption of human nature. The first believed that if man could be saved from tyranny he would take care of himself; the second believed that if man could be saved from himself a great society would arise in America. The first were necessarily for a frugal government, which would do as little as possible; the second were necessarily for an active, creative government, which would bend events to the purpose of the wise rulers.*

The spirit of America, the hope and faith in man that put zest into building a new world in a wilderness, were given by Jefferson and his followers; the economic core of America, the hard sense and the toughness, were given by the Hamiltonians. Without the commercial and industrial competence of the latter, and the financial daring, America would not have been able to grow and prosper; without the spirit and the optimism of the former, she might not have cared to do so. Since both are necessary neither is unworthy, and neither should be described as better or worse than the other. Dryden is not better than Shelley; the Romantic Revival is not better than the Restoration. Both are needed in the life of a great people; but each is likely to speak unkindly of the other.

* In 1773 and 1774, when Hamilton was sixteen and seventeen, he kept a volume of "school exercises" in which he copied his favorite passages from the books he was reading. From the *First Philippic* of Demosthenes he copied the following: "As a general marches at the head of his troops, so ought the politicians . . . to march at the head of affairs; insomuch that they ought not to wait the *event,* to know what measures to take; but the measures which they have taken, ought to produce the *event.*" It would be hard to find a clearer statement of the theory of government which Hamilton followed and which Jefferson hated.

6

Just as the exact powers of the Executive were left vague in the Constitution, so were the exact powers of the Judiciary. Article III, Section 1, reads: "The judicial power of the United States, shall be vested in one supreme Court, and in such inferior Courts as the Congress may from time to time ordain and establish. . . ." Section 2 reads: "The judicial power shall extend to all cases, in law and equity, arising under this Constitution, the laws of the United States, and treaties made, or which shall be made, under their authority." The first question to arise was whether the Supreme Court has the power to declare acts of Congress null and void if they are found to be inconsistent with the Constitution. This power was soon assumed by the Court; yet because of the ambiguity of the written document it has always been challenged by those who are dissatisfied with a decision.

It was wise for the delegates to leave this, like so many other problems, to be settled by life rather than by words. And in this case the verdict of experience has been exactly what the delegates expected. In spite of continual complaint, the Court has exercised the power they intended it to exercise; and because of continual complaint, the Court has usually exercised the power with discretion. If the Constitution had been more precise in conferring the power, the discretion with which it has been used might have been less noteworthy.

Yet most of the strong and popular Presidents have fought the Supreme Court, and have sought either to deny or to curb its powers. It is therefore worth noting that the makers of the Constitution were clear in their own minds that the Court must have such powers. During the debates at Philadelphia, Madison said: "A law violating a constitution established by the people themselves, would be considered by the judges as null and void." Luther Martin said: "As to the constitutionality of laws, that point will come before the judges in their proper official character." There were no recorded objections to these flat statements. What else could a people believe, who had quoted Justice Coke against the Stamp Act?*

---

* In his very old age Madison stated that he had always thought the supremacy of the federal judiciary essential. Dealing with this weighty question, Professor McLaughlin (*The Foundations of American Constitutionalism,* pp. 154–55) calls attention to the second paragraph of Article 6 of the Constitution: "This Constitution, and the laws of the United States which shall be made in pursuance thereof; and all treaties made, or which shall be made, under the authority of the United States, shall be the supreme law of the land; and the judges in every state shall be bound thereby, anything in the Constitution or laws of any state to the contrary notwithstanding." This paragraph, he points out, rests on the old principle, so often argued during the days of the Revolution, that "any legislative act beyond the

While urging the Constitution upon the people of America, during the period of ratification, Hamilton wrote:

> The complete independence of the courts of justice is peculiarly essential in a limited Constitution. By a limited Constitution, I understand one which contains certain specified exceptions to the legislative authority; such, for instance, as that it shall pass no bills of attainder, no *ex-post-facto* laws, and the like. Limitations of this kind can be preserved in practice no other way than through the medium of courts of justice, whose duty it must be to declare all acts contrary to the manifest tenor of the Constitution void. Without this, all the reservations of particular rights or privileges would amount to nothing. . . .
>
> It can be of no weight to say that the courts, on the pretense of a repugnancy, may substitute their own pleasure to the constitutional intentions of the legislature. . . . The courts must declare the sense of the law; and if they should be disposed to exercise WILL instead of JUDGMENT, the consequence would be . . . the substitution of their pleasure to that of the legislative body. The observation, if it prove anything, would prove that there ought to be no judges distinct from that body.[12]

Some of the most interesting storms in American history have arisen because the people felt the courts were exercising "will" instead of "judgment." Hamilton had foreseen the danger and had decided it was unavoidable. It is implicit in the nature of a written constitution, and we shall not understand American history, or American government, unless the danger with all its implications is kept in mind.

7

In his pamphlet, *Common Sense,** Thomas Paine wrote: "Yet that we may not appear defective in earthly honors, let a day be solemnly set apart for proclaiming the charter; let it be brought forth, placed on the divine law, the work of God; let a crown be placed thereon, by which the world may know that so far as we approve of monarchy, in America the law is

---

competence of a legislative body is not law. . . . The reign of law, the fundamental principle which we have seen to be a part of the old compact-philosophy and of Puritan theology—the principle which was the basis of Revolutionary argument against the Parliament—was now made the essential principle of federalism. The states were to be held together, the Union was to be conserved, and essential harmony of the system was to be maintained, not by a new doctrine, but by the old. The courts of the states and (it would seem as a logical sequence) the courts of the Union are bound by law not to give their assent to 'acts of pretended legislation'— those words which appear in the Declaration of Independence as the groundwork of the charges against George III."

* January, 1776.

king." Paine's words are an amusing prophecy of what has happened. The American people have put the Constitution on an altar, and have worshiped it with incense and song and the sacrifice of innumerable goats.

They have worshiped it rather more diligently than they have read it. Many of them assume it is a precise document laying down a precise order of government from which no good man would care to deviate. Except for the various amendments* they assume that it stands unchanged, embodying the deathless wisdom of the Fathers. Yet it is a question whether the massive party system which was soon to develop, and which was unforeseen by the Fathers, is not more important in determining the form of government than the Constitution itself. Perhaps it is for this reason that a Harvard professor annually warns his class in Constitutional Law not to read the document, since it would only "confuse their minds."[13]

One result of the deification of the charter is that political strife in America tends to take the form of a debate as to whether or not certain powers are permitted. From Washington to Franklin Roosevelt, every strong president has been accused of seeking to overthrow the Constitution. And whenever the Supreme Court declares a popular law null and void it is attacked on the ground that a group of wicked old men are imposing their view upon the country in the name of the sacred text. The argument is not so barren as it sounds, for it makes for caution and conservatism, qualities which are perhaps essential if a country the size of the United States is to maintain both unity and free government.

Some of the attributes of the American government which are most often satirized at home and abroad can be understood and perhaps forgiven if we keep in mind the difficulty, for any political society, of being not only united and free but also huge. When a nation divides horizontally, on class lines, it runs the risk of revolution. When it divides vertically, on sectional lines, it runs the risk of secession, of breaking into pieces. All nations are threatened with the first division, which must be the primary care of any government; but only nations of a very large size are steadily threatened with the second division. In an immense country the economic interests of the sections must often clash. If the will and the self-interest of a distant majority are imposed upon a minority region, the first impulse is to withdraw from the Union. The problem of maintaining unity, in a large free country, is as constant as the problem of avoiding class strife. It can only be met by compromise, by a tenderness for minority interests even when the minority lives thousands of miles away, even when it is obstructive and tiresome, even when the majority has the legal "right" to insist on its decision.

---

* The first ten amendments, declared in force November 3, 1791, comprise the Bill of Rights. These amendments were requested by several of the states at the time of ratification.

The American political system, especially the party system, has assumed its present form largely because of the need to insure such compromise. The result is a clumsy, slow, self-thwarting system, easy to criticize but hard to improve. After bitter experience, it has solved the problem of unity and liberty over an imperial area. It has been helped until recently by America's remoteness from the world's worst strains and pressures. If it needs reform today in the way of speed and efficiency, so that the public business may go forward on time in an age when there is very little time, we should at least understand why it has grown into its present shape, and why it has proved a blessing, even if an awkward blessing.

It was the political system, the party system, which achieved these results. As we proceed down the decades it will become more and more important to distinguish between the reality of the system and the theory of the Constitution. The system makes the Constitution work. The system is abused and the Constitution is revered, just as in a limited monarchy the government is abused and the king is revered; but it is the system which we must study if we are to understand America.

IV

The First President

THERE WERE almost four million people in the United States when Washington became President; most of them were farmers, and most of the white farmers were freeholders. Among the New England States, slavery had been abolished in Massachusetts and Vermont, while in New Hampshire, Connecticut, and Rhode Island, less than ten per cent of the people were slaves. The same was true in the so-called Middle States: New York, New Jersey, and Pennsylvania. The southern boundary of Pennsylvania, which separated that state from Delaware and Maryland, was the Mason and Dixon line. It was the boundary between the farming and commercial states to the north, and the plantation states to the south. Within a few years it became the boundary between the free and the slave states.* South of the Mason and Dixon line, slaves formed from thirty to fifty per cent of the population in most of the heavily settled districts.

Although agriculture was everywhere the main occupation, trade was not negligible. Exports, during the first decade of the new government, amounted to forty-five million, and imports to fifty-five million dollars. Most of this commerce was in the hands of New England, where the climate was harsh, the soil poor, and the harbors excellent. "God performed no miracle on the New England soil," writes Samuel Eliot Morison. "He gave the sea. Stark necessity made seamen of would-be planters."[1]

The two dominant, expansive forces in American life—the Industrial Revolution and the winning of the West—had scarcely made themselves felt in 1789. It was still possible for wise men to assume that America would remain an agrarian country, taking many generations to populate the seemingly vast stretch from the mountains to the Mississippi. Only in Kentucky were there considerable settlements west of the mountains, and there the density of population ranged from two to seventeen per square mile. In the entire country there were only six cities with more than eight

---

* West of Pennsylvania, the Ohio River became the dividing line between freedom and slavery. The new states north of the line (and east of the Mississippi) were free from the time they were created. All of the old states north of the line, except New Jersey, had adopted gradual abolition by 1799. New Jersey had adopted it by 1821. The Mason and Dixon line takes its name from the two English surveyors who ran it in 1763.

thousand inhabitants; Philadelphia was the leading city, with about sixty thousand.

It was not yet certain that the white man could conquer the vast and gloomy forests of the West. It was not yet certain, if he did so, that the West would remain part of the Union, since its natural outlet (the mouth of the Mississippi) was in the hands of Spain. It was still believed by many Englishmen that Britain might break up the Union with a combination of tariff wars, navigation acts, and special concessions to discontented states. Three quarters of America's commerce was with Britain, and it was only a few years since Vermont had been negotiating for a separate return to the Empire.*

Foreign travelers were inclined to rate America's chances low, and her amenities nonexistent. They gave a depressing picture of bad roads, filthy inns, ugly houses, inefficient agriculture, and quarrelsome people. Yet there was something wrong with the picture. The plain people of America would not have known what the pessimists were talking about, and if they had known they would not have cared. Indeed, it was the self-confidence of these plain people which the foreign traveler found peculiarly irksome; for there was already at work the force (was it climate, diet, landscape, or the idea of liberty?) which was to make generations of immigrants from the worst slums and ghettos of Europe into sanguine patriots as soon as they landed and breathed the new air.

Henry Adams describes the impatient surprise of foreigners in the face of this irrational hope:

"Look at my wealth!" cried the American to his foreign visitor. "See these solid mountains of salt and iron, of lead, copper, silver, and gold! See these magnificent cities scattered broadcast to the Pacific! See my cornfields rustling and waving in the summer breeze from ocean to ocean, so far that the sun itself is not high enough to mark where the distant mountains bound my golden seas! Look at this continent of mine, fairest of created worlds, as she lies turning up to the sun's never-failing caress her broad and exuberant breasts, overflowing with milk for her hundred million children! See how she glows with youth, health, and love!" Perhaps it was not altogether unnatural that the foreigner, on being asked to see what needed centuries to produce, should have looked about him with bewilderment and indignation. "Gold! Cities! cornfields! continents! Nothing of the sort! I see nothing but tremendous wastes, where sickly men and women are dying of homesickness or are scalped by savages! mountain ranges a thousand miles long, with no means of getting to them, and nothing in them when you get there! swamps and forests choked with their own rotten ruins! nor hope of better for a thousand years! Your story is a fraud, and you are a liar and swindler!"[2]

* Vermont was still negotiating at London for recognition as an independent state.

There was something else wrong with the pessimistic picture, beyond the failure to make allowance for the New World's dazzled hope. A culture can be judged by its style more accurately than by the impressions of a tourist. In spite of the bad roads and inns and sanitation, in spite of the litter in the back yard and the stumps in the cornfield, the style of the men who built America was good. There were in fact two styles: the style of romantic republicanism, of those who saw freedom in every blue hill on the horizon; and the style of tolerant realism, of those who met at Philadelphia and who explained their plans in *The Federalist*. The style of Jefferson and John Taylor, and the style of Hamilton and John Marshall. Both styles were later to be debased by a superstitious faith in progress, which was perhaps always implicit in romantic republicanism; but it was not only in America that they were debased. In France, the home of romantic republicanism and of tolerant realism, of Rousseau and of Montesquieu, the spell of the progress-myth became so strong that Victor Hugo could write:

> Oh! L'avenir est magnifique!
> Jeunes Français, jeunes amis,
> Un siècle pur et pacifique
> S'ouvre à vos pas mieux affermis.
> Chaque jour aura sa conquête.
> Depuis la base jusqu'au faite,
> Nous verrons avec majesté,
> Comme une mer sur ses rivages,
> Monter d'étages en étages
> L'irrésistible liberté!

This was only a few years before Europe began her trek back toward blood, barbarism, slavery, and rubble. If the nineteenth century could weaken a Frenchman into such words, who can blame the lucky children of the West for thinking progress (steady, inevitable progress) a reasonable hope?

2

The first task of the new government was to set some precedents and to fill in the blank spots of the Constitution.

To begin with, what was to be done about the heads of the Executive departments: the men who have since come to be known as the President's Cabinet? Congress might have made them responsible to itself; instead, it made the Secretaries of State and of War responsible to the President alone, an example which was followed (except in regard to the Treasury Department) when new Cabinet posts were created.

Congress could not decide whether the Secretary of the Treasury was the servant of the Executive or of the Legislature. Elbridge Gerry of Massachusetts felt that the Secretary ought "to recommend general systems of finance without having anything to do with actual administration of them, because if he engages in the executive business, we shall be deprived of his talents in more important things." There was also long debate as to whether the Secretary should report in person on the floor of Congress, or whether he should send his recommendations in writing. In the end, all was left ambiguous.* The bill creating the department was amended so that instead of requiring the Secretary to "digest and report plans for the improvement and management of the revenue," it required him to "digest and prepare plans." Since nobody knew what that meant, nobody was dissatisfied—until Alexander Hamilton sought to impose his own creative interpretation on the words.

Another vital decision of the first session was the Judiciary Act of September 24, 1789. This act created a Supreme Court consisting of a chief justice and five associate justices; thirteen district courts, each with a single federal judge; and three circuit courts consisting of the district judges in the circuit plus two Supreme Court justices. The act also laid down the procedure for judicial review, and the conditions under which disputes may be taken from the state courts into the federal courts. This latter section is as essential to the federal system as the Constitution itself. "Without it, every state judiciary could put its own construction on the Constitution, laws, and treaties of the Union. With it, a case involving any of these three factors may originate either in the state or lower federal courts; but its final determination belongs to the Supreme Court of the United States."[3]

Two other precedents of great importance were established during Washington's presidency. The first concerns the Senate and its characteristic crankiness. According to the Constitution, the President has the power to make treaties, appoint foreign service officers, Supreme Court judges, and other major officers of the United States "by and with the advice and consent of the Senate." It was hoped this might lead to the use of the Senate as a privy council, thus building a bridge between the Executive and the Legislature and reassembling in practice some of the powers which had been divided in plan.

Washington tried to make such use of the Senate. For example, he entered the chamber one day and took the Vice-President's chair, saying he had come for their advice and consent regarding an Indian treaty, and that he had brought with him General Knox, the Secretary of War, who knew all about the treaty. Knox produced the papers, which were read;

* Fifty years later Congress was still debating whether the Treasury was an "executive" department.

Washington then waited for some advice or some consent. The Senate was unwilling to give either in the presence of the President and his Cabinet Minister. The feeling seemed to be that the Senators were under pressure, and that their dignity was being violated.

After delay and awkwardness, a motion was made to refer the matter to a committee. Washington "started up in a violent fret," according to Senator Maclay. "This defeats every purpose of my coming here," he said, adding that he had brought General Knox so that the Senate could learn everything that had been done, and why it had been done, and could then advise in the light of complete knowledge. He was prepared to postpone consideration, he said, but he could see no point in referring the matter to a committee. The Senate did not want information from General Knox; it wanted to be left alone to act in its own inscrutable fashion. "We waited for him to withdraw," wrote Senator Maclay. "He did so with a discontented air."*

The discontent was so extreme that Washington soon gave up trying to treat the Senate as a privy council. He did what all other Presidents have had to do: he made his treaties first and then submitted them to the Senate, to be accepted or rejected or mangled, on the basis of some knowledge or none, but at least with no infringement of the Senate's rights. This does not seem the ideal way to conduct foreign relations. The day came (May 27, 1898, during the Spanish-American War) when John Hay, Ambassador to England and Secretary of State under President McKinley, wrote to Henry Adams: "The weak point . . . is the Senate. I have told you many times that I did not believe another important treaty would ever pass the Senate. What is to be thought of a body which will not take Hawaii as a gift, and is clamoring to hold the Philippines? Yet that is the news we have today."[4]

On another occasion John Hay said that the clause requiring the concurrence of two thirds of the Senators present, for the ratification of a treaty, was the "irreparable mistake" of the Constitution. It is interesting to recall why the "mistake" was made. The authority to ratify treaties was given to the Senate, rather than to the entire Congress, in the hope of making the Senate a privy council and in the belief that the treaty-making power concerned the states rather than the people. The states had equal representation in the Senate, the people in the lower House. And ratifica-

---

* That night Senator Maclay wrote in his *Journal:* "I cannot be mistaken, the President wishes to tread on the necks of the Senate. Commitment will bring the matter to discussion, at least in the committee, where he is not present. He wishes us to see with the eyes and hear with the ears of his Secretary only. The Secretary to advance the premises, the President to draw the conclusions, and to bear down our deliberations with his personal authority and presence." This is not the attitude of a normal man, possessed of normal abilities, when approached for advice and offered all the relevant information.

tion was made subject to concurrence by two thirds of the Senators present in order to insure a minority veto over treaties. At the time the Constitution was made, one section of the country was deeply concerned to secure the right to navigate the Mississippi, and another section was deeply concerned over the right of New Englanders to their fisheries. Neither section would have accepted the Constitution if a mere majority of the states had the power to make a treaty bartering either of these interests in order to secure the other.[5] It did not seem to the Fathers that they were making an "irreparable mistake" by including this clause, and permitting a sectional veto, since it did not occur to them that the United States would develop political parties. Only when the certainty of a partisan vote is added to the possibility of a sectional vote does it become obstructive to allow each vote in the negative to carry twice the weight of each vote in the affirmative. It was this certainty which John Hay faced.

The first effort to make a working team of the Executive and the Legislature had failed. One effect of the failure was to add to the prestige of the Cabinet. Professor Ford writes:

> It was generally supposed at the time of the adoption of the Constitution that the administration would practically consist of the President and the Senate acting in conjunction. If the President had found in the Senate a congenial body of advisers, so that treaties and appointments to office would have been made in conference with it, so much of the policy of the administration would thus have been brought within the habitual purview of the Senate that the natural tendency would have been to draw in the rest likewise. The language of the Constitution would favor that tendency, while on the other hand the Constitution is altogether ignorant of the President's Cabinet, which actually became his privy council. The idea that the heads of executive departments are the personal appointees of each President, the chiefs of party administration, did not at first exist. It was assumed that their position was nonpartisan and that their tenure of office would be the same as that of other officials, which was then regarded as one of permanency during good behavior.[6]

Ford adds, in a footnote:

> This explains why neither Jefferson nor his opponents thought there was anything dishonorable in his retention of office while stirring up opposition to the policy of the administration. Jefferson continued in office from a sense of public duty for some time after he wanted to retire. The idea that by so doing he precluded himself from carrying on an agitation in support of his views of public policy did not occur to him or to his friends, even the most high-minded of them. . . . The same observations apply to Hamilton's conduct in maintaining a secret control over Adams's administration by his influence with the Cabinet officials.

The Senate had overreached itself. The Cabinet became the President's council, with the result that by 1795 Washington had decided that he would not "bring a man into any office of consequence knowingly, whose political tenets are adverse to the measures which the general government are pursuing." This became the presidential practice; but it was not Washington's view in 1789.*

The second effort to bring the Executive and the Legislature together, so that the public business might go forward, was made by Hamilton, and was defeated by the House of Representatives. During the first session Congress asked Hamilton to prepare a financial program. At the beginning of the second session Hamilton was ready to report. Ignoring the fact that the Secretary of the Treasury was authorized to "digest and prepare plans," rather than to "digest and report" them, Hamilton assumed that he would appear in person before the House to defend and explain his proposals. The House thought differently, and after a brief debate decided that the report should be made in writing. This was a momentous decision. Professor Binkley comments:

> We reach the fundamental question here involved: Shall the leadership of Congress be provided internally or shall that body frankly accept leadership from without? The agrarians, including Jefferson, who was soon to be their chieftain, were not even aware of the existence of this problem. They believed that public policies were to be evolved from the free and unrestricted discussions of the Committee of the Whole. . . . The Federalist leaders, Washington, Hamilton, Marshall, and Ames, both in word and deed, were giving expression to a more realistic and businesslike view of the necessities of the case. They would have preferred the frank and free appearance of the secretaries before the Congress in order to keep responsibility in the full light of publicity and discourage intrigue and backstair methods.[7]

The decision to exclude the Secretaries was not immediately harmful; for Hamilton, denied access to the House, met with a caucus of his Congressional supporters and persuaded them to enact his financial plan. He kept his control long enough to lay the economic foundations on which the United States have since reposed; yet his daring program soon bred an Opposition. When the Opposition became organized, the formation of national parties had begun. When the Opposition became strong enough to thwart his measures, Hamilton resigned. It did not seem worth his while to continue preparing plans which he was not allowed to defend, or even to explain to the hostile majority.

The second attempt to unite the Executive and the Legislature had

---

* At a time of mortal danger, President Franklin Roosevelt put members of the opposition party at the head of both War and Navy Departments; but there was no political controversy as to the need for national survival.

failed. As early as 1794, the House had stopped calling upon the Executive departments for help and guidance in formulating measures. For a time the Representatives floundered about in the Committee of the Whole; in 1795 they began to develop special standing committees to do the work which they would not allow to be done by the competent agencies. These committees are of such importance in determining the real (as opposed to the written) government of America that their history must be told in some detail.

The First Congress set up only one standing committee in the House of Representatives—that on elections.* The recommendations of the President and the reports from heads of departments supplied the subjects for legislation during these early years. The House of Representatives considered the recommendations and reports in Committee of the Whole. When the sense of the House became clear, a select committee was appointed to prepare the bill. This made for close relations between the House and the Administration; but the House, as we have seen, soon came to resent the closeness, feeling that it was too much influenced by the Executive.

The Third Congress had only two standing committees—elections and claims; but the Fourth Congress (meeting in December, 1795) added two more. And in 1796, when the breach between the House and the Administration was complete, the Standing Committee on Ways and Means was created to watch over the national finances. Thenceforth, the proliferation of committees was rapid. Under Jefferson and Madison, when the House was alleged to be the seat of administration, the list of standing committees grew to cover every Executive department and every function of the government (such as Indian Affairs, Foreign Affairs, etc.). Meanwhile, the appointment of these all-important committees was vested with the Speaker of the House.

The Senate, being less unwieldy and less concerned (during the early years) with originating legislation, did not appoint standing committees until 1816. Thereafter the system grew as rapidly in the Senate as it had grown in the House, with the difference that the Senate appointed its own committees in party caucus, refusing to hand this vast power to one man.

All these committees were the result of the jealous tension between Executive and Legislature. The tension was bound to develop, since the Constitution made possible a legislature with a majority hostile to the

---

* A standing committee is one appointed under standing regulations, and therefore regularly formed at the beginning of each new Congress. A select committee, appointed on a particular subject of current interest, expires with the Congress that appointed it. A joint committee, composed of members of both the House and the Senate, is appointed to iron out differences between the two Houses on a specific bill. It may also be appointed to report on policy, as in the case of the Joint Committee on Reconstruction, created by the 39th Congress in 1865.

Executive. A parliamentary government, as in England, has one large strong committee (the ministry of the day) which is backed by the majority of the legislature, and which controls all the more important business and shapes the important legislation. Such a government has no need for a mass of standing committees. But as Lord Bryce points out, when the attempt to produce an unofficial parliamentary government, in spite of the Constitution, broke down in America, there were only two courses possible: first, to create a ruling committee of the majority party which would act like a ministry; second, to "divide the unwieldy multitude into small bodies capable of dealing with particular subjects."[8] A "ruling committee" would have been hated as undemocratic and tyrannical, so the second choice had to be made.

The standing committees, unhappily, combine power with irresponsibility. A bill presented to the House, for example, will be given its first and second reading without debate and will then be referred to a committee. The committee can amend the bill, or report it favorably or adversely, or delay reporting it until too late in the session, or not report it at all. The committee's decision is usually final, although the House can move for a report at any moment, and can amend or restore the bill at its will. But the House seldom has time. Yet the committee, in theory, is simply the agent of Congress, appointed for its convenience; so the committee has no responsibility. And since the committee, being one of scores of similar committees, cannot be carefully watched by press or citizen, the public seldom knows where to attach praise or blame.

Lord Bryce comments:

> It is through these committees chiefly that the executive and legislative branches of government touch one another. Yet the contact, although the most important thing in a government, is the thing which the nation least notices, and has the scantiest means of watching.[9]

And he quotes from Woodrow Wilson's *Congressional Government:*

> Constituencies can watch and understand a few banded leaders who display plain purposes and act upon them with promptness; but they cannot watch or understand forty-odd standing committees, each of which goes its own way in doing what it can without any special regard to the pledges of either of the parties from which its membership is drawn. . . . The more power is divided, the more irresponsible it becomes. The petty character of the leadership of each committee contributes towards making its despotism sure by making its duties uninteresting.[10]

Yet the work of the Congress does go forward, and in spite of the seeming chaos with fair efficiency. And we shall see that the committee system— dilatory and irresponsible as it is—has made possible the incessant delicate compromise between regions and interests upon which the life of the huge American Commonwealth depends.

When the committees first developed, when they first set themselves up as policy-makers in rivalry with the Executive, they were viewed with a natural alarm by the supporters of the Administration. In 1797 Fisher Ames, who had refused re-election to the House and was about to retire, wrote to Hamilton:

> The efficiency of government is reduced to a minimum—the proneness of a popular body to usurpation is already advancing to its maximum; committees already are the ministers; and while the House indulges a jealousy of encroachment in its functions, which are properly deliberative, it does not perceive that these are impaired and nullified by the monopoly as well as the perversion of information by these committees.[11]

Fortunately for the life of the Republic, Ames's predictions were usually too gloomy even for the world of politics; but this time he was right. It took thirty years for the House to prove, to the people's satisfaction, that it was constitutionally incapable of making policy except at the cost of weakening the government beyond the danger point. By that time the original plans for building a working unit had been broken. Something new had to be devised. It turned out to be the most far-reaching, professional party system ever seen in a free country.

3

Since Washington did not know that the Cabinet was to become a group of party leaders responsible solely to the President, he chose in 1789 to have a representative Cabinet: representative of the geographical regions and of the main currents of political thought. General Henry Knox of Massachusetts, who had been Washington's chief of artillery, was given the War Department; Edmund Randolph, ex-Governor of Virginia, was made Attorney General; Thomas Jefferson, still Minister to France, was asked to become Secretary of State on his return home; and on the advice of Robert Morris,* Alexander Hamilton of New York was put in charge of the Treasury. Two Northerners, two Southerners; two centralizers, two believers in states' rights.

Washington sought advice as to the Treasury because that department was of prime importance during the formative days. He was doubtless pleased with the advice he received, for Hamilton had been close to him during the war and had a mind which he trusted and respected. This mar-

---

* The able finance minister of the Confederation. He financed the Revolution and the Revolution financed him.

velous youth (he was thirty-two when he became Secretary of the Treasury) was born in the island of Nevis,* in the Leeward Group of the West Indies. At the age of twelve he became a storekeeper's clerk at St. Croix. Three years later the Leeward Islands were devastated by a storm; Hamilton wrote a description which so impressed his relatives that funds were raised to send him to the mainland for an education. He spent a year at a grammar school and then entered King's College (now Columbia) in New York City. This was in 1773, two years before the outbreak of the Revolution. Hamilton was sixteen. After three years at college, where he seems to have won his mastery over the problems of government and finance (unless he learned it all as clerk in a store), he was made captain of a New York company of artillery. The next year he was appointed A.D.C. and Military Secretary to General Washington, with the rank of lieutenant colonel. He stayed with Washington until 1781, when he insisted on returning to active duty. He was in time to play a splendid part in the capture of Yorktown.

During the war Hamilton found time to marry a daughter of General Schuyler, thus securing his social position in New York, and to write a number of political pamphlets, including a memorandum to Robert Morris on the establishment of a national bank. He was twenty-six when the war ended, thirty at the time of the Philadelphia Convention and the first numbers of *The Federalist,* thirty-one when single-handed he secured the ratification of New York State for the new Constitution. This latter deed is a sign of his power over the minds of men—he never tried to assert power over their affections.

If New York failed to ratify, the federal government would collapse, for the Union would be divided into two parts, separated from each other by Hamilton's state. All the years of fighting and planning, all the work at Philadelphia, would go to waste. The states would lapse into disunity and weakness; they would probably fall one by one into the hands of foreign powers. Yet when the New York Convention met, Hamilton knew that more than two thirds of the delegates were against ratification.** Governor Clinton was also against it, a strong and stubborn politician who controlled forty-six votes, against nineteen on which Hamilton could count.

Hamilton fought every point; yet for weeks he was always beaten. He spoke for hours on end, with the force and wisdom he had shown in *The Federalist;* yet the vote stayed forty-six to nineteen. Twice the Convention voted for absolute rejection; but somehow Hamilton kept the delegates in session and kept them listening to his arguments. He told a friend, "The Convention shall never rise until the Constitution is adopted." That was easy to say; no one has ever explained how it was accomplished.

* He was of illegitimate birth.

** They did not take the foreign danger seriously; they did take seriously the danger of strong government.

Finally a few of the forty-six were won over; but Hamilton was still in a minority. His last hope lay in holding the Convention until news came of the decision of Virginia, where the immense influence of Washington was fighting against many of the state's most popular leaders. The Convention did *not* rise until word arrived that Virginia had accepted; then, after five and a half weeks of seemingly hopeless defensive fighting, Hamilton won by three votes. It was a victory of will power and persuasion on an occasion which may have decided the fate of the nation, for in retrospect one cannot see much hope of a second chance if the states had taken the wrong turning in 1788. Only a few years later they were face to face with Napoleon (more formidable than the brothers Howe and the sickly George Germaine), who had planned to rebuild the French Empire in the West, and who had therefore taken from Spain the vast lands across the Mississippi. It seems unlikely that he would have relinquished this prize to a League of quarrelsome neighbors. And if France had still held Louisiana at the time of the Congress of Vienna, it seems even more unlikely that it would have been conferred upon the universally disliked democrats across the Atlantic. Without Louisiana, where were the United States?

4

Such was the young man who set himself to build a financial system on the chaos left by the Confederation, and an economic system which would give power and permanence to the frail Union. Although he had worked harder to secure ratification than any other man, Hamilton was convinced the Constitution would not endure unless it was made stronger by interpretation, and unless it was buttressed by all the wealth and influence in the community. At the Philadelphia Convention he had said:

> One great error is that we suppose mankind more honest than they are. Our prevailing passions are ambition and interest; and it will ever be the duty of a wise government to avail itself of those passions in order to make them subservient to the public good. . . . All communities divide themselves into the few and the many. The first are the rich and well-born; the other the mass of the people. . . . Turbulent and changing, they seldom judge and determine right. Give therefore to the first class a distinct, permanent share in the Government.

This is exactly what Hamilton did, and by so doing he probably saved the Union; but it is easy to see why he did not win the hearts of the democracy.

The First Congress under the new Constitution met for its second session on January 7, 1790. On the fourteenth, the House of Representatives took up Hamilton's report, which was chiefly concerned with the support of the public credit. At the time, neither the national nor the state governments could be said to possess credit. Hamilton asked that the federal debt, foreign and domestic, should be funded at par, and that import duties and excise taxes be provided to meet interest and amortization.* Further, he asked that the war debts of the states be assumed by the federal government, in order to bind the creditors of the states to the national interest. Finally, he asked that a Bank of the United States be created, with powers similar to those of the Bank of England except that it should be allowed to establish eight branches.** By the summer of 1791 the entire program had been accomplished; United States securities, which had been almost worthless, were selling above par in London and Amsterdam.

When the bills for funding the debt came before the House of Representatives the two great partners of *The Federalist* papers began to be aligned against each other. Madison, representing a typical agrarian district in Virginia, led the opposition to parts of Hamilton's plan. It was Madison, after all, who had instructed the Constitutional Convention on the deeper facts of the relation between politics and class interest. He saw at once what Hamilton was doing; but he could not educate his followers in time.

The assumption of the national debt went through easily; but the bill for the assumption of the state debts caused a sectional division. On the face of it, the plan was unfair to the South. The federal government would assume $18,000,000 of state debt, two thirds of which was owed by the Northern states, and would then tax the whole country for interest and repayment; but this was only the superficial injustice. If the South had understood the plan more fully, it would have felt more aggrieved; for the assumption of the state debts was urged partly for honor and the public credit, and largely to build a centralized money-power. The latter is precisely what the Jeffersonians did not want; yet Jefferson became an agent in promoting the plan. He thought the minor hardship to the South, resulting from the payment of more than its share of the debt, could be remedied by bartering one favor against another. So he urged the Southerners to accept assumption in return for a promise that the new capital city would be built on the banks of the Potomac.

Later, when he had learned more about Hamiltonian finance, Jefferson

---

* In other words, the government should offer to redeem its debt, and to pay interest, not at the market price but at the price of issue. This would make a number of people rich, and well disposed to the new federal state.

** The Bank of the United States had its main office at Philadelphia. The government was its principal client. One fifth of its ten million dollars of capital was subscribed by the government—the rest by private investors. The Bank could issue notes up to the amount of its capital. It could carry on a commercial banking business but could not deal in commodities or real estate. When Congress refused to renew its charter in 1811, the Bank paid off its shareholders above par.

said the result of the Assumption Bill was "twenty millions of stock divided among the favored states and thrown in as pabulum to the stock-jobbing herd." This was a harsh description of the bargain; yet it expressed a truth.* Hamilton's economics had a political aim: to bind the moneyed classes to the central government, to persuade them that the security of their property depended on the federal rather than the state power. Accepting the doctrine of *The Federalist,* that power follows property and cannot be dissociated from it, Hamilton hoped to ensure that property would be on the side of the Union. He could do no other, since he and all his moneyed friends believed that strong central government was the one hope for America, and since it was clear that there would be no strong government if property looked to the states for support.

5

A few months after his financial plan had been accepted by Congress, Hamilton submitted to the House of Representatives his famous Report on Manufactures.** This was his plan for industry, intended to supplement his financial measures and to lead to the same end. It was an end which a growing number of representatives from rural areas had come to understand and to abhor. Hamilton did not want a quiet agrarian America slowly filling up its empty spaces; he wanted a dynamic, aggressive America, quickly exploiting its resources while offering opportunities to its more able citizens and security to all. He believed in liberty, but he did not believe in equality.*** He would have agreed with "Paddy Divver": "All men are born equal, but some of them are lucky enough to get over it."

In order to help them get over it as fast as possible, Hamilton proposed a system of duties for industry; bounties for agriculture; roads and waterways to be built or improved by the national government; generous copyright laws for inventors; inspectors of produce to ensure the highest quality

---

* There is no truth, however, in Jefferson's statement that he had been innocently misled by Hamilton. It is doubtful whether Jefferson was ever innocent; it is certain that he knew as much about politics as anyone in American history, with the possible exceptions of Abraham Lincoln and Franklin D. Roosevelt. He knew exactly what he was doing when he made the bargain with Hamilton. "In the present instance," he wrote to Monroe, "I see the necessity of yielding for this time to the cries of the creditors in certain parts of the union for the sake of the union, and to save us from the greatest of all calamities, the total extinction of our credit in Europe." While agreeing to save his country from "the greatest of all calamities," he managed to extract for his own region a very handsome plum. We shall see more of this type of innocence when we come to Jefferson's presidency.

** December, 1791.

*** At the Philadelphia Convention Hamilton said that "an inequality would exist as long as liberty existed, and that it would unavoidably result from that liberty itself."

of goods; and a national board with ample funds to promote agriculture, industry, commerce, and the arts. His program was a combination of eighteenth-century mercantilism and twentieth-century planning. His Report has been used ever since as a mine for arguments favoring tariffs and other forms of paternalism.

Since Congress had accepted the first half of Hamilton's plan, it might have done better to accept the whole and give it a fair trial; but by 1792 the Jeffersonians were strong enough to defeat this far-reaching government intervention. Hamilton thought that the government should act as the trustee for the people; the Jeffersonians thought that the more the government acted the more the people must suffer. Government interference, they said, will benefit a privileged class at the expense of the rest. Jefferson had seen the slums of Paris and London and was frightened at the thought that such afflictions might spread to his own country; Hamilton had never been abroad and was eager to make America into a larger and more prosperous England. Each represented one of the new forces, as yet scarcely understood, which were to form the nation's future; and each to his misfortune ignored the other force. Hamilton was the harbinger of the industrial and financial revolutions; but he knew nothing of the democratic way of life, the pattern of a new society, which was coming into being along the frontier. Jefferson knew and loved that life; he had grown up on the edge of the frontier; he feared the coming of factories and the "dark Satanic mills," but he did not understand them and could never control or combat them successfully. For the time being, however, he and Madison and their friends defeated Hamilton's plan for federal encouragement of business. They were less successful in suggesting an alternative, since their negative attitude became increasingly vain with the spread of industrialism and the wars of Napoleon. Yet they found a brilliant defender for their doomed cause in Jefferson's guide and friend, John Taylor of Caroline County, Virginia.

Taylor was one of the best farmers in the South. He spent most of his life on his plantation, improving the methods of agriculture and brooding over the sad state into which industry and finance were plunging his people. In 1794 he made an attack on the Hamiltonian system which gave arguments and a philosophy to the whole opposition. In 1814, when it was too late, he published his great work: *An Inquiry into the Principles and Policy of the Government of the United States*. The book had little practical effect; but the author was the soul and brains of the Southern agrarians.

John Taylor was at one with *The Federalist* on the relation between property and power. "Wealth," he said, "like suffrage, must be considerably distributed, to sustain a democratic republic; and hence, whatever draws a considerable proportion of either into a few hands, will destroy it. As power follows property, the majority must have wealth or lose power."

The Federalists agreed, concluding that the majority must lose power; Taylor concluded that the majority must have wealth. Hence his fear and detestation for large-scale industry, for finance and banking, for centralized power, for everything which supported what he called the "aristocracy of paper and privilege." The life of democracy depended on the wide distribution of "natural" property: land for the farmer, tools for the craftsman, a ship for the trader. Tariffs would destroy the farmer and deprive him of his land; big industry would destroy the crafts and make the artisan a wage slave; finance would drive the little man out of commerce. It was all true; but Taylor was unable to suggest a remedy except the repeal of the whole Hamiltonian plan. For this, it was too late; the Industrial Revolution was on the side of Hamilton, and nobody could repeal that singular event.

John Taylor's deepest rage was reserved for those who used the sacred word "property" for the new pieces of paper, the apparatus of high finance, which were destroying his "real" property. "If the fruit of labor is private property," he wrote, "can stealing this fruit from labor, also make private property? By calling the artillery property, which is playing on property, the battery is masked. Tythes and stocks, invented to take away private property, are as correctly called private property, as a guillotine could be called a head." And again, "We know death very well, when killing with one scythe, but mistake him for a deity, because he is killing with four."

What could they do about it—the agrarians who joined Jefferson in creating an Opposition? The event proved that they could do very little; yet they had to try. They felt that Hamilton's plan would turn America into an economic copy of the Old World. They saw slipping from under them what they believed to be the one solid basis for a free society. They put the blame on the use by selfish men of the too-great powers of the central government. They thought Hamilton's talk of trusteeship and enlarged opportunity nothing but a mask for the plots of the money-power.* They thought Hamilton himself had been bought and corrupted. The works of John Taylor of Caroline explain the fierce passion with which the Jeffersonians organized, fought Hamilton, seized the national government—and then found themselves unable to make the necessary reforms.

In the summer of 1792 Washington made a last effort to reconcile the two fiery opponents, who were both still members of his Cabinet. In reply, Jefferson again asked to resign,** and added that he did not wish his retirement "to be clouded by the slanders of a man whose history, from the

---

* Hamilton described his national bank as a device for uniting "the interest and credit of rich individuals with those of the State." (*Works,* III, p. 332.) To him this seemed plain common sense; to the agrarians it seemed cynicism bordering on dishonor.

** He was not allowed to do so until the last day of 1793.

moment at which history can stoop to notice him, is a tissue of machinations against the liberty of the country which has not only received and given him bread, but heaped its honors on his head." Yet in 1816, long after Jefferson had retired from the presidency, when Congress was at last beginning to enact Hamilton's Report on Manufactures, Jefferson wrote: "Experience has taught me that manufactures are now as necessary to our independence as to our comfort." He saw at last that the agrarian paradise of his hopes had been doomed by life itself, not by the plots of Hamilton.

6

It is hard, in writing of this period, to do sufficient justice to the personal influence of Washington, which was exercised with such dignity and such aloofness that it is often overlooked. We have seen that during the revolutionary war there might have been no army without Washington. Similarly, there might have been no Constitution, at least in 1787, without his weight on the side of those who favored a federal government. In the following year, Virginia would probably not have ratified the Constitution, and the new government would thus have been still-born, except for Washington's influence in that state. And the men who breathed life into the written document during the decisive first four years, the men who passed the laws and made the administrative decisions upon which the country's life rests, would have wasted most of their energy in fighting each other if Washington had not held them to the task of building a nation.

When we speak, therefore, of "Hamilton's financial policy," we must remember that not one word of it would have been written into law if it had not been Washington's financial policy as well. The Jeffersonians railed at Washington for being under Hamilton's influence; but it has yet to be shown that he was ever under any man's influence. He had a slow and accurate mind, with unsurpassed judgment. He listened to both sides; he solicited the opinions of Hamilton's foes; and he concluded that Hamilton was right, that the country needed the strengthening of government, the centralizing of influence, for which Hamilton's measures were designed. Hamilton's brilliance in argument would have availed him nothing if the Congress had not known that Washington was behind him.

In the field of foreign affairs, where Washington had to make the most painful and unpopular decisions of his life, the two men also saw alike. And here, too, there was a sharp and bitter difference between Hamilton and Jefferson. Indeed, the passions and prejudices stirred by the foreign relations of America were identical with the passions and prejudices stirred by domestic policy. From the spring day in 1793 when news arrived (three months late) that France had killed her king and had declared war on

England and Spain, it was inevitable that men who believed human nature could only be saved by wise paternal government and conservative customs should turn toward England, and that men who believed human nature would save itself if freed from shackles and discouragement should turn toward France. Furthermore, since three quarters of America's commerce was with England, and ninety per cent of her imports came from England, the capitalist and commercial classes naturally favored the British cause, while for precisely the same reasons the Southern agrarians hated Britain, and hence favored France. British merchants were as unpopular among the Southern planters after the War of Independence as they had been before; the London factors were still felt to be distant anonymous exploiters, knocking down the price of farm goods and providing manufactured necessities on their own terms.

The strife caused by these divisions on foreign policy, coinciding with divisions which had already arisen at home, was intensified by two facts: first, the United States had made a treaty with France in 1778 which, if applied literally, would bring her into the war against England; and second, the deeds and manners of the British Government were such that it was hard for England's friends to defend her effectively.

The first crisis came with the arrival of Citizen Genet as Minister from the French Republic, an event which coincided with Washington's neutrality proclamation.* Genet's instructions were to use America as a base for privateering, and to recruit troops for the conquest of Louisiana and Florida, "and perhaps . . . Canada." Luckily he was a silly man who overplayed his hand and tried openly to turn the American people against Washington and against the neutrality proclamation. Had he been wiser he might have created enough trouble to make war with England a certainty; but within a few months even Jefferson turned against him, fearing that he might discredit the whole anti-Hamilton party if they allowed him to attach himself to their cause. In August, 1793, the Cabinet voted unanimously to request his recall. Since the French Government showed that it would be pleased to execute him, he was allowed to settle in New York state, where he married the daughter of Governor Clinton.

Jefferson was firm for the policy of peace, knowing that America might be destroyed if she went to war divided and weak, and with her new government not yet strongly founded; but he was equally firm for the cause of France, which he called "the most sacred cause that ever man was engaged in." Hamilton, on the other hand, saw the French Revolution as the return of anarchy and night. He feared Jefferson would create a similar

* April 22, 1793. The Administration accepted Hamilton's thesis that the French, having changed their form of government and killed their king, could not demand the fulfilment of contracts made with the abolished government and the murdered king. Jefferson, although he persuaded Washington not to use the word "neutrality," agreed that the United States should not go to war to help France.

chaos in America, if he were allowed to try out his theories as to man's natural goodness; whereas Jefferson feared the Federalists would create a miserable copy of the mother country—king, aristocracy, national debt, military burdens, and hopelessness for the poor. Only the presence of Washington prevented the immediate clash of parties.

Meanwhile, it was a question whether England would allow Washington to have peace, would allow America the necessary years to found herself solidly. The British Government did not want war, but seemed incapable of behaving toward America in a way to make peace possible. If the British had planned to reconquer America they might have been wise to hamper American commerce with irritating restrictions, to impress American sailors, to insult American diplomats, and in general to keep the pot of hatred boiling; but the British did all these things, not as a policy, but as a mannerism. They simply could not bring themselves to take the ex-colonies seriously, which was a pity, because there is no one who would rather be taken seriously than an ex-colonial unless it be a colonial.

Similarly, if the British had planned to reconquer America they might have been wise to behave as they did about the Northwest army posts. According to the Treaty of 1783, the British were to evacuate these posts at once. They had not done so by 1794. They had excuses for remaining, since the Americans had also failed to live up to all the terms of the treaty. Nevertheless, it was not wise to remain unless they wanted war, for so long as British troops were in those posts the Indians would feel encouraged to resist the encroachment of the white man. If the world were the just world of Jefferson's imagination, no people would ever treat their neighbors as the Americans treated the Indians; but the world is cruel. It was clear that the Indians were doomed to suffer the customary fate of the weak, and that the Americans intended to take from the Indians any land they wanted at any time. Indian resistance could only take the form of occasional massacre and torture; by clinging to the frontier posts for a few years the British gave courage to the Indians and thus increased the frequency of such outbreaks. It was not the way to improve Anglo-American relations.

For reasons such as these Washington saw little hope of peace unless he could negotiate a fair treaty with the British. In the spring of 1794 he sent John Jay, Chief Justice of the United States and one of the authors of *The Federalist,* as envoy extraordinary to the Court of St. James's. It was not an ideal choice. Jay was a good and wise man; but he was vain and easily flattered, a defect in a diplomat. The British report on Jay said: "He can bear any opposition to what he advances, provided that regard is shown to his abilities. Mr. Jay's weak side is *Mr. Jay.*" Taking advantage of this information, and of some wholly unauthorized statements made by Hamilton to the British Minister at Philadelphia, the British negotiated a treaty which was a victory for their diplomacy and which has harmed the relations between the two countries ever since, for it started the American legend that English diplomats are inhumanly competent and never to be trusted.

The treaty did secure the evacuation of the Northwest posts; it wisely referred boundary problems, uncollected debts, and British spoliations on American commerce to settlement by mixed commissions; but it said nothing about impressment, or about indemnity for slaves seized during the Revolutionary War, or about the Orders in Council whereby the British exercised the right to capture French property in American vessels and the right to treat food as contraband. It was these Orders in Council which seemed, to the pro-French party in America, to make the United States an unwilling ally of Britain in her war upon the Revolution. The Jay Treaty was harsh. It would not have been accepted by a nation which felt itself strong enough to fight. Washington had to make a grim decision before submitting it to the Senate.

He knew that if he did so the Francophiles would accuse him of treason, and many moderate men would accuse his Administration of incompetence. The people sensed that the summer of 1794 was a favorable time for making a treaty with England, because her war against France was going badly. If an onerous treaty emerged from a promising situation, it must be somebody's fault; and there was no doubt who would be blamed. Yet Washington feared that if he suppressed the treaty and announced that it was unacceptable war would result. He was doubtful whether his five-year-old country could survive a war. "Sure I am," he wrote, "if this country is preserved in tranquillity twenty years longer, it may bid defiance in a just cause to any power whatever; such in that time will be its population, wealth and resources."

In sadness, and in knowledge of what was to come, he sent the treaty to the Senate. Needless to say, although the Senate met in secret the terms were quickly divulged. A cry of rage and pain went up from the country. Washington was execrated; Jay was burned in effigy; Edmund Randolph, who had succeeded Jefferson as Secretary of State, opposed ratification.

Bad as the treaty was [writes Henry Adams], both in its omissions and in its admissions, as a matter of foreign relations, these defects were almost trifles when compared with its mischievous results at home. It thrust a sword into the body politic. . . . Nothing could have so effectually arrayed the two great domestic parties in sharply defined opposition to each other, and nothing could have aroused more bitterness of personal feeling. In recent times there has been a general disposition to explain away and to soften down the opinions and passions of that day; to throw a veil over their violence. . . . Such treatment of history makes both parties ridiculous. The two brilliant men who led the two great divisions of national thought were not mere declaimers; they never for a moment misunderstood each other; they were in deadly earnest, and no compromise between them ever was or ever will be possible. Mr. Jefferson meant that the American system should be a democracy, and he would rather have let the world perish than that this principle, which to him represented all that man was worth, should fail. Mr. Hamilton considered democracy a fatal curse, and meant to stop its progress. The partial truce which the first Administration of Washington had imposed on both parties, although really closed by the retirement of Mr. Jefferson from the Cabinet, was finally broken only by the arrival of Mr. Jay's treaty.[12]

In the end, the majesty of Washington's influence prevailed. The treaty was accepted by the Senate, but without a vote to spare. The treaty, however, contained provisions which could only be carried out by an appropriation from Congress. The House of Representatives caused a constitutional crisis by claiming the right to refuse the appropriation unless it too were satisfied that the treaty, though harsh, was a necessity. Here was one of the weak points in the theory of the division of powers. According to the Constitution, Congress possesses all legislative powers; but the President, with the consent of the Senate, has the power to make treaties which, like the laws of Congress, are the supreme law of the land. So it would seem that the Congress does not possess all legislative powers. As Albert Gallatin said during the House debate on the Jay Treaty, in March, 1796:

> If the treaty-making power is not limited by existing laws, or if it repeals the laws that clash with it, or if the Legislature is obliged to repeal the laws so clashing, then the legislative power in fact resides in the President and Senate, and they can, by employing an Indian tribe, pass any law under the color of a treaty.

The argument could not be met, so for the time being it was dodged. After months of wrangling, the House passed the necessary appropriations. It was not until 1868, when the treaty for the purchase of Alaska came before the House on the question of appropriating the necessary money, that the constitutional point was settled. The Administration in 1868 admitted the right of the House of Representatives to call for papers, to discuss the merits of the treaty, and to refuse appropriations if it considered the treaty inconsistent with the Constitution or with the policy of the country.* Presumably the precedent stands. Presumably the outside world, which was surprised in 1919 to learn that the President could not make a treaty alone, may one day have to acquire the further knowledge that the President and the Senate cannot make a treaty together, if enabling legislation is required.

* Washington's Administration had tried, inconclusively, to stand on the assertion that "The House of Representatives have nothing to do with the treaty but provide for its execution."

The Jay Treaty was negotiated in November, 1794; it received the assent of the Senate in June, 1795; the House voted the necessary appropriations at the end of April, 1796. During all those months George Washington was repeatedly accused of having betrayed his country. Today, we can salute the President who chose to be called a traitor rather than risk needless danger for his country. What shall we say of the British statesmen who thought it clever to put George Washington in such a position? We shall see other examples of this cleverness; but we shall never know what trouble the world might have been spared if Parliament had followed the younger Pitt in 1783, immediately after the War of Independence, when he introduced a bill for unconditional free trade between England and America. If relations had begun with such a brilliant gesture of friendship there would never have been a Jay Treaty; there might never have been a War of 1812; there would probably never have been an anti-British tradition in America.*

7

In the fourth summer of his first term, Washington wished to announce that he was not a candidate for re-election. He wrote Madison a letter outlining the message he would like to give to the country, and received a long reply. His friends and advisers then persuaded Washington to accept a second term. Four years later he sent to Hamilton his original letter, and also Madison's reply, asking Hamilton to draft a message. In the end Hamilton made two drafts, one with the help of Jay. Washington preferred the first, and after further corrections and omissions he issued his Farewell Address on September 17, 1796.** In these last words of advice to his people, Washington makes clear the main dangers which the new government had met.

* The Jay Treaty did one favor for Washington: it secured him a satisfactory treaty with Spain. Ever since the close of the Revolutionary War, Spain had denied America's right to navigate the Mississippi, and of course had denied the right of deposit and reshipment in the Spanish port of New Orleans. The result was a western discontent so violent that it threatened to lead either to secession or to a war with Spain. Jay's treaty made the Spaniards fear that Britain and America might one day get together to attack Spain in the New World. So in 1795 Godoy, the prime minister, made a treaty granting the right of navigation, and even the right of deposit for three years—with the stipulation that if the latter right should be withdrawn in New Orleans, Spain would assign to the Americans "on another part of the banks of the Mississippi, an equivalent establishment." This calmed the fears of the Westerners—until France appeared at New Orleans with a new and more deadly threat.

** It is interesting that the three authors of *The Federalist* collaborated once again on this remarkable document, although Madison and Hamilton were now in opposite camps. The ideas in the address were all chosen and imposed by Washington, yet Hamilton must have agreed on every point.

The first was the danger of secession.

It is of infinite moment [he says] that you should properly estimate the immense value of your national union to your collective and individual happiness; that you should cherish a cordial, habitual, and immovable attachment to it; accustoming yourselves to think and speak of it as the palladium of your political safety and prosperity; watching for its preservation with jealous anxiety; discountenancing whatever may suggest even a suspicion that it can in any event be abandoned, and indignantly frowning upon the first dawning of every attempt to alienate any portion of our country from the rest or to enfeeble the sacred ties which now link together the various parts.

The second was the danger of weakening the central government.

Remember especially [he says], that for the efficient management of your common interests in a country so extensive as ours a government of as much vigor as is consistent with the perfect security of liberty is indispensable. Liberty itself will find in such a government, with powers properly distributed and adjusted, its surest guardian. It is, indeed, little else but a name where the government is too feeble to withstand the enterprise of faction, to confine each member of the society within the limits prescribed by the laws, and to maintain all in the secure and tranquil enjoyment of the rights of person and property.

The third was the danger of political parties.

I have already intimated to you [he says] the danger of parties in the State, with particular reference to the founding of them on geographical discriminations. Let me now take a more comprehensive view, and warn you in the most solemn manner against the baneful effects of the spirit of party generally. . . . It serves always to distract the public councils and enfeeble the public administration. It agitates the community with ill-founded jealousies and false alarms; kindles the animosity of one part against another; foments occasionally riot and insurrection.

The fourth was the danger of playing favorites among foreign nations.

Permanent, inveterate antipathies against particular nations [he says], and passionate attachments for others should be excluded. . . . In place of them just and amicable feelings toward all should be cultivated. The nation which indulges toward another an habitual hatred or an habitual fondness is in some degree a slave. It is a slave to its animosity or to its affection, each of which is sufficient to lead it astray from its duty and its interest. . . . Against the insidious wiles of foreign influence (I conjure you to believe me, fellow-citizens) the jealousy of a free people ought to be *constantly* awake. . . . But that jealousy, to be useful, must be impartial, else it becomes the instrument of the very influence to be avoided, instead of a defense against it. . . . The great rule of conduct for us in regard to foreign nations is, in extending our commercial relations to have with them as little *political* connection as possible. So far as we have already formed engagements let them be fulfilled with perfect good faith. Here let us stop. . . . It is our true policy to steer clear of permanent alliances with any portion of the foreign world, so far, I mean, as we are now at liberty to do it.

These are not the sole themes of the Farewell Address; but they are the major themes. We have seen that each of them is based on the experience of Washington's two terms. The advice could not be literally followed. America has not been spared secession, or weak government, or party passion, or foreign entanglements of a type to create disunity at home. But in her earliest, weakest days Washington prevented any of these dangers from destroying her. The West did not secede; the powers of the central government were not diminished; the country was not distracted by party hatreds before she had the strength to resist those fierce fires; and neither worship for France nor suspicion for England was allowed to create a needless war. Washington gave America the time to grow, to find herself, which he so clearly saw she required. He thus became the father of his country in peace as well as in war.

On March 4, 1797, Washington attended the inauguration of John Adams as President, and five days later he left Philadelphia* for Mount Vernon. The following year, when war with France threatened, Washington accepted the appointment as Commander-in-Chief of the American Army; but the war did not come, so Washington had no further military duties. He gave the last two years of his life to restoring order on his estates.

In December, 1799, at the age of sixty-seven, he developed an inflammation of the throat, following on a bad cold. Within two days he was dead.

---

* Congress adjourned at New York in the summer of 1790, and met for the first time in Congress Hall, Philadelphia, in December, 1790. Philadelphia remained the capital city until November, 1800, when the government moved to the emptiness and mud of Washington, on the Potomac. The city had been planned on an imperial scale by Major L'Enfant, a French engineer; but in 1800 it was still a clearing between the forest and the river, with one wing of the Capitol finished, a few brick houses, and a scattering of wooden huts: "This famed metropolis," as Tom Moore called it, "where fancy sees Squares in morasses, obelisks in trees."

V

The Birth of Parties

T HE CONSTITUTION, as we have seen, was made at Philadelphia by men who had a common economic interest. They were mostly merchants, shippers, lawyers, planters, speculators in land and in paper. Such men prefer a government with sufficient authority to enforce contracts at home, and with sufficient standing abroad to raise loans and make commercial treaties. The frontiersmen and the small farmers (who were usually in debt) were satisfied with the weak Confederation; but they were little represented at Philadelphia, and their efforts to defeat ratification were a failure.

The economic interests of the constitution-makers were not identical. They clashed at many points; but the delegates were astute enough "to disregard differences and concentrate on the one thing essential to their several purposes, in this case an integrated, national, economic society of which the *sine qua non* was the central authority the Constitution provided."[1] The disregarding of differences lasted until the Constitution was ratified and the government was safe. Then new alignments began to form —the first sign being Madison's opposition, in the House of Representatives, to the plans of the co-author of *The Federalist*.

Such opposition need not have bred political parties. Madison, who feared parties and thought them unnecessary, knew that there could be no free government without pressure groups; but he thought the groups would form brief coalitions to deal with issues on which their interests were alike, and would then dissolve the partnership, ready for new alignments and new issues. He hoped that the clash of sectional interests between the pressure groups would make it impossible to form a coalition for radical aims. The size of America would enforce conservatism, for by the time each group in a coalition had made the compromises which were necessary for unity the surviving program would be cautious and unalarming.

Such were the hopes not only of Madison but of the majority of the Fathers. They were right in predicting loose associations of pressure groups and regional interests; they were right in predicting that such associations would make for conservatism; but they were wrong in thinking that when a group had come together to form a majority for a single bill or a single protest it could then afford to dissolve. Because of the growing power of the presidency, and the need to control that office if a national policy was to be defended or defeated, the groups found that they had to maintain their uneasy partnerships, that they had to form permanent parties, each with its own traditions, its own saints and martyrs, its own fierce battle-cries. The centrifugal forces in American life were so strong that nothing could have held these groups together except the prize of power, the knowledge that if they did not compose their differences and find a common ground they would never control the Administration and never get even a fraction of a loaf. The same knowledge kept them from forming many parties, and held them to two. For if the President was an astute politician (as often happened) he could gather into the party which was in power such a coalition of interests that it could not be upset except by a coalition of all the dissenting interests. And it soon became clear that a successful party, in spite of its saints and slogans, must be so flexible, so little committed to dogmas or to programs, that it could accommodate any group which was willing to make concessions to the prejudices of the other groups in order to acquire or to retain office.

Conservatism, compromise, deference to regional bias, these were the prerequisites for a successful national party. The local groups which composed the party might be as extreme as they liked in their own districts; but when they joined with the other local groups to act nationally they had to leave their fanaticisms at home. This was the price of unity in so huge a nation. By learning to unite themselves, the parties learned to preserve the Union. When the party compromises broke down in the name of principles, the Union was shattered.

2

The Constitution was made by the gentry, and the Administrations of Washington and Adams were the rule of the gentry. Had it been possible for this class, which had seized power with the conservative reaction of 1785 to 1788, to "keep the people in their place," to repel successfully the new forces of democracy, the country would soon have known civil war. America was saved by a split within the ruling class itself, and the consequent birth of an opposition party. "It was the great unconscious achievement of Thomas Jefferson," writes Henry Jones Ford, "to open constitutional channels of political agitation, to start the processes by which the development of our constitution is carried on."[2] Immediately the tensions and the regional grievances, which might have bred revolution, found relief in party activity. Both parties were soon bidding for democratic support. "This was the salvation of the government. Change became possible without destruction."[3]

Jefferson sensed all this, at least by the year 1790. He was not disturbed by the violence of party politics, because he felt confident that so long as opposition was not suppressed the violence would resolve itself in moderate action and in compromise. He was almost alone, however, in his refusal to be alarmed. Most of the leaders of the day agreed with Vice-President Adams when he said: "There is nothing I dread so much as the division of the Republic into two great parties, each under its leader. . . . This, in my humble opinion, is to be feared as the greatest political evil under our Constitution."[4] Since the first warning of the coming division was the appearance of a rancorous political journalism, the Fathers can be excused for some of their fears.

The trouble began in the autumn of 1790, when the Virginia Assembly adopted a resolution opposing the assumption by the federal government of the wartime debts of the states. Patrick Henry introduced the resolution, denouncing assumption as "repugnant to the Constitution of the United States, as it goes to the exercise of a power not expressly granted to the general government." This was followed a few days later by an even stronger Protest and Remonstrance, which said that all powers not expressly given in the Constitution were reserved to the states. "In an agricultural country like this," said the Remonstrance, ". . . to erect, and concentrate, and perpetuate a large monied interest, is a measure which your memorialists apprehend must in the course of human events produce one or other of two evils, the prostration of agriculture at the feet of commerce, or a change in the present form of federal government, fatal to the existence of American liberty."

Here was the first revolt of Virginia, directed against the first act of the Hamiltonians: a clear statement of the conflict between South and North, the farmers and the slaveholding planters against the merchants and bankers, the men with a feudal disdain for money against the men who understood business, credit, finance. Hamilton saw at once the farthest implications of the Virginia Remonstrance. This was nullification, the doctrine that each state can decide for itself whether an act of the federal government is constitutional. The sanction for nullification is secession: war, or the death of the federal plan. Hamilton wrote to Chief Justice John Jay of the Supreme Court: "This is the first symptom of a spirit which must either be killed, or it will kill the Constitution of the United States. I send the resolutions to you, that it may be considered what ought to be done." Jay did nothing. There was nothing he could do; but he comforted himself (and vainly sought to comfort Hamilton) with the thought that such talk would weaken the influence of the states rather than of the federal government. He did not know that nullification, and "strict construction" of the Constitution, were to be rallying cries for the political party which Jefferson was building and which Hamilton regarded as a deadly threat to America.*

In the same autumn of 1790, Hamilton took steps to counter the threat. In October of that year, and again in January, 1791, Hamilton's cash book shows loans of $100 to a certain John Fenno, editor of the *Gazette of the United States.* Shortly thereafter Fenno began to receive Treasury contracts for government printing.[5] The *Gazette,* which had been founded in 1789, was supposed to be a semi-official newspaper, devoted chiefly to government affairs. Before the end of 1791 it had become a defense of Hamilton and his works and plans, and thus an attack on Jefferson and Madison.

In May, 1791, Jefferson wrote to Thomas Mann Randolph, enclosing a copy of the *Gazette,* which he described as a "paper of pure Toryism, disseminating the doctrines of monarchy, aristocracy, and the exclusion of the influence of the people." He added that he and Madison were trying to persuade Philip Freneau, the poet, to move to Philadelphia and set up "a weekly or half-weekly paper" in support of their program. They were successful, and Freneau became editor of the *National Gazette.* He also became a clerk at the Department of State, with a salary of $250 a year.**

There was now a party press, although there were as yet no official parties. With the advent of political journalism, all restraint and all politeness departed from politics; minor differences became major; small hostilities became lifelong feuds; the genial air of Philadelphia was poisoned by pumped-up hatreds. Washington saw the deterioration with sad-

* For the most part, the group which is out of power in America tends to favor "strict construction." (New England talked nullification and threatened secession when Jefferson became President.) A written, federal constitution, which divides power between local governments and a limited central government, incites the Opposition to declare that every act it dislikes is unconstitutional. If such an act is disliked by a majority throughout a state or region, the temptation is strong for the citizens to say that they will disobey the act, not out of lawlessness but out of a special reverence for law, out of zeal to protect the Constitution. Yet the lesson of the ruinous Civil War has been so well learned in America that it is many years since regional discontents have led to talk of secession. The political parties have learned to minimize such discontents, sometimes by concessions, sometimes by ignoring the evasion of the law. As usual when a political problem has been allayed, the absence of friction is now taken for granted. The party system is given no credit; it is merely abused for the delays, the seeming inefficiencies, the endless regional compromises, which are the cost of exorcising the demon of secession.

** The *Gazette of the United States* was founded in 1789 and moved from New York to Philadelphia with the federal government. At first it was a semi-weekly; but in December, 1793 (after two months of suspended publication because of yellow fever in Philadelphia), it became a daily. The maximum circulation was about 1400. The year it moved to Philadelphia the *Gazette* was printed in three columns on a single sheet of paper, 17 by 21 inches. Freneau's *National Gazette,* first issued on October 31, 1791, was a semi-weekly with a maximum circulation of about 1500. In the year 1790 there were 92 newspapers in the United States, of which 8 were dailies; in 1800 there were 235 newspapers, of which 24 were dailies.

ness, and with forebodings of trouble; but not even Washington's influence could prevent party strife or could make such strife pretty. Only Jefferson, who understood politics by instinct, knew that the turmoil and the abuse would diminish tensions and make for peace, not anarchy.

In the summer of 1792 Hamilton himself turned journalist and wrote savage attacks on Jefferson, which appeared in the *Gazette of the United States.* He was quickly answered by Madison in the *National Gazette.* Although both men used pseudonyms the public was not fooled; it watched with mixed emotions while the Secretary of the Treasury made vicious accusations against the Secretary of State, and was answered with equal viciousness by the co-author of *The Federalist,* now the most important member of Congress.* When Washington sought to impose a little dignity on the brawl, Jefferson and Hamilton offered to resign. They were with difficulty persuaded to continue serving the President whom they both honored; they could not be persuaded to pretend agreement with each other.

Under such conditions nothing but dictatorship could have prevented the birth of parties. The opposed interests existed; the opposed theories of federal government existed; the natural leaders (also opposed in temperament and in philosophy of life) existed; and foreign relations, which might have cut across domestic feuds, in fact exacerbated them. The only remaining problem was how the parties would be organized, and when. The answer was determined by the fact that New York State became the first critical battleground.

3

It was clear that Virginia would follow Jefferson and the agrarians who feared a strong central government; it was clear that Massachusetts would follow Hamilton and the friends of commerce and capitalism. Much of the South could be expected to go along with Virginia, and much of New England with Massachusetts. In Pennsylvania there was a majority of true democrats, who understood what Jefferson meant, and there was one great

---

* Years later, Madison explained the split with Hamilton on the ground that the latter had made plain "his purpose and endeavour to administrate the Government into a thing totally different from that which he and I both knew perfectly well had been understood and intended by the Convention which framed it, and by the people adopting it." (Schachner, *Alexander Hamilton,* p. 457.) This is doubtless true. Hamilton on the one side, Jefferson and Madison on the other, felt that the nation's life depended on molding the federal government according to their own theories. There could be no better ground for disagreement; but only the rash and irresponsible childhood of journalism could explain the fury with which the disagreement was expressed.

leader, Albert Gallatin, who became Jefferson's Secretary of the Treasury. But what of New York? As usual, the politics of that state were involved and murky—a fact which did not trouble Jefferson, for he was as comfortable in the midst of political complications as Br'er Rabbit in the midst of a briar patch.

The two Senators from New York were Rufus King, a wise and moderate Hamiltonian, and General Schuyler, Hamilton's father-in-law. Their votes were vital for the support of the Treasury measures in Congress. In the spring of 1791, General Schuyler (who by lot had drawn the short term when the Senate first met*) expected to be reappointed by the New York legislature. To everyone's surprise, and to Hamilton's fury, Schuyler was rejected and Aaron Burr—"the Mephistopheles of politics," the man who was to be the central figure in the two great political melodramas of Jefferson's presidency—was chosen in his place. Hamilton assumed that this mortal threat to his program must be the result of plots and tricks by Burr. He responded with a violence which led by successive steps to his own death, in 1804, on the dueling-ground at Weehawken.

What had happened, in fact, was something very simple, and very characteristic of New York State politics: the powerful Livingston clan, who had supported Hamilton in the fight against Governor Clinton for ratification of the Constitution, and who had hitherto backed his bills in Congress, changed sides because they had not received the patronage they expected. Rufus King, instead of a Livingston, had become the second New York Senator; John Jay, instead of a Livingston, had become Chief Justice of the Supreme Court. The family felt neglected even in local appointments; so with the help of a little urging by the wily Burr they struck at Hamilton through Schuyler, joining hands with his old enemy, the Governor.

As a result of this turnabout by one of the baronial houses, the spring of 1791 saw two factions of almost equal importance in New York State: the aristocratic faction of the De Lanceys, the Van Rensselaers, and General Schuyler; and the somewhat more professional faction of Governor George Clinton, the Livingstons, and Aaron Burr. The second group was both anti-Hamiltonian and discontented, and thus of double interest to Jefferson. Although Clinton was governor, his opposition to the Constitution (and to Hamilton personally) had been so inveterate that he received no patronage from Washington's Administration. He was prepared, therefore, to help Jefferson put his new party into power in return for a reasonable share of loaves and fishes. So in the summer of 1791, Jefferson and Madison took what they described as a "botanizing excursion" up the Hudson

---

* The Constitution required that one third of the Senate be chosen every second year; so the first Senate had to divide itself into two-year men, four-year men, and six-year men.

river—the river of New York politics which runs from Albany (the state capital) in the north to Tammany Hall in the south.* There they laid the foundation for the longest-lived, the most incongruous, and the most effective political alliance in American history: the alliance of southern agrarians and northern city bosses.

Jefferson and his Virginians stood for a theory of government; so did Massachusetts and the Hamiltonians; but New York, as Henry Adams points out in a famous passage,

> cared little for the metaphysical subtleties of Massachusetts and Virginia. . . . New York was indifferent whether the nature of the United States was single or multiple, whether they were a nation or a league. Leaving this class of question to other states which were deeply interested in them, New York remained constant to no political theory. There society, in spite of its aristocratic mixture, was democratic by instinct; and in abandoning its alliance with New England in order to join Virginia and elect Jefferson to the Presidency, it pledged itself to principles of no kind, least of all to Virginia doctrines. The Virginians aimed at maintaining a society so simple that purity should suffer no danger, and corruption gain no foothold; and never did America witness a stranger union than when Jefferson, the representative of ideal purity, allied himself with Aaron Burr, the Livingstons and Clintons, in the expectation of fixing the United States in a career of simplicity and virtue. George Clinton, indeed, a States'-rights Republican of the old school, understood and believed the Virginia doctrines; but as for Aaron Burr, Edward Livingston, De Witt Clinton, and Ambrose Spencer— young men whose brains were filled with dreams of a different sort— what had such energetic democrats to do with the plough, or what share had the austerity of Cato and the simplicity of Ancus Martius in their ideals? The political partnership between the New York Republicans and the Virginians was from the first that of a business firm; and no more curious speculation could have been suggested to the politicians of 1800 than the question whether New York would corrupt Virginia, or Virginia check the prosperity of New York.[6]

Was Jefferson wrong in seeking help from men who pledged themselves "to principles of no kind, least of all to Virginia doctrines?" The question may be put another way: would Jefferson have been right to prefer purity to power, when he believed that his country's fate was at stake? Pending an answer to the riddle, it is worth noting again that the coalition of local groups which Jefferson created is the standard pattern for American political parties. The national party is always a loose alliance of local parties,

---

* Aaron Burr was already discovering the possible political uses of the Sons of St. Tammany. Tammany had begun as a benevolent organization. Burr induced it to become less benevolent and more of an organization. Although never a member he controlled Tammany from 1797 until his removal from politics, teaching it how to "get out the vote" and how to circumvent property qualifications for voters.

held together precariously by self-interest or by a shared hostility. In every presidential election countless votes are determined by state politics, neighborhood politics, church, trade union, or racial-minority politics—none of which may have any bearing upon the alleged issues of the campaign. The President, after he is elected, must do his best to impose upon innumerable local groups (chiefly concerned with their parochial troubles, demands, and hatreds) a policy which is in the national interest.

This conflict between central authority and local government is a problem in all free countries; but it is a problem of special acuteness in the United States because the size and the federal structure of the nation make for the autonomy and the self-absorption of state and county machines. Also, the American Constitution denies to the President authority over his party-associates in Congress. He is the chief executive, and he is charged with recommending national policy; but he has no official power to enforce his recommendations. The members of Congress represent particular districts, or particular states. They are elected by the local party, not by the national party. It is their business to know the local problems, not the national problems. The best policy for the nation may be a troublesome and unpopular policy in certain districts. In that case the members for those districts will either oppose the policy or they will cease to represent the districts. From Jefferson (the first party manager) to Franklin Roosevelt (the most ingenious), all Presidents have struggled to find a working relationship between the national view and the views of the Congressional districts. To help them in this Sisyphean task they have a loose party machine and loose party discipline.

4

On December 31, 1793, Jefferson at last resigned from the Cabinet, and thenceforth gave all his time to political organization. The following year Hamilton resigned. He was a poor man and he wished to return to his law practice in New York. He also wished to have more freedom for the active work of politics. He knew that his useful days in the Cabinet were done.

Meanwhile, as soon as it had become clear that the Jeffersonians would have a majority in the lower House when the Third Congress convened in March, 1793, Hamilton's enemies began an attack against him* which

---

* William Branch Giles of Virginia, who was to quarrel with all men but Jefferson, and who in his last days was to betray even that loyalty, introduced the famous House resolutions inquiring into Hamilton's conduct of the Treasury (January 23 and February 27, 1793). The resolutions were drafted by Jefferson, and one of Giles's major points was based on a memorandum by Madison. (Schachner, *Alexander Hamilton,* pp. 312–13.) The result was a complete vindication for Hamilton, but also a heavy burden on his time and health. If the Virginian trio could not disgrace him, they intended at least to wear him down.

must be admired for its power and unscrupulousness, and which did not
slacken until its victim retired from office. The purpose of the attack was
both to blacken Hamilton's character and to prevent him from doing his
work. The Jeffersonians in Congress harrassed the Treasury with demands
for information, and with investigations for incompetence and thievery;
they carried on a whispering campaign against Hamilton's honor; they
accused him of turning the country into a monarchy, of turning himself
into a Prime Minister, and of destroying the federal system with his unconstitutional money bills. If the fury and the vindictiveness seem strange
today, it is only because we have forgotten the stakes.

The real object of the attack was the Executive, of which Hamilton was
the symbol. Sensible politicians who were seeking the votes of their neighbors did not often attack Washington by name; but Hamilton was of
foreign and illegitimate birth; he was openly contemptuous of the masses;
and he was domineering toward his opponents. He also held the most important executive job under Washington, so he became the ideal target.

Hamilton and his friends believed that the government must fail without effective, concentrated leadership; they believed that the heads of
departments under the President should constitute a ministry and should
give policy guidance to the Congress. Such guidance, they thought, would
receive full publicity, full criticism from the Congress and the public, and
would thus attain to full responsibility. Any other form of liaison between
Executive and Legislature must take place in the darkness or semi-dark-
ness, must consist of political pressures, promises, or deals, and must therefore be irresponsible. This was the Federalist solution to the problem of
enforcing national policy upon a parish-minded Congress.

During Washington's first term the Jeffersonians were slow to see the
dangers of the Federalist doctrine. They did not fear a powerful Executive
until Hamilton proved what the Executive could do for commerce and
finance. When they woke to their danger, Hamilton's plans were half-
completed; but the agrarians were in time to prevent the second half—the
plan for industry. They then sought to ward off future surprises by demanding that Congress become the policy-making body. They wanted the
federal government to be inactive. They did not want its help; they
wanted to be safe from its harm. They felt that Congress, composed of the
representatives of innumerable communities, would be a passive policy-
maker, would be laissez-faire, whereas the Executive had already proved
itself centralizing, dominating, and aggressive. So by way of breaking the
power of the President and his Cabinet they undertook to break Hamilton.

Such were the motives for the fierce onslaught. The stakes were the control of the federal government during its formative years. Each side felt
that if it could hold power it could set the pattern for the American
future. Life was not in fact so simple, nor the future so easy to control;

but neither group can be blamed for straining to seize what seemed a magic chance. Against the background of such a hope, the passions of those days of party-building are not inordinate.

5

The presidential election of 1796, the third such election, was the first to be contested by formal, or semi-formal, parties with regular party candidates. There were no official nominations. The candidates were chosen by consultation among the national and state leaders; the gentry, in other words, were still in control. The anti-Hamiltonians were now officially known as Republicans (or Democratic-Republicans); they supported Jefferson and Burr for President and Vice-President. The Hamiltonians, who kept the name of Federalists, nominated John Adams of Massachusetts and Thomas Pinckney of South Carolina. In so far as there was a popular campaign issue, it was Jay's treaty, which the Federalists defended and which the Republicans called a national disgrace.

Legally, the members of the electoral college had freedom of choice; but it was impossible for them to exercise that choice if there were to be effective parties, so it was expected that men nominated by Federalist legislatures would vote for Adams and Pinckney, while men nominated by Republican legislatures would vote for Jefferson and Burr. The plain purpose of the Constitution was already disregarded. The first step had been taken toward making the President, not the choice of an oligarchy, but the tribune of the people. This was not yet understood; indeed, the party organization was still so primitive that Jefferson told Madison he preferred not to have the nomination in case the decision had to be made by the House of Representatives.[7] He was afraid his party might not be well enough knit to bear the burden of government after so close an election.

On the basis of this half-acknowledged party system, Adams won the presidency with seventy-one electoral votes; but some of the second votes of Federalist electors had been wasted on local favorites, instead of going to Pinckney, so Jefferson received the next largest number of votes, and became Vice-President.*

* See Appendix for the constitutional provisions for the election of Vice-Presidents. These provisions were changed, by constitutional amendment, in 1804.

VI

The Failure of the Federalists

On March 4, 1797, when John Adams was inaugurated President of the United States, Washington's noble bearing overshadowed the dumpy, pompous little lawyer from Massachusetts. Yet Adams was undoubtedly the second most important man in the making of the Revolution and the winning of independence. And he shared with Washington a burning faith in American destiny, not as an idle hope, but as a call to work and to responsibility. "The people in America," Adams wrote in 1787, in the preface to his *Defence of the Constitutions of Government of the United States of America,* "have now the best opportunity and the greatest trust in their hands that Providence ever committed to so small a number since the transgression of the first pair; if they betray their trust, their guilt will merit even greater punishment than other nations have suffered, and the indignation of heaven."

Adams's Puritanism, though seemingly typical in its effect on his character, was by no means orthodox Calvinism; it was closer to the Unitarianism of the younger generation in New England. At the age of twenty he wrote in his diary:

> . . . spent an hour in the beginning of the evening at Major Gardiner's where it was thought that the design of Christianity was not to make men good riddle-solvers, or good mystery-mongers, but good men, good magistrates, and good subjects, good husbands and good wives, good parents and good children, good masters and good servants. The following questions may be answered some time or other, namely—Where do we find a precept in the Gospel requiring Ecclesiastical Synods? Convocations? Councils? Decrees? Creeds? Confessions? Oaths? Subscriptions? and whole cartloads of other trumpery that we find religion encumbered with in these days.

The passage is Miltonic in its rejection of institutions and its insistence on an individual approach to the Bible. And in the letters of his old age, after he had renewed his long-lapsed friendship with Jefferson, he wrote:

> You and I have as much authority to settle these disputes as Swift, Priestley, Dupuis, or the Pope; and if you will agree with me, we will issue our bull, and enjoin it upon all these gentlemen to be silent till they

can tell us what matter is, and what spirit is, and in the meantime to observe the commandments, and the sermon on the mount.

It is clear that no reverence for other men's opinions would restrain John Adams from revolution.

2

Adams was born in 1736, in Massachusetts, where a certain Henry Adams had been granted land a hundred years before. For three generations the family had bred competent yeomen, but with John Adams it became a nursery of greatness. During the next hundred and fifty years it produced in direct descent two of America's chief statesmen, one of her leading diplomats, and a great historian. And from John Adams to his great-grandson they have had a common character: sarcastic, self-critical and equally critical of others, learned, tireless in work, thin-skinned, stubborn, suspicious, disinterested in public service.

John Adams was graduated from Harvard in 1755. He was intended for the Church, but his temperament was wholly secular, and his distaste for ecclesiastical forms or tradition would have made him a recalcitrant member of the ministry. He chose the law instead. A few years later he married Abigail (Quincy) Smith—a woman of learning, humanity, spiritual elevation. She also had powerful family connections, so the law practice began to prosper. Adams would soon have grown rich—something which none of his descendants for the next two generations could take time from the public service to accomplish—if all his energies had not soon been absorbed in the quarrel with England.

In 1765 the courts were closed as a result of a protest against the Stamp Act. Adams wrote in his diary:

> I was but just getting under sail . . . and an embargo is laid upon the ship. Thirty years of my life are passed in preparations for business; I have had poverty to struggle with, envy and jealousy and malice of enemies to encounter, no friends, or but few to assist me, so that I have groped in dark obscurity till of late, and had but just become known, and gained a small degree of reputation, when this execrable project was set on foot for my ruin as well as that of America in general, and of Great Britain.

It is amusing to compare this outburst with the facts: Adams had received the best education Massachusetts could offer and had married the most remarkable woman in the colony. He had rich friends and patrons. England, having asked for aid from the colonies and having received nothing, was trying (unwisely, to be sure) to raise money to help carry her debt of £140,000,000—much of it incurred in the defense of the American colonies. But to John Adams it was all a plot on the part of King and Parliament to frustrate his young career, already hideously handicapped by "envy and jealousy and malice of enemies." Such are the suspicions and easy grievances which create a good leader of revolution.

In 1774 Adams attended the First Continental Congress at Philadelphia, where little was accomplished except the Declaration of Rights and a non-exportation, non-importation, and non-consumption agreement. Adams was impatient of such moderation, and fiercely impatient of the long-drawn-out debates. "I am wearied to death," he wrote, "of the life I lead. The business of the Congress is tedious beyond expression. This assembly is like no other that ever existed. Every man in it is a great man, an orator, a critic, a statesman; and therefore, every man upon every question, must show his oratory, his criticism, and his political abilities. The consequence of this is, that business is drawn and spun out to an immeasurable length." This seems a fair description of all political meetings, in spite of Adams's hopeful statement that it was "like no other that ever existed." Yet the talk and the lack of action were almost more than he could bear. "Should the opposition be suppressed," he wrote, "should this country submit, what infamy and ruin! God forbid! Death in any form is less terrible." In a letter to his wife he says: "Frugality, economy, parsimony must be our refuge. . . . Let us eat potatoes and drink water. Let us wear canvas and un-dressed sheepskin, rather than submit to the unrighteous and igno-minious domination that is prepared for us."

Adams curbed himself as best he could during the meetings of the First Congress. He knew that the other colonial leaders were not so impetuous as himself and that he might scare them into inaction if he kept reminding them that they were headed for war. The following year, when the Second Continental Congress met and he could at last talk openly of independ-ence, Adams became the leader of the war party. He was a member of the committee to draw up the Declaration of Independence, and although he suggested that Jefferson with his ready pen should do the writing, Adams himself was the strength of his side in the debate. He then commented characteristically:

> If you imagine that I expect this Declaration will ward off calamities from this country, you are much mistaken. A bloody conflict we are destined to endure. . . . If you imagine that I flatter myself with happi-ness and halcyon days after a separation from Great Britain, you are mistaken again. I do not expect that our new government will be so quiet as I could wish, nor that happy harmony, confidence and affec-tion between the Colonies, that every good American ought to study and pray for, for a long time. But freedom is a counter-balance for poverty, discord, and war, and more.

Adams's expectation of trouble and pain was never an expectation of failure. On the strong rock of his pessimism he built a faith in the possibilities of the future; but he knew that good could only be attained by hard and bitter work. He did not want his fellow countrymen to have too much help in their travail, for fear they should not learn the lesson of such work. In May, 1777, months before the British defeat at Saratoga and the consequent French alliance, he wrote from Philadelphia:

> I must confess that I am at a loss to determine whether it is good policy in us to wish for a war between France and Britain. . . . I don't wish to be under obligations to any of them, and I am very unwilling they should rob us of the glory of vindicating our own liberties.
> It is a cowardly spirit in our countrymen which makes them pant with so much longing expectation after a French war. I have very often been ashamed to hear so many Whigs groaning and sighing with despondency and whining out their fears that we must be subdued unless France would step in. Are we to be beholden to France for our liberties?

He wanted the Americans of his time to feel responsibility not only for their country's freedom but for its farthest future. In his *Defence of the Constitutions*, written when he was the first American Minister in London, he describes the huge and populous country which he foresees, adding:

> When we recollect that the wisdom or the folly, the virtue or the vice, the liberty or servitude, of those millions now beheld by us . . . are certainly to be influenced, perhaps decided, by the manners, examples, principles, and political institutions of the present generation, that mind must be hardened into stone that is not melted into reverence and awe.

There was small room for relaxation or delight in the world of John Adams.

> I must study politics and war [he wrote from Paris in 1780], that my sons may have liberty to study mathematics and philosophy. My sons ought to study mathematics and philosophy, geography, natural history and naval architecture, in order to give their children a right to study painting, poetry, music, architecture, statuary, tapestry and porcelain.

It is typical of the Puritan to feel that the arts are a decoration to life, which may be studied after the hard work has been done, rather than a revelation of the spirit and the needs of man, without a knowledge of which the study of politics may prove unrewarding. Poetry precedes prose in the history of civilizations; a little painting and music, a little tapestry and porcelain, might have given to John Adams and to his heroic son the two qualities they lacked: humor, and sympathy for the frail flesh.

3

After a brief trip to France in 1777–78, where he decided that Benjamin Franklin needed no help in representing America, Adams became engrossed in the work of the Massachusetts Constitutional Convention. He was largely responsible for the constitution which was accepted by the citizens of his state in 1780, and was almost wholly responsible for its Bill of Rights. Three years later the supreme judicial court of the state declared that by virtue of the first article in that bill of rights slavery could no longer exist in Massachusetts.

Late in 1779 Adams returned to France, thinking that peace negotiations might soon be opened. When this proved a vain hope he went to Holland, where he was recognized as Minister from the United States. This was an important diplomatic victory which gave a new standing to America in the eyes of Europe. In 1783 the peace conference was finally convened and Adams returned to Paris, where he headed the American mission which included Franklin and John Jay. Adams discovered that his French allies, who had been glad to help split the British Empire, did not wish the ex-colonies to grow too great. Their policy, he said, was "to deprive us of the grand fisheries, the Mississippi river, the western lands, and to saddle us with the tories." So he ignored the French, whom he had been told to consult on every point, and made a very favorable peace. The terms are surprising in view of the fact that the British Navy still ruled the seas and the British Army held New York, Charleston, Savannah, and seven northwestern posts. Although several boundary lines were drawn vaguely and ignorantly (and thus caused subsequent trouble), the Americans secured the Mississippi as their western boundary and the fishing privileges in the waters of British North America which they had enjoyed as British subjects. For this point Adams fought long and alone, and his victory made him a hero in New England.

Adams's next mission was to make a commercial treaty with the British. The negotiations were unsatisfactory; but in 1785 he was appointed American Minister at the Court of St. James's.* He was treated coldly, for he was not only an ex-rebel but he represented a government which, in its foreign relations, was absurd. The hostile British Ministers could fairly raise the question whether America under the Articles of Confederation was a government at all, or whether Adams was merely the agent of a league of jealous states. One thing only was clear: Whether America was a nation or league, whether Congress was a government or a group of

---

* There is a plaque today on the bomb-ruined house at the northeast corner of Grosvenor Square where Adams, the first American Minister, lived.

ambassadors, the Confederation was bankrupt, a fact which added to the troubles of Adams and sharpened the contemptuous manners of his British hosts. Yet Adams combated England's official attitude as fiercely as if he represented the greatest power on earth—which he probably did, in his own mind, for he never forgot those countless millions who were to inhabit the country in the future and whose welfare was "to be influenced, perhaps decided, by the manners, examples, principles, and political institutions of the present generation."

In 1788, at the age of fifty-three and after nine years abroad, Adams returned to America, arriving in time to be chosen Vice-President in the first election held under the new Constitution, and also in time to endanger the plans and ambitions of Alexander Hamilton. Circumstances had doomed Adams and Hamilton to rivalry, and their own characters made certain that the rivalry must be bitter. Each man expected, for what seemed to him good reasons, to be the second figure in the country, subordinate only to George Washington; and there was not room for two second figures. When Adams landed after his long exile, Hamilton was already Washington's favorite, and was hoping to become chief adviser and to mold the institutions of the nation according to his own clear plans. His foreign birth would prove a bar to the presidency;* but he intended to dominate the politics of America and to make himself the unofficial if not the official prime minister for as long a time as Washington would stay in office. John Adams, by his mere existence, was a threat to all these hopes.

Hamilton could not expect to sweep Adams into his train through the clarity and precision of his own political thinking. Many men followed Hamilton almost with a sense of awe, because he could make easy the tortuous subjects of government and finance; but Adams was not given to awe in the presence of his neighbors, rather to a crabbed criticism. And he had his own sharp views on government, just as clear as Hamilton's and more deeply based in knowledge of the past.

The two men agreed on the need for a strong state, with a very strong Executive, and with a financial system which would make the well-to-do identify their own security with that of the Union. They also agreed on a pessimistic view of man's nature. This pessimism led them both to favor rigid institutions in order that man might be protected from himself.

I think with you [wrote John Adams to his cousin Samuel, in October 1790], that knowledge and benevolence ought to be promoted as much as possible; but, despairing of ever seeing them sufficiently general for the security of society, I am for seeking institutions which may supply in

* Not a constitutional bar (since Hamilton was a citizen of the United States at the time the Constitution was adopted), but a political bar, another argument for his enemies to use.

some degree the defect. . . . All projects of government founded in the supposition or expectation of extraordinary degrees of virtue are evidently chimerical. . . . Human appetites, passions, prejudices, and self-love will never be conquered by benevolence and knowledge alone, introduced by human means.

In a similar mood he had written a few months earlier to his old friend, Benjamin Rush:

> I own that awful experience has concurred with reading and reflection to convince me that Americans are more rapidly disposed to corruption in elections than I thought they were fourteen years ago.

With all of this Hamilton agreed. The chief difference was that Adams had as little faith in the rich as in the poor, whereas Hamilton did not seem to fear the aggressions of the wealthy as much as the follies of the masses. "As to usurping others' rights," wrote John Adams, "they are all three (i.e., the democratical, aristocratical, and monarchical portions of society) equally guilty when unlimited in power." Hamilton thought that a strong capitalist state, insuring the prosperity of the few, would automatically insure at least the reasonable well-being of the many, whereas Adams felt that there could be no justice and no stability unless each class were prevented from exploiting the other. Adams was an intense believer in divided powers, in setting one group to watch another so that none could ever use the government for its own unhindered purpose. His lengthy *Defence of the Constitutions of Government of the United States of America* was a defense of the balance of powers which Adams himself had written into the Constitution of Massachusetts.*

Discussing the danger of a legislature with a single chamber, Adams said the well-to-do would always dominate such an assembly.

> The only remedy [he wrote] is to throw the rich and the proud into one group, in a separate assembly, and there tie their hands; if you give them scope with the people at large or their representatives, they will destroy *all equality and liberty, with the consent and acclamations of the people themselves.* . . . But placing them alone by themselves, the society avails itself of all their abilities and virtues; they become a solid check to the representatives themselves, as well as to the executive power, and you disarm them entirely of the power to do mischief.

---

* The first volume of this work, which was published in London in 1787–88, reached America at the time the Constitutional Convention was assembling at Philadelphia; so Adams may be said to have had an indirect part in those famous debates. Benjamin Rush wrote to Richard Price: "Our illustrious minister in this gift to his country has done us more service than if he had obtained alliances for us with all the nations of Europe."

This may not seem, especially in its last clause, an accurate description of the modern American Senate; but it shows the faith which Adams, and indeed most of the makers of America, had in the power of the machinery of government to affect the behavior of man. If the political mechanism were correctly constructed, they believed that many of the faults and failures of the past could be avoided. There is a passage in the same volume where Adams gives classic expression to this faith:

> The first magistrate [he writes] may love himself, and family, and friends better than the public, but the laws, supported by the senate, commons, and judges, will not permit him to indulge it; the senate may love themselves, their families, and friends more than the public, but the first magistrate, commons, and judges, uniting in support of public law, will defeat their projects; the common people, or their representatives, may love themselves and partial connections better than the whole, but the first magistrate, senate, and judges can support the laws against their enterprises; the judges may be partial to or factions, but the three branches of the legislature,* united to the executive, will easily bring them back to their duty.

In retrospect this may seem rather too simple, and rather too hopeful for so unoptimistic a writer; yet it is a statement of the faith which has been held by most Americans from that day to this, and it is not possible to understand the people or their government without keeping the faith in mind.

> Longitude [wrote Adams], and the philosopher's stone, have not been sought with more earnestness by philosophers than a guardian of the laws has been studied by legislators from Plato to Montesquieu; but every project has been found to be no better than committing the lamb to the custody of the wolf, except that one which is called a *balance of power.*

This is the basic political dogma in the American mind. The fact that it may be untrue has no effect upon the importance of the dogma in history. The dogma explains the cry of alarm which goes up each time the President is forced by circumstance to exert new powers and thus to threaten the balance; it explains the cry of alarm which goes up each time the Supreme Court is attacked, as it has been attacked by almost every strong

---

* Adams includes the President in "the three branches of the legislature," because the President has the veto power and must therefore pass upon every law. Adams believed that the President's power of veto should be absolute, and that the Constitution did wrong in giving to the Congress the power to pass, by a vote of two thirds of both Houses, a bill which the President had rejected. (Letter to Roger Sherman, July 18, 1789.) He also believed the Senate should not have the power to veto the President's appointments to office. (Letter to Richard Rush, May 14, 1821.)

President from Jefferson to Franklin Roosevelt; it explains the cry of alarm which goes up whenever the powers of the states are diminished— for the American feels that his liberties are safeguarded almost as much by the balance between the state and federal authorities as by the balance within the federal authority itself.

4

In 1792, when Washington was persuaded to accept a second term, Adams was re-elected Vice-President, receiving a little more than half the electoral votes;* Washington again received them all. The reorganization of Washington's Cabinet which took place during this term had a profound and evil effect on Adams's political future, and on his relations with Hamilton.

The reorganization was made necessary by the resignations of Jefferson and Hamilton, and by Washington's own disagreements with Edmund Randolph, who at first took Jefferson's place. When Randolph left the government, Washington wrote to Hamilton: "What am I to do for a Secretary of State? I ask frankly, and with solicitude, and shall receive kindly any sentiments you may express on the occasion." Hamilton suggested Rufus King, who refused the job; he then suggested Timothy Pickering of Massachusetts, who had succeeded General Knox as Secretary of War. Pickering accepted, and at once asked Hamilton's help in choosing his own successor at the War office. Hamilton nominated James McHenry of Maryland, one of his closest friends since the days when he and McHenry served together on Washington's staff. These two men, along with Oliver Wolcott, who had been made Secretary of the Treasury on Hamilton's advice, turned to Hamilton for guidance and instruction on all public matters. This gave a curious and hitherto unknown unity to the opinions of the Cabinet; but it did not make for tranquillity after Washington had retired and the same Cabinet served John Adams.

At the election of 1796, Hamilton had schemed among the electors with the hope of preventing Adams from becoming President. Hamilton wanted Thomas Pinckney of South Carolina, instead of Adams. He dared not come out openly for Pinckney, for fear of splitting the Federalist Party in New England; but he tried to have Pinckney's election appear an accident —a chance result of the constitutional provision that the electors were to vote for two candidates without specifying which was intended for President and which for Vice-President. Hamilton's plot failed; but it led to

* As a result of the Jefferson-Madison "botanizing excursion" up the Hudson River, New York (in addition to Virginia and North Carolina) gave her second electoral votes to George Clinton.

Adams being elected by a very few votes. Also, as a result of the double-dealings within the Federalist Party, Thomas Jefferson, leader of the Opposition, became Vice-President. So on the day of the inauguration, in addition to feeling wounded because the people so obviously ignored him in favor of Washington, Adams was full of rancor against the chief figure in his own party. The rancor would have been far greater if Adams had known the relations between Hamilton and the Cabinet.

The Constitution of the United States says nothing about a Cabinet; it merely remarks that the President "may require the opinion, in writing, of the principal officer in each of the executive departments, upon any subject relating to the duties of their respective offices." We have seen that the Congress made the executive departments responsible to the President, with the exception of the Treasury Department, which had an ambiguous status; and we have seen that with the refusal of the Senate to act as a privy council the President turned more and more to his Cabinet for advice and help. In 1797, however, no one knew whether the Cabinet should be regarded as a body of civil servants, holding office during good behavior and removable only by impeachment, or whether they were the President's personal appointees, representatives of the major regions and interests within the party. If they were the latter, they would go out of office with the President; if they were the former, they would be a bureaucracy of experts, able to serve any administration but owing personal loyalty to none.

When Adams decided to keep Washington's Cabinet he must have thought he was setting a precedent which would make for good government by diminishing party spirit. He must have thought that the Cabinet was composed of non-partisan civil servants; in fact it was composed of bigoted Hamiltonians intent on carrying out the policies, not of the President, but of the ex-Secretary of the Treasury. Adams's first act was to ask these men for their opinions on America's relations with France— the problem which was to plague his Administration.

By 1797, Danton and Robespierre, friends of America, were dead; France was under the Directory, venal and aggressive. She regarded the United States Government as an enemy, or at best as a willing tool of England. She thought the Jay Treaty, whereby America agreed to order French privateers out of her harbors, was the sign of an Anglo-American entente. She did not know that the treaty was accepted out of necessity, with a bitter heart, and with a resentment toward England which was to fester for a century.

To make matters worse, the Jeffersonians had not yet learned that France had changed, that the sentimental transatlantic ties of the early revolution had been broken; they thought Washington and Adams and all the Federalists were needlessly suspicious of a friendly government, and they thought the reason was pro-British bias. In their rage, some of the extremists urged the French Minister at Philadelphia to persuade his government to attack the shipping of Federalist New England. The suggestion appealed to the Directory; so the French began seizing American merchantmen on a scale which made the depredations of the British seem trivial.

Finally, when Adams came to power there was no American Minister in France, for Washington had withdrawn Monroe in 1796 and the Directory had refused to receive a successor. So the new President turned to his Cabinet for advice, and his Cabinet turned at once to Hamilton. It was perhaps fortunate that they did so, for on this occasion Hamilton was moderate whereas the members of the Cabinet if left to themselves would have urged hostilities. Hamilton wanted to send a commission to France, making one last effort to avoid war. McHenry relayed Hamilton's suggestions to Adams, almost word for word; but Wolcott and Pickering were inclined to argue back, for they knew that many of the extreme Federalists wanted war and that some were even talking secession, and a return to the Empire, in case the Jeffersonians became too pro-French.[1] Hamilton, however, remained firm and the two Cabinet members gave way to the private citizen, Wolcott writing a remarkable letter of submission in which he said: "I am not so ignorant of the extent of your influence upon the friends of government, as not to be sensible, that if you are known to favor the sending of a commission, so the thing must and will be."

And so the thing was. Adams sent Elbridge Gerry, John Marshall, and C. C. Pinckney to France, and there was a relaxation of tension until the strange news of their reception reached America. Also, the Cabinet made no further efforts to resist the directions of Hamilton. When the President asked for advice on what to do in case the mission failed, McHenry and Pickering gave him almost exact copies of the letters they received from their master in New York.

The American commissioners reached Paris in October, 1797, when the Directory had just made peace with Austria. The unacknowledged war against American shipping was profitable, and Talleyrand, the Minister of Foreign Affairs, was avaricious; so he sent three negotiators, referred to as X, Y, and Z, to demand a loan of ten million dollars for France and a bribe of $250,000 for himself as a prerequisite to further talks. When the money was refused the Americans were threatened with the power of the French party in their own country, and it was vaguely hinted that the days of French Empire in North America were not necessarily ended. After some months of useless talk, Marshall and Pinckney returned home to report to the President. Their dispatches were made public in April, 1798. The effect on public opinion appeared to be a triumph for the Adams administration and the Federalist Party; but the triumph was brief.

Hamilton advised his friends in the government to prepare for war, to begin fighting back on the sea, and to wait for a declaration of hostilities from France, which he felt sure would come and which would unite the country. Congress created the Navy Department, put three frigates into service, bought some smaller ships, and abrogated the treaties with France of 1778. War began on the sea, chiefly a war against merchant shipping, though in February, 1799, the American frigate *Constellation* captured the French frigate *L'Insurgente.*

So far, Hamilton's desires were similar to those of John Adams; but when it came to military preparations at home a rift appeared which was to end in the destruction of the Administration. Acting on the advice of Hamilton, Congress increased the regular army, and made plans for a large emergency army. Washington agreed to head the army, on condition that he be allowed to choose his general staff and that he should not take active command till war broke. This meant that the second in command would in fact be in charge of the army. McHenry and Pickering persuaded Washington to nominate Hamilton for this position. Adams rebelled, but Washington was induced to write a letter suggesting that he would resign his own commission unless he were allowed to choose his generals.

At last Adams awoke to what was happening. The whole of his Cabinet served Hamilton, not the President; the Federalist leaders in Congress served Hamilton, and conferred with Hamilton, not with the President. Under pressure from all these friends of Hamilton, Washington too ignored the man who had once made him Commander-in-Chief and did the bidding of the New York lawyer. Adams had to give in, allowing Hamilton to become the actual commander of the new army; but the Federalist Party was broken. The strife between the titular leader and the real leader was thenceforth steady, and open, and implacable. No party under such conditions could hope to hold the presidency against an opposition headed by the suave Thomas Jefferson.

The one thing which might still have saved the Federalists was a declaration of war from France; but Talleyrand was not interested in saving the Federalists, or in providing England with a new ally.* He induced the Directory to explain away the X, Y, Z episode as a mistake, to stop the attacks on American shipping, and to make plain their willingness for peace. Nothing could have been more frustrating to Hamilton, who by this time had dreams of leading his army against New Orleans, seizing the mouth of the Mississippi, and dividing with Great Britain the spoils of Spanish America. None of these spirited events could take place unless the

* It is possible that war with France, instead of uniting the country behind the Federalists, might have destroyed the Union. The extreme Hamiltonians were planning repressive measures against their pro-French neighbors in case of war. A little too much of the strong hand might have broken the frail ties which held the new country together.

French were willing to provide a war. The extreme Federalists might have tried to force the French to oblige—but not John Adams. Military adventure made no appeal to him. He believed in a strong government; but unlike Hamilton he did not think that a standing army constituted strength. Now that he saw what had been going on behind his back, and who had been making policy, he felt that his country was threatened with a needless war. Without warning, with one dramatic gesture, he destroyed the war party and broke the power of the Hamiltonian wing of the Federalists. He did so by sending to the Senate on February 18, 1799, the nomination of William Vans Murray as minister to the French republic. In view of the recent friendliness of the Directory it was obvious there could be no war if America was willing to reopen negotiations. No one, therefore, dared reject the nomination outright; but Hamilton's friends in the Senate substituted a commission for the single envoy and then delayed the sailing so that the commissioners did not reach France until 1800, when they were received by Napoleon as First Consul. They signed a commercial agreement, and for a time there was peace.

In a letter to Benjamin Rush, in December, 1811, Adams referred to "the partial war with France, which I believed, as far as it proceeded, to be a holy war." He felt that the firmness of the United States after the X, Y, Z incident, and the undeclared naval warfare, had made peace possible; there was no act of his life of which he was more proud than the nomination of Murray and the averting of further hostilities. There was probably no act for which he received less immediate credit; instead of a war-President's popularity he won for himself the anger of his own party and the derision of his opponents. As he neared the end of his first term he had only one hope left: if he were re-elected he might redeem the negative record, rid himself of the incubus of Hamilton, and build a party which truly represented his high principles of government. He had already reorganized his cabinet, dispensing with McHenry and Pickering but retaining Wolcott, who had betrayed Adams so skillfully that he was still thought to be a friend.

It was too late. Although Adams became the Federalist candidate for a second time, Hamilton saw to it that he was defeated—by publishing an arraignment of the Administration[2] which clearly implied that Adams was unfit for public office. Seventy-three electors voted for Jefferson and Burr, sixty-five for Adams, and sixty-four for Pinckney. That Adams should have done so well, in spite of Hamilton's quaint contribution to the campaign, suggests that his character and his devotion to public service were better understood by the people than by the Federalist leaders. The people were represented by the state legislatures which named the Adams electors; the leaders would have been glad to drop Adams altogether.

During the campaign Adams had been caricatured as a puffed-up tyrant, a monarchist at heart, whose one interest was the accumulation of honors. Unaccustomed to the new ferocity of politics, Adams took this to heart. In his grief he felt that Jefferson had betrayed the past, and all the years of their generous work together. He sat signing documents until the last hour of his presidency, and then left Washington* at dawn, to avoid his old friend's inauguration.**

Among the final acts of his administration was one of the most important which Adams ever performed, and one of the most annoying to Jefferson. After his dismissal of Pickering, Adams had appointed John Marshall Secretary of State; then, toward the end of his presidency, he made Marshall Chief Justice of the Supreme Court. The last Federalist President thus insured that for the next thirty-five years an arch-Federalist would mold and interpret the Constitution. Adams knew exactly what he was doing. He had first offered the chief justiceship to John Jay, writing: "In the future administration of our country, the firmest security we can have against the effects of visionary schemes or fluctuating theories will be in a solid judiciary." Jay refused, on the ground that the whole system of government had proved so defective that the courts would not be able to supply "the energy, weight, and dignity which are essential."*** Marshall accepted the post and proved that Jay was wrong. Mr. James Truslow Adams writes: "By his nomination of Washington as Commander-in-Chief, Adams had made a nation possible. By his nomination of Marshall he gave, for centuries following, the fundamental law to that nation."

5

The Federalist Party lingered on as the only opposition until it destroyed itself during the War of 1812. During these years it continued to win local elections, especially in New England; but its great days on the national stage were ended in 1801. There were several reasons for the decline. In the first place, the Federalists did not believe in political parties and were thus handicapped when it came to building an effective one. They organized only under pressure from the Opposition, and never as well

* The government had moved from Philadelphia to Washington in November, 1800.

** Time was to soften his feeling about Jefferson. On Christmas Day, 1811, Adams wrote to Benjamin Rush: "You exhort me to 'forgiveness and love of enemies,' as if I considered, or had ever considered, Jefferson as my enemy. This is not so; I have always loved him as a friend. If I ever received or suspected any injury from him, I have forgiven it long and long ago." Shortly afterwards he wrote to Jefferson, suggesting that they might renew their old friendship. The result was an interesting and touching correspondence which lasted until 1826.

*** John Jay had already served as Chief Justice from 1789 to 1795.

as the Opposition. Also, the party was dominated by a ruling class which was certain of its own right to rule, and equally certain that the humble voter should be pleased and proud to take orders. In Massachusetts, for example, the Federalist members of the legislature appointed the county committees, which in turn controlled the town committees and thus the nominations to office. The organization was kept secret, since the Federalists condemned the Jeffersonians for their party machine; so the voter merely knew that from time to time he was told to vote for someone chosen by his lords and masters. This did not make for solidarity, or party loyalty. Jefferson could produce equally autocratic results while allowing the people to feel they were in control.

Until after the turn of the century, however, the Federalists were able to hold their working-class support in New England, and the support of the Negroes in New York City, where the recently freed slaves held the balance of power in a close election, and where they voted for the party of the masters who had liberated them and against the party of the Jeffersonian workingmen who had fought abolition on the ground that they did not want to meet the competition of the Negro. Jefferson's phrases about "the mobs of great cities," whom he called "panders of vice," and who, he said, "add just so much to the support of pure government, as sores do to the strength of the human body," were used against him with some success by the Federalists in the Northern towns. Also, in New England the ship caulkers and many other artisans were inclined to vote Federalist on the ground that the prosperity of the merchants and shippers meant the prosperity of the worker.

These advantages were slowly frittered away as the ruling Federalist gentry proved that in an era of change and upheaval they thought society should be changeless. They also proved that they had no knowledge of the West except as a vague place where the workman could take up land if he was dissatisfied at home. The failure to court the West, or to find new recruits anywhere, doomed the Federalist Party in a rapidly expanding nation. The Federalists might hold all their original strength and still be ruined, if they allowed the Jeffersonians to get the new voters.

6

The Federalists left behind them in 1801 a working government machine, far more durable than they thought, fully impervious to the "visionary schemes or fluctuating theories" of their enemies. They left behind them a constitutional theory (as to the powers of the federal government and the responsibilities of the Supreme Court) which for the most part has prevailed to this day. They did not, however, succeed in establishing their view—or any view—of the relation between the executive and the legislature, a relation which was not defined in the Constitution and which presumably was not definable. Here was a problem which had to be solved by experience and the Federalists failed to solve it. Their plan was to give to the department heads, and thus to the Executive, the initiative in the making of policy and the shaping of laws. It seemed a workable plan so long as there were no political parties; it might have led to an American form of parliamentary government, with the President less important than at present and the cabinet far more important.

The plan became discredited, partly because of the rise of parties (since the Constitution made possible an Executive belonging to one party and a legislature belonging to another), and partly because of the failure of the Federalists to understand politics and to respect the Opposition. To them the Opposition was little better than a band of rebels, to be treated firmly and if necessary roughly; so the people began to look upon the Federalists as would-be autocrats. Their plan for concentrating energy and responsibility in the executive was interpreted as a threat to the people's liberties. Colonial experience had made Americans feel that the Executive was the natural tool of tyranny, the local legislature the natural friend of the people. Some of the Federalist measures seemed to support this theory.

In 1794, for example, they made an immense show of power to put down a minor uprising in western Pennsylvania known as the Whisky Rebellion. The one way to transport and sell the surplus corn of the Westerners was to distill it and sell it as whisky; so Hamilton's excise tax of 1791 seemed as unjust beyond the mountains as the British stamp tax had seemed to the colonies of the seaboard. The law was resisted, and a federal marshal at Pittsburgh was prevented from serving writs against distillers. The revolt created an interesting problem for Washington, since the essence of the new federal government, as compared to the old confederacy, was its power to operate directly upon the individual and not merely upon the state. Hamilton, always eager for a show of strength, urged Washington to use the authority given him by Congress and to call out the militia of four states. This was done; fifteen thousand militiamen were marched across the mountains and the authority of the central government was established; but the Federalists paid a heavy price. Such an army, sent to quell so small a revolt, seemed to confirm Jefferson's repeated charge that the Federalists were "monocrats" bent on using the Executive to enslave the people. The Opposition never allowed the charge to rest, never allowed "Hamilton's army" to be forgotten.

The Alien and Sedition Acts of 1798 were even more harmful to the Federalist cause than the Whisky Rebellion. These were passed at the height of the French crisis, when it was feared that in case of war the more violent Jeffersonians might give aid to the enemy.* The Alien Act gave the President power to expel foreigners from the country by Executive decree. The Sedition Act provided stiff penalties for conspiracies, or libels on high officials, and declared that any speech or writing against the President or the Congress "with intent to defame," or to bring them "into contempt or disrepute," was punishable by fine or imprisonment. A number of Republican editors were convicted under this act, a sign of the inability of the Federalists to distinguish between political opposition and treason.**

This time the extreme Jeffersonians did more than call the Federalists names: they threatened revolution. They declared, in effect, that it was the duty of the states to resist these laws of the central government. Their protest took the form of two sets of resolutions in the year 1798— one drafted by Jefferson and offered to the Kentucky legislature by John Breckenridge, the other drafted by Madison and offered to the Virginia Assembly by John Taylor of Caroline County. It would not have been possible to find four men who carried more weight in the South.

The resolutions charged the federal government with a dangerous usurpation of power; they declared that "the States composing the United States of America are not united on the principle of unlimited submission to their general government";[3] and they concluded that when the central government overstepped its powers the states were the proper authorities to decide that the Constitution has been violated. What then was to be the redress? Kentucky called upon her fellow states to "concur . . . in declaring these acts" void and "in requesting their repeal"; Virginia talked about "interposing" state authority between the citizen and the unconstitutional acts of his federal government.

The replies from other states were not favorable; but Kentucky was undeterred, and in the following year adopted a further resolution which stated: "That the several states who formed that instrument [that is, the Constitution] being sovereign and independent, have the unquestionable right to judge of the infraction; and, *That a nullification of those sovereignties, of all unauthorized acts done under color of that instrument is the rightful remedy."* In Virginia, in 1798 and 1799, there were preparations for resistance by force. Characteristically, the most extreme view was taken by young John Randolph of Roanoke, who first stepped upon the national stage in the latter year, standing for Congress on a platform which demanded armed resistance if the laws were not repealed. He made a speech at Charlotte Court House, where he boldly

* Hamilton, for all his belief in strong government, disapproved of these acts, describing them as "violence without energy."

** The First Amendment to the Constitution, drafted to protect critics of the government, and declared in force December, 1791, forbids Congress to pass a law abridging freedom of speech or of the press.

opposed the dying Patrick Henry. In a last great speech, Henry warned his state not to lift her hand against the national government. Henry had disliked the Constitution on the ground that it took too much power from the states; but he also disliked civil war. He warned his Virginians that Washington himself would lead an army against them if they resisted. "Where is the citizen of America," he asked, "who will dare lift his hand against the father of his country? No! you dare not do it! In such a parricidal attempt, the steel would drop from your nerveless arm!" John Randolph—long to be the scourge of every compromiser and the center of every resistance to federal power—won the election with his radical views.* Henry, who was a Federalist candidate for the State Senate, was also elected;** but he died a few months later.

The problem raised by the Virginia and Kentucky Resolutions, like most of the important problems of government, can never be solved. It can only be allayed. In a federal union the central government has certain clear powers and the states have certain clear powers; but there is a shadowy and ill-defined borderland between the two. An aggressive majority, especially a majority of reformers, will be tempted to encroach on this borderland in the name of efficiency, saying that only the federal power can act throughout the country with speed; but when such a majority makes laws which are felt to be hurtful by a region, the region will appeal to states' rights, will discover that the laws are unconstitutional and that it is a duty to resist. Within a few years of the Virginia and Kentucky Resolutions, the Federalists of New England, feeling themselves harmed by President Jefferson, were quoting his resolutions back at him, threatening to nullify, threatening to secede.

States' rights are the support of a minority in resisting the will of a distant majority. There can be no federal government without states' rights, or with too much states' rights; and no one has ever been able to define what "too much" means. Only compromise, delay, inefficiency, the willingness of a minority not to obstruct beyond the limits of human patience, only such fruits of political experience can make a large federal system work. Nothing is more fatal to federalism than the insistence on

* We shall hear much of this young man during the next few years. A Virginian, and a distant cousin to Jefferson, he was not yet twenty-six when he faced Henry at Charlotte Court House. When the Jeffersonians came to power in 1801, Randolph was appointed chairman of the standing committee on ways and means, and became in effect the administration leader in the House. Brilliant, erratic, arrogant, incapable of compromise, Henry Adams called him "a Virginian Saint Michael— almost terrible in his contempt for whatever seemed to him base or untrue." He was an "old Republican" with all his passionate being, believing utterly in the principles of the Resolutions of 1798, and in the promises made by the Jeffersonians in 1800. His break with Jefferson, in 1806, because that practical leader was prepared to compromise, was one of the stormiest episodes in early American history.

** Distaste for the French Revolution, and perhaps his growing fortune from law practice and land speculations, caused Henry to change parties in his old age.

logic and definition; for it is not logical to seek to divide power, and it is not possible to define with clarity the areas of division. The problems of federalism cannot be solved; but subtle, human, compromising, undogmatic, and boldly illogical political parties can sometimes allay them. This they have done in the United States since the end of the Civil War; this they will cease to do the day they become clear and exclusive in their ideas, rigid in their principles, impatient in their desire to do good without delay. Jefferson was the natural politician who could make a federal system work because he did not expect it to work reasonably; John Randolph was the natural reformer who would drive his country toward civil war rather than allow it to rest in its imperfections.

VII

Mr. Jefferson and His Methods

THE JEFFERSONS were among the early settlers in Virginia; but they remained relatively obscure until the time of Peter Jefferson, the father of Thomas, who acquired fourteen hundred acres of land in the wilderness at the foot of the Blue Ridge Mountains, and who then married Jane Randolph, thus allying himself to one of the leading families in the colony. Thomas Jefferson, the third child but eldest son of this marriage, was born in 1743. His earliest years were spent at "Tuckahoe," the William Randolph estate on the James River; but at the age of nine he moved to his father's land in what was then the wild West: only a hundred miles from the coast, yet inhabited by backwoodsmen to whom democracy was not a theory of politics but an inescapable fact. To the end of his fastidious and privileged life, Jefferson was influenced by the egalitarianism of these early surroundings.

As he grew toward manhood he became a member of the democratic group in Virginia, which was led by Patrick Henry. The strength of the democrats came from the twenty-one western counties and from minority groups in the conservative East: "small farmers along the upper rivers, tobacco-growers from the ridges between, hunters and trappers from the slopes of the Alleghenies, and the hitherto inert and unorganized mass of small proprietors and slave-owners from the old counties."[1]

Jefferson's father died in 1757, and the boy of fourteen inherited 2750 acres. Three years later he entered William and Mary College, and began to enjoy life among the planters of the Tidewater. In appearance, Jefferson was a blend of the border and the planter types. He was well over six feet tall, and ungraceful. On horseback he was splendid; in the drawing-room he stood, or sat, awkwardly. His forehead and his cheekbones were high (the Randolphs had Indian blood); his mild eyes were blue; his hair sandy, verging on red; his mouth large and sensitive. He was negligent in his dress (carefully so, according to his enemies); but his dignity was deep and unshakable, and his cold reserve with strangers was a surprise to those who idealized him as the great democrat. He never sought to mix with the public; indeed, he was seldom seen in public except on horseback. He never sought to move his fellow men by oratory; his voice was weak and hoarse; his shyness made public speaking hateful. He was a democrat in all his public deeds, in all his policy; at home, he was a quiet, friendly patrician.

At college Jefferson perfected his knowledge of the classics and laid the basis for a love of modern letters. In mind and temperament he belonged to the pleasant band of eighteenth-century dilettanti: the men who thought it possible to have a knowledge of all art, all literature, all applied science. With his exuberant health, his power for day-long, year-long application, Jefferson made his dilettantism a form of genius. Most men who sought to know so much, so gracefully, would never know anything well; but in literature, politics, architecture, agriculture, mechanics, Jefferson had a mastery which time has only made more evident. And in several branches of science, such as paleontology and botany, he was a pioneer.

After leaving college Jefferson studied law, and was soon earning a good income. He also made a profit from his farms, having greatly increased his landholdings and become the master of fifty-two slaves.* In 1772 he married Martha (Wayles) Skelton, a twenty-three-year-old widow. Her father soon died, leaving her a considerable property in land, but also leaving large debts which were a permanent burden to her husband.

At the age of twenty-six Jefferson became a member of the Virginia House of Burgesses. He soon joined the more aggressive rebels against British policy, and in 1774, unable because of illness to attend the Virginia Convention on colonial grievances, he forwarded the paper which was published as *A Summary View of the Rights of British America.* It was an eloquent expression of the faith in natural law which was to govern Jefferson's life and to inspire his most famous deed: the Declaration of Independence. The *Summary View* ended with some comments to the King:

> These are our grievances, which we have thus laid before His Majesty, with that freedom of language and sentiment which becomes a free people, claiming their rights as derived from the laws of nature, and not as the gift of their Chief Magistrate. Let those flatter who fear: it is not an American art. To give praise where it is not due might be well from the venal, but it would ill beseem those who are asserting the rights of human nature. They know, and will, therefore, say that Kings are the servants, not the proprietors of the people.

The *Summary View* was not kindly received in London, where Jefferson's name was included in a bill of attainder. Yet for all his strong words he still felt that American independence was unnecessary. Two

---

* A little later in his life, Jefferson owned 10,000 acres and considerably more than a hundred slaves.

years later, long after John Adams had known that war, hard war, was ordained, Jefferson could write to his Randolph relative, the loyalist Attorney General of Virginia: "I would rather be in dependence on Great Britain, properly limited, than on any other nation on earth, or than on no nation." By "limited" dependence he meant self-government within a commonwealth of nations, a federal empire. No such plan was possible in London, so there was no stopping short of war; but the ever-sanguine Jefferson preferred to hope for peace. It was a hope which he indulged in later life with startling results.

In June of 1775 Jefferson attended the Second Continental Congress at Philadelphia—his first trip north. The impatient and sarcastic John Adams was charmed by him. "Though a silent member in Congress," said Adams, "he was so prompt, frank, explicit and decisive upon committees and in conversation—not even Samuel Adams was more so—that he soon seized upon my heart." There were no differences, in 1775, between the two men who were to become bitter political foes. During the previous years, Adams, like Jefferson and James Wilson, had published articles demanding for the colonies a status almost as free as that of Dominions in the modern British Empire.[2] He was not disturbed to find that Jefferson thought such a policy consonant with peace, because he knew that Jefferson would abandon peace, rather than the policy, on finding that he could not have both.

In 1776, when independence had finally to be proclaimed, the Continental Congress appointed a committee to draft a statement of the colonial case, addressed to all men and to all times. The committee asked Jefferson to do the writing. His draft received a number of minor corrections from Adams and from Franklin. Adams then defended it on the floor of Congress with such eloquence that again the great work was not importantly altered. One of the changes made by Congress was to strike out a passage denouncing George III for the slave trade—a fortunate excision, since the trade was carried on by New England shipowners and supported by Southern slaveowners.

Meanwhile, in Virginia, a new constitution was being made for a new and sovereign state. From Philadelphia, Jefferson sent home a draft embodying his own far-reaching hopes. "Our revolution . . ." he said many years later, "presented us with an album on which we were free to write what we pleased. We had no occasion . . . to investigate the laws and institutions of a semi-barbarous ancestry. We appealed to those of nature, and found them engraved on our hearts." What Jefferson found engraved on his heart was an annually elected lower House with representation in proportion to population and with the duty of choosing the senate and the governor. The plan was not adopted. In the end, the new constitution left the rich eastern part of the state overrepresented as compared with the frontier west, left power concentrated in the hands of property and privilege, and defeated the first chance to create a model democracy in America.

Jefferson's reply to the failure of his proposals was to resign from the Congress, return to Albemarle County, and become a member of the Virginia House of Delegates. There he fought for the changes which his constitution would have made inevitable. He did away with entails and with primogeniture; he was partly successful in removing the privileges of the established church. He failed in his two remaining efforts: to found a system of free public schools and to secure the gradual abolition of slavery.* Without free schooling, he felt, democracy would not have a fair chance; and without the abolition of slavery, the freedom-loving men of the western counties would one day find themselves defending an obnoxious form of property.

2

In 1779, after his work in the Virginia legislature, Jefferson became governor of the state. He served for two terms,** attempting the thankless task of finding men, arms, money, and provisions for Washington's armies outside the state, and at the same time making Virginia strong to resist British invasion. The latter was impossible; at least it was impossible for Jefferson, who lacked ruthlessness, quick decision, and military knowledge. The state was overrun by the British; Jefferson himself was almost captured, and one of his plantations was plundered. He was a feeble war governor.

After these disheartening years Jefferson withdrew to his plantation. Like Washington, he far preferred the running of his own farms to the grandeurs and miseries of public life; and like Washington, he was an agricultural reformer, feeling that there was no more useful work than the improvement of a nation's husbandry. When making a list of his major achievements, he included the disestablishment of the church in Virginia, the ending of entails, the drafting of the Declaration of Independence, and the importing of olive plants from Marseilles and of heavy upland rice from Africa.

His retirement to the land brought him no peace on this occasion; for his wife, having given birth to her sixth child, became seriously ill and soon died. This was a heavy grief to Jefferson, who was already sadly familiar with death, since only two of his children survived infancy.

---

* This was to be combined with a gradual deportation.
** Each term was a year in length.

Three daughters and a son died; two daughters remained. After the death of his wife, Jefferson took charge of the education of the girls. He wished them to be prodigies of learning and of charm, of worldly graces and of unworldly goodness. Astonishingly, his wishes were in large part granted.*

In the summer of 1784, Jefferson went as special envoy to Paris, where he later succeeded Franklin as American Minister. It was while he was in France that his bill for establishing religious freedom, which had been introduced into the Virginia House of Delegates in 1779, was finally passed.** Jefferson always felt that the statute was one of his chief contributions to history; it stated that the mind is not subject to coercion, that "rights" are not dependent on opinions, and that opinions are not the concern of civil government.

Jefferson's duties in France were undemanding, so he spent much time traveling the country, sometimes to study architecture, sometimes to study the tragic needs of the nation.*** "Of twenty millions of people supposed to be in France," he wrote, "I am of the opinion there are nineteen millions more wretched, more accursed in every circumstance of human existence than the most conspicuously wretched individual of the whole United States."**** By the time Jefferson left France, in 1789, his belief in American isolationism had become a passion. If the liberties of the New World were to be preserved, if the corruptions of the Old were not all to be repeated, America must keep herself clear of Europe and must keep Europe clear of the western hemisphere.

In 1785 he wrote Charles Bellini:

> You are, perhaps, curious to know how this new scene has struck a savage of the mountains of America. Not advantageously, I assure you. I find the general fate of humanity here most deplorable. The truth of Voltaire's observation offers itself perpetually, that every man here must be either the hammer or the anvil. It is a true picture of that country to which they say we shall pass hereafter, and where we are to see God and his angels in splendor, and crowds of the damned trampled under their feet.

* One of the daughters, Maria, died in April, 1804. "I, of my want," he wrote sadly, "have lost even the half of all I had."

** Madison was largely responsible for getting the bill through the House of Delegates.

*** He also visited England and northern Italy, the former on an unsuccessful mission to help Adams negotiate a treaty.

**** This was not a snap judgment, for Jefferson had studied France as he studied everything new that came his way. We find him advising Lafayette to learn more about his own countrymen, to "ferret the people out of their hovels, as I have done, look into their kettels, eat their bread, loll on their beds under pretense of resting yourself, but in fact to find if they are soft."

The fear of contamination with which Jefferson viewed Europe was not lessened by his love for the beauties of that continent. In the same letter to Bellini, he said:

> Were I to proceed to tell you how much I enjoy their architecture, sculpture, painting, music, I should want words. It is in these arts they shine. The last of them, particularly, is an enjoyment the deprivation of which with us cannot be calculated. I am almost ready to say it is the only thing which from my heart I envy them, and which, in spite of all the authority of the Decalogue, I do covet.

Jefferson will not be understood—neither his foreign nor his domestic policies, his hopes nor his wounding disappointments—unless this dread of Europe and her poisons be kept in mind. He almost despaired of Europe; he thought America the last hope of man; he believed that the hope would be extinguished if America saw herself as a copy, or even as a potential partner, of Europe; he was willing to be deprived of the joys of Old-World art for as long as necessary, rather than run the risk of Old-World contagion. In 1820 he wrote to William Short:

> The day is not distant when we may formally require a meridian of partition through the ocean which separates the two hemispheres, on the hither side of which no European gun shall ever be heard, nor an American on the other; and when, during the rage of the eternal wars of Europe, the lion and the lamb, within our regions, shall lie down together in peace. . . . The principles of society there and here, then, are radically different, and I hope no American will ever lose sight of the essential policy of interdicting in the seas and territories of both Americas, the ferocious and sanguinary contests of Europe.

And in 1823, when President Monroe asked him whether the United States should join with England in opposing the intervention of the Holy Alliance in South America, Jefferson wrote:

> The question presented by the letters you sent me is the most momentous which has ever been offered to my contemplation since that of Independence. That made us a nation; this sets our compass and points the course which we are to steer through the ocean of time opening on us. . . . Our first and fundamental maxim should be, never to entangle ourselves in the broils of Europe. Our second, never to suffer Europe to intermeddle with cis-Atlantic affairs. . . . One nation, most of all, could disturb us in this pursuit; she now offers to lead, aid, and accompany us in it. . . . Great Britain is the nation which can do us the most harm of any one, or all, on earth; and with her on our side we need not fear the whole world. . . . The war in which the present proposition might engage us, should that be its consequence, is not her war, but ours. Its object is to introduce and establish the American

system, of keeping out of our land all foreign powers, of never permitting those of Europe to intermeddle with the affairs of our nations. It is to maintain our own principle, not to depart from it.

Jefferson's isolationism, his longing that America should be let alone to build a new and better life, was honorable, and sensible, and doomed. It was sensible because there did seem reason for thinking that "the principles of society there and here are radically different," and it did seem true that America was a safe distance from the Old World. Morally, the hope seemed justified, since it was based on a wish for self-improvement, so that America could help her neighbors by example. And physically the hope seemed possible. The industrial revolution was to change both appearances. The difference between "there and here" turned out to be one of good fortune, not of morals or of economic wisdom; and the size of the Atlantic turned out to be negligible.

America was luckier than Europe. Her neighbors were weak and therefore unrapacious; her natural resources were large; her politics, being freshly made, took advantage of the past two hundred years of European thought and work in the cause of freedom; but her economics were the same as other people's. She enjoyed no special favors there, save size and wealth, which are also special temptations. She had to face the dangers of the industrial revolution on the same terms as everyone else: its destruction of social relationships, its frustration of the spirit, its tendency to make men cruel and to make them shortsighted, so that slavery seems justified by the production of wealth, and the pillaging of the resources of one's own country seems justified by the gaudiness of the spoils. Here America was on an equal footing with her neighbors. And here she did no better and no worse than the rest. And here she lost her youth and her Jeffersonian dream. The industrial revolution, as accepted and applied, quickly made impossible the America which Jefferson preached when he became president. And within a century or a century and a half—some time between the sinking of the *Maine* and the ruin of Hiroshima—it made impossible the isolation which Jefferson preached till he died: the deep, the decent wish to escape "from the contagion of the world's slow stain." It is no wonder that the wish lingered for a few years, beyond hope or reason.

3

When he returned home in 1789, Jefferson thought it was only for a visit; but Washington persuaded him to become Secretary of State. As we have seen, he was not long in the Cabinet before he felt impelled to build a political party to oppose the Hamiltonians. Years later, in *The Anas* papers, Jefferson recalls his disillusionment when he first landed from France:

> The President received me cordially, and my colleagues and the circle of principal citizens apparently with welcome. The courtesies of dinner parties given me, as a stranger newly arrived among them, placed me at once in their familiar society. But I cannot describe the wonder and mortification with which the table conversations filled me.
>
> Politics were the chief topic, and a preference of kingly over republican government was evidently the favorite sentiment. An apostate I could not be, nor yet a hypocrite; and I found myself for the most part the only advocate on the republican side of the question, unless among the guests there chanced to be some member of that party from the legislative Houses.

This picture of official society was doubtless distorted; but it was not the years which had caused the distortion, it was a quality in Jefferson's mind which translated any slighting remark about the Constitution, or about the people, into a request for a king. He coined a language of his own to express his distaste for the crypto-monarchists he imagined all about him: the "monocrats," he called them; the "Anglomen." Washington tried to assure him that the town was not really filled with such monsters; but not even Washington could quiet his fears. So he set to work building his party with the zest of a man who felt he was rescuing the people from slavery. He called it the Republican Party, for he felt that he and his followers were the sole friends of the republic.

"The Republican party"* [in Congress], he wrote to Washington in 1792, "who wish to preserve the government in its present form, are fewer in number than the monarchical Federalists. They are fewer even when joined by the two or three or half-dozen anti-federalists,** who though they have not owned it are still opposed to any general government: but being less so to a republican than to a monarchical one, they naturally join those whom they think the lesser evil." Putting aside Jefferson's extreme fears of "Anglomen," it is typical of American politics that the Republicans should describe themselves as the men "who wish to preserve the government in its present form." It is the result of a written constitution that political controversies become an argument as to who is saving, and who is debauching, the sacred text. Crawford of Georgia commented on this in the Senate, in 1811. "It has become so extremely fashionable," he said, "to eulogize this Constitution, whether

---

* Later the party became known as the Democratic-Republican Party. In the time of Andrew Jackson the word "Republican" was finally dropped, and from that day to the present it has been the Democratic Party.

** The anti-Federalists had been opposed to the adoption of the Constitution, preferring to continue under the Articles of Confederation.

the object of the eulogist is the extension or the contraction of the powers of the government, that whenever its eulogium is pronounced I feel an involuntary apprehension of mischief."

Fortified by his conviction that the life of the nation was at stake, Jefferson built his party, took advantage of the Federalist war between Hamilton and Adams, and won the election of 1800. The farsightedness of his "botanizing" trip of 1791 was shown by the fact that the New York City elections, in the spring of 1800, decided who was to be made President the following autumn. The electors were still chosen by the legislatures of the several states, so a Federalist legislature meant electors presumably pledged to Adams, a Republican legislature meant electors certainly pledged to Jefferson.* The two parties were so equal that the electors of New York State were expected to decide the result; the electors would be Federalist or Republican, depending on who held the majority in the legislature, and that majority depended on the vote of New York City in May. There Hamilton and Burr were again pitted against each other, knowing that their struggle was the turning-point of American political history for a generation.

In the local elections of 1799 Burr and Tammany Hall had been beaten by Hamilton and the Federalist merchants. Confident that he could win again in 1800, Hamilton allowed his hatred for Adams to push him into a rash act: instead of choosing the strongest possible Federalist candidates for the legislature, Hamilton chose candidates who would take orders from himself. He thought he could win with these candidates, keep the Federalists in power, and contrive to make Pinckney of South Carolina the President instead of Adams. It was dangerous to seek so much, to grasp at such a complicated victory, when dealing with Aaron Burr.

In opposition to the colorless candidates of Hamilton, Burr persuaded the best Republicans in the city to offer themselves. He not only perfected the organization of Tammany, but he saw to it that a number of voteless members were given sufficient property to qualify as voters. When all plans were laid, Matthew Davis wrote to Gallatin, Jefferson's leader in Congress: "Never have I observed such an union of sentiment, so much zeal, and so general a determination to be active."[3]

On the day of the election Hamilton rode a white horse from polling

---

* The distinction is important. Candidates were chosen at a meeting of the Congressional representatives of each party—known as a party caucus. Early in 1800 it was clear that the Republican caucus would nominate Jefferson, and probably Burr for Vice-President. The Federalist caucus would nominate Adams, and C. C. Pinckney of South Carolina; but the strife within the Federalist Party was so intense that the Hamiltonian faction, if they saw a chance for victory, would try to persuade one or two electors to vote for some local favorite instead of Adams. In that case, so long as everyone made Pinckney his second choice, Pinckney would become President—for the electors merely chose two men; they did not say which man was for which office.

booth to booth, exhorting the voters; Burr stayed in his office, making
sure that the Tammany men did their duty. Davis wrote to Gallatin
that the election "will decide in some measure on our future destiny. The
result will clearly evince whether a republican form of government is
worth contending for. On this account the eyes of all America have been
turned toward the city and county of New York. The management and industry of Colonel Burr has effected all that the friends of civil liberty
could possibly desire."[4] The rest of the letter is a plea that Burr should
be rewarded with the nomination for the vice-presidency.

The next day Gallatin was sent the good news: complete Republican
victory.

> That business [wrote his informant] has been conducted and brought
> to issue in so miraculous a manner that I cannot account for it but
> from the intervention of a Supreme Power and our friend Burr the
> agent.
> On the day on which we learned . . . the vote of the city of New
> York [wrote Jefferson to Benjamin Rush, in 1811], which it was well
> known would decide the vote of the state, and that, again, the vote
> of the Union, I called on Mr. Adams on some official business. He
> was very sensibly affected, and accosted me with these words: "Well,
> I understand that you are to beat me in this contest, and I can only say
> that I will be as faithful a subject as any you will have."
> "Mr. Adams," said I, "this is no personal contest between you and
> me. Two systems of principles on the subject of government divide
> our fellow-citizens into two parties. With one of these you concur, and
> I with the other. As we have been longer on the public stage than
> most of those now living, our names happen to be more generally
> known. One of these parties, therefore, has put your name at its head,
> the other mine. Were we both to die today, tomorrow two other names
> would be in the place of ours, without any change in the motion of
> the machinery. Its motion is from its principle, not from you or myself."

Jefferson undoubtedly believed these words. He undoubtedly thought
his election was the triumph of good principles over bad, and that such
a triumph was ordained by Providence. Yet he never made the mistake
of trusting Providence to do its own work without the help of someone
like "our friend Burr the agent." Nine years before the election he
saw that the hurt feelings of the Livingston family might one day be
turned to account, so he began to inflame and to flatter those feelings.
Despising Aaron Burr, prepared in the course of time to break Burr's
power and drive him into virtual exile, he nevertheless realized that
Burr's manipulation of Tammany Hall was something from which a
wise Providence might profit. Playing every card astutely, writing from
his Vice-President's chair endless letters to politicians great and small,

letters of help, encouragement and sage guidance, taking advantage of every local quarrel or prejudice, of every folly on the part of his opponents, Jefferson managed to win by 73 votes to 65. And then he told the sardonic John Adams that "the motion of the machinery . . . is from its principle, not from you or myself." And he believed it; and it was partly true, though the historian may be pardoned for pointing out that it was not the whole truth and that the tendency among Jefferson's enemies to call him a hypocrite can at least be understood.

4

There was one point on which Providence and Mr. Burr may not have seen eye to eye: when the electoral votes were counted it was discovered that the Republican candidates for President and Vice-President had the same number of votes; but according to the letter of the Constitution there were no such things as candidates for President and Vice-President. The electors were to vote for the two best men, "of whom one at least shall not be an inhabitant of the same state as themselves." In case two men turned out to have a majority, "and an equal number of votes, then the House of Representatives shall immediately choose by ballot one of them for President." So it was still possible that "our friend Burr the agent" had overdone his helpfulness and had made himself President. The decision would have to be made, not by heaven, but by the Federalist majority in the House of Representatives. This majority naturally saw that it would be a pleasing political joke to put Aaron Burr, whom nobody wanted, in the presidency, and to send Jefferson, the creator of his party, back to the obscurity of the Vice-President's office. Hamilton, however, was still capable of large-mindedness on a matter that did not concern Adams, so he used his influence to help Jefferson's election. In doing so he took one more step toward the fatal field at Weehawken.*

While urging Jefferson's cause, Hamilton gave a description of the mind and character of his old adversary which displays the passions of the day but which also displays the Hamiltonian realism in judging political action.

> I admit [he wrote] that his [Jefferson's] politics are tinctured with fanaticism, that he is too much in earnest with his democracy; . . . that he is crafty and persevering in his objects; that he is not scrupulous about the means of success, nor very mindful of the truth, and that he is a contemptible hypocrite. But it is not true, as is alleged, that

* The Twelfth Amendment to the Constitution, proposed in 1803 and ratified in 1804, provides that the electors shall name the person voted for as President, and the person voted for as Vice-President. The confusion of 1800 cannot recur.

he is an enemy to the power of the executive. . . . While we were in the Administration together, he was generally for a large construction of the executive authority and not backward to act upon it in cases which coincided with his views. . . . I have more than once made the reflection that, viewing himself as a revisioner, he was solicitous to come into the possession of a good estate. Nor is it true that Jefferson is zealot enough to do anything in pursuance of his principles which will contravene his popularity or his interest. He is as likely as any man I know to temporize—to calculate what will be likely to promote his own reputation and advantage; and the probable result of such a temper is the preservation of systems, though originally opposed, which, being once established, could not be overturned without danger to the person who did it. . . . Add to this that there is no fair reason to suppose him capable of being corrupted.

It is interesting to compare this with John Marshall's picture of Jefferson's political character. Hamilton asked Marshall, who was then Secretary of State, to use his influence with the House of Representatives to make Jefferson President instead of Burr. Marshall refused.

Mr. Jefferson [he wrote in explanation] appears to me to be a man who will embody himself with the House of Representatives. By weakening the office of President, he will increase his personal power. He will diminish his responsibility, sap the fundamental principles of government, and become the leader of that party which is about to constitute the majority of the legislature.

The two estimates appear to be contradictory; yet within a few years they were both proved to be true. Jefferson did, seemingly, "diminish his responsibility" and "embody himself with the House of Representatives"; but he also showed himself capable of "a large construction of the executive authority and not backward to act upon it in cases which coincided with his views." He came to office as leader of a party which fiercely condemned the Federalists for saying that the Executive should make policy.* Yet his Administration was faced with the relentless fact that the public business must somehow go forward. If the Executive did not make policy, who would? If the separation of powers were taken literally, and if the Republican talk about legislative policy-making were taken literally, where would the government of the United States reside?

The new Republican majority in the House of Representatives consisted

---

* Article II, Section 3, of the Constitution says that the President "shall from time to time . . . recommend to their [the Congress's] consideration such measures as he shall judge necessary and expedient." According to the Federalists, this meant that the President should control and direct policy. According to the Republicans, it meant that he should occasionally report on the state of the Union, and make such suggestions as he chose. But he should not then use the patronage, or any other power, to press for action. Luckily for the country Jefferson, while talking like a Republican, controlled policy like a Federalist.

of a swarm of undisciplined individualists who had neither the unity of interests, nor the knowledge of administration, which had given cohesion to the Federalists. Journalists and politicians might talk about the "constitutional duty" of returning control over policy to the House; but when Jefferson surveyed the House he did not see anyone to whom he could return anything. He saw a number of talkative and touchy men, self-assured, steeped in the prejudices and problems of their districts, intent on staying in office by airing the prejudices even if they could not solve the problems. How was policy, national policy, to emerge from the frictions of such a group? The question did not dismay Jefferson, for he had a short-term political answer. He knew how policy would be made during his own administration, and he was content to leave problems in the theory of government unexamined, at least until he had retired from the practice.

In his first Inaugural Address, Jefferson spoke the appropriate party language. "Nothing," he assured the Congress, "shall be wanting on my part to inform, as far as in my power, the legislative judgment, nor to carry that judgment into faithful execution." Here, it seemed, was the division of powers in all its naïveté. The President, if asked a question by the Congress, would do his best to answer it (he might even volunteer information from time to time) ; and the President, if Congress passed a bill, would do his best to execute it. For the rest, all was apparently to be left to "the legislative judgment": but only in appearance, not in fact. We have seen that Jefferson would not trust Providence to win an election without the help of Mr. Burr; similarly, he would not trust "the legislative judgment" until he or his friends had told the legislature what to judge.

When the new House of Representatives had organized itself, the world noticed that the Speaker and the committee chairmen were all aids and close associates of Jefferson. He did not appoint them; he merely saw to it that they were appointed. He did this, not as President, but as leader of the party. The Federalists, for all their administrative competence, had failed to find a workable relation between President and party—perhaps because they did not believe in parties. Washington behaved like a reluctant, short-term, constitutional monarch, and he allowed Hamilton to behave like a far from reluctant Prime Minister. No one could usurp Washington's position, or in any way diminish his authority, so the arrangement was satisfactory during his two terms; but John Adams, who still tried to pretend there were no parties, awoke one day to find that Hamilton was running his Administration because Hamilton was the party boss. Vice-President Jefferson, presiding over the Senate, writing his endless political letters, compiling his *Manual of Parliamentary Practice,* blandly watched the Federalists attack each other, and thereby learned that the head of the Administration and the leader of the party must be the same man. From that day on, all successful Presidents have filled the two rôles. In 1801 the parties began their long and never-ending task of reassembling the powers which the Fathers in their wisdom had sundered.

This is exactly what John Marshall feared. As a Federalist, he agreed that the powers had to be reassembled if government was to function; but he thought it should be done openly, by a general admission that the Executive should make policy subject to the criticism and the permission of the legislature. He feared a system whereby the Executive would make policy in the darkness, by intrigue, by party pressure, by the quiet and irresponsible use of personal influence. Such policy-making could not be criticized effectively, because it could not be discovered in time. Yet this was Jefferson's system. "What is practical must often control what is pure theory," he wrote in 1802. The pure theory, in his case, was the complete division of powers whereby the Congress made laws in one vacuum and the President administered them in another. Jefferson saluted the theory in public; but in private he turned to "what is practical." In private he told the Congress what laws the Administration wanted, and did not want. "His whole system of administration," wrote John Quincy Adams in his *Memoirs,* "seems founded on the principle of carrying through the legislature measures by personal or official influence." And Senator Pickering said that Jefferson tried "to screen himself from all responsibility by calling upon Congress for advice and direction. . . . Yet with affected modesty and deference he secretly dictates every measure which is seriously proposed."[5]

There was one flaw to Jefferson's plan: it was not a permanent system of government; it could only be worked by one remarkable man, the like of whom has never been seen again. "This well-organized system," writes Professor Binkley, "worked with almost infallible precision, despite the fact that the machinery and its operation were concealed from the public. Through a hint dropped here, a diplomatic letter sent there, and a suggestion made to another the President had his way."[6] The virtuosity was admirable; yet the Federalists were right in pointing out that their rejected system would work without a magician in the White House, and would work in broad daylight where the whole country could watch. They were also right, or at least very human, to be annoyed at the readiness with which the Republicans took over Federalist methods which they had criticized unmercifully. The new Secretary of the Treasury was soon being consulted by Congress as Hamilton had been consulted, and was soon steering his bills through the House of Representatives with a Hamiltonian authority. Also, the Republicans made effective use of the much-abused caucus—the device for bringing together President, Cabinet, and party members of Congress to decide on policy and to frustrate the constitutional division of powers. When Jefferson's party caucus approved a measure, and Jefferson's party floor leader was on hand to make sure that wavering members voted correctly or suffered the swift consequences of Jefferson's displeasure, there was little danger that "the legislative judgment" would either surprise or pain the president.*

5

James Madison became Jefferson's Secretary of State, and Albert Gallatin his Secretary of the Treasury. Gallatin was Swiss. He had moved to America at the age of nineteen, and had finally settled in western Pennsylvania. Although descended from a proud and ancient family in Savoy, he was both a natural and an intellectual democrat; he had Jefferson's purity of motive without the guile; he had Hamilton's clarity of mind without the arrogance. And like Hamilton he was a nationalist before he was a local patriot. Perhaps this was because both men were born abroad. No early memories—no spires, no farms, no "blue remembered hills"—anchored them to a state rather than to the nation. They were Americans who happened to live in New York or Pennsylvania, not Pennsylvanians or New Yorkers who happened to have joined a federal union.

Gallatin was elected to the Fourth Congress, taking his seat in 1795 and serving until he became Secretary of the Treasury in 1801. A foreigner, with a foreign accent, representing a frontier district at a time when the nation was still sending many of her best men to Congress, Gallatin within two years became Republican leader of the lower House, taking that position without contest when Madison resigned in 1797. He did this by the power of his mind, and by the goodness and restraint of his character. Gallatin had exact knowledge, where most of his confrères had vague prejudice; Gallatin was disinterested, balanced, calm, where a man like Giles (who became party leader in the House in 1801) was unfair, partisan, and noisy.** It is a tribute to the Jeffersonians in the Fifth and Sixth Congresses that they naturally took Gallatin as their leader.

During the first year of his Congressional service he began to train his party in the financial ideas which underlay the Republican creed. With the whole of his mind and spirit he believed in Jefferson's "frugal government." As strongly as Hamilton stood for binding the rich to the government through public debt and through privilege, Jefferson and Gallatin stood for a government which should get along on its annual revenue, and

* There seems to be no proof that Jefferson himself ever attended a caucus, although the Federalists accused him of doing so as if it were a crime. But the important point is that whether or not he was present his plans were accepted and his influence was paramount.

** William Branch Giles of Virginia retired from Congress in October, 1798, and did not return until 1801. He retired again, because of ill health, in 1802. In 1804, he became Senator from Virginia, serving until 1815.

which should make sure that the revenue was as modest as possible, so that "labor may be lightly burdened." They agreed that payment of the public debt should have precedence over any other expenditure. This, they thought, was the one road toward equal rights, economic justice, and the abolition of special privilege. It was worth paying any price in commercial inconvenience, and in temporary humiliation abroad, to be allowed to travel this road.

Like Jefferson, Gallatin believed in an almost Arcadian isolationism. Arguing against appropriations for a navy in 1798, he said:

> I know not whether I have heretofore been indulging myself in a visionary dream, but I had conceived, when contemplating the situation of America, that our distance from the European world might have prevented our being involved in the mischievous politics of Europe, and that we might have lived in peace without armies and navies and without being deeply involved in debt. It is true in this dream I had conceived it would have been our object to become a happy and not a powerful nation, or at least no way powerful except for self-defence.[7]

And years later he wrote to Jefferson, almost in despair, when it was becoming plain that the demands of "self-defence" alone were enough to thwart all their hopes for Republican purity:

> I cannot, my dear sir, consent to act the part of a mere financier, to become a contriver of taxes, a dealer of loans, a seeker of resources for the purpose of supporting useless baubles, of increasing the number of idle and dissipated members of the community, of fattening contractors, pursers, and agents, and of introducing in all its ramifications that system of patronage, corruption, and rottenness which you so justly execrate.[8]

Here is the basic faith of the triumvirs who were now to rule the country: Jefferson and Madison and Gallatin. Simplicity, thrift, and the liquidation of debt at home, isolation (and if necessary the acceptance of insult) abroad, until America had shown that a new type of nation, a new type of Great Power, could exist. It was to establish this faith that the three leaders had sought office; it was because the people believed their promises (as well as because of Jefferson's extreme political dexterity) that the party had been put in power. "A wise and frugal government," they promised again in Jefferson's First Inaugural, "which . . . shall not take from the mouth of labor the bread it has earned." They stressed frugality, not because they were misers but because they were moral philosophers. They believed that debt, public or private, leads to the vices associated with the rule of the "mere financier"; above all they believed that debt, public or private, tends to concentrate property and power in the hands of a small group.

To the Federalists, of course, the whole Republican faith was absurd. No nation could survive, they said, in this harsh world, except by the sword. No weak government could escape robbery abroad and disorder at home. America was capable of being strong; but she would perish if Jefferson imposed weakness upon her. To this the triumvirate answered that there was more than one type of strength with which to impress the outside world, and that order at home depended less on power than on the consent of the governed. To strengthen and secure this consent they proposed (as soon as the national debt was so reduced that its extinction became a certainty) vast public works to help both the body and the brains of the nation. Early in Jefferson's second term it seemed that the great plan might succeed. In 1806 the President was able to tell Congress that the debt would soon be gone, and that then, with only the lightest of tax burdens, he planned to build roads and canals running from Maine to Georgia, and connecting the eastern rivers with the Mississippi, and that he planned also to build a great national university.*

A prosperous rural community ("the encouragement of agriculture, and of commerce as its handmaid," in the words of Jefferson's First Inaugural), and an educated public: these, said the Republican leaders, were the basis for a free state. These, and not the sword, could save America. A great and pure society which might reform the world by its example; a nation capable of choosing happiness and knowledge instead of armed power: for what else was the new republic given her isolation, given her resources, given her faith in natural law? Was nothing new intended? Was nothing new ever to be tried? The world had grown gray watching the results of pure force. From the eagles of Rome to the eagles of Napoleon, everything that could be done by the sword had been done, and it was not enough. Poverty and ignorance still ruled the world; but according to the Jeffersonians they need not rule America.

The Federalists replied that it was a good and decent dream, but still a dream; that nations were ruled by circumstances, not by principles, and still less by hopes; and that the circumstances which were personified in Napoleon and George Canning did not make for Arcadian tranquillity, or democratic purity, or freedom from debt.

A few months after Jefferson laid his noble hopes before Congress, the friendly Charles James Fox died, and the next year Canning became British Foreign Secretary. Henry Adams comments:

> From the moment Mr. Canning and his party assumed power, the fate of Mr. Jefferson's administration was sealed; nothing he could do or could have done could avert it; England was determined to recover

---

* Disagreeing with Gallatin, Jefferson felt a constitutional amendment would be needed to authorize this program; but he thought that the amendment would be easy to procure.

her commerce and to take back her seamen, and America could not
retain either by any means whatever; she had no alternative but submission or war, and either submission or war was equally fatal to Mr.
Jefferson's Administration.*

Not only was either choice fatal to the Administration, it was fatal to the
whole Republican theory of government, to the hope that the new country
might find a substitute, in human relations, for force.

6

When Jefferson came to power in 1801 he was the leader of an odd as-
sortment of interests and groups: the small farmers of the South and of the
western borders everywhere; many of the great Southern landowners and
slaveowners (notably the arch-conservative seaboard aristocracy of South
Carolina, who had been alienated by Hamilton's financial system); many
of the mechanics in the northern towns, to whom Jefferson had to explain
that he had meant only the European laborers when he wrote about "the
mobs of great cities"; and the Clinton-Burr-Livingston machine in New
York State.

If New York voted for this coalition because it wanted spoils and power,
and if South Carolina joined (in spite of deploring the ideas in Jefferson's
Declaration of Independence) because it feared the aggressiveness of
Northern capitalism, Pennsylvania supported Jefferson for the eccentric
reason that she believed in him. She believed in that same Declaration
which made the lords of South Carolina shudder, and the lords of the
Hudson Valley laugh. "In Pennsylvania," said Albert Gallatin, "not only
have we neither Livingstons nor Rensselaers, but from the suburbs of
Philadelphia to the banks of the Ohio I do not know a single family that
has any extensive influence. An equal distribution of property has rendered
every individual independent, and there is among us true and real equality."

Jefferson referred to his election as "the Revolution of 1800"; but it is
easy to understand, after making a list of his supporters, why the revolution
was not very revolutionary. The immense conservative influence of American parties, deriving from the fact that they are always coalitions of local

---

* Canning was probably unaware that such a thing as Jefferson's theory of government existed, or could exist. He sensed that America was reluctant to fight for
her interests, and the knowledge may have increased his rudeness though it did not
affect his policy. This was based on the sensible conviction that in order to beat
Napoleon England must strengthen her commerce and take back every deserting
seaman. If this meant injustice toward America, so much the worse for America.
If she wished to save her money, and the lives of her young men, she could not
expect delicate treatment in the midst of world carnage.

interests, was never better shown than in these first years of the first well-organized party. Jefferson was able to impose his money-saving, debt-paying financial policies; he was able, in the face of heavy protest, to get rid of a small number of Federalist civil servants and to install some of his own clamoring friends; he was able to send the much-abused Federalist Navy to fight the Barbary pirates in the Mediterranean, thus abandoning the ancient and shameful system of paying tribute to those thieves; but there was nothing very shocking or upsetting in any of this. The old ladies in New England who hid their Bibles at the inauguration of the Infidel, and the businessmen who would have liked to hide their gold, found that life proceeded with a surprising tranquillity and absence of change.

The same discovery was made by the more sincere and whole-souled of Jefferson's followers. The reassurance of the Federalists was paralleled by the disillusionment of men like John Randolph and John Taylor of Caroline, who expected an agrarian anti-capitalist economy to be substituted for the Hamiltonian "aristocracy of paper and privilege." They did not understand the party which they had helped to build. They did not see that the price of power in the United States is eternal compromise, for any attempt to force a radical program will mean that the coalition of regional groups will break. Then the party will go out of power or the states will cease to be united. Jefferson knew this instinctively. He led his curious team with unhurried confidence. "His academic views," writes Charles A. Beard, "assiduously circulated by his partisans pleased the temper of the agrarian masses and his practical politics propitiated rather than alienated the capitalistic interests."[9] If the foreign world had left Jefferson alone, his administrations would have been tranquil and widely popular; but his presidency lay in the years between Marengo and Wagram. It was not a happy time for the heads of states. Jefferson had hardly come to office before Napoleon began plotting his ruin.

VIII

The Tyranny of Circumstance

In the year 1801, Lucien Bonaparte was sent as French Ambassador to Madrid. His first act was to negotiate a treaty, the sixth article of which provided that the retrocession of Louisiana to France should be carried out at once. Later in the year Napoleon signed preliminary articles of peace with Great Britain, putting an end for the time being to war on the seas. He was now ready for Talleyrand's most cherished project, ready to regain the lost glories of the French Empire in North America. Europe was to have a rest from carnage; the sufferings of the United States were to begin. Preliminary to this vast plan, Napoleon sent his brother-in-law, General Leclerc, with a large army, to break the power of the Negro, Toussaint L'Ouverture, and to re-establish France and the institution of slavery on the island of San Domingo. The expedition sailed toward the end of 1801.

In the years before the French Revolution, "nearly two thirds of the commercial interests of France centered in San Domingo."[1] Only the small western end of the island belonged to France; but even so it was the most valuable of her colonial possessions. There were about six hundred thousand inhabitants of San Domingo, five sixths of whom were Negro slaves. During the Revolution they revolted and massacred the whites. The French National Assembly then abolished slavery, with the result that the native genius, Toussaint, took service under the Republic. He soon subdued and controlled the island, and was made a general by the National Convention in Paris. In 1795, Spain ceded her part of San Domingo to France; but for years Toussaint was inevitably let alone, and he came to think of himself as the ruler of a sovereign state. When Napoleon rose to power, Toussaint refused to take his orders and defied him to restore slavery. Toussaint claimed independence, counting on the breadth of the sea to save him from Europe's master; but San Domingo was essential to the building of a new French empire. Without the island Napoleon could not support his troops in Louisiana, so Toussaint had to be destroyed.

Early in 1802, the world began to realize what a fateful decision rested with the Negro leader of the little West Indian island. "If he and his blacks," writes Henry Adams, "should succumb easily to their fate, the wave of French empire would roll on to Louisiana and sweep far up the

Mississippi; if San Domingo should resist, and succeed in resistance, the recoil would spend its force on Europe, while America would be left to pursue her democratic destiny in peace."[2] After three months of bitter fighting, which destroyed one French army, Toussaint was taken prisoner by trickery and sent to Europe to die in the cold of the Jura Mountains. It seemed that Napoleon had once again triumphed. He gave orders to return the Negroes to slavery and prepared an expedition, ostensibly for San Domingo, but in reality to occupy Louisiana. France was about to become the greatest power in the New World as well as in the Old.

Jefferson saw the deadly danger to America, and in April, 1802, he wrote to Robert Livingston, the American Minister at Paris:

> It [the cession of Louisiana to France] completely reverses all the political relations of the United States. . . . There is on the globe one single spot the possessor of which is our natural and habitual enemy. It is New Orleans, through which the produce of three eighths of our territory must pass to market. . . . The day that France takes possession of New Orleans . . . we must marry ourselves to the British fleet and nation. We must turn all our attention to a maritime force, for which our resources place us on very high ground; and having formed and connected together a power which may render reinforcement of her settlements here impossible to France, make the first cannon which shall be fired in Europe the signal for the tearing up any settlement she may have made, and for holding the two continents of America in sequestration for the common purposes of the united British and American nations.

Those are bold words; but they would have had small meaning if ten thousand veteran troops under a marshal of France had been stationed on the Mississippi. In October, 1802, Jefferson learned that the Spanish governor had withdrawn the American "right of deposit" at New Orleans. Three months later James Monroe was sent as envoy extraordinary, to join Robert Livingston at Paris. His instructions were to buy New Orleans and the Floridas, or New Orleans alone, or some other space on the east bank where the Americans could transship their goods. If all was refused, Monroe should press for a perpetual guarantee of the rights of navigation and deposit; if that too failed, he was to open conversations with the British. Bold words again; but their strength depended, not on anything which Jefferson could do, but on the Negroes of San Domingo.

The expedition to Louisiana, headed by a general of division and three generals of brigade, was to have sailed in September, 1802. It did not sail because "as fast as regiments could be named they were consumed in the fiery furnace of San Domingo."[3] The treacherous capture of Toussaint had not ended the war; it had only made the fighting more bloodthirsty. In January, 1803, news reached Paris that General Leclerc was dead, that

fifty thousand French troops and vast supplies had been consumed in a
year of slaughter, that San Domingo was ruined, its plantations destroyed,
its population returned to barbarism. The French army now dreaded
service in that cursed island, whence no man came home, and where
money accomplished nothing but to increase the ruin.* Napoleon waited
another three months, while the news grew more savage and more bloody:
the white men burning Negroes, and Negroes massacring the whites; then
he abandoned his imperial dream, telling Talleyrand to sell Livingston the
whole of Louisiana. This was the week in which Toussaint L'Ouverture
died in his mountain dungeon.

> Toussaint [wrote Henry Adams] never knew that San Domingo had
> successfully resisted the whole power of France . . . ; but even when
> shivering in the frosts of the Jura, his last moments would have glowed
> with gratified revenge had he known that at the same instant Bonaparte
> was turning into a path which the Negroes of San Domingo had driven
> him to take and which was to lead him to parallel at St. Helena the fate
> of Toussaint himself at the Château de Joux. . . . The prejudice of
> race alone blinded the American people to the debt they owed to the
> desperate courage of five hundred thousand Haytian Negroes who
> would not be enslaved."[4]

2

On April 30, Livingston and Monroe bought the province of Louisiana
for sixty million francs ($11,250,000), the United States Government agree-
ing to assume an additional twenty million francs of debts which were owed
by France to American citizens ($3,750,000). The boundaries of Louisiana
were not defined, and the treaty of cession contained the promise that "the
inhabitants of the ceded territory shall be incorporated in the Union of the
United States, and admitted as soon as possible, according to the principles of the Federal Constitution, to the enjoyment of all the rights, advantages, and immunities of citizens of the United States." Monroe had
been instructed by Secretary of State Madison to make no such promise,
on the ground that it would be unconstitutional; but the dazzled envoys
did not dare prolong the negotiations, lest haggling should cause Napoleon
to change his mind once more. Soured by the losses in San Domingo, and
bored at the thought of further waiting, he had suddenly abandoned
Talleyrand's policy of peace in Europe and expansion in North America;
but if the next ship brought good news from the West Indies, he might as
suddenly take it up again.

* General Rochambeau, who succeeded Leclerc, wrote that he must have 35,000
fresh troops at once, to save the island.

It was this sense of urgency when dealing with an erratic tyrant which led Jefferson to confirm the purchase without waiting for a constitutional amendment. He believed that the act was unconstitutional, since it involved a far-reaching change in the relations between the states and in the balance of power within the country. It also involved an interpretation of the treaty-making power which would permit the President and Senate to annex the whole of Europe. Jefferson, who had recently been pleading for the strictest of strict constructions of the Constitution, rightly ignored logic in order to make sure of Louisiana; but he wished to repair the damage by asking for a constitutional amendment after the fact. Both Gallatin and Wilson Cary Nicholas* thought this unnecessary; but Jefferson stuck to his point, writing to Nicholas on September 7, 1803:

> When I consider that the limits of the United States are precisely fixed by the treaty of 1783, that the Constitution expressly declares itself to be made for the United States . . . I do not believe it was meant that [Congress] might receive England, Ireland, Holland, etc., into it,— which would be the case on your construction. . . . I had rather ask an enlargement of power from the nation, where it is found necessary, than to assume it by a construction which would make our powers boundless. Our peculiar security is in the possession of a written Constitution. Let us not make it a blank paper by construction. I say the same as to the opinion of those who consider the grant of the treaty-making power as boundless. If it is, then we have no Constitution.[5]

In spite of this clear statement, Jefferson in the end allowed his friends to persuade him to do nothing, to accept the annexation without raising the question of constitutional propriety. He abandoned what he described as his country's "peculiar security"; he acquiesced in making blank paper of the Constitution. And the following year he went even further in repudiating the ideas of 1798, of the Kentucky and Virginia Resolutions, by accepting a bill creating a territorial government in which the people of Louisiana were to have no share. According to this bill, the governor and secretary of Louisiana were to be appointed by the President, the legislative council was to be appointed by the President, and the judges were to be appointed by the President.

John Quincy Adams, in the Senate, raised the awkward question whether the Constitution gave the federal government power to tax the citizens of Louisiana without their consent. The question was ignored. The "inalienable rights" of 1776 were apparently not shared by French Catholics.

> Within three years of his inauguration [wrote Henry Adams] Jefferson bought a foreign colony without its consent and against its will,

---

* Senator from Virginia and one of Jefferson's close friends. Jefferson had consulted with Nicholas when framing the Kentucky Resolutions.

annexed it to the United States by an act which he said made blank paper of the Constitution; and then he who had found his predecessors too monarchical, and the Constitution too liberal in powers—he who nearly dissolved the bonds of society rather than allow his predecessor to order a dangerous alien out of the country in time of threatened war, made himself monarch of the new territory, and wielded over it, against its protests, the powers of its old kings.[6]

Strict construction had been abandoned, for the best of reasons, without apologies, by an Administration of strict-constructionists. The theory that the government must be kept weak, as a protection to liberty, that the powers of the central government must be severely limited by the most rigid interpretation of the written document, has never wholly recovered from this event. If Jefferson and his Virginian Republicans could not adhere to the theory, nobody could. The theory has been revived many times by minorities that have felt themselves oppressed; it is the theory on which the Southern Confederacy was built; yet for better or worse the dominant American practice has been to construe the Constitution broadly, to find therein the powers deemed necessary. Sometimes the Supreme Court has speeded this development; sometimes it has stood in the way; but when the Court has aggrandized the power of the federal government, as it did under Chief Justice Marshall, the new power has never been withdrawn; whereas when the Court has restricted the power of the federal government, as it did under Marshall's successor, Chief Justice Taney, the restrictions have not endured. The tendency to find more and more leeway within the Constitution has triumphed; and the moment when this first became a predictable development was 1803–04, when the Jeffersonians found they could not meet the responsibilities of office if they held to their constitutional theories.

The Louisiana Purchase was the most popular act of Jefferson's presidency. It ensured the allegiance of the Western country, and hence the dominance of the new party. The Western states of those days were Tennessee, Kentucky, and Ohio. They were democratic communities, Jeffersonian in principle and practice; but they would not have been Jeffersonian on election day if the Republicans had allowed legal theory to interfere with buying the port of New Orleans. Free navigation of the Mississippi, and the right of deposit, were essential to the existence of the Western states; by acquiring Louisiana and the great port of New Orleans Jefferson consolidated his party and began the alliance of South and West which was to dominate politics for more than half a century. He also doubled the size of the country. He also sacrificed his favorite theory on the cruel altar of necessity. The Supreme Court was soon to show the importance of the sacrifice.

3

In the dying days of the Adams Administration, Congress increased the number of federal courts, and reorganized the judiciary in the District of Columbia. The President quickly filled the new places with judges who were strongly anti-Jeffersonian, and as we have seen he gave the chief justiceship to Jefferson's deep enemy, John Marshall.* After the "Revolution of 1800," therefore, the Republicans who had come to power found their opponents securely in control of one main branch of the government. In their annoyance they repealed the act creating the new federal judgeships, and they refused to deliver the commissions of the four new justices of peace for the District of Columbia.

These appointments had been made on March 2, 1801, and confirmed by the Senate on March 3—the last day of office for John Adams. The commissions had then been signed by the President, and sealed by Marshall as Secretary of State; but they had not been delivered. They were found in the Department of State, and Jefferson ordered that they be withheld. The four appointees then applied to the Supreme Court for a writ of mandamus, to compel Madison (the new Secretary of State) to deliver the commissions. The basis of the application was Section 13 of the Judiciary Act of 1789, which authorized the Supreme Court to issue such a writ "to officers of the United States." The case was presented in the name of William Marbury, one of the plaintiffs, and thus became known as *Marbury* v. *Madison.*

The unanimous decision of the Court, written by John Marshall, was given in February, 1803. The first question was whether Marbury had a right to the commission. The Court found that he had such a right. The second question was whether the laws provided a remedy for the violation of this right. The Court found that the laws did provide a remedy, and that the writ of mandamus was the proper form of remedy. The third question, which contained John Marshall's joker, was whether the Supreme Court had the authority to issue such a writ. The authority was not conferred by the Constitution, which was precise in its grants of original jurisdiction to the Supreme Court. "In all cases," says Article III, Section 2, "affecting ambassadors, other public ministers and consuls, and those in which a state shall be a party, the Supreme Court shall have original jurisdiction. In all other cases before mentioned the Supreme Court shall

---

* Marshall assumed the new office on February 4, 1801. He continued as Secretary of State until the end of the Adams Administration, though he did not draw the salary of that office.

have appellate jurisdiction. . . ." The power to issue a writ of mandamus rested solely on the Judiciary Act of 1789, and Marshall held that Congress was not permitted by the Constitution to expand the original jurisdiction of the Court. Section 13 of the Judiciary Act was invalid, since an act conflicting with the Constitution could not become the law of the land. The writ, therefore, could not issue from the Supreme Court.

Politically and legally, this was a remarkable decision. By holding that Marbury had a right to his commission, Marshall was able to admonish the President and the Secretary of State, picturing their deed as both illegal and unjust. By holding that the Supreme Court had no jurisdiction, Marshall was able to combine a seeming act of restraint with a real assertion of power. At the time, the chief interest centered on the statement that Jefferson had no legal right to withhold the commissions; but the drama of the case for later generations was that it affirmed for the first time that the Supreme Court might declare an act of Congress null and void. The decision "brought to the support of the Union, while the memory of the Virginia and Kentucky Resolutions was still green, the ineffably important proposition that the Constitution has one final interpreter, at the same time seizing for the Court its greatest prerogative."[7] The power then seized has never been withdrawn, although several of the strongest presidents have fought to curb it.

We have seen that the members of the Constitutional Convention were in apparent agreement that the Supreme Court should possess this power. Ever since the adoption of the Constitution, state courts had undertaken to declare state laws invalid, and in colonial days the acts of the assemblies had been subject to disallowance by the courts. Most modern scholars would probably agree with Justice Oliver Wendell Holmes, who stated bluntly in 1927 that "research has shown and practice has established the futility of the charge that it was a usurpation when this court undertook to declare an act of Congress unconstitutional."[8] Nevertheless, this was not the popular view at the time of the campaign of 1800, and it was certainly not the view of Jefferson. As Senator Beveridge pointed out in his life of Marshall, there was much discussion in 1800 as to what power, if any, could annul acts of Congress. "During these years popular opinion became ever stronger that the Judiciary could not do so, that Congress had a free hand so far as the Courts were concerned, and that the individual states might ignore national laws whenever those states deemed them to be infractions of the Constitution."[9] That was the theory which underlay the Virginia and Kentucky Resolutions of 1798; it must lead to a weak central government, and perhaps in the end to disunion. It was the theory to which Jefferson hoped to return, even after his immense assumption of federal power in the Louisiana Purchase. It was the theory which Marshall felt he must scotch if the nation was to survive.

Marshall had been a member of the Virginia Assembly from 1782 to 1784. Professor Corwin writes:

> This was the period when governmental power was concentrated in the state legislatures; and they speedily forfeited the confidence of those elements of society whose views or interests transcended state lines, playing fast and loose with the treaty obligations of the Confederation, starting commercial wars among the states, and finally becoming in the majority of instances the abject tools of the numerous but bankrupt small-farmer class.[10]

It was to save society from the radicalism and the debtors' laws of those days that men like Marshall, Washington, and Hamilton had fostered the conservative movement which ended in the making of the Constitution. If the Constitution itself was now to be annulled or overridden by the state legislatures, Marshall felt the entire effort would have been vain. Having established the power of his Court to annul acts of Congress, he went on to establish the same power to annul acts of the states when they conflicted with the written document.* Only then did he feel that the nation was safe. The Supreme Court and not the states, the Supreme Court and not the Congress, would decide what powers the central government possessed. And so long as John Marshall influenced the Supreme Court, those powers would be sufficient.

The measures which spelled safety to Marshall spelled tyranny to Jefferson and his friends. They wanted freedom, not order; individualism, not authority; agrarian self-sufficiency, not the centralizing march of commerce and finance. And they were in power after 1801. So Beveridge was right in saying that the issue raised by the Jeffersonians—whether the Supreme Court could enforce the essentially conservative and authoritarian Constitution, or whether radical state legislatures or a radical Congress could ignore it—"must be settled at the time or abandoned perhaps forever. The fundamental consideration involved must have a prompt, firm, and, if possible, final answer. Were such an answer not then given, it was not certain that it could ever be made. . . . For the reasons stated, Marshall resolved to take that step which, for courage, statesmanlike foresight, and, indeed, for perfectly calculated audacity, has few parallels in judicial history."[11] And a few pages later Beveridge describes the opinion in *Marbury* v. *Madison* as "a *coup* as bold in design and as daring in execution as that by which the Constitution had been framed."

This was precisely Jefferson's view of the decision, only it moved Jefferson to hatred, not to praise. Marshall had staked his claim; but the

---

* *M'Culloch* v. *Maryland,* 1819. The second power was implicit in the first. In this decision Marshall also gave a very broad, Hamiltonian interpretation to the powers of the central government.

decisive battle with the President was still to come. Beyond all other centralizing forces, Jefferson feared what he once described as "the consolidation of our government by the noiseless and therefore unalarming
instrumentality of the Supreme Court." And Jefferson's opinion of his
cousin, John Marshall, was such that he dared not hope the Court would
be restrained by reason or by scruples. "The judge's [Marshall's] in-
veteracy is profound," he wrote to Gallatin in 1810, "and his mind of that
gloomy malignity which will never let him forego the opportunity of
satiating it on a victim." Nothing but a final test of strength would decide
between these two great Virginians, both with Randolph blood. If it was
a question of "the noiseless and unalarming" use of power, Jefferson
should have been at his most formidable; yet strangely he failed.

Jefferson thought his election marked a revolution. He thought he and
his Republicans could cancel the evil precedents of the Federalists, re-
directing the government toward that decentralization, political and economic, which he believed to be the one hope for democracy. Clearly, after
Marbury v. *Madison,* none of this would be possible unless Jefferson could
either reform or diminish the Supreme Court. The Jeffersonians were
temporary; but the decisions of the Court were permanent. Short of revolution, they could only be undone by another Court. If Jefferson truly
meant to set the republic on a new track, he must either procure another
Court or curb the newly claimed powers of the existing one.

> The question how to deal with the Judiciary [wrote Henry Adams]
> was, therefore, the only revolutionary issue before the people to be met
> or abandoned; and if abandoned then, it must be forever. No party
> could claim the right to ignore its principles at will, or imagine that
> theories once dropped could be resumed with equal chance of success.
> If the revolution of 1800 was to endure it must control the Supreme
> Court. The object might be reached by constitutional amendment, by
> impeachment, or by increasing the number of judges. Every necessary
> power could be gained by inserting into the United States Constitution
> the words of the Constitution of Massachusetts, borrowed from English
> constitutional practice, that judges might be removed by the President
> on address by both Houses of the Legislature.[12]

Federalists would say this was revolution; but what of it? Jefferson claimed
that his party came to power in order to change the whole Federalist plan
of government. "Serious statesmen could hardly expect to make a revolution that should not be revolutionary."

The easiest of the three methods of attack would have been to increase
the number of judges, thus swamping the Federalist members of the
Court. Jefferson could have done this, or he could have amended the Constitution, at any time between 1801 and 1804, when his power was at its
height. Randolph and John Taylor of Caroline urged him to radical

action; but all that happened was the impeachment of inebrious Judge Pickering* in 1803. The next year the House voted articles of impeachment against Justice Samuel Chase of the Supreme Court, a violently indiscreet and overbearing enemy of Republicanism. The case did not come to trial before the United States Senate until February, 1805, in the last hours of the first term, when it was already too late for unity among the Republicans. And Randolph—overbearing, eccentric, and intolerant—was put in charge of the Administration forces: Randolph, who was perhaps the only man in public life as indiscreet, and as happy to make enemies, as Justice Chase himself. Furthermore, Jefferson's "judge-breaking" friends began to talk about impeachment as "an inquest of office," which suggested that if they were successful with Chase they would make a clean sweep of the Court.

At the time of the trial, twenty-three votes in the Senate were needed to convict. The Republicans had twenty-five Senators, the Federalists nine. Five Republican Senators were doubtful, chiefly because the loose talk of the Virginians made it clear that Chief Justice Marshall was the real object of attack, rather than Associate Justice Chase. Having chosen a bad battleground, a bad time, and a bad leader, the Jeffersonians had to abide by the result. The Chase trial decided for a long time to come whether the Supreme Court should keep the powers John Marshall had won for it. The decision was in favor of the Court; the Senate said, in effect, that it was not prepared to remove a judge because his manners were bad or his rulings unpopular. The Senate refused to become a court of appeals.

The Chase trial was a grievous blow to Jefferson's theory of government. The Louisiana Purchase and its aftermath had weakened the theory; but the acquittal of Justice Chase ruined it. "Chief Justice Marshall at length was safe; he might henceforward at his leisure fix the principles of Constitutional law. . . . Henceforward the legal profession had its own way in expounding the principles and expanding the powers of the central government through the Judiciary."[13]

In 1820 Jefferson made his final comment on the failure of 1805.

> The Judiciary of the United States [he wrote] is the subtle corps of sappers and miners constantly working underground to undermine the foundations of our confederated fabric. . . . Having found from experience that impeachment is an impracticable thing, a mere scarecrow, they consider themselves secure for life: they skulk from responsibility; . . . an opinion is huddled up in conclave, perhaps by a majority of one, delivered as if unanimous, and with the silent acquiescence of lazy or timid associates, by a crafty judge who sophisticates the law to his mind by the form of his own reasoning.[14]

* Judge of a federal district court in New Hampshire.

Such appears to have been Jefferson's view from the beginning of his presidency to the end of his life. For years Jefferson enjoyed as much power as any man ever held in America; yet it was not until the power had begun to wane that he took action against the Court. It was not until the power was wholly gone, in the final days of the embargo fight, in 1807 and 1808, that Jefferson took the obvious course of proceeding against the Court by constitutional amendment. Introduced in both houses and endorsed by many state legislatures, the amendment provided that federal judges should hold office for a term of years, and should be removed by the President on address by two thirds of both houses. Nothing happened; the amendment died of the general inertia which had fallen upon the last days of Jefferson's second term.

4

Early in 1804, when it became obvious that Jefferson would be elected for a second term, some of the Federalist leaders grew desperate. Justice Chase announced that freedom and property were about to be destroyed; and Timothy Pickering, the senior Senator from Massachusetts, wrote: "The people of the East cannot reconcile their habits, views and interests with those of the South and West. The latter are beginning to rule with a rod of iron." Pickering wished to move at once toward disunion; but the wiser leaders of New England, such as George Cabot and Justice Parsons,* knew that it was not yet possible to carry the people with them. They told Pickering to wait, assuring him that bad as things were they would soon be worse, and that only then could the misguided common folk be turned from Jefferson. "A separation is now impracticable," wrote Cabot to Pickering in February, 1804, "because we do not feel the necessity or utility of it. The same separation then will be unavoidable when our loyalty to the Union is generally perceived to be the instrument of debasement and impoverishment. If it is prematurely attempted, those few only will promote it who discern what is hidden from the multitude."

The soundness of Cabot's judgment was shown later in the year, when Massachusetts and New Hampshire voted for Jefferson. There was not yet sufficient discontent to make secession popular. Pickering, however, was unconvinced by Cabot's letter. He saw that he could not go the whole way toward secession without the support of the great leaders in his own section; but he went part way, dabbling in the tenebrous politics of New York, encouraging Aaron Burr in the plot that ended with the death of Hamilton.

* Theophilus Parsons, who became chief justice of Massachusetts in 1806, was one of the most learned lawyers in America. Like Pickering, he was an Essex County man and a devout Federalist.

Burr was still Vice-President in the spring of 1804. The Virginians had paid him for his efficiency and adroitness in helping them to win the election of 1800; but they did not like him or trust him. They knew that his ambition was fierce and they suspected that his scruples were nonexistent. He was also a threat to Jefferson's plan to elect Madison as his successor, thus keeping the presidency in Virginia for at least sixteen years. As early as 1802 Jefferson and his friends were suggesting to the Clinton family* that the vice-presidency could be theirs after the next election, if they would be kind enough to break Burr's power in New York State. The Clinton newspaper** then set about Burr with a violence and a lack of scruple which was unusual even for the political journalism of those days. In January, 1804, Burr went to Jefferson and offered friendship or enmity. He intended to retire as Vice-President in 1805, he said; but he wanted Jefferson to appoint him to some important office. Jefferson refused, and Burr turned to the intrigues of Pickering.

The plan was a simple one: if the Federalists could help Burr to become governor of New York, Burr might then be able to take his state out of the Union and to join it to New England in a Northern confederacy. Burr could not hope for the Republican nomination in New York, since the party machinery was in the hands of the Clintons and Livingstons; so his friends in the state legislature held a caucus and named him an independent candidate. Pickering and his New England Federalists then sought to persuade the New York Federalists to vote for Burr. The party was disorganized in that state, and without a candidate; also many of the Federalists liked Burr because he was hated by Jefferson and the Virginians. The plan was partly successful, and might have been wholly so except for Burr's old, implacable enemy.

When Hamilton heard what was afoot he was alarmed and angry. He

* George Clinton, many times governor of New York State, vigorous opponent of the Federal Constitution and therefore of Hamilton, Vice-President of the United States during the second term of Jefferson and the first term of Madison; and De Witt Clinton, the nephew of George, who retired from the United States Senate in 1803 in order to become mayor of New York City and who succeeded his uncle as the most powerful political leader in the state. He was the farsighted promoter of the Erie Canal, on which so much of New York's prosperity was built, and Professor Dixon R. Fox has described him as "perhaps the most effective personal force for public education in the history of the state." He was also a ruthless friend of the spoils system in state politics. As we have seen, the Clintons joined with Burr and the Livingstons in 1800 to put Jefferson's party in power; but by 1804 Burr was excommunicated by the Clintons and Livingstons, and by 1807 De Witt Clinton and the Livingstons were again enemies, and by 1812 De Witt Clinton was himself allied with the New England Federalists, who would have elected him President if they could have won the state of Pennsylvania. The politics of New York were not always easy to predict.

** The *American Citizen*, a daily newspaper run by James Cheetham, in partnership with a cousin of De Witt Clinton's. Cheetham was an Englishman who had been forced to leave his country at the time of the Manchester riots of 1798.

thought Burr was a cheap demagogue whose rise to power would encourage all the worst vices of democracy. And he thought his New England friends were wrong to attempt secession, which would make for weakness, and then anarchy, and in the end for the ruin of the whole American cause. A few hours before he died he wrote to his friend Theodore Sedgwick of Massachusetts, one of the Federalist leaders: "Dismemberment of our empire will be a clear sacrifice of great positive advantages, without any counterbalancing good; administering no relief to our real disease, which is democracy; the poison of which, by a subdivision, will only be the more concentrated in each part, and consequently the more virulent." The enemy, in other words, was not union, but democracy; the remedy was not secession, but oligarchy.

Feeling as he did, Hamilton must fight the Burr plot. At a Federalist meeting in Albany he explained with clarity and violence why no man should help Burr; yet it was obvious that a majority of Federalists intended to reject his advice. This only spurred him to harsher measures. Throughout the election, wherever Hamilton went, he denounced Burr unrestrainedly. Whether or not as a result, Burr was beaten by the Clinton-Livingston candidate, in April, 1804. This was the end of Burr, politically. He had no future in the Republican Party, because Jefferson and the Clintons feared and hated him; he had no future in the Federalist Party, because Hamilton barred his way. He might have been elected President in 1801 by the Federalist House of Representatives; but Hamilton had begged his friends to support even Jefferson rather than Burr. He might have been elected governor in 1804, and then become president of the Northern states; but Hamilton had argued tirelessly with every Federalist not to trust this adventurer. It is no wonder that the adventurer felt aggrieved.

On June 18, Burr wrote Hamilton a brief letter, calling attention to some of the expressions which Hamilton was said to have used about him, and adding, "You must perceive, sir, the necessity of a prompt and unqualified acknowledgment or denial." Two days later Hamilton answered, without giving Burr the denial he sought, and ending with the ominous words, "I trust on more reflection you will see the matter in the same light with me; if not, I can only regret the circumstance, and must abide the consequences." These were the words with which men made clear that they were willing to accept a duel.

The duel took place early in the morning of July 11, across the Hudson River from New York, under the heights of Weehawken. As clearly as any Northern soldier in the Civil War, Hamilton fought for the Union. He believed that if he refused the duel his own political influence would be destroyed, and that at some future date Burr might break the nation. He believed that if he accepted the duel but refused to fire, and if Burr then killed him, Burr would ruin himself as well. So he went to Weehawken, and threw away his fire, and died from Burr's first bullet.* He had been right in one belief: Burr fled the state, never to have political influence in New York again.**

Hamilton died at the age of forty-seven. He may well have been the greatest genius of his time and country—not the greatest character, who was certainly Washington; and not the greatest political leader, who was certainly Jefferson; but the greatest genius in government, in law, in economics. Talleyrand, in his *Etudes sur la République*, makes a larger claim. "Je considère Napoléon," he wrote, "Fox, et Hamilton comme les trois plus grands hommes de notre époque, et si je devais me prononcer entre les trois, je donnerais sans hésiter la première place à Hamilton. Il avait deviné l'Europe." He had divined more than Europe. After a few years as a shop assistant, and before the first copy of Adam Smith had crossed the Atlantic, he had divined the science of economics; and after a little schooling and a few years in the army, he had divined political philosophy, and the art and practice of government; after a few months of study, he had divined the law. Chancellor Kent*** once referred to his "mighty mind"; it was the speed as well as the power of that mind which made his genius.

The Federalists, especially in New England where they had refused his advice, felt that the death of Hamilton was the death of hope. From that moment they were as despairing before Jefferson, as the Irish were before Cromwell after the death of Owen Roe O'Neill; and they mourned Hamilton with as wild a melancholy:

> Sheep without a shepherd, when the snow shuts out the sky—
> Oh, why did you leave us, Owen? why did you die?

---

* Hamilton left a paper explaining his intention to waste his first shot. Nathaniel Pendleton, his second, testified that Hamilton did not fire until after he had been hit, when an involuntary tightening of his finger set off the pistol. The leaves of the tree above him showed the erratic course of the bullet. Hamilton admitted that he might have injured Burr unduly, which is why he "reserved" his fire. He did not seek death, but he knew that if it came Burr's power to do harm would die also.

**He presided as Vice-President, over the trial of Justice Chase. After finishing his term of office, he went down the Ohio and the Mississippi Rivers on his mysterious mission to detach the western states from the Union. In 1807 he was tried for treason, was acquitted, and then sought exile in France.

***James Kent, the first professor of law at Columbia University (1793–98; 1824–26), author of the famous *Commentaries on American Law*, chief justice of the Supreme Court of New York State, and chancellor of the New York Court of Chancery. He has been described as "practically the creator of equity jurisdiction in the United States." He thought Hamilton the greatest lawyer he had known. "I have little doubt," he wrote, "that if General Hamilton had lived twenty years longer, he would have rivalled Socrates or Bacon, or any other of the sages of ancient or modern times, in researches after truth and in benevolence to mankind."

The more extreme Federalists may well have persuaded themselves that Jefferson was as ruthless as Cromwell, and that it would not be long now before the massacres began. In fact, the good days were almost over for that gentle philosopher-president, not because he was about to war on his enemies but because France and England were about to war on him and to expose the weakness of all his hopes and plans for government.

5

After the death of Hamilton a number of minor troubles beset Jefferson, leading up to the major trouble that was to overthrow his system. First came the failure of the Chase trial, which meant victory and power for John Marshall; then came the failure of a dubious effort to acquire West Florida by stealth.

From the beginning, Jefferson had been discontented with his bargain on Louisiana. He did not foresee the effect of the Industrial Revolution upon westward expansion in America, so he did not believe this new land would be needed within measurable time. He was interested in it as a geographer, and as an amateur of natural history; he knew the importance of the Mississippi, but not of the immense country beyond. He would have preferred to have bought the little strip of Spanish land known as West Florida, which included the good harbor of Mobile Bay and the lower courses of the rivers that drained the Mississippi Territory. He tried, unsuccessfully, to persuade Spain that West Florida was part of Louisiana and had already been sold; then he tried, unsuccessfully, to buy or to threaten the Spanish into parting with the territory. Finally, he hit upon a plan which did justice neither to his brains nor to his morals: he undertook to bribe Napoleon into extorting West Florida from the Spaniards and handing it to America. For this, he wanted a secret appropriation of two million dollars.

Nothing was more remarkable about Jefferson than his capacity for adapting principles to reality without cynicism and without pain. A sincere believer in strict construction and the least possible government, he was prepared to stretch the Constitution to the breaking-point in order to seize the powers necessary for the Louisiana Purchase; a sincere believer in economy, he was willing to spend money faster than the Federalists when it seemed to him wise; a sincere believer in simple and open government which all men could understand and criticize, he was willing to keep the House of Representatives in secret session for two months in order to wring a furtive appropriation from his reluctant followers; a sincere believer in the separation of powers, he was not only willing to guide the Congress at every point, promoting the faithful and diminishing the disobedient with suave efficiency, but he often seemed incapable either of permitting a rebellion or of noticing that he was suppressing it. This time, however, he had to notice what he was doing, for the Two Million Act led to a major revolt by John Randolph of Roanoke, the Administration leader in the House.

To understand the seriousness of such a revolt, we must recall Randolph's dazzling success, in 1804 and after, in defending the cause of principle against party expediency over the labyrinthine Yazoo claims. The claims went back to 1795, when the Georgia legislature authorized the sale of thirty-five million acres of western land to four companies, for five hundred thousand dollars.* It was then proved that every member of the legislature who voted for this bill, except one, had been corrupted and had a personal interest in the sale. The citizens of Georgia were annoyed. They elected a new legislature, annulled the sale, expunged the sale from the record, and by means of a special convention made the expunging act a part of the state constitution. Meanwhile the four companies had paid their money and sold large tracts of the land to unsuspecting citizens throughout the Union. In many cases these buyers had resold the land; so the vengeance of the Georgians against their venal legislature created a nice problem for the courts. Some of the purchasers surrendered their titles and were paid back their money; others did not.

The case soon became far more tortuous, for the United States Government intervened as protector of the Indians who in fact owned and occupied most of the land in question. In 1802 Georgia ceded to the federal government her nebulous rights over this area, which now comprises most of the states of Alabama and Mississippi; she also ceded the privilege of settling the claims of the purchasers who had retained their titles. Years later the Supreme Court declared in favor of these titles, saying that the rescinding act of 1796 impaired the obligation of contract and was therefore invalid under the Constitution of the United States. Meanwhile, although Jefferson and his Cabinet did not believe the titles were good, they wished to make a settlement to quiet the political uproar of the claimants.

The importance attached to a settlement is shown by the fact that the commissioners for arranging terms were the Secretary of State, the Secretary of the Treasury, and the Attorney General. These eminent men agreed that five million acres should be put aside to settle all claims. So when the Yazoo question came before the House in 1804 in the regular course of business, the whole force of the Administration was behind a quick and quiet compromise—except John Randolph. He attacked the report of the three commissioners on moral grounds, saying that the Georgia legislature did not have the power to alienate territory except "in

* The claims received their name from the Yazoo River, which ran through part of the territory.

a rightful manner and for the public good." He offered a long series of resolutions directed toward destroying the compromise. Alone, against a hostile and irritated House, against the entire Administration of which he was a leading member, he succeeded in postponing the question for another year.

When the matter came up again in 1805, he returned to the attack with a violence the House had never yet heard, and which it has seldom heard since. The whole government, he said, was being corrupted by these monstrous frauds. All the vices which the Republicans had come to office to abolish were refreshed by such compromise with sin. The unhappy Postmaster-General, who had undertaken (unwisely) to act as agent for the claimants, was pictured as the worst man alive. "His gigantic grasp," said Randolph, "embraces with one hand the shores of Lake Erie, and stretches with the other to the bay of Mobile. Millions of acres are easily digested by such stomachs! The retail trade of fraud and imposture yields too slow and small a profit to gratify their cupidity. They buy and sell corruption in the gross, and a few millions, more or less, is hardly felt to the account."[15]

Amazingly, he again postponed legislation for a year, and in 1806 he procured the rejection of the bill. In 1810, in the case of *Fletcher* v. *Peck*, Supreme Court Justice Marshall held in favor of the claimants and their property rights. And at last, when Randolph was absent from Congress in the session of 1813–15, the House of Representatives passed the measure for the Yazoo compromise. Such was the man—a fury and a confusion of energy and moral reprobation—who prepared to turn from the Administration when Jefferson asked for secret money to buy West Florida.

Jefferson got the two million dollars, and Randolph for the most part confined his opposition to the secret sessions; but this was the last breaking of the strict Republican code which the fiery Virginian purist would permit. The two million dollars did no good, and the next time the Administration asked for something which Randolph regarded as unprincipled he went into opposition and attacked with maniac rage. The break came on the Non-Importation Bill, a mild effort to retaliate against Great Britain for her impressment of American sailors and her interference with American trade. This was avowedly a halfway measure which would lead to nothing except further talk, and Randolph despised all halfway measures just as he despised all compromise. "A milk-and-water bill," he called the Non-Importation Act; "a dose of chicken broth."

Either America meant to go to war, he said, in which case she was betraying Republican principles, or she didn't mean to go to war, in which case she was either lying or fooling by such pinprick measures against Britain. Speaking four and a half months after the battle of Trafalgar, Randolph asked with reason, "Shall this great mammoth of the American forest leave his native element and plunge into the water in a mad contest with the shark? Let him stay on shore, and not be excited by the mussels and periwinkles on the strand!" So far he was on sure ground, and might have won his case, and might even, because of his large influence in Virginia, have been forgiven; but before he sat down his pent-up rage led him to abandon safety and to attack Jefferson's whole method of conducting the government:

> I have protested, and I again protest, against secret, irresponsible, overruling influence. The first question I asked when I saw the gentleman's resolution was, Is this a measure of the Cabinet? Not of an open declared Cabinet, but of an invisible, inscrutable, unconstitutional Cabinet, without responsibility, unknown to the Constitution. I speak of back-stairs influence—of men who bring messages to this House, which, although they do not appear on the Journals, govern its decisions. . . . When I behold the affairs of this nation—instead of being where I hoped, and the people believed they were, in the hands of responsible men—committed to Tom, Dick, and Harry, to the refuse of the retail trade of politics, I do feel, I cannot help feeling, the most deep and serious concern. . . . I know, sir, that we may say, and do say, that we are independent (would it were true!), as free to give a direction to the Executive as to receive it from him; but do what you will, foreign relations, every measure short of war, and even the course of hostilities, depends upon him. . . . You give him money to buy Florida, and he purchases Louisiana. You may furnish means; the application of those means rests with him. Let not the master and mate go below when the ship is in distress, and throw the responsibility upon the cook and the cabin-boy! I said so when your doors were shut; I scorn to say less now they are open.

This seems a far cry from the gentle words of the First Inaugural, in which Jefferson told Congress that "nothing shall be wanting on my part to inform, as far as in my power, the legislative judgment, nor to carry that judgment into faithful execution." Randolph was complaining that Jefferson had done exactly what John Marshall predicted he would do: under the guise of careful adherence to the separation of powers, the government had become "invisible, inscrutable . . . without responsibility." Randolph did not suggest what else could happen, short of returning to the Federalist theory of Executive responsibility. Randolph was never willing to subject theory to fact, principle to circumstance. Jefferson was always willing. He did it so easily that he seemed not to notice he was doing it, which irritated his opponents almost beyond endurance; but for a grateful posterity the important point is that he did it.

As the debate on non-importation proceeded, Randolph grew wilder and wilder. Tall and thin and gawky, with a dead-white desperate face and shrill voice, he seemed to be whipping himself to madness. At last, on April 7, 1806, he made the fatal break. "I came here," he said, "prepared to co-operate with the government in all its measures. I told them so. But I soon found there was no choice left, and that to co-operate in them would be to destroy the national character. I found I might co-operate, or be an honest man. I have therefore opposed, and will oppose them."

There is something frightening about the quiet way in which, when Randolph made this final challenge, Jefferson took up the fight and broke the strength of his former, and formidable, ally. The day before his April 7 speech, Randolph was a hero in Virginia, a great party leader, a man who stood for principles and possessed power, a man with a boundless future. Within a few weeks of challenging Jefferson, he was left with half a dozen disgruntled followers, no power, and no hopes. Joseph Nicholson,* the most important man who went into opposition with Randolph, was gently detached by Jefferson and given a seat on the Bench as judge of the Sixth Maryland Circuit. And when the Ninth Congress came to an end, in 1807, Randolph was deposed as chairman of the Ways and Means Committee.

What else could the President do? The first duty of a government is to govern. The riddle of politics is how to keep both principles and power. Randolph's method made it easy to keep principles but impossible to keep power. Assuming that he wished to accomplish something in public life, other than the proof of his own virtue, his method was self-defeating.**

6

The failure of the Chase impeachment, the failure to acquire West Florida, the Randolph schism, the ambiguous but alarming Burr conspiracy—all these were but preludes to the final heartbreak of Jefferson's second term. In April, 1807, while the Burr trial for treason was still under way, the nation's attention was distracted from that singular event by something far more striking and more dangerous. The American frigate *Chesapeake,* under orders for the Mediterranean, shortly after leaving Norfolk Roads with her decks littered with stores and few of her guns

---

* A Marylander of high character, and Randolph's closest friend in the House. Like Randolph and John Taylor, he was an "old Republican"; i.e., he believed in the principles of 1798 and the promises of 1800.

** It is interesting that Jefferson, who could so quickly break Randolph's national influence, had no control over his position in his own Virginia district. Except for the session of 1813–15, when he was defeated because of opposition to the war, Randolph remained in Congress until he resigned voluntarily in 1829. He was a lone voice, without power and without patronage; but he pleased his district and his district was faithful to him. The autonomy of the local groups which compose a national party has seldom been better shown.

mounted, was attacked by the British frigate *Leopard* and forced to strike her flag. The attack took place because the *Leopard's* commander believed that there were British deserters aboard the *Chesapeake* and the American commander would not permit a search.* It seemed that the old problem of impressments might have to be settled at last. Had Jefferson called a special session of Congress he could have had war for the asking; and it would have been a more reasonable and a more defensible war than the one which finally came in 1812.

Jefferson, however, believed he could get redress without war, by the use of purely commercial weapons. This was a favorite theory with him and with Madison and he advanced almost gaily to the test that was to break him. He told Monroe, who was in London,** to demand reparation; but he made reparation from the stubborn Canning impossible by adding that the United States would accept nothing less than the end of the system of impressment. Jefferson thought he was playing a strong hand. "I verily believe," he wrote at the time, "that it will ever be in our power to keep so even a stand between England and France as to inspire a wish in neither to throw us into the scale of his adversary."[16] This might have been the case if Jefferson had spent the previous six years building frigates instead of gunboats, and if he had been pouring money into the army instead of proving how cheaply a government could be run. As it was, he had nothing with which to oppose the British or the French except commercial threats and moral lectures.

> Whatever the errors or faults of Mr. Canning may have been [wrote Henry Adams], timidity was not one of them, and the diplomatic ingenuity of Mr. Jefferson, with its feeble attempts to play off France against England and England against France, was the last policy he was likely to respect. Even the American who reads the history of the year 1807, seeing the brutal directness with which Mr. Canning kicked Mr. Jefferson's diplomacy out of his path, cannot but feel a certain respect for the Englishman mingled with wrath at his insolent sarcasm.[17]

The first step in "kicking Mr. Jefferson's diplomacy out of his path" was a royal proclamation of October 17, 1807, directing the navy to intensify in every way possible the impressment of British sailors from neutral shipping. The second was the Orders in Council of November 11, 1807 (designed as reprisals against the Continental System of Napoleon), which subjected

* There was one British deserter aboard, also three Americans who had been falsely impressed by the British and who had escaped and returned to their own service.
** Monroe was Minister Resident in London. He and William Pinkney of Maryland, a special envoy, had negotiated a treaty with the British in the autumn of 1806. The treaty had been intended to afford relief from commercial restrictions and from impressments. It was so unsatisfactory that Jefferson did not send it to the Senate.

the whole of American shipping to British control. As Spencer Perceval, the Chancellor of the Exchequer, pointed out:

> British produce and manufactures, and trade either from a British port or with a British destination, is to be protected as much as possible. For this purpose, all the countries where French influence prevails shall have no trade, but to or from this country or from its allies.[18]

The British did not choose to argue the legal basis of their action; they merely pointed out that they meant to win the war against Napoleon and that in order to win they must protect British commercial shipping which was suffering both from the French regulations and from the American competition. England intended, as we have said before, "to recover her commerce and to take back her seamen." What would America intend?

Jefferson had three choices: he could fight; he could try his commercial intimidation; or he could admit the British thesis that the war on Napoleon was a war for mankind and that America should not be too touchy about her "rights" until that war was won. The third course, which doubtless seemed reasonable in London, was unthinkable in Washington. American politics had long been distorted by the loves and hates inspired by the politics of Europe. Since the outbreak of the French Revolution the United States had divided into two camps: those who saw France as the hope of the world, and England as monarchical reaction; and those who saw France as anarchy and irreligion, and England as the hope of the world. News was not only slow but sparse in those days. Long after France had become a military dictatorship, her lovers in America thought of her as the symbol of freedom, her detractors as the symbol of anarchy. Long after England had become the last defender of the liberties of Europe, she was regarded by her enemies in America as the bulwark of privilege and corruption. The fact that there was little information on which these passions could feed helped them to remain more passionate. No Administration could afford to be convicted of subservience to either group. The charge was always made; but it would be fatal if the charge could be proved. It was a political necessity to try to hold the balance even between France and England, to assert America's rights equally against both— even if the assertion must be made in words, not deeds. So the third course was impossible to Jefferson, as it would have been to any president at that time. He was left with war, or with commercial retaliation.

He refused war on the ground that "peace is our passion." No ruler has ever proved a better right to make that boast. Jefferson chose peace, and clung to it in the face of the most wounding injuries from both the warring powers—injuries made worse by impudence from France, by arrogance from England. He not only chose peace; he succeeded in persuading the quick-tempered American people to choose it with him.

In December, 1807, Jefferson asked the Congress for an absolute em-bargo on all American commerce: no vessels were to clear for any foreign port,* no exports were to move by sea or by land. The Senate debated for one day, the House for two days; both met in secret session. The bill passed on the twenty-first of December, and Jefferson signed it on the twenty-second. Henry Adams comments: "Of all President Jefferson's feats of political management, this was probably the most dexterous. On his mere recommendation, without warning, discussion, or publicity, and in silence as to his true reasons and motives,** he succeeded in fixing upon the coun-try, beyond recall, the experiment of peaceable coercion. His triumph was almost a marvel; but no one could fail to see its risks. . . . If Jefferson's permanent embargo failed to coerce Europe, what would the people of America think of the process by which it had been fastened upon them? What would be said and believed of the President who had challenged so vast a responsibility?"[19]

The Embargo did not coerce Europe; and what the American people thought may be inferred from the measures which had soon to be taken to enforce this law. Gallatin, with his usual prescience, had urged that a time-limit be put on the Embargo. He knew that if it did not bring results quickly it must cause trouble at home. "In every point of view," he wrote to the President on December 18, "privations, sufferings, revenue, effect on the enemy, politics at home, &c., I prefer war to a permanent embargo. Governmental prohibitions do always more mischief than had been calcu-lated; and it is not without much hesitation that a statesman should hazard to regulate the concerns of individuals as if he could do it better than themselves." He was overruled; and it was not long before Gallatin, who had always preached and practiced that the least government was the best, found himself enforcing rules so oppressive that Napoleon might have hesitated to impose them.

The first effect of the Embargo was to do for Canning precisely what he had undertaken to do for himself: diminish American shipping and commerce,*** force American sailors into British employ, and generally rehabilitate British merchant shipping. It also provided a certain amount of amusement abroad. Napoleon confiscated all American ships that put into French ports, saying that he was helping Mr. Jefferson to enforce his law; and when the American Government approached the British Gov-

---

* To avoid retaliation, foreign ships in harbor at the time were allowed to depart.

** The President said he wanted the Embargo "to aid him in the negotiations with England." (J. Q. Adams, *Diary.*)

*** Canning did not wish to destroy all American shipping and commerce, but only that part of it which was inconvenient to Great Britain. Under the Orders in Council there was much trade still open to Americans who would accept British inspection and license, which explains the special hatred for the embargo on the part of the New Englanders whose interests it was designed to protect.

ernment with an offer to withdraw the Embargo if the British would withdraw the Orders in Council, Canning regretted that he could not do so, adding that His Majesty "would gladly have facilitated [the Embargo's] removal as a measure of inconvenient restriction upon the American people."

The second effect of the Embargo was the partial ruin of Virginia. Jefferson's own state obeyed the rules loyally; but the plantation society, the easy hospitality, the four hundred thousand slaves who had to be fed, who could not be laid aside like farm machinery until good times returned, the dependence of the tobacco-growers on the foreign market—all conspired to make her the chief sufferer. The old life of Virginia was undermined; Jefferson himself did not recover financially from the disaster of those two years.

The third effect of the Embargo was to breed corruption, repression, and political hatreds. This is interesting, because it was to evade such evils that Jefferson chose peace instead of war. He believed that a free country, if it accepted war, must lose its liberty and its civic virtue either in victory or defeat. The chief reason for his rooted isolationism was his conviction that America must become as miserable as Europe unless she could escape the eternal wars of Europe. He was prepared, in order to prove war unnecessary, to meet New England's evasions of the Embargo with force and to endure political hatreds; he was not prepared for the discovery that the corruption and crime attendant on his peaceful coercion were comparable to the corruption and crime accompanying war. He gave up all his theories of government for peace, and peace betrayed him. The triumvirate of Jefferson and Madison and Gallatin, who had set out to prove that government could be frugal, that government could leave men alone, found themselves interfering grossly with business and commerce, bankrupting themselves and their neighbors, jailing their constituents—and all for nothing, because the Embargo did not work. It did not coerce France or England—though one may argue that if it could have been given a longer trial it might eventually have succeeded.

The dilemma which faced the triumvirate, and the bravery with which they met it, is shown in the following two letters.

I am perfectly satisfied [wrote Gallatin to Jefferson on July 29, 1808] that if the embargo must be persisted in any longer, two principles must necessarily be adopted in order to make it sufficient: First, that not a single vessel shall be permitted to move without the special permission of the Executive; second, that the collectors be invested with the general power of seizing property anywhere, and taking the rudders, or otherwise effectually preventing the departure of any vessel in harbor, though ostensibly intended to remain there—and that without being liable to personal suits. I am sensible that such arbitrary powers are equally dangerous and odious; but a restrictive measure of the nature of the embargo, applied to a nation under such circumstances as the United States, cannot be enforced without the assistance of means as strong as the measure itself.

Jefferson replied:

I am satisfied with you that if Orders and Decrees are not repealed, and a continuance of the embargo is preferred to war (which sentiment is universal here), Congress must legalize all means which may be necessary to obtain its end.[20]

The last, and the most derisive, effect of the Embargo was to force New England into the position of Virginia and Kentucky in 1798, and to induce the Republican Party to sponsor an Enforcement Act* which made the Alien and Sedition Laws seem niggardly in their grants of authority. The Federalists now flung back at Virginia the state rights doctrines of Jefferson and Madison; the Virginians now insisted on a use of power which Justice Joseph Story** of the Supreme Court later described as "a measure which went to the utmost limit of constructive power under the Constitution." Because of the Embargo and the necessary rigors of the enforcement act, Pickering was able to stir the New England town meetings to bitter protests and to threats of disunion; the New York legislature nominated Vice-President George Clinton for the presidency as an anti-Embargo Republican; John Randolph's group in Virginia nominated Monroe as an anti-Administration Republican. Jefferson's party seemed in tatters as it approached the election of 1808; but Jefferson's candidate, Madison, was saved because the opposition was divided into three parts —the Federalists having failed to get together with the dissident Republicans. Madison's victory was thus assured; but it seemed that he might find himself head of a broken federation.

Three days before he left office, Jefferson bowed before the storm of protests and signed the repeal of the Embargo. The whole of his first term had been blessed by good fortune and the whole of his second term had been poisoned. The four lean kine, said John Randolph, ate up the four fat kine. The failure was by no means so absolute; but it must have seemed absolute to Jefferson as he rode horseback through the snows of March toward his much-loved Monticello.*** He lived for another seventeen

* January, 1809.

** Joseph Story of Massachusetts, author of the famous *Commentaries*, was appointed to the Supreme Court by Madison in 1811, when he was thirty-two years old. He was a Republican in politics, but during the one session he served in Congress (1808–1809) he urged the repeal of the Embargo on the ground that it had failed of its object. Jefferson accused him of being personally responsible for the repeal: "I ascribe all this to one pseudo-Republican, Story."

*** His home in Albemarle County, Virginia.

years; he continued to give advice and direction to his followers, while pro-
fessing to have no part in politics and to disbelieve in leadership; he was the
guide and philosopher for the next two presidents; but he never again went
outside his own corner of Virginia. He died on the Fourth of July, 1826, the
fiftieth anniversary of the Declaration of Independence. John Adams died
a few hours later on the same day.

7

There was not much left of Jefferson's political philosophy by the time of
his death. He had been forced to override all his own theories of government, and to watch history override all his plans for maintaining republican liberties. He was opposed to the concentration of wealth and
power; but such concentration, which has been one of the most notable
features of American life, was under way by 1826. He was opposed to government interference with the economy, confident that such interference
must always be in the interest of one class and at the expense of the commonwealth; but he lived to see the revival of Hamilton's bank and the
application of Hamilton's Report on Manufactures. He almost lived long
enough to see the famous Tariff of Abominations. He was opposed to the
growth of cities, and feared the effect of city "mobs" on political virtue;
but he was forced to admit that America, to save her life in a brutal world,
must promote manufactures. He was opposed to slavery; but he lived to
see King Cotton breathe new life into the slave system. He was the prophet
of democracy, political and economic. He knew that the first was unlikely
to flourish without the second; but it was his fate to watch America, under
the influence of his own ideas, move steadily toward the first, and under
the influence of the Industrial Revolution move steadily away from the
second.

Jefferson knew only one weapon with which to fight the tendency of
the new industrialism to breed new forms of oligarchy and political corruption. The weapon was education, free education for the masses. The
most important work of Jefferson's last years was the founding of the University of Virginia, which was chartered in 1819. This was a lifelong
ambition, for it was part of his creed that men could not be free if they
were denied knowledge. He did more than any other man to induce the
Virginia legislature to create and support the University. He selected the
best teachers he could find, in the United States and in Europe, for the
first professorships; and he was largely responsible for the design and for
the location of one of the finest and most appropriate groups of buildings
in North America. The University was opened in 1825.

The Rotunda, which he modeled on Palladio's Villa Rotunda at

Vicenza, and the colonnades with alternating two-story and one-story buildings which form the east and west boundaries of the lawn at the University, are Jefferson's design. Here, in these lovely neo-classic forms, here and in his prose style, can the spirit of the man be traced. It was a cool spirit, benevolent and intelligent and calm, without the deep passions of Washington, without the alarming intellectual intensity of Hamilton. Professor Becker writes as follows of the style of the Declaration:

> One might say that Jefferson felt with the mind, as some people think with the heart. He had enthusiasm, but it was enthusiasm engendered by an irresistible intellectual curiosity. He was ardent, but his ardors were cool, giving forth light without heat. . . . All his ideas and sentiments seem of easy birth, flowing felicitously from an alert and expeditious brain rather than slowly and painfully welling up from the obscure depths of his nature. . . . There are in his writings few of those ominous overtones charged with emotion, and implying more than is expressed.

And again:

> If the style is always a bit fragile, and sometimes in danger of becoming precious, is it not because the thought is a bit fragile also, too easily satisfied with what is open and visible, and therefore lacking depth and subtlety, ignoring all that must be ignored if the life of man is to be understood and described, even with the felicity of genius, at the level of common sense?[21]

This does not do full justice. No one has described Jefferson's elusive spirit with full justice; but some of its refreshing quality can be felt by anyone who will sit on the steps of his Rotunda and contemplate the colonnades and the lawn of his design. It is the spirit of the Enlightenment, of eighteenth-century liberalism, charming even in the harsh glare of today.

IX

The Frustration of a Foreign Policy

IN THE LAST exhausted days of Jefferson's second term, when Congress was struggling with the repeal of the Embargo, when the faithful Jeffersonians were reeling under attacks by Randolph, by half their Northern friends, and by the revived Federalists, Josiah Quincy* of Massachusetts wrote: "Jefferson is a host; and if the wand of that magician is not broken, he will yet defeat the attempt." The magician was tired. He was discouraged by failure. He no longer waved a wand; from the moment the election was decided he refused responsibility and put the whole burden of policy-making on his unhappy successor.

Nobody could accuse James Madison of being a host, or a magician. He was a learned and industrious man who knew everything about government except how to govern. At the Constitutional Convention he was a hero; in the Executive Mansion** he was almost a nonentity. As a result of his weakness, the weakness of the Republican theory was displayed. Now that there was no magician and no wand, the Administration could no longer make policy; the Congress attempted to take over that task and almost ruined the country in the process of proving that such was not its function. The first step was to deny Madison the excellent Secretary of State whom he had chosen, and to foist upon him a nonentity. John Quincy Adams, who had resigned as United States Senator from Massachusetts the previous year, left an account of this episode.

Madison, he wrote,

> had wished and intended to appoint Mr. Gallatin, who had been Secretary of the Treasury during the whole of Jefferson's Administration, to

* The gay and charming young Federalist from Quincy, Massachusetts. He was elected to the House of Representatives in 1804, at the age of thirty-two. He quickly became the minority leader, opposing the Embargo and Non-Intercourse Acts as cowardly, useless, and unconstitutional. He and John Randolph became fast friends. They were nominal opponents; but they shared a love of letters, a firm belief in states' rights and fear of centralized government, a distaste for Jefferson and for democracy, and an irritating habit of applying logic to politics just when their leaders were prepared for a vast and salutary act of inconsequence. Hating and opposing the war, Quincy resigned from Congress in 1813 to serve happily in local Boston politics and as president of Harvard College. He lived to support Lincoln and the Civil War, dying on July 1, 1864.

** It did not come to be called the White House until after it had been burned by the British, and repaired.

succeed himself in the Department of State, and Mr. Robert Smith, who had been Secretary of the Navy, he proposed to transfer to the Treasury Department. He was not permitted to make this arrangement. Mr. Robert Smith had a brother in the Senate. . . . Mr. Madison was given explicitly to understand that if he should nominate Mr. Gallatin he would be rejected by the Senate. Mr. Robert Smith was appointed [Secretary of State].

J. Q. Adams then compares "this dictation to Mr. Madison, effected by a very small knot of association in the Senate," to the intrigues which had destroyed his father's Administration.

In both instances [he adds], it was directly contrary to the spirit of the Constitution, and was followed by unfortunate consequences. In the first it terminated by the overthrow of the Administration and by a general exclusion from public life of nearly every man concerned in it. In the second its effect was to place in the Department of State, at a most critical period of foreign affairs and against the will of the President, a person incompetent, to the exclusion of a man eminently qualified for the office. Had Mr. Gallatin been then appointed Secretary of State, it is highly probable that the war with Great Britain would not have taken place . . . If the people of the United States could have realized that a little cluster of Senators, by caballing in secret session, would place a sleepy Palinurus at the helm even in the fury of the tempest, they must almost have believed in predestination to expect that their vessel of state would escape shipwreck. And he ends by saying that even when these conspiring Senators had made such pests of themselves that the people forced their retirement, "they left behind them practices in the Senate and a disposition in that body to usurp unconstitutional control, which have already effected much evil and threaten much more."[1]

The failings of Madison as a political leader were an invitation to "much more" of such evil.

When Jefferson had made it clear that he intended to enforce the succession of his Secretary of State,* John Randolph's bitter protest contained the following comment on Madison's career: "We ask for energy, and we are told of his moderation, we ask for talent, and the reply is his unassuming merit, we ask what were his services in the cause of Public Liberty, and we are directed to the pages of *The Federalist.*" The indictment is not so harsh as Randolph took it to be, for the pages contributed

---

* When Washington retired from the presidency at the end of his second term, he did so on the grounds of health and personal inclination; but when Jefferson retired, also after two terms, he did so on the ground that he thought no president should serve for more than eight years. He established a precedent which was followed until 1940.

by Madison to *The Federalist* are an achievement of rare worth. They are
an education in the economics of politics and in the relation between economics and history; they are remarkable for their steady grasp of reality,
their avoidance of the usual abstractions about government; they are a
steady warning against the danger of tyranny inherent in popular rule,
and against the danger to liberty of an economic system in which fewer
and fewer people owned real property.* Their hard matter-of-factness,
their bluntness about the nature of man, and about the nature and temptations of power, would seem to fit their author for the work of governing—just as the sentiment of the Declaration of Independence, the aspir-
ing hopefulness as to life and reality, suggest the amateur rather than the
party organizer. Yet Jefferson seldom made a mistake in the handling of
men, and Madison seldom made anything else.

In 1811, Washington Irving attended a presidential reception and wrote
the following impression of the Madisons: "Mrs. Madison is a fine, portly,
buxom dame, who has a smile and a pleasant word for everybody. Her
sisters, Mrs. Cutts and Mrs. Washington, are like the two Merry Wives
of Windsor; but as to Jemmy Madison—Ah! poor Jemmy!—he is but a
withered little apple-John." The description was unkindly true. Madison
was a neat, modest little man in black breeches and black silk stockings.
He seemed to shrink from asserting himself in action. His writings were
clear and exact and authoritative; but he showed no such qualities as
President during three years of drifting into war and two and a half years
of misdirecting it.

2

The Madison family had settled in Virginia in the middle of the seventeenth century. James Madison's father made his home in Orange County,
where the boy was later to inherit the twenty-five-hundred-acre estate
of Montpelier. At school he was taught the classics, French, and Spanish;
in 1769, at the age of eighteen, he went north to the College of New Jersey
(later Princeton University). After finishing the classical course, he stayed
on for a year studying Hebrew and ethics under President Witherspoon,
and also studying Montesquieu, Locke, Hobbes, and James Harrington.
It was a good course for the future maker of governments; and John
Witherspoon, with his impatient Scots emphasis on common sense and
practicality, was probably a good guide. After this northern interlude
Madison returned home, where he continued his studies in theology and
Hebrew.

* On the relations between power and property, Madison (like most of the
Americans of his day) agreed with Harrington's *Oceana*.

In 1776, Madison was a delegate to the Virginia Convention to make a new constitution. He became a member of the first Assembly under that constitution, and failed of re-election the following year—according to tradition, because of his refusal to distribute rum and punch. He became a member of the governor's council, and a delegate to the Continental Congress, where he stood firmly for securing the free navigation of the Mississippi—a fight which he never abandoned and which won him the loyalty of the Western country. He returned to Montpelier in 1783 and was at once elected to the Virginia House of Delegates, where he opposed paper-money inflation and the attempt to prevent the payment of pre-Revolutionary debts to British creditors. He also secured the passage of Jefferson's bill for freedom of religion and for the final disestablishment of the Anglican Church. During this period in the House of Delegates he learned the need for greater unity among the thirteen states, if they were not all to be ruined and reabsorbed by Europe. He took an important part, therefore, in the series of conferences which led to the Constitutional Convention at Philadelphia in 1787.

Just before the coming together of this convention, Madison returned to the Continental Congress for a few months in order to combat what he decribed as "Mr. Jay's project for shutting the Mississippi." A number of Northern states had voted, in 1786, to authorize John Jay,* in dealing with the Spanish Minister, to offer to forego the use of the Mississippi for twenty-five years in order to gain commercial concessions useful to these states. Madison secured the defeat of this plan. If he had not done so the United States might have been split in two almost before they began their national life, for the western settlers cared more about their use of the Mississippi than about their nebulous ties with the friends they had left behind, east of the mountains.

At the Constitutional Convention, as we have seen, Madison became the leader of the group favoring a strong government. From May 25 to September 17, he was in daily attendance, seldom missing so much as half an hour. His notes on the debate, first published in 1840, are by far the best record of those secret meetings. And he was second only to Hamilton in the subsequent work to secure ratification. Not only did he make a momentous contribution to *The Federalist;* but in the Virginia Convention he played a leading part, with George Washington, in persuading that powerful state to join the Union. Without Virginia, as without New York, there could have been no attempt at building a new country.

*

* Jay was Secretary of Foreign Affairs from 1784 until after the new government was organized under the Constitution. Then he administered the Department of State until March, 1790, when Jefferson took over as the first Secretary of State.

3

Madison served in the first House of Representatives. We have seen that he quickly understood the meaning of Hamilton's measures and that before the end of the First Congress he had become a recognized leader of the agrarian opposition to the capitalistic, centralizing plans of the Secretary of the Treasury. It was the capitalism of the Federalists that drove Madison into Opposition, not their tender care for property. On the latter point he was in agreement—only, as a Virginia gentleman, he thought of property in terms of land and animals, not in terms of pieces of paper.

In 1794, Madison married Dorothy Payne Todd, a young widow from Philadelphia. This was the "fine, portly, buxom dame" of Washington Irving's description. It was a completely happy marriage; Dolly Madison had a social charm which more than compensated for the mousiness of the "little apple-John." Since Jefferson was a widower, she was the First Lady in Washington society throughout his two terms as well as throughout her husband's, and she did much to make that desolate and fever-ridden clearing in the forest seem habitable.

In 1797, Madison retired voluntarily from Congress, expecting (like Washington and Jefferson before him) to lead the life of a Virginia planter, overseeing his twenty-five hundred acres and his more than a hundred slaves,* giving his mind and energies to the development of scientific agriculture, for his own pleasure and for the good of the community. But it was not the time for rural peace. The next year he was writing those Virginia Resolutions which, with Jefferson's Kentucky Resolutions, defined the principles of 1798 which the "Old Republicans"** defended all their lives, and which they were to accuse Jefferson and Madison of betraying. Many years later, when the doctrines of 1798 were used by South Carolina to justify nullification and even secession, Madison insisted that there was no threat of nullification, and no suggestion of the use of force, in the Resolutions. Yet Kentucky, in Jefferson's words, declared her determination "tamely to submit to *undelegated and consequently unlimited* powers in no man or body of men on earth," adding that acts of undelegated power, "unless arrested on the threshold, may tend to drive these states into revolution and blood." And Virginia, in Madison's words, said that "in case of a deliberate, palpable, and dangerous exercise of other powers not granted by the said compact, the states, who are the parties thereto, have the right, and are in duty bound, to *interpose* for

---

* Madison's father did not die until February, 1801; but the administration of Montpelier was already in Madison's hands.

** Such as John Randolph, John Taylor, Joseph Nicholson.

arresting the progress of the evil, and for maintaining, within their respective limits, the authorities, rights, and liberties appertaining to them."

This was the essence of the Republican doctrine: that there existed a force to prevent the steady growth of power at the center of government, that the states were the custodians of that force, and that the states had the right, and were "in duty bound" to take action when they found the central government using "undelegated and consequently unlimited powers." This was the meaning of the dispute between Jefferson and Marshall, between Madison and Hamilton. The Jeffersonians believed that if the central government were allowed to define its own powers (or if a Federalist Supreme Court were allowed to define them) America must repeat the old story of corruption, usurpation, and tyranny which had been the normal lot of man. It is hard to see how they could believe that the states had a "right" to prevent this, unless the "right" had a sanction of force. A right without such sanction is no right at all. Whatever Madison may have thought in his old age, this was the view of Virginia in 1798 and 1799, where preparations were afoot for armed resistance to the "tyranny" of the government of John Adams.*

4

The "Revolution of 1800" brought Madison back into public life. Even before the outcome of the election was known, Jefferson had asked him if he would become Secretary of State. It was a natural appointment because of Madison's vast knowledge of government and complete agreement with Jefferson on matters of political principle; but it was an appointment which led to divisions within the party—divisions which were to embitter, almost to destroy, Madison's presidency, but which were kept quiet so long as the wand of the magician ruled at Washington.

There were two reasons for the anti-Madison faction among Republicans. Men like Randolph and the noisy William Branch Giles of Vir-

* In January, 1817, John Randolph—who was first elected to Congress as an enthusiastic supporter of this resistance—said: "There is no longer any cause for concealing the fact that the grand armory at Richmond was built to enable the state of Virginia to resist by force the encroachments of the then administration upon her indisputable rights." (Henry Adams, *John Randolph*, p. 28.) Madison and Jefferson, unlike Randolph, did not reach spontaneously for the sword; but they used strong words at times. They may have thought that power can be controlled by strong words. If so, this would explain the failure of their foreign policy; for power can only be controlled by stronger power. If the states truly had a "right" to resist the Alien and Sedition Acts, it was a duty to build, and at need to use, the grand armory at Richmond. The "natural right" of Americans to leave the Empire was stated in the Declaration of Independence; but it did not exist in fact until after Saratoga and Yorktown.

ginia, who had returned to the House and was soon to move to the Senate, distrusted him because of his old association with the men who wanted a strong government. How, they wondered, could the same Madison who had framed the Constitution, and who had collaborated with Hamilton in writing *The Federalist,* draft the Virginia Resolutions of 1798? They decided that he was still a crypto-Federalist, and they blamed him for the moderation of Jefferson's program. Instead of rooting out the Federalist heresies, and establishing an Arcadian, agrarian, anti-capitalist, states'-rights paradise, Jefferson was administering the government as if it made little difference which party was in power. Madison could have told them why this was happening, and why he was not to blame. It was Madison who had explained to the Constitutional Convention that although a nation-wide coalition of local groups and interests may sound dangerous and radical in opposition, when it comes to power its members can agree only on a moderate program. In opposition, they can add together all the grievances of all the regions, and make a tremendous noise; in power, they can only add together the very few policies on which all the regions and all the interests agree. It was not the Federalist background of his Secretary of State which made Jefferson move cautiously, it was the conservative influence of the size and diversity of America.

The second reason for the anti-Madison faction was that he, like Albert Gallatin at the Treasury, refused to remove as many Federalist office-holders as the hungry Republicans wished. Especially bitter on this point was William Duane* of Philadelphia, editor of the *Aurora,* the most powerful of the Jeffersonian papers. When the Republicans came to power Duane descended on Washington, urging sweeping removals from office and a full-fledged spoils system. "He was coldly received at the State and Treasury departments, which gave him contracts for supplying paper, but declined to give him offices; and Duane returned to Philadelphia bearing toward Madison and Gallatin a grudge which he never forgot."[2] His paper became the organ for Madison's enemies, a group which was soon to be strengthened by the able Senator Samuel Smith of Maryland ("rather mischievous than alarming," according to Henry Adams) and his commonplace brother, Robert, "the sleepy Palinurus" who was to become Secretary of State as part of the revenge against Madison.**

* Duane was born in northern New York, of Irish parentage. He drifted to India, where he founded a paper and whence he was deported. He became a parliamentary reporter in London, then moved to Philadelphia and helped Benjamin Franklin Bache to edit the *Aurora,* a daily paper. When Bache died, Duane married his widow, who was the owner of the *Aurora.*

** Duane may also be responsible for the hostility of Michael Leib (Representative from 1799 to 1806, and Senator from 1809 to 1814), who shared with Duane the political dictatorship of Philadelphia.

During Madison's years in the Department of State he showed small initiative. Jefferson was responsible for the Louisiana Purchase, for the unsuccessful efforts to acquire West Florida, and for the Embargo. Madison agreed on all points; he wrote a number of able arguments against the depredations of the British and the French—one of which was described by John Randolph as "a shilling pamphlet hurled against eight hundred ships of war"; and he gave support to Jefferson's belief that France and England were acutely in need of the commerce of the United States. It was on this faith that they built the embargo policy. In January, 1801, Madison wrote to the incoming President that England, "however intoxicated with her maritime ascendency is more dependent every day on our commerce for her resources, must for a considerable length of time look in a great degree to this Country, for bread for herself, and absolutely for all the necessaries for her islands. . . . Besides these cogent motives to peace and moderation, her subjects will not fail to remind her of the great pecuniary pledge they have in this Country, and which under any interruption of peace or commerce with it, must fall under great embarrassments, if nothing worse."[3]

This did not prove to be true. The whole plan for "peaceful coercion" was dismissed by Canning with sarcasm and rude scorn. The question arises, Why should two sensible statesmen have believed it to be true? We should remember that Madison was one of the first writers on government to keep always in the front of his mind the economic springs of action; this habit may have misled him in judging the course of a great nation in the midst of a war for survival. And Jefferson's burning belief that America must have peace, in order to save herself and the world, may have helped him to think that America would therefore be allowed to have peace. Madison's realism and Jefferson's hopefulness may have led to the same conclusion.

5

The election of 1808, as we have seen, was Jefferson's last success. He easily had his way with the Republican caucus in Congress, which dutifully nominated Madison: and he was able to elect his candidate because the anti-Madison Republicans put two men in the field,* and because the efforts of the Federalists to get together with one of these men failed. Jefferson then tried to put the burdens of government upon Madison before Madison was inaugurated, with the result that for a time there

* Vice-President George Clinton of New York, and James Monroe of Virginia. Missing the presidency, Clinton was nevertheless re-elected Vice-President. So Madison had an enemy presiding over the Senate.

was no government at all, except such as could be contrived by the unruly Congress, where the Republicans were divided into the friends of Madison and Gallatin, and the friends of Giles, Clinton, Duane, and the brothers Smith—with John Randolph circling the two camps like a wild Indian, emitting occasional war whoops and poisoned arrows.

The Federalists of New England, meanwhile, were again flirting with secession, under the old leadership of Timothy Pickering. Although the movement did not come to a crisis for several years, a series of town meetings throughout New England early in 1809 adopted resolutions violently opposing the Embargo and the anti-British policy of the government, and in many cases pointing out that if such policies were continued patriotic citizens would be driven to consider disunion. "Oppression did sever us from the British Empire," said a petition from the town of Alfred, in Maine, "and what a long and continued repetition of similar acts of the government of the United States would effect, God only knows." Such was the state of the nation which Madison faced on March 4, 1809. "Under such circumstances," wrote Henry Adams, "until then without a parallel in our history, government, in the sense hitherto understood, became impossible."[4]

When the Embargo was repealed on March 1, 1809, the Non-Intercourse Act was put in its place. This prohibited trade between the United States and France or England, or any of their colonies or dependencies; but American goods and ships were otherwise free. The Non-Intercourse Act was to expire in the spring of 1810, at the end of the next session of Congress. The Act diminished the discontent in New England, where ships were no longer compelled to rot at their wharves; but it did little to help Virginia whose best tobacco markets were still denied her. George Washington Campbell,* who had succeeded to Randolph's position as chairman of the Ways and Means Committee, opposed the bill eloquently on the ground that it was a sectional bribe.

> The non-intercourse [he said] would press most severely on the Southern and Western states, who depend chiefly on the immediate exchange of their productions for foreign goods, and would throw almost the whole commerce of the nation into the hands of the Eastern states, without competition, and also add a premium on their manufactures at the expense of the agricultural interest to the South and West. Foreign goods being excluded, the manufacturing states would furnish the rest of the Union with their manufactured goods at their own prices.

* Campbell was born in Scotland, son of a physician. His family brought him to North Carolina when he was three years old. He was educated at Princeton, then studied law and moved to Tennessee. He entered the House of Representatives in 1803, resigned in 1809, and in 1811 returned to Congress as a Senator. Toward the end of the war he served briefly and unsuccessfully as Secretary of the Treasury. In 1818 he was appointed Minister to Russia.

The argument could not be answered; it was merely ignored. The Congress was afraid of war, afraid of decisiveness. The Administration, which for eight years had disciplined the unruly and taught the rest to obey, suddenly refrained from leadership. The hungry sheep looked up, and were not fed. As in the poem, they soon began to "rot inwardly, and foul contagion spread." Non-intercourse must ruin the South; non-intercourse was a bribe to quiet the revolt of the New England townships, at the expense of the rest of the country; yet non-intercourse was supported by forty-one Southern members, and by only twelve New Englanders. Sometimes, apparently, men do not vote from economic interest, or from any motive which can be made intelligible; sometimes they seem to vote from helplessness, from weakness and confusion, and a wild wish to do something, anything. Sometimes, to return to Milton, the sheep became "swollen with wind, and the rank mist they draw," and then there is no telling what will happen.*

Among all the ironies and inconsistencies of those years, the most unexpected was that Jefferson should become the chief promoter of the Industrial Revolution in America. Jefferson, who hated factories as a Puritan hates a witch, who felt that if Americans became crowded into great cities they would repeat in their green and pleasant land all the dismal experiences which had ever degraded the race, who fought Hamilton chiefly because Hamilton fostered industry and its handmaid finance, Jefferson was compelled, in order to keep America pure from war, to infect her with manufactures.

Never in the days of McKinley and Mark Hanna, never even in the mad nineteen-twenties, did the manufacturing interests dare to ask for such protection as was thrust upon them by the Embargo and the Non-Intercourse Act. The most selfish capitalist who ever trod Wall Street never suggested that the whole of the South should reduce itself to poverty in order to confer a monopoly upon his factories. Yet this is what the South did, in response to the pleading of her greatest and her most favored son. Then came the war, to prolong the period of complete protection for another two and a half years. By that time the balance of strength was determined. The South was growing poorer and the North was growing richer. Agrarianism was on the defensive and capitalism was dominant. New England was by no means grateful, for New England did not yet see what was happening. Another decade passed before New England understood that her industry was to outstrip her commerce in the production of wealth.

Another odd result of the Non-Intercourse Act was the pleasure it gave in London. Under the guise of retaliation for the Orders in Council, the

* Or was the Deep South already eager for war with England, and her ally Spain, in order that Florida might be seized? This seems unlikely as early as 1809.

Act was a complete submission to those orders.* "I conceive that great advantage may be reaped from it by England," wrote Erskine, the British Minister at Washington, "as she has command of the seas and can procure through neutrals any of the produce of this country, besides the immense quantity which will be brought direct to Great Britain under various pretences; whereas France will obtain but little, at a great expense and risk." Perhaps the one inconvenience of the Act to Great Britain was that it permitted American ships to sail the seas once more, thus diminishing the incentive which had been driving American sailors into the British marine. Canning, however, did not complain.

6

In spite of non-intercourse and the follies of Congress, Madison's Administration appeared to open with a triumph. On April 7, when the President had been in office a month, the British Minister in Washington received from Canning instructions which he took to be conciliatory. David Montague Erskine, Minister Plenipotentiary, was the son of the famous orator and Lord Chancellor, Thomas Erskine; he had married the daughter of General John Cadwalader of Philadelphia. With a Whig background and an American wife, Erskine was eager to settle the differences between the countries. He had been appointed in 1806 by Charles James Fox, who sincerely wished to improve relations, and he did not seem to know the change that had come over British policy with the death of Fox.

Interpreting his new instructions freely, and assuming that he was to offer redress of outstanding American grievances in case the United States would lift all restrictions on trade with England and retain the prohibition on trade with France, Erskine quickly and easily reached an agreement with Secretary of State Smith.** On April 19, he informed the Department of State that he was "authorized to declare that His Majesty's Orders in Council of January and November, 1807, will have been withdrawn as respects the United States on the tenth of June next." Smith replied that the President's proclamation in regard to British and French

---

* British Orders in Council are executive edicts, in the name of the King, "by and with the advice of his privy council." They have the force of law unless superseded by acts of Parliament. The Orders in Council of January 7, 1807, put French commerce under a blockade and forbade neutrals to trade from one port to another under French jurisdiction. The Orders of November 11, 1807, far more dubious in international law, said that neutral ships might not enter any ports from which the British flag was excluded, "and all ports or places in the colonies belonging to his majesty's enemies, shall, from henceforth, be subject to the same restrictions . . . as if the same were actually blockaded by his majesty's naval forces, in the most strict and rigorous manner."

** The Non-Intercourse Act allowed the President to restore trade relations with whichever belligerent first withdrew its Orders or Decrees.

trade would be issued immediately; two days later the proclamation and the Smith-Erskine notes were published.

The long trouble appeared to be at an end. The United States had in effect become a silent partner of Great Britain. Without admitting it openly she seemed to have accepted the thesis that Britain's victory was essential for the liberties of Europe; and in return England seemed willing to forego the destruction of American commerce. It was assumed that she needed the goods and was therefore willing to permit the trade. It was assumed that the Embargo and Non-Intercourse policies must have been a success after all, and that it was only the presence of the Francophile Jefferson which had prevented an accommodation with England. The Erskine agreement would doubtless mean war with France; but the Americans did not seem to care. They were happy to be on cordial terms with England. Federalists and Republicans alike congratulated Madison; for a few deluded weeks he was the most popular President the country had known.

The Erskine dispatches, containing the good news, reached Canning on May 22, 1809. On May 25, Canning recalled his Minister and repudiated the agreements. Erskine's disgrace could be explained on the ground that he had gone far beyond his authority; but it is not easy to see why Canning turned down a settlement which had already made America a passive ally and must soon make her an active one. The repudiation was accompanied by a deed equally hard to explain, except on the ground of inveterate enmity: the appointment of Francis James Jackson* as the new Minister to Washington, in Erskine's place. Commenting on the harsh and peace-defying terms of Jackson's instructions, Henry Adams wrote:

> While England waited impatiently for news from Vienna, where Napoleon was making ready for the battle of Wagram, Canning drew

---

* Rufus King, the most moderate-spoken and one of the wisest of the Federalists, was American Minister in London in 1802, when it seemed possible that the British were about to appoint Francis James Jackson to Washington, instead of Anthony Merry. King wrote to Secretary of State Madison: "It was not without some regret that I heard of the intention to appoint Mr. Jackson in lieu of Mr. Merry. . . . I have been led to make further inquiry concerning their reputations, and the result has proved rather to increase than to lessen my solicitude. Mr. Jackson is said to be positive, vain, and intolerant. He is moreover filled with English prejudices in respect to all other countries, and as far as his opinions concerning the United States are known, seems more likely to disserve than to benefit a liberal intercourse between them and his own country." Jackson's wife was a Prussian baroness, whom he had married while he was Minister at Berlin. Her "opinions concerning the United States" were even more likely to "disserve a liberal intercourse" than were her husband's. It was Jackson who had been sent with the British fleet to deliver the ultimatum at Copenhagen before the bombardment; Canning supplied him with instructions for his trip to America which were scarcely more ingratiating than his instructions for Denmark. He was to propose nothing whatever, and he was not even to refer back to London any American proposals which did not bind the United States to serve the policy of Whitehall. Under such conditions a man of gentler manners than Jackson, and with warmer feelings toward America, might have had trouble in reaching an agreement.

up the instructions to Jackson—the last of the series of papers by which, through the peculiar qualities of his style even more than by the violence of his acts, he embittered to a point that seemed altogether contrary to their nature a whole nation of Americans against the nation that gave them birth. If the famous phrase of Canning was ever in any sense true —that he called a new world into existence to redress the balance of the old—it was most nearly true in the sense that his instructions and letters forced the United States into a nationality of character which the war of the Revolution itself had failed to give them.[5]

Jackson reached Washington September 8. The President was at Montpelier, and did not return until October 1. Immediately thereafter, Jackson and Robert Smith began negotiations; but the Secretary of State was so incompetent that the President had to take charge, writing all of Smith's notes himself. He soon reached the only conclusion which was possible in dealing with Jackson, whose instructions forbade conciliation even if his character made it possible. On November 8, the President wrote, and Secretary Smith forwarded, the final note: "Sir . . . Finding that in your reply of the fourth instant you have used a language which cannot be understood but as reiterating and even aggravating the same gross insinuation, it only remains, in order to preclude opportunities which are thus abused, to inform you that no further communications will be received from you."

While refusing to argue further with Jackson, Madison expressed his continuing desire to establish friendly relations with Great Britain. There was no official change in relations, therefore. The American Government, lacking Executive or any other leadership, remained unable to act; and the British Government continued to seize American trade and sailors. Not until the Congress which was elected in 1810 came together in the spring of 1811 did the new mood of hostility find expression in deeds. Thereafter, the march toward war was steady. It was also unnecessary, for the British had done their worst and were soon to improve. Canning was out of office by September, 1809, and an adjustment might have become possible; but as British folly diminished, American folly took hold. The arrogance of Canning was to give way to the boastfulness and land-greed of the frontier. Whatever might have been done with better men or better luck, the Erskine disagreement was in fact the decisive moment, the point from which there was no returning. After the Erskine case, each government ascribed bad faith to the other. Madison felt he had been trapped into showing that he would go to almost any length for British friendship, and had then been struck in the face. The British felt that Madison had deliberately cast a spell over Erskine and persuaded him to exceed his authority. It was Jackson's repetition of this charge—this "gross insinuation," as Madison called it in the final note—which brought to an end his relations with the Department of State.

7

Meanwhile, something had to be devised to take the place of the Non-Intercourse Act, which would expire automatically at the end of the existing session of Congress. Madison seemed unable or unwilling to make a suggestion; but Gallatin tried to supply the leadership which the chief Executive shunned. In December, 1809, Nathaniel Macon, of North Carolina,* chairman of the committee on foreign relations, reported a bill which had been inspired by Gallatin and which would exclude all French and British ships from American harbors, and restrict all importations of French and British goods to ships owned wholly by American citizens. The bill authorized the President to remove the restrictions against either country, if that country should first remove the hostile decrees or orders in council. Non-exportation had failed; non-importation had failed; so it was now proposed by Gallatin to try a strict navigation act. The bill passed the House but was defeated in the Senate by a combination of the Federalists with Gallatin's personal enemies: Smith, Giles, and Leib, backed by Duane and the *Aurora*. Once again, Congress had failed either to follow the Administration or to produce a policy of its own. The country was wobbling toward war, while government seemed powerless either to prevent the war or to prepare for it.

In the last days of the session Congress passed an act known as Macon's Bill No. 2.** This repealed the Non-Intercourse Act, leaving American shipping to go where it could, and authorized the President to reimpose non-intercourse with either Great Britain or France in case the other should cease to interfere with American commerce. It was a silly act, lacking in dignity, lacking in courage, and strong only in its power to create mischief. It handed American trade to Great Britain on her own terms,

---

* An "old Republican" who supported Randolph's revolt in 1806, but who soon made friends again with Jefferson. Educated at Princeton, Macon studied law in North Carolina, entering state politics in 1781. He was opposed to the Constitution of 1787, but accepted a seat in the Federal House of Representatives in 1791. He served until 1815; then he was transferred to the Senate, where he served until 1828. He was known as the greatest economizer and the greatest opponent of new legislation who had ever sat in Congress. He was said to have voted "no" more often than any ten other members. He was a strict and devout Jeffersonian who really believed in the least possible government; he was also a thorough supporter of the Jefferson-Madison foreign policy.

** It was not prepared by Macon, or even approved by him. He merely reported it, as chairman of the relevant committee. It was passed on May 1, 1810.

abandoning all resistance and all restrictions, and it thereby tempted Napoleon to make a dupe of Madison by pretending to revoke the French decrees.

On August 5, 1810, the American Minister in Paris was informed that the Berlin and Milan decrees would cease to have effect on November 1—on the understanding, of course, that the United States would then reimpose non-intercourse with Great Britain.* John Quincy Adams warned the President that this was a trap, but Madison walked into it obstinately, and on November 2, he announced that non-intercourse would be revived against England if she did not repeal the Orders in Council within three months. The British Government pointed out that there was no evidence the French decrees were really repealed, that American ships were still being seized and sunk by French authorities and French privateers, and that Napoleon did not even pretend to have repealed the Rambouillet Decree, which was perhaps the most burdensome to America; but Madison insisted on being gulled, and in February, 1811, he forbade all trade with Great Britain.

This time, by chance, non-intercourse became a serious blow to Britain. Napoleon's power was at its height and the trade of Western Europe was denied England; warehouses were crowded and factories were closing; a crop failure led to food shortage during the winter of 1811–12. The result was heavy pressure on the British Government to withdraw the Orders in Council and revive the American trade. On June 16, 1812, the House of Commons heard the Orders would be withdrawn; but two days later, long before this news had crossed the Atlantic, the American Congress declared war on England.

Jefferson had embittered his country and ruined his popularity in order to show that peaceful coercion would work; but it didn't work. Then a floundering Congress passed a law which has been described as having "strong claims to be considered the most disgraceful act on the American statute-book,"[6] and a floundering president allowed the French emperor to trick him, and suddenly peaceful coercion had the effect which was intended five years before. But by that time the needless war had started. The declaration was received with indignation in London. The British could not believe that Madison had truly been fooled by Napoleon. It seemed to them that Madison had seized the thinnest of excuses for forcing a war at the time of Britain's greatest need, when she was defending

* This was the "Cadore letter." Napoleon's Continental Decrees were the Berlin Decree of November 21, 1806, which imposed a paper blockade of the British Isles; the Milan Decree of December 18, 1807, which declared that ships submitting to the British Orders in Council became lawful prey; the Bayonne Decree of April 17, 1808, wherein Napoleon pretended that he was helping Jefferson to enforce the Embargo by seizing all American ships in French ports; and the Rambouillet Decree, effective on March 23, but published on May 14, 1810, which legalized the seizing of American shipping in retaliation for the Non-Importation Act.

Europe. The Marquess Wellesley, who had succeeded Canning as Foreign Secretary, said in Parliament "that a more unjust attack was never made upon the peace of any nation than that of the American Government upon England," and that "the American Government had long been infected with a deadly hatred toward this country, and (if he might be allowed an unusual application of a word) with a deadly affection toward France."

This was what the Federalists of New England had been telling their British friends for years: that Jefferson and Madison were irrationally pro-French, and therefore anti-English; but it was not true. Madison's willingness to throw himself into England's arms at the time of the Erskine agreement is proof that it was not true. Until that tragedy of crossed purposes and disappointed hopes, England could have had America's glad friendship in return for a little politeness, a little respect. After the Erskine failure, new men with new ambitions seized control of Congress: men who wanted war. They represented a small minority; but they had their way because every injury received from Britain had been exacerbated by sarcasm and contempt. A young, weak country is naturally sensitive to bad manners. The French had done America more harm than the British; but there was no Canning in Paris to rub gunpowder into every small wound. For years the United States could have gone to war justly, with either of her tormentors or with both; in the end she went to war unjustly, with the nation which had at last decided to cease doing her harm. If the British must be blamed for the embittered emotional background which made this possible, the Americans must be blamed for the leaderless chaos of government which allowed a few young men to push their country into an unwanted fight.

8

In February, 1810, when Senators Leib and Smith and their friends were emasculating Macon's Bill No. 1, young Henry Clay from Kentucky rose to urge strong measures. Not yet thirty-three years old, Clay had been sent to fill an unexpired term in the Senate. His remarks on Macon's bill struck the note which was to be dominant in the next House of Representatives, where Clay himself was to be elected Speaker.

> The conquest of Canada [he told the Senators] is in your power. I trust I shall not be deemed presumptuous when I state that I verily believe that the militia of Kentucky are alone competent to place Montreal and Upper Canada at your feet. . . . I call upon the members of this House to maintain its character for vigor. I beseech them not to forfeit the esteem of the country. Will you set the base example

to the other House of an ignominious surrender of our rights after they
have been reproached for imbecility and you extolled for your energy?

It was time to extol energy, and to condemn the imbecility of Congress;
but where did the conquest of Canada fit into an argument over impressments and orders in council? The surprising answer is that the young men
of the West were land-hungry. Although the country had recently been
doubled in size by the Louisiana Purchase, they wanted Canada to the
north and Florida to the south in order to have room to expand.* And
they wanted Canada for still another reason: the Indians east of the
Mississippi and north of the Ohio were at last organizing themselves into
a desperate confederacy, trying to save the remnants of their hunting
grounds. The Westerners believed that the British in Canada were supplying the Indians with arms and with moral backing. So the war to protect
the New England merchants and sailors (who did not want protection,
who saw their trade and their livelihoods ruined equally by embargo and
by fighting) was changing into a war to take Canada and the Floridas.

The Congressional elections of 1810–11 removed almost half of the
absurd House of Representatives which had passed Macon's Bill No. 2,
substituting a young and pushing membership. This was the start of a
new age, when the men who were assuming leadership could scarcely, if
at all, remember the Revolution. Gerald W. Johnson comments:

> The first three Presidents all dealt with a country dominated, and
> largely inhabited, by men who were familiar, through personal experi-
> ence, with the horrors and dangers of war against a powerful enemy.
> Madison was the first to face a different population, a people who were
> born freemen and emotionally conditioned to regard the republic, not
> as a strange and doubtful experiment, but as part of the natural order
> of things. They knew nothing else, and only by a deliberate effort could
> they imagine anything else. It never occurred to them that the United
> States of America existed, so to speak, only by sufferance and that it
> could be expected to survive only as long as it carefully avoided the
> shock of battle.[7]

Chief among the new men, and the first to assume very high position,
was the young and charming and still impetuous Henry Clay, who had
left the Senate at the end of the Eleventh Congress and had returned to
assume the House leadership in the Twelfth. Clay was thirty-four, a
Virginian by birth, who had followed his mother and stepfather to Kentucky in 1797. First, however, he had spent four years in the office of

---

* This is not as silly as it sounds. The pioneers were woodsmen. Neither their
tools nor their training were yet adequate for the treeless prairies of Illinois and the
trans-Mississippi. Their way of life was to waste land fast, and then find some more.

Chancellor George Wythe, at Richmond. Wythe was the teacher and friend of Jefferson, Marshall, Monroe; he was one of the makers of the Federal Constitution and one of the greatest of Virginians. Among all the lawyer-politicians who went out from Wythe's office to build and to preserve the new nation, none was more promising, and none more quickly famous, than Henry Clay. After fourteen years in the untamed West, he was sent back East to Washington with a reputation for irresistible success, and was at once elected Speaker of the House. His first act was to use his power of appointment to organize the main committees for war.*

On the Committee of Foreign Affairs Clay placed three men whom he could trust to support strong action: Felix Grundy, brought up on the Kentucky frontier and recently moved to Tennessee; Peter Buell Porter, an ardent "war hawk" who had moved from Connecticut to the banks of the Niagara River in western New York; and John Caldwell Calhoun from the South Carolina uplands, a man whose life, like that of Clay himself, was to color the life of his country for the next forty years.

These young men from the West had no concern with the sea; they had never been incommoded by orders in council; but they intended war.** John Randolph complained that their speeches lacked variety: "like the whip-poor-will, but one eternal monotonous note—Canada! Canada! Canada!" Faced with Madison, such men were certain to get what they wanted: a war for Canada and Florida (though ostensibly for the rights of the seamen), and a war in which Congress (at least at first) assumed no unpopular burdens of taxation or preparedness. On February 7, 1812, the President wrote to Jefferson: "The newspapers give you sufficient insight into the measures of Congress. With a view to enable the executive to step at once into Canada, they have provided, after two months' delay, for a regular force, requiring twelve [months] to raise it, on terms not likely to raise it at all for that object." Yet Madison, who saw that he would soon be fighting, not a defensive war against British outrages, but

---

* James Bryce, in *The American Commonwealth* (2d edition, 1889, vol. I, p. 136), wrote that the Speaker of the House of Representatives has a "power which in the hands of a capable and ambitious man becomes so far-reaching that it is no exaggeration to call him the second, if not the first political figure in the United States, with an influence upon the fortunes of men and the course of domestic events superior, in ordinary times, to the President's, although shorter in its duration and less patent to the world." There were three reasons, in Bryce's day, for this immense power: first, the Speaker had been authorized, since 1790, to appoint the standing committees of the House, and also to appoint their chairmen; second, the Speaker had been a member, since 1858, of the Committee on Rules (which determines what business may come before the House), and was usually chairman of the committee; third, the Speaker had the right to recognize or refuse to recognize members seeking to address the House—a right which was only qualified, as Bryce explained, by "the line which custom has drawn between ordinary and oppressive partisanship."

** Some of the Westerners blamed the agricultural depression which had begun in 1808 on England's interference with American trade.

an offensive war to dismember two empires, did nothing to secure adequate forces.

In January, 1812, Gallatin asked for a war budget. The Congress debated his request, off and on, until June 26, eight days after the declaration of war; it then decided to postpone the matter until the next session. The previous year, February, 1811, the Senate had been divided evenly on Gallatin's recommendation to recharter the national bank. In spite of the fact that the Secretary of the Treasury believed the impending war might be a financial disaster without this bank, Vice-President George Clinton cast the decisive vote in the negative, and the President did nothing to rescue Gallatin, who was the one man he thoroughly respected in the entire Administration. No wonder that Randolph said Madison was a "president *de jure* only," and that Professor R. V. Harlow wrote: "Madison could hardly have played a less important part during those eight uncomfortable years if he had remained in Virginia."[8]

The declaration of war was supported by 79 votes to 49 in the House, and by 19 votes to 13 in the Senate. The only New England state which lacks a sea coast is Vermont, which was the only New England state to give a majority for war. The rest were strongly for peace. New York, New Jersey, and Delaware, also sea-faring states, were for peace. Congressional majorities from Pennsylvania, Maryland, Virginia, North Carolina, South Carolina, Georgia, Kentucky, Tennessee, Ohio, and the new state of Louisiana were for war. Josiah Quincy was accurate in stating, "This war, the measures which preceded it, and the mode of carrying it on, were all undeniably Southern and Western policy, and not the policy of the commercial states."

A war in 1807 would have been popular, and perhaps right; a peace in 1812 would have been sensible, and easy. The popular war was refused by Jefferson, out of his magnanimous strength; the sensible peace was sidetracked by Madison, out of his weakness. When it was clear that the evil must come, Gallatin wrote to Jefferson: "Our hopes and endeavors to preserve peace during the present European contest have at last been frustrated. I am satisfied that domestic faction has prevented that happy result."[9] Domestic faction would have been powerless, had Madison been a President *de facto* as well as *de jure*.*

* In 1836, Madison told George Bancroft, the historian, that in 1812 he had known the unprepared state of America, "but he esteemed it necessary to throw forward the flag of the country, sure that the people would press onward and defend it." (Letter from Bancroft, quoted by Henry Adams, *Gallatin*, pp. 460–61.) Madison was eighty-six when he made this statement, and he may have confused the year 1809, when the war would still have been just and when Madison would have been prepared to go forward if Congress had not held back, with the year 1812, when the war had become an excuse for land-grabbing and when Congress "pressed onward" without any pushing from Madison. "Our President," wrote Calhoun at the time, "though a man of amiable manners and great talents, has not I fear those commanding talents, which are necessary to control those about him."

9

Two months before the declaration of war, Congress admitted the state of Louisiana to the Union. This was a more important act than the war itself. For the first time the Union accepted into membership and full equality a state carved out of territories which had not belonged to the Union at the time it was formed. It was thereby decided, irrevocably, that states would multiply throughout the vast Louisiana Territory, that the new states would soon outnumber and outvote the old, that the American empire (at least within the continental boundaries) would offer federal union to its colonial areas.

The precedent was not accepted lightly. A number of Eastern states protested that such a momentous act should not be done by a mere majority vote, without at least the consent of all the original thirteen states. Josiah Quincy went so far as to say that if Louisiana were admitted without such consent, "I am compelled to declare it as my deliberate opinion that . . . the bonds of this Union are virtually dissolved; that the states which compose it are free from their moral obligations; and that as it will be the right of all, so it will be duty of some to prepare definitely for a separation—amicably, if they can; violently, if they must." Quincy's argument was logical; when the Constitution was adopted, and the federal Union formed, it was known that the land which then belonged to the Union (between the Appalachian Mountains and the Mississippi River) would one day be divided into states and welcomed into membership; but if the same was to be done with the measureless land beyond the river, and with any other land which might be acquired by the greedy Westerners, the nature of the Union was indeed changed. Yet the good sense of the people rejected the logic, rejected the impossible demand for unanimous approval, and welcomed the unacknowledged birth of a federal empire.

A week later Congress did something even more high-handed, this time with Spanish territory instead of American. We have seen that Jefferson and Madison tried to pretend that they had bought West Florida* along with Louisiana. When Spain objected, they tried to buy West Florida again. When Spain refused, they tried to bribe Napoleon into giving it to them. When this failed, they were obliged to wait until Napoleon reached such a point in the rape of Spain that it was safe to

---

* The territory along the Gulf of Mexico, from the Mississippi River on the west to the Perdido River on the east, but not extending south of the Iberville River and Lake Pontchartrain: in other words, the Gulf coast as far east as the Perdido, but not including the strip of land immediately north of New Orleans, between the Mississippi and the two lakes.

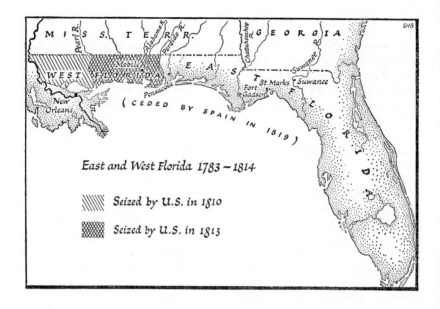

East and West Florida 1783 – 1814

\\\\\\ Seized by U.S. in 1810

▓▓▓ Seized by U.S. in 1813

seize the territory by force. The time had now arrived. In 1810 a section
between the Mississippi River and the Pearl River had been incorporated
by presidential proclamation into the Territory of Orleans, soon to become
the state of Louisiana. And on April 14, 1812, Congress formally divided
West Florida into halves at the Pearl River, annexing the western half to
the new state of Louisiana. A month later the eastern half was added to
the Mississippi Territory, and the following year an American army forced
the Spanish garrison at Mobile to surrender, and took possession formally.
A touch of gallantry was added to the scene by the fact that the American
general was the fabulous Wilkinson, who had long been in the pay of the
Spanish king.* And in 1819, to complete the curious picture, this land,

---

* James Wilkinson of Maryland first showed his style during the Revolutionary
War, when he was forced out of his post as clothier-general because of serious irregularities in his accounts. After the war he drifted west to Kentucky, then down
the river to New Orleans, where in order to acquire a trading monopoly he took an
oath of allegiance to the Spanish king. He convinced the Spaniards that he would
induce Kentucky, and perhaps other Western states, to secede from the Union; in

which according to the Americans had already been bought once and seized once, was ceded to the United States by Spain, along with East Florida, in return for five million dollars. One way or another the territory today belongs to the three states of Louisiana, Mississippi, and Alabama; but nobody knows how.

10

Madison was renominated for the presidency by the congressional caucus of his party in May, 1812. The Federalists insisted, then and thereafter, that Clay and his friends had made the President promise to send a war message to Congress as the price of nomination. The story is still repeated in history books, but it does not seem to be true.[10] Madison had two rivals for the nomination: De Witt Clinton (whose uncle, the Vice-President, had died in office on April 20, 1812), and James Monroe (who had recently deserted Randolph, rejoined the orthodox Republicans, and become Secretary of State in place of the absurd Smith).* It is not necessary to assume a blackmail plot in order to explain why the caucus would choose Madison in preference to either of those men. Monroe, as Secretary of State, would presumably have his chance in 1816; and Clinton—although he had been nominated, unofficially, by the Republicans in the New York State legislature—was known to be flirting with the New England Federalists, posing in that region as an enemy of war. In September, 1812, an unpublicized Federalist convention, meeting in New York, endorsed Clinton as a lesser evil than the President.

Madison won by an electoral vote of 128 to 89, in spite of losing all the votes east of Delaware except the eight from Vermont. If Pennsylvania had voted with New York, New Jersey and New England, Madison would

---

return, he was granted an annual salary of two thousand dollars. He continued to draw this money long after he had become the senior general in the American army. He was also involved in the obscure Burr conspiracy, and in the end betrayed Burr. He was three times tried by courts-martial, but never convicted. When in 1814 he was finally relieved from active duty, the American army became a safer place. In the last year of his life, at the age of sixty-eight, he represented the American Bible Society in Mexico City, where he managed to obtain an option on Texas lands for himself.

* Monroe later returned to the fold. In regard to Madison's troubles with his first Secretary of State, Henry Adams, in the *Formative Years,* vol. II, p. 588, comments: "The more he had to do with Robert Smith, the more intolerable became the incubus of Smith's incompetence. He had been obliged to take the negotiations with Erskine and Jackson wholly on his own shoulders. The papers drafted by Smith were, as Madison declared, brought from the Department of State in a condition 'almost always so crude and inadequate that I was, in the more important cases, generally obliged to write them anew myself, under the disadvantage sometimes of retaining through delicacy some mixture of his draft.' "

have been beaten and "Mr. Madison's war" (as it was called in Massachusetts) would have ended almost before it got under way. The new Vice-President was Elbridge Gerry, a signer of the Declaration of Independence, one of John Adams's commissioners at the ill-fated "X, Y, Z" negotiations in France, and famous in history as the father of the gerrymander.*

The sectional nature of the opposition to Madison at the election of 1812 was a warning of what was to come. Massachusetts in particular was beginning to question the worth of the Union. She did not yet know that the new factories which were being forced upon her by the commerce-killing policies of the Virginians would one day be more profitable than all her ships, than all her fisheries; and she was contemptuous of the Westerners who talked about the impressment of her sailors when they meant the conquest of Canada. Josiah Quincy referred to the invasion of Canada as a "cruel, wanton and wicked attack . . . upon an unoffending people, bound to the Americans by ties of blood and good neighborhood."

Furthermore, the war was wretchedly mismanaged. The militia of Kentucky, to Henry Clay's chagrin, proved very unlike the conquering armies of Napoleon, and the militia of other states did not resemble armies at all. "In the conduct of this strange contest," according to Charles A. Beard, "the United States called out about fifty thousand regulars, ten thousand volunteers, and four hundred and fifty thousand militiamen to cope with the British forces which at the moment of greatest strength did not exceed seventeen thousand disciplined soldiers." Yet the British army was not destroyed; in fact, it captured and burned the federal capital. And no part of Canada was ever conquered. The only resounding victory was won by Andrew Jackson at New Orleans; but this was after peace had been signed.

On the sea, the tiny American navy and the numerous privateers did superbly well; but the result was to rouse the British Admiralty to blockade the Atlantic coast. Until 1814 Massachusetts was exempted from this blockade, on the ground that New Englanders were more friends than foes, and that they might return to their British allegiance.

Angry at her financial losses, disgusted by the hypocrisy of the warmakers, half-pleased and half-pained at the humiliating failure of the war, Massachusetts at last seemed ready to listen to Timothy Pickering. In the spring of 1813 the legislature attacked the federal government for

* In February, 1812, when Gerry was governor of Massachusetts, the state was redistricted so as to insure more Republican state senators than Republican votes would justify. It was not a new idea to distort the shape of an election district in order to secure party advantage; but no one had previously gone to such absurd lengths. Among the new districts was an unusually odd one in Essex County, which was drawn by a cartoonist to resemble a flying monster, and named the gerrymander.

its injustice toward England and its partiality toward France, and a few days later a committee of the state senate brought out a strange report on a naval victory by Captain James Lawrence. The senate, said the report, must refrain from approving Lawrence's success lest it seem to encourage an unjust, unnecessary, and iniquitous war. "And to the end that all misrepresentations on this subject may be obviated," continued the report:

> *Resolved,* as the sense of the Senate of Massachusetts, that in a war like the present, waged without justifiable cause, and prosecuted in a manner which indicates that conquest and ambition are its real motives, it is not becoming a moral and religious people to express any approbation of military or naval exploits which are not immediately connected with the defense of our seacoast and soil.

Town meetings, as in the early months of 1809, adopted resolutions against the government; but this time the tone was more bitter. The temper of Boston was shown in April, 1814, when government brokers were trying to float a new loan authorized by the Treasury. Advertising the loan in the Boston *Chronicle,* the brokers promised that the names of subscribers would be kept secret! On the same day the Boston *Gazette* wrote: "Any man who lends his money to the government at the present time will forfeit all claim to common honesty and common courtesy among all true friends to the country." New England contributed less than three million dollars in loans during the war, while the rest of the country contributed thirty-eight millions.

In view of such a mood, and of the continued failure of American armies, it is not surprising that Pickering and his friends thought the time was ripe to take New England out of the Union. The first attempt to accomplish this, in 1804, had ended in the death of Alexander Hamilton, the Federalist Party's hero and philosopher. The second attempt, in 1814, ended in the death of the Federalist Party itself, for the timing of events was unfortunate.

In October, 1814, Massachusetts sent an invitation to the other New England states for a meeting to discuss the war, and to plan their future course in case the federal government became so discredited or so defeated that it could no longer protect its members. The result was the Convention which met at Hartford, Connecticut, on December 15—Massachusetts sending twelve delegates, Connecticut seven, Rhode Island four, New Hampshire two, and Vermont one. Every delegate was a Federalist. The cautious George Cabot was made president, so there was no likelihood of extreme measures; nevertheless, the Convention recommended a series of far-reaching constitutional amendments, among which were the following: that no new state be admitted to the Union without the concurrence of two thirds of the members of both houses of Congress; that Congress should not have the power to lay an embargo for more than sixty days; that the concurrence of two thirds of the members of both houses should be necessary to pass an act for commercial non-intercourse with any nation, or to declare war except in case of actual invasion; and that "the same person shall not be elected president of the United States a second time; nor shall the president be elected from the same state two terms in succession." The Convention also resolved that if nothing was done about these amendments, and the war dragged on unsatisfactorily, another convention should meet at Boston the following June "with such powers and instructions as the exigency of a crisis so momentous may require."

January 5, 1815, the Hartford Convention adjourned. The legislatures of Massachusetts and Connecticut approved the proposed amendments and sent commissioners to Washington to urge their adoption. The commissioners set out in the hope of arriving at the capital of a beaten and discredited government. Napoleon was on the island of Elba, and Wellington's veterans were free to pay attention to the United States; the blockade had become absolute; the British held part of the Maine coast (which still belonged to Massachusetts) and the island of Nantucket; also, it was known that a large British force had either attacked New Orleans or was about to attack it. The Administration of "the withered little apple-john" seemed undone, and the New Englanders thought they could extort any promise they wished.* So the Hartford commissioners took their way at leisure and did not arrive in the capital until after February 13. There they discovered, to paraphrase Professor Samuel Morison, that their mission was abortive and themselves ridiculous. For on February 4, word had come of the immense American victory at New Orleans,** and a week later it was learned that peace had been signed, on the day before Christmas, at Ghent.

The Federalist Party did not recover from the Hartford Convention, for its leaders could thereafter be accused, plausibly if not fairly, of plotting treason. In the election of 1816 it played a negligible part; and after that it played no part at all on the national scene. Its economic plans, its view of the nature of the federal government, its methods of administration—all these survived unimpaired; but they were to be defended by new leaders, under new names. And the Federalist contempt for democracy, the proud and open demand for government by an élite, disappeared from New England with the Federalist Party. Thenceforth, in the land of Fisher Ames, Quincy, and Pickering, those who despised democracy either dissembled their feelings or refrained from politics.

---

* "If the British succeed in their expedition against New Orleans," wrote Pickering, "and if they have tolerable leaders I see no reason to doubt their success—I shall consider the Union as severed."

** The battle of New Orleans was fought on January 8, 1815.

11

A strange, anomalous peace had been contrived at Ghent, ending an anomalous war. The American negotiators were John Quincy Adams, Henry Clay, Albert Gallatin, Jonathan Russell of Rhode Island (the American Minister at Stockholm), and James Asheton Bayard of Delaware, a moderate Federalist. The British began by offering conqueror's terms, which the Americans, according to their instructions, could not even discuss. The Americans were told to insist on satisfaction in regard to impressments, which the British would not discuss. Then the American delegation split on sectional lines (over the relative importance of the Newfoundland fisheries and the navigation of the Mississippi), and in the end spent more energy contending with itself than with the British.

The Treaty of 1783, at the insistence of the elder Adams, had secured for Americans the right to fish on the Grand Bank, on the other banks of Newfoundland, in the Gulf of Saint Lawrence, "and at all other places in the sea where the inhabitants of both countries used at any time heretofore to fish." In return for this large concession, the treaty also provided that "the navigation of the river Mississippi, from its source to the ocean, shall forever remain free and open to the subjects of Great Britain. . . ." By 1814 the Mississippi had become a wholly American river, with the result that the Westerners, represented at Ghent by Henry Clay, objected to renewing the British right of navigation. Yet the New Englanders, represented by Adams, objected to abandoning the fisheries. And the British, naturally, objected to discussing either right except in connection with the other.

Albert Gallatin, soothing and patient, first persuaded his fellow delegates and then persuaded the British to say nothing about either the fisheries or the Mississippi. This singular system was later applied to all points of disagreement, with the result that the treaty settled no problems, answered no questions, but merely said that hostilities were to cease. Every claim on either side was left open for future discussion, while four commissions were created to determine the boundary between Canada and the United States. This was an odd conclusion to a war which should not have happened; a war which few people wanted, which nobody won, which began after the chief *casus belli* had been withdrawn, and which ended before the chief battle was fought.*

---

* It was predicted in both countries that such an inconclusive treaty must lead to a new war. Yet with time every problem was settled peacefully. In 1817, the Rush-Bagot Agreement provided for naval disarmament on the Great Lakes, where each side had been busily building warships in 1815. The eastern boundary, between Maine and New Brunswick, was settled by the first of the treaty commissions.

Yet the Peace of Ghent brought joy to America. The treaty which settled nothing was received with an enthusiasm suitable for Athens after Marathon, Rome after Zama. The Americans felt, correctly, that at last they were escaping from Europe. Nothing could give more pleasure than such a release. For twenty-six years, ever since Washington's first term, domestic politics had been distorted and embittered by foreign affairs. Many nations would have accepted this as the normal fate of man; but it did not seem normal to the United States, whose lucky citizens believed with Jefferson that their fate was to go their own way, and find their own salvation, at peace, protected by the broad seas. Yet whenever America had tried to go her own way she had been prevented by some new explosion in Europe. These interferences, she sensed, were now to end, at least for a long time. It was natural that she should ascribe her new freedom to the Peace of Ghent, that she should decide the war had been a great victory, and that in the flush of victory she should temporarily forget sectionalism, condemn the Hartford Convention, and unite in a national pride which would have pleased George Washington. In one important sense, true American history (as opposed to colonial history) begins with the Treaty of Ghent.

Perhaps victory was a useful illusion. Perhaps it is well that no one told America that her new freedom depended not on the Treaty of Ghent, but on the Treaty of Paris which had been signed on May 30, 1814, after Napoleon's abdication at Fontainebleau.* It was not the little war against England which won for America the blessing of being let alone; it was the enormous war against Europe's conqueror. With Napoleon beaten, and England supreme at sea, the world was to know relative peace for a hundred years; and within that peace the United States was safe, and grew strong. She made the mistake of thinking the safety was conferred by nature, rather than by the vigilance of men. She was therefore surprised to find, when new conquerors arose in a new century, that her strength did not keep her isolated and comfortable, any more than her previous weakness.

The northern and western boundaries of Maine caused trouble, and were not set-tled until 1842. The third boundary commission made a satisfactory arrangement as far west as Lake Superior. Their line was carried to the Lake of the Woods in 1842. From there, the Convention of 1818 had made the forty-ninth parallel the boundary as far west as the "Stony Mountains" (i.e., the Rockies), and had agreed to leave the question of Oregon open for future debate. There was much debate, as we shall see, and almost a war; but that, too, was settled in 1846. The Newfound-land fisheries were dealt with, imprecisely, in the Convention of 1818. This led to the usual result of imprecision in diplomacy: long and needless recriminations. The question of British rights on the Mississippi River settled itself by default. The prob-lem of impressments did not arise again; and the problem of "neutral rights" on the high seas had a future which was more pleasing to the satirist than to the moralist.

* The Hundred Days did not begin until March 1, 1815; they had no effect on the mood or the fortunes of America.

12

For the time being, the War of 1812 brought the ruin of the "Old Republican" resistance, and of the Jeffersonian hopes for simple government. The measures to avoid the war had been harmful to these hopes, but the measures to fight the war were worse. Sixteen years of rule by the authors of the Kentucky and the Virginia Resolutions had brought concentration of power instead of diffusion, a larger (though still trifling) national debt instead of economy, a free and easy stretching of the Constitution instead of strict construction, the beginnings of industrialization instead of the triumph of agrarianism, a reluctant use of authority instead of a mild government which should put to shame the authors of the Alien and Sedition Acts. After such an experience, the youth and bloom had gone from the Republican dream. John Randolph of Roanoke and John Taylor of Caroline might go on pretending that the United States, if she were not perverted by wicked rulers, could become an Arcady; but most politicians, when they had struggled with harsh fact in the person of Napoleon, with cruel circumstance in the shape of the British fleet, found themselves driven to respect the old forms of power, the Hamiltonian power which they had derided. From the simple standpoint of survival, it seemed clear that the future did not belong to agrarianism and purity of heart, but to nationalism and the Industrial Revolution.

In his message to Congress on December 5, 1814, Madison recommended liberal spending for the army, navy, and military academies, a protective tariff, a national bank, a budget of twenty-seven million dollars instead of the ten millions his party had once thought ample. This was a Hamiltonian program, and the Republican Congress responded with an enthusiasm which would have made Hamilton surprised but proud. His once-rejected Report on Manufactures was revived, and from it his old enemies learned the arguments for their new policy. The tariff bill was signed by Madison on April 27, 1816. The rates were low—but high enough to whet the appetite of industry for further favors. Early in the same month the President had approved the bill for a new national bank,* and before the close of the month the Congress appropriated a million dollars a year for three years, to build ships-of-war. This was perhaps the most drastic break of all with "Old Republican" principles.

In the following December, John Caldwell Calhoun—soon to be the

---

* Cp. Binkley, *American Political Parties,* p. 98: "Republican newspapers in 1816 reprinted in support of the second Bank of the United States Hamilton's argument for the first bank. . . . Thus cavalierly was Jefferson's historic opinion against the chartering of the first bank, including his classic statement of the dogma of strict construction, given the *coup de grâce* by his own disciples."

prophet of a revived states' rights, nullification, and if need be secession—introduced a bill for internal improvements at federal expense. He warned America that her size exposed her to "the greatest of all calamities, next to the loss of liberty, and even to that in its consequences—*disunion*." The bill passed both houses of Congress; but characteristically Madison chose this moment to do one last deed for the "Old Republican" cause. It was one of his most important deeds and one of his most baneful: he vetoed Calhoun's bill, in language which recalled the arguments of 1798.

> I am not unaware of the great importance of roads and canals and the improved navigation of water courses [he said at the end of his veto message], and that a power in the National Legislature to provide for them might be exercised with signal advantage to the general prosperity. But seeing that such a power is not expressly given by the Constitution, and believing that it cannot be deduced from any part of it without an inadmissable latitude of construction and a reliance on insufficient precedents; . . . I have no option but to withhold my signature from it.

Madison must have known as much about the Constitution as any man alive, and his interpretation was doubtless logical. Yet Madison was Secretary of State at the time of the Louisiana Purchase, for which no one even pretended there was written constitutional authority; he was Secretary of State at the time of the Embargo Act, which with its enforcing legislation strained the Constitution to bursting-point; he was President when Louisiana became a new state on terms which seemed to violate the original compact, and which according to Josiah Quincy dissolved the Union. If he did not boggle at any of these acts, he was crotchety to veto a bill setting aside the Bank bonus of a million and a half dollars, and the future dividends from Bank stock, as a fund for building roads and canals. One cannot help feeling that he was performing an act of purification, rather than of statesmanship, that he was burning a little incense at the altar of the lost cause: a pretty gesture, but in this case an expensive one, for the veto imposed new burdens and in the end a new inferiority upon the South, the unhappy South which had been so grievously hurt by the Embargo.

New York, with the help of De Witt Clinton and his friends, was able to promote her own internal improvements and to build the Erie and the Champlain Canals which were to bring her exhaustless treasure. Pennsylvania, likewise, could find the money to build her own roads and canals, and so could Massachusetts; but the South was too poor to equip herself for the competition which was about to begin. The new trade routes were to have a determining effect on the westward march of empire, and that vast expansion was to breed many of the new problems which would soon torment America. The South, with help from the federal government denied her on constitutional grounds, was to become an underprivileged region, seemingly dependent on slavery for her waning economic strength. It was a pity that a Virginian President could accept the Embargo, which impoverished the South, but not Calhoun's bonus bill, which might have brought new strength to the region. "We are under the most imperious obligation," said Calhoun in defending his bill, "to counteract every tendency to disunion." And again, "Little does he deserve to be entrusted with the liberties of this people who does not raise his mind to these truths."

The veto message was sent to Congress on March 3, 1817; it was Madison's last official act. The next day he attended Monroe's inauguration; then shortly he retired to Montpelier, where he lived in peace for another nineteen years. Like Jefferson, he became an elder statesman whose views were often sought. Like Jefferson, he was deeply interested in the founding of the University of Virginia, and served as its rector. Also like Jefferson, he was nearly ruined by his own Virginian hospitality;* but he managed to avoid the complete collapse that overtook his friend's fortunes. He lived to see the rebirth of sectionalism in 1820, and the rebirth of nullification and secession threats between 1828 and 1832. During the latter crisis he claimed that his famous Resolutions of 1798 gave no support to the doctrines of Calhoun. This was not a claim which could be defended in logic.

---

* In 1820, Mrs. Madison wrote to her sister: "Yesterday we had ninety persons to dine with us at one table, fixed on the lawn, under a large arbour."

X

The One-Party Period

The DEFEAT of Napoleon, with the consequent easing of European pressure on America, marked the end of the days when domestic politics were twisted and embittered by foreign affairs. Americans no longer called each other "Anglomen," or "Gallomaniacs"; they were free at last to concern themselves exclusively with their own interests and problems. This they gladly did. New and vastly upsetting forces were at work throughout the land, and the next twenty years would display with copybook clarity the influence of economics upon politicians. Fiery nationalists would become equally fiery nullifiers, pompous secessionists would become equally pompous defenders of the Union, following the shifting business interests of their communities.

The Industrial Revolution and the rise of the new West were the two mightiest forces of the day. They had long been gathering; but men's attentions had been turned abroad, so the full impact had not been felt. Generous efforts were now made to harness industry and westward expansion to the new nationalism; but it soon became sadly clear that both were fated to promote sectional bitterness: industry because it demanded tariffs which would hamper the crop-exporting states, and the westward march because it created rich new areas for whose control the older regions must contend. The precarious balance of power between the regions was threatened each time a new state grew to manhood, and the insoluble problem of minority rights was posed in a fresh form each time Northerners and Southerners brought their differing institutions to the same frontier.

2

The Industrial Revolution first came to the South in the form of the world-upsetting cotton gin. The inventor, Eli Whitney of Massachusetts, had been gifted with mechanic's fingers from the time he was little. He was useless on his father's farm; but he repaired violins, and made nails, and before he was eighteen had almost cornered the hatpin business in his district. After graduating from Yale College he went to Georgia as a private tutor. While visiting on a friend's plantation he discovered the need of a machine to separate the seed from short staple cotton (or green seed cotton). This was in the early winter of 1793. Southern agriculture was in its customary state of depression, and the ingenious Yankee was told by his Georgian friends that such a machine would save the region. The long-staple, or sea-island, cotton had been grown along the Carolina coast since about 1778; but it would not grow far from the sea, and the short-staple cotton which flourished inland could not be cleaned at a profitable price: a slave could only separate one pound of lint from its seed in the course of a day.

In England, meanwhile, the cotton textile business had become the most dynamic part of the Industrial Revolution. The demand for the new cheap cloth seemed insatiable, although England's imports of raw cotton rose from about 5,000,000 pounds in 1775 to 56,000,000 in 1800. Most of this came from Brazil, the West Indies, and the Middle East. So Georgia and the Carolinas were faced with the irritating combination of an immense demand for a crop which they could grow, and an inability to market the crop at a fair price. When all this had been explained to Eli Whitney, he designed a cotton gin within less than a fortnight; and within two months he built a machine which could clean fifty pounds of cotton a day. He then hoped to return to his quiet life, and to preparation for the law; but he had harnessed forces which were to destroy the quiet of much of the world, and he was to have no more tranquil studying. In 1794, the year Whitney patented his gin, the southern states of America produced about 2,000,000 pounds of cotton; in 1826 the South (including the new states of the Southwest) produced 330,000,000 pounds, and within a few years this was increased to 450,-000,000 pounds.*

No such fierce change can take place politely, or without wide destruction of human values. The first subversive effect of the cotton gin was to turn slavery from a dying to a vigorous institution. Less was heard, thenceforth, about slavery as a transitional state for the Negro; more and more, at least in the South, it came to be looked upon as his permanent lot. With the exhaustion of the land in tidewater Virginia, and with the ruinous effect of the Embargo even upon the inland districts, slavery had in many cases become a burden on the masters. The old Virginia planter was being bankrupted: witness the financial troubles of Jefferson and Madison, and the still greater disaster that overtook Monroe. John Randolph prophesied the time was coming when masters

---

* Whitney, needless to say, made little money from his invention. He soon turned to the manufacture of firearms, wherein he perfected the system of interchangeable parts. The idea of interchangeability may have been Whitney's own, or it may have come from another Connecticut arms manufacturer, Simeon North.

would be running away from their slaves and the slaves would be advertising for them in the newspapers. The sudden new cotton prosperity did not affect the Virginians directly, for they lived too far north to grow this crop; but it offered them a market for their surplus slaves, and it tempted the more adventurous to move with their human capital to the fabulously rich lands along the Gulf.

As we shall see, most of these lands belonged to Indians, and some of the Indians were irritatingly peaceful and civilized, so that it was hard to find excuses for defrauding them. Nevertheless, the speed and rapacity with which they were expelled parallels the speed and rapacity with which England's green and pleasant land was turned black in order that the factories might expand as fast as the cotton fields. The betrayed and banished Cherokees, the Negroes who would now not be freed, the English farm families driven from their lands into the dark satanic mills, all were caught up in the stream of power liberated by the young Yankee visitor who only wanted to be helpful to his hosts. Meanwhile, the price of cotton goods was rapidly lowered, a fact which may or may not outweigh the honor of the American Government and the happiness of the English workman. And in the Southern states, political leadership followed economic leadership from Virginia to the Deep South; Crawford of Georgia and Calhoun of South Carolina replaced Washington, Jefferson, Madison. Monroe, a Virginian, remained President; but for the time being makers of opinion and of domestic policy were in Congress, not in the White House.*

3

In the North, during the same years, the Industrial Revolution was sowing another crop of dragon's teeth. The Embargo and the war had not only stimulated manufacturing,** it had also depressed shipping to the point of extinction. By the eighteen-twenties, the mercantile interest was waning, and by the end of that decade New England and Pennsyl-

---

* The leader of the Cherokees, in their peaceful resistance to plunder, was the astonishing John Ross, whose father was a loyalist Scot who had settled among the Cherokees during the Revolutionary War, and whose mother was also a Scot, but with one fourth Cherokee blood. Ross won every legal and diplomatic engagement, but was defeated in the end by the refusal of President Jackson to put force behind the decisions of the Supreme Court. So he had to lead his people away from their rich, well-watered country, across the Mississippi, beyond Arkansas, out to the edge of the Great Plains where the timber and the water disappear and there is nothing left but land. The white man could not farm this land until he had invented barbed wire and the metal windmill, so for a few years the Cherokees had only the savage nomads of the plains to fear: the Apaches and the terrible Comanches.

** In 1807 there were 8000 cotton spindles in the United States; in 1815 there were 500,000.

vania had discovered their industrial future and were uniting behind a demand for high tariffs—just when the South had come to believe that its hope lay in free trade. The South wished to sell raw cotton unhampered to the world; New England wished to prevent the world from selling finished cotton unhampered to the United States. The South wished to buy manufactured goods at the lowest possible world price; New England and Pennsylvania wished to sell manufactured goods at the highest possible domestic price. The politicians were to have trouble in reconciling these wants.*

At the same time, to the west of the Appalachian Mountains, the Industrial Revolution was bringing an even more startling change. In 1811 the first steamboat had been launched in the western waters. By 1825, the Erie Canal was completed, connecting the East, via the Hudson River, with the West, via the Great Lakes. The flow of population into the Ohio Valley became a torrent; the mountains were no longer an unconquerable barrier to trade.

Kentucky and Tennessee, which are western extensions of Virginia and North Carolina, had become states while Washington was still President; so had Vermont, after settling its relations with New York and New Hampshire. Between 1803 and 1819, six more states were added to the Union: Louisiana, Mississippi, and Alabama along the Gulf of Mexico; Ohio, Indiana, and Illinois along the Lakes. This made twenty-two states: eleven to the north of the Mason and Dixon line, eleven to the south. The agrarian slaveholding South and the capitalist North were thus evenly balanced in the Senate. Each district had western appendages which might break off and form new alliances; but so far, if the slave issue should arise, the new Northwest and the new Southwest would vote with its eastern neighbors, from whom most of its immigrants had come. Whenever a twenty-third state were to apply for admission to the Union, this equilibrium must be broken.** And in addition to exacerbating the slave issue and upsetting the balance of power, the rise of the new West forced upon the country another explosive problem: the disposition of the imperial public domain.

* One way of reconciling them would have been to promote industry in the South, making of that region a mixed economy, capitalist and agrarian. This seems to have been Calhoun's plan in 1816. It was defeated in part by Madison's constitutional scruples (which frustrated the first effort to equip the South for the new form of competition), in part by the difficulty of creating an industrial proletariat side by side with agricultural slave labor, and in part by the English country-gentleman ideal which was for years accepted by most Southern leaders.

** In 1820 the population of the United States was 9,638,453. The most populous state was New York (1,372,812); the most populous southern state was Virginia (1,065,366); the most populous state west of the Appalachians was Kentucky (564,317). Since 1790 the center of population had moved from a point east of Baltimore to a point in West Virginia.

4

Ever since the birth of the republic there had been two main attitudes toward the Western lands. Hamilton and his friends, eager for the rapid growth of manufactures and for a society of the conventional European type, wished to retard the settlement of the West until the East was fully populated and its potential wealth fully exploited. They thought the federal lands should be sold sparingly, in large units, and at a high price. Democrats like Jefferson and Gallatin, on the other hand, felt that the health and liberty of the country depended on creating a maximum of agricultural freeholders; they thought the federal lands should be made available to any genuine settler, at a price which would not discourage the pioneer. Each group attracted selfish interests: some manufacturers, fearing that wages must rise if the discontented had a place of refuge, wanted the lands withheld; some speculators, confident of their own ability to get the better of farmers and pioneers, wanted the lands offered cheaply and in large quantities. In spite of such camp followers, however, this division on policy was simply another form of the honest and deep division, symbolized by Hamilton and Jefferson, throughout American life.

The first Land Act passed by the new government, in 1796, was a compromise. The Act applied to most of the territory in the present state of Ohio. The township six miles square was made the unit of public land, each township being divided into 36 sections of one square mile, or 640 acres. One township was to be sold in sections of 640 acres and the next in lots of eight sections each, or 5120 acres. All land was to be sold at public auction, with a minimum price of two dollars an acre. It was hoped that this price would be too high for the speculator; in fact it was too high for the settler.

In 1800 Congress lowered the size of the minimum tract to 320 acres, and gave four years' credit. In 1804 the unit of sale was made a hundred and sixty acres; and finally in 1820, the price was reduced to a dollar and a quarter and the minimum tract to eighty acres.* The same system of land sale had meanwhile been extended to each new acquisition of land from the Indians, and to the Louisiana Purchase. Also, when Ohio was admitted to the Union in 1802, the federal government set the precedent of retaining title to all unsold land within the state, except for one section in each township which was given to the state as an endowment for education.

The general pattern for an orderly disposal of the lands had thus been

* This law of 1820 also put an end to the credit system established in 1800.

set by 1800. With the reduction, in 1820, of the minimum unit to eighty acres the really poor settler was for the first time given a chance. It only remained, if the policy of promoting rapid settlement for the sake of democracy and freedom was to be a success, to lower the price still further and to find some form of land tenure which would be a protection against the speculator. Good land at a dollar and a quarter an acre was a blessing for the speculator, who could afford to wait for a profit running from a hundred to a thousand per cent; but such a price was not cheap for the man with a family and a wagon and a few farm animals, who wished to try the great Western adventure. In many cases such a man had no cash; and if he began his adventure by borrowing, the result was likely to be that the moneylender inherited the land. Free land, combined with tenure laws to thwart speculation, would have made for free farmers and democracy; but land at a dollar and a quarter an acre, with no protective tenure laws, was bound to make land speculation (and its consequent rural booms and collapses) a national vice.

The problem was soon to be posed in an interesting form, for the national debt was about to be extinguished. What, then, should the government do with its profits if it continued to sell land? Should it give the land away, and if so, to whom, and on what conditions? Or should it return to the Hamiltonian plan and withhold land sales, at least until the older parts of the country were settled? Since the acreage involved would have made several good-sized nations, the avarice and acrimony which were aroused gave a new meaning to Hamilton's comment that a national debt is a national blessing. Had the nation remained in debt, had the government needed the money from land sales, it might have continued to evade the awkward political issue; but when the government did not need the money, and dared not face the issue, one more sectional trouble arose, and one more source of corruption. The evil would be felt from the days of Andrew Jackson to the days of Ulysses Grant.

5

The nationalism, the pride in continental unity and in strong government with which Monroe's Administration began, was for the most part short-lived; but it was not short-lived in John Marshall's Supreme Court. Long after sectional strife had returned to plague the politics and the economics of the country, long after the arguments of 1798 were being revived by Calhoun with clearer logic and more unyielding passion, Marshall and his Court were still quietly building the legal foundations for the American nation of today. As Jefferson feared, they were "ever acting with noiseless foot and un-alarming advance, gaining ground step by step

. . . engulfing insidiously the special governments into the jaws of that which feeds them." James Bryce gave a more friendly description of the same process when he said of John Marshall, "No other man did half so much either to develop the Constitution by expounding it, or to secure for the judiciary its rightful place in the government as the living voice of the Constitution."[1]

In 1819 the "living voice" announced an opinion which has had as much influence on American government as any deed by President or Congress. The opinion concerned the Second Bank of the United States, which had been chartered in 1816 and which began business in 1817. The Bank's powers were similar to those of the First Bank of the United States (which had expired in 1811) except that the capital (and the limit for note issue) was increased from ten to thirty-five million dollars.* The Bank was allowed to establish branches in the main towns. These branches were feared by the state banks doing business under state charters. The Maryland legislature taxed the notes of the Baltimore branch of the Bank of the United States, planning to drive it out of business. The tax was upheld, as constitutional, by the state court of appeals and the problem was then taken to the Supreme Court of the United States. The case was *McCulloch* v. *Maryland;* it gave Marshall his chance to intervene in the states'-rights controversy, putting the slow but weighty influence of the Supreme Court on the side of centralized government.

> The counsel for the State of Maryland [wrote Marshall] have deemed it of some importance, in the construction of the Constitution, to consider that instrument not as emanating from the people, but as the act of sovereign and independent states. The powers of the general government, it has been said, are delegated by the states, who alone are truly sovereign; and must be exercised in subordination to the states, who alone possess supreme dominion.

This was the view of Jefferson and the Virginia school. It was to become the view of Calhoun and the South Carolina school, and finally of the Southern Confederacy. It was not the view of John Marshall. "It would be difficult," he wrote, "to sustain this proposition"; and he proceeded to demolish it, so far as the Court was concerned, by pointing out that although the convention which framed the Constitution was elected by the state legislatures, "the instrument, when it came from their hands, was a mere proposal, without obligation, or pretensions to it." The instrument was then submitted to the people who assembled in conventions.

> It is true [said Marshall] they assembled in their several states; and where else should they have assembled? No political dreamer was ever

* See above, for the First Bank. The new bank, like the old, had a twenty-year charter.

wild enough to think of breaking down the lines which separate the states, and of compounding the American people into one common mass. Of consequence, when they act, they act in their states. But the measures they adopt do not, on that account, cease to be the measures of the people themselves, or become the measures of the state governments.

From these conventions [concludes Marshall] the Constitution derives its whole authority. . . . The government of the Union, then . . . is emphatically and truly a government of the people. In form and in substance it emanates from them, its powers are granted by them, and are to be exercised directly on them, and for their benefit.

No statement could have been more hateful to Jefferson or to John Randolph. If the people of the national community are sovereign, and not the separate states, it follows that the states have no right to nullify an act of Congress. If such an act is constitutional, it is binding; if it is not constitutional, the Supreme Court must so decide.

Having disposed of states' rights to his own satisfaction, Marshall attacked the doctrine of "strict construction." Discussing the constitutionality of the act creating the Second Bank, Marshall relied on the arguments used by Hamilton in 1791. At that time, as we have seen, Madison and Jefferson were bitterly opposed to the First Bank—although Madison was to sign the bill for the Second Bank, in 1816, with the strange explanation that he yielded to an overwhelming "public judgment, necessarily superseding individual opinions."* The original argument against the Bank had been that the power to charter such a corporation is not expressly granted by the Constitution and cannot be inferred from the clause in Section 8, Article I, which gives Congress permission "to make all laws which shall be necessary and proper for carrying into execution the foregoing powers . . ." A national bank, said Jefferson and his Virginian friends, is clearly not necessary, even if some people may consider it useful. In meeting this argument Marshall made two statements which have not been successfully challenged, and which have therefore determined one aspect of America's constitutional growth.

The first statement dealt with the "implied powers" of Congress.

Let the end be legitimate [wrote Marshall], let it be within the scope of the Constitution, and all means which are appropriate, which are plainly adapted to that end, which are not prohibited, but consist with the letter and spirit of the Constitution, are constitutional.

This goes a long way; but it also raises the question, who is to decide whether the end is "within the scope of the Constitution," and whether the means "are plainly adapted to that end"?

* This justification, if such it be, was given years later.

Marshall's second statement answers the question.

> Should Congress [he wrote] in the execution of its powers, adopt
> measures which are prohibited by the Constitution; or should Con-
> gress, under the pretext of executing its powers, pass laws for the ac-
> complishment of objects not intrusted to the government, it would
> become the painful duty of this tribunal, should a case requiring such a
> decision come before it, to say that such an Act was not the law of the
> land. But where the law is not prohibited, and is really calculated to
> effect any of the objects intrusted to the government, to undertake
> here to inquire into the degree of its necessity, would be to pass the
> line which circumscribes the judicial department, and to tread on
> legislative grounds.

This is clear, and it seems to follow logically from the existence of a
written constitution; yet it suggests that the nature of the American
government depends upon the opinions and the principles of the men
who constitute the Supreme Court. The scope within which the Congress
may operate, the means which it may choose, are to be decided by those
men. Since they are men, not gods, they are presumably subject to mundane influences, and a study of American government must therefore
include a study of the tastes and temptations of judges.

Having dissolved states' rights and strict construction, Marshall concluded by declaring the law of the state of Maryland, imposing a tax
on the Bank of the United States, unconstitutional and void, on the
ground that "the states have no power by taxation or otherwise, to retard,
impede, burden, or in any manner control, the operations of the constitutional laws enacted by Congress to carry into execution the powers
vested in the general government." *McCulloch* v. *Maryland,* from beginning to end, was one continuous refutation of the Virginia and Kentucky Resolutions of 1798. The "Old Republican" creed of government—
states' rights, strict construction, nullification, and if need be secession
—could not finally be defeated by a court which disposed of no physical
power. John Marshall could only say what he believed the law to be; it
took the armies of Grant and Sherman to establish what the law was.
And even then, even after the final sanction of force, local rights and
decentralization proved so necessary to a land the size of America that
we shall find the political parties devising new ways, unwritten ways,
of restoring to the states some of the power of resistance which was taken
from them by *McCulloch* v. *Maryland,* followed by Shiloh, Gettysburg,
and Appomattox.

In addition to its nationalizing tendencies Marshall's Court was notable
for its defense of property rights. For example, in *Fletcher* v. *Peck* (1810),
Marshall had undertaken to settle the Yazoo land fraud which was driving

John Randolph to the verge of mania. The Constitution provides that no state shall pass a law imparing the obligation of contracts; it was the unanimous opinion of the court, therefore, that Georgia had no right to rescind her corrupt sale of western lands. The state of Georgia had entered into a contract with the land companies, and these in turn had sold much of the land to innocent men and women. These private purchasers would be defrauded if Georgia were allowed to declare her contract void.

This was the first case in which the Supreme Court had held a state law void because it conflicted with the Constitution.

> Georgia [wrote Marshall] cannot be viewed as a single, unconnected, sovereign power, on whose legislature no other restrictions are imposed than may be found in its own constitution. She is part of a large empire; she is a member of the American union; and that union has a constitution, the supremacy of which all acknowledge, and which imposes limits to the legislatures of the several states.

In a similar case a few years later, Marshall decided that the legislature of New Hampshire had no right to rescind the prerevolutionary royal charter of Dartmouth College and to place the college under state control. The opinion that a corporation charter is a contract, and thus unbreakable by a state legislature, has been important both for good and ill in American economic history. It was modified by Marshall's successor; but even in its limited form it remained a vital influence.

The world has often wondered that a country seemingly so volatile, a country whose national life is rooted in revolution, should be as politically conservative as the United States. For this there are several reasons, most of them connected with the size of the nation and with the party system which has been developed to deal with the problems of federalism and of bigness; but one simple reason is that the Constitution, until amended by the people, is what the Supreme Court says it is,* and that the legal mind is conservative and tends to cherish the rights of property.

6

James Monroe, under whose presidency these forces of division and of consolidation developed without hindrance, or guidance, or any sign of Executive leadership, was the last of the "Virginia dynasty." Born in Westmoreland County in 1758, he went to William and Mary College at the age of sixteen, but soon left to join the War of Independence. He

---

* Charles Evans Hughes, before he became Chief Justice of the United States, made this statement in almost these words.

became a lieutenant in a Virginia regiment and saw much fighting for three years. In 1780 he retired to the study of law.

When the war ended, he was sent to the legislature of the Confederation, where he became chairman of the committees dealing with Western interests: the committee on the free navigation of the Mississippi, and the committee on forming a temporary government for the Western lands. In the course of his duties he made two long trips to the trans-Appalachian country. His knowledge of that country, and the faith of its people that he understood their needs and hopes, helped him throughout his career; for the conflict within his own state of Virginia between the democratic men of the mountains and the great slaveholders of the East, which was one day to split the commonwealth in two, was bitter from the beginning. Yet Monroe's most enduring act during his three years in the Congress of the Confederacy was more pleasing to his Eastern friends than to his Western. It was a negative but decisive act: he was absent on the famous occasion when the attempt to bar slavery forever from all the West failed by a single vote. "Heaven was silent," wrote Jefferson, "in that awful moment." So, unfortunately, was James Monroe.

Monroe did not attend the Philadelphia Convention of 1787; but he was a member of the state convention called to ratify the Constitution in 1788. He opposed the new form of government, but accepted defeat tactfully, and in 1790 was appointed to the Senate of the United States by the Virginia legislature. He quickly became a leading opponent of the Hamiltonian plan, and a personal enemy of its author. Yet in 1794 Washington appointed him Minister to France. Madison and Livingston had refused the mission, and Washington wished to send a member of Jefferson's pro-French party. In Paris Monroe was well liked, with his democratic ideas, and his undisciplined habit of explaining that Washington and Hamilton and their friends did not represent the "real" (and Francophile) feelings of America. In 1796 he was recalled, under something of a cloud.

The state of Virginia, where the majority shared Jefferson's friendliness toward Monroe, assuaged his hurt feelings by electing him governor for three successive terms. Then Jefferson sent him back to France, early in 1803, to help Robert Livingston negotiate for the purchase of New Orleans. By the time he arrived, Livingston had already been offered the whole of Louisiana. Instead of thanking Toussaint and the other unconquerable Negroes of San Domingo for this startling good fortune, Jefferson seems to have given credit to his friend Monroe. So the next year he sent Monroe to Madrid, with instructions to produce another miracle by duping or frightening Spain into giving up the Floridas. The mission failed, and in 1805 Monroe was transferred to London on an even more hopeless task. Here he was joined by William Pinkney of

Maryland. As we have seen, their effort to make a treaty which would settle the problem of impressments was defeated—largely because of the death of Fox and the imminent reappearance of Canning at the Foreign Office. Monroe's latest biographer writes:

> Something like a panic seems to have seized [Monroe and Pinkney] as the Tory Majority in Parliament rapidly increased. Aware of the futility of insisting upon the ultimatum he had been directed to present, Pinkney seems to have taken the part of encouraging Monroe to abandon even the slight advantages he had wrenched from Fox. Thus it was that on the last day of December, 1806, Monroe and Pinkney affixed their signatures to a treaty wholly incompatible with the instructions both had received.[2]

Jefferson rejected the treaty out of hand; yet Monroe had probably secured all that could be won from the British Government at that moment. Lord Holland, with whom he negotiated, believed that if the treaty had been accepted the War of 1812 would not have occurred. Lord Holland's opinion of Monroe was that "he was plain in his manners and somewhat slow in his apprehension; but he was a diligent, earnest, sensible, and even profound man." This is very far from the impression of flightiness which he had made in Paris ten years before. Monroe, in the meanwhile, had experienced almost every form of public service and had developed into one of the first of America's national politicians who could be called a professional. Public employment was his chief source of livelihood. Political leadership was soon to pass from the gentry to the professionals, and Monroe was a transition figure. He belonged to the gentry, and he could live without office; but he could live better with it. His years in office were not an interruption to what he considered his real life; his years out of office were the interruption.

After working with Monroe for eight years, John Quincy Adams described him in the famous diary as having "a mind anxious and unwearied in the pursuit of truth and right, patient of inquiry, patient of contradiction, courteous even in the collision of sentiment, sound in its ultimate judgment, and firm in its final conclusions." This is notable praise from J. Q. Adams, and the praise seems deserved. Monroe possessed neither the imagination of Jefferson nor the knowledge of Madison; but he developed into an experienced and reliable public servant. Even in his youthful army days Washington had called him "a brave, active and sensible officer." He seems to have lacked humor, charm, and any form of impressiveness; yet the great men of his day not only honored and respected him, they liked him.

In 1807 Monroe once more returned to the United States in an aggrieved mood, feeling that his good work abroad had been misrepresented and underestimated. Yet he must have known that the results of his diplomacy were not impressive.

> His disasters [wrote Henry Adams] came, not in any ordinary form of occasional defeat or disappointment, but in waves and torrents of ill-luck. . . . In many respects Monroe's career was unparalleled, but he was singular above all in the experience of being disowned by two presidents as strongly opposed to each other as Washington and Jefferson, and of being sacrificed by two secretaries as widely different as Timothy Pickering and James Madison.[3]

Smarting from these rebuffs, Monroe allowed the dissident Republicans of the Randolph and Taylor faction to support him for the presidency in opposition to Jefferson's candidate. As usual with those who opposed Jefferson, he was badly defeated; and also as usual, Jefferson made every effort to placate him and to bring him back into the fold as soon as the defeat was consummated. Monroe had never spoken or felt with Randolph's utter bitterness, so it was easy for him to return to good relations with Jefferson. In the autumn of 1810 he served again in the Virginia House of Delegates, and in the following year became governor for a fourth term. This puzzling man, who seems so colorless in retrospect, and whose diplomatic career was so unfortunate, had never the least trouble in obtaining high appointive office from his friends or high elective office from his public.

Madison and Gallatin, meanwhile, were being driven beyond their gentle patience by the ineptitude of Robert Smith, the Secretary of State. In March, 1811, Gallatin forced the issue by resigning from the Treasury. Madison refused the resignation and at last brought himself to defy the Senate cabal and to discharge Smith. As we have seen, during two vital years this foolish, bumbling man had held the most important office in the state, next to the presidency, because the President was afraid of Giles of Virginia, Leib of Pennsylvania, Samuel Smith of Maryland, and Vice-President George Clinton. Jefferson, if thwarted by such people, would have broken them almost before they knew he had given them his attention; but Madison allowed them to poison his Administration and to endanger the country because he did not know how to meet their plots. He could write a constitution of divided powers, but he could not administer one.

Needing Monroe's help and influence in Virginia to offset these newly challenged enemies, Madison offered him the Department of State, and with it the prospect of succession to the presidency. Monroe resigned from the governorship in order to accept. The appointment of the new Secretary, the new heir apparent, did not mean a new policy; it merely meant a new efficiency in one part of Madison's ramshackle Administration. Monroe had for some months been explaining away his connection with Randolph, lest that should impede his return to high office; he had been making it clear that he was no longer an "Old Republican" of 1798, but a practical man of 1811, ready to accept everything Randolph hated: war, loans, a navy, conscription. He had gone so far in these explanations that Randolph had broken with him in two characteristically bitter letters.[4]

During the war Monroe hoped for a military command; but he could not be spared from Washington, where he and Gallatin were the only competent administrators.* After the burning of Washington, in the summer of 1814, Madison dismissed General Armstrong, the Secretary of War, and allowed Monroe to run the War Department as well as the Department of State—the change coming just in time for Monroe to receive credit for the victories with which the war ended. In spite of this good fortune, and in spite of receiving the support of both Jefferson and Madison, Monroe was nearly defeated for the presidential nomination by William H. Crawford of Georgia. In the Congressional caucus of 1816, Monroe won by only eleven votes. The caucus, which in the days of the magician from Monticello had been used to serve and strengthen the Executive, was about to try to make the executive the servant of Congress.

7

Crawford of Georgia was a veteran of a rough school of politics. A brilliant young lawyer from the uplands, he became a leader of the conservative faction in his state, supported by the planters of the coast and the wealthy farmers inland. He was hated by Governor John Clark, an almost illiterate demagogue, defender of the Yazoo men, and idol of the small farmer and the frontiersman. An attempt was made to kill Crawford in a duel, or a series of duels. The first man who tried was killed himself; then Clark challenged, and wounded Crawford seriously. The following year Crawford was sent to the comparative safety of the United States Senate, where he became one of the most popular members and a special favorite of John Randolph because of his anti-Yazoo record.

He was a huge, genial man, and an amusing storyteller. He was also efficient and hard-working, with an understanding of finance which made him a help to Albert Gallatin at the Treasury. When Vice-President Clinton died, in 1812, Crawford was elected president *pro tempore* of the Senate. The following year he was sent as Minister to France, and from 1815 until the end of Madison's Administration he was Secretary of the Treasury. His popularity with Congress was so great that he could have

* After May, 1813, Gallatin was abroad on diplomatic missions.

had the caucus nomination in 1816, and with it the election, if he had
been willing to oppose Monroe. He felt, however, that Monroe was the last
of the Revolutionary worthies with a claim to the presidency, and he believed (mistakenly) that he himself would have time to become President
later; so he told Monroe's friends to announce publicly that he was not a
candidate. Nevertheless, he received 54 votes, and Monroe 65.

The Federalists, meanwhile, nominated their last presidential candidate,
Rufus King. Monroe and Governor Tomkins of New York (the Republican candidate for Vice-President) received the electoral votes of
every state except Massachusetts, Connecticut, and Delaware: 183 votes,
to 34 for Rufus King. This was the end of the Federalist Party, and the
beginning of the so-called Era of Good Feelings. For more than eight
years there was no official opposition; but every ambitious man conspired
stealthily for his own advancement, hating his rivals with a fury which
made party bitterness seem affectionate. Since there was no opposition,
there could be no party discipline, which meant that the President had no
control over Congress. A member of the lower House expressed the general
disregard of the Executive as follows:

> We have lately given a pretty strong proof of the little influence pos-
> sessed by the Administration over the House of Representatives by the
> passage of the Army Bill. The Secretary of War and all his friends, in
> and out of doors, opposed by every expedient in their power—the
> President was known to be against it—and probably other members of
> the Cabinet—but it was carried notwithstanding many defects in the
> details of the bill by an overwhelming majority. A similar proof was
> given last year in the refusal of the House to proceed with the Yellow
> Stone Expedition, after the President had informed us that it was a sub-
> ject of very great importance in which he took a particular interest and
> was willing to incur great responsibilities to secure its success.[5]

This is the language of a schoolboy rejoicing at having discomfited the
Latin master; but more serious men observed the same lack of co-ordina-
tion in government and were not amused. John Quincy Adams quotes
Clay as saying that

> he considered the situation of our public affairs now as very critical and
> dangerous to the administration. Mr. Monroe had just been re-elected
> with apparent unanimity, but he had not the slightest influence on
> Congress. His career was considered as closed. There was nothing
> further to be expected by him or from him. Looking at Congress, they
> were a collection of *matériels,* and how much good and how much evil
> might be done with them, accordingly, as they should be well or ill
> directed. But henceforth there was and would not be a man in the
> United States possessing less personal influence over them than the
> President.[6]

Crawford spoke of the deadly atmosphere, "with ambitious and crafty and disappointed men on the watch for every mischief, and welcoming every disaster,"[7] and Adams wrote in his diary that "the rankling passions and ambitious projects of individuals, mingling with everything, presented a prospect of the future which I freely acknowledged was to me appalling."[8]

Here was a result of that freedom from party spirit which the Fathers in their innocence had desired, and which John Quincy Adams still thought must somewhere, somehow, lead to purity in public life. The illusion died hard. After Monroe had been elected President, Andrew Jackson wrote him:

> Now is the time to exterminate the monster called party spirit. By selecting characters most conspicuous for their probity, virtue, capacity and firmness, without any regard to party, you will go far to, if not entirely eradicate those feelings, which, on former occasions, threw so many obstacles in the way of government; and perhaps have the pleasure of uniting a people heretofore divided. . . . Consult no party in your choice.[9]

Monroe consulted no party. He chose the best men he could find, and although Clay and Jackson refused his offers he appointed a very good Cabinet: John Quincy Adams, Secretary of State; John Caldwell Calhoun, Secretary of War; William H. Crawford, Secretary of the Treasury; B. W. Crowninshield of Massachusetts (a temporary holdover from Madison's Cabinet), Secretary of the Navy; and William Wirt, Attorney General.*

Yet this Cabinet of high talents was effective only in foreign affairs (where the interference of Congress was not constant, and therefore not quite disastrous), and in political intrigue. "Petty factions grouped themselves about Crawford, Clay, Adams, Calhoun, De Witt Clinton, and General Jackson, and political action was regulated by antipathies rather than by public interest. If any one of these leaders seemed to be gaining an advantage, the followers of all the others combined to pull him down."[10]

The personal bitterness, the intrigues and the jockeying for position among members of the same government, the decline in the authority of the Executive, all were the result of the absence of party opposition. In-

---

* Son of a Swiss tavernkeeper who lived at Bladensburg, Maryland, Wirt moved to Virginia at the age of nineteen and practiced law in Culpeper County. Author of the immensely popular *Letters of the British Spy* (1803), Wirt was a gregarious, humorous, much-loved minor figure in literature and the law. In 1816 Madison appointed him United States attorney for the district of Richmond, and the next year Monroe made him attorney general. He held this office for twelve years, under Monroe and John Quincy Adams. He was one of the few men in high position during the Era of Good Feelings who did not make bitter, vindictive enemies.

stead of dividing the country, as Jackson thought, the political parties had canalized discontents, discouraged their own extremists and perfectionists in order to hold together as many interest groups as possible, and given form and order to the government. Instead of uniting the country, the decline of the Federalist Opposition led to a chaos from which only tyranny or the reappearance of parties could rescue the state.*

When there is no Opposition there is no incentive for politicians to co-operate on a consistent policy. Each man is free to maintain his popularity at home, among his own voters, by stating the extreme demands of his region or his interest group. When there is no Opposition, discipline is impossible and the President cannot require the support of his party members in the legislature, neither can the legislature impose sufficient unity upon itself to make or carry out policy. A tyrant can demand unity from his servants and can abolish the Opposition; but in a free system unity is achieved only when disunity means the loss of power. When there is an orderly and effective alternative, the government must either dis-cipline itself, and hold together, or accept defeat. When there is no alter-native, no threat of defeat, there is no incentive to hold together, and in the end no policy, merely a scramble for special privileges. The members of Monroe's Administration had nothing to fear except each other, so they spent their time seeking to frustrate each other's hopes and plans. The result was interesting, but it was not useful.

It is equally true, of course, that free institutions will not work unless the parties agree on fundamental aims. An Opposition which seeks to destroy the foundations of the state can only provoke a civil war. So free government requires at least two parties, both of which are competent to take over the Administration and neither of which aspires to revolution. The United States, in Monroe's day, was threatened not with revolution, but with constitutional collapse for lack of an Opposition. Only the birth of a vigorous party system could supply the government with enough strength to govern. The first step was the creation of a single, strong, pro-fessionally organized party. The politicians who were excluded were then driven by the instinct for survival to build another party of their own.

The new party which began to form toward the end of Monroe's eight years was built in the name of Andrew Jackson, who had advised Monroe "to exterminate the monster called party spirit." It was built by men who did not care in whose name they organized, but who understood the virtues of organization for its own sake. They had no cause, no plan for saving or remodeling the country; they merely had a plan for putting themselves into office. They had learned in local government how to build a political machine, and how to defeat opponents who did not possess such

* "Party organization," said Walter Bagehot, "is the vital principle of representa-tive government."

a machine, or who did not keep it in good order. They had also observed that the gentry, who had long run the federal government, were losing touch with the constantly expanding electorate, and that a new type of popular leader was needed. After the election of 1824 they found the leader, built the first national political machine, won power within four years, and incidentally restored health to the government.

8

Meanwhile, during the years of drift, during the cantankerous Era of Good Feelings, history was not marking time while America learned her political lessons. The West and the Industrial Revolution continued to expand, breeding new dangers incessantly. The first explosion came on the frontier, across the Mississippi, when in 1819 the legislature of Missouri applied for admission into the Union as a slave state. This not only disturbed the balance of power in the Senate, where there were eleven Northern and eleven Southern states, but it raised the question whether slavery was to be allowed throughout the Louisiana Purchase. The Ohio River had become the boundary between freedom and slavery in the old West; but there was no boundary in the new West, beyond the Mississippi. Which set of institutions was to inhabit that empire? Missouri lay far north for a slave state. Would her admission mean that Southern ways, and the Southern economic system, must expand at the expense of the Northern?

The question had not yet become moral and impassioned; it was still chiefly a struggle for power. Aggressive industrial capitalism did not wish to be outvoted in the Senate by an agrarianism made newly aggressive through the cotton gin and its rehabilitation of slavery. Wherever slavery spread, the Southern way of life went with it; if Missouri were admitted, might not the whole West be overrun by the land-hungry planters? It was already known that slave labor and one-crop cotton culture were having a deadly effect on Southern land. The cotton kingdom was exporting its top-soil to Liverpool, along with the ever-mounting millions of pounds of fiber. If slavery was to remain profitable, it must expand; if cotton was to supply the South with a counterpoise to the new manufacturing wealth of the North, it must cross the great river. This knowledge fired both Southern and Northern representatives during February, 1819, when the bill to admit Missouri came before the House. When the North supported an amendment offered by a New York member, providing for the gradual abolition of slavery in Missouri, Cobb of Georgia prophesied: "You have kindled a fire which all the waters of the ocean cannot put out, which seas of blood can only extinguish."[11] The House, nevertheless, passed the bill thus amended; but the Senate rejected it, and since Congress dissolved in March, the question was held over until the next session.

During the summer and autumn the Missouri problem was debated bitterly by the people, with many threats of secession from the North and from the South. Senator James Barbour of Virginia proposed to call a convention of the states to dissolve the Union and to agree upon the terms of separation and the disposal of the public debt and public lands. And J. Q. Adams, convinced that slavery must be abolished if the nation were to survive, wondered whether a temporary dissolution of the Union could be arranged, until such time as the South would free its Negroes.[12]

In March, 1820, the new Congress accepted a compromise. The district of Maine, which had detached itself from Massachusetts, was admitted as a free state, and Missouri was admitted as a slaveholding state, thus keeping the balance even. Also, slavery was prohibited in any other part of the Louisiana Purchase north of latitude 36° 30′; that is, north of the southern boundary of Missouri. Many fiery Southerners, including his son-in-law, urged the President to veto the compromise on the ground that Congress had no constitutional right to ban slavery in the territories. Although he prepared a veto message, Monroe finally signed the bill March 6, 1820, rather than risk civil war. "The President," wrote J. Q. Adams in his diary, "thinks this question will be winked away by a compromise. But so do not I. Much am I mistaken if it is not destined to survive his political and individual life and mine. . . . I take it for granted that the present question is a mere preamble—a titlepage to a great tragic volume."

Henry Clay, who was still Speaker of the House, was responsible for the success of the Compromise Bill. He had learned a lot since the confident days of 1811 when he believed in pushing issues to a clear-cut conclusion, even though the conclusion should be war. He had watched his country driven not only to the edge of defeat, but to the edge of disunion and treason, by the rash policy of his Western War Hawks, and he had seen the value of compromise if the great regions of America were to live together in amity. "All legislation," he was to say years later, "all government, all society is founded upon the principle of mutual concession, politeness, comity, courtesy; upon these everything is based. . . . Let him who elevates himself above humanity, above its weaknesses, its infirmities, its wants, its necessities, say, if he pleases, I never will compromise; but let no one who is not above the frailties of our common nature disdain compromise."[13] So Clay put his strength and his cunning behind the Missouri bill (securing a vote of 90 to 87 in the House), not because he thought that it would settle the slave question, or that it was eternally "right," but because he hoped it would diminish tension, creating an atmosphere in which the problems of the federal empire could be discussed in friendliness. The contrast between Jefferson and Randolph, the politician and the dogmatic perfectionist, was scarcely more sharp than the contrast between Clay and John Quincy Adams.

On March 3, the day after Clay had persuaded the House to accept the compromise, Adams devoted pages of his diary to clarifying his own views.

> The impression produced upon my mind by the progress of this discussion [he concludes] is that the bargain between freedom and slavery contained in the Constitution of the United States is morally and politically vicious, inconsistent with the principles upon which alone our Revolution can be justified; cruel and oppressive, by riveting the chains of slavery, by pledging the faith of freedom to maintain and perpetuate the tyranny of the master; and grossly unequal and impolitic, by admitting that slaves are at once enemies to be kept in subjection, property to be secured or restored to their owners, and persons not to be represented themselves, but for whom their masters are privileged with nearly a double share of representation*. . . . I have favored this Missouri Compromise, believing it to be all that could be effected under the present Constitution, and from extreme unwillingness to put the Union at hazard. But perhaps it would have been a wiser as well as a bolder course to have persisted in the restriction upon Missouri, till it should have terminated in a convention of the states to revise and amend the Constitution. This would have produced a new Union of thirteen or fourteen states unpolluted with slavery, with a great and glorious object to effect, namely, that of rallying to their standard the other states by the universal emancipation of their slaves. If the Union must be dissolved, slavery is precisely the question on which it ought to break.

The moral issue had played a very small part in public discussion of the Missouri question; but the leaders were aware of the issue and rightly feared it, for if the day came when the nation was split along moral and economic lines which coincided, the bonds of union would dissolve.

9

Monroe took no part in the Missouri controversy. Although deeply troubled over the future of the country, he did not feel the Executive should attempt to lead, or to make domestic policy. This was probably just as well, for the Congress was in no mood to listen to Monroe and the breakdown of party discipline had left him without power to command a hearing.

In foreign affairs, however, the Executive was forced to accept leader-

* Article I, Section 2, of the Constitution provides that three fifths of the slaves shall be counted in apportioning representation.

ship. Not even Monroe with his Virginian scruples could deny that the
Constitution expected the President to be responsible for foreign relations;
if he had sought to deny it, he would have met resistance from his able and
pushing Secretary of State. John Quincy Adams had inherited his father's
belief that since America was destined to be strong, she was in fact strong,
and that the great powers should treat her as an equal. The belief was not
shared abroad; but it gave to Adams's dispatches a unique flavor, a combination of power and impertinence.

In February, 1819, Adams finally persuaded Spain to cede the whole of
the Floridas to the United States. As we have seen, America had been
taking progressive bites out of West Florida ever since 1810. East Florida,
meanwhile, was so poorly governed by Spain that it had become a refuge
for escaped slaves and a base from which Indians could attack the white
men who were steadily forcing the Creeks out of their lands between
Georgia and the Mississippi. The Americans took the view that if Spain
was unable to govern Florida she should leave it to someone who could,
and in 1817 Monroe gave General Andrew Jackson permission to pursue
marauding Indians into Spanish territory.* Jackson did not need to be
prodded into offensive action. He crossed the Florida border with his
Tennessee militia, seized St. Marks, hauled down the Spanish flag, hanged
two Indian chiefs, and also executed two Englishmen who had been encouraging the Indians. He then marched on to Pensacola and removed the
Spanish governor.

In London this typical outburst of Jacksonian energy might have led to
war; but fortunately Lord Castlereagh was Foreign Secretary, and after
examining the reports he decided that Jackson's two victims "had been
engaged in unauthorized practices of such a description as to have deprived them of any claim on their own government for interference."** In
Washington the news from Florida shook Monroe's Cabinet; but in the
end J. Q. Adams had his way and was allowed to justify every act of
Jackson on the ground of the failure of Spain to keep order in her colony.
There was small enthusiasm for this view in Madrid; but even there it
was recognized that America would not much longer refrain from East
Florida and that the province had better be sold unless Spain was prepared

---

* Monroe later denied that he gave permission for Jackson's invasion of Spanish
land; but Congressman John Rhea swore that he himself carried the President's
message to General Jackson.
** Morison and Commager, *The Growth of the American Republic*, vol. I, p. 347.
Commenting on Lord Castlereagh, the authors say that he "coined no phrases about
Anglo-Saxon solidarity during his long career. In England his achievements were
eclipsed by the plausible Canning; in America he is known chiefly through Byron's
savage verses. Yet, judged by his deeds, this great and silent statesman must be
placed beside Washington, Hamilton, Peel, and Bright as a promoter of Anglo-
American concord. He was the first British statesman to regard friendship with
America as a permanent British interest." (*Ibid.*, pp. 341–43.)

both to govern it and to protect it. Ruined by Napoleon, struggling help-lessly against the loss of her whole South American empire, Spain was in no state for extra effort, so she relinquished all her lands east of the Missis-sippi, together with her nebulous claims to the Oregon country, for five million dollars.* The treaty also provided that the southwestern boundary of the United States should leave Texas within Mexico. For this reason the Senate held up the treaty for two years; but it was finally ratified in Feb-ruary, 1821. A year later President Monroe recognized the independence of the Latin American republics which had formed the Spanish Empire. The destruction of that empire in the Americas was complete,** unless Spain could persuade a great power to intervene and win back the colo-nies.

When France invaded Spain in 1823, to "save" Ferdinand VII, and when the French were welcomed by the Spanish people, it seemed to many observers that a Franco-Spanish invasion of Latin America might follow. This would have been equally unwelcome in Washington and in London, where George Canning had returned to power after the death of Castlereagh. Canning had not recognized the new American republics, and was in no hurry to do so; but he meant to keep Spain and France from re-establishing a colonial monopoly in lands where England hoped to ex-

---

* Adams's official note to the American Minister at Madrid (Department of State, 28 November, 1818), defending Jackson and putting the blame for every unpleasantness upon Spain, is one of the most charming examples of self-righteous-ness in diplomatic history. National pride backed by a New England conscience produced a masterpiece of pained superiority. "Is this narrative of dark and com-plicated depravity," he asked, "this creeping and insidious war . . . these political filters to fugitive slaves and Indian outlaws, these perfidies and treacheries of vil-lains incapable of keeping their faith even to each other . . . is all this sufficient to cool the sympathies of his Catholic Majesty's government, excited by the execu-tion of these two 'subjects of a Power in amity with the King'?" And in conclusion, after the moralistic surprise, the cold threat: "If the necessities of self-defence should again compel the United States to take possession of the Spanish forts and places in Florida, we declare, with the frankness and candor that become us, that another unconditional restoration of them must not be expected; that even the President's confidence in the good faith and ultimate justice of the Spanish govern-ment will yield to the painful experience of continual disappointment; and that, after unwearied and almost unnumbered appeals to them for the performance of their stipulated duties in vain, the United States will be reluctantly compelled to rely for the protection of their borders upon themselves alone. You are authorized to communicate the whole of this letter, and the accompanying documents, to the Spanish government. . . ."
The Spanish Government, in its time, had given many strange excuses for the seizing of many people's lands. The one thing that would have surprised them about John Quincy Adams's note would have been the knowledge that he meant exactly what he said. He really thought America was wholly right, Spain wholly wrong. His father, after all, had written on the day before the Declaration of Independence, "Britain has been filled with folly, and America with wisdom." Few men, especially in tired, cynical Spain, could hope to inhabit so clear a world.

** Except for the valuable islands of Cuba and Puerto Rico which Spain held until 1899.

tend her trade. So in August, 1823, Canning asked the American Minister in London, Richard Rush,* whether the United States would join with Great Britain in ordering France to leave Latin America alone.

Rush preferred not to answer the momentous question (especially since Canning refused to recognize the South American republics), so he referred it to Monroe, who in turn referred it to Jefferson with the suggestion that the answer should be yes. We have already seen Jefferson's reply; the high priest of American isolationism was willing, in such a cause, to urge an Anglo-American alliance. So, too, was Madison, whom Monroe had also consulted; but not John Quincy Adams. The suspicious and fiercely patriotic Secretary of State did not believe there was danger of French intervention. In this he was right, for in October, 1823, while the ex-presidents were consulting together, France had renounced all designs against Latin America.** Furthermore, Adams felt that the real threat to the United States came from Russia in the Pacific, not from France in the Atlantic where British power was supreme. And lastly, as he told the Cabinet, he did not think it fitting to the dignity of the United States "to come in as a cock-boat in the wake of the British man-of-war." So Adams urged an independent American statement which would concentrate on the problem of Russian expansion down the Pacific coast, from Alaska into the Oregon territory. Adams wished to embody such a statement in one of his own thorny notes to the Russian Government.

In the end Monroe compromised. He agreed with Adams on a separate American statement; but he insisted that it include the problem of European intervention in Latin America, and instead of making the statement in a note to a foreign power, he chose the quieter method of inserting it into his annual message to Congress, on December 2, 1823. In two widely separated passages of this message the President laid down what has come to be known as the Monroe Doctrine. Early in that document, while discussing American relations with Russia, he said that "the American continents, by the free and independent condition which they have assumed and maintain, are henceforth not to be considered as subject for future colonization by any European power." And in the closing paragraphs he dealt with the Spanish colonies, saying that, since the political

* Rush was one of the most pleasant and unambitiously able men of his day. A Philadelphian, a Princetonian, son of a famous physician, he had been attorney-general of Pennsylvania, Attorney General of the United States (under Madison), Secretary of State for a few months while Monroe waited for John Quincy Adams to return from Europe, and then Minister to Great Britain. He was the first American Minister to the Court of St. James's who was both efficient and well liked. Later he served as Secretary of the Treasury for J. Q. Adams, and as Minister to France for President Polk. Aside from a quarrel with John Randolph, who said his appointment to the Treasury was the worst appointment since Caligula made his horse a consul, Richard Rush led a tranquil, uncontentious, gratifying life.

** This was the Polignac Agreement, made under British pressure.

system of the powers composing the Holy Alliance differed radically from that of America,

> we owe it to candor, and to the amicable relations existing between the United States and those powers, to declare that we should consider any attempt on their part to extend their political system to any portion of this hemisphere as dangerous to our peace and safety. With the existing colonies and dependencies of any European power we have not interfered and shall not interfere. But with the governments who have declared their independence and maintained it, and whose independence we have, on great consideration and just principles, acknowledged, we could not view any interposition for the purpose of oppressing them, or controlling in any other manner their destiny, by any European power in any other light than as the manifestation of an unfriendly disposition towards the United States.

The statement was received with great enthusiasm in America, and with distaste in Europe. To many Europeans it seemed a gratuitous insult, for the message was directed against an imaginary menace. "Not one of the Continental powers cherished any designs of reconquest in the New World in November or December of 1823."[14] In his history of the Monroe Doctrine, Professor Dexter Perkins says that the Europeans,

> innocent of nefarious designs . . . could hardly be otherwise than resentful of the imputations of the President. Without any preliminary warning or exchange of views, without any effort to establish the facts, in a document intended only for the American national legislature, Monroe and Adams had laid down the principles on which they expected the policy of the Old World to be governed in relation to the New. These doctrines were nothing more nor less than a challenge to the monarchies of Europe. . . . "Blustering," "monstrous," "arrogant," "haughty," "peremptory"—these were some of the terms applied to the message.[15]

The importance of the Monroe Doctrine lay chiefly in the future; but even at the time, even though there was no genuine danger to overcome, the statement of a clear and popular foreign policy, which soon became so widely accepted that no later President could retreat from it, was a weighty deed. It was this which Adams and Monroe intended, and which they achieved. They also achieved something which they did not intend, and which was less useful: they helped to mislead the American people as to the relation between policy and power. For many decades the chief guarantee of the Monroe Doctrine was to be the British fleet. The nations of Europe refrained from colonial experiments in South America, not because a President and a Secretary of State had admonished them, but because they knew the British would fight rather than lose those new expanding markets. In his nationalistic pride, Adams had concealed from the American public the dependence of the Doctrine on British sea power; by so doing he made it easier for Americans to believe that foreign policy can be created by speeches and pronouncements, or by mere benevolence. The delusion was to prove baneful in the future.*

10

In the election of 1820, meanwhile, Monroe had received every electoral vote but one—a sign of public indifference rather than of praise. The election came shortly after the fiery conflict on the Missouri question, and it came after a financial panic which shocked and scared the country during 1819 and 1820. Yet there was no demand to turn Monroe out, not because the country trusted him, but because it knew he had nothing to do with the making of domestic policy. The country did not care whether Monroe was President or not. Public interest, for the time being, centered on Congress, and especially on the House of Representatives where policy was made, or where it failed to be made.** The Jeffersonian theory (but not practice) of Congressional government, of executive self-denial, was now fully applied; the result was to show the incapacity of the representative assembly to direct a government. The Administration of John Quincy Adams was soon to show the incapacity of the Executive itself to govern in the absence of a party system and party discipline. Then, with the coming to power of the Jackson men, the lessons of the twelve years following 1817 were applied; the government and the uses of the Constitution were radically changed.

* The South Americans were not fooled. They knew they owed their safety to the Polignac Agreement, and thus to British power.

** "In the first three decades of national history," writes Allan Nevins (*Ordeal of the Union,* vol. I, pp. 163–64), "when the Senate was too small to carry great weight and the House was still a truly deliberative body, public interest had centered in the lower chamber. It was in the House that Madison and Gallatin, Randolph and Webster, Clay and Calhoun, had won their first parliamentary fame. But the debates on the Missouri Compromise in 1820–21 had signalized a shift in popular attention. The Senate had by that time risen to a membership of forty-four. William Pinkney of Maryland, Rufus King of New York, and others had given it lustre, while before long Clay and Webster would enter it, and Calhoun would preside over it as Vice-President. For the next forty years, down to the Civil War, the Senate enjoyed a much greater prestige than the House."

XI

The President Without a Party

SINCE THE PUBLIC in 1820 had no strong feelings about Monroe, his jealous heirs did not mind leaving him in office for another four years. If he was not an asset, neither was he a menace, and he could be counted on to depart politely when the time came. In 1824 the time had come. Even if the country had wished to keep Monroe as a symbol of concord, the two-term tradition made this impossible; so the political malice which had been seething for eight years in the hearts of the ambitious was at last released. There were no parties in the campaign; there were supposed to be no issues and no disagreements; but there were four bitter candidates, each with numerous bitter friends.

Crawford of Georgia should have been the strongest candidate. He had refused the caucus nomination in 1816, out of respect for Monroe. In the midst of the new nationalism he had adhered to the states' rights of 1798 and the doctrine of nullification, so he was supported by Randolph and by the powerful Representative Nathaniel Macon of North Carolina. He had been a faithful servant of the Virginia dynasty, so he was supported by Madison, and had the benevolent approval of Jefferson. He had kept the good will of the planters, as a "safe" Southerner; and on the ground that he was the most "Jeffersonian" of the candidates he was backed by Martin Van Buren, the future President, who had come to Washington in 1821 as junior senator from New York.* Hoping to please his Northern followers without alienating the South, Crawford had modified his states'-rights position by endorsing a mild tariff and the national bank. His popularity seemed secure and his friends were confident. He was so far the favorite that he was attracting the united hostility of all the other candidates, when suddenly, in the autumn of 1823, he was stricken with paralysis. For a year he was almost blind, and helpless, and although he then grew better he was never again well. In spite of the disaster his friends persuaded the caucus to nominate Crawford in 1824; but only 68 senators and representatives voted, while 261 abstained.

* Cp. Van Buren's *Autobiography,* pp. 139–40, and p. 131. Van Buren was already a leader in the "Albany Regency," the New York State political machine which was so smooth and effective that it had acquired national fame. His support brought into the Crawford camp other Regency leaders, such as William L. Marcy: the future Secretary of War, Secretary of State, and Governor of New York.

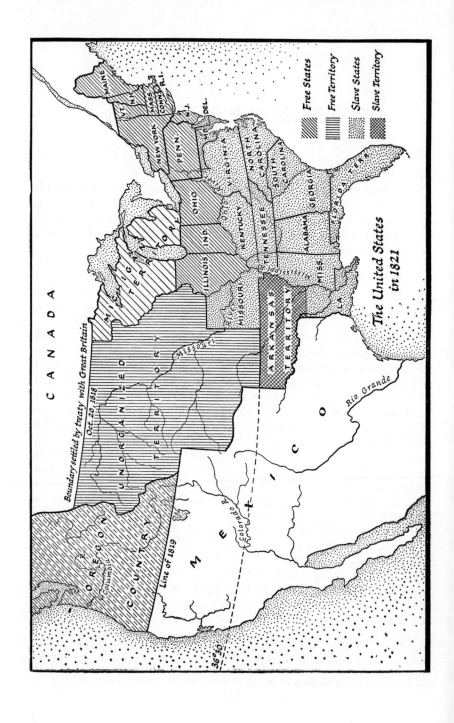

The United States in 1821

Free States
Free Territory
Slave States
Slave Territory

CANADA

Boundary settled by treaty with Great Britain
Oct. 20, 1818

OREGON COUNTRY

Columbia R.

Line of 1819

UNORGANIZED TERRITORY

MISSOURI River

MICHIGAN TERRITORY

MAINE

VT. N.H.

NEW YORK

MASS.
CONN. R.I.

PENN.

N.J.
DEL.

OHIO

ILLINOIS IND.

OHIO R.

VIRGINIA

MD.

KENTUCKY

MISSOURI

TENNESSEE

NORTH CAROLINA

SOUTH CAROLINA

MISSISSIPPI R.

ARKANSAS TERRITORY

ALABAMA

GEORGIA

MISS. LA.

FLORIDA TERR.

MEXICO

Colorado R.

Rio Grande

36°30'

This was not only the end of Crawford's hopes; it was the end of the caucus system. Jefferson had used it to secure his own nomination in 1804, and then to impose Madison as his successor in 1808; but with the decline of the Federalist Opposition the Republican caucus became too powerful. Its nominee automatically became the President, and there was no appeal from its decision, since the majority in the electoral college could only ratify what its party leaders had done. The makers of the Constitution had turned down the suggestion that the legislature should elect the President, on the ground that the Executive would become subservient. The system which they had rejected was establishing itself by accident, in spite of the danger that if the caucus chose the Presidents, the caucus would some day choose their policies as well. We have seen that the caucus had already been accused of such usurpation—of demanding that Madison promise to declare war on England before granting him a renomination.

Of all possible ways of solving the basic constitutional problem, of re-assembling the powers which the Fathers had divided, the worst would be to reassemble them in the hands of Congress. The inability of that large amorphous body to make and administer policy had been shown during the Administrations of Madison and Monroe. From 1809 to 1812, faced by a hostile France and England, the country drifted and whirled like a barge in a tidal rip; then a new and seemingly strong Congress decided on war. The Congress found that it could compel a war but could not get ready to fight, that it could compel the invasion of Canada but could not provide an army capable of invading a rabbit-hutch, that it could compel the spending of much money but could not bring itself to raise the needed taxes.

When America by magic or by the grace of Providence avoided defeat, avoided disunion, and achieved the Treaty of Ghent, her troubles were no longer mortal but they were still acute. New forces had bred new problems which should have been faced during the eight drifting years under Monroe, instead of being postponed until they became uglier. Yet except for the Missouri Compromise, when Congress was compelled to act because the nation had come again to the brink of secession, nothing happened outside of foreign affairs except an occasional negative deed by the President. Just as Madison had unhappily vetoed the bill for internal improvements, so Monroe roused himself to veto the Cumberland Road Bill, also on constitutional grounds. Although feeling was high, and the West believed its economic hopes were at stake, the Congress could neither pass the road bill over the President's veto nor arrange for a constitutional amendment.* When the Executive fails to make policy, the Congress is

* The road had been completed as far as Wheeling, on the Ohio River, in what was then the state of Virginia but is now West Virginia. The proposal was to extend the road to the Mississippi, which would have given the West its first commercially practical land route to the Atlantic.

not qualified to take on the burden. Left to itself, it can obstruct but it cannot create; it becomes "a scuffle of local interests," in the words of Professor Ford.

   After sixteen years of weak or negative presidents, there was little popular support for the system of nomination by Congressional caucus. None of the rival candidates, therefore, felt that the caucus nomination of Crawford in 1824 was decisive, or that there was an obligation to withdraw. Each of them allowed his friends to "nominate" him in state legislatures or in mass meetings. This was an admissible system only because there were no national parties; the presidential electors could declare for whichever candidate was the favorite in their own state, or (as in the case of New York) they could divide their votes among the favorites of the local factions. As soon as disciplined parties were reborn, it was necessary to find a more orderly method of nomination, so that the full party strength could be put behind one man.

2

Next to Crawford, the candidate with the strongest claims in 1824 was John Quincy Adams. Like Jefferson, Madison, and Monroe, he had served as Secretary of State, and unlike the two latter, he had served with high distinction. "Of the public history of Mr. Monroe's administration," Adams wrote to his wife on October 7, 1822, "all that will be worth telling to posterity hitherto has been transacted through the Department of State." The claim may have been immodest but it was largely true. Adams was fifty-seven; he had been steadily in the public service for thirty years, since Washington had appointed him Minister to the Netherlands in 1794. Relying upon this record, he expected the presidency to be conferred as a right. He was not prepared to ask for it. His wife wrote him that friends in Philadelphia thought he should visit that town for a week, in order to gain new supporters. He treated the suggestion as if it were somehow dishonorable, writing to his wife to tell the unfortunate Philadelphians "that I am *not* bound to be President of the United States, but that I *am* bound to perform the duties of Secretary of State so long as I hold that office, and that Washington and not Philadelphia is the place where those duties must be performed." If his friends replied that he must make concessions to public opinion, "Tell them that I am going by another road and to another temple."*

   The third candidate was Henry Clay of Kentucky, with a program

* October 7, 1822. Unfortunately for Adams's peace of mind, it was not entirely another temple. He very much wanted to be President; he was, therefore, at least in part, seeking the temple of worldly ambition. It is an attractive temple; but it is not easy to attain, or to abide in, if it is mistaken for something else.

which he called the "American System" and which he thought would unite the major sections. The plan was simple: a protective tariff, plus a widespread building of highways and canals (to be financed by the proceeds of the tariff). The purpose was to promote industry and to enlarge the home market for farm goods. The wool, hemp, and flax of the Middle States and of Kentucky wanted protection; so did the iron of Pittsburgh and the cotton mills of New England. All the farmers everywhere wanted better communications, to enlarge their markets and lower their costs. Clay's plan was a politician's catch-all; but this time it caught very little. The nationalism of 1816 was already giving way to revived sectional jealousies which bred fear of internal improvements at federal expense. The New England shipping interests were still more powerful than the manufacturers, so Daniel Webster,* the mirror of Massachusetts, announced coldly that he could see nothing "American" about Clay's plan. Even the West did not rally wholly to the Kentuckian, for the West was producing a more popular and more Western candidate: Andrew Jackson.

In 1821, when General Jackson saw himself mentioned as a possibility, he exclaimed, "Do they think I am such a damned fool as to think myself

---

* Parts of the career of Daniel Webster might have been written by an artless German professor, to prove the economic theory of politics. Born in New Hampshire and educated at Dartmouth College, Webster was admitted to the bar in 1805. A strong Federalist, he was sent to the House of Representatives, where he refused to vote taxes for the War of 1812 and denounced the Conscription Bill as unconstitutional. If it were passed, he thought the states should nullify the law, "to interpose between their citizens and arbitrary power." In 1816 he voted against the Bank of the United States, and he opposed the protective duties of the tariff bill of that year. New England was still a free-trade shipping region, in favor of states' rights as a protection against the "tyranny" of the Jeffersonians. Webster then moved to Boston and for a time dropped politics for the law, becoming one of the leading practitioners before the Supreme Court. He returned to the House of Representatives in 1822, and in 1824 again opposed protection, and with it the whole of Henry Clay's "System." By 1828, however, Massachusetts had decided that protected factories would bring more wealth than ships, so Webster, by now in the Senate, argued that the tariff, whether good or bad in theory, must not be diminished. When Jackson attacked the Bank, Webster was its most active supporter, and also one of its pensioners. And when Calhoun revived nullification to defend a Southern interest, Webster, whose constituents now wanted the largest possible domestic market, became a moving and eloquent defender of the Union.

This bald recital is, of course, unfair to Webster, who, as we shall see, had great deeds to his credit. Yet the obvious economic base for his policy, and the bland shamelessness with which he often acknowledged it, may explain why he was not loved as Clay was loved, or trusted as Calhoun was trusted. Like sensible politicians, all three of these men changed their ideas to fit the economic needs of their constituents; but Webster alone seemed to revel in the fact. "His character was complex," writes Gerald W. Johnson (*America's Silver Age*, p. 110), "but not his ideas. He was frankly the servant of big business, but he served it excellently, and there is no conclusive evidence that there was any conscious hypocrisy in his course." The unforgiving John Quincy Adams commented on the same qualities less kindly, in 1841. "Such is human nature," he wrote in his *Diary* for September 17, "in the gigantic intellect, the envious temper, the ravenous ambition, and the rotten heart of Daniel Webster."

fit for the presidency? No sir, I know what I am good for. I can command a body of men in a rough way, but I am not fit to be a president."[1] A year later he had changed his mind, and when he failed of election in 1824 he spoke as if the dearest and the wisest hope of the American people had been thwarted.

The panic of 1819, and hard times lasting until the election, had given Jackson his first chance, and his first taste of the sparkling delights of political hero-worship. High prices after the war of 1812, plus the four-year credit offered by the Public Land Act of 1800, plus the pressing sales-manship of the speculators, had led settlers to push into the West faster than the roads or the markets could follow them. They borrowed money from "wild-cat" local banks, which in turn were in debt to the Bank of the United States. The latter did nothing to discourage reckless Western loans until the end of 1818, when it ordered its branches to present all state bank notes for payment and to renew no mortgages. Within a few months, inevitably, the depression came; the Western banks collapsed, and vast tracts of land became the property of the Bank of the United States. It was at this moment that John Marshall's Supreme Court gave the decision in *McCulloch* v. *Maryland*, affirming the constitutionality of the Bank, and forbidding the states to tax it out of business. To the West, the Bank became "the Monster," engulfing all men's property and hopes. Not only the Supreme Court, but the old ruling class, the gentry, were felt to have betrayed the interests of the common man. A new type of popular leader, a new type of noisy appeal, suddenly became possible. Among the first men to know it were the Tennessee politicians who put forward Andrew Jackson as the champion of the people, the friend of the oppressed.*

---

* Thomas Hart Benton, who in his unregenerate Tennessee youth had tried to kill Jackson, and who later, as the famous senator from Missouri, became Jackson's floor leader in the "war" on the Bank, was first elected to the Senate in 1820 and took his seat in 1821. Describing the state of the nation when he arrived in Washington, he wrote (*Thirty Years' View*, vol. I, pp. 5–6): "The Bank of the United States was chartered in 1816, and before 1820 had performed one of its cycles of delusive and bubble prosperity, followed by actual and wide-spread calamity. The whole paper system, of which it was the head and citadel, after a vast expansion, had suddenly collapsed, spreading desolation over the land, and carrying ruin to the debtors. . . . No money, either gold or silver: no paper convertible into specie: no measure, or standard of value, left remaining. . . . The Bank of the United States, created as a remedy for all those evils, now at the head of the evil, prostrate and helpless, with no power left but that of suing its debtors, and selling their property, and purchasing for itself at its own nominal price. No price for property, or produce. No sales but those of the sheriff and the marshal. . . . No employment for industry—no demand for labor—no sale for the product of the farm—no sound of the hammer, but that of the auctioneer, knocking down property . . . DISTRESS, the universal cry of the people: RELIEF, the universal demand thundered at the doors of all legislatures, state and federal."

The description shows what the West thought of Eastern finance, and of the old ruling class. It shows the mood in which the Jackson men built their new party,

Jackson was a national figure because of the battle of New Orleans; but he was the special hero of the West because of his hatred of the Indians, his rough treatment of the Spaniards and the British in Florida, and his own frontier youth. He had no strong convictions in politics; but he was disinterested, and he had prodigious powers of leadership and of stubbornness. The people believed he was their friend, and that he would be a hard man to fool or to coerce. If he alone could beat the foreign enemies, perhaps it was he alone who could defeat hard times at home. He was the first popular hero in American politics, and he was destined to transform the presidency. Jefferson had been revered and obeyed; but Jackson was loved.

In New York, Vermont, Delaware, Georgia, South Carolina, and Louisiana the members of the electoral college were still appointed by the state legislatures, so popular enthusiasm could not yet express itself with full force in a presidential election. Nevertheless, Jackson led the field in 1824, receiving 99 electoral votes to Adams's 84, Crawford's 41, and Clay's 37.* Adams had captured the whole of New England, 26 out of 36 votes in New York, part of Ohio and of Maryland. Jackson's vote came from the West, the upland South, and parts of Pennsylvania and Ohio. Since no candidate received a majority of the electoral votes, the choice of President devolved upon the House of Representatives, where each state cast one vote. Since the House must choose among the three highest candidates, Clay was out of the running; but as Speaker of the House, and its most influential member, he could decide the contest. As a Western man, he was inclined toward Jackson; but John Quincy Adams's domestic policies were almost identical with Clay's American System, so in the end he supported the New Englander, who was thereupon elected.

Jackson's friends at once raised the cry that the people had been cheated out of their choice. But when, according to the Constitution, did "the people" come into the picture? What had they to do with the choice of President? They had thrust themselves into the picture most unconstitutionally, and because of Andrew Jackson they were soon to solidify their position.

3

John Quincy Adams, born in 1767, was the eldest son of John and Abigail Adams. At the age of eleven he began to accompany his father on hazardous wartime trips to Europe. Precocious both in learning and in maturity

---

and it explains why one of the most popular acts of the party was its attack on the Bank.

* Calhoun was elected Vice-President.

of mind, he worked hard during these travels, becoming a good classical student and learning to speak French, Dutch (and later Italian) fluently. When he was fourteen he spent a year at St. Petersburg as secretary to the American Minister. In 1783 he joined his father in Paris. John Adams, after wrangling all day with the British peace commissioners, spent the evenings teaching his son geometry, trigonometry, conic sections, and the differential calculus.

On graduating from Harvard, John Quincy studied law and was admitted to the Massachusetts bar. In 1791 he attacked the views of Tom Paine in a series of articles. Paine, defending the sovereignty of the majority, had written: "that which a whole nation chooses to do, it had a right to do." John Quincy opposed this by appealing to natural law much as Antigone had appealed against the commands of the tyrant. It was the task of the statesman, said Adams, to learn and apply this higher law; therefore, he could not bow to the whims of the people who put him in office. "The eternal and immutable laws of justice and morality," he wrote, "are paramount to all human legislation. The violation of those laws is certainly within the power, but is not among the rights of nations."

These articles pleased Washington, who appointed the twenty-seven-year-old Adams as American Minister to The Hague. He was later sent to London on a diplomatic mission, where he married the daughter of the United States consul. When John Adams became President, Washington wrote him expressing "a *strong hope* that you will not withhold merited promotion from Mr. John [Quincy] Adams because he is your son. For without intending to compliment the father or the mother, or to censure others, I give it as my decided opinion that Mr. Adams is the most valuable public character we have abroad, and that there remains no doubt in my mind that he will prove himself to be the ablest of our diplomatic corps." So John Quincy spent four years as Minister in Berlin, returning home in 1801, after his father's defeat for re-election. He was soon sent to Washington as United States senator from Massachusetts.

Ignoring party politics, and to the rage of the Federalists who had given him office, John Quincy voted with Jefferson's followers on the Louisiana Purchase and the Embargo Bill.* Timothy Pickering, the other Senator from Massachusetts, denounced Adams and persuaded the Massachusetts legislature to elect his successor nine months ahead of time. The legislature also adopted resolutions against the Embargo, making it clear that they expected Adams to vote as he was told. Adams immediately resigned.** "As to holding my seat in the senate of the United States," he wrote,

* Adams voted for the appropriation to pay for Louisiana, although the other Federalist Senators opposed it, and although he himself condemned the plans for governing the new territory and felt that the acquisition was unconstitutional. The vital point, he felt, was to get the territory while Napoleon was still willing to sell it.

** June 8, 1808.

"without exercising the most perfect freedom of agency, under the sole and exclusive control of my own sense of right, that was out of the question."

In an autobiographical letter to Skelton Jones (April 18, 1809) Adams wrote:

> In the Senate of the United States, the part which I acted was that of an *independent* member. My fundamental principles, as I have told you, were *Union and Independence.* I was sworn to support the Constitution of the United States, and I thought it my duty to support the existing administration in every measure that my impartial judgment could approve. I discharged my duty to my country, but I committed the unpardonable sin against *Party.* . . . It was not without a painful sacrifice of feeling that I withdrew from the public service at a moment of difficulty and danger, but when the constituted organs of that country, under whom I held my station, had discarded me for the future, and required me to aid them in promoting measures tending to dissolve the Union, and to sacrifice the independence of the nation, I was no representative for *them.*

Adams was acting precisely as the men who made the Constitution expected all good Americans to act, with the result that he was driven from office. When he became President he acted in the same way, again ignoring party politics, with the result that his Administration was hamstrung and he himself was denied re-election.

A year after Adams resigned, President Madison appointed him Minister to Russia. The Senate refused confirmation, ostensibly because the mission was unnecessary, but really because Adams was now a man without a party, hated by the Federalists and suspected by the Republicans. Madison, however, taking advantage of his own brief days of popularity when the Erskine Agreement had seemingly put an end to strife with England, sent Adams's name to the Senate a second time. In the benign mood of those happy deluded days the Senate confirmed the nomination, showing once more the good will that followed on the settlement which Canning so coldly disavowed.

In 1814 John Quincy left St. Petersburg for Ghent, where he presided over the American peace commission. The result was the peace that settled nothing, except that it freed both countries from an unpromising war. Adams and his fellow commissioners did well to win such a treaty, as the Marquess Wellesley testified when he said in the House of Lords that the Americans "had shown a most astonishing superiority over the British during the whole of the negotiations."

Like his father in 1783, John Quincy became the first American Minister to the Court of St. James's after the making of the peace. In 1817, when Monroe asked him to become Secretary of State, he at last returned home to stay. He was fifty years old, and since the age of eleven had lived half his life abroad. Perhaps this is why his intense patriotism was always national, never local, and why his plans and policies were always intended to serve every region, not merely New England.

4

Adams's Cabinet appointments, in 1825, gave immediate notice to the country that he would not admit the existence of party strife, or ask for party support in his Administration. He revived Washington's theory of a Cabinet, and sought the men of greatest capacity irrespective of their opinions or their political associations. The result, as every politician fore-saw, was frustration.*

Adams wanted Jackson as Secretary of War, in spite of Jackson's belief that Adams and Clay had made an "unholy coalition"; and he offered to make Crawford, another defeated candidate, Secretary of the Treasury. Both men refused, so Adams brought Richard Rush home from the Lon-don mission to the Treasury, made Senator James Barbour of Virginia Secretary of War, and kept Monroe's Secretary of the Navy (Samuel Southard of New Jersey), Postmaster General (John McLean of Ohio), and Attorney General (William Wirt).** The most interesting appoint-ment was McLean—a good man, who was well known to be a friend of Jackson, and who was soon using his official position to work against the President and in favor of his chief rival. The most damaging appointment, however, was perhaps the best and strongest from the point of view of the public interest: Henry Clay for Secretary of State. Adams knew that the Jackson men were saying he made a "corrupt bargain" with Clay, promis-ing the Department of State in return for the necessary votes in the House of Representatives. He ignored the gossip for no better reason than that it was untrue, a fact which has little relevance in politics, as the Jacksonians quickly proved. For four years they never let up on the reiterated slander that Clay had sold himself to Adams and that the two men had flouted the will of the "sovereign people." Clay asked for an investigation, but it was not granted—the Jackson forces preferring to let the charges fester.

* Adams took the same non-partisan view of all federal appointments, saying he was determined "to renominate every person against whom there was no complaint which would have warranted his removal." He was disgusted at the suggestion of certain Senators "to introduce a principle of change or rotation in office. . . . which would make the government a perpetual and unintermitting scramble for office. A more pernicious expedient could scarcely have been devised."

** Although the office of Postmaster General was created by Congress in 1794, it was not officially a Cabinet position until 1829, when Jackson invited the Post-master General to Cabinet meetings.

The attack on the new Administration was not a purely cynical and negative act. The politicians gathering from every state under the banner of Jackson were of course seeking office; but they were also seeking a more effective way of organizing the government. The methods of nomination and election in 1824 were clearly impossible. They were bound to create the maximum of envy and malice among the country's leaders. The hatreds established that year, between Calhoun and Adams, Jackson and Adams, Jackson and Clay, Crawford and Calhoun, embittered politics for a generation and prevented America from getting the best service from these men. The Federalist Party had at least been decently interred; but the Republican Party, unopposed and therefore unhealthy, was dying in the streets and becoming a nuisance. It had long been kept alive by the magic of Jefferson's name and by his mysterious influence. Jefferson was now in the last year of his life and neither the magic nor the mystery would any more suffice. A new type of party was needed. It might use Jefferson's name but it could not use his methods; they were methods appropriate to an oligarchy, not to a people's party. The members of an oligarchy could maintain the needed unity by writing letters to each other; but a popular movement, to be effective, needs discipline, needs imposed loyalty, needs an organization strong enough to reward the faithful and punish the dissident, to fatten the sheep and starve the goats. It also needs the worldly wisdom to define sheep as tolerantly as possible, and to welcome home, at the first sign of softening, even the most obdurate goat.

In the spring of 1825 the Jackson men undertook to build such a party. Had Adams been willing, he and Clay could have done the same and thereby saved their program from destruction. They had many skillful supporters, like the young Thurlow Weed who was to become a dictator in New York State politics and who worked devotedly for the Adams cause from 1824 until after the disaster of 1828. Weed, who was allied with the conservative forces of the state, had prevented Van Buren from delivering the state to Crawford in 1824 and had held 26 electoral votes for Adams. Van Buren, with his Albany Regency, then began to move toward the Jackson camp.* If the New York conservatives were to make way against this formidable combination, they needed patronage and encouragement from the federal administration. Weed made two trips to Washington,

* The Albany Regency was a tightly knit, well-disciplined caucus. It was a central organization at the state capital, with no subsidiary branches in the counties or the precincts. It was so well disciplined that the members supported each decision unanimously, even if there was strong difference of opinion in the caucus. Among the chief members of the Regency were Martin Van Buren, William Marcy, Silas Wright, and Edwin Crosswell (editor of the Albany *Argus*). For years the Regency ran the state, distributed offices, directed the dominant party. Thurlow Weed, the most powerful adversary of the Regency, said (*Autobiography*, p. 103): "They were men of great ability, great industry, indomitable courage and strict personal integrity."

where he got little help from Clay and none from Adams. "Mr. Adams," he commented sadly, "during his administration failed to cherish, strengthen, or even recognize the party to which he owed his election; nor so far as I am informed, with the great power he possessed did he make a single influential friend."[2] The Adams men, and the other anti-Jackson groups, had to wait until John Quincy was out of the White House before they could attempt a serious organization, whereas the General's friends set to work vigorously, even before Adams was inaugurated, to build the disciplined party which took the name Democratic.*

They defined their task clearly: first, to reach the plain man with the message that Adams's election had been a fraud, that the people had been cheated, that Jackson was their friend, and that in the interest of democracy Jackson must be elected the next time; second, to organize in every district of the country a group of men who were prepared (in the hope of future favors) to work for Jackson throughout the whole four years of Adams's presidency. They undertook, that is, to build a party of common soldiers to take the place of the party of generals and other high officers which was all that Jefferson had attempted.

The number of common soldiers available for such a party had been greatly increased during the previous fifteen years. Beginning with Maryland in 1810, there had been a movement among the older states to wipe out the property qualifications for the franchise. Connecticut, New York, and Massachusetts soon followed Maryland's lead, and the new Western states, as they entered the Union, helped to spread electoral democracy. By 1828 the country was well on its way toward white adult male suffrage.** And at the same time, the state legislatures were ceasing to appoint the presidential electors and were arranging for them to be chosen by popular vote. By 1824 only six states preserved the older method; by 1832 only one—South Carolina. Inevitably this increased the people's feeling that the President was their own man.

Long before the end of Adams's four years, the Jackson men had built a

---

* The Democrats claimed descent, of course, from the Jeffersonian Republicans, and since in the end the Opposition contained most of the old Federalists the claim was reasonable. The Adams-Clay followers were for a while called National Republicans; but after Jackson was elected a second time they chose the name Whig, on the ground that the eighteenth-century Whigs had fought King George III and the new Whigs would fight King Andrew.

** Vermont had universal male suffrage from the beginning. By 1830, Maine had the same; Maryland, New York, Kentucky, Indiana, Illinois, Missouri and Alabama had universal white male suffrage; Louisiana, Mississippi, Georgia, Ohio, Pennsylvania, Delaware, Connecticut, Massachusetts and New Hampshire had a tax-paying qualification; Tennessee had a light property qualification; only South Carolina, North Carolina, Virginia, New Jersey and Rhode Island maintained a heavy property qualification. In 1790, on the other hand, before Vermont was officially admitted, all but three states had a heavy property qualification, and those three had a tax-paying qualification.

party able to keep close and steady contact with the new mass of voters: through a party press, through local clubs and committees under the leadership of men who were hungry for federal patronage, through the wide distribution of speeches made in Congress for the purpose of being read in the constituencies rather than for the purpose of being heard in the Capitol. This new national machine, however, was really a bundle of local factions and local machines, prepared to co-operate in national politics under the pressure of strong leadership and large favors but otherwise fiercely protective of local interests and pride. The same has been true of every major party in America from that day to this.

Propaganda and discipline were the cement for this imposing structure. The propaganda could be supplied by the leaders; the discipline had to be improvised. The quickest way to do this was by appealing to self-interest, which is why the Jackson men practiced "rotation in office," or the spoils system. From the days when Jefferson complained that very few officeholders died and none resigned, the political uses of patronage* had been admitted. John Quincy Adams might refuse to soil his mind with such thoughts; but men who were building a nation-wide party could not be so disdainful. They had gathered an army which was expected to do hard and steady work in the districts. To keep the soldiers on their toes, to keep them from straying off into rival camps, it was necessary to offer them rewards. So the Jacksonians accepted as inevitable, and defended as good, the system of political appointments in the civil service. They themselves used the promise of patronage sparingly; later Administrations were less restrained.

5

At the very best, a contest between the amorphous Adams following and this new machine must have resembled a contest between a rabbit and a weasel; but the odds became even more unequal when John Randolph, greatest of free-lance fighters, flung himself with lunatic rage against the Adams men. Randolph had scorned the elder Adams and he deplored the son; but these were mild emotions compared with his hatred for Henry Clay. Ever since the Missouri Compromise Randolph had dreamed of uniting the South, on the basis of states' rights, to resist Northern interference with slavery. This was a consistent plan. He had fought for states' rights since 1798, implacably and without compromise; now at last he saw a chance to convince his neighbors that only by states' rights could they

---

* Patronage—federal and local—includes all forms of largesse at the disposal of officeholders: jobs, contracts, and personal favors such as tickets to a convention or the quashing of a police charge.

save their property and their way of life. The chief danger to this, his earliest and his latest cause, was Henry Clay of Kentucky, whose immense popularity divided the South, winning many of her most influential citizens away from states' rights, away from regional unity, toward nationalism, a tariff, and internal improvements at federal expense. Clay was a formidable opponent, for Kentucky united within herself the South and the West, and Clay, with his Virginia background and his expansive manner, was equally the Southerner and the Westerner. He was equally at home in the land of the mint julep and dueling sword, or in that of the coonskin cap and long rifle. If he could hold South and West together in his "American System," if he could step from the Department of State to the presidency as four of his predecessors had done, there would be no room in the future for Randolph's extreme states' rights. So Randolph set himself to break Clay, who could not fight back from his new office with the deadly competence he would have shown as Speaker of the House of Representatives.

When James Barbour of Virginia became Secretary of War, Randolph was sent to fill the vacancy in the Senate. There he launched his attack. The myth of a "corrupt bargain" between Adams and Clay was well contrived to undo Randolph's wandering judgment; brilliant and desperate and by this time half-deranged, he was the man to believe such a libel and to enlarge it in words which could not be forgiven. Soon, in the course of a debate on the President's nomination of envoys to a proposed Congress of American Nations at Panama, Randolph whipped himself into a fury, attributing every bad motive and every meanness to the President and to the Secretary of State, referring to them as "the coalition of Blifil and Black George—the combination, unheard of till then, of the Puritan and the blackleg."* In conclusion he lamented that Clay's parents had brought into the world "this being, so brilliant yet so corrupt, which, like a rotten mackerel by moonlight, shines and stinks." Clay challenged Randolph to a duel, but only succeeded in shooting him through the coat, or rather through the white flannel wrapper which he strangely wore.**

In the face of such tactics, against an Opposition which combined every strength, from that of the disciplined machine to that of the wild guerrilla, the Adams Administration foundered. In his Inaugural Address the innocent President had said: "There remains one effort of magnanimity, one sacrifice of prejudice and passion, to be made by the individuals throughout the nation who have heretofore followed the standards of political party. It is that of discarding every remnant of rancor against each other,

---

* The allusion to Fielding was borrowed from Lord Chatham.

** The United States was not represented at the Panama Congress. The Senate reluctantly and belatedly approved an American mission. One delegate died en route. The other arrived after the meeting was over.

of embracing as countrymen and friends, and of yielding to talents and virtue alone that confidence which in times of contention for principle was bestowed only upon those who bore the badge of party communion." The pathetic wrongness of this hope, the vanity of this desire, explains the failure of every measure upon which Adams had set his heart.

In his first annual message to Congress he announced that "the great object of the institution of civil government is the improvement of the condition of those who are partners to the social compact." He asked for a system of roads and canals which "by multiplying and facilitating the communications and intercourse between distant regions and multitudes of men, are among the most important means of improvement." Such public works, he felt, would lead to an increase in the price of federal lands which would make possible an endowment of education and science on a scale never previously dreamed by man. He foresaw a republic of informed men and women administered by trained and conscientious servants such as himself; and though his Adams pessimism must have kept him from believing in this vision completely, he felt that he could surely lead the nation toward a fairer future. "While foreign nations," he said in the same message, "less blessed with that freedom which is power than ourselves are advancing with gigantic strides in the career of public improvement, were we to slumber in indolence or fold up our arms and proclaim to the world that we are palsied by the will of our constituents, would it not be to cast away the bounties of providence and doom ourselves to perpetual inferiority?"

Here was the most vigorous challenge to strict construction ever issued; here was a proposal to strengthen the federal government beyond the hopes of Hamilton or Marshall. It was a brave plan, which might have been accomplished by a strict party machine backed with the popularity of a Jackson or a Roosevelt. Proposed by a man without a party and without a large personal following, it merely became a rude joke to the Opposition. Especially funny and foolish seemed the President's request for a national university and an astronomical observatory. The practical men from the local political clubs, who had set themselves to destroy Adams, could hardly believe their luck when they heard him say: "While scarcely a year passes over our heads without bringing some new astronomical discovery to light, which we must fain receive at second hand from Europe, are we not cutting ourselves off from the means of returning light for light while we have neither observatory nor observer upon our half of the globe and the earth revolves in perpetual darkness to our unsearching eyes?" This, they felt, was not the stuff of which votes are made.

6

Denied all of the measures which he hoped would heal antagonisms and advance the health of the nation, Adams was presented by his Congress with one major deed: the "Tariff of Abominations." This ugly miscarriage of an act was the cause of the chief disunion crisis between the Hartford Convention and the Civil War.

The first protective tariff, in 1816, was largely the work of Lowndes* and Calhoun, both from South Carolina. It was then thought that the South, with waterpower and cotton, would profit from industry at least as much as New England. Slave labor, however, proved a bar to Southern industry; by 1820, when an attempt was made to raise the rates, the South was weakening on protection, and by 1824, when a new act proposed duties on hemp and cheap woolens, the South began to talk about "injustice" and "unconstitutionality." John Randolph put the case with his usual violence:

> We [of the South] are the eel that is being flayed, while the cookmaid pats us on the head and cries, with the clown in King Lear, "Down wantons, down!" . . . If, under a power to regulate trade, you prevent exportation: if, with the most approved spring lancets, you draw the last drop of blood from our veins . . . what are the checks of the Constitution to us? A fig for the Constitution! When the scorpion's sting is probing us to the quick, shall we stop to chop logic?[3]

During these years Calhoun was being driven from protection to free trade, step by step, while Webster of New England was being driven from free trade to protection; but Calhoun, after 1825, was fortunate in being the presiding officer of the Senate, where he need not express an opinion day by day. Then in 1828 came the Tariff of Abominations, the first purely politician's tariff to insult the statute books. The Jackson men, heedless of commerce, industry and agriculture alike, hoping to force the Administration to defeat its own plans for protection, piled higher tariffs on raw materials than on manufactures. If this absurdity was defeated, it

---

* William Lowndes was first sent to the House of Representatives in 1810, along with Calhoun. Like Calhoun, he became a leading "war hawk" and an intense nationalist. Six feet six in height, grave and dignified, he was one of the few men in America who could debate even the slave question dispassionately. It was his habit in the House, before giving his own cool logical arguments, to present his opponent's case so fairly that on one occasion John Randolph said, "He has done that once too often; he can never answer that." He had ill health all his life, and died at the age of forty, a heavy loss to the nation. Henry Clay said, in his old age, "I think the wisest man I ever knew was William Lowndes."

was thought that industry would blame the President. Reluctantly, however, the Adams men accepted the bill rather than deny aid to New England at the very moment when her leading citizens were turning to industry instead of commerce. "Its enemies," said Daniel Webster of this ridiculous act, "spiced it with whatever they thought would render it distasteful; its friends took it, drugged as it was."*

From South Carolina, in June 1828, came a cry of revolt which boded ill for America:

> The day of open opposition to the pretended powers of the Constitution cannot be far off. . . . If you are not prepared to follow up your principles wherever they may lead, to their very last consequence—if you love life better than honor—prefer ease to perilous liberty and glory, awake not! stir not! . . . Live in smiling peace with your insatiable oppressors, and die with the noble consolation that your submissive patience will survive triumphant your beggary and despair!

This was the first startling speech of Robert Barnwell Rhett, the original fire-eater, "the father of secession." It was sad that the Administration of Adams, whose life was based on love of the Union, should have produced a bill so biased that it made sectional hate seem almost sensible.**

The Tariff of Abominations, which made Webster a nationalist, finally drove Calhoun to the defense of states' rights. The wasteful cotton culture, which was ruining South Carolina and driving her most ambitious sons to the new Southwest, could not support this final burden of a subsidy to the North. Anonymously, Vice-President Calhoun wrote the South Carolina *Exposition*, in which he developed the doctrines of 1798 to their extreme limit. Jefferson and Madison had recommended a collective nullification, whereby a number of states would resist the encroachment of the federal government. Calhoun proposed nullification by a single state, on the ground that the sovereignty of the original states was indestructible, that the federal government could never be more than the agent of the states, and that the deeds of the agent could always be disallowed. The South Carolina *Exposition* was a plan for the future; Calhoun urged his state to take no immediate action, since Jackson would soon replace Adams and might prove a friend of the South.

* Morison and Commager, *The Growth of the American Republic*, vol. I, p. 372. The "friends" of this tariff may not have been as reluctant as Webster would like us to think. When the bill was before Congress, Abbott Lawrence, a Massachusetts manufacturer, wrote to Webster: "This bill if adopted as amended will keep the South and West in debt to New England the next hundred years." As Professor Walter Prescott Webb comments (*Divided We Stand*, p. 19): "The hundred years have passed and the prediction has been fully confirmed."

** Craven, *The Coming of the Civil War*, pp. 63–64. The name was Robert Barnwell Smith in 1828; it was changed to Rhett, the name of a distinguished ancestor, in 1837, at the instance of Robert Barnwell's brothers.

7

The election of 1828 had been lost by Adams in 1825, when he decided to make no political appointments, to build no party, to oppose the combination of democracy and smooth professionalism with the other-worldliness of a Platonic philosopher-king plus the prickliness of a churl. During the election, the friends of Adams in the local districts vied with the friends of Jackson in disgracing free institutions by their wild talk and their unworthy charges; but the friends of Adams were discouraged by four years without patronage, whereas the friends of Jackson were on tiptoe with the eager hope of spoils. There were no issues, only the scurrilous attacks on the two candidates. The result was more favorable to the somber and much-abused President than might have been expected: Adams won popular majorities in New England, New Jersey, Maryland, half of New York, northern Ohio, southern Louisiana, and parts of Kentucky. Jackson won the rest, including the whole of Pennsylvania and almost the whole South and West. Adams won 44 per cent of the popular vote; but in the electoral college he had only 83 votes to 178 for Jackson.*

When the election returns were in, Adams felt despairing. He knew his friends believed he had ruined them by refusing to adopt the new methods in the use of patronage, and he probably knew he could have made a better fight if he had possessed more personal charm, if he had been less "reserved, cold, austere, and forbidding," as he once called himself in his diary. The weight of his grief was not caused by personal failure, by the loss of office or fame; it was caused by the country's dismissal, almost with contempt, of his vast plan for internal improvements. He wanted a second term so that he could build those roads and canals without which he feared America must decline into weakness and civil war, so that he could promote science and education, without which he feared free government must fall into disgrace.

* At first, many of the states which arranged for electors to be chosen by popular vote provided that they should be chosen by districts, like members of the House of Representatives. According to this system, the electoral vote of a state could be divided. Soon, under pressure from the dominant party in each case, the states began choosing electors by a single popular vote, with the result that all the electoral votes of the state go to the candidate who has a majority of one. By 1828, Maryland was the only state to preserve the older system of district voting. This explains the discrepancy between the popular vote and the electoral vote which is so common in American politics. In 1828, for example, Adams won nearly half the vote of New York State, but he lost the whole of the vote in the electoral college; 1828, incidentally, was the first year in which the people of New York voted for members of the electoral college. In 1947 and 1949 a bill was introduced into the Congress, but not passed, providing that each state's electoral vote be divided in proportion to the popular vote of the state.

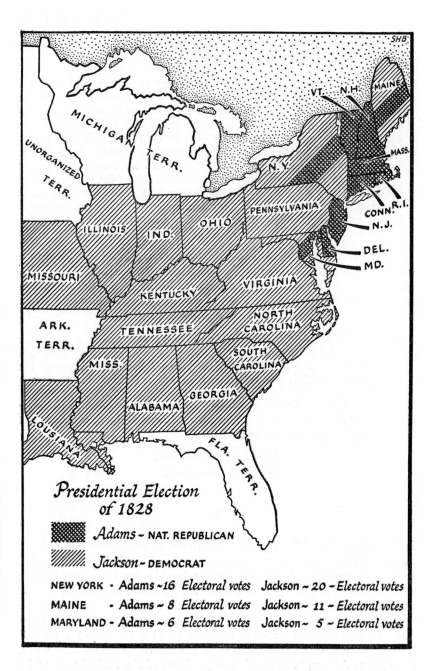

SHB

MICHIGAN TERR.

UNORGANIZED TERR.

VT. N.H. MAINE

N.Y.

MASS.

CONN. R.I.

ILLINOIS IND. OHIO PENNSYLVANIA

N.J.

DEL.

MD.

MISSOURI

KENTUCKY VIRGINIA

ARK. TERR.

TENNESSEE NORTH CAROLINA

MISS. SOUTH CAROLINA

ALABAMA GEORGIA

LOUSIANA

FLA. TERR.

Presidential Election of 1828

Adams – NAT. REPUBLICAN

Jackson – DEMOCRAT

NEW YORK · Adams ~16 *Electoral votes* Jackson ~ 20 – *Electoral votes*
MAINE · Adams ~ 8 *Electoral votes* Jackson ~ 11 ~ *Electoral votes*
MARYLAND - Adams ~ 6 *Electoral votes* Jackson ~ 5 ~ *Electoral votes*

In 1837, he wrote to Charles Upham, a Salem clergyman who had asked for material on his life:

> The great effort of my administration was to mature into a permanent and regular system the application of all the superfluous revenue of the Union to internal improvements. . . . In ten years from this day the whole Union would have been checkered over with railroads and canals. It may still be done half a century later and with the limping gait of state legislature and private adventure. I would have done it in the administration of the affairs of the nation. . . . The great object of my life, therefore, as applied to the adminstration of the government of the United States, has failed. The American Union, as a moral person in the family of nations, is to live from hand to mouth, and to cast away instead of using for the improvement of its own condition, the bounties of Providence.[4]

All the rest of his life Adams held to the heartbreaking faith that it might have been done, that if he had been a better man he might have bequeathed to his beloved country wisdom and health and wealth and peace. A few days before he died he was still lamenting in his diary that his intellectual powers had not been equal to the task.

> I should [he wrote] have been one of the greatest benefactors of my country and of mankind. . . . But the conceptive power of mind was not conferred upon me by my Maker, and I have not improved the scanty portion of His gifts as I might and ought to have done.[5]

It was reflections such as these which caused him to be haunted throughout the year 1829 by a song from the opera, *Coeur-de-Lion*, which he had heard forty-five years before in Paris:

> O Richard! O, mon Roi!
> L'Univers t'abandonne.

8

In 1830 the voters of the Plymouth District in Massachusetts asked him to be a candidate for the House of Representatives. He said he would be glad to do so on two conditions: first, that he should never be expected to ask for their votes, and second, that if elected he would do and say exactly what he chose and would not feel himself under obligation to follow the whims or to consult the wishes of the men who elected him. On these terms he was chosen by a great majority (1817 votes, out of a total of 2565), and was kept in Congress until the day of his death. This was a deep joy to Adams. "My election as president of the United States," he wrote, "was not half so gratifying to my inmost soul. No election or appointment conferred upon me ever gave me so much pleasure."[6]

Adams's free-lance career in Congress won him more influence on the public mind, at least in the North, than he had attained as President. He worked unceasingly for education and for science; he urged Congress to create a naval academy, and he continued to urge his observatory. He also became a center of resistance to the slave power. When Southern members forced through a "gag-rule" that petitions against slavery should be laid on the table without being printed, or referred, or acted upon in any way, Adams led a long fight against the restriction; and in 1845, when he was seventy-eight years old, he had the rule repealed. As a result of this battle, Adams, who was not an abolitionist, received anti-slavery petitions from all over the country, and his insistence on presenting them made him an object of hate in the South.*

Even when he had passed the age of eighty, nothing could keep Adams from Washington when Congress was in session. There he continued until the end, fighting alone for the ways of a vanished America: the America of his father and of George Washington, ruled by an oligarchy, fearful of political parties, fearful of the rude democracy which was coming into its own with Andrew Jackson, but strong with patriotism and the sense of public duty. On the twenty-first of February, 1848, John Quincy Adams lost consciousness while trying to rise from his seat in the House of Representatives. Two days later he was dead.

---

* His position was that which he had taken at the time of the Missouri Compromise: that slavery was a curse, but a constitutional curse, which could not lawfully be interfered with in the old states but which should be kept out of the new territories so far as possible. Adams was such a hard and bitter fighter in the House that Ralph Waldo Emerson described him as "an old roué who cannot live on slops but must have sulphuric acid in his tea."

XII

Jackson and the New Type of Presidency

ANDREW JACKSON was born in 1767, on the frontier—the upland country at the dividing line between North and South Carolina.* His parents were Scotch-Irish immigrants. His father died a few months before Jackson was born. His mother was left with no money and three children, so the young Jackson saw backwoods life at its hardest.

He also saw the Revolutionary War at its hardest. His eldest brother was killed in action; he and the other brother were captured by the British after taking part in a local battle; they both caught smallpox in jail, and the brother died. Then in 1781, Jackson's mother, who had gone to Charleston to nurse the sick, died of prison fever. Jackson was alone in the world at the age of fourteen, alone with his hatred of the English. This hatred had been made personal and abiding when, as a prisoner, the boy was beaten across the face with the flat of a sword because of his distaste for cleaning an officer's boots. Andrew Jackson became a vindictive man; he could not pursue the officer, but he pursued the British army. He had the satisfaction, at New Orleans in 1815, of killing more than two thousand veterans of Wellington's army with the loss of thirteen of his own troops.**

* Both states have claimed him; but it seems that he was born on the South Carolina side. Cp. Marquis James, *Andrew Jackson, the Border Captain,* p. 12.

** Implacable hostility toward the English was in any case a tradition among Jackson's ancestors. Large numbers of Presbyterian Lowlanders went to Ireland at the time of the Ulster Plantation, in 1610. After the Revolution of 1688 another 50,000 Scotch Presbyterian families poured into Ulster. Not only did they have to pay tithes in support of the Established Church, whose ministrations they neither desired nor received, but they were forbidden, after 1699, to export manufactured wool; most forms of linen export were denied them; hempen manufacture was discouraged until it ceased; and after 1717 and 1718 (when the original leases began to fall in) the tenant farmers were rackrented by their landlords. Naturally, and in spite of prohibitions, they began to escape to America, taking with them an enduring load of hatred. Thirty-eight ships sailed from Ireland to New England between 1718 and 1720. The famine years of 1740 and 1741 increased the emigration from Ulster to about 12,000 annually. Most of the latter group made for Pennsylvania, whence they pushed their way south along the Shenandoah, the Valley of Virginia. They became hardy upland farmers who found the cruelest frontier life an improvement upon Ulster. As Lecky wrote: "They went with hearts burning with indignation, and in the War of Independence they were almost to a man on

In 1787, the year of the making of the American Constitution, Jackson was admitted to the bar in North Carolina. He knew little law, but during his two hard years as a student he had become an authority on horse-racing, cock-fighting,* and shooting. He had also acquired a horse of his own. A horse, and no family, and no possessions: it was easy for Jackson, in 1788, to move west across the Appalachian Mountains to the new frontier in the wilderness which would soon become the state of Tennessee. He was then twenty-one, and he became a frontier hero. He had every quality which men in such surroundings admire. He was brave, loyal, impetuous, and revengeful. He was quarrelsome, honest, sentimental, and indiscreet. He accepted and lived the simple morality of a simple people. He was a gambler; fighting came naturally to him, whether in duels or brawls or warfare. He showed early in his career that when provoked he was prepared to kill. Because of this he has often been misjudged. Jackson was not a border ruffian; he was not a wild man from the frontier. He was a man born to command, with the dignity inseparable from the birthright; but no man could command on the frontier who did not possess the virtues and the severity of the hero in a primitive epic.

In his old age, when he was President of the United States, Jackson was furious because a member of his Cabinet left Washington to avoid a duel with another Cabinet officer. "What a wretch!" cried Jackson. "My creed is true—there was never a base man a brave one." There was another side to this hardness; when one of his major policies was under attack, after he had left the presidency, Jackson wrote to his successor, "I say, lay on; temporize not, it is always injurious." The sentence is a summary of Jackson's career. He invariably laid on; he could not temporize. There may be a relation between this trait and the love which the American people felt for him.

"He called himself the people's friend and gave proofs of his sincerity," said a Senator to a German visitor who was perplexed by this hero-worship. "The people believed in General Jackson as the Turks in their prophet. With this species of popularity it is vain to contend; and it be-

---

the side of the insurgents. They supplied some of the best soldiers of Washington." (Quoted by Henry Jones Ford, *The Scotch-Irish in America*, p. 208; and cp. pp. 165–208.) Jackson became not only the representative but the hero of these unforgiving Scotch-Irish, "these bold and indigent strangers," as Penn's agent called them in 1724, complaining that they all asserted "it was against the laws of God and nature that so much land should be idle while so many Christians wanted it to work on and to raise their bread." The ease with which the followers of John Knox identify their well-being with "the laws of God and nature" is not unimportant in American history.

In spite of this heritage, and in spite of his childhood experiences and his vindictive nature, Jackson's rancor toward the English subsided in middle age. As President, he was notably friendly to Great Britain.

* Senator Benton (*Thirty Years' View*, vol. I, p. 737) claimed that Jackson was never interested in cock-fighting; but the weight of evidence is against the Senator.

trays little knowledge of the world and the springs of human action to believe that those who possess it [are] men of ordinary capacity."[1] And Thomas Hart Benton, describing the scene when Jackson left the Capitol, on his way to final retirement after eight years in the presidency, says that when the General started toward his carriage a great shout came from the crowd, a cry "such as power never commanded, nor man in power received. It was the affection, gratitude, and admiration of the living age, saluting for the last time a great man. It was the acclaim of posterity, breaking from the bosoms of contemporaries."[2]

No man in politics could inspire such love without inspiring hatred also. With the possible exceptions of General Washington and Franklin D. Roosevelt, Jackson was the best-abused President; but the plain people knew he was their friend. They had been in awe of Washington; they never saw Jefferson, the most withdrawn of presidents; but Jackson was their own man. They knew he could not equivocate or trim; they knew he was disinterested; so he became the spearhead of the change from oligarchy to democracy, a change which revolutionized the office of President.*

At the beginning of that revolution, America was already a land which George Washington would not have recognized. He had ruled over a nation of four million people; when Jackson became President there were more than twelve million. The Industrial Revolution was in full blast. Although there were only twenty-three miles of railway in the United States in 1830, there were two thousand eight hundred in 1840, and nine thousand in 1850. When Washington gave his Farewell Address, westward expansion was still so slow that a thousand years might have been consumed in filling the country east of the Mississippi; yet by 1821 there were two flourishing states on the far side of the river. And in addition to industry and the winning of the West, immigration, the third great force that was to alter the old America, was booming by 1830. Between 1789 and the year Jackson went to the White House, there had been less than 400,000 immigrants into the United States; in the next decade there were 599,000; between 1840 and 1850, there were 1,713,251; and between 1850 and 1860, more than two and a half million. These new citizens went to the North and West, avoiding the slave-ridden South.

---

* The people, by 1830, felt themselves sorely in need of a friend. The Industrial Revolution was producing its first crop of woes for labor: slums and long hours and insecure jobs. The old ruling class was not interested, any more than it was interested in the sorrows that followed on imprisonment for debt. The gentry were out of touch with the masses who were beginning to vote. A new type of leadership was wanted.

2

Tennessee became a state in 1796, and Jackson quickly rose to power in the new community. By 1806 he had been a judge on the Tennessee Superior Court and had represented his state first in the lower House in Washington and later in the Senate. His appearance was in keeping with his character. He was tall and very thin, with a long stern face and lantern jaw, high cheekbones and a strong mouth. His deep-set blue eyes were terrifying in anger. His face was crowned with a shock of intractable hair, soon to turn gray. His whole person expressed strength of passion and resolve, but not great physical strength, for he was flat-chested and had a slight stoop. He suffered throughout life from the effect of gunshot wounds acquired during his various fights.

In 1792 he married. His wife had been married before, and it had been reported that her husband had divorced her in Virginia. Two years later the report was proved to be untrue. The injured husband then sued successfully for divorce on the grounds of his wife's adultery with Jackson. Thereafter a second marriage took place. Jackson was devoted to his Rachel with all the strength and sentiment of his nature. There is no doubt he acted in good faith at the time of his first marriage; but the episode, and the rude comments which were often made upon it, rankled throughout his life. He killed one man for referring to the Jackson "adultery" and fought many others. He was an easy man to anger. In 1813, when he was forty-six, he got into a brawl in a Nashville tavern with the Benton brothers. They fought with pistols and knives, and with the help of the bystanders they nearly exterminated each other. Jackson was seriously hurt, and this injury, added to many previous ones, plagued him the rest of his life. Neither wounds nor age, however, nor the opposition of the most powerful men in the country, ever halted him in his implacable drive to get his own way. Since he had the power of attracting popular worship, it is a lucky thing for America that on the whole his own way was good.

During the War of 1812, Jackson first led Western militiamen against the Indians of Georgia and Alabama. He was then made a major general in the Regular Army and put in charge of the defense of New Orleans. Here he became a national hero by destroying General Sir Edward Pakenham and his troops. In 1818 came his stormy invasion of Florida, which almost provoked war with both England and Spain. And again in 1821, when Jackson was military governor of Florida (which by that time belonged to the United States), he had trouble with the civil authority. On both these occasions he was saved by John Quincy Adams.

In 1824, therefore, when he first became of major importance in na-

tional politics, Jackson was a war hero to the people at large and a veteran
of government, law, and fighting in the state of Tennessee. If he had a
reputation for rashness which might excuse his more cautious fellow citizens for viewing him with fear, he also had a reputation for success. In
addition, his struggle for worldly goods was behind him; Jackson was no
longer one of the unprivileged. Tennessee had grown from a frontier into
a settled, prosperous state, and Jackson had become a ruling landowner,
with two plantations, many slaves, and financial connections of the most
conservative and respectable order. In border language, he had become a
"nabob," having begun as a "leathershirt." If he had any political opinions, they were probably conservative, for he had aligned himself with the
conservative group in his own state. Yet the people were right in sensing
that his opinions were less important than his prejudices, and that his
prejudices were popular: he hated Indians,* Englishmen, people who
thought themselves superior, and institutions (whether legal, financial, or
social) which tended to regiment life or to diminish freedom of choice and
conduct. This was an agreeable set of hatreds, to the mind of the new
democracy.

3

In his *Autobiography,* Martin Van Buren wrote:

> Within three months after the commencement of Mr. Adams's ad-
> ministration [I decided] that as Mr. Crawford was removed from fur-
> ther competition by the state of his health my next candidate would be
> Andrew Jackson. . . . By adding the General's personal popularity to
> the strength of the old Republican party which still acted together . . .
> we might, I thought, be able to compete successfully with the power and
> patronage of the Administration.[3]

This decision on the part of the "Red Fox" of New York State was one
of the most fortunate events in Jackson's long and lucky career.

Van Buren was of Dutch descent. He was born at Kinderhook, near
Albany, New York. When he joined the camp of General Jackson he was
forty-three years old, and the most successful of the political bosses whose
struggles for power had made the politics of New York State too complicated for the average citizen to follow. He was as suave as Aaron Burr,

---

* In 1796, as Tennessee's first member in the House of Representatives, Jackson
made himself popular at home by securing compensation for militiamen who had
marched under Sevier of Tennessee on an Indian raid which was not only unauthorized by the government but which had actually been forbidden. "This accom-
plishment," said Mr. Abernethy in his article on Jackson in the *Dictionary of American Biography,* "must have required some ability."

without the tormenting ambition or the twisted sense of honor; he was as forceful as the Clintons, without their tendency to make enemies and generate friction. Short and straight and very correct in his dress, wary and self-contained in his expression, yet friendly and amusing, he never grew angry or emphatic. And he never argued. John Quincy Adams, annoyed at Van Buren's caution and his refusal to make enemies, called him *"l'ami de tout le monde"*—which is perhaps not as bad a fault as Adams thought. He was the first of the new type of political organizer to move from state politics to the national stage. He would have come to power with Crawford in 1825, had not fate intervened. He chose Jackson as the next best hope.

He chose Jackson cold-bloodedly, believing that there was nothing against him, and confident that he could be made into a popular myth. Jackson was a weapon with which to beat Adams, and also a center around which to build a new and properly conducted party. Van Buren, as a professional, deplored the inefficiency of the Adams Administration, and he was also opposed to the Adams plan for internal improvements at federal expense—whether on constitutional grounds, or because such improvements would detract from the monopolistic advantages of New York's Erie Canal, no one will ever know. One of Van Buren's amusing qualities was his refusal to explain, to retract, or to deny. When his enemies accused him of malfeasance, he smiled cheerfully and continued to treat them as friends. Silence and indifference, he discovered, were more disconcerting than the best-reasoned reply.*

This was the man whose serene touch brought New York into the Jackson fold, soothed Calhoun into postponing his fierce ambitions and accepting second place on the Jackson ticket, charmed the Jeffersonians of Virginia and the planters of South Carolina into forgetting their fears of the wild Westerner on horseback, and (most marvelous of all) persuaded Macon of North Carolina and John Randolph—the two men who were always opposed to everything—to serve the General's cause.** Nobody with Van Buren's orderly mind would have expected such a team to hold together for long; but he had to conjure them into a brief unity before he could start on his main design, which was to create a national party as

---

* In his *Autobiography* (p. 367) he speaks of "the course which I have always preferred, that of living down calumnies unsupported by proof, instead of attempting to write them down." One charge, however, he denied indignantly (*Autobiography*, p. 199): the charge that when asked whether the sun rose in the East he had answered that he presumed so, but, as he invariably slept until after sunrise, he could not speak from his own knowledge.

** In the long irony which was Randolph's life there was nothing more cruel than the fact that he had to help Andrew Jackson in order to hurt Henry Clay. As the true meaning of the Jacksonian revolution emerged, Randolph found that he had helped the man who was to abolish the America in which Randolph believed and for the sake of which he had turned against all his friends.

frictionless and effective as the Albany Regency. To do this he must control the patronage, and to control the patronage he must put his candidate in the White House. So the first step was to win an election by any means available—hence the strange coalition which he briefly used. As soon as possible he would impose party discipline, say farewell to anarchists like Randolph, accept good-naturedly the secession of all who refused to conform, and build a government capable of carrying out a policy. Incidentally he and his friends would transform the President into a tribune of the people—a change which was only possible because Jackson was a born master of men. We do not know when Van Buren realized that he had an untamable leader on his hands; but we know that the discovery did not frighten him, or make him jealous, and we also know that when he first dropped Crawford and turned to Jackson he saw the General as a man who stood for almost nothing except integrity and military success.[4]

In the work of electing Jackson the first time, of creating the coalition which made possible the new party and the new era, Van Buren had the help of three men from Nashville who banded together as early as 1821 to make their beloved general President, and who secured his first nomination by the Tennessee legislature: John Overton, William Berkeley Lewis, and John Henry Eaton. Overton was a year older than his hero. He had left Virginia for Kentucky in 1787, then moved to Nashville, where he found himself not only in the same boarding-house but in the same bed with Andrew Jackson. He became Jackson's partner in land speculation, and before long he was the richest citizen of Tennessee.* From 1821 until the triumph in 1828, Overton gave his time, money, and driving energy to making Jackson President. He then refused all favors and all jobs, remaining an adviser and a friend until his death but never sinking into the swirl of mere followers.

The other two members of the Nashville trio, Lewis and Eaton, were many years younger. They were brothers-in-law, their wives being wards of General Jackson. Eaton wrote a second-rate life of Jackson in 1817; the next year he went to the United States Senate, where he arrived just as his hero burst into Florida, carrying fire and sword against Indian, Englishman and Spaniard. Eaton remained in the Senate until after Jackson's election, becoming liaison officer between the Nashville clique and the Eastern politicians. During this period his first wife died, which was a pity, for his second wife became a national joke and a tempest in the Washington pot.

Lewis, the last of the faithful three, had been Jackson's quartermaster

---

* In 1819 Overton and Jackson, who had bought land along the Mississippi River, founded the city of Memphis, which grew into the largest town of Tennessee. In 1940 it had a population of over 330,000.

during the Indian campaigns of 1812 and 1813. He was the first man to suggest Jackson for President, and he became a combination of secretary, errand boy, and political "fixer" for the Jackson men. From his earliest days in politics he was a friend and admirer of Van Buren, and he may have helped to bring that smooth and imperturbable boss into the alliance.

4

It was easy for these enthusiastic Westerners to believe, in 1825, that their candidate had been cheated of office by a corrupt bargain between Henry Clay and a man from Massachusetts. They hated Clay because he sought to divide the West with their candidate; and they expected no good from Massachusetts, which from earliest days had been willing to sacrifice the Mississippi Valley for the sake of her own fishing rights. With the help of Van Buren (who did not ask whether a story was true, but only whether it was useful) they made the fight to oust Adams a personal fight, to undo a personal wrong which had been inflicted by the gentry upon the people's friend. This was an issue which had wider appeal than the problems of a tariff or a national bank.*

An immediate result of the new type of campaign was the defeat of the Administration in the mid-term elections of 1826. For the first time in American history the House of Representatives had a strong majority against the President and his policies. There followed a futility which was shocking, even to a nation inured to governments which could not govern. Ever since the breakdown of responsible leadership under Madison, the Washington scene had been one continuous proof of Hamilton's statement to the New York Convention, when fighting for the ratification of the Constitution: "There are two objects in forming systems of government—safety for the people, and energy in the administration. . . . If the latter object be neglected, the people's security will be as certainly sacrificed as by disregarding the former." Since the repeal of the Embargo in 1809 the American Government had displayed no "energy in the administration," with the result that the nation blundered into an unnecessary war, blundered into an increase in sectional tension, and finally, under Adams, failed either to accept the Administration's plans for internal improvements and the use of the public lands, or to put other plans in their place.

---

* There is no doubt that Jackson believed the story of a corrupt bargain, for which a strong case can be made, as may be seen in Marquis James's *Andrew Jackson: Portrait of a President*. Glyndon Van Deusen makes an equally strong case against the story in his *Life of Henry Clay*. Since there is little written evidence—unless some is contained in the Adams papers which are still withheld by the family—one can only judge by a knowledge of the people concerned, and such a knowledge makes the tale seem wildly improbable.

The American taste for weak government had been indulged too thoroughly.

Commenting on Hamilton's remarks to the New York State Convention, Henry Jones Ford writes:

> Hamilton held that since in every form of government power must exist and be trusted somewhere, able to cope with every emergency of war or peace, and since the extent of emergency is incalculable, therefore, public authority is not really susceptible of limitation. If limitation be imposed, the effect is not to stay the exertion of power under stress of public necessity, but is rather to cause it to become capricious, violent, and irregular. The true concern of a constitution is therefore not limitation of power, but is provision of means for defining responsibility. The constitutional ideal aimed at by Hamilton may be fairly described as plenary power in the administration, subject to direct and continuous accountability to the people, maintained by a representative assembly, broadly democratic in its character.[5]

As we have seen, Congress refused to allow Hamilton to propose and defend his Treasury measures in the open, with full responsibility, on the floor of the House, and drove him to meet and plan secretly with a party caucus. A little later Jefferson carried the irresponsible making of policy behind closed doors to its extreme, presenting Congress with conclusions to be accepted, not criticized.* The system broke down when the triumvirate of Jefferson, Madison, and Gallatin failed to find a policy which could meet the French and British threats. Thereafter Jefferson bowed himself out; Madison and Monroe refused to make policy; the Congress refused to allow Adams to make policy; and for a period of twenty years the government drifted, or in moments of necessity or anger it committed sudden acts which can fairly be described as "capricious, violent, and irregular."** The chief exception was in the field of foreign affairs, when

---

* Supreme Court Justice Joseph Story, in his *Commentaries on the Constitution of the United States* (1833), argued that the exclusion of Cabinet members from the floor of Congress made for back-stairs government. "If corruption ever eats its way silently into the vitals of this government," he wrote, "it will be because the people are unable to bring responsibility home to the executive through his chosen ministers." And he added that without the right to urge its measures openly before the Congress, "the executive is compelled to resort to secret and unseen influences, to private interviews, and private arrangements . . . instead of proposing and sustaining its own duties and measures by a bold and manly appeal to the nation in the face of its representatives. . . . Measures will be adopted or defeated by private intrigues, political combinations, irresponsible recommendations, and all the blandishments of office, and all the deadening weight of silent patronage."

** Cp. the War of 1812; the self-defeating conflict between nationalist legislation and a states'-rights veto in 1816; the similar conflict between Monroe's Cumberland Road veto and the nationalism of Marshall's Supreme Court and of Henry Clay; the stagnation of government under Adams, with the exception of the Tariff of Abominations. When the President, as in 1825, had a clear plan, the Congress

Adams was Secretary of State and Monroe made some useful and far-reaching decisions.

The Federalist plan for working the government had been rejected; the Jeffersonian plan had broken down; the modesty and weakness of Madison and Monroe had exposed the fact that neither Congress as a whole nor the standing committees of that body were capable of making policy—so the third, or Congressional, plan was also discredited. What next? The disorder of the Adams Administration could not long endure. A government whose most constructive act was the Tariff of Abominations could scarcely expect to survive. Fortunately, the new forces of democracy were to provide a partial answer. By seizing the presidency and rejuvenating its powers they were to make possible new forms of growth within the old Constitution. And by building political parties of a size and complication never before imagined, they were to create an agency for reassembling the scattered parts of government and for supplying (at least occasionally) Hamilton's "energy in the administration."

The first step was to elect Jackson, "the people's friend." In 1828, as we have seen, he had an easy victory in the electoral college; but the sign of his coming strength was the aggregate popular vote throughout the country, which in four years had tripled. In 1824, 361,120 votes were cast; in 1828, 1,155,340.[6] The concentration of popular interest on the presidential election had begun. During the years between Jefferson and Jackson, the Congressional election had been the important event; but from 1828 the question of who was to be President overshadowed the rest of politics. This is interesting, since in 1828 no one had the least idea what Jackson stood for; the people merely knew he was their "friend," that he had been "betrayed," and that they must undo the wrong. The Jackson men had invented the modern presidential campaign: a combination of sport, cynicism, and zeal.

"It was a proud day for the people," wrote Amos Kendall* when the

---

would permit nothing; when the Congress, as in 1816, had a policy, the President vetoed it and the Congress accepted the check. If this is division of powers, it is also neurosis. The government of the United States might have cried with Endymion:

> Do gently murder half my soul, and I
> Shall feel the other half so utterly.

Hamilton was right: because there was no "energy in the administration," there was no "safety for the people," who got nothing from this long chaos but the wounding financial crisis which began in 1819 and the negative pleasure of not being governed too much.

* Kendall was the chief figure in Jackson's "kitchen cabinet." Born on a Massachusetts farm, educated at Dartmouth, he moved to Kentucky in 1814 and became a newspaper editor. He supported Clay until 1826, when he joined the Jackson camp, helping to carry Kentucky for the General in 1828. He then moved to Washington, and was given a job in the Treasury. In 1835 he became Postmaster General, rescuing that department from incompetence and corruption. His chief work,

returns were in; "General Jackson is *their own* president." Justice Story took a different view. "The reign of King 'Mob' seemed triumphant," he wrote. Both statements were true. Jackson was indeed the people's President, and the people are indeed a mob if one chooses to regard them as such. The interesting question, on the March day in 1829 when Jackson was inaugurated, was whether the American people (or the American mob) were capable of self-government. Many of the revered founders of the Republic had thought they were not; and the base tone of the 1828 election would have made the founders shiver. But the people had laid their hands upon the presidency, and they were never to relinquish that hold. It was not then known that the change was irreversible, that it was part of a movement toward democracy throughout the Western world which must either justify itself or bring ruin, that there was no road back toward the oligarchies of the eighteenth and early nineteenth centuries.

5

The first sign of the political revolution was the open acceptance of the spoils system,* or rotation in office. This was not a new idea; it had been recommended for centuries as a cure for political corruption. Harrington's *Oceana* (a book which influenced most of the Constitution-makers) proposed that every executive and representative should be returned to private life for a term of years equal to his term in power, and Jefferson himself had favored rotation in office as the best way to prevent the rise of bureaucracy. In 1820 Congress passed the Four Years Act, establishing a fixed term for numerous federal officials. This helped the Jackson men to speed the turnover in office and to fix party regularity as the price of favors, thus welding their discordant followers into an effective team.

> The wrangling factions [writes Professor Ford] were rapidly aligned in party ranks. There was no opening for an independent role. Factions had to choose one side or the other, or be cut off from present enjoyment or future possibility of office. Appropriate party issues were shaped by executive policy. The administration of the patronage on party grounds carries with it the power of defining party issues, for it implies

---

however, was as private adviser, and as drafter of speeches, for Jackson. In the last year of Van Buren's Administration, Kendall resigned to become once more the editor of a newspaper. Silent and audacious, with a brilliant pen and an utter devotion to General Jackson, he had been a major power in the capital for eleven years.

* William L. Marcy, Van Buren's colleague in the Albany Regency, gave the system its name. Marcy was sent to the United States Senate in 1831. There, while defending Van Buren against the charge of having debauched the public service, he somewhat incautiously remarked that he and his friends could see "nothing wrong in the rule that to the victor belong the spoils of the enemy."

on the part of the appointing power a conception of what constitutes party membership. . . . Dissenters may contend that they represent the true party tradition, but that does not help their case. They must submit or go into opposition.[7]

In spite of the effectiveness of the system, the first large-scale removals from office caused shrieks of anger and pain. Van Buren thereupon intervened to make the machine work more smoothly, by which he meant more secretly. As Marquis James points out in his biography of Jackson, Van Buren "regarded all this clatter attending Federal removals as the clumsy work of amateurs. In New York thrice as many public servants as Jackson had sent on their way might vanish into the void without awakening so much as an echo. Moreover, small as the number of Federal replacements had been, too many offices had fallen to the friends of John C. Calhoun." So Secretary of State Van Buren began to teach the uncouth Westerners how to bathe the machinery in oil. The noise of friction hurt his ears; it was a sign that somebody was doing a job awkwardly. Suavity and silence were his ideal: never answer questions, never make excuses, never get angry. When a delegate from the Florida territory protested to Jackson that twelve good officials had been turned out to make way for worthless men, Jackson hotly replied that no man had been turned out except for oppression or defalcation. The delegate took this story to Van Buren, asking what crime the twelve men had committed. Van Buren blandly replied, "The President's recollection must be at fault. We give no reasons for our removals."

There were fewer removals after Van Buren took charge; but each one counted. And the friends of Calhoun—Van Buren's obvious rival for the succession to the presidency—began to find it hard to get jobs, and impossible to get explanations for their unemployment.

So far as numbers were concerned, the Jackson record was moderate. A hostile Senator, in a speech attacking the "proscription," charged that there had been nineteen hundred and eighty-one removals in twelve months. The Administration press replied that there had been only nine hundred and nineteen removals in eighteen months. At the most this would be one in six of the civil service jobs available—a figure which later Administrations would have thought Utopian in its restraint.* Senator Benton claimed that even in the executive departments at Washington Jackson left a majority of his opponents in office; nevertheless, he made enough changes to establish discipline in his party by proving that the Administration could both reward and punish, and he thereby fastened the system of spoils upon the country.

* According to Professor Erik Eriksson, Jackson during his eight years replaced only one fifth of those whom he found in office.

6

Van Buren's appointment as Secretary of State caused no surprise, for the "Little Magician" was the most powerful of Jackson's backers. John McLean, who had supported Jackson while serving as Postmaster General under Adams, refused to stay in the Cabinet because of the wholesale political removals; he was therefore made Associate Justice of the United States Supreme Court, and his place was given to William T. Barry of Kentucky, who had deserted Clay and helped to carry the state for the new President.* Jackson's old friend, John Eaton, became Secretary of War, and the other posts were distributed among Calhoun's followers. Since Calhoun, as Vice-President, was Van Buren's rival for the succession, the Cabinet broke into two factions. Strife between these factions was soon exacerbated by the farcical social war against Eaton's second wife.

A few months before his inauguration Jackson had been consulted by Eaton, who wanted to marry the beautiful, notorious Peggy O'Neale.** Believing that Jackson planned to offer him a Cabinet position, Eaton wanted to know whether the marriage would stand in his way. Naturally, he pictured his loved one as a misunderstood and maligned woman. Jackson's own wife, Rachel, was still shocked and wounded from the gross treatment she had received during the campaign; so Jackson attached all his fierce loyalty to Peggy O'Neale, turning his rage against those whose evil tongues were "wronging" her. He told Eaton that of course he must marry the woman, if he loved her. Eaton cheerfully acted on the advice. Mrs. Eaton was then received by Rachel Jackson, which in the General's eyes bestowed the final mark of goodness. Shortly thereafter Mrs. Jackson died, and her husband's wrath against gossip-mongers grew still more bitter, for he ascribed her death to the slanders of the political press. Immediately after the inauguration, he appointed Senator Eaton Secretary of War.

Peggy O'Neale had served as barmaid in her father's tavern in Washington. She had been married to a man called Timberlake, a drunken purser in the navy, by whom she had three children. Timberlake cut his throat in 1828, while on duty in the Mediterranean. Senator Eaton, who had boarded at the O'Neale tavern since 1818, was said to have been Peggy's lover both before and after the suicide. Mrs. Calhoun, a member of one of the best families in South Carolina, refused to meet Mrs. Eaton, and the Cabinet wives (whose husbands belonged to the Calhoun faction) followed her lead. There is no telling whether this conduct was

---

* It was Barry from whose administration Kendall rescued the post office in 1835.
** Her name is sometimes spelled O'Neil or O'Neill.

caused by a passion for virtue or by the hope of driving John Eaton, Van Buren's best ally, out of the Cabinet. If anyone indulged the latter hope, he did so out of an ignorance of Andrew Jackson. The General, feeling that he was championing his own departed angel, would not hear of Eaton's resignation, but undertook to force the unwanted Peggy upon Washington society.

The headlong tactics that had triumphed in Indian warfare and border raids proved ineffective in social combat. Jackson held a Cabinet meeting at which he announced—presumably as official policy—that Mrs. Eaton was "as chaste as a virgin";* but still the women would not call on her. Even the President's niece, Mrs. Donelson, who lived with Jackson and acted as his hostess, would not call. She left the White House rather than abandon the pleasures of sanctified impoliteness. There was only one person for whom all the nonsense was delightful: Van Buren, a widower, who really liked to treat men and women with courtesy, and who also liked to make his political rivals look silly. Van Buren enjoyed being kind to Mrs. Eaton, and he enjoyed watching Jackson's wrath at the Calhouns (and at their friends and their friends' wives) grow until the South Carolinian had lost all hope of the royal favor; then he intervened to settle the problem, lest the country should decide that Jackson and his friends were a joke.

In April, 1831, Van Buren resigned, making it clear that he did so in order to help the President get rid of a cantankerous Cabinet. Then Eaton resigned. Then it was easy for Jackson to force Calhoun's friends to follow; so by the summer he was free to start afresh, with no Peggy Eatons to plague him and no warring sects within his family. Van Buren was sent as Minister to England, and at that point Calhoun made a mistake which kept him from the presidency. While Van Buren waited gratefully in London, the Vice-President conspired in the Senate to produce a tie vote on confirming the appointment, and then cast his deciding vote for rejection. Not content with ruining himself once, Calhoun arranged for the vindictive show to be repeated. "It will kill him, sir, kill him dead," he exulted, unaware that the pronoun applied to his own presidential hopes.[8] Senator Benton, a smaller but wilier statesman than Calhoun, commented as follows:

> I was opposed to Mr. Van Buren's going to England as minister. He was our intended candidate for the presidency, and I deemed such a mission to be prejudicial to him and the party, and apt to leave us with a candidate weakened with the people by absence, and by a residence at a foreign court. I was in this state of mind when I saw the combination formed against him, and felt that the success of it would be his

* "Age cannot wither," said Henry Clay, "nor custom stale, her infinite virginity."

and our salvation. Rejection was a bitter medicine, but there was health
at the bottom of the draught.[9]

So Benton did not vote to save his friend, Van Buren, explaining, "I was
not the guardian of Messrs. Clay, Webster, and Calhoun, and was quite
willing to see them fall into the pit which they were digging for another."

The result, easily foreseen by the new school of professionals, was that
Van Buren returned home to be acclaimed in New York, and to be elected
Vice-President on Jackson's ticket in 1832, and President in 1836.*

7

One more change had to be made before Jackson's unwritten reform of
the Constitution was complete. It was clear that in the future each political party, struggling for the great national prize of the presidency and held
together by federal patronage or the hope of patronage, must choose a
single candidate. There could be no return to the chaos of 1824, when the
anti-Adams votes were divided between Crawford and Jackson, with the
result that a candidate with no organization and a minority of supporters
was finally successful. The unified party which had since been built by the
Jackson men must compel a unified Opposition; yet the question remained, How were the parties to choose their candidates?** Nomination
by Congressional caucus was discredited; nomination by state legislatures
made for a scattering of strength; nomination by the President himself was
acceptable only to the gentry, and only when the President was Mr. Jefferson who practiced an unknown sorcery upon his followers.

Jackson, of course, meant to choose and impose his successor, just as he
meant to impose Van Buren as Vice-President in 1832. Jackson was an
autocratic democrat, who believed that the people could have no greater
good fortune than that he himself should always get his way. Yet a certain concealment was needed, so the problem arose as to what machinery
he should use to gloss his autocracy. He wisely chose the machinery of the

---

* Peggy O'Neale lived until 1879, her life remaining unusual until the end. After
suffering the disdain of Washington, she had four years of social triumph at the
Court of His Catholic Majesty at Madrid. She then returned home, and after the
death of Eaton she married an Italian dancing master, who not only stole all her
money but eloped with her granddaughter. Her last years were poor and angry;
but she left behind her an autobiography, published in 1932, which is a defense
of her honor and morals and an odd picture of Washington in the days of Andrew
Jackson.

** In 1836, the Whig Party put forward several candidates, in the hope of preventing anyone from getting a majority, so that the election might be thrown into
the House of Representatives. This was a sign of weakness. Four years later, when
the Whigs had gathered strength they concentrated on one man.

nominating convention. Such conventions had been suggested in state elections as early as 1792, but had been opposed on the ground that the members of the convention would become all-powerful, dictating the choice of the electorate. The growth of parties, however, disposed of the naïve theory that the voters could vote for anyone they chose. If they did, they would disperse their strength and ensure perpetual defeat at the hands of any unified minority. If the majority was to assert itself, the majority must be organized, which meant it must accept orders (or at least decisions) from the politician.

Calhoun saw exactly what was happening, and why it must happen; it was one of his reasons for deploring a "government of the numerical majority." Under majority rule, he wrote, the parties would find it "indispensable to success to avoid division and keep united;—and hence, from a necessity inherent in the nature of such governments, each party must be alternately forced, in order to insure victory, to resort to measures to concentrate the control over its movements in fewer and fewer hands, as the struggle became more and more violent."[10] It is not customary, however, for democratic politicians to admit that they must seize more and more power; they prefer to suggest that they are in fact conferring more and more power upon the voters. So it was in 1832, when the Jackson men adopted the nominating convention. They did it in the name of free discussion, but for the sake of party discipline. The Whigs (or National Republicans) had held a loosely organized convention the previous year, and had chosen Henry Clay for their candidate. Following Calhoun's rule that "each party must be alternately forced to concentrate control," the Jackson men created a far more efficient and tightly run convention. Its avowed purpose was to secure a democratic representation of the party will; its real purpose was to make sure that Jackson was obeyed and that Van Buren was nominated for the vice-presidency. It was here that the federal patronage counted. Since Jackson was certain to be President for the next four years, his managers had only to suggest that local organizations desiring federal favors had better vote for Jackson's friend. Van Buren was liked by the politicians and respected for his success; but he was little known to the nation and would not have been the free choice of the people. The power of the federal patronage and the smoothness of the new machine were shown by the vote: Van Buren, 208; Philip Pendleton Barbour of Virginia, 49; Richard Johnson of Kentucky, 26. Incidentally, Van Buren was the best man for the job.*

---

* A strong and popular President, such as Jackson, can expect to dominate the convention which meets at the end of his first term, since he is likely to be the source of political favors for another four years. At the end of a second term, when the President is about to go out of office (or whenever the party is out of power), the convention is less easy to handle. The delegates are free to register a popular choice, if such a choice exists and has made itself vocal. The fact that conventions

When this first Democratic Convention met, Jackson had already been nominated by state legislatures and by popular acclaim, so aside from choosing the Vice-President the important work was to adopt rules of procedure. The convention consisted of delegates from the local party machines, each state having been asked to send delegates equal to the number of presidential electors from that state.* The legislature of New Hampshire issued the invitation for the first meeting, and every state responded except Missouri. The decisions of the convention were binding upon nobody, except that the national leaders could withhold patronage from the local groups who rebelled. This was a strong influence, but not strong enough to force a state machine to accept a locally unpopular decision, or to work hard for a locally unpopular candidate; so early in their history the conventions undertook the task of weeding out the men and the issues that might cause dissent in any important region, of toning down all demands which might lose votes anywhere, of ratifying the compromises and the diplomatic adjustments which make co-operation possible between local party machines—in other words, of doing all the work which Madison foresaw must be done in a large federal union, and which he knew must make American politics cautious and conservative.

These balances and compromises, which find expression in the party platform** (or statement of party principles), plus the federal patronage, plus the national popularity of the President or the candidate, are all that hold the party together. For the rest, it is a congeries of local and state groups, intent upon local and state interests, electing local and state candidates, from aldermen to United States senators. The national party only elects two men: the President and the Vice-President.

The desire of the state organizations to be protected against a national majority found expression in the rule that "two-thirds of the whole num-

---

are usually run by political bosses is perhaps more a sign of popular apathy than of a defect in the system. Yet it is interesting that Senator Benton grew to hate the nominating convention. He described it as "an irresponsible body—juggled, and baffled, and governed by a few dextrous contrivers, always looking to their own interest in the game which they play in putting down and putting up men." (*Thirty Years' View,* vol. I, p. 122.) This is a fair description of what normally happens, yet it seems that the voters could prevent it from happening if they took a lively interest in their local party affairs. Failing such an interest, the political bosses do a sensible job at balancing sectional antipathies and class or economic antipathies, and at producing candidates and programs which annoy the least number of voters. Such candidates and programs are not always heart-warming.

* According to the Constitution, the presidential electors from each state shall be "equal to the whole number of senators and representatives to which the state may be entitled in the Congress." Today, at the major party conventions, each state has approximately twice as many delegates as it has members of the two houses of Congress.

** The first Democratic Party platform was adopted in 1840. In 1848 the Democratic National Committee was created: a central party agency with the authority to call conventions.

ber of votes in the convention shall be necessary to constitute a choice." This rule, peculiar to the Democratic Party, was accepted by every convention until 1936, when it was repealed at the request of Franklin Roosevelt, the great centralizer of power. For over a hundred years, the two-thirds rule gave to minorities the right to block a nomination, a right which was sometimes used with startling results. Yet it is in keeping with the spirit of American federal government, which tends to prevent action in order to placate minorities, rather than to make action efficient or responsible.

With the growth of the convention system the thwarting of the constitutional plan for the presidency was complete. The electoral college had become a party agency, automatically registering the party votes for the candidates chosen by the party convention. The President, instead of being selected by a few dozen wise men deliberating at leisure, was chosen by the whole electorate from a list of two, or sometimes three, candidates nominated by the party bosses. And the "whole electorate" was no longer merely the well-to-do; it was very nearly equivalent to the adult white male population. The President had become the spokesman of the will of the nation;* but he still lacked constitutional authority for carrying that will into effect. A popular President, in his first term, with the full power of federal patronage and of public approval behind him, might often get his way, especially if he had a genius for political combinations. Otherwise, the written Constitution, devised to prevent action, still triumphed over the unwritten constitution, devised to make action possible. As Professor Ford put it with careful understatement:

> The nomination of a presidential candidate is accompanied by a declaration of party principles which he is pledged to enforce in the conduct of the administration; but no constitutional means are pro-

---

* There were four main steps by which the people captured the presidency: first, the members of the electoral college were forced by unwritten law to vote not for the candidates of their choice but for the candidates of their party's choice. This change was generally accepted by 1796, and was binding by 1800. It did not seem important while the party's choice of candidate was still made by the gentry, either in unofficial caucus or in correspondence with one another. Second, members of the electoral college began to be elected by the voters instead of being appointed by the legislatures of their several states. By 1832, only one state clung to the system of appointment. This change gave to the voters the feeling that they themselves chose the President, even if they had nothing to say about the candidates. Third, the suffrage was steadily extended. By 1832 most of the adult white males could vote. Fourth, the major parties adopted the nominating convention, which took the choice of candidates away from the old ruling class and gave it to the democratic politicians—or, in theory, to the people.

Woodrow Wilson wrote that since the candidate chosen by the convention "is the only man for whom the electors of his party can vote . . . the expression of the preference of the convention of the dominant party is practically equivalent to election, and might as well be called election by anyone who is writing of broad facts, and not of fine distinctions." Cp. *Congressional Government,* p. 245.

vided whereby he may carry out his pledges, and it is due solely to the extra-constitutional means supplied by party organization that the presidential office is able to perform the function imposed upon it of executing the will of the nation. Party organization acts as a connective tissue, enfolding the separate organs of government, and tending to establish a unity of control which shall adapt the government to the uses of popular sovereignty. The adaptation is still so incomplete that the administrative function is imperfectly carried on and the body-politic suffers acutely from its irregularity.[11]

These words were written fifty years ago; but they are still largely true. The adaptation is still incomplete and sometimes the body politic still "suffers acutely from its irregularity." The talent for government with which the Americans of the Jackson era changed a semi-oligarchy into a full democracy, amending the written Constitution with unwritten and extra-legal devices such as the party system and the nominating convention, may need to be exercised still further in our time.

XIII

The Jackson Men in Action

WITH ONE EXCEPTION, Jackson's new Cabinet (appointed in 1831, after the Peggy O'Neale excitement) was more peaceful than the old. Edward Livingston* took Van Buren's place, Lewis Cass** became Secretary of War, and Roger B. Taney, who was to play a stormy part in the war on the Bank and to succeed Marshall as Chief Justice of the Supreme Court, became Attorney General. Finally, in order to make room for Van Buren in London, Louis McLane*** was recalled from that post and appointed

* Edward was the younger brother of the Robert R. Livingston who was American Minister to France at the time of the Louisiana Purchase. Edward served in the House of Representatives from 1795 until 1801. It was this Livingston family whose members became outraged because Washington did not give them high office, and which changed camps in 1791, joining with the Clintons to make Aaron Burr Senator instead of reappointing General Schuyler, the father-in-law of Hamilton. Shortly after leaving Congress, Edward Livingston found his finances hopelessly involved and went to New Orleans to recoup his fortune. This he did not do; but he served as Jackson's aide-de-camp at the battle of New Orleans, and later made himself a world reputation by the penal code which he constructed for the state of Louisiana. In 1824 he returned to the House of Representatives, and in 1828 he became United States Senator from Louisiana. He had worked for Jackson in 1824, and again in 1828, and was a natural candidate for office in the Administration. The renown of Livingston's contribution to penal law is shown by the oration delivered before the Academy of the Institute of France at the time of his death: "America," said François Mignet, the historian, "has lost her most powerful intellect, the Academy one of its most illustrious members, and Humanity one of her most zealous benefactors."

** Lewis Cass, born and educated in New Hampshire, had been for eighteen years governor of the Territory of Michigan when Jackson brought him to Washington as Secretary of War. He knew the old Northwest as few men have known it, for he traveled as much as five thousand miles a year, mostly by canoe, through his vast wild territory. His frontier life had made him an imperialist who felt there was no limit to America's need for land, an enemy to all Indians who dared claim a right to their ancestral hunting-grounds, and a bitter foe of the British. He lived to become United States Senator from Michigan, presidential candidate for the Democratic Party in 1848, and Secretary of State under Buchanan.

*** Louis McLane of Delaware was one of the Crawford men who switched to Jackson after 1824. He had served in both the House and the Senate, where he was known as a strong friend of the Bank of the United States. Since Jackson meant to destroy the Bank, his choice of McLane as Secretary of the Treasury seems eccentric. When the inevitable trouble came, McLane contrived an elaborate plan whereby Livingston went as Minister to France, he himself became Secretary of State, and the Treasury was given to William John Duane (son of William Duane of the *Aurora*, Gallatin's inveterate enemy). This left Jackson as harassed as ever, since young Duane also refused to make war on the Bank.

Secretary of the Treasury. Yet, in spite of these more harmonious helpers, Jackson continued to seek strength and encouragement and clarification of his ideas and prejudices from unofficial advisers such as Kendall, and Kendall's friend Frank Blair, whom Jackson had called from Kentucky to edit the Washington *Globe*.* It was these men who saw that the General's greatness lay in his sense of what the people wanted and his fiery desire to procure them justice; it was these men who gave the aging autocrat a philosophy of democracy and helped him to become a national hero. They loved him because his heart was right, and they served him by making him see the implications of that rightness. Inevitably, they met the jealousy which follows royal favorites; they were reviled by Jackson's foes, and appreciated only by the wisest of his political friends, such as Benton and Van Buren.

With a reorganized Cabinet, a strengthened presidency, a party organization which gave some unity to the Administration, an aroused public opinion expecting great deeds in the name of democracy, what did the Jackson men do? Strangely enough, they did very little of permanent importance. Their mission was to create fresh institutions and a fresh hope, not to solve the problems that bedeviled the country. Everything they touched they left unsettled—except the powers of the presidency.

One of the most explosive things they touched was the currency problem, which they made a popular issue through their battle against the Bank. It was a battle in the old war between the "little man" and monopoly, and we may doubt whether Jackson would have been found on the side of the little man if it had not been for the influence of his friends in the Kitchen Cabinet.**

As we have seen, the charter of the First Bank of the United States— Hamilton's Bank—expired in 1811, and Gallatin was unable to secure a renewal. In 1816, the Second Bank was chartered for twenty years, with a capital of thirty-five millions, of which the government subscribed seven. The control was vested in a board of twenty-five directors, five of whom

---

* Francis Preston Blair founded the *Globe* in 1830, when he was thirty-nine years old. Few political journalists have rivaled the influence wielded by Blair between 1832 and the end of Van Buren's presidency in 1841. In his *Autobiography* (p. 323), Van Buren complains of his troubles in persuading Jackson to keep anything quiet until the appropriate time: "He [Jackson] was entirely unreserved in his public dealings—the People, he thought, should know everything and 'give it to Blair' (or *Blar* as he pronounced it)—was almost always his prompt direction whenever any information was brought to him which affected or might affect the public interest." It is no wonder that Frank Blair was the envy of journalists. The *Globe* was a semi-weekly in 1830, and became a daily in 1833.

** In 1821 Jackson was apparently in favor of the Bank, for in that year he forwarded a petition for a branch of the Bank of the United States at Pensacola, Florida. It was not until he had become the mouthpiece of the democratic movement that Jackson began to think the Bank had too much power for an institution which was in no way responsible to the popular will.

were appointed by the President of the United States and the rest by the outside stockholders. The Bank was named as the depository of all government funds, though the Secretary of the Treasury had the right to put funds elsewhere provided he gave Congress his reasons. The Bank paid no interest on these funds; but it gave the government a bonus of a million and a half dollars,* and it was required to transfer the funds free of charge. The Bank could issue notes, to be redeemed in specie on demand. Such notes, like the notes of state banks which were redeemable in specie, were receivable for government dues.

At the request of President Monroe, the elegant and brilliant young Nicholas Biddle** had accepted one of the five government directorships, and in 1823, at the age of thirty-seven, he was elected president of the board. By the time Jackson went to the White House, Biddle's Bank had twenty-seven branches and agencies throughout the country. By devising the system of "branch drafts" the Bank had taken to itself the power to extend (or contract) the currency far beyond the limits which the charter was meant to impose. In a nation which responded joyfully to the temptations of easy credit the Bank had become a dominant influence in industry, commerce, and agriculture. Inevitably, the magnitude of this influence made the Bank hated by all who suffered from the long depression of the eighteen-twenties. We have already seen what Senator Benton thought.

In return for its large powers the Bank had given good service, handling the government's funds efficiently and providing a stable currency for the first time in American history. The chief objection which could be made was that the Bank's powers were not subject to control by government. The longer Biddle remained head of the Bank, the stronger this objection became, for with all his graceful talents and his competence Biddle was proud, strong-willed, and when hardened by power, ruthless. In addition to the enemies which it earned, the Bank could also count on the hostility of the strict constructionists, who thought it unconstitutional, and of the New Yorkers who hoped to make their city the financial

* This was the money which Madison would not allow the Congress to spend on internal improvements.

** This remarkable man became the center of such passionate hates and friendships that his story has never been told convincingly. He always appears either too wise or too wicked for this world. Born in Philadelphia of an old Quaker family, he went to Paris at the age of eighteen as secretary to the American Minister, General John Armstrong. The following year he began extensive travels throughout Europe, which ended in 1806 when he was called to London to be secretary of legation under James Monroe. On returning home he studied law and was admitted to the bar; but he gave most of his time to scholarship and to writing. He was reluctant to accept the appointment in the Bank, having already refused to become a director for the majority stockholders; but once he had taken the job he became an expert on finance, and he seems to have found the immense power of his position agreeable. He may have overestimated that power, or he may have underestimated the tenacity of Jackson; in any case, he challenged the strongest man and the hardest fighter in America, which proved a mistake.

capital of the country, promoting Wall Street to the position which Chest-
nut Street* then held. It was suggested that Van Buren's distaste for the
Bank might have such roots.

The Bank's charter did not expire until 1836; but Biddle approached
the Administration in 1829 with an offer to help extinguish the national
debt within four years, in return for a new charter. This was a shrewd
plan, for the abolition of the debt was one of Jackson's dearest designs.
He hated speculation, and feared debt of all kinds, public and private.**
But he believed that the Bank's power over the paper currency was a
power to create or cancel debt, and that in private hands such power must
always be used to help the rich at the expense of the poor. He therefore
refused Biddle's offer, and in his annual message he warned the people
to consider carefully whether they wished such a privileged institution
as the Bank to survive.

The problem was what to put in its place. Granting that the Bank was
a dangerous monopoly, might it not be a necessary danger? In 1829 Jackson spoke vaguely of a "bank founded upon the credit of the government
and its revenues"; but when he asked J. A. Hamilton (son of Alexander
Hamilton, and an enemy of his father's favorite institution) to work out
a plan for such a bank, Hamilton could not do so. The government might
run a bank of deposit in which everyone would have confidence; but what
was needed was a bank to advance credits as well as to receive deposits,
and Hamilton pointed out that such a bank in the hands of the government could become a more tyrannous monopoly than the Bank of the
United States. If private bankers could play politics with the credit system, so could the politicians. Early in 1831 Senator Benton attacked the
Bank as an autocracy with frightening power over the people and over
their servants. Yet Benton, also, had trouble finding a substitute; he could
only suggest that paper money was not necessary, and that the country
could get along, for all common purposes of life, on gold and silver. By
"paper money" Benton and the other Jacksonians appear to have meant
actual paper bank notes, rather than commercial paper or credit money.***

---

* In Philadelphia, the headquarters for the Bank of the United States.

** His own early experiences with gambling and speculation may have helped
breed this hate.

*** There are three types of money in common use. First, there is hard money—
metallic coins—the issuing of which is usually a government monopoly. Second,
there is the bank note, the "paper money" of Benton and the Jacksonians. This was
issued, in the eighteen-thirties, both by the Bank of the United States and by other
banks operating under state charters. The bank notes were supposed to be redeemable in specie; but since each state had its own banking laws, some of the local
banks were less than careful in maintaining a safe relationship between their paper
and their supply of gold and silver coins. Third, there is commercial paper—or
check money, or credit money. During the financial revolution of the nineteenth
century this bank credit became a far more important part of the money system
than coin or notes. In the United States, for example, in 1934, there was about

"Note issue was regarded as the characteristic function of banks," writes Arthur Schlesinger, Jr., "and an attack on the 'banking system' or on 'banks' meant generally an attack on the power of private note issue. It did not mean the elimination of the functions of discount or deposit."[1]

It is easy to see why the notes of irresponsible state banks were feared, especially by the poor and by people of small fixed income. "The working classes," says Schlesinger, "believed that they were regularly cheated by paper money. A good portion of the small notes they received in wages were depreciated, worthless, or counterfeit. Unscrupulous employers even bought up depreciated notes and palmed them off on their workingmen at face value."[2] Such conditions were bad; but they were not the fault of the Bank of the United States, which by its example and by the stability of its own notes had a moderating effect on the state banks. Yet it was doubtless inevitable that a revolt against the banking system should include a revolt against the most powerful and notorious example of that system.

The arguments for and against the Bank were repeated in Congress, in the press, and throughout the country. The Jacksonians could make an emotionally effective attack, but only by attributing to the Bank of the United States the evils which resulted from the misconduct of the local banks. Biddle could make a sound defense; but he could not escape the fact that in bad times his Bank was feared and hated, and blamed for countless misdeeds which were none of its doing. Meanwhile a decision had to be made. Since there seemed to be no answer in terms of logic or science, the question became one of personalities and politics. Here the Bank played its cards badly, in spite of having the advice of Henry Clay, who in 1831 returned to Washington as senator from Kentucky.

Clay came back from two years' retirement to take charge of the opposition to Jackson, confident that he could defeat his fellow Westerner and capture the presidency. He wanted an issue, and it seemed to him that the rechartering of the Bank would suit his purpose, for the business world and most of the press favored the charter, the people seemed apathetic, and the Administration had no sensible alternative. So Clay induced Biddle, in January, 1832, to ask Congress for an immediate recharter. In the following July, Congress passed the required bill and sent it to the President, who decided to veto it. Attorney-General Taney worked on the veto message; so did Amos Kendall; and so, at great length, did Jackson himself.

$40,000,000,000 of this credit money on deposit, as against about $5,000,000,000 of currency. Bank-credit had not reached such importance in the eighteen-thirties; but it is surprising that the "hard-money" reformers did not take it into account. They directed the whole of their attack against the irresponsible creation of bank notes.

Distinctions in society will always exist under every just government
[said the message]. Equality of talents, of education, or of wealth, cannot be produced by human institutions. In the full enjoyment of the
gifts of heaven and the fruits of superior industry, economy, and virtue,
every man is equally entitled to protection by law. But when the laws
undertake to add to these natural and just advantages, artificial distinctions . . . to make the rich richer and the potent more powerful, the
humbler members of society, the farmers, mechanics, and laborers,
who have neither the time nor the means of securing like favors to
themselves, have a right to complain of the injustice of their government. . . . There are no necessary evils in government. Its evils exist
only in its abuses. If it would confine itself to equal protection, and, as
heaven does its rains, shower its favors alike on the high and the low,
the rich and the poor, it would be an unqualified blessing. In the act
before me, there seems to be wide and unnecessary departure from these
just principles.[3]

This was good Jeffersonian doctrine, and so was the rejection of
Marshall's claim that the Supreme Court could decide finally on the
constitutionality of an act. Jackson in his veto message declared flatly
that the Bank was unconstitutional, although the Supreme Court had
already held the reverse. "Each officer who takes an oath to support the
Constitution," said Jackson, "swears that he will support it as he understands it, and not as it is understood by others."

Biddle professed to be "delighted" with the message. "It has all the fury
of the unchained panther," he wrote, "biting the bars of his cage. It is
really a manifesto of anarchy, such as Marat and Robespierre might have
issued to the mob of the Faubourg St. Antoine; and my hope is that it
will contribute to relieve the country from the domination of these miserable people." Biddle's defeat could have been predicted from that one
statement. He did not know that the days of Fisher Ames were gone
forever, that allusions to Marat made no man cringe, and that it was inexpedient as well as demeaning to refer to the heroes of the new electorate
as "miserable people." Nobody so ignorant of politics should have attempted to fight Andrew Jackson.

Webster in the Senate made a strong reply to the veto message, with
the result that his loan from the Bank was increased from twenty-two
to thirty-two thousand dollars.* Yet the veto was upheld, first by Congress and later by the American people, who re-elected Jackson in 1832
with Van Buren as Vice-President. Henry Clay with his National Republican Party was a very poor second.

---

* It is not unfair to recall this fact, for Webster was consistently grasping in his
relations with the Bank. At the height of the battle, in December, 1833, he wrote to
Biddle: "I believe my retainer has not been renewed or *refreshed* as usual. If it be
wished that my relation to the Bank should be continued, it may be well to send
me the usual retainers. Yours with regard, Danl. Webster."

Strengthened by success, Jackson decided not to wait until the charter expired but to deprive the Bank of government business at once. The Secretary of the Treasury, Louis McLane, objected; so he was promoted to the Department of State, and Duane was put in his place. Duane also objected, so he was dismissed, and Taney was put in his place. Then at last the President had his way, and the government ceased depositing funds with the Bank of the United States. The existing balances were left in the Bank until exhausted; but all new funds were deposited in state banks.

At this point Biddle lost his head and began restricting credit, thus promoting a panic. "Nothing," wrote Biddle to the head of his Boston branch, "but the evidence of suffering abroad will produce any effect in Congress. . . . A steady course of firm restriction will ultimately lead to . . . the recharter of the Bank." He was wrong for two reasons: first, he was fighting a man who could not be frightened; second, he was fighting with weapons which justified the popular fear of the Bank. The good will which the Bank had earned was nullified by a cold conspiracy to induce a depression.

Biddle and his friends insisted that the collapse in values was the result of Jackson's ignorant money policy, that by refusing the charter and withdrawing the funds he had forced the Bank into a restrictive course. Countless petitions were sent to Washington by victims of the economic storm, and delegation after delegation pleaded for a new policy. The reply was characteristic: "Is Andrew Jackson to bow the knee to the golden calf? I tell you, if you want relief go to Nicholas Biddle." Biddle's comments did not endear him to the country. "The Bank," he said, "has taken its final course and it will not be frightened nor cajoled from its duty by any small drivelling about relief." And again: "The Bank feels no vocation to redress the wrongs of these miserable people. Rely upon that. This worthy President thinks that because he has scalped Indians and imprisoned Judges, he is to have his way with the Bank. He is mistaken." After a few months of such talk, people who at first were undecided agreed that the Bank might really be the "Monster" which Jackson called it.

By June of 1834 the Bank was beaten. Admitting defeat, it relaxed the credit policy, thus proving that the suffering and destruction had been imposed upon the country from Philadelphia. Yet Jackson's victory was negative. The Bank had behaved stupidly and had lost its fight; but the Bank had been useful to the country, and its enemies had nothing with which to replace it. The condition of the currency became alarming, for there was no adequate control over the state banks. Paper money was printed on little or no security—or on the security of the country's faith that tomorrow must always be richer than today.

Land settlement and land speculation, canal-building in the twenties
and railway-building in the thirties—these had formed the basis for another boom. Between 1829 and 1837, bank loans increased from about
$14,000,000 to $525,000,000; note circulation increased from $48,000,000
to $149,000,000; the number of banks increased from 329 to 788. By 1836
the government was receiving $25,000,000 a year from the sale of public
lands. Foreign money was pouring into the country, adding to the instability—for the foreign money might be suddenly withdrawn because of conditions at the other end of the world.

Even the rapid increase in real wealth could not keep pace with the
increase in paper money and in loans. Jackson realized early in 1836 that
the nation was moving toward disaster.[4] And Benton declaimed in the
Senate: "I did not join in putting down the Bank of the United States,
to put up a wilderness of local banks. I did not join in putting down the
paper currency of a national bank, to put up a national paper currency
of a thousand local banks. I did not strike Caesar to make Antony master
of Rome."[5] This was all very well; but Benton had in fact done exactly
what he said he did not do. And with all Caesar's shortcomings, he was
a better man than Antony.

The Administration—unable to control the state banks directly, and
having destroyed the one agency which could influence them indirectly—
decided that it must at least cease encouraging the state banks to speculate on the federal lands. Benton introduced a resolution requiring that all
payment for public lands be made in specie rather than in bank notes. This
was defeated in the Senate; but after the adjournment the President issued
the "specie circular" as an Executive order. This was a proper step for
anyone who believed, with Jackson, that hard money was the friend of
the plain man, and that speculation and a fluctuating currency were his
enemy; but the step, though proper, came much too late to restore financial health. It could only precipitate a panic, which doubtless had to come
but which was now blamed on Jackson, his policies and his friends. The
crash began in May, 1837, when the New York banks suspended specie
payments. By that time the unhappy Van Buren was President. "Check
the paper mania," Jackson wrote him, "and the republic is safe and your
administration must end in triumph." The advice was good, but Van
Buren could not act upon it. He could make sure that the money issued
by the federal government was sound; but he could not interfere with
the state banks.*

When he destroyed the Bank of the United States, Jackson did away

---

* After the Civil War, the Republican Party was able to tax the wildcat state
bank notes out of existence. It is unlikely, in view of the economic illiteracy of the
country in 1837, that the Western states would have supported Van Buren in such
a measure.

with the only existing brake on credit expansion. When he removed the federal deposits from Philadelphia and distributed them among state banks, Jackson encouraged both a credit and a paper-money inflation. When he and "Old Bullion," as Benton came to be called, urged hard money as the one cure, they were ignoring the fact that their cure would not control the volume of credit money, or check money, and they were also ignoring the fact that their cure could not be enforced upon the states. So the destruction of the national Bank did as much harm as Jackson's enemies predicted, whereas the hard-money policy did very little good. It was left to Van Buren to apply the latter policy under the most trying conditions, with great bravery and stubbornness.

When the panic broke, Van Buren had three choices: he could do nothing, leaving the federal funds with the incompetent state banks; he could admit defeat for Jackson's dearest cause and restore the Bank of the United States; or he could make the federal government, its funds and its currency, independent of all banks. He chose the third course. In a message to Congress on September 4, 1837, he recommended that government funds be stored in an "Independent Treasury" at Washington, and in sub-treasuries throughout the country, and that the government issue its own currency: gold and silver for small units, notes for large units.

> By removing the public funds from the banks [writes Schlesinger], it [the independent Treasury policy] reduced the amount of specie on which paper could be issued and thus had a sobering tendency on the economy. By rejecting bank notes in payment of the revenue, it considerably restricted the power of the banks over the currency. By confining banks to the needs of the commercial community, it held them to "legitimate" economic operations and limited their capacity for redistributing wealth in favor of a single class.[6]

The conservative press of the day took a less cheerful view. "The message is a heartless, cold-blooded attack upon our most valuable and most cherished class of citizens," said the New York *Gazette*. And according to the *National Gazette* of Philadelphia, "It is the incarnation of the Bentonian-Jacksonism—a sophistical sermon on the favorite text of 'Perish commerce —perish credit,' and an ungenerous appeal to the irrational passions of the worst party in the country."[7]

Conservative Democrats, combining with the Whigs, prevented the passage of the Independent Treasury Bill until 1840. The following year, the Whigs repealed the law; but the Democrats revived it in 1846 and it remained in effect until the Civil War. If it was not a solution, at least it was not an aggravation to the vexed money problem of a federal society wherein banks operating under state charters could create a partial chaos no matter how careful and how orthodox was the policy of the central government. In any case, whatever its merits, Van Buren's plan had an interesting effect on the new political alignments, North and South.

Calhoun, as we shall see, had been flirting with the Whigs for several years before 1837; but he had too clear a head to be happy in that camp.* He knew the Whigs wanted a policy of centralized government and aid to capitalism. He believed they were as dangerous to agrarianism as Hamilton himself, except that their power for harm was mitigated by the woolliness of their minds. Calhoun shared the Whig distaste for Jackson; yet he knew that if the South put the Whigs in power the South would be sorry. On the other hand the Democratic Party under Jackson's leadership had shown signs of believing in democracy, and this, he felt, was a fatal creed. The word "democrat," he wrote to Robert Barnwell Rhett in 1838, "as usually understood means those who are in favor of the government of the absolute majority to which I am utterly opposed and the prevalence of which would destroy our system and destroy the South."[8]

What should Calhoun do? The old Democratic Party, built by Jefferson, had at least affirmed states' rights (however much it betrayed them under the pressure of events), and states' rights meant that the majority in one community would be allowed to block the will of the national majority; but Jackson's Democratic Party, with its immensely strengthened presidency, seemed likely to assert the absolute power of the national majority. That way, Calhoun felt sure, lay the death of the nation; but the other way, the Whig way, lay triumphant capitalism and the subjection of the South to the needs of Northern industry. Calhoun could not support either group fervently; but after Van Buren's message to Congress in September, 1837, he did support the Democratic money policy, thus giving unexpected aid to his old rival. He did this because he agreed with the New York and Philadelphia newspapers that the system of divorcing the banks from the state would prove bad for business. Anything which was bad for business would diminish, he hoped, the pressure of Northern capitalism upon the agrarian South.

The Independent Treasury policy also won for Van Buren the backing of the Locofocos of New York.** Throughout the East, farsighted mem-

---

* By 1833 and 1834 the National Republicans (who had held together since John Quincy Adams's Administration in support of the "American System"), plus the states'-rights men who felt that Jackson was wrong on nullification, plus the Northerners who opposed Jackson on the Bank, had become sufficiently numerous and widespread to form a true national Opposition. They began during these years to call themselves the Whig Party, and by 1836 the new name was accepted throughout the country.

** The radical wing of the Democratic Party in that state. In 1828 there had come into being an amorphously organized Workingman's Party, asking for such reforms as free education and the abolition of imprisonment for debt. Like all minor parties, or parties seeking social legislation, this was hampered by the federal system. Constitutionally, only the state legislatures could pass the type of law desired by

bers of the labor movement, and radicals in general, were in favor of "hard money" on the sensible ground that a workman who was paid in state bank notes might find that his wages had no purchasing power. The conservative New York Democrats, on the other hand, cared less for the workman's wages than for the fact that they themselves had profited from Jackson's deposit of federal funds in the state-chartered banks. They were glad to destroy the Bank of the United States; but a plan for really sound money was going too far. Many of them left the Democratic Party in disgust over Van Buren's policy, joining with the Whigs to elect William H. Seward* governor of New York in 1838. In the West, also, many of the old Jacksonians opposed the Independent Treasury. They, too, had profited from the lush days of paper inflation, and they deplored Van Buren's notion that money should have a definable value. Like many of the well-to-do in the East, they wanted to take their chance in a gambler's economy. The industrial workers, and the men with small fixed incomes, and the Southern agrarians, preferred "hard" money. Strangely, because the Locofocos favored it, this became known as a "radical" demand.

Hard money was the nearest approach to a policy which the Jacksonians produced. In so far as they stood for anything consistent, they stood for helping the poor by hindering the money gamblers. And on this issue they found their chief support in the industrial East, not the frontier West. As Mr. Schlesinger has written:

> Eastern ideas rose to supremacy in Washington as Jacksonianism changed from an agitation into a program. . . . The great illusion of historians of the frontier has been that social equality produces economic equalitarianism. In fact, the demand for economic equality is generally born out of conditions of social inequality, and becomes the more passionate, deeply felt, and specific as the inequalities become more rigid. The actual existence of equal opportunities is likely to diminish the vigilance with which they are guarded, and to stimulate the race for power and privilege. The fur capitalists of St. Louis and the land specu-

the Workingman's Party; yet only a national party could survive under the new, rigid, presidential system which put more and more emphasis on "voting the straight ticket." Hence the more practical and politically effective members of the Workingman's Party in New York State merged with the Jacksonian Democrats and became ardent supporters of the "hard-money" policy. In October, 1835, these radicals attended a party caucus at Tammany Hall to protest against the "regular" candidates. At the height of the meeting the gas lights were turned out: the normal Tammany system for quieting dissent. This time the protesters were equipped with candles and with the new friction matches, known as "locofocos." They lit their candles and continued the meeting.

* The brilliant young man from Auburn, New York, who was to become Lincoln's Secretary of State. Seward was thirty-seven when he became governor. He was a lawyer, and a friend and protégé of Thurlow Weed, the Whig "dictator" of New York State. His family were Democrats; but Seward had chosen the Whigs because of his distrust of the Southern slaveholders, and because of his strong belief in internal improvements at federal expense.

lators of Mississippi were as characteristic of the West as Andrew Jackson.[9]

2

Jackson's second important effort, the fight on nullification, suffered from the same weakness as the fight on the Bank: Jackson knew what to attack, but he had no remedy to offer. He could destroy the Bank, but he could not build a just money system; he could oppose nullification, but he could not diminish the sectional injustices and jealousies which were poisoning the national life. He did not know how to build a government which would give enough power to the sections to protect them from oppression, and yet leave enough power in Washington to conduct the public business.

Unhappily, the struggle over nullification was discussed in terms of what was constitutional, not in terms of what was wise. The constitutional argument could satisfy nobody, for it was well known that Jackson, like Webster and like most Americans, was himself a nullifier whenever it suited him—as in the case of the unhappy Cherokees. Relying on the treaties which concluded Jackson's Indian campaigns in 1813 and 1814, the Cherokees had settled peacefully on the lands left to them. Because of their rapid advance in civilization and the arts of peace, and because the cotton gin was giving a new value to their lands, they were soon hated by their white neighbors. Hostile and savage Indians were a nuisance— but only a temporary nuisance, because they could be defeated and ousted. Peaceful and friendly and settled and civilized Indians were more than a nuisance, they were a catastrophe, for if they persisted in behaving themselves it might be difficult to take the land which had been guaranteed them by the United States Government—especially since one of the federal treaties which gave this guarantee had been signed by Andrew Jackson.

Just before Jackson became President, the state of Georgia tore up the federal treaties and annexed the land of the Cherokees and the Creeks. Mississippi and Alabama followed suit, expropriating the Choctaws and Chickasaws. The Cherokees engaged William Wirt of Baltimore, former Attorney General, to take their case before the federal court on the ground that it is unconstitutional for a state to annul a federal contract, whereupon Jackson made a trip into the Indian country to tell the chiefs that their case was hopeless, that even if they won in the courts they would be robbed by their white neighbors. It was a question of robbery with or without murder, and a wise chief would choose the latter.

The Chickasaws and Choctaws gave in; they abandoned seventeen million acres of land in Mississippi and Alabama and moved west across the river. The Cherokees put their faith in the Supreme Court of the United

States and stayed where they were. The state of Georgia extended its jurisdiction over their territory. The Supreme Court upheld the rights of the Indians and ordered Georgia to desist. Georgia paid no heed, and neither did the President.

Another case, arising when Georgia for the second time extended its power over the doomed Cherokees, came before the Supreme Court in 1832. The Court held that Georgia was without authority over the Indians. It is on this occasion that Jackson is reported to have said, "John Marshall has made his decision, now let him enforce it." There is some doubt as to this neat statement of the nullifier's creed; but there is no doubt that Jackson wrote: "The decision of the Supreme Court has fell still born, and they find it cannot coerce Georgia to yield."

It would seem to follow that if the federal government made a law, a decision, or a treaty, which was disliked by the citizens of a state, those citizens might refuse to obey and the President would do nothing. Yet when Calhoun urged the South Carolinians to refuse to obey a federal tariff, Jackson talked of treason and of hanging. The sanction of a law, in other words, depended upon whether the President liked the law. Jackson might have had trouble putting the idea into philosophic terms, yet it was good American doctrine. Jefferson, Madison, Webster, Jackson, Calhoun himself, all found that the demands and decisions of the federal government were sacred when they agreed with them, tyrannous when they didn't. Or to use the language of the American Revolution, they found these demands and decisions backed by natural law when they agreed with them, and opposed by eternal principles when they didn't.

The Tariff of Abominations, as we have seen, led Vice-President Calhoun to write the South Carolina *Exposition;* but he kept the authorship secret and urged his followers to wait for an attempt at peaceful repeal. He thought Jackson, the incoming President, would prove a friend and ally, and it was two years before he knew he was wrong. Meanwhile, in 1829, the *Exposition* was defended in the Senate during a debate on Western land.

The North and the South were bidding for Western votes—the first to maintain, the second to abolish, the tariff. The West wanted cheaper land, or free land if possible. The North could not offer free land, for fear too many of its own factory hands should turn pioneer; so it proposed as an alternative to distribute the proceeds from land sales among the states, with a bonus to those states wherein the lands lay. The ingenious Henry Clay thought this would satisfy the West and at the same time get rid of the surplus revenue, so that the high tariff could not be attacked on the ground that it brought in too much money. The South, on the other hand, felt free to support the West in throwing open the public domain if the West would vote for a reduction in the tariff. "On the outcome of this sectional balance," wrote Professors Morison and Commager, "depended the alignment of parties in the future: even of the Civil War itself. Was it to be North and West against South, or South and West against North?"[10]

In December, 1829, this momentous question came before the Senate. Foot* of Connecticut suggested restricting the sale of public lands to those already on the market. Benton of Missouri opposed the resolution as a typical piece of Eastern hostility toward the West, and called upon the South for help. Hayne of South Carolina responded, precipitating the most famous debate in Congressional history. Hayne quickly got away from the problem of public land onto the problem of the Constitution. He defended the Calhoun doctrine that a state may defy a federal law if it is convinced that the law is unconstitutional. If the federal government was the judge of its own power, argued Hayne, the states were impotent; and if the states were impotent a numerical majority of voters living in the industrial Northeast might impose unbearable conditions upon the entire southern region.

Here was the old problem which had called forth the resistance of Kentucky and Virginia to John Adams, and the resistance of New England to Jefferson: men might submit to a majority of their neighbors, but they would not submit to a majority living a thousand miles away. "Of what value is our representation here," said Hayne, attacking the tariff, when "the imposition is laid, not by the representatives of those who pay the tax, but by the representatives of those who are to receive the bounty?" South Carolina, he argued, was trying to save herself from federal laws which had wrecked her economy and which would soon reduce the South to ruin. By devising means to frustrate an unjust majority, South Carolina was safeguarding the Union.

On January 26, 1830, Daniel Webster replied. The power which Senator Hayne would bestow upon the states, said Webster, belonged to the federal Supreme Court. The Court alone should decide whether Congress had the power to make a law, otherwise the federal government became a rope of sand. In one state the tariff would be null and void; in another state it would be legal; there could be no consistency, and in the end no Union Nullification was treason, and neither a state nor a man could commit treason with impunity. Webster, whose amazing presence made his speeches far more important than the arguments they contained,** concluded with the peroration about "Liberty and Union, now and forever, one and inseparable." Generations of school children were to recite those

---

* Senator Samuel Augustus Foot, like his father before him, spelled the name without a final *e*. His descendants have adopted the longer form.

** Carlyle described Webster's "crag-like face; the dull black eyes under the precipice of brows, like dull anthracite furnaces, needing only to be *blown;* the mastiff

sonorous lines. They helped to attach men's patriotism, in the North and West, to the national rather than the local community. They may well have helped to turn the sentimental Andrew Jackson from the support of state rights, which he had once seemed to favor, to the support of the Union.

On April 13, 1830, a few months after the Hayne-Webster debate, the leaders of the Democratic Party attended a Jefferson Day dinner. It was expected that Jackson, when he spoke, would make clear which side of the debate he favored. The question was vital for the assembled politicians; Jackson's choice would settle whether Calhoun was to be the next President, and whether for the immediate future the Constitution was to be administered according to the logic of Webster or of Hayne. When the time came for the President to give a toast, Jackson rose and pledged "Our Federal Union, it must be preserved!" The nullifiers were undone. Calhoun's plan to unite the South in resistance to centralization was delayed for twenty years, until the slave question had overshadowed the problem of government. The Democratic Party was committed, temporarily, to a nationalism as complete as that of Clay and Webster and John Quincy Adams.

Although Jackson's toast meant that Calhoun would not yet rule the Democratic Party, he still ruled the state of South Carolina. Nullification was defeated as a national solution to the problem of minorities; but it was not defeated in its birthplace. During the summer of 1831 Calhoun issued an *Address to the People of South Carolina,* a restatement of the argument in the *Exposition.* When in July, 1832, Clay won the votes of the West for a new high tariff, Calhoun abandoned passive resistance. In the autumn elections the nullifiers swept the state. The legislature called a convention which passed an "Ordinance of Nullification" declaring that neither the "Tariff of Abominations" nor the new tariff of 1832 was binding upon the people of South Carolina. The legislature also decreed that if goods were seized by federal officers for nonpayment of duties, the owners of the goods might recover twice their value from the officials who seized them. The governor was authorized to call out the militia, and early in 1833 he summoned ten thousand citizens to be ready to repel invasion.

Jackson was the last man in America to be impressed by a threat of

---

mouth accurately closed." Robert Lytton saw Webster when he visited America as a youth in 1850–52. Years later he wrote (*Personal and Literary Letters of the Earl of Lytton,* vol. I, p. 32): "Webster I think on the whole the greatest speaker, or rather the greatest orator, I ever heard. . . . He had a singularly musical and mellow voice. . . . He had a wonderful, an awful, face, with eyes set in caverns, and one might certainly say of him what Sydney Smith said of Lord Thurlow, that the Almighty never made any man as wise as he looked." It was Fox, not Sydney Smith, who made the remark about Lord Thurlow.

force. He prepared the Navy and the Army, talked bravely about hanging Calhoun,* and in December, 1832, issued his Proclamation to the people of South Carolina (the work of Edward Livingston).

> Admit this doctrine [said the Proclamation] and every law for raising revenue may be annulled. . . . I consider, then, the power to annul a law of the United States, assumed by one state, incompatible with the existence of the Union, contradicted expressly by the letter of the Constitution, unauthorized by its spirit, inconsistent with every principle on which it was founded, and destructive of the great object for which it was formed. . . . To say that any state may at pleasure secede from the Union is to say that the United States is not a nation. . . . Disunion by armed force is treason. Are you really ready to incur its guilt? If you are, on the heads of the instigators of the act be the dreadful consequences.

Those are strong words. They did not lead to strong deeds because the country was averse to treating Calhoun and his followers as traitors. South Carolina stood firm; but the rest of the country was of divided mind. In Virginia the powerful group represented by John Tyler was in sympathy with the nullifiers. Opinion in New York was divided. Georgia, Mississippi, and Alabama would not have supported Jackson against South Carolina had he not recently helped them nullify the federal treaties which favored the Indians. Except for the fiery President, there were few who would have executed the leaders of South Carolina with a clear conscience. The country wanted a compromise.

Clay, the skilled and happy compromiser, used his influence to secure a bill which would reduce the tariff over a period of nine years until it stood at twenty per cent. At the same time, as a sop to the nationalists, a "Force Act" was passed, giving the President authority to call out the army and navy to enforce the laws of Congress. South Carolina, having won the reduction of the tariff, repealed her Nullification Ordinance but declared the Force Act null and void. Temporarily the crisis was at an end.

The crisis was at an end, and there was no comment from John Randolph. For the first time in thirty-four years an important political event was not annotated by that singular mind. Randolph of Roanoke was dying. The most faithful of the "Old Republicans," he had broken his career and denied his friendships out of loyalty to the principles of 1798. All his life he had labored to weaken the power of the central government,** and all his life he had watched that power grow: sometimes at the hands of his fellow Virginians, sometimes at the hands of a hated North-

* Marquis James and Hugh Russell Fraser have shown that Jackson was not the cheerful swashbuckler he has often been pictured, when he threatened to hang Calhoun. On the contrary, he was much worried as to what might happen to the country if he was driven to strong measures.

** Except when he supported the Louisiana Purchase.

erner, but most of all at the hands of "this wretched old man," as he described Jackson during the nullification fight. In his last days he saw the start of a new challenge to central power, led by a man as implacable as himself and far more competent. Perhaps he took hope from knowing that the fight would go on; but probably not, since he had long foretold that the fight was lost, that centralization must conquer, and that "my country," as he called Virginia, must fall. Nevertheless, he offered to join the army of South Carolina if Calhoun went to war. Instead of such melodrama, he lived just long enough to see his detested Henry Clay make another compromise. He was too tired to fight. We do not know what baleful flashes of vision and of invective the nation was spared; but we do know that Randolph was not the man to praise a compromise.*

At the height of the conflict Calhoun had resigned the vice-presidency, and in January, 1833, he replaced Hayne in the Senate. The day he took his oath he was looked upon as a brave man who might soon pay with his life for his opinions; but two months later he emerged from the shadow of the gallows with a new prestige. He also emerged as the ally of a new political party. With several of his disciples, Calhoun made overtures to the Whigs. He was warmly welcomed by Henry Clay, for the only conviction demanded of a Whig was that he should dislike Andrew Jackson. Nevertheless Calhoun's association with the new party was to be brief and embarrassed. As we have seen, it was virtually at an end by 1837.

3

Calhoun was born in the South Carolina uplands where Jackson had been born fifteen years before. They both had the same dour Scotch-Irish blood. Unlike the Jacksons, the Calhoun family had been settled for two generations and had begun to prosper. The ambitious boy, therefore, did not push West but stayed at home and married his cousin, Floride, whose mother was Floride Bonneau of the tidewater aristocracy. Calhoun was educated at Yale College and became a lawyer. After his marriage he had enough money to devote himself to public life. He began his Congressional career as a "war-hawk," a nationalist, a promoter of internal improvements to avoid "that greatest of all calamities . . . disunion." During the eighteen-twenties he watched with distress the growth of economic and cultural antagonism between North and South. He sought constitutional means for protecting his minority region. With all his ardent being he still hoped to hold the nation together—but not at the sacrifice of South Carolina. If nationalism meant the exploitation of the farm by the factory, he

---

* He was buried at Roanoke with his face to the West. According to legend, this was so he could "keep an eye on Clay."

must abandon nationalism and give allegiance to his state. It was the greatness of Daniel Webster that he could feel (and make others feel) the beauty and the hope for man that lay in the federal Union; it was the strength of Calhoun that when the choice had to be made his heart had to be given to the hills and villages of his youth. For him, South Carolina was the only unit small enough to be known the way a man should know his country, small enough to be loved. And it may not be irrelevant that the Union, for Massachusetts, meant wealth, but for South Carolina, poverty. Or so it seemed to Calhoun, unless he could exempt his people from the laws passed to benefit other regions, with other interests, climates, institutions.*

He saw America as a nation of dangerous and growing diversity, stretching from the sub-tropical Gulf to the sub-arctic continental plains and containing many races, religions, and economies. The clash of these interests must either split the Union, or subject some regions to a colonial economic status, or else the clash must be restrained. It could not be restrained by force, since if the use of force were permitted those who controlled it would run the country for their own advantage and suppress dissent. How, then, could man's lust for power and wealth be kept from ruining America? Only, he decided, by an agreement that each important interest and each important region must consent to every act of government which impinged upon its affairs. This might be done by giving to each state the right to nullify federal laws which displeased it, or it might be done by constitutional amendment. In either case, the result would be what Calhoun called the rule of the concurrent majority: rule by the agreement of all interested parties.

The fact that such a rule, embodied formally in the Constitution, would thwart all government action did not bother Calhoun. As a traditional American he felt that a government incapable of acting at all would be better than a government free to act as it chose—especially if a mere numerical majority was to do the choosing.** In this, he was a devout "Old

---

* Calhoun exaggerated when he spoke as if the South was suffering "oppression." After the North had accepted Clay's compromise tariff bill of 1833, the South had no serious economic grievance. And in any case, she was to control the federal government most of the time until the Civil War. But Calhoun was alarmed by the growing population of the North, and wished to ensure a minority veto for his state or region while there was still time. In speaking of a future danger as if it were already present, he had good American precedent. Colonial discontent, beginning with the Stamp Act and culminating in the Revolution, was based more upon fear of what Great Britain intended than upon anything that had been done. Professor Samuel Eliot Morison writes (*The American Revolution, 1764–1788, Sources and Documents*, p. xiv): "It is a fair question whether potential rather than actual oppression did not produce the ferment in America."

** In the *Address to the People of South Carolina*, July 26, 1831, he wrote that the "dissimilarity and, as I must add, contrariety of interests in our country . . . are so great that they cannot be subjected to the unchecked will of a majority of

Republican," a faithful son of 1798. But he allowed his logic to triumph over his political wisdom when he asked that the federal government formally commit itself to impotence. The rule of the concurrent majority is a fair description of how the government of a federal empire must operate; it is a fair description, as we shall see, of how in normal times the modern American Government does operate—but only informally, only by custom, and gentlemen's agreements, and the subtle refinements of the party system. All these can be overridden in time of emergency; but in an emergency Calhoun's rigid plan would have condemned the nation to death. Calhoun was a doctrinaire, not a politician in the Anglo-American tradition of practical compromise.

Calhoun was the stern, pessimistic leader of a doomed cause. He was the sleepless enemy of Leviathan; but Leviathan could not be destroyed. If Webster looked too wise for this world, Calhoun looked too tragic. It was not a pose, for he foresaw accurately the ruin of his hopes. Henry Clay pictured him as "tall, careworn, with fevered brow, haggard cheek and eye, intensely gazing, looking as if he were dissecting the last and newest abstraction which had sprung from some metaphysician's brain, and muttering to himself, in half-uttered words, 'This is indeed a crisis!' "

Clay did not believe in crises or in abstractions. He did not believe in the logic by which Calhoun learned that day by day the nation moved closer to disunion. Clay was the assured politician, adept in the conciliations whereby "inevitable" crises were postponed, "inevitable" issues evaded. This time he seemed to be wrong; this time the issue could not be dodged. America was either a nation or a cluster of sovereign states, and some day she must decide which. Yet even so, even where Calhoun's logic was right, Clay was to triumph in the end by temporizing and compromising and denying the plain facts until it was too late for Calhoun to get his way without force, and too late for the force to be effective. Calhoun would have had the South a free nation by 1850; but Clay and the other compromisers postponed the issue until the North was strong enough to win a civil war. Clay did not plan it that way. He merely planned to avoid head-on collisions as long as possible, in the hope that something might turn up. By so doing he became a savior of the Union.

4

The problem of the public domain had been exacerbated rather than settled by the Hayne-Webster debate. The Land Act of 1820, as we saw,

---

the whole without defeating the great end of government, without which it is a curse—justice."

had allowed settlers to buy tracts as small as eighty acres, and for a dollar and a quarter an acre. This was a victory for the Western school (which wanted to dispose of the lands quickly, for the benefit of settlers and speculators alike) over the school of John Quincy Adams (which wanted to hold the lands for a fair price and to use the money for internal improvements and education). Yet even a dollar and a quarter an acre seemed excessive to the West, as the day approached when the national debt would be extinguished. According to the school of Benton, when the federal government no longer needed the money it should either give the land away or give the proceeds to the states. So in 1832 six states asked Congress to sell them the public domain within their own borders and to divide the money among all the states in the Union. The request led to a show of political chicanery which was a warning to the new democracy.

The Jackson men in the Senate referred the matter to the Committee on Manufactures, of which Clay was chairman, rather than to the Committee on Public Lands. "I felt," said Clay, quite correctly, "that the design was to place in my hands a many-edged instrument which I could not touch without being wounded." It was in this report that Clay, unable to persuade his Eastern allies to lower the price of the lands, suggested distributing the proceeds among all the states with a bonus to the states in which the lands lay. The suggestion was ingenious; but the Jackson politicians had only played half their hand. When the Clay report was in, the Senate voted to refer the whole matter, for reconsideration, to the Committee on Public Lands, where it should have gone in the first place. That committee brought in a report written by Thomas Hart Benton, attacking Clay for putting revenue ahead of the interests of the settlers. The Benton report said the price of the lands should be reduced to a dollar an acre, and in five years to fifty cents an acre.

Clay defended his plan in a good speech, and again nothing was done except to reduce the size of the minimum tract from eighty to forty acres. The Jackson men, however, had procured a Clay-Whig report and a Benton-Democratic report to circulate through the Western country, so that the settlers could see which party was willing to offer them the best terms. "The old school of politicians," wrote Claude G. Bowers in discussing this episode, "still gauged public opinion by the roll-calls of the Congress. The new school, which came in with Jackson, were least of all concerned with the views of the politicians at the capital. They were interesting themselves with the plain voters, and were devising means for reaching these in the campaign to follow."[11] Unhappily, the "new school" did not interest itself in the plain voters with an eye to what would do them good, but with an eye to what would trick them into voting for the members of the school.

Nothing useful resulted from the elaborate game which had been played upon Clay. The moment when the proceeds from the public lands were no longer needed to pay the national debt was the moment to face the problem of a permanent land policy. Instead of seeking to deal with the problem, the "new school" treated itself to some low japery and left the matter where it was. Neither the Adams plan nor the Benton plan was adopted. The lands were not used to endow a democratic educational system for the entire nation. Neither were they made secure, at the lowest price, for genuine settlers. They were left at the mercy of the speculator. And the land problem was left, like other major problems, to become entangled with the slavery fight and thus help promote the catastrophe of war.

As late as the decade of 1840–50 the question of free land was discussed apart from the question of slavery. "Hayne of South Carolina, Thomasson of Kentucky, Smith and Ficklin of Illinois, Murphy of New York, Mc-Connell of Alabama, and Andrew Johnson of Tennessee all advocated the principle in one form or another. The important point . . . is that the demand came from every quarter; . . . but in the next decade the question became strictly sectional."[12]

In 1851, Andrew Johnson introduced a homestead bill* which was supported by thirty-three Southern members of the House and opposed by thirty. In 1859 the same bill received only three Southern votes—one each from Kentucky, Tennessee, and Missouri. The merits or demerits of free land no longer mattered. The Southerners were against it; the new Republican Party was solidly for it; slavery had made even the use of land into a sectional struggle. The reason usually given is that the South awoke to the knowledge that the Homestead Act would favor the small farmer rather than the planter, and thus encourage free labor rather than slave labor. It is hard to see why this should have become clear in the eighteen-fifties if it was not clear in the eighteen-forties. Professor Webb offers a more plausible reason. Profitable large-scale slavery, on the whole, was confined to the cotton plantation, and by 1850 the cotton kingdom in its westward march had almost reached the 98th meridian—that fateful divide in American climate, geography, and life. West of 98° lay the Great Plains, where there was no timber and the rainfall dropped to less than twenty inches a year, and in places to less than ten. West of 98° the animals, the plants, the Indians, the life of the white man, changed radically; in fact, the white man jumped this vast region at first, carrying the frontier straight to the Pacific Ocean, not seeking to settle the Plains until he had devised new institutions and new machinery: the cattle ranch, the stock farm, barbed wire, the tin windmill, and the Colt six-shooter.

There was no place for the cotton kingdom, with its pampered institu-

* Granting free land to genuine settlers.

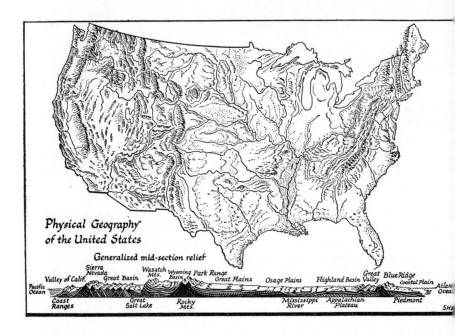

Physical Geography
of the United States

Generalized mid-section relief

Pacific Ocean — Coast Ranges — Valley of Calif. — Sierra Nevada — Great Basin — Great Salt Lake — Wasatch Mts. — Wyoming Basin — Park Range — Rocky Mts. — Great Plains — Osage Plains — Mississippi River — Highland Basin — Appalachian Plateau — Great Valley — Blue Ridge — Piedmont — Coastal Plain — Atlantic Ocean

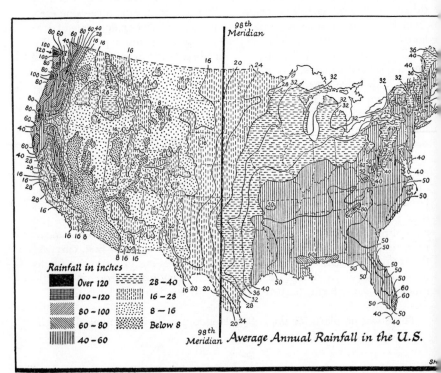

98th Meridian

Rainfall in inches

Over 120	28 – 40
100 – 120	16 – 28
80 – 100	8 – 16
60 – 80	Below 8
40 – 60	

Average Annual Rainfall in the U.S.

tion of slavery, in the rough world west of 98°; and the cotton plantation was already prevented from spreading north, both by law and by climate.

> The southern opposition to the Homestead Act [wrote Professor Webb] grew out of the fact that it was to apply in a region from which plantations, and therefore, slaves, were barred by the laws of nature. By 1850 the cotton kingdom had expanded about as far as it could go to the West. . . . It was bounded on the north by cold; it was bounded on the west by aridity. . . . Had the southern portion of the Great Plains been suitable to cotton, the South would have had possession of it before an issue arose, and would have continued in favor of free land as it was in the beginning. The point that has been overlooked is that the land was useless to the South, even though it was free.[13]

In 1832, however, the frontier was well east of the 98th meridian. In 1832, the land question might have been solved forever, without sectional bitterness, if the politicians had been less crafty.

When the South turned decisively against free land, in the eighteen-fifties, the North espoused it. The long opposition of Eastern industry was silenced by the argument that free land was the price of Western votes for a high tariff. "Vote yourself a farm" and "Vote yourself a tariff" became the campaign cries during the election which put Lincoln into the White House. The South had bought almost thirty years of low tariff by offering very cheap land; the North was now to buy generations of high tariff by offering land for nothing. So the final alignment was North and West against South: an alignment which created desperation in the South and thus made disunion more likely.* The difficulties of maintaining a federal empire had been needlessly aggravated by the failure to deal with the Western lands in time.

5

The first task of the politicians gathered about Jackson was to please as many groups as possible in the loose coalition which had put the Democrats in power. There was reason to hope that the Eastern workers, and the poor in general, would be pleased by the war on the Bank, that the North and most of the West would be pleased by the attack on nullification, and that the West would also be pleased by the demagogic treatment of the public land question. The planters of Alabama and of inland Georgia were unquestionably pleased by the betrayal of the Indians; but what of the tidewater planters, a number of whom Van Buren had lured

---

* As we shall see, this alignment was greatly strengthened by the Southern failure to compete with the North in railway-building.

into the Jackson coalition? The further the President turned from states' rights toward the Webster view of the Union, the more these men would feel cheated. What could be done to cheer them? For the sake of party unity and discipline Van Buren was ready to lose some of the original Jackson votes, but never by default, never without making a fight to hold them. The planters, with their immense social influence, represented many votes and much power. Such a group must not be allowed to feel forgotten. The best way to calm their fears at the drift away from states' rights would be to perform some symbolic act in praise of states' rights—such as the veto of a bill for internal improvements at federal expense. For Jackson, such a veto would have the added charm of undermining Henry Clay and his American System.

Internal improvements, however, were popular among the Western grain-growers, so the veto should apply to as small a project as possible: something which would sound important in the South, unimportant in the West. Such political gems are hard to find, so the search was assigned to the past-master, Van Buren. "It was understood between us," wrote Van Buren, "that I should keep an eye upon the movements of Congress and bring to his [Jackson's] notice the first Bill upon which I might think his interference would be preferable."[14]

Biding his time, Van Buren found the perfect article: a bill authorizing federal subscription of stock for a twenty-mile highway lying entirely in Kentucky, Henry Clay's state. By ignoring the fact that the little "Maysville Road" was intended to be a link in the long road to New Orleans, Jackson could attack it as a selfish local project which could not possibly come under the head of the "general welfare." The bill was so exactly what the Administration wanted that Van Buren was afraid Clay's friends would learn what was afoot and would "substitute a bill for a work more national in its pretensions."[15] He begged the General for once to be discreet, and three pages of his *Autobiography* are given to a description of Jackson's droll but unsuccessful efforts to take his advice. The veto, nevertheless, was a success.* The Democrats lost votes to Clay in Kentucky and Ohio; but most of the country was indifferent, and the Southern planters were temporarily placated. Even Hayne of South Carolina spoke of the veto as "the most auspicious event which had taken place in the history of the country for years past." Van Buren had achieved the *grand coup* of American politics: he had gratified a powerful group of supporters, in an important region, at the cost of a minimum of votes elsewhere, and without disturbing the country as a whole. This is a maneuver which must frequently be attempted by American national leaders. It is the price of such unity as they can impose upon their precarious coalitions; but it does not make for logic or consistency.

* May 27, 1830.

The Maysville Bill was one of twelve bills vetoed by Jackson. His six predecessors, during a period of forty years, had vetoed only nine bills between them. The change is a sign of the new type of people's presidency. Jackson told the Senate that he alone was "the direct representative of the people, elected by the people, and responsible to them," whereas the Senate itself was "a body not directly amenable to the people." It followed, in Jackson's mind, that he must if necessary protect the people from the acts of the legislature; not merely from such acts as were unconstitutional but from such acts as were unwise.

The Senate cried out against this novel view of the President's office; but it cried in vain. "Really and in practice," said Henry Clay a few years later, "this veto power drew after it the power of initiating laws, and in its effects must ultimately amount to conferring on the executive the entire legislative power of the government. With the power to initiate and the power to consummate legislation, to give vitality and vigor to every law, or to strike it dead at his pleasure, the President must ultimately become the ruler of the nation."[16] And again he said, "the veto is hardly reconcilable with the genius of representative government. It is totally irreconcilable with it if it is to be employed in respect to the expediency of measures, as well as their constitutionality." Under such circumstances, "the government will have been transformed into an elective monarchy."*

Webster and Calhoun protested as bitterly, and to as little effect. What Clay said about the power of the presidency was true, so long as the people were willing to support the President as they supported Jackson. The veto messages, written by the Kitchen Cabinet for popular consumption, became an effective form of campaign literature and a device for carrying the President's ideas into every cottage. No member of Congress could command such an audience. If the Senate felt itself diminished by the Jacksonian presidency, which in Clay's words was an "elective monarchy," the House of Representatives mourned its own decline with even more reason.

> The democratic revolution [wrote Ford] overthrew the pillars of its greatness. It ceased to make Presidents; it ceased to control them. Instead of being the seat of party authority—the motive force of the administration—it became in this respect merely a party agency. National party purposes, having to seek their fulfilment through the presidential office, had nothing to ask of the House but obedience to party demands, and at once began the task of devising machinery to enforce submission.[17]

* President Franklin Roosevelt vetoed 631 Acts of Congress.

6

At the end of his second term, in 1837, Jackson retired to "The Hermitage," his farm near Nashville, Tennessee. He did not seek to maintain in retirement the influence over his old associates which Jefferson had kept up until the end. Perhaps he felt that his work was done, that his task had been to alter institutions, rather than to make policy. He and his friends had remodeled the Executive and the political parties; they had changed the nature of the American Government; but they had not succeeded in using the new forms to deal effectively with the old problems. They failed to solve the money question, though at least they prevented it from being solved badly. They failed to solve the question that lay back of nullification—how to run a country the size of an empire, on democratic principles, without sacrificing regional minorities to the greed of the people who can muster the most votes. They failed to solve the tangled problem of the public lands. And for the most part they failed even to admit the problem of slavery.

One intangible asset they bequeathed to the future: the symbolic figure of Jackson. In the American mind the word "Jackson" means the buoyant and hopeful youth of democracy. It means a fighting friend for the people, a friend who could not be terrorized. It means a proper contempt for the power of mere finance. From the time of Jackson, no American has doubted that a man working for the people's good can be as relentlessly stubborn as any tyrant.

Andrew Jackson died in 1845. It is a legend in Tennessee that one of his slaves was asked if he thought the General had gone to heaven. The reply came without hesitation: "Of course he went to heaven—*if he took a mind to.*"

XIV

The Rise of the Whigs

The election of 1836 was unusual in several ways. The Democratic nominating convention—the second in the history of the party—had been held eighteen months before, during the spring of 1835. Jackson had insisted on this because his health was declining and he feared that he might soon be too tired to dominate his own party. State legislatures and state conventions were already putting forward a variety of candidates; but Jackson meant to prove that there was only one Democratic Party, of which he was the master, and that the party had only one choice for the presidency: Van Buren.

Strict discipline, backed by federal patronage, was imposed upon the delegates. In theory, these delegates were "fresh from the people," representing the considered wishes of the electorate; in fact, they were a collection of docile party workers, representing nothing but the orders which the local machines had given them. The rule of 1832, that each state should send as many delegates as it had presidential electors, was not observed; each state sent as many delegates as could be trusted to do what they were told. Maryland, for example, sent 181 delegates (out of a total of 626), whereas Illinois, South Carolina, and Alabama sent none.*

Van Buren was unanimously nominated on the first ballot. Colonel Richard Johnson of Kentucky,** his most powerful rival, was chosen for

---

* The convention met in Baltimore. The figures are taken from Frank Kent's *The Democratic Party.*

** Johnson was born in 1780, at Beargrass, a settlement on the site of Louisville, Kentucky. He was one of the first national figures to be a native of the new West. He went to the House of Representatives, where he supported the War of 1812. During the war, as colonel of a regiment of mounted Kentucky riflemen, he was a popular and successful leader. He was badly wounded at the battle of the Thames. When he recovered he returned to Congress, serving in the House until 1819, and then in the Senate until 1829. After 1825 he became a faithful follower of Jackson; but he never did or said anything of importance. As a candidate for the presidential nomination, he was chiefly interesting because of his illegitimate daughters by a mulatto slave whom he had inherited from his father. Johnson, who was unmarried, made no concealment of the affair. He brought his girls up as educated and privileged young women. They both married white men, and inherited from their father. As a result of this openness, Virginia disapproved of Johnson, even as a vice-presidential candidate, and in 1836 he failed to get a majority of the electoral vote. He thus became the only Vice-President ever elected by the Senate—under Article II, Section 1 of the Constitution. He served inconspicuously, and retired to private life in 1841.

the vice-presidency. There were no nominating speeches, the chairman remarking that "the rule against them is intended to prevent any violent, angry and unnecessary discussion that might otherwise arise." He flattered the patient sheep, who had been sent to do Jackson's bidding, by assuming that they could rouse themselves to violence or anger. Yet in spite of the autocracy, and of the humbug inseparable from such a boss-ridden convention, there is little doubt that Van Buren was the best man available. Jackson insisted on his own way to the end, and his own way continued useful for the nation.

The Whigs, meanwhile, decided not to spend their frail strength on one candidate, but to back a local favorite in several of the main regions. They hoped to keep Van Buren from receiving a majority, and thus throw the election into the House of Representatives. In the Southwest they chose Senator Hugh Lawson White of Tennessee, an old friend and supporter of Jackson who had been alienated by the dwindling of Western influence in the Democratic Party, and by the ascendancy of the Easterner, Van Buren, and of the radical Locofocos. In the Northeast, Daniel Webster was the Whig candidate. In the Southeast, Calhoun was expected to be cold to Van Buren even if he was not warm to the Whigs. And in the Northwest, a truly remarkable candidate was unearthed: William Henry Harrison, clerk of the court of common pleas in Cincinnati, a quiet, unsuccessful gentleman of sixty-three who in 1811 had led a thousand troops against the Indians at Tippecanoe Creek and had lost 188 of his own men in the course of the indecisive engagement. This harmless ex-Virginian was destined to become the symbol for all that was absurd in the new type of democratic politics. No sooner had Harrison been nominated by his friends, in the summer of 1835, than Nicholas Biddle wrote a set of instructions for the campaign:

"Let him say not one single word about his principles, or his creed—let him say nothing—promise nothing. Let no Committee, no convention —no town meeting ever extract from him a single word, about what he thinks now, or what he will do hereafter. Let the use of pen and ink be wholly forbidden as if he were a mad poet in Bedlam."

Here was a course of action well suited to Harrison's taste and training. He adopted it literally, and with striking success. Whereas White carried only Tennessee and Georgia in the election, and Webster only Massachusetts, the silent and penless Harrison won seven states. This was not enough to deprive Van Buren of a majority (he won 170 electoral votes to 124 for all his opponents); but it was plenty to set the politicians thinking about the value of a candidate who was so little known that nobody disliked him and so ambiguous that nobody could attack him with clarity. It had hitherto been assumed that popularity was useful in a candidate; it now dawned on the professionals that the absence of unpopularity might be more important. The new party machines could "get out the vote" for any-one who was not actively disliked, and by the simplest process of ballyhoo they could make a nonentity into a national figure within a few months. Failing an uncommonly popular candidate like Jackson, whose friends were so numerous that they could overwhelm his foes, might it not be better to have a synthetic candidate like Harrison, with no friends and no foes? Might it not be better to elect a Harrison, who could be invented to suit the needs of the moment, than a Clay or a Webster—men of recalci-trant reality, who were widely known, widely loved, and widely hated? The questions were to be well explored in 1840.*

2

Van Buren's Inaugural Message was a gentle and sensible sermon in praise of democracy, combined with an attempt to persuade both North and South that there was no reason why they should not live together amicably. Van Buren was to show courage and character when he finally came to see that the slave question could not be dodged; but in 1837 his political training still made it impossible for him to believe that both sides would not compromise if properly soothed and flattered. At the famous Jefferson Day dinner during the nullification crisis (when Jackson de-clared his enmity to Calhoun and the South Carolina doctrine by the toast, "Our Federal Union, it must be preserved"), Van Buren's toast had been, "Mutual forbearance and reciprocal concessions." In this he was true to his calling. It is a major task of American politics to promote reciprocal concessions.

In addition to his faith that good politics meant avoiding crises, Van Buren held that good government meant doing as little as possible. In his message to Congress on the Independent Treasury Bill (September 4, 1837), he wrote:

Those who look to the action of this Government for specific aid to the citizen to relieve embarrassments arising from losses by revulsions in commerce and credit lose sight of the ends for which it was created and the powers with which it is clothed. It was established to give security to us all in our lawful and honorable pursuits. . . . It was not intended to confer special favors on individuals or on any classes of them, to

* "Since 1840," say Professors Morison and Commager (*The Growth of the American Republic*, vol. I, pp. 451–52), "successful presidential candidates have not been prominent and experienced statesmen, but military heroes or relatively obscure men who have not had time to make enemies. Only by inadvertence, as in the case of Lincoln and the Roosevelts, did the President prove to be a man of out-standing ability." This is a sobering thought. The same system of party politics which gives untold powers to the President tends to insure that the President shall

create systems of agriculture, manufactures, or trade. . . . All communities are apt to look to government for too much. Even in our own country, where its powers and duties are so strictly limited, we are prone to do so, especially at periods of sudden embarrassment and distress. But this ought not to be. The framers of our excellent Constitution and the people who approved it . . . wisely judged that the less government interferes with private pursuits the better for the general prosperity. . . . Its real duty—that duty the performance of which makes a good government the most precious of human blessings—is to enact and enforce a system of general laws commensurate with, but not exceeding, the objects of its establishment, and to leave every citizen and every interest to reap under its benign protection the rewards of virtue, industry, and prudence.

This is pure Jefferson. It is the doctrine implicit in the optimistic philosophy of natural rights. This philosophy denies that man is by nature given to evil and to error, denies that he can only be saved by institutions and by authority; it affirms that he is sufficiently endowed with reason and with conscience so that if government will let him alone (will confer upon him "the blessings of liberty") he can find his own way to a good life. Liberty, for the eighteenth-century believer in natural rights, meant civil liberties and the absence of government interference. It meant, in Carl Becker's words, "the happy idea that the best way to serve the inalienable rights of man is just to leave the individual as free as possible to do what he likes, and that accordingly no form of government can secure them so well as the one that governs least."[1] This "happy idea" grew up in the pre-industrial world, when man suffered more from the officiousness of church and state than from the insecurity, the unemployment, and the breadlines which have accompanied the machine age. Van Buren was the first American President to learn that in a time of fear and want men do not appreciate lectures on laissez-faire.

The Panic of 1837 lasted throughout Van Buren's term, which explains why he found it necessary to protest that people "are apt to look to government for too much." Van Buren sat tight, divorced the government from all connection with the banks, and hoped that his party organization would see him through. He went much farther than Jackson in the use of federal patronage, and in readiness for 1840 he prepared an elaborate, smooth, and disciplined machine.

---

be unfit to use them; yet in that case the powers are not conferred upon anybody else, so it is no wonder if the public business sometimes lags. By a remarkable series of accidents the system has so far worked without disaster, for not only did Lincoln and Franklin Roosevelt turn out to be strong when they were expected to be feeble, but Theodore Roosevelt was put into the White House by the accident of death, and James K. Polk, a typical politician's "dark horse," proved a winner. It is a question whether the United States should continue to stake the future on such haphazard strokes of good fortune.

The Democratic Party had become more homogeneous, more easy to manage, since the days when Van Buren had built it out of whatever bits and pieces were available. The party had begun as a crazy coalition of anti-Adams men who were prevailed upon to vote for Jackson, not because they liked him but because they thought he might beat the New Englander. Little by little, as Jackson defined his views, he lost sections of his following; but his knowledge of the people's mind, and of their hopes, was so acute that he never lost ten votes without winning a dozen. His party was stronger than ever when he stepped down, and more united.

He lost the missionaries and the Quakers when he betrayed the Indians; he lost the more ardent friends of internal improvements with the Maysville veto; he lost the followers of Calhoun when he made Van Buren his heir; he lost the states'-rights men in Virginia, and many of the planters throughout the seaboard, when he made bitter war on nullification; his hard-money policy lost him all the gamblers who had supported the attack on the Bank because they preferred a wildly fluctuating currency. The same money policy, however, won him the mass of the new urban workers; the Indian policy won him the Northwestern wheat farmers as well as the inland Southern planters; the fight against nullification won him the many simple Northerners and Westerners who were growing steadily more distrustful of the slave power. Without intending it, Jackson was building a farmer-labor party, a party predominantly of the plain people. When Van Buren went "locofoco" with his Independent Treasury Bill, this class alignment became clearer; the Democrats were the party of the poor, the Whigs the party of property. Within a very few years, however, regional strife was to prove stronger than the economic bond of interest, and was to break the Jacksonian alliance.

"Jacksonian Democracy," as a people's movement, was born about the time of the destruction of the Bank, after the election of 1832; it was dead, or dying, by 1844, when the Democratic National Convention refused to endorse the Declaration of Independence in the party platform. The Declaration, as an epitome of the natural-rights philosophy, had been the battle cry of the Jacksonians. In 1840, Van Buren and the Locofocos could still force it into the national platform; but it was not praised again by the Democratic Party until long after the Civil War. By the end of the decade, the farmer-labor party of Jackson had been captured by the slave power and made to serve a cause that would not have been owned by the author of the Declaration. Jacksonian Democracy perished; but the Democratic Party machine remained.*

Party organization was by this time completed. Except for the addition of women, it has changed little from Van Buren's day to the present. The

---

* In 1932 and 1936 the Democratic Party of Franklin Roosevelt had many resemblances to that of Jackson.

essential feature of the party machines was that they operated in three spheres simultaneously: the federal sphere, the state sphere, and the municipal or county sphere. Nothing should be said or done in any one sphere which would prejudice the party's chances in either of the other spheres. Hence the preference for saying and doing very little. At every moment the professional party worker had to consider national interests, parochial interests, regional interests, and class interests. Nobody could reconcile these interests completely; but it was the task of the politician to reconcile as many as possible, or better still to alienate as few as possible. Victory would belong to the party which either appealed to the maximum of interests in the maximum of regions, or which succeeded in annoying nobody, so that it received the votes of all the people who disliked any part of the opposition program. On the whole, the politicians felt safer in this negative position. They felt that less could go wrong. Hence the charm of a candidate such as William Henry Harrison. Since he did not, in any real sense, exist, he could be "filled in" by the local party workers to fit the emotions of the day and the place. A man like Clay—even a man like the tranquil Van Buren after he had been long in public life—was known to have certain ideas and plans. There was no use promising that he would go counter to all the causes for which he had stood; but in the name of a man like Harrison, who stood for zero, anything (and indeed everything) could be promised. The strength of a Harrison depended on his capacity to keep quiet, and on the energy and inventiveness of the local party workers.

The party workers, meanwhile, were becoming steadily more numerous as the new state constitutions created more and more elective offices, and in many cases decreed shorter and shorter terms of office.* The more jobs were available, and the more rapid the turnover in each job, the easier it was to hold the machine together and to reward the faithful. Also, the system of the nominating convention was being extended into local politics, with useful results in the way of multiplying jobs and titles.

> Local caucuses sent delegates to county conventions for nominating candidates to county office; county conventions sent delegates to state conventions for nominating state candidates, and to district conventions

---

*It is no wonder that Bryce, writing in 1887, was struck by the number of people in America who made political work the chief business of their lives. He estimated that there were hundreds of thousands of such people (there would of course be far more today), whereas in England (including editors and other political writers) he thought there were about 3500. The chief reason for the difference is that a rigid and numerous political organization is needed to make the American Constitution, with its division of powers, workable, and that the only device which has been found for holding such an organization together is the spoils system, which produces even more politicians than are needed.

for nominating congressional candidates; state conventions sent delegates to the quadrennial national conventions for nominating the presidential candidates and drafting the platform. . . . Every state had its captains of hundreds and captains of thousands, working for the party every day in the year, and looking for reward to the spoils of victory.[2]

3

William Henry Harrison was born in Charles City County, Virginia, in 1773. On both sides of the family his ancestry was distinguished. His father was Benjamin Harrison, a member of the Continental Congress, a signer of the Declaration of Independence, and three times governor of Virginia. Harrison was educated at Hampton-Sidney College, and then studied medicine under the famous Dr. Benjamin Rush at Philadelphia. His father died in 1791. Finding himself in financial difficulties, Harrison entered the army as an ensign. He had an uninspired but blameless military career, in the course of which he married Anna Symmes—daughter of the pioneer, John Cleves Symmes, who was largely responsible for the founding of Cincinnati. In 1798, having risen to the rank of captain, Harrison resigned to become Secretary of the Northwest Territory. The next year he was elected the territory's first delegate to Congress. As chairman of the House Committee on Public Lands, he reported the bill which became the Land Act of 1800.

The year the bill became law, John Adams appointed Harrison governor of the Indiana Territory, an office which he held until 1812. He was expected by the federal government to look after the interests of the Indians and at the same time to make sure that they ceded as much land as possible to the United States. He can scarcely be blamed for failing in this double task and for incurring the hostility of the Indians whom he had done his best to help. When the Indians attempted to form a league to fight for their lands, Harrison led a combined force of militia and regular troops against them. The result was the battle of Tippecanoe, famous in politics but inconclusive in warfare, for although the Indians withdrew they reoccupied the land a few months later.*

In the course of the War of 1812, Harrison rose to the rank of major general and to the command of the Army of the Northwest. In September and October, 1813, troops under his command reoccupied Detroit and won an important victory against Major General Proctor on the River Thames. It was at this battle that Colonel Richard Johnson of Kentucky,

---

* During the period when he was governor of the Indiana Territory, Harrison's eldest son was born—a boy who was to have a minor political career and to become the father of the twenty-third President of the United States.

Van Buren's Vice-President, made his name. Harrison's reputation was not enhanced, although the criticisms brought against him may have been unjust.* In any case, he soon fell out with the Secretary of War and resigned from the Army.

After the war Harrison settled at North Bend, on the Ohio River below Cincinnati, where he ran his farm and engaged in a number of unsuccessful commercial ventures. From 1816 to 1819 he served inconspicuously in the House of Representatives, and in 1825 was elected to the United States Senate. Three years later President Adams made him the first United States Minister to Colombia. In 1829, after Jackson had sent a successor to take his place, he stirred up so much trouble that the Colombian Government threatened to arrest him. Returning to America, he retired once more to North Bend where he suffered further financial reverses, becoming dependent for a living on his farm and on his salary as clerk of the court of common pleas. There seemed every reason to think that his modest career was at an end; but suddenly the Whigs unearthed him to serve as their Northwestern candidate in 1836.**

As we have seen, he won seven states and seventy-three electoral votes. He and Clay were therefore the leading candidates when the next Whig nominating convention met at Harrisburg, Pennsylvania, in December 1839. The party was unencumbered with ideas or principles. It was devoted to the single and simple task of rounding up everyone in the country who could be induced to vote against Van Buren—just as the Jackson men in 1828 had been devoted solely to collecting the enemies of John Quincy Adams.

Clay was too well known, too strong a leader, too positive a character, to satisfy the party bosses at Harrisburg. They were afraid that Clay might alienate somebody, somewhere, who might otherwise cast a Whig vote. And they knew that Clay would talk, if he were nominated. He would make speeches; he might even put something in writing. Every time a candidate said anything which could be understood, he was likely to lose somebody's vote. If Van Buren had been a popular and dynamic figure, it might have been necessary to oppose him with a man like Clay; but Van Buren was a pedestrian President, burdened with the long depression which had begun in 1837. He had nothing but his party machine to help him, and in a contest of machines the Whigs preferred not to be handicapped by a candidate with a known record. Under the guidance of Thurlow Weed of New York (the Whig counterpart of

* The *Dictionary of American Biography* deals with them in the following cautious words: "He was not a great general, but he served to the best of his ability in the face of great difficulties; and the controversies over his valor and ability . . . were regrettable rather than conclusive."

** Presumably they chose him because his name was linked with the Land Act of 1800, a famous and popular measure in the Northwest.

Van Buren), they chose the mouselike Harrison.* For the vice-presidency they nominated John Tyler of Virginia, a leader of the states'-rights group who had opposed Jackson's removal of the bank deposits, and also his stand on nullification, and who was therefore considered an honorary Whig.

4

Needless to say, the campaign of 1840 was absurd. Neither Harrison nor any party leader was to say "a single word about what he thinks now or will do hereafter"; so it was necessary to find some other topic for speech-making. This was supplied by a Democratic editor. The farmhouse where Harrison had been living for ten years had formerly been a log cabin, and the General was said to drink cider with his meals. So a foolish Baltimore newspaper called him the "log cabin and hard cider" candidate. Delighted with the phrase, the Whigs pictured Harrison as a son of toil who could be trusted to understand all humble men, and whose life proved how cynical was the suggestion that the Whigs favored the moneyed classes. On the contrary, the Whigs were happy only in the simplest surroundings and with the simplest drinks.

Not only was Harrison made into the frontiersman's friend, but he became a military hero. It seemed that the battle of Tippecanoe was the crisis in American history. "Tippecanoe and Tyler too," was the chief campaign slogan, varied at times with the more practical statement: "Harrison, two dollars a day, and roast beef." The campaign songs were on the order of the following:

> Let Van from his coolers of silver drink wine
>> And lounge on his cushioned settee.
> Our man on his buckeye couch can recline,
>> Content with hard cider is he,
> The iron-armed soldier, the true-hearted soldier,
> The gallant old soldier of Tippecanoe!

Or, more briefly:

> Farewell, dear Van,
> You're not our man;
> To guide the ship
> We'll try old Tip.

* Webster had withdrawn his name before the convention, knowing that he had no chance. Clay sat drinking and cursing in a Washington hotel, waiting for the bad news. When it came he cried out, "My friends are not worth the powder and shot it would take to kill them!"

The fact that Harrison had been born into the wealthy planter class in Virginia, and that his family had held the highest positions for generations, did not interfere with the success of the log-cabin nonsense. Nobody knew anything about Harrison—and nobody ever would, if the Whigs had their way. A committee was set up to answer all his letters, and to make sure that the answers were meaningless. When the old gentleman appeared in public, which was seldom, he put aside his silk hat and wore a broad-brimmed rustic model.[3] Having contrived, by persistent inability, to sink from the top of the pile to well down toward the middle, Harrison found himself transformed into a proof of how men rise by merit in America. Van Buren, meanwhile, was transformed into an aristocrat who scented his whiskers with cologne, drank nothing but champagne, and laced himself in corsets. Yet Van Buren's father had been a tavern keeper at Kinderhook, without the means to give his son an education.

At the age of fourteen, Van Buren had begun to study law in his spare time. At the age of nineteen he went to New York City, where he suffered from extreme poverty, until at twenty-one he was admitted to the bar and began to make a difficult living. In 1807, at the age of twenty-five, he married his childhood sweetheart, who died in 1819 after bearing four sons. In the year after his marriage Van Buren got his first political job. Thereafter his rise was rapid, as state senator, attorney-general for New York, member and then leader of the "Albany Regency," United States Senator, and finally backer of Andrew Jackson. He was in fact the self-made "man of the people" that Harrison was praised for being; he was also the inventor of the political methods which the Whigs were turning against him. He had played all these tricks, and more, on John Quincy Adams; yet there is no record that he was amused to have them played on himself.

The result of the lying, diverting, irrelevant campaign was that Harrison received 234 electoral votes and Van Buren 60.* J. Q. Adams's comment was as follows: "If Harrison is not found time-serving, demagogic, unsteady, and Western-sectional, he will more than satisfy my present expectations." Adams knew more about Harrison than most of the voters, for Adams (at Clay's request) had sent him to Colombia.

The world has seen many curious campaigns since 1840, but nothing quite like this. The entire performance might have been invented by a satirist to show how silly democratic politics can be. Every weakness of the American party system was exaggerated: the tendency to choose

---

* The Van Buren machine had not done as badly as the electoral votes suggest. Van Buren lost Pennsylvania by 349 votes out of more than 287,000. He lost Maine by 401 votes out of 93,000; New Jersey by 2317 votes out of 64,385; and New York by 13,000 votes out of half a million (figures compiled by Hugh Russell Fraser). So a change of about 8000 votes would have made the electoral college result: Van Buren 154; Harrison 140.

inconspicuous and feeble candidates; the tendency to substitute songs, or other loud noises, for a discussion of issues; the tendency to promise, in private, all things to all people, while avoiding in public any language which could be construed to mean anything, in the hope that commitments made to New England manufacturers will not be heard south of the Potomac, while commitments made to the planters will never reach the West; the swirling, roaring atmosphere of circus, football game, and county fair; the joyful feeling that the election matters more than anything else in the world, combined with the still more joyful feeling that it is just a sport and does not really matter at all. The Harrison campaign was the first to combine all these features, and it combined them in a more preposterous form than has ever since been attained. Perhaps this is because America has never again been quite so lighthearted. The many unsolved problems, whose existence the politicians denied, produced a mounting tension after 1840. The country could no longer ignore all the storm warnings. And after the storm had passed, after the Civil War, the country had lost its innocence. There were to be many imitations of 1840; but they did not seem so exuberant or so funny.

5

What was the Whig Party which won its first victory through these comic-opera methods? A partial answer may be found by asking, who was left out of the loose alliance which formed the Democratic Party? Who felt threatened, or challenged, by the mildly radical mass-movement of the Jacksonians?

First and most obvious, there were the old followers of Adams and Clay, who had begun to call themselves National Republicans before the election of 1828. They became the solid center of the Whig Party, for they were not merely anti-Jackson men. They believed in something positive, the "American System": a tariff to help the Eastern manufacturer, and internal improvements (financed by the tariff) to bind the country together and incidentally to help the farmer reach the growing urban markets. The well-to-do grain growers; the sheep and cattle farmers of the Northwest; the tobacco farmers of Tennessee and Kentucky; the sugar planters of Louisiana—these had remained faithful to the "American System," and when added to the Eastern manufacturers they made a good beginning for a party.

They were only a beginning, however, as had been shown in the election of 1832 when the National Republicans fought their last campaign. Henry Clay was the candidate, and he challenged Jackson on the Bank charter. He thought he had found a popular issue, yet he did less well than John

Quincy Adams had done in 1828. The party of the "American System"
clearly needed new allies, if not a new name.

A number of the allies were attracted, as we have seen, on negative
grounds. They were people who disliked something Jackson had done,
rather than people who had a plan of their own. Some of them thought
"King Andrew" was making himself a tyrant, which was untrue, and that
he was upsetting the balance of the American Government, which was
a fact. Some of them, like Tyler and his states'-rights Virginians, thought
he was too much of a nationalist. Some of them, like the coastal cotton
planters (the old Crawford men whom Van Buren had wheedled into
the Jackson camp), thought he was too much of a radical; they were disgusted with the talk about the Declaration of Independence, and about
man's natural rights. Some of the Whigs were angry because Jackson
had destroyed sound money by his attack on the Bank and by distributing
the Treasury surplus among the state banks; others were angry because
he had destroyed unsound money with his "specie circular" and his encouragement of Van Buren in Locofoco Independent-Treasury heresies.

Little by little, the anti-Jackson group grew. Each time it absorbed a
new set of allies, it had to say less about its policies for fear of losing some
of the old allies. This is typical of American parties. If the men who like a
fluctuating currency are to be kept in the same fold with the men who
like a steady currency, the less said about the money problem the better.
And if the men who dislike Jackson because he is making himself a
dictator are to work happily with the men who dislike Jackson because
he believes in democracy, the less said about theories of government the
better. In the end there is not much to discuss, except an old man's love
of log cabins.

As the party grew, and began to prepare for the election of 1836, the
Southern planters refused to call themselves National Republicans. They
didn't like the word "national." It reminded them of the Adams family
and the Federalists. They began calling themselves Whigs, and within a
few years the name was established. It suggested patriotism, and a distaste for tyranny; and it had the advantage of meaning nothing definite.
It could not frighten the most delicate voter.

During Van Buren's presidency the Whigs acquired the last, the strongest, and the strangest-named of their converts: the Anti-Mason Party.
In September, 1826, a brick and stone worker called William Morgan,
who had promised to publish the secrets of the first three degrees of
Masonry, disappeared from the town of Canandaigua* in western New
York and was never seen again. He was thought to have been murdered
by vengeful Masons. The prosperous farmers of the neighboring counties
were inclined to be anti-Mason in any case, since most of them were

---

* He had been taken there, under false arrest, from his home in Batavia.

of New England descent and their Puritan background gave them a prejudice against secret societies. Also, they favored the "American System," because they wanted canals and roads to take their goods to market, and a tariff to maintain high prices. Furthermore, it happened that Jackson was a Mason, whereas John Quincy Adams, the friend of the "American System," was not. Out of these seemingly unrelated facts, politicians were able to build a local political movement which combined the economic with the religious appeal, offering the delights of intolerance in addition to a program of government aid. Thurlow Weed at once saw the possibilities in the new party, and set to work wooing the anti-Masons into the Adams camp.

With these new allies, the National Republicans (later the Whigs) began to win elections in New York. We have already seen that in 1838 the Whigs made William H. Seward governor, with the help of disgruntled conservative Democrats who abandoned Van Buren to his Locofoco friends. It was the anti-Masons who really turned the election, and from that time on they were completely absorbed into Thurlow Weed's Whig Party. They brought with them not only a majority of voters in western New York, but an important group of Scots and Germans in Pennsylvania, who were anti-Mason for religious reasons, and a number of temperance enthusiasts from New England who disapproved of wine-drinking at Masonic meetings. The history of the party is a lesson in how the professional politician can find uses for the most unlikely causes and the most unusual prejudices.[4]

The Whig Party was now complete. It was a typical collection of regional special-interest groups which were prepared to collaborate so long as each group received an agreed favor. In return for this favor, each group refrained from demanding other favors which would upset the balance and make compromise impossible. The East was to receive a tariff and a revived National Bank; the West was to receive internal improvements, plus the suppression of the specie circular (which would encourage cheap paper money); Louisiana was to receive a tariff for her sugar, a National Bank to help her large commercial interests, and the pleasure of ousting the friends of Andrew Jackson, who had left a bad name behind him in New Orleans;* the Eastern planters were to receive a market for their cotton in New England, favorable prices on the cotton textiles sold them by New England (a promise easier to make than to keep), and the support of the national Whig Party against the "leveling" tendencies of the Jacksonians and against anybody anywhere who raised the slave question.

New England was so closely tied to the planters that her Whigs came to be known as "Cotton Whigs." Her textile mills received their raw

* After the War of 1812 he had ruled the city as if it were a conquered province.

material from the cotton kingdom, and sold a large part of their cheap goods to the plantations. Her bankers financed the profitable trade, and her shippers, along with those of New York, flourished on the two-way traffic. "Cotton thread holds the union together," wrote Ralph Waldo Emerson. "Patriotism [is] for holidays and summer evenings with rockets, but cotton thread is the union." Calhoun had not yet convinced his Southern friends that they must be the losers in any political bargain with the business world. The rich planters believed that "cotton was king"; they believed their Northern allies would always treat them gently, for the sake of what they bought. Until well into the eighteen-forties, they were Whigs to a man.*

6

When the precarious alliance of local groups which made up the Whig Party is examined, the campaign of 1840 becomes comprehensible. There were two interests unrepresented in the Whig camp, and both had to be placated. The first was the states'-rights interest in Virginia, led by John Tyler. The Whigs dared not pretend that they stood for the principles of 1798, for if they were overheard in the North they might lose their business and banking associates. Having nothing to offer the Virginians in the way of policy, the Whigs offered them the vice-presidency which was accepted with thanks. This seemed a harmless way out of the trouble; but it proved to be the death of the Whig hopes.

The second unrepresented interest was that of the plain people, who were unfortunately very numerous. In New York State Thurlow Weed understood the plain people, and he was able to give the Whig Party a solid foundation of working-class votes. In New York City, oddly enough, the Negroes who had once voted Federalist now voted Whig, on the grounds that the Democrats were the party of the immigrant laborer who resented and ill-treated the Negro, not being in a position to ill-treat anyone else. And in New England the native workman was inclined to vote Whig as a sign of his superiority to the Irish immigrant who was sure to vote Democratic. Yet this was not enough. It might serve to win New York and Massachusetts; but if the poor elsewhere were faithful to the Jacksonians, the Whigs would lose the election. Hence Harrison and the mad campaign of 1840. Log cabins instead of democracy; hard cider instead of radicalism; songs instead of natural rights. The Whigs were rich and they spent a fortune on sheer entertainment during the campaign. The people had great fun out of the fireworks and

* When Varina Howell of Mississippi met Jefferson Davis, whose wife she was to become in 1845, she wrote that he was the first Democrat she had seen who was a gentleman.

the blarney. Van Buren was beaten partly by the depression, partly by his own laissez-faire philosophy which kept him from offering aid to the victims of the depression, partly by the sensible votes of the Whigs who knew and approved their own program, and partly by the bemused votes of people who had been taught that Van Buren lived in oriental splendor and selfishness, whereas Harrison gave laborious days to thinking how to help the poor.

The election re-established the normal pattern of American politics. Jacksonian Democracy had shown signs of developing into a class party, cutting across regional lines; but it lacked a philosophy of class warfare, and it lacked a class-conscious electorate. After 1840 the party went back to the usual method of seeking votes by regional bribes and balances, and of bolstering the Union by regional compromise. The economic struggle between the sections was still the most acute, dangerous struggle, and was about to impose a truce between the classes within each major section.

It was perhaps just as well that the economic and political problems of the Industrial Revolution could be temporarily shelved, for in neither party did the leaders show a capacity for thinking about democracy in a machine age. The founders of America, as we have seen, had a realistic basis for their politics. They believed there was a direct relation between power and property, and thus between political responsibility and property. Most of them, like Adams and Hamilton (and Madison in *The Federalist*), believed that the mass of mankind must always be without property; so they believed that the same mass should be without political power. Others, like Jefferson and John Taylor, believed that America could become a nation of small property holders, and could thus spread political power safely. These are sensible beliefs, relating to sensible premises, and admitting of many applications—including the application that in an industrial, proletarianized society all property and thus all power should be given to the state. Since the days of Hamilton and Jefferson, however, two changes had occurred: first, America was committed to becoming a great industrial power, which meant that she was committed to becoming a nation with a large class of factory workers owning no part of the means of production. (They might own a house, or a horse; but they wouldn't own anything with which they could earn a living—like a farm, or a machine shop.) And second, America was committed to becoming a political democracy. She had gone so far along the road to universal white male suffrage that there was no returning.

Both the Federalist and the Jeffersonian philosophies had thus been denied. The one said there could be no democracy because there could be no widespread ownership; the other said that there must be widespread ownership because there must be democracy. So America compromised by adopting political democracy from the Jeffersonians and adopting the factory system from Europe. Already by the eighteen-forties, it was too late to undo either. It was impossible to take the vote away from those who had received it; and it was impossible to cancel, or even control, the Industrial Revolution. It was also impossible, therefore, to derive further help or counsel from the wisdom of the Fathers. Everything which they feared, and against which they had warned the nation, had come to pass. The new America was on her own; she had to find a new way of reconciling power and property in the world of the machine. She had made a political democracy and she was making an economic oligarchy, and what was she to do with them?

Fortunately, the problem was not yet acute; for the Jacksonians had no answer except a few simple reforms (they advocated the ten-hour day, and permission for the workers to build unions); and the Whigs not only had no answer, they had no question. They did not admit that a problem had arisen. In order to maintain this innocence of mind, they created a social picture of America which was so unreal, but so pleasing to contemplate, that it has handicapped the conservative cause to this day. The new Whig sociology was based on three assertions: first, that it was wrong to think there could be any difference between the interests of the propertied and the unpropertied classes; second, that it was wrong to think there were any classes in America at all, since everyone was both a capitalist and a worker (unless he was a Negro slave, who didn't count); third, that it was wrong to agitate for what they called "external reform," since the only reform worth a wise man's attention was inner, or spiritual, reform. Mr. Arthur Schlesinger, Jr., comments: "This complex of attitudes—the identity of interests between the classes, the unimportance of class, the non-existence of class, the superior happiness of the laborer, the necessity for internal reform—satisfied the feeling of the business community in all the shades of ambivalence, from the compulsions toward power to the lurking intuitions of guilt."

It was just as well, since this was the level of her political thinking, that America could postpone class problems for the time being and devote herself to the familiar problem of sectional strife.*

---

* The class problems, however, were not far below the surface. Professor Allan Nevins writes (*Ordeal of the Union*, vol. I, p. 56, note): "When Jackson entered the White House, hours of labor in America had averaged twelve and a half a day. By 1850 at least a third of the population were working only eleven hours a day. One student who has investigated the question of vacations concludes that very few enjoyed such a luxury in this period. . . . Thomas Low Nichols wrote in *Forty Years of American Life:* 'In no country are the faces of the people furrowed with harder lines of care. In no country that I know of is there so much hard, toilsome, unremitting labour: in none so little of the recreation and enjoyment in life.' "

7

One important legacy of the Jacksonians was the result of chance: during the eight years of the General's presidency, seven justices of the Supreme Court died and one resigned. Jackson appointed what was almost a new court. Like the Federalists in 1800, he left behind him men who were to determine the law of the land for the next generation.

The most important appointment was that of Roger Brooke Taney to succeed John Marshall as Chief Justice. Taney had been born on a tobacco plantation in southern Maryland in 1777. On both sides of his family he came from the privileged class. He was a Roman Catholic, a lawyer, and a politician who had begun his career as a Hamiltonian Federalist. After the death of the Federalist Party, Taney became a supporter of Andrew Jackson, joining his Cabinet as Attorney General in 1831. During the war on the Bank Taney was among the most aggressive of the Jacksonians, urging the President to veto the new charter, and accepting an interim appointment as Secretary of the Treasury in order to insure that future government funds should be deposited in the state banks. He thus became the symbol of radical Jacksonism. The Senate refused to confirm his appointment as an Associate Justice of the Supreme Court, and refused to confirm his appointment as Secretary of the Treasury. But in 1836 a number of new Democratic Senators were elected and the next year Taney was accepted as Chief Justice.

The Whigs mourned the appointment as loudly and as bitterly as Jefferson had mourned the appointment of John Marshall. They thought the last stronghold of conservatism had fallen to the Jacksonian mob. And Taney's first opinion as Chief Justice strengthened their fears, for he liberalized John Marshall's definition of contract.

Article I, Section 10, of the Constitution says: "No state shall . . . pass any . . . law impairing the obligation of contracts." In the famous Yazoo case, *Fletcher* v. *Peck,* we have seen Marshall decide that a state might not rescind any of its grants, and in the Dartmouth College case he added that a charter is a contract as understood by the Constitution. In a relatively static economy these decisions might have been harmless; but in the midst of the first wild rush of the Industrial Revolution they could have put the American business system into a strait-jacket. What would happen, for instance, if a stagecoach company possessed a charter to carry passengers between two cities and a railway company requested a charter for the same route? An analogous problem came before the Supreme Court in the Charles River Bridge case.

In 1785 the Massachusetts legislature had granted to the Charles River

Bridge Proprietors the right to build and maintain a toll bridge between Boston and Charlestown. In 1792 the charter was extended for seventy years. In 1828 the legislature granted to the Warren Bridge Company the right to erect a bridge a few rods from the first. The Warren Bridge was to become free to the public within six years. The Charles River Company at once sued on the ground that the competing bridge constituted an impairment of contract.

The case was first carried to the Supreme Court of the United States in 1831, Chief Justice John Marshall presiding. Marshall wished to hold the second grant invalid; but because of absences from the Court, and because of disagreements, no decision was made until 1837, when Taney had succeeded to Marshall's position. With two dissenting votes the Court now upheld the constitutionality of the charter. The minority opinion, which would have been Marshall's opinion, was written by Justice Story, and stated that the action of the legislature was confiscatory and a breach of contract. Taney, speaking for the majority, upheld the new charter on the ground that rights granted by charters must be narrowly construed and that no charter could imply powers which were clearly opposed to the public interest. "While the rights of private property are sacredly guarded," he said, "we must not forget that the community also have rights, and that the happiness and well being of every citizen depends on their faithful preservation." This rule that corporate charters are to be construed with an eye to the public interest has proved a blessing in American constitutional law. It is only by accident, however, that the case was not decided in 1831, with the rule in reverse. The Charles River Bridge case is an interesting gloss on the statement that the Constitution is what the Supreme Court says it is.

On the whole, in spite of Whig fears, the new Chief Justice proved cautious, intelligent, and statesmanlike. On the whole, he turned out to be a Maryland gentleman with the states'-rights and anti-Negro prejudices of the South, rather than the wild Jacksonian radical of Whig imagining. In this he was a true representative of his time. Sectional interests and the race question were more important than the division into Left and Right, and the decision which will be forever associated with Taney's name was one of black reaction, in which he sought to render meaningless the "natural rights" clauses in the Declaration of Independence in order that Negroes might be defined as simple property.

XV

New Alignments and New Passions: 1844

THE WHIG PARTY asked only two favors of Harrison: that he say nothing and that he stay alive. The first he could grant; but the second was not for him to decide. On April 4, 1841, a month after taking office, the new President died of pneumonia. But even before this crowning act of inconvenience, Harrison was making trouble for his masters. Having been silent during the campaign, he seemed to think free speech was restored to him by the election. To the surprise of the men who had invented him, and who thought he could not move unless they wound him up, he wrote a florid inaugural address all by himself. He not only wrote it, he became fond of it, and he baulked when told it had to be rewritten. It was with difficulty that Daniel Webster got permission even to revise this inflated work. After a day at the task, he arrived late and weary to a dinner party. When his hostess asked whether anything had happened, he answered, "Madam, you would think something had happened, if you knew what I have done. I have killed seventeen Roman proconsuls as dead as smelts!"

Behind the demise of the proconsuls lay plans and ambitions which might have changed history; for Webster and Clay[1] put into Harrison's weak hands an address which would have meant constitutional revolution if the old man had lived. The new type of presidency, the privileges and the prestige gathered into the office by Jackson—all were repudiated. Congress was handed back the power to control policy which the impatient Westerner had wrested from it. If Harrison had ruled for eight years, instead of the stubborn Tyler and the strong-willed Polk, the President might not have become the tribune of the people and the dispenser of party favors; the presidential form of government might not have developed in the United States; and the states might not now be united. Of Harrison, as of few men, it can be said that the one important thing about him was the date of his death.*

The Webster-Clay-Harrison Inaugural Address said that "the great danger to our institutions . . . appears to me to be . . . the accumulation

---

* Jackson's comment on Harrison's death was characteristic: "A kind and over-ruling Providence has interfered to prolong our glorious Union. . . . Surely Tyler [will] stay the corruptions of this clique which has got into power by deluding the people with the grossest of slanders . . . and hard cider."

in one of the departments of that which was assigned to the others."
The address pointed out that many patriots feared the government was
moving toward monarchy, and admitted that "the tendency for some
years past had been in that direction." But the danger was now at an
end; Harrison would not aggrandize the presidency; on the contrary, he
would undo the recent damage. "It is preposterous to suppose," he said,
"that a thought could be entertained for a moment that the President,
placed at the capital, in the center of the country, could better understand the wants and wishes of the people than their own immediate
representatives who spend a part of every year among them." Jackson's
behavior in regard to the Bank and the federal funds was condemned.
"The delicate duty of devising schemes of revenue," said Harrison, "should
be left where the Constitution has left it—with the immediate representatives of the people." And again, referring to Jackson's removal of
Duane and the appointment of Taney as Secretary of the Treasury:
"It was certainly a great error in the framers of the Constitution not
to have made the officer at the head of the Treasury Department entirely independent of the Executive. He should, at least, have been removable upon the demand of the popular branch of the legislature. I
have determined never to remove a Secretary of the Treasury without
communicating all the circumstances to both houses of Congress."

No wonder a modern historian has written, "In this inaugural address
are passages which raise the suspicion that designing Whig leaders may
have practically persuaded the aged President-elect to prepare a mortgage
of his office to Congress."[2]

2

John Tyler was born in 1790, in Charles City County, Virginia. His
father was a man of position, and the boy was educated at William and
Mary College. He finished his course at the age of seventeen, and two
years later was admitted to the bar. He soon became a member of the
Virginia House of Delegates and of the Council of State. During the
War of 1812 he served briefly as captain of a company of volunteers, but
saw no action. In 1816 he was sent to the House of Representatives in
Washington. Here he rivaled John Randolph in the firmness of his states'-
rights views. He was opposed to the Bank of the United States, to a
protective tariff, and to Calhoun's bill for internal improvements at
federal expense. He was also opposed to the Missouri Compromise, on
the ground that the federal government had no right to control slavery
in the territories.

In 1821 Tyler left Congress because of ill health; but he continued to take part in state politics. In 1824—like most of the old Jeffersonians and states'-rights men in Virginia—he supported Crawford for the presidency. In 1825 and 1826 Tyler was governor of Virginia, and the next year he was sent to the United States Senate to succeed Randolph of Roanoke. He supported Jackson in 1828, and again in 1832, as the "least objectionable" candidate; but he was never a Jacksonian. He favored the Maysville veto and the war on the Bank; but he opposed the Nullification Proclamation as subversive of the Constitution; he was the only Senator to vote against the Force Bill;* and he bitterly attacked the removal of the deposits by Jackson and Secretary Taney. He backed the Senate resolution censuring the President for this act, and in 1836 he resigned office rather than follow the instructions of the Virginia legislature to reverse his stand.

No man ever made a more consistent record. The Whigs who nominated Tyler for the vice-presidency had no excuse for misunderstanding him. From his first to his last public deed, he had proved that states' rights were his guiding star, and that for him states' rights meant opposition to all but the most limited use of federal power. It was not presidential power he disliked, but centralized power, whether in the hands of President or Congress. And the Whigs would discover to their chagrin that there was one Jacksonian power which Tyler wholly approved: the power to deny, to use the veto.**

The first sign that Tyler was to be a disappointing substitute for the pliant Harrison came with his insistence that he was President of the United States, and not merely Vice-President filling in for the remainder of the term. The Constitution is perhaps ambiguous on this point;*** and in view of the number of Presidents who have since died in office the precedent set by Tyler was important. The Whig leaders thought he should have been content with the more humble position; yet they tried to take comfort from a passage in his Inaugural Address which said:

> In view of the fact, well attested by history, that the tendency of all human institutions is to concentrate power in the hands of a single man, and that their ultimate downfall has proceeded from this cause, I deem it of the most essential importance that a complete separation

* The other opponents of the bill discreetly left the chamber.

** John Quincy Adams, who detested Tyler, at least understood that the new President was not a back-sliding Whig but an old-fashioned Republican. "Tyler is a political sectarian," wrote Adams (*Diary,* April 4, 1841), "of the slave-driving, Virginian, Jeffersonian school, principled against all improvement, with all the interests and passions and vices of slavery rooted in his moral and political constitution."

*** The relevant passage, from Section 1, Article II, of the Constitution, reads: "In case of the removal of the President from office, or of his death, resignation, or inability to discharge the powers and duties of the said office, the same shall devolve

should take place between the sword and the purse. No matter where or how the public money shall be deposited, so long as the President can exert the power of appointing and removing at his pleasure the agents selected for their custody the commander-in-chief of the army and navy is in fact the treasurer.

Webster and Clay hoped this meant that the Whig Congress would have a free hand to make financial policy; but in fact it meant that the new President would be vigilant at every point to construe the powers of the government narrowly. He believed in a diffusion on power, not in Executive abdication to the Senate. When he realized that Clay intended to introduce bills reviving the whole "American System," Tyler asked the Kentuckian to a conference, hoping to avoid a public break. But Clay pushed on with his program, saying "I'll drive him before me." He could not believe that behind Tyler's mild manners and aristocratic calm —a gentleness found in many of the "Old Republicans" of Virginia— lay a strength of will which made him one of the hardest men to "drive" in all America. Clay had bad luck with his presidents; his attempts to break Tyler's stubbornness were as futile as his previous assaults on Jackson.

Tyler signed a bill abolishing Van Buren's sub-treasury system, and he accepted an upward revision of the tariff.* This was as far as he would go to redeem Whig promises—few of which had been made in the open. He vetoed all bills for internal improvements, or for harbor works. He vetoed a bill for a new Bank of the United States, and when the bill was rewritten to meet his constitutional objections he vetoed it again.** The Whig program was in ruins. Tyler's own following in Congress was so weak that it was known as "the corporal's guard"; but there were enough old Jacksonians to support his vetoes. In January, 1842, Clay, in despair, proposed a constitutional amendment empowering Congress to pass a bill over the President's veto by a majority vote. He argued, with force, that the veto as used by Jackson and Tyler made the President "the ruler of the nation"; but he received no popular support. The people, it seemed, were content to have the President rule the nation. In 1844, the Democratic platform approved the veto power, and the Whig platform dared do no more than urge "a reform of executive usurpations." That was the end of political attacks on the Jacksonian use of the

on the Vice President, and the Congress may by law provide for the case of removal, death, resignation or inability, both of the President and Vice President, declaring what officer shall then act as President, and such officer shall act accordingly, until the disability be removed, or a President shall be elected."

* The tariff compromise of 1833, which ended the nullification crisis, applied only until 1842.

** September 9, 1841.

veto. The power to veto is the power to compel alternatives. Thenceforth a popular President was equal in legislative strength to anything short of a two-thirds majority of both Houses.

Tyler, meanwhile, was having almost as much trouble with Daniel Webster in the Cabinet as with Clay in the Congress. The new President had retained the whole of the Harrison Cabinet, including Webster as Secretary of State. At the first full meeting, Webster said: "Mr. President, it was the custom of our cabinet meetings with President Harrison that he should preside over them. All measures relating to the administration were to be brought before the cabinet and their settlement was to be decided by the majority of votes, each member of the cabinet and the President having but one vote." Here was the Whig theory of the presidency in extreme form: the President was chairman of his Cabinet; he had a vote like everyone else, but no authority, no command over the party machinery, no power to make policy and to enforce it. If Tyler accepted the proposal, the Jacksonian changes in the government would be canceled.

Jackson and his friends had called in the people to upset the balance of power and to give the President strength to enforce policy: the people, plus the political machine. Were the Whig leaders to undo this work, through a palace revolution? With Harrison to take their orders they would have turned the country back to government by Congressional committee, which had proved itself to be government by drift and log-jamb. But Tyler, to their rage, refused to play the part allotted him. Although he preferred a weak central government, sharing Jefferson's faith that the least government was the best, he knew that within even the weakest government the Executive must lead. "I am the President," he replied to Webster; "and I shall be held responsible for my administration."

In September, 1841, after five months of Tyler's presidency, the whole Whig Cabinet resigned, except for Webster. The resignation was a protest against the veto of Clay's second bill for a National Bank. Webster remained in office, partly to show that he was independent of Clay, and partly because he was deep in negotiations with the British.

The boundary between Maine and Canada had been vaguely defined by the Treaty of 1783, and as always in diplomacy the vagueness had made trouble. In 1814 the Treaty of Ghent created a joint commission to settle the trouble; but the commission failed. The King of the Netherlands was asked to arbitrate; but the compromise he recommended was refused by America. The problem was then neglected until 1837, when rebellion broke out in Upper and Lower Canada against the British Government. America saw the rebellion as a repetition of her own fight for freedom. Along the border, therefore, the rebels were given illegal and unneutral aid. Then the rebellion quieted; Lord Durham, sent from England, contributed his famous report, and the experience of 1763 to 1775 bore fruit. The British Empire began its evolution toward a Commonwealth of Nations.

The border incidents, however, left hard feelings behind them, and the situation was not improved by the presence of Lord Palmerston at the Foreign Office. Whenever that interesting character lacked larger or more dangerous game, he amused himself by bearing down on the Americans.* Under such conditions the old boundary dispute became a danger to peace, so Tyler pressed for a new effort at settlement. His chance came when the Melbourne Ministry resigned, in August, 1841, and Sir Robert Peel became Prime Minister with Lord Aberdeen at the Foreign Office. Early in 1842 Aberdeen sent Lord Ashburton to Washington, and within a few months the Webster-Ashburton Treaty had been negotiated, establishing the present boundary and settling other minor disputes.

When it came to explaining the compromise to a belligerent Senate and an irascible Parliament, the treaty was saved by the famous "battle of the maps."[3] Through strange good fortune Webster possessed an early French map which was assumed to be the one mentioned by Franklin at the time of the peace negotiations and which justified the extreme British claim, whereas the Foreign Office possessed a map formerly belonging to George III which justified the extreme American claim. Each side, therefore, could happily pretend that it had cheated the other. When Palmerston attacked the "Ashburton capitulation," he was shown the British map; when the ever-restive Senate sought to reject the treaty, it was shown the American map. The real map, meanwhile, had been seen by nobody. Years later, when it was discovered in Spain, it proved that America had received less than had been intended in 1783; but at the time of the settlement everyone was satisfied, since everyone thought he was getting the best of his neighbor.

* Palmerston, for example, was justly annoyed at slave traders who claimed immunity under the American flag. In August, 1841, he insisted on the "right of visit" in regard to such ships. There is little doubt that America would have fought rather than admit this "right"; but Palmerston left office before the month was out, and the new ministry dropped the claim. In his chapter on Palmerston's foreign policy in *Crimean War Diplomacy, and other Historical Essays*, Gavin Burns Henderson writes: "To Palmerston the sense of power was always more important than the purpose for which that power was being exercised; and contemporaries and posterity, in praising Palmerston, have praised him not for himself but for his incarnation of Britain at her peak of glory." As we shall see when discussing the next election, "Britain at her peak of glory" was cordially disliked in the United States during the early forties; and Palmerston, with his simple pleasure in power for power's sake, was wholly indifferent to what America did or didn't like. As a result, there was real danger of war. The agreement reached between Tyler and Webster on the one hand, and the Peel Ministry on the other, was a triumph of diplomacy over human folly. Such triumphs are rarely praised.

3

The resignation of the Cabinet left Tyler a President without a party. After twice supporting Jackson for the presidency, he had turned against the Jacksonians; and now that his new friends, the Whigs, understood what Tyler really thought, they had turned against him. When he appointed his own Cabinet, it contained three Southerners who felt as strongly as Tyler himself about states' rights. This was the camp where he belonged: not with the radical Jacksonian Democrats, not with the business-and-banking Whigs, but with the remnant of the "Old Republicans," the men who had preserved Jefferson's philosophy of government without his belief in natural rights. This group was about to receive a large increment in strength. As Jacksonian Democracy weakened under the pressure of revived sectionalism, the states'-rights men were to take over the Democratic Party. Meanwhile, in 1842, that party won a majority in the House of Representatives. The next year, Webster finally left the Cabinet, and after a brief interval John Caldwell Calhoun became Secretary of State. The appointment completed the political upset which had begun with the death of Harrison.*

In 1841 the Whigs had come to power after an overwhelming victory. Three years later they found themselves with a President who had in fact returned to the Democratic Party, a Secretary of State who had not only returned to the Democratic Party but was dominating the thinking of that party, a Cabinet which would follow the lead of these two Democrats, and a Democratic majority in the House. Not a single important law proposed by the Whigs had escaped the President's veto. And to complete the confusion, the Democratic Party which was coming to power in this unusual manner had little except the political machine to identify it with the party which had so recently triumphed under Jackson. The brief alliance of Locofocos and Southern and Western farmers had lost control of that machine; it was to be taken over by a new alliance, contrived by Calhoun.

Calhoun had long been working toward two ends: to capture the Democratic Party for the states'-rights group, and to bring all the leading Southerners, especially all the planters, into this reformed party. The first aim was now virtually accomplished; the second was under way, although a majority of the great Southern landowners still called themselves Whigs. For them the Democratic Party was still tainted with democracy, with

* Abel Parker Upshur of Virginia succeeded Webster as Secretary of State; but he died the following February in an accident on board the battleship *Princeton*. Calhoun succeeded him in March, 1844.

Jeffersonian natural rights and Jacksonian urban radicalism. Calhoun's mission, from 1844 until his death, would be to persuade the Southern Whigs that the South could not be defended against capitalist aggression unless Southerners united and took the leadership of the dominant Democratic Party. Many of the Whig planters accepted Calhoun's teaching when they discovered, at the time of the Tyler crisis, that Clay and Webster meant to restore a Hamiltonian Bank, a Hamiltonian tariff, and a more than Hamiltonian program of federal expenditures. The rest of the Southern Whigs joined Calhoun after the Texas question and the Mexican War had made slavery the dominant and inescapable issue.

4

During the years between the death of Jefferson, in 1826, and the appointment of Calhoun as Secretary of State, in 1844, the South had changed radically. Because of his long fight against power and privilege in Virginia, and indeed throughout the country, Jefferson was disliked by many of the old Tidewater families; yet on the whole he had been a hero, during his lifetime, throughout the South. The great majority of Southern people had thought themselves followers of Jefferson, accepting his hopeful view of human nature and his optimism about the future of democracy. They had even believed that in a short while they would follow his teaching on the Negro question.

The South, after all, was a land of small farmers, most of them poor. Andrew Jackson and John Caldwell Calhoun were the sons of such farmers in the South Carolina uplands; Abraham Lincoln and Jefferson Davis were the sons of such farmers in Kentucky. Except for slavery, which was assumed to be dying, Western egalitarianism was more characteristic of the South, in 1826, than the privileged life in the mansions along the Potomac. And the South of the small farmer seemed more likely to survive than the aristocratic South, for the old families of the tidewater were falling on bad times. Their lands were losing fertility; their slaves were multiplying so fast that no profitable employment could be found for the surplus—yet they all had to be fed. When man-made disasters such as the Embargo and the War of 1812, or the depression of 1819, were added to the disasters provided by nature, the Old South seemed doomed. Until the imperial booty of rich soil was taken from the Indians in Georgia, Alabama, and Mississippi, the once rich slaveowners could not even emigrate unless they abandoned most of their human property. They were not allowed to take slaves into the country north of the Ohio, and neither the Appalachian uplands (where corn and wheat were the usual crops), nor the valleys of Kentucky and Tennessee (where tobacco-growing was established), lent themselves to the plantation type of agriculture with its hordes of slaves.

The South seemed on its way to becoming a land of poor farmers and of moderate-sized plantations, with slavery moribund. Soil conservation began to be practiced, and plans were laid for the introduction of small-scale industries and the diversification of the region's economy. Then, in the twenties and the thirties, came the change we have already seen: the plantation system renewed its youth with the theft of the Indian lands.* But the departing red man left behind him a curse from which his dispossessors have not yet wholly recovered. Soil conservation became less interesting when abundant new land was offered for destruction. Diversification of the economy ceased (a decision which proved fatal to the South between 1861 and 1865) when a profitable outlet for capital was found in the service of King Cotton. Negroes were no longer a liability to their seaboard masters; the more they multiplied the better, for they could be sold on a rising market. By 1850 the value of a strong, healthy Negro had risen to fifteen hundred dollars, so the attempt to deal with slavery was postponed.

An unusual type of emigrant left the southern seaboard for the new cotton country during these years. Some were the unsuccessful or the naturally adventurous; some were the hopelessly poor, who moved from shiftlessness rather than ambition; but a considerable number were the well-to-do (or the children of the well-to-do), taking with them a fortune in slaves. They were accustomed to gracious living and to a high cultural standard. They were either learned themselves, or they had respect for learning. Almost overnight they produced a sumptuous life in the wilderness: a life notable for the sense of security that seemed to rise out of that rich soil.** Yet the system, though spectacular, was brief. It was based not only on the wasteful institution of slavery, but on a destruction of the

* The settling of the state of Louisiana also helped, and in the forties came the vast new opportunities in Texas.

** Compare the story of Thomas Dabney, who left Virginia for the Southwest in the middle thirties. "He had been one of the most successful wheat and tobacco farmers in his part of the state. But the cost of living in the Old Dominion, for a man with a growing family and many slaves, was too heavy. Therefore, Thomas made a trip through a large part of Alabama, Louisiana and Mississippi, and finally bought from a half dozen small farmers a tract of four thousand acres in Hinds County, Mississippi. Returning home, he called his Negroes about him and offered to buy or sell where intermarriage on neighboring estates threatened to divide families. No one, he announced, was to leave Virginia who did not wish to do so. Such careful preparations for the removal were made that the long trip was completed in comfort and health. Old lands were planted at once and a hundred new acres cleared each year. Cotton crops ran a bale and a half to the acre. The Dabney plantation, with a well-organized labor force competing for prizes and assigned to tasks according to ability, raising its own stock and provision, and widening its acres as opportunity offered, became a model in the kingdom of cotton." (Avery Craven, *The Coming of the Civil War*, p. 108.)

land so ruthless and so short-sighted that even without the Civil War the
new cotton kingdom would have been in ruins within seventy years of its
birth. Had it possessed endless space across which to expand, it might
have had a long if migratory history—moving ever westward and leaving
behind it the disgrace of ruined fields. But we have already seen that by
the fifties the cotton planters were face to face with destiny: "bounded on
the north by cold and bounded on the west by aridity." Unless they
embarked on overseas colonial adventures they had all the land, suitable
to their system, which they could ever acquire. And they had not learned
to use it without consuming it.

These few thousand plantation owners, with their tens of thousands of
slaves, not only bequeathed to the world its picture of the Old South but
during their short day of power they fastened their views, their prejudices,
and their desires upon the entire region. By the middle forties they and
their kinsmen along the seaboard had given the South a new philosophy
and a new political faith. They had brought the back-country farmers, the
men from the hills and the remoter valleys who had been born to distrust
and oppose the coastal aristocrats, to unlearn their Jeffersonian principles and to accept the leadership of an oligarchy. The South had never
before been a unit; it had been a society divided against itself, largely on
class lines; but these men made it a unit in defense of the institution of
slavery. They probably would not have succeeded if the Northern abolitionists had been less bitter and less provoking in their attacks on all things
Southern.

The new leaders did not hide the fact that they were seeking a revolution in thought, that they were tearing up the teachings of the "Virginia
dynasty." In 1838, Chancellor William Harper of the Supreme Court of
South Carolina said of the Declaration of Independence:

> Is it not palpably nearer the truth to say that no man was ever born
> free and that no two men were ever born equal, than to say that all men
> are born free and equal? . . . Man is born to subjection. The procliv-
> ity of the natural man is to domineer or to be subservient. . . . If
> there are sordid, servile, and laborious offices to be performed, is it not
> better that there should be sordid, servile, and laborious beings to per-
> form them?

Already in 1837 Calhoun had stated bluntly that he held slavery to be a
positive good and that the South should cease apologizing for it. And as
early as 1832 Thomas R. Dew, in Richmond, had put the new creed forcefully:

> The exclusive owners of property have ever been, ever will and per-
> haps ever ought to be the virtual rulers of mankind. . . . It is the order
> of nature and of God that the being of superior faculties and knowledge,

and therefore of superior power, should control and dispose of those who are inferior. It is as much in the order of nature that men should enslave each other as the animals should prey upon each other.

When the poor men's churches went over to slavery and to the anti-democratic philosophy, the great change was complete. In 1846 the Methodist Church split on the slavery issue, the Southern Methodists forming their own organization. The same split had already come to the Baptists. Even among the poor, no one could hold his job as a Christian minister if he defended the brotherhood of man. The South had been changed into a complacent oligarchy.

It was this new, proud, briefly prosperous, anti-democratic South which Calhoun finally united in the Democratic Party. It is unlikely, however, that either Calhoun or the pressure of economic interest could have reconciled the Scotch-Irish of the back country to the lordly slaveholders of the coasts if it had not been for the violence of Northern abuse.

5

At the time of the Missouri Compromise there was little moral passion in the anti-slavery argument. The discussion, for the most part, dealt with the cold-blooded problem of preserving the balance of power in the Senate so that neither the Northern nor the Southern interest could command a majority. Yet there was talk on both sides of secession, and Senator Rufus King of New York appealed ominously to the higher law, saying that "no human law, compact, or compromise can establish or continue slavery." This welding of morals and economics, on a sectional issue, frightened the aging Jefferson. He had made a revolution himself; he knew the strength of the explosion which follows when personal interest and eternal principles are fused.

Soon another fiery element was added to the mixture, as industrial discontents made the Northern public more quarrelsome, readier to throw stones at its neighbors. With the spread of the factory system many manual workers felt their security threatened and their hopes for the future dimmed.* It was natural, as tensions in the North increased, that cranks

---

* The misery was acute in many Northern cities. Describing New York during the depression of 1837–43, Horace Greeley wrote (*Recollections,* p. 145) : "I saw two families, including six or eight children, burrowing in one cellar under a stable, —a prey to famine on the one hand and to vermin and cutaneous maladies on the other, with sickness adding its horrors to those of a polluted atmosphere and a wintry temperature. I saw some men who each, somehow, managed to support his family on an income of five dollars a week or less, yet who cheerfully gave something to mitigate the sufferings of those who were *really* poor. I saw three widows, with as many children, living in an attic on the profits of an apple stand which

and busybodies should increase also. And when neither the women's-rights movement nor the pacifist movement nor the temperance movement nor Owenism nor prison reform nor the Fourier phalanx showed signs of making life more agreeable, it was natural that the South and its peculiar institution should receive increasing censure. The appeal for emancipation within reasonable time began to give way to the clamor for abolition at once. It was the clamor of a small minority, yet by the eighteen-thirties it came with troubling eloquence from such men as William Lloyd Garrison in New England and Theodore Weld in the Northwest. The first issue of Garrison's *Liberator,** after appealing to the Declaration of Independence for authority, continues in these words:

> I will be as harsh as truth and as uncompromising as justice. On this subject, I do not wish to think, or speak, or write, with moderation. No! No! Tell a man whose house is on fire, to give a moderate alarm; tell him to moderately rescue his wife from the hands of the ravisher; tell the mother to gradually extricate her babe from the fire into which it has fallen;—but urge me not to use moderation in a cause like the present. I am in earnest—I will not equivocate—I will not excuse—I will not retreat a single inch—AND I WILL BE HEARD. The apathy of the people is enough to make every statue leap from its pedestal, and to hasten the resurrection of the dead.

One may admire the language and applaud the sentiments while recognizing that they are the language and sentiments of war, not of democratic politics. These are not the terms in which men argue with each other, or persuade each other; they are the terms in which they prepare to kill each other. Long before Garrison and his followers were taken seriously in the North, they had changed the tone of the discussion in the South. While the "Cotton Whigs" of Boston were dismissing Abolition contemptuously as another crotchety movement, like Prohibition, and Peace, the South responded as men always respond when they are simultaneously called immoral and threatened with the loss of property: The South replied that it was morally superior to its neighbors, and that it would hold on to its property. If the South was morally superior, then slavery must be a positive good, instead of the misfortune which it had long been thought; and if the South was to hold on to its property, then slavery must be a permanent institution, and not the transition stage

---

yielded less than three dollars a week, and the landlord came in for a full third of that. But worst to bear of all was the pitiful plea of stout, resolute, single young men and young women: 'We do not want alms; we are not beggars; we hate to sit here day by day idle and useless; help us to work,—we want no other help; why is it that we have nothing to do?' " As usual during such periods, the nascent labor unions withered away and collective bargaining was abandoned.

* Boston, January 1, 1831.

which it was once considered. Hence the new anti-Jeffersonian philosophy, and the new unity throughout the southern region.

Since Garrison appealed to the Declaration of Independence, the South denied its validity, denied that it was part of the American political system, and finally attacked the whole theory of natural rights—either on the ground that such rights were "glittering generalities," or on the subtler ground that natural law if properly understood would lead to a respect for slavery. The latter doctrine, characteristically, was the work of Calhoun.

> It is a great and dangerous error [he wrote in the *Disquisition on Government*] to suppose that all people are equally entitled to liberty. It is a reward to be earned, not a blessing to be gratuitously lavished on all alike;—a reward reserved for the intelligent, the patriotic, the virtuous and deserving;—and not a boon to be bestowed on a people too ignorant, degraded and vicious, to be capable either of appreciating or enjoying it. . . . An all-wise Providence has reserved it, as the noblest and highest reward for the development of our faculties, moral and intellectual. This dispensation seems to be the result of some fixed law. . . . The progress of a people rising from a lower to a higher point in the scale of liberty, is necessarily slow;—and by attemtping to precipitate it, we either retard, or permanently defeat it."[4]

In any case, whether natural rights were nonexistent or whether their nature had been misunderstood, Jefferson and his Declaration were wrong. On that, the entire South seemed agreed.

6

The new Southern unity in defense of the slave system was first proved by the harassing problem of Texas. In 1836 Texas had seceded from Mexico, and the same year a small Texan army led by Sam Houston defeated a Mexican army and captured its commanding general, Santa Anna. Houston was elected first president of the Lone Star Republic. He secured American recognition, and would have asked for annexation to the United States had not President Van Buren discouraged him. Texas, if she entered the Union, would bring a huge new area where slavery and the plantation system could prosper. Texas was so large that she might be carved into half a dozen moderate-sized states, upsetting the Senate balance between the North and South permanently. At first nobody wished to force the issue, lest compromise prove impossible. Then in 1843 it was rumored that England might lend money to Texas, and that both England and France planned an alliance with the new republic guaranteeing her independence.

Large and dangerous hopes were stirring in the minds of Aberdeen, and

Guizot, the French Prime Minister. If Texas could be made permanently independent, and guaranteed against the United States, a balance of power in North America might be created, the further expansion of the United States might be thwarted, and an independent source of supply for cotton and tobacco might be found—a source closely bound by self-interest to the two European powers. In 1844 France and England approached Mexico with a plan for a joint guarantee of both the independence and the boundaries of Texas and Mexico against the United States and all the world; but Mexico foolishly refused to recognize Texas as an independent state, thus losing her last chance to keep the United States from dismembering the Mexican Empire. Yet as late as June, 1845, after the annexation of Texas was a certainty, Guizot returned to Talleyrand's old dream of thwarting the expansion of the United States. "France has a lasting interest," he said, with obvious reference to Texas, "in the maintenance of independent states in America, and in the balance of forces which exists in that part of the world."*

By 1844, therefore, the South could no longer assume that Texas must some day inevitably join the Union, so Secretary of State Calhoun negotiated a treaty of annexation.** The treaty was defeated in the Senate, so the Texas question became the leading issue in the presidential campaign. And the question who was to run the Democratic Party—Calhoun or Van Buren, the Southern planters or the Northern radicals—was settled at the same time.

In spite of his defeat in 1840, Van Buren remained a leading candidate for the next nomination. His hold over the machine was such that he was almost sure to be chosen unless he said something indiscreet, something which would be unpopular in one of the major regions. Since it was his habit to say nothing at all, this seemed unlikely—until the Texas question rose to destroy him. Shortly before the Democratic Convention met in Baltimore, in 1844, Van Buren was asked by his political enemies where he stood on Texas. Passions were so high that he could not refuse to answer. If he opposed annexation, he would lose the South; if he favored it, he would lose his own supporters in New York State, where politics were as complicated and as bitter as usual and where Van Buren's long association with the Jacksonians had broken his ties with the conservative wing of the party and left him dependent on the Locofocos of the city and on their rural allies, known as Barnburners.

The Barnburners were the reform element within the state party. They were deeply in earnest—hence their name, given them by derisive oppo-

---

* The balance of forces to which Guizot referred had already ceased to exist; but if Mexico had been less stubborn or self-assured in 1844 she might have altered the course of modern history.

** Most of the work had already been done by Secretary of State Upshur; but Calhoun concluded the arrangements.

nents who said they were such fanatics for reform that they could only be compared to the Dutch farmer who burned down his barn to kill the rats. They were originally formed to combat the indifference to public welfare of Van Buren's own Regency.* No Democrat could count on carrying New York State in 1844 without the Barnburners, and they would support no one who favored annexing Texas. They represented the serious, conscientious, anxious group in the North which would not follow the abusive abolitionists but which would no longer tolerate the extension of slavery. They became one of the ancestors of the Republican Party which elected Abraham Lincoln.

Since one of Van Buren's few firm beliefs was his opposition to the spread of slavery, and since his remaining supporters in New York State felt the same way, he answered the question about Texas by saying (with as many qualifications as possible) that he opposed annexation. The South turned strongly against him. Even his loyal friend Andrew Jackson cried, "I wish to God I had been at Mr. V. B.'s elbow. . . . I would have brought to his view *the proper conclusion*. We are all in sackcloth and ashes." The old General then called James K. Polk and other friends to "The Hermitage," where he announced that Van Buren had killed himself politically, that the party must have a candidate from the Southwest who stood for annexation, and that Polk was the man.

Van Buren's last hope was that his friends might rescind the two-thirds rule at Baltimore. His friends tried; but Robert J. Walker of Mississippi, a party manager almost as able as Van Buren himself, defeated the attempt. Walker also induced Tyler to withdraw as a candidate and to lend his strength to Polk. Although Van Buren had a majority of the votes on the first ballot, he lost ground steadily on each succeeding ballot, and on the ninth Polk was nominated.** Walker then contrived a regional compromise which was a masterpiece of American political art. Jacksonian Democracy had been an alliance of Northern radicals with farmers throughout the Mississippi Valley. The rejection of Van Buren and the choice of a pro-Texas man from Tennessee clearly endangered the alliance. How could it be revived? Walker's answer was to attack Great Britain and to offer an enlarged Oregon territory as a prize to the North, balancing the Southern prize of Texas. Fortunately for the plan, the Canadian-American boundary in the far Northwest was undetermined; it was still possible to push the claims of the United States hundreds of miles

* Their opponents, the "practical" wing of the party—the remains of the old Regency led by Marcy and supported by Tammany—were known as Hunkers, on the ground that they hungered, or "hunkered," after office. It was chiefly Van Buren's hard-money policy and his Independent Treasury Bill which lost him the Hunkers and won him the Barnburners and Locofocos.

** The first telegraph line in America carried the news of the nomination from Baltimore to Washington.

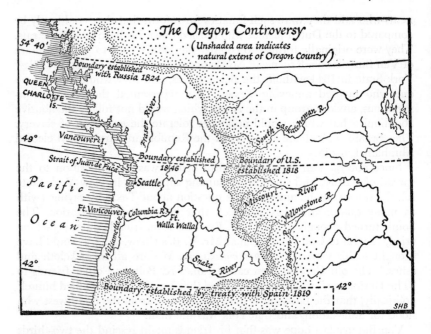

to the north, while complaining about British selfishness and British aggression. This would please the expansionists of the West; it would please the Irish of Tammany Hall; and it would please the farmers of New York and the upper Ohio Valley who were in revolt against the British Corn Laws which shut their grain out of England and which they blamed for the lean years of the long depression. It was not the old Jacksonian alliance; but it appealed to the same sections, and Walker hoped it would suffice.

"The *re*annexation of Texas and the *re*occupation of Oregon" was Walker's slogan for the Democratic campaign. The two prefixes were intended to suggest that Texas had been included in the Louisiana Purchase and then basely abandoned to Spain by John Quincy Adams in his Florida Treaty of 1819, whereas Oregon had been American by manifest destiny until the British came perfidiously upon the scene.* Senator Allen

* The land known as Oregon included British Columbia plus the present states of Oregon, Washington, Idaho, and a bit of Wyoming and Montana. England and America both claimed the whole of this territory, the northern boundary of which was latitude 54° 40′, at which point Russian Alaska began. By the treaty of 1818 the two countries occupied Oregon together. John Quincy Adams, as Secretary of State and as President, had three times offered to accept latitude 49° as the boundary; but the British refused to settle. By actual occupation they had a valid claim as far south as the Columbia River; on the other hand, the longer they waited to make a final settlement, the larger the American population would

of Ohio—"Foghorn Bill," one of the silliest senators ever to become chairman of the Committee on Foreign Relations—heightened the slogan for the Middle West by cutting it to "Fifty-Four Forty or Fight." This left out the delicate problem of Texas, while strengthening the anti-British appeal. Finally, having contrived an "issue" which might help the Northern Democrats to forget that they were electing a Southern President pledged to annex an empire of slave land, Walker completed his diplomatic task by giving the vice-presidential nomination to George Dallas, a high-tariff man from Pennsylvania, who was considered the ideal running-mate for Polk, a low-tariff man from Tennessee.

While the Democrats were producing this triumph of double or triple dealing, the Whigs were nominating Henry Clay for the presidency, in spite of the fact that he took the same stand as Van Buren on Texas. This willingness to annoy the slaveholders showed that the Whigs now felt their strength lay in the North. Southern Whigs, taking note of the fact, prepared to follow Calhoun's advice and join the Democratic Party. Hoping to hold these Whigs, Clay hedged on Texas. In the course of the campaign he made it clear that he was both for and against annexation—depending on what his audience preferred. He did not, thereby, win the votes he wanted in the South; but he lost the votes he needed in New York, where a group of anti-slavery Whigs turned to a third-party candidate.* Clay lost New York State, and with it the election, by five thousand votes.

---

become. Webster and Ashburton discussed the matter in 1842, but came to no agreement. The next year "Oregon fever" struck the northwest frontier, and the caravans of covered wagons a hundred strong began the long haul from Independence, Missouri.

* James Gillespie Birney, of Kentucky, an ex-slaveholder who had first worked to make the institution more humane, and who later advocated gradual emancipation and colonization. Finally, and reluctantly, he had become a moderate abolitionist—never violent enough to be trusted by Garrison. The Liberty Party, which nominated Birney for the election of 1844, received 62,300 votes.

XVI

Calhoun and the Meaning of 1850

JAMES KNOX POLK was born in North Carolina in 1795. When he was eleven his parents crossed the mountains into Tennessee. His adolescence was spent on the frontier; but when he was ready for college he went back east to the University of North Carolina. After taking his degree he studied law in Nashville, Tennessee, and was admitted to the bar in 1820. Three years later he began his political career in the state legislature.

During the presidencies of John Quincy Adams, Jackson, and Van Buren, Polk was a dull and diligent member of the House of Representatives at Washington. He proved a faithful partisan of Jackson, and was made the Administration leader in the lower House during the war on the Bank. From 1835 to 1839, he was Speaker of the House. He was then persuaded, somewhat against his will, to become candidate for governor of Tennessee, as the only man who could "redeem" the state from the Whigs. He won the election, but was defeated in 1841 and went into retirement, to emerge as the successful "dark horse" of the convention of 1844. In spite of his long career as a "safe" party man, Polk had no national fame at the time of his nomination. The convention which chose him not only passed over an ex-President and the President then in office, but refused John C. Calhoun, Lewis Cass of Michigan, and Silas Wright, who had been Senator from New York since 1833 and who was about to be made governor of that state.*

"Who is James K. Polk?" was the campaign cry of the Whigs. It is a question that many Americans today might echo if they chanced to hear the name. Although some of the most important episodes in the nation's history took place during his Administration, and as a result of his policies, and although he was a strong, stubborn, and dominating man, he was so colorless that he left nothing behind him but a few facts. He was without intimate friends and without charm. Formal and punctilious in bearing, stiff and angular in appearance, he looked as insignificant as people mistakenly believed him to be.

---

* Unlike the others, Wright did not want the nomination. He was an ardent Jacksonian, a member of the radical wing of the Democratic Party, a close friend and adviser of Benton and Van Buren. He had just refused an appointment to the United States Supreme Court and was campaigning for Van Buren's nomination, convinced that only by maintaining the Jacksonian alliance of Western farmers and Eastern radicals could the party save itself and the nation.

A month after the election, Polk wrote to a friend that he hoped for party harmony, but "in any event I intend to be *myself* President of the U. S." He appointed James Buchanan of Pennsylvania Secretary of State, Robert J. Walker Secretary of the Treasury, William L. Marcy (the leader of the Hunkers) Secretary of War, and George Bancroft, the historian, Secretary of the Navy. Years later, Bancroft wrote that on the day of the inauguration Polk said he had four clear objectives: to reduce the tariff, to re-establish the Independent Treasury (which had been suppressed by the Whig-Tyler Administration), to settle the Oregon boundary, and to acquire California. Three of these aims were accomplished within a year. The fourth took a little longer, since California belonged to Mexico and could only be had by war; yet before the end of Polk's term California was American property. This Administration, wrote Bancroft, "viewed from the standpoint of results, was perhaps the greatest in our national history, certainly one of the greatest. He [Polk] succeeded because he insisted on being its center and in overruling and guiding all his secretaries to act so as to produce unity and harmony."

The Independent Treasury Bill of 1846 revived Van Buren's favorite plan and displeased the New York Hunkers. They were placated by an extra share of the federal patronage. The Walker Tariff Bill of the same year put import duties on a revenue basis. Webster and his friends insisted that it would ruin industry and bankrupt the Treasury. In fact, it was a financial success; yet it was disliked by many Northern Democrats who described it as a cotton planter's measure and a sign of Southern dominance in the party.* The repeal of the English Corn Laws,** however, delighted the Northern grain-growers, with the result that in 1857 another Democratic Administration was able to make America a truly free-trade nation. "Wheat and cotton might have kept her in that column through the nineteenth century, had not the secession of the Southern states given the protectionists a new opportunity."[1]

2

The Oregon boundary was settled in the same momentous year of 1846, and it too was settled in a fashion that did not please the North. After all the rant about "Fifty-Four Forty or Fight," and after an inaugural ad-

* The vote on the bill was ominously sectional. Regardless of party, not a single Congressman from Massachusetts, Connecticut, Rhode Island, or New Jersey supported it, and only one from Pennsylvania. Fifty-seven Southern Democrats voted for the bill, and one against. The West supported the South in the expectation of return favors.

** 1846. Duties on wheat entering the United Kingdom were reduced immediately, and it was provided that they were to become purely nominal by 1849.

dress which stated that "our title to the country of the Oregon is clear and unquestionable," Polk told Secretary of State Buchanan to suggest to Great Britain that the territory be shared by extending the forty-ninth parallel as the boundary all the way to the Pacific. The British Minister, Pakenham, refused the offer. Polk reasserted America's claim to the whole of Oregon, and war seemed probable. The British Government then disavowed Pakenham's act, offering to accept the Polk plan with the proviso that the island of Vancouver was to remain British. The treaty was signed in June, 1846.

It was a good settlement; but it had a rough passage in the Senate. Western expansionists attacked Polk for sacrificing their interests and for being a tool of the planters. They had been promised Oregon as a reward for allowing the South to have Texas. They had been cheated of their prize; but the South had already received full payment—for after the election of Polk, in the last days of Tyler's Administration, the annexation of Texas had been authorized by a joint resolution of both houses of Congress, and on July 4, 1845, the Texas legislature had agreed to join the Lone Star Republic to the American Union.*

"Oh, Mountain that was delivered of a mouse!" cried Thomas Hart Benton, "Thy name shall be fifty-four forty." And Senator E. A. Hannegan of Indiana proclaimed that "Texas and Oregon were born the same instant, nurtured and cradled in the same cradle—the Baltimore Convention—and they were at the same instant adopted by the Democracy throughout the land. There was not a moment's hesitation until Texas was admitted; but the moment she was admitted the peculiar friends of Texas turned and were doing all they could to strangle Oregon." In the end the treaty was accepted. Polk had assured this by suddenly and surprisingly treating the Senate as a privy council and asking its advice in advance as to whether he should decline England's reluctant offer to accept the forty-ninth parallel as the boundary. The Senate dared not advise rejection, at the possible cost of war, and was therefore denied the pleasures of indefinite delay and inordinate abuse when the treaty came before it for ratification. This was the first time the Senate had been consulted in such a fashion since Washington's unhappy experience. It was characteristic of Polk to seize all means, new or old, to impose his will.

As the Northerners and Westerners well knew, beyond Texas Polk saw California, which he intended to take. And between Texas and California lay an enormous Mexican province, seven hundred miles wide, which he would have to take too, and most of which would make slave states if the Missouri Compromise line were extended to the Pacific. The breaking of Walker's bargain between the sections was good foreign politics, for Polk could scarcely have afforded two wars at a time; but it was bad domestic

* Formalities were completed on December 29, 1845.

politics and the North and West retaliated after the Mexican War by acts which helped to split the nation in two.*

The West soon acquired another grievance. When she gave her votes for the Walker Tariff she understood that the South would support improvements at federal expense for Western harbors, rivers, and roads. Senator Hannegan had sent word to Calhoun that if the South would promise this help, the West would "go with the South on the tariff." So in 1844 Calhoun argued strongly for the improvement of the navigation of the Mississippi, insisting that the federal government could do this under the power to regulate commerce. He had also renewed his support for the Western plan to reduce the price of public lands. In the summer of 1846 a river and harbor bill passed Congress, providing for large improvements on the Great Lakes and on Western rivers. In spite of Calhoun, the South did not rally to the support of this bill; and as if to discredit Calhoun, Polk vetoed it on constitutional grounds. Calhoun's program was ruined. He had stretched his strict-construction conscience to the breaking point in order to outbid the North for Western support, and the President had made him look like a crooked dealer. The Western press was furious and Western Congressmen began plotting revenge. They had been fooled on Oregon; they had been cheated on internal improvements; but the South had been paid in full, with Texas and with the Walker Tariff. "Hereafter," wrote the Chicago *Democrat,* "the West must be respected, and her commerce must be protected as well as that of other portions of the Union: and the iron rod wielded over her by Southern despots must be broken."[2]

Step by step, the South's ability to barter for Western votes was being diminished. All she had left to offer was free land, and we have seen that in the next decade this offer was withdrawn. The long contest between North and South for the allegiance of the new third region was ending in Southern defeat. Incidentally, Polk was the third Southern President to frustrate the hopes of his section by vetoing an internal improvements bill. The first and the last of those bills had been backed by Calhoun. The inventor of "rule by concurrent majorities" knew that the South could not ask for a veto to protect her own interests unless she was ready to confer positive favors upon the interests of others.

* Calhoun must have foreseen this danger, for he warned against the war of expansion which was so popular in the South. "Mexico is to us the forbidden fruit," he said in the Senate, whither he had returned after his service in the Tyler Cabinet; "the penalty of eating it would be to subject our institutions to political death." In this (and perhaps in this alone) he agreed with Ralph Waldo Emerson, who declared that "Mexico will poison us."

3

Since the late eighteenth century the merchantmen of Massachusetts had been trading with California, exchanging anything from Chinese fireworks to New England rum for hides and tallow whose cheapness more than repaid the long voyage. In the early years the trade had been illegal and irregular; but after 1822, when California revolted from Spain and became a province of the Republic of Mexico, the trade was legitimate. Meanwhile the growth of a shoe-manufacturing industry in New England increased the demand for hides. Yet Mexican duties were from eighty to a hundred per cent, and Mexican regulations were onerous, so it seemed clear to Polk that destiny intended the United States to own this rich and underpopulated country.

After telling the American consul on the Pacific coast that the United States would protect the people of California if they cut loose from Mexico, Polk turned his attention to acquiring the land between Texas and California. This could only be done by purchase or by war. Mexico refused to sell and was reluctant to fight, in spite of the annexation of Texas. Polk hesitated—as Bismarck or Cavour might have hesitated—to attack Mexico on the bare and open ground that he wanted to steal her land. Fortunately for Polk's plans, there was a dispute as to the southern boundary of Texas —the Texans claiming it was the Rio Grande, the Mexicans claiming it was the Nueces, which lay considerably farther north. The facts were disappointingly pro-Mexican, for until the young Republic of Texas made her large claim the Nueces River had been the established boundary of the province for a hundred years. Polk, however, ordered General Taylor to lead an American army across the Nueces and to occupy the left bank of the Rio Grande. Even then the exasperating Mexicans would not start a war.

Early in May, 1846, Polk told his Cabinet that he was about to send a war message to Congress. The United States had some claims against Mexico for repudiated bonds and damage to American property during civil disturbances. When Mexico, being virtually bankrupt, suspended payment on these claims, Polk prepared to use them as an excuse for war. He had first tried to force Mexico to cede all the land he wanted in return for a cancellation of the claims and a payment of fifteen or twenty million dollars. The Mexicans refused to sell their country and insisted on mentioning honor, a point of view which seemed both obstructive and backward to Polk. The claims, when they were finally adjudicated in 1851, amounted to a little more than three million dollars.

The Cabinet agreed to Polk's message, but regretted that Mexico had not committed some overt act, for as things stood American benevolence might be questioned by a cynical world and the war might be thought aggressive. That very afternoon, the welcome news arrived that a Mexican force had crossed the Rio Grande and killed some American soldiers. Polk could go ahead happily. "The cup of forbearance had been exhausted," he told Congress, "even before the recent information from the frontier. . . . But now, after reiterated menaces, Mexico . . . has invaded our territory and shed American blood upon the American soil." Congress promptly declared that "by the act of the Republic of Mexico, a state of war exists between that Government and the United States."

This was not a triumph of duplicity, but of bigoted stubbornness. It is hard to convey the combination of smallness and strength, triviality and importance, that went to the making of James K. Polk. Bernard De Voto writes:

> Polk had come up the ladder, he was an orthodox party Democrat. . . . But sometimes the belt line shapes an instrument of use and precision. Polk's mind was rigid, narrow, obstinate, far from first-rate. He sincerely believed that only Democrats were truly American, Whigs being either the dupes or the pensioners of England—more, that not only wisdom and patriotism were Democratic monopolies but honor and breeding as well. "Although a Whig he seems a gentleman" is a not uncommon characterization in his diary. He was pompous, suspicious, and secretive; he had no humor; he could be vindictive; and he saw spooks and villains. . . . But if his mind was narrow it was also powerful. . . . If he was orthodox, his integrity was absolute and he could not be scared, manipulated, or brought to heel. No one bluffed him, no one moved him with direct or oblique pressure. Furthermore, he knew how to get things done, which is the first necessity of government, and he knew what he wanted done, which is the second.[3]

If Polk could not attribute patriotism, or even good manners, to an American Whig, the thought that a Mexican might have rights which should be honored and protected could clearly find no lodgement in his narrow brain.

The Americans in California, meanwhile, had taken Polk's hint and had declared themselves an independent state. The Mexican War, to which the Whig minority in Congress was bitterly hostile, was brief and successful, the American Army proving a more useful force than it had been during the last expansionist attempt in 1812. Early in 1848 Mexico accepted a peace which recognized the annexation of Texas and ceded to the United States the provinces of Upper California and New Mexico—a territory larger than France and Germany combined.* The United States paid fif-

* This included the present states of California, Nevada, Utah, Arizona, New Mexico, and parts of Colorado and Wyoming.

teen million dollars and assumed the damage claims. At the time the treaty
was being prepared, gold was discovered in California.

On accepting the nomination in 1844, Polk said that he had "a settled
purpose of not being a candidate for re-election." Much to everyone's surprise, this was still his purpose when his first term drew to an end. On
March 4, 1849, he left Washington for his home in Nashville. Three
months later he was dead.

4

Polk was accused by the Whigs of forcing a war in order to extend the institution of slavery, and many Americans were sick at what they took to be
their country's dishonor. When Lewis Cass claimed the nation needed
more room, Thomas Corwin of Ohio attacked him in the Senate. "This,"
said Corwin, "has been the plea of every robber chief from Nimrod to the
present hour. . . . If I were a Mexican, I would tell you, 'Have you not
room in your own country to bury your dead men? If you come into mine,
we will greet you with bloody hands and welcome you to hospitable
graves.' " Herman Melville, bitter at the smugness with which his countrymen condoned aggression, compared them unfavorably to the honest can-
nibals of the South Seas. And Abraham Lincoln, serving as a young Whig
Congressman from Illinois, asked that the President indicate the exact spot
where the war began, so the nation could decide for itself whether the
United States had been invaded. And on January 3, 1848, Lincoln voted
for a resolution which referred to the war as "unnecessarily and unconstitutionally begun by the President of the United States."

Unnecessary the war may have been, but only on the assumption that
there was no need for the United States to have more land. Polk was not
bent on extending slavery, but on extending America. He had caught the
expansionist fever* which raged through the West in the middle forties,
and since he was a President of rare force he had his way both with Mexico and with Congress. He not only, as Bancroft said, imposed his will
upon his Cabinet, but he imposed it upon his legislature, which is more
difficult for an American President. He was the strongest man in the

---

* De Voto (*The Year of Decision,* pp. 8–9) lists the obvious economic reasons
for this fever, and then wisely adds: "Expansionism contained such other and un-
analyzable elements as romance, Utopianism, and the dream that men might yet
be free. It also contained another category of ingredients—such as the logic of
geography, which the map of January 1st, 1846, made quite as clear to the Americans then as it is to anyone today. You yourself, looking at a map in which Oregon
was jointly occupied by a foreign power and all the rest of the continent west of
Texas and the continental divide was foreign territory, would experience a feeling
made up of incompletion and insecurity. . . . The Americans had always devoutly

White House between Jackson and Lincoln. He consolidated the Jacksonian changes in the presidency and made certain that they would endure. There have been many weak Presidents since his day, who dared not use the formidable power that had been handed them; but for all who wished to use it, the power was there.

Polk, incidentally, was the first President to reassert the Monroe Doctrine, thus helping to establish it in the public mind as permanent national policy. His own plans for acquiring territory in North America were so ambitious that there was obviously no room for other nations. In a message to Congress on December 2, 1845, he not only reaffirmed the Doctrine, he stretched it to apply to any European protectorate or to any foreign interference with the dealings between American nations. Having in mind Guizot's provocative statement of the previous June, Polk wrote:

> Jealousy among the different sovereigns of Europe . . . has caused them anxiously to desire the establishment of what they term the "balance of power." It cannot be permitted to have any application on the North American continent, and especially to the United States. We must ever maintain that people of this continent alone have a right to decide their own destiny. Should any portion of them, constituting an independent state, propose to unite themselves with our Confederacy, this will be a question for them and us to determine without any foreign interposition. We can never consent that European powers shall interfere to prevent such a union because it might disturb the "balance of power" which they may desire to maintain upon this continent.

The final step in the annexation of Texas was about to take place, and France and England had clearly decided not to interfere, so the words at the time seemed uncalled-for; but later, when the United States had more power with which to back such words, the fact that they had been spoken, and repeated, became important.

5

The steady attacks upon Polk by the Whigs, the repeated statements that his use of the presidential authority was unconstitutional, led to a stern

---

believed that the superiority of their institutions, government, and mode of life would eventually spread, by inspiration and imitation, to less fortunate, less happy peoples. That devout belief now took a new phase: it was perhaps the American destiny to spread our free and admirable institutions by action as well as by example, by occupying territory as well as by practising virtue. . . . For the sum of these feelings, a Democratic editor found, in the summer of '45, one of the most dynamic phrases ever minted, 'Manifest Destiny.' " This is true; yet one may regret that "the logic of geography" so often leads to theft and battle.

reply. In his last annual message to Congress Polk read that body a lecture on the Executive office.

> Any attempt [he said] to coerce the President to yield his sanction to measures which he cannot approve would be a violation of the spirit of the Constitution. . . . The people by the Constitution have commanded the President as much as they have commanded the legislative branch of the Government to execute their will. . . . If it be said that the Representatives in the popular branch of Congress are chosen directly by the people, it is answered, the people elect the President. . . . The President represents in the executive department the whole people of the United States as each representative of the legislative department represents portions of them.

It was this last statement, when made by Jackson, which infuriated the Senate and drove Clay to his loudest cries of protest. Yet it was simply the truth. The people had seized the presidency and made it the agent of their will. They had circumvented the Constitution, substituting popular election of the President for the elaborate scheme of the Fathers, and thereby giving to the office a direct representative character. No speeches by Whig Senators could undo that fact. So long as the people supported the President, he could make policy and he could defeat a Congressional policy of which he disapproved. Without the strong support of the people, he could still defeat Congressional policy but he could do nothing positive. Professor Ford writes:

> The agency of the presidential office has been such a master force in shaping public policy that to give a detailed account of it would be equivalent to writing the political history of the United States. From Jackson's time to the present day it may be said that political issues have been decided by executive policy. . . . While all that a President can certainly accomplish is to force the submission of an issue to the people, yet such is the strength of the office that, if he makes a sincere and resolute use of its resources, at the same time cherishing his party connection, he can as a rule carry his party with him, because of the powerful interests which impel it to occupy the ground taken for it by the administration. . . . If, in default of a definite administrative policy vigorously asserted, Congress is left to its own devices, issues are compromised and emergencies are dealt with by makeshift expedients. . . . The evidence which our history affords seems conclusive of the fact that the only power which can end party duplicity and define issues in such a way that public opinion can pass upon them decisively, is that which emanates from presidential authority. It is the rule of our politics that no vexed question is settled except by executive policy.[4]

The President, according to this statement, must "cherish his party connection" if he is to exert his strength. This was the second part of the

Jacksonian revolution: not only was the new power of the popularly elected President asserted, but a new form of party organization was built to help the President to exercise the power in concert with the legislature. As Professor Ford comments:

> Party organization continues to be the sole efficient means of adminis-
> trative union between the executive and legislative branches of the
> government, and . . . whatever tends to maintain and perfect that
> union makes for orderly politics and constitutional progress; while what-
> ever tends to impair that union, disturbs the constitutional poise of the
> government, obstructs its functions, and introduces an anarchic condi-
> tion of affairs full of danger to all social interests. This is the cardinal
> principle of American politics.[5]

It is a principle which first became clear in the days of Jackson and his friend Polk. Thenceforth the President, to be successful, must not only represent the people as a whole, defending the national interest against sectional and class interests, he must also guide and control and wheedle the party leaders who are the representatives of sectional and class interests. The party leaders, in Congress and in the state machines, know the compromises which must be made if national policy (however necessary) is not to breed bitterness and disunion. The President knows the compromises he dare not make if the nation is to be served. Yet it is not enough to win a majority of all the people to his support; he must also win the specially affected local majorities and class majorities—for it is the representatives of local and economic interests who will pass upon his measures in Congress. Silver Senators or Farm Senators or Labor Senators or Southern white-supremacy Senators may have to be placated before a bill desired by most of the voters can pass. If they are not placated, if they are merely overridden by the will of a distant and unknown majority, the American federal system may begin to break.

It is not easy to be the one national leader in a country the size of America, the one man elected by all the people and expected to understand their common needs, and at the same time to be the party leader, presiding over the incessant and essential party compromises—never giving more than necessary, but never giving less. Yet this is what a successful President must attempt, which is why the American Government seldom runs well or easily. Yet one tribute must be paid to the system which developed during the Jackson days: it can be worked successfully by any very able and very popular politician. The system devised by Jefferson, on the other hand, could only be worked by himself. And the no-party system, envisaged by the Constitution, cannot be worked at all.

6

The first of the Northern retaliations against Southern expansion, foreseen by Calhoun, came in 1846. During the discussion of an appropriation
bill for "extraordinary expenses"—that is, for inducing Mexico to cede
land—Representative Wilmot (a Pennsylvania Democrat) offered an
amendment providing that no territory acquired from Mexico should be
open to slavery. The Wilmot Proviso was accepted by the House but not
by the Senate. The Proviso was reintroduced in 1847, and was again defeated in the Senate. The country was divided and angry, North against
South; the final struggle had begun.* Meanwhile, the time approached
for the next presidential campaign.

Undeterred by their recent experience with Tyler, the Whigs nominated
another strong-willed man: General Zachary Taylor, the hero of the
Mexican War. They sought to compensate by giving him the weakest possible running-mate: Millard Fillmore of New York State. Taylor, who was
sixty-four years old, was born in Orange County, Virginia. His father, who
had been a colonel in the War of Independence, moved to Kentucky, near
the present Louisville, when the boy was a year old. Zachary grew up on a
small, not very successful, plantation, and received almost no formal education. When war with England threatened, and the Army was being enlarged, Taylor was given a commission as first lieutenant in an infantry
regiment. At the end of the War of 1812 he left the service with the rank
of major; but he returned to it in 1816. At the time of the Black Hawk
War in 1832, he was in command of a regiment. About this time a young
officer in the regiment, named Jefferson Davis, fell in love with the
colonel's daughter. Taylor forbade the marriage; the girl went to visit an
aunt in Kentucky; Davis resigned his commission, followed Miss Sarah
Taylor to Kentucky, and there married her. They set out at once for
Davis's plantation in Mississippi; but the romance had a bad ending, for
Sarah Davis died of malarial fever three months after her marriage.

In 1845 Taylor was stationed in Louisiana and had become a brigadier
general and the owner of an unprosperous plantation in Mississippi. In
that summer he received orders from President Polk to march his troops
into Texas, across the Nueces, and in 1846 he was told to advance to the
Rio Grande. In the war which ensued he became a major general and
conquered the northeastern states of Mexico. He was liked by his troops,

---

* On January 4, 1847, the day the Proviso was reintroduced, Polk wrote in his
diary: "The slavery question is assuming a fearful and a most important aspect."
He added that if the Proviso was pushed it "will be attended with terrible consequences to the country, and cannot fail to destroy the Democratic party, if it
does not ultimately threaten the Union itself."

who called him "Old Rough and Ready," and his success made him a hero with the people. Since he was a Whig in politics, and since the wily Thurlow Weed had begun to push him for the presidency as early as 1846, his popularity may not have pleased Polk. In any case, Winfield Scott was sent to take Mexico City and Taylor's army was depleted to supply Scott with troops. Taylor believed this was a plot to break him. If so, the plot misfired, for when Taylor's force had been reduced to 5000 men it was attacked by Santa Anna with 20,000. Taylor made a magnificent stand in the glaring heat at Buena Vista—February, 1847—finally beating off the Mexicans and adding the finishing touch to his own reputation. Within a month, a Whig convention in Iowa had nominated him for the presidency.*

Taylor, though a Whig, had never voted for a President or taken an active part in politics. At first he was unwilling to accept the nomination, but he gave in to the flattering popular clamor. He insisted that he did not want to be a party candidate, but he discovered there was no other kind. He was emphatically the people's choice, the politicians (except for Weed) being afraid of him. He had dogmatic views in private; but the public was not told of them. And the Whigs were careful not to handicap him by expressing any opinion or suggesting they had any policies or plans for the future. Taylor ran, and triumphed, as a military hero whom the people wished to reward. He could count on his full party strength in the North, outside of Ohio and Indiana, and as a slaveowner and the father-in-law of Jefferson Davis he could hope to hold some of the Southern Whigs whom Calhoun was luring into the other camp. Nevertheless, the Democrats might have won the election had they been able to hold their party together and sidestep the slavery issue. They failed to do either of these desirable things—largely because of Van Buren.

The Barnburner faction of the Democratic Party in New York State controlled the legislature and in 1844 had elected the governor, Silas Wright.** Because they approved the Wilmot Proviso, the federal patronage was withdrawn from the Barnburners by Polk's Administration. The jobs all went to Hunkers, and with the help of this patronage the Hunkers were able to run the New York State Democratic Convention at Syracuse, in 1847. The convention rejected a Barnburner resolution expressing "uncompromising hostility to the extension of slavery into territory now free." The Barnburners thereupon seceded and called their own meeting at

---

* Another future President established a national reputation at Buena Vista. Colonel Jefferson Davis of the "Mississippi Rifles" had saved the day with a gallant defense against a Mexican cavalry charge, and his name was almost as widely applauded as his general's.

** Among their other leaders were "Prince John" Van Buren, the ex-President's son, and Samuel J. Tilden of post-Civil-War fame. Wright failed to be re-elected governor in 1846.

Herkimer, New York, to discuss their wrongs and to plan their future. This Herkimer meeting is the first step toward the creation of the modern Republican Party. It agreed on a blunt statement that the New York State Democracy would not vote for any presidential candidate who favored the extension of slavery into the territories.

In 1848 the Barnburners met at Utica to choose delegates to the Democratic National Convention. They issued a statement—the work of the two Van Burens and of Tilden—affirming that slavery contradicted the principles of the Democratic Party and the traditions of the American people. Meanwhile, the Hunkers chose their own delegates; so when the National Convention met at Baltimore (in May, 1848) two sets of delegates appeared from New York State. The convention offered to let each of them cast half the state's vote; but the compromise was refused by both groups. The Barnburners withdrew. The convention then nominated Lewis Cass of Michigan—the man who had become Jackson's Secretary of War after the resignation of the too-much-married Eaton. The party platform said nothing about the slavery issue, but spoke highly of the late war with Mexico and referred disparagingly to European monarchs.

Cass was America's leading imperialist. After he had failed to receive the presidential nomination in 1844, the Michigan legislature appointed him to the United States Senate. There he favored appropriating most of the North American continent. The annexation of Texas he of course approved. "The Oregon I claim," he said, "is all Oregon, and no vote of mine in this Senate will surrender one *inch* of it to England." Similarly, the Mexico he claimed appeared to be all Mexico, for in 1847 he announced, "We must continue our occupation of Mexico, and push the invasion still farther." He was opposed to the Wilmot Proviso, and anticipated the doctrine of "squatter sovereignty" which was later put forward by Stephen A. Douglas. "Leave to the people who will be affected by this question," said Cass, "to adjust it upon their own responsibility and in their own manner."

With these views, Cass was acceptable to the South, but not to the Barnburners. After walking out of the Democratic Convention at Baltimore they called for a convention to meet at Buffalo, in August, 1848, inviting all who were opposed to the further extension of slavery. Van Buren sent a letter in which he reviewed the long argument as to whether Congress had the power to exclude slavery from the territories, urged forcefully that it had, and asserted that he could not vote for Lewis Cass. The Buffalo Convention thereupon created the Free Soil Party, nominating Van Buren for President and Charles Francis Adams (the son of John Quincy Adams) for Vice-President. There were four main planks to the party platform: the prohibition of slavery in the territories, the free distribution of public lands to actual settlers, internal improvements, and a protective tariff.* The Barnburner Convention not only assured the defeat of the Democratic Party in 1848, it led to the birth of the Republican Party a few years later. When that party came to power in 1860, it was with the four planks from the Free Soil platform plus the Whig demand for a National Bank.

Van Buren, as Free Soil candidate, won about 300,000 votes but no electors. In New York State he got 121,000 votes against 114,000 for Cass. General Taylor got 218,000 votes in New York. Cass might have won the state if it had not been for the Free Soil Party, and if he had won New York he would have won the presidency.** So Van Buren, the inventor of party "regularity," had broken his party. The first "organization man" had betrayed the organization which he himself had built. No one could be more cool or forgetful than Van Buren toward a man who did not "play the game" in politics, so he cannot have been surprised to find himself reviled by his old friends. In 1833 Van Buren was the favorite of the all-conquering Jackson; Calhoun was in danger of being hanged for a traitor. In 1848 Van Buren was the party apostate, with no political future; Calhoun was master of the South, and the South was master of the Democratic Party. The stage was set for the last great effort of the Cotton Kingdom to control the nation's destiny. "A population of two and a half millions in the lower South," writes Professor Dodd, "with only a tenth of them directly connected with slavery, would guide a nation of twenty millions, nine tenths of whom were either outspoken or silent opponents of slavery and all it connoted."

Van Buren played no further part in high politics. He returned to the Democratic Party in 1852, but could do nothing to prevent the mistakes which he felt the party was making. He lived to see the outbreak of the Civil War, dying at Kinderhook in 1862.

7

The second Whig President lived a little longer than the first, but not long enough to matter. Taylor's Inaugural Address was a proper, self-denying Whig document.

> The Executive [he said] has authority to recommend (not to dictate) measures to Congress. Having performed that duty, the Executive department of the Government cannot rightfully control the decision of

* A neat combination of sops to the East and to the West. Van Buren had not submerged his old cunning in his new righteousness.
** That is, if he had held Indiana and Ohio. It is probable that without a Free Soil Party Taylor would have taken these states, and thus the election.

Congress on any subject of legislation until that decision shall have been officially submitted to the President for approval. The check provided by the Constitution in the clause conferring the qualified veto will never be exercised by me except in the cases contemplated by the Fathers of the Republic. I view it as an extreme measure, to be resorted to only in extraordinary cases, as when it may become necessary to defend the executive against encroachments of the legislative power or to prevent hasty and inconsiderate or unconstitutional legislation.

This was all very well, and Taylor undoubtedly meant it, for he had expressed the same opinions in letters to Jefferson Davis and others in 1847; but the presidency had by this time become an office in which it was difficult to refuse power. No strong-willed man like General Taylor, accustomed to rule, could any longer be a Madisonian President. Taylor was faced immediately with the Wilmot Proviso, which he had thought was an unimportant issue in the days when he was only a general. He now found it of vital importance, and on studying it he discovered that he was in total disagreement with the leaders of the Whig Party. If a bill containing the Wilmot Proviso was presented him, he would sign it. He told the Northern people that they "need have no apprehension of the further extension of slavery." When Southern Congressmen threatened secession, he told them he would take the field in person and hang anyone guilty of rebellion. Clay and Webster were soon as bitter against Taylor as they had been against the previous Whig President. And Taylor had begun to understand why the country laughed when he urged Congress, in his first message, to "abstain from the introduction of those exciting topics of sectional character which have hitherto produced painful apprehensions in the public mind."

While learning that the major problem in American life could not be dissolved in words, he was also receiving instruction in one of the minor problems of politics. Like most amateurs, Taylor had been contemptuous of all forms of jobbery, and as a candidate he insisted he saw no reason why Whigs should be preferred to Democrats when it came to making appointments. On taking office he was quickly shown that he must be either a John Quincy Adams, virtuous and impotent, or he must be a party leader, maintaining party discipline and thus securing Congressional help for his measures. And how, he was asked, would he maintain party discipline if he refused to distribute the patronage among his loyal followers?

The heads of the large custom houses and post offices, the federal attorneys, marshals, and land officers, the lucky recipients of government printing contracts which often yielded fifty per cent profits—these were the men (or the friends of the men) who manned and directed the state and city machines, dominated the state conventions, selected many of the candidates for House and Senate. If the President and his executive aids did not appoint their friends to these positions, how could they expect faithful support for their policies? And if they did appoint their friends to the top posts, how could they object if the thousands of minor jobs were distributed for the same purposes and in the same fashion? Because of the size and diversity of the country, the national party was nothing but a skeleton organization, a communications center for the powerful state and city machines. If the state and city leaders were dissatisfied, the national party fell to pieces and the Administration could not govern. Even with the firmest discipline and the strongest party machine, and even when the President's party had majorities in both Houses, Congress could be counted on to water down the Administration measures, to delay almost unbearably, and to introduce many regional and special-interest compromises. This was proper; it was an intentional result of the federal system and the division of powers; it was a needed protection against government by a mere majority. But it was one thing for Congress to impose delay, to impose compromise, to insist on a hearing for every economic and regional interest; it was another thing for Congress to refuse all Executive leadership and even advice, and to revert to the chaos of government by standing committees. Yet this was what happened whenever the President failed to "cherish his party connection."

These facts were explained to the innocent General Taylor, with the result that during his first few months in office 3400 Democratic officeholders were replaced by Whigs.

On July 4, 1850, Taylor became a victim of the Washington climate. At a public ceremony in the boiling heat he drank too much cold water. He contracted a fever, and in five days he was dead. It is possible that his death was a blessing both to himself and to his country, for he was on the verge of a Cabinet scandal involving a lighthearted attitude toward the public funds on the part of the Attorney General, the Secretary of the Treasury, and the Secretary of War, and he was also on the verge of a sectional conflict which might well have led to fighting. On July 5 Taylor would have sent to Congress a message demanding the immediate admission of California and New Mexico as free states, and the settlement of the border dispute between Texas and New Mexico in favor of the latter, if necessary with the help of federal troops. Professor Allan Nevins comments:

> Had Taylor lived, his defiant message on the dispute with Texas would have gone to Congress. He would have remade his Cabinet with a decided Northern preponderance. . . . Conflict in the Southwest, coupled with a general Southern revolt against the naked California and New Mexico bills, would have given the country stormy months and perhaps bloody scenes. It may be said that a stern Jacksonian policy in 1850 would perhaps have cowed the secessionists into submission, and

thus possibly have averted the Civil War which came a decade later. But this seems so unlikely that we may well rejoice that death intervened; that the clash of two civilizations was postponed until the North was relatively much stronger, and a far wiser leader sat in the White House.[6]

8

Taylor had been opposed to dodging the issue presented by the Wilmot Proviso. In this he was supported by John C. Calhoun, who also did not want a compromise. Calhoun pressed for a final decision as to where the South stood. Superficially, the problem of the new territory seemed to have settled itself by 1850, for by that time New Mexico was known to be a dry land where no slaveholder could prosper, and California had declared her desire to be a free state.* But Calhoun was looking to the future. He countered the Wilmot Proviso with the doctrine that Congress had no power to prohibit slavery in the territories, since slaves were common-law property. It was Congress's duty, he said, to protect the lawful property of American citizens, not to take their property away from them. If this doctrine were accepted (and in 1857 it was endorsed by the Supreme Court), the Missouri Compromise of 1820, which prohibited slavery in the territories north of 36° 30′, would become null and void.

Calhoun knew he would raise a storm in the North; but he wished to force the issue, being prepared for one of two results: secession (before the North was too strong to be resisted), or a constitutional amendment which would insure what he called "the rule of the concurrent majority." He wished to make certain that the South, which was already heavily outnumbered, could never be subjected to the domination of a numerical majority resident elsewhere. One way to accomplish this, he believed, would be to create a dual Executive: one President elected by the North and another by the South, each with a legislative veto. If this were deemed impractical, the South would accept any constitutional change which made sectional compromise a necessity.

Such compromise, Calhoun felt, was the dominant theme in American political life, and the unique contribution of the United States to the political thought of the free world; but the South could no longer count on the political good sense of the North to insure compromise. The ravings of anti-slavery fanatics had clouded that good sense and the South must now insist on a form of protection which was written into the constitu-

---

* The South had hoped, originally, that California might be divided in two, the southern half of it being saved for the plantation system.

tional bond. This was her last chance. The North was far more wealthy than the South and far more populous.* In a few years the railways would have built a new Northwest, tied to the Northeast by lines of commerce and by a common aversion to the "peculiar institution" of slavery. When that happened, the North would win final control of the government at Washington and would reinstate all the Hamiltonian policies, meanwhile interfering in every possible way with the slave system. To Calhoun this meant the doom of Southern agriculture and Southern life. If Southerners waited for secession until all this had happened, they would find themselves too weak, and would be constrained to remain in the Union under Northern domination. Now was the time to force a decision. If Union sentiment in the North was strong enough to secure a constitutional amendment protecting the South forever against exploitation, so much the better. That was the one compromise the South could afford to accept. The argument was logical, but fatally doctrinaire and unbending.

Unfortunately for Calhoun's plans, a very different compromise was accepted. Henry Clay, who had patched up the sectional quarrel in 1820, and again in 1833, returned to the Senate to face the new crisis and produced his last and greatest effort. In January, 1850, he brought forward compromise resolutions containing prizes and bitter pills for both sides. California was to be admitted at once as a free state, and the slave trade in the District of Columbia was to be stopped. Those were the Northern prizes. They were balanced by two other resolutions: that the rest of the land taken from Mexico was to be organized into territories with no provision as to slavery or its absence, and that a more strict fugitive-slave law was to be passed.** A week later Clay defended the proposals in two of his finest speeches. He begged the North to understand the South's pride and the South's fears, and to accept the substance of the Wilmot Proviso without insisting that it be written into law. He begged the South to remember the benefits of Union, and not to forget that secession must mean war— "furious, bloody, implacable, exterminating." The millions who lived in the upper Mississippi Valley, he said, would never permit the mouth of that river to be held by a foreign power. Throughout the long debate he returned to these points disarmingly and beguilingly. It was obvious why the public had loved him beyond all his contemporaries. In July he made the last great speech of his career.

Early in March Calhoun made his reply to the proposals. He was a dying man, and his cause was dying with him. He was so weak that he had

* In 1850 there were 23,191,876 people in the United States. Of these, the eleven states which were to form the Southern Confederacy had seven and a quarter million.

** There was a fifth resolution, that the boundary dispute between Texas and New Mexico be settled, with assumption of the Texas debt by the federal government.

to sit grimly watching while his speech was read by Senator Mason of Virginia. In the early days of the Union, he wrote, there had been an equal distribution of power between the North and the South. That equality was gone. In wealth and population the North had forged ahead, and the disparity would grow greater. The change had not come for natural reasons, but because of three pernicious policies of the federal government: first, the exclusion of slavery from most of the territories (under the Northwest Ordinance and the Missouri Compromise), with the result that the Southern economic system had been deprived of its proper chance to spread; second, the protective tariff, making artificially high prices for what the South had to buy, and subsidizing the Northern factory; third, the consolidation of power in the hands of the federal government, with the result that any regional majority which took charge at Washington would find an all-too-efficient weapon for oppression.

To these old wrongs a new grievance had been added: the anti-slavery agitation which openly sought to overturn the social system of the South. Unless scotched at once, this must grow stronger as the North grew stronger, until the South was forced to choose between abolition and secession.

And why should the South be forever on the defensive? The South was not seeking to impose adverse economic conditions on other regions; she was only seeking to keep other regions from imposing such conditions upon herself. The South was not trying to change the social system of Boston, or to improve the lot of wage-slaves in the factories of Fall River; the South was asking to be let alone.

Henry Clay's compromise met none of the Southern grievances. The North had taken the offensive, and that offensive must cease. If the South were given protection against exploitation or interference from without, the Union could endure forever, and for the good of all. If the South were denied this protection, she must secede.

Until the publication of his posthumous books, this was the last word from Calhoun. He died within the month. He is said to have died murmuring, "The South! The poor South! God knows what will become of her!" One of the South's devoted sons commented in 1939:

> What has become of her? God knows! She went out to battle and she fell. She has lain in economic bondage longer than the republic had lasted when Calhoun was in his prime. She has felt the lash of the taskmaster, and has made bricks without straw. She has been perverse, and froward, and indomitable, foul and magnificent. She has produced Robert E. Lee and Huey Long, *Deep River* and *Tobacco Road,* John Wilkes Booth and Sergeant York, Woodrow Wilson and *The Memphis Blues.* In the matter of Negro enfranchisement she has defied the Constitution of the United States and she has flung her sons by thousands

on the bayonets of its enemies. She has given us lessons in lynching and courtesy. Distracted, violent and tender, she is filled with loveliness and horror and drives her sons to revile while they adore her.[7]

The decisive speech was made by Webster on the seventh of March. New England would never accept a new and more punitive Fugitive Slave Act unless it were backed by the whole power of Webster's prestige. And if the Fugitive Slave Act were rejected, the South would reject the rest of Clay's measures and Calhoun would have his way. Webster's first sentence showed that he favored the proposals: "I speak today for the preservation of the Union. Hear me for my cause." This speech, and the arduous subsequent debates, were to be his last great effort also. The speech was given added dignity by the knowledge that the men of letters and the younger men of politics in the North would turn on Webster and call him traitor for recommending the Compromise. Once again the Senate was under the spell of that conquering presence. Old age had destroyed none of Webster's impressiveness; and when, with a weakened voice but undiminished oratory, he pleaded for conciliation in the name of patriotism, it must have been hard even for a Southerner to remember the reasoning of Calhoun. "No speech more patriotic or evincing a higher degree of moral courage had ever been made in Congress," writes Professor Nevins. "For once Webster rose to the highest level of statesmanship. In the fierce light of the history written by events during the next generation, hardly a line of his address failed to meet the test of truth and wisdom."[8]

Webster, nevertheless, did not reach men's hearts as Clay had reached them. For too many years Webster had made a parade of his service to business. When he talked of the glory of the Union, his enemies had learned to compute the dividends the Union was paying to the Cotton Whigs of Massachusetts. In 1850 those dividends were high. Both maritime and manufacturing Massachusetts flourished on the Southern trade.

Year by year [writes Samuel Eliot Morison] the wealthy Cotton Belt wore out more boots and shoes, purchased more cottons for her slaves, used more Quincy granite in her public buildings, and consumed more Fresh Pond ice* in her mint juleps. The New England mills, on their part, were calling for more cotton; and every pound of it that they received, before the Civil War, came by sailing vessel from Charleston, Savannah, Mobile, and New Orleans. The factory hands were equally hungry for cheap food. . . . In the period from September 1, 1841, to May 1, 1842, one-quarter of the lard, more than one-quarter of the flour, nearly half the pork and more than half the corn shipped out of New Orleans went to Boston.[9]

---

* The trade in ice (cut from New England ponds) with the South, the West Indies. and even the Orient, was an interesting example of Yankee enterprise.

Yankee ships also took cotton from New Orleans to Lancashire, Nor-
mandy, Flanders, Prussia, and the Baltic Provinces. Cotton, in fact, had
become

> the most important medium in our carrying trade, replacing colonial
> rum and codfish, and the Oriental goods of Federalist days. Few con-
> verts were obtained by the abolitionists in Boston counting-rooms.
> Society, business, and politics in Massachusetts were dominated by a
> triple entente between "the Lords of the Lash and the Lords of the
> Loom"—and the Lords of the Long Wharf.[10]

In 1850, with the relatively low Walker Tariff and with hopes for a still
lower tariff if the Democrats returned to power, this two-way trade
profited the South as well as New England; but Southerners knew that
Webster's ideal Union would be one in which Massachusetts sold her
manufactures to the Cotton Kingdom at artificial high-tariff prices and
bought her raw materials from the South at world prices. The South saw
the threat of economic colonialism in Webster's Union; the Northern Free
Soilers saw the shadow of State Street across Webster's noble sentiments.
These suspicions do not diminish the splendor and the truth of the seventh
of March speech; but they do explain why many good citizens refused to
be moved by it.

Senator Seward of New York represented the younger generation of the
North in the great debate. He spoke for the future: the ominous future,
foreseen by Calhoun, wherein the South must choose abolition or secession.
Seward spoke for the "Conscience Whigs," as opposed to the "Cotton
Whigs"; he spoke for the Barnburners; he spoke for the men who were to
form the Republican Party. He admitted that under the Constitution Congress could allow slavery in the territories "but there is a higher law than
the Constitution which regulates our authority over the domain." "A
higher law"—America was back again at her beginnings, back with Jefferson, and Locke, and Blackstone. "This law of nature . . . dictated by
God himself . . . binding over all the globe . . . no human laws are of
any validity, if contrary to this." It is hard to argue with people who know
that their deeds correspond to the "higher law." And it is impossible to
compromise with them.

Such certainty was not yet the mood of the majority, North or South.
A number of influential Southerners, such as Alexander Stephens and
Robert Toombs, were still in the Whig Party and worked loyally for the
compromise.* After months of debate the necessary measures passed in

---

* In 1852 both Stephens and Toombs joined the Democratic Party. In the same
year, Henry Clay died and those of his followers who had remained with the Whigs
out of personal loyalty felt free to join the Democrats. At last, Calhoun's work
of uniting the Southern leaders in a single party was accomplished—posthumously
and too late.

September, 1850. Calhoun had died meanwhile; and a Southern convention had met in Nashville to decide whether to take Calhoun's advice and demand special guarantees as the price of staying in the Union. Nine states were represented. South Carolina and Mississippi were for strong measures; but the majority chose moderation, and in the end the convention merely asked that the old Missouri Compromise line be extended to the Pacific.

It was fortunate for the Compromise that Zachary Taylor took his overdose of ice water while the debates were still in progress. He had come under the influence of Senator Seward, and he threatened to veto any agreement which did not contain the Wilmot Proviso. Clay protested that the President and his friends had declared "war, open war, undisguised war" against the Compromise. Fillmore, on the other hand, had said that in case of a tie vote in the Senate he would exercise his privilege as Vice-President and cast the deciding vote in favor of the Compromise. Once again, therefore, the death of a Whig President meant a reversal of Executive policy.* On succeeding to office Fillmore at once changed the course of the debate by urging that Texas be paid ten million dollars for her boundary claim against New Mexico. Texas state securities, which were well distributed throughout the country, rose nine hundred per cent in value, and a new set of pressures were brought to bear on Congress. "The Texas Surrender Bill," wrote Senator Salmon P. Chase of Ohio, "was passed by the influence of the new administration which is Hunker and Compromise all over. The message of Fillmore . . . did the work."[11]

9

Calhoun's predictions as to what would happen were so accurate that some have blamed him for the subsequent tragedy, as if he had brought it to pass by mentioning it. Others have felt that the great Compromise was the culprit, and that Calhoun's proposal for a constitutional amendment should have been accepted. Yet this would only have aggravated what we have already seen to be a main problem of the American form of government: the problem of getting positive action in time. The government was devised to prevent action. With great difficulty and ingenuity (and with the able help of Marshall's Supreme Court and Jackson's advisers) it had cast off some of its chains, gained a little freedom and strength. Calhoun would have riveted the chains back on, and added a few more for safety. His "rule of the concurrent majority" meant that each

---

* The first time the change had been away from Whig Party policies, the second time it was toward them. The death of Taylor was almost as much of a blessing for the party leaders as the death of Harrison had been a calamity.

major region, class, or economic interest must have a formal, constitutional right to veto action.

Like Jefferson and like most Americans of the early days Calhoun was certain that increased powers for the government meant decreased liberties for the people. Hence his fear of the Mexican War and of the doctrine of "manifest destiny"—of America's mission to spread liberty even by force. War kills liberty, said Calhoun. So does the rule of an unchecked majority. Liberty can only flourish when man is protected from the rulers of his own choice.[12] The ruled, therefore, must be given "the means of making peaceable and effective resistance." And the one effective resistance is for each major interest and each section to have a veto. Obviously, if this were accepted, government would become impossible. Only in Jefferson's lost Arcadia could such a system work.

The nation was wise, therefore, to reject Calhoun's constitutional amendment. And it was also wise to adopt—extra-constitutionally, informally—many of Calhoun's proposals. The dilatory rule of the concurrent majority is a fair description of how, in normal times, the American party system operates. Out of the continent-wide welter of hopes and desires the parties build a compromise on which many diverse interests can agree. They do not ignore minorities, they incorporate and placate them. Each major party, in fact, is a league of minority groups—class, race, and regional. Such parties cannot afford to have hard and fast ideas, or to be Left, or Right, or even Middle. They must be all three at the same time, in different parts of the country. And they must make gentlemen's agreements (and committee rules) in Congress to prevent coalitions of enthusiasts from brushing aside minority protests. So, in truth, the party system provides for concurrent majorities, but in a subtler and more flexible form than Calhoun demanded.

Government by concurrent majority, however, would be death if it were written into the Constitution, for it must always break down at two points: it cannot act fast (so it must be overridden in an emergency), and it cannot deal with a conflict of principles. It can ward off unnecessary conflicts of principles. It can even pretend for a very long time that a conflict which clearly exists, and which cannot be dodged, does not exist at all—thus aggravating the problem deplorably. But it is a negative system, a system of inaction. And matters of principle, if they are so important that they must be settled, cannot be settled by inaction. This is what Jefferson feared, when he said that if the day came when a disagreement on moral principle was also a disagreement between sections the nation might fall.

PART TWO
1850–1909

XVII

The Parties on the Verge of Failure

THE COMPROMISE OF 1850 was the valiant last effort of the Webster-Clay generation to avoid disunion. It seemed to succeed. Threats of secession seemed to be overwhelmed by a renewed national goodwill. The Compromise was celebrated throughout the land as a glorious victory; yet within a few years it broke, and shortly thereafter the Union also broke. The divisive forces which are active in any large, rambling federal structure had triumphed over the forces making for prudence and concession. The party system had temporarily failed.

In seeking the reasons for failure[1] we should remember that the United States had never known a time of rest, of calm self-possession. Whenever the young nation seemed about to reach an equilibrium of forces, the circumstances shifted and the balance was again upset. From the day of her birth America lived among storms which she could neither control nor dodge. The storms of Napoleon coincided with her childhood, and were succeeded by the storms of the Industrial Revolution. Uneasy and insecure as the world may always have been, the United States surely faced uncommon troubles when she sought to found her new political and social institutions at a time when the conditions of life were changing more radically in a single generation than they had previously changed in a thousand years. Throughout the Western world for several decades each new invention brought a confused swirl of blessings and woes, until life lost whatever stability it had known. And if this was true even in Europe, the ferment must have been at its greatest in America, where the all-changing magic of the new technology was revealed during a period of wide westward expansion and of heavy immigration. The United States, for example, had by no means digested or even explored the whole of the Louisiana Purchase when the empire of Texas was added to the Union, and then Oregon, and the vast booty of Mexico. At once, gold in California, and discontent in Europe following the outbreaks of 1848, increased the torrents of new settlers. During the eighteen-forties the country received 1,713,251 immigrants; during the fifties 2,598,214.

This was exciting and inspiring, but it did not make for ease or political rest. Meanwhile the spoils of Mexico, as Emerson and Calhoun predicted, came close to poisoning the land—for with every new push toward the

West, every new territory opened for settlement, the rivalry between
Northern and Southern institutions was revived, and either the fear or the
stubborn defense of slavery was strengthened. And then, at last, under a
President who praised the Compromise but failed to grasp its spirit, the
lust to reach the gold fields of California in a hurry spurred on a sectional
struggle for control of the first transcontinental railway which helped to
explode the long-restrained hatreds. Yet the federal system as it had developed by 1850, with the party machinery which had been invented to
make it work, might have preserved the Union for many years, half slave
and half free, and might even have allowed the slow forces of social and
moral pressure to dispose of slavery and dissolve the tragic tension, if the
country had remained relatively quiet, subject only to normal vicissitude.
But in the boiling, churning welter of change which America had in fact
to endure, no palliatives could cloak the ever-renewed divisions, no concessions were given time to diminish ill will. This need not mean that the
Civil War was inevitable. Bonar Law may have been right when he said,
"There is no such thing as inevitable war. If war comes it will be from
failure of human wisdom." Nevertheless, among the reasons for the failure
of American wisdom during the eighteen-fifties, one of the most compelling may be that the rate of change had for some time been too rapid
for man-made systems to control.

The same hurry, the same derangement of inner peace, sharpened and
made dissonant the "cultural federalism" of America. When the United
States spread across thousands of miles of land, pushing into strange
climates and into regions like the Great Plains, which are so dry and high
and difficult that few plants or animals from the humid forest-country
could settle there (and no white men, until they invented new machinery
and new methods), the cultural similarity of the old seaboard days was
broken. And when non-English immigrants (chiefly the Irish, the Germans, and the Scandinavians during the forties and fifties) began in some
sections to outnumber the "native" stock, there ceased to be a solid cultural similarity to break.*

> The task of the political leaders, therefore [writes Professor Roy
> Franklin Nichols in defining the problems of cultural federalism], was
> more subtle than keeping slave and free states in a political union; it
> was the task of finding ways and means to hold citizens dominated by a
> variety of attitudes in one body politic. . . . Politicians must forever be

* The word "non-English" might suggest that the original citizens of the United
States were overwhelmingly of English blood. This was not the case. In colonial
days the New World was already a "melting pot." The Dutch were there in considerable numbers, and the French, the Welsh, the Swedes, the Irish, the Scotch-
Irish, the Germans. Yet during the first thirty years of her independence only about
a quarter of a million immigrants reached America. And during the next decade
only 143,439. So the growth in population, from about three millions at the time

busy composing formulas, organising through legislation, patronage, and power, political combinations strong enough to insure continued cooperation in the federal union.[2]

To combat the forces of division which were latent in cultural federalism politicians recommended a variety of cures, among which three were outstanding. Any one of the cures might in itself have been helpful; but the three taken together made everything worse. The first was an ardent nationalism which transcended state allegiance—gallantly preached by Webster. By the time the great orator died millions of his fellow-citizens, mostly but not solely in the North and West, had learned to base their patriotism and pride upon America as a whole, and upon American destiny.

Side by side with this, however, the eighteen-forties and fifties saw a strengthening of regionalism under the influence of the logical Calhoun. This, too, was an attempt to save the Union—a last effort to prevent secession. Calhoun was as firm a patriot as Webster. But he did not think the United States could survive the unchecked tendency toward concentration of power. So he made his rigid plans for fastening upon the Constitution for all time what he took to be the undefiled federalism of the Fathers. He wished to preserve the Union, not merely by reversing the drift of history, but by making the act of reversal everlasting. He chose to face the crisis in his country's life with the absolutism of a Plato (who never tried to govern) rather than with the give-and-take of a politician who has known the shifting sands of power. Daniel Webster was a weaker character than Calhoun, with a mind less cold and clear; but he understood better than his adversary the need for fluidity and imprecision if a federal system is to endure.*

This revived regionalism and this waxing nationalism might have conflicted in any case; but the conflict was made sure by reason of the third idea put forward for the preservation of the Union: the idea of democracy, or majority rule. As Professor Nichols points out, the ambiguous

---

of the Revolutionary War to more than twelve millions by 1830, came almost wholly from the reproduction of "native" stock. And although these "natives" were themselves of mixed blood, their institutions derived mostly from England and their culture was an American development from an English archetype. The language of England, the literature, the prayers, the nursery rhymes, the common law, the many shared political beliefs and practices, the background of a century and a half of political association—all these make it reasonable to speak of the early America as chiefly English, in spite of the rich variety of stock. Since the presidency of John Quincy Adams the country never again has been so homogeneous. (Cp. Professor Carl Wittke, *We Who Built America,* pp. xvi, 3–97, 101.)

* Neither regionalism nor nationalism, of course, was invented as a "cure" by Calhoun or Webster. Each, from earliest days, had been a strong force in the life of the nation. Each was now praised and put forward as the answer to the nation's troubles if everyone would only agree upon it. But everyone refused to agree.

word "democracy" was used in the early days of the republic to describe a political party rather than a national way of life: Jefferson's "Democratic-Republicans" for example, or Jackson's "Democrats," or "the American Democracy" as a name for Jackson's party. In most of the states, meanwhile, both life and politics were growing steadily more democratic, not in the party sense, but in the sense of manners and of popular government. Yet even as late as the age of Jackson popular government, or majority rule, was regarded as a matter concerning the states, and only the states—as a form of suffrage and a way of using their local powers which the states might adopt or reject, as they saw fit. No one had dared suggest that federal decisions should rest on nation-wide head-counting; the Senate alone seemed sufficient protection against such heresy. Then in the eighteen-fifties "democracy" began to assume new meanings, all distasteful to the South. Some suggested that the vexed question of slavery in the territories should be settled on democratic principles, rather than by federal bargains—that the settlers should be allowed to decide for themselves, by majority vote, whether this type of property was to exist. But many Southern leaders objected that under the Constitution no man could be deprived of property in any form, in any of the land which was held as a common trust. If a man from Ohio could take his horse into the territories, a man from Georgia could take his slave.*

Finally, and most bitter of all to the regionalists, radicals in some of the populous Northern states began to suggest that the federal Union was itself a "democracy" in the sense that the will of the national majority should prevail. "Pleas were heard," writes Professor Nichols, "for the acceptance of the democratic principle as the means of substituting fair play for the fractious negativism of minorities. . . . Such sporting words, however, did not make southerners forget the warning of the census. If the voice of the majority became the will of the Republic, they might well be at the mercy of their free-state neighbors. They feared the tyranny of numbers."[3]

People on all sides of the debate seem to have forgotten that a federal state must be an ever-renewed compromise between "the fractious negativism of minorities" and "the tyranny of numbers." If the majority demands its way too harshly the federal principle is broken, for the essence

* During the campaign of 1852, John A. Quitman of Mississippi, who had recently served as governor of that state and who had told the legislature that "prompt and peaceable secession" was better than acceptance of the Compromise of 1850, wrote that a slaveholder had a right to take his human property into any territory and to demand federal protection. Congress, he said, should "pass such laws as may be necessary to protect such property as well as any other. When the common government refuses such protection, it would disregard the object which called it into existence." As Professor Nevins points out, such a demand would seem "preposterous and horrifying" to many Northerners; yet in the South it was soon to be accepted as normal and moderate.

of federalism is the power of regional minorities to protect their interests. Yet if the minorities are too tediously fractious, they too can destroy federalism by abusing their privilege of obstruction. No group, whatever its constitutional "rights," can afford to forget the Hamiltonian maxim that the public business must somehow go forward. Throughout the eighteen-fifties in America the balance of forces, the delicate federal equilibrium between the power of the many to insist and the power of the few to deny, was increasingly threatened. The attempts to find a cure only made matters worse. Nationalism led to a strengthened regionalism; regionalism led to a demand for democracy; and the mere mention of democracy led the South to new insistence upon minority rights and local veto powers.

2

With the nation's mind so bedeviled, and with vast new lands to quarrel about (in addition to the old quarrels which had made trouble from the beginning), it seemed that the political parties with their nation-wide membership were the chief safeguard of the Union and that if they should break the Republic must be destroyed. Yet few men foresaw that they were in danger of breaking, for the party machinery seemed formidably strong in 1850—both Whigs and Democrats having perfected party organization in almost its modern form. A complete hierarchy of conventions had been established, beginning with ward and precinct conventions, proceeding through county and state conventions, and culminating in the National Convention which met every four years to select the party's leader and to write its platform. The Democrats had begun issuing a party platform in the campaign of 1840, and the Whigs in 1844.

By 1848 the Democrats had invented a hierarchy of committees, ostensibly to act as the party executive at every level of politics. Each ward and precinct had its committee, each county and state, and the national party was served by a national committee.* The President, or in the case of the Opposition the most recent presidential candidate, is the head of the party. If the President is the head in fact as well as in name, if he is so gifted politically and so popular with the country that he can unite and control this ungainly machine and keep it lumbering in the general direction toward which he wishes it to go, he can conquer the Congress and impose a policy. But if he cannot control his party, or if the majority

---

* Today the National Committee consists of one man and one woman from each state and from most of the territories. The chairman and a small executive committee are the effective members. The new Republican Party copied this committee system from the Democrats during its first presidential campaign in 1856, and both parties have maintained it ever since.

in Congress does not belong to his party, there can usually be no domestic policy and there may be no foreign policy either—a situation which would not have troubled eighteenth-century Americans, who feared government more than they feared anarchy, but which sometimes causes qualms today.

Since the breakdown of the party system during the eighteen-fifties was the prelude to the Civil War, and since the system was restored after the war and gradually reassumed its old form, learning to perform ever more smoothly its old functions, it may be useful to state as clearly as may be the structure of these unique machines.[4] As often happens in government, the chart of organization is wholly misleading. The pyramid of committees and conventions may suggest that authority and discipline flow downwards from the party chief. But in fact, instead of autocracy, logic and order, the American political party is a chaos of democratic confusion. The National Committee, for example, which forms the crown of the pyramid, is an advisory agency with no power to dictate to the state committees. The chairman of the National Committee, who would seem from the chart to be the executive head of the party, cannot send orders to the rank and file, or to the county and state committees. He cannot send orders to anybody, except himself and his private secretaries. Yet his importance is incalculably great. On his wisdom and experience may depend not only the election of the presidential candidate but the success of the Administration. Without co-operation between President and Congress the Administration stalls; without the repeated skillful greasing and mending of the party machine no co-operation is possible. And the greasing is primarily the job of the chairman of the National Committee.*

His strength lies in his friendships. He has no power; but as the servant of a popular President he has vast influence, which cannot be used effectively on the bristling and jealous leaders of the state and city machines unless he is known and liked and trusted by those leaders. He can offer not only jobs and prestige but policy concessions to their local needs which may help them to remain in power. He must learn from them what the nine-and-ninety machines making up the national party want, and he must try to persuade the President to adopt policies which will not override too many of those wants. If local bosses become bitter and obstructive because the Administration neglects them, he must either woo them back to the fold or he must conspire with other factions within their feudal territories and seek to drive the dissident bosses from power—a maneuver, incidentally, which rarely succeeds. And all this he must do without authority. His office is a communications center through which the lines of power run; but it does not possess power, except the power to destroy the party by annoying too many of the great lords of the cities and the states.

* Today, when his party is in power, the chairman of the National Committee is usually made Postmaster General.

The national party is a ramshackle alliance, held together by prayers and promises. The essence of the chairman's job is to build a network of personal friendships throughout the country. His informal private organization, resting upon these friendships, will have a unity and a temporary effectiveness which the formal party structure cannot attain.

The members of this private organization—the true state leaders and the true leaders of the city machines—are not necessarily the men whose titles would mark them for eminence. One of the most trying tasks for an observer of American politics is to learn who belongs to this private organization. The man who knows that, knows everything—though he will need to freshen his knowledge continually, for the members change from year to year if not from month to month. The question is, whose advice does the national chairman take on all matters affecting a state (or city) party; with whom does he "clear" all decisions of patronage? It may be the Senators from that state, or some member of the House of Representatives, or the governor, or the chairman of the state committee, or a boss who is little known to the public. If the Administration works with tolerable smoothness, the national chairman and the President are consulting the right people; if it jerks and grinds and backtracks, they must have got athwart too many local leaders, ignored too many prejudices, overridden too many interests. They are being punished, and the country with them. All this, which may sound bizarre, is a logical result of federal politics.

The Opposition often amuses itself by attacking the President for his dependence on bosses or on selfish state leaders. The people grin and do not listen, because they know it is like attacking the President for breathing or for requiring food. He cannot do his job if he alienates the state machines. The nature of those machines is not his business; it is the business of the citizens of the states. He may quarrel with one or two of the most obnoxious bosses, and seek to supplant them with his own friends; but if he quarrels with all the politicians whom sensitive reformers dislike he had better resign his office, for he can be only a nuisance to the country. During his first term, for example, Franklin Roosevelt (and the national chairman, James Farley) not only stood aloof from the high-flavored machine of Curley in Massachusetts, but fought the Huey Long machine in Louisiana. They denied all patronage to Senator Long and to either of his henchmen in the lower House. They gave aid and encouragement to all who opposed the Senator on his home ground. Yet they never weakened Long's position in his state. He remained not only Senator but national committeeman, to say nothing of popular hero. The quarrel was settled by an assassination which even the genial Mr. Farley must have had difficulty in condemning. If Mr. Roosevelt had made similar war on Tammany in New York, on Boss Hague in Jersey City, on Kelly-Nash in Chicago, on Crump in Memphis, and so on round the country, he would have hamstrung his Administration, ruined his relations with Congress, and presumably failed of re-election in 1936. As a contribution to "clean government" the gesture would have been inadequate.

Later, Mr. Roosevelt's strength with the country became so great that he was able without injury to break with James Farley, his national chairman. Normally such a break would be most harmful, since the real national machine is built on the friendships and personal dealings of the chairman and must begin to disintegrate when he leaves his post. But when Mr. Roosevelt stood for a third term, in 1940, the Democratic Party stood or fell with him. No one could take his place. It had not been possible for an alternative leader to grow up under the shade of that great oak. Revolt was impossible, except by party suicide; so the machine was handed from Mr. Farley to Mr. Flynn and continued to function, if not happily at least with fair effect. Yet the disgruntled memoirs which have lately begun to appear show the hazards of such a transfer, hazards which no one less popular than Mr. Roosevelt would willingly incur.

The power to give orders, therefore, the effective discipline, lies not with the national machine but with the many local groups which compose it. There, in the states and the cities, is the rigid organization, the system of rewards and punishments, the insistence on obedience and "regularity," which only a genius like Thomas Jefferson has been able to impose at the center and which not even Jefferson could maintain for eight years. Judging by the results of such local discipline, the amorphousness of the national party may have been a blessing. "The strength of our local party organization," writes Professor Herring, "is in marked contrast to the protean character of the party viewed nationally. We have escaped in this wider realm the rigidities that have made democracy a mockery in our cities."[5]

The price of escaping centralized party control from the top down is the unbuttoned inefficiency which surprises many newcomers to Washington. When Lord Elgin was negotiating a reciprocity treaty in 1854 he wrote home: "There was no government to deal with. . . . It was all a matter of canvassing this member of Congress or the other." And many a President, coming to his intricate task from the simpler world of war, or of diplomacy, or of state management, has been surprised to learn not only that there is no "government" in the British sense, but that there is no party—only an aggregation of parties, each stubbornly clinging to its local pride and privilege. To call the national machine a loose alliance is to exaggerate its unity. Instead of resembling the cruel car of Juggernaut beloved by the cartoonists and feared by the fathers of the republic, the machine is so fragile that it almost ceases to exist (except in a crisis) unless tended by the most delicate diplomacy. It is a typical American creation, for by its very nature it is a guard against the centralizing pull of power. Although, when united, it can help the President to rule, it will not be united unless the President, or his national-committee chairman, woos and pleases all (or nearly all) its constituent parts. So the policy which it helps him to make must be a common factor, a federal bargain. This is another reason why the politics of the United States tend toward conservatism. No major party can be truly radical, any more than a common factor can be immoderate.

A skillful President may often pretend to rule his party and to get what he wants, when in fact he is content to want what he gets. For the masters of the state and the city machines can for the most part only be cajoled when they need favors, or when they need the President's help for their local candidates.* They live by local victories, not national. They join together nationally, not to serve a political theory but to win jobs. In many states they prosper even if the national party is out of office for twenty years—so even a President from their own party has no hold over them except through his control of the patronage. If this were taken from him, as many desire, the American Government might become unworkable. Professor Patterson, who deplores what he calls "this extra-constitutional system of government," comments as follows:

> As long as he [the President] undertakes to control the Congress in legislative matters he must have important positions with which to purchase . . . support. Public works and unearmarked appropriations may also be necessary. The main reason why we do not have a real merit system in national administration is that the President must have control of these positions to enable him to play a role which the Constitution does not provide for him. He was not intended to be a prime minister, a chancellor of the Exchequer and the real head of all the executive departments.[6]

Whatever one may think of the presidential form of government, the system rests heavily on the man who must be both the constitutional and the political Executive, both the head of the state and the head of the party, both the king and the prime minister. And unfortunately, as we have seen several times already, the same system which imposes this responsibility tends to ensure that the man chosen for President shall not be capable of exercising it. Woodrow Wilson said of the American Government, "its President is chosen, not by proof of leadership among the men whose confidence he must have if he is to play an effective part in the making of affairs, but by management—the management of obscure men —and through the uncertain chances of an ephemeral convention which has no other part in politics."[7] Yet the national nominating convention, which has been condemned by political leaders from Thomas Hart Benton

---

* Or when the nation faces (and knows that it faces) a dire emergency.

to the present day, should not be dismissed too cavalierly. The fact that it has survived these repeated attacks, and that no one has presented a plausible alternative, suggests that it has virtues as well as weaknesses.

The convention mirrors the anomalous character, the conflicting interests, and the divided counsels of the party. It is a "parley of state bosses accompanied by their henchmen carrying with them local jealousies and favoritisms."[8] Its chief job is to find a candidate who is not too much disliked by any of the state, city, or county machines; but it has three important subsidiary jobs. First, it must try to unify the party, at least until the following November when the election takes place. Since normally the party has no unity of ideas and principles, these must be kept as far as possible in the background and the stress must be on common loyalties, common prejudices and ambitions, common distaste for the other party. Second, it must give to the rank and file a sense of taking part in great enterprises—taking part with their hearts and all their emotions as well as with their physical presence. The simple followers of a cause are held by enthusiasm and a sense of self-importance quite as much as by a sense of self-interest. When men have met and sung and conspired and abused the enemy together, they can return to their villages and prairies, their factories and mines, two thousand miles apart, and still feel a residue of unity. Third, the convention must catch the interest of the whole people and direct it upon the selection of a presidential candidate. It is not easy, even in the days of radio and television, to make a nation of a hundred and fifty millions pay heed to what you are doing—and it was perhaps more difficult before these inventions to be noticed by even forty millions. Yet if a party's candidate is launched quietly and with dignity in the dark, he will sink forever. It is this that makes irrelevant some of the complaints against the clownishness of conventions. They are meant to attract attention and they succeed in doing so.*

Once the purposes of the convention are understood its methods appear less ludicrous. This is especially true of the party platform, the insincerity and flabbiness of which are a stock subject for sarcasm. If the platform were as meaningless as it sounds, the politicians would not strain over it so tensely. But the meaning is lost if the platform is taken literally as the program for the party. It must be read first as a picture of who is up and who is down in the struggle for dominance between the interest groups, and second as a sign of who has made bargains with whom. All this becomes clear when the party is seen, not as a group of like-minded men united to forward an idea, but as a jumble of representatives from diverse

---

* Woodrow Wilson suggested a national primary election as an alternative to the nominating convention. This might prove a satisfactory way of choosing among the candidates, and it might even attract sufficient attention; but it would do nothing to unify the party and nothing to give the men and women who carry on the dreary daily work a sense of participation.

interests, occupations, classes, climates and philosophies, assembled in order to help each other to office.

The platform tells, not what a party will do, but who is pushing and pulling for what, and with how much success. It explains, to those who can read its cryptic language, the equilibrium which the leaders have established among the warring energies and ambitions represented at the convention. It may even forecast the name of the candidate who has yet to be chosen, for if the platform leans unexpectedly far in one direction it is possible that the candidate will lean unexpectedly far in the other. It is not unusual for a conscientious nominee, in his acceptance speech, to repudiate some part of the platform. But even if he does not, nobody expects him to be bound by the document.

The reason for constructing the platform first, and choosing the candidate later, is that thus the writing of the platform offers the widest possible scope for making bargains. Bargains must be the food and drink of a convention which is designed, among other things, to bring unity where chaos previously ruled. In a free world, where the gallows and the concentration camp are ruled out as persuaders, bargains are the price of agreement. A Senator, or a state legislator, or a city boss, can go proudly home to his people as a power in the party, as a man who must still be reckoned with, if he can show that although he did not get the presidential or the vice-presidential candidate of his choice, his favorite "plank" was included in the platform.

The alternative to this odd system of conventions which are a combination of bazaar and sporting event, and of national parties which are held together by incantation, compromise, and the hope of favors, would be a disciplined authoritarian machine, able to impose its will from the top so long as most of the voters support it. Such a machine would tell the state parties what to do, instead of wheedling them; it would select the most strong-minded and able candidate for the presidency, instead of the man who can best unite the wrangling factions and who is least likely to annoy an organized group of voters; it would write a platform which was a clear statement of policy to be imposed by the party leader with the help of the party whip. This would be efficient, orderly, and easy to understand. It would be what many Americans are in fact recommending. Yet the price of making policy by such methods might prove too high, since it would mean bowing to that unchecked rule of a national majority which the American people have so long fought and feared.

Up to the present, however, in view of the party structure which has prevailed, and of the uses to which the conventions have been put, it is not strange that the average presidential candidate is less than a heroic figure. Yet the problem of selecting better candidates cannot be solved by making fun of the convention system. Perhaps (like many problems of government) it cannot be solved at all. So long as the United States remains a rambling, easygoing and enormous federation, it is doubtful whether the parties can nominate first-class candidates except by mistake. The number of such mistakes in the past has been notable; but unhappily for the Union there was no mistake in the year 1852, or in 1856. At the time of the nation's greatest stress the party system produced masterpieces of "availability" and weakness.

3

In 1852 the Democratic Convention at Baltimore astonished itself by nominating Franklin Pierce of New Hampshire. The plan had been to nominate James Buchanan of Pennsylvania; but it was one of those plans, dear to politicians, which are so intricate and so dark that they easily undo themselves.[9] No one was much concerned at the undoing, because Buchanan had been picked for his pliability and it was clear that Pierce would comfortably meet the requirement. He had no enemies and almost no convictions. He was graceful, attractive, kind, and softly inebriate. At a time when the nation and the party needed a firm, calm hand, this was not the ideal candidate.

Franklin Pierce, whose father was a farmer, an officer in the Revolutionary Army, and two times governor of New Hampshire, was born in 1804. He was educated at Bowdoin College, Maine, and was admitted to the bar at the age of twenty-three. In 1833 he went to the House of Representatives, and in 1837 to the United States Senate. When he resigned in 1842—partly because of his wife's health and partly because the drinking temptations of Washington were too compelling—he had shown himself a Yankee with an unusual respect for Southern interests. He served inconspicuously in the Mexican War, and on returning to New Hampshire became a supporter of the Compromise of 1850, including the hated Fugitive Slave Law. When the leading candidates at Baltimore had frustrated each other, and the elaborate Buchanan plan failed, Pierce emerged as so dark a horse that even the nominee for the vice-presidency was vexed at such a running-mate, and complained, impolitely, against the tendency of the convention system to choose men who are unfit for the job.

Pierce made no speeches during the campaign and appeared to have no plans. If he possessed a belief of any sort—aside from that respect for the Southern point of view which had won him the nomination—it was the un-Jacksonian conviction that the Executive should be retiring and meek. "The dangers of a concentration of all power in the general government of a confederacy so vast as ours," he said in his Inaugural

Address, "are too obvious to be disregarded. You have a right, therefore, to expect your agents in every department to regard strictly the limits imposed upon them by the Constitution of the United States."* This was good Whig doctrine; but it came strangely from the leader of the party of Jackson and Polk. In fact, the Democratic Party in the last sad years of drift toward war rejected the new tools for power and efficiency which had been devised during the age of Jackson. The Southerners who mastered the party and its mild Northern Presidents from 1853 to 1861 distrusted the Jacksonian methods, which were democratic and nationalistic.

The strength which Jackson and his friends had given the presidency was the strength of a popular national leader. But the South was convinced that it could only protect itself by regionalism and by resisting popular rule. Calhoun, when dictating his book on government, told his secretary that if the North would read this disquisition, "then we shall never have any more unmeaning talk about the false assertion that the *majority shall govern.*" To the followers of Calhoun, the Jacksonian presidency was the enemy. It was the people's centralizing weapon, to impose their majority will. So during the years when the Southerners controlled the Democratic Party, they made sure that there were no Jacksonian Presidents.

4

The Whigs in 1852 were unable to profit from the weakness of Pierce, for their own inner struggles led them to choose a candidate equally unfit. The only Presidents they had ever elected were generals, and although both had quickly died the Whigs stubbornly decided to nominate a third. This time the general survived; but the Whig Party didn't.

The convention was a melancholy autumnal meeting for those who had known the great days of the party. Henry Clay, their hero and their much-defeated candidate, lay dying in Washington. Webster, who in Fillmore's Cabinet had once more become Secretary of State, had only a few months to live, and those months were to be poisoned by his old hope for the nomination and his old disappointment. He thought Fillmore would step down in his favor, and that the President's following among the Southern Whigs would join with his own following in New England to bring him at last to the White House: the prophet of Union, the nation's answer to all radicals whether of the North or of the South. But first-term Presidents do not often step down, and Fillmore was no exception. His friends told him that he could have the nomination for the asking, and although

---

* Like most weak men, Pierce could not be consistently unassuming. Suddenly, and at the wrong time, he would become rashly vigorous.

his friends were wrong the mere fact of his candidacy dashed Webster's chances.

Millard Fillmore, an obscure ex-Congressman from New York State, had been nominated for the vice-presidency in 1848 as a concession to the friends of Henry Clay, who were in a vengeful mood when General Taylor was given the first place on the ticket. Since hardly anyone had heard of Fillmore it was assumed that he would not lose the party many votes. He was a large man with a big, smooth, kindly face and impressive manners. He looked like a President and much to his surprise he had become one, and he did not see why he should give way to Webster.

Fillmore was not gifted with political insight. After the election of 1848, when the country was torn with the most intense strife it had known, he said: "I regard this election as putting an end to all ideas of disunion. It raises up a national party, occupying a middle ground, and leaves the fanatics and disunionists, North and South, without the hope of destroying the fair fabric of our Constitution." Later, as we have seen, he did his best to make these cheerful words come true by giving to the great Compromise the full support of his Administration, and he thought the party should therefore help him to a second term. The convention thought otherwise. For fifty-two ballots Fillmore and Webster divided the moderate pro-Compromise vote. Neither could win and neither could hand his following to the other. So in the end the Seward Whigs (the "Conscience Whigs," who were soon to become Republicans) were allowed to nominate Winfield Scott, the general who had led American troops to Mexico City.*

Fillmore was to make one last eccentric appearance on the national stage in 1856, and was then to retire into innocuous philanthropy in western New York. Perhaps his most striking and unusual act came in 1855, when he refused the degree of D.C.L. from Oxford University on the ground that he had no literary or scientific attainments.

The South distrusted General Scott because of Seward's backing, yet so far as politics and opinions were concerned he seemed as colorless as a man may be. It was for this that the convention accepted him, and this was the sum of the Whig hopes: that nobody would discover whether Scott stood for anything at all, and that the people might be content to vote for him because of his war record. But the Whig Party was dying, along with the two men who had made it great. Clay, who might have put spirit into the slack campaign, died on June 29. Webster, who had repudiated Scott's nomination and prophesied his party's doom, died on October

---

* On the first ballot Fillmore received 133 votes, Scott 131, and Webster 29. The vote remained much the same until the break on the fifty-third ballot. There were 396 delegates, and since the Whigs nominated by a simple majority 149 votes were needed for a choice. If Fillmore and Webster could have come together, either could have been nominated.

24. Boston mourned him, and most of Massachusetts; but throughout the nation there was no such wave of tenderness and respect as had been roused by the death of Clay.

Webster had left instructions for a simple funeral. "My heart swelled," wrote one of his friends, "when I saw the eminent men all passed by, and six plain men of Marshfield called out to be pallbearers. Was not that beautiful?" It would have been well for Webster's career if he had made the gesture while he was still alive. Truly, he might have claimed to be a friend of the plain men of Marshfield most of his days, for he had long defended the Union, which was the hope of democracy; but while breath was in his body Webster could not pass by the eminent men. The new leaders of industry, the factory-rich, were his clients, and the masses may be forgiven for thinking that where his fees lay, there lay his heart. Yet even the masses, who had judged him coldly, may have felt forsaken at times during the autumn of 1852. Clay and Webster had gone with Calhoun to the grave. These were the men who had given strength and continuity and many a touch of grandeur to the politics of the country ever since the far-off days of the second war with England—ever since America grew up and cut loose from Europe and set out in isolation on westward-walking paths to follow her strange new destiny. "Eastward I go only by force," said Thoreau; "but westward I go free. . . . I must walk toward Oregon and not toward Europe." Yet the Oregon Trail could be lonely—lonelier than ever when the old leaders had departed. Fillmore and Pierce and Scott were no substitute, nor Seward with his "higher law," nor the rising star of Illinois: Stephen A. Douglas. In the nation's life it was one of the hours of low vitality, during the midnight watch, when man is shaken with fears he does not own.

5

Even before election day of 1852 the Whig Party was crumbling. General Scott's Northern friends induced him to say nothing in his acceptance letter about the Compromise of 1850—although the platform had promised that the entire Compromise, including the Fugitive Slave Law, would be accepted and maintained. At once an important group of Southern Whig Congressmen, led by Robert Toombs and Alexander H. Stephens of Georgia, rejected Scott and seceded from the party. This was an act of decisive importance because of the character of the two leaders. Toombs and Stephens between them had been the symbols of Union sentiment in the Deep South. They were moderate Whigs who could work loyally with Webster of Massachusetts. They were opposed to expansion at the expense of Mexico; but when the war had been fought and won, and an attempt was then made by means of the Wilmot Proviso to prevent the spread of slavery into any part of the new land, both men insisted that such an act must lead to secession. They were serving in the House of Representatives, and they warned the Northern members. "Appropriate this common property to yourselves," said Toombs, "it is then your government, not mine. Then I am its enemy, and I will then, if I can, bring my children and my constituents to the altar of liberty, and like Hamilcar I would swear them to eternal hostility to your foul domination." And Stephens said that if the Proviso passed, the result would be "desolation, carnage and blood."

The two Georgians worked for the Compromise measures of 1850, and when these were passed they joined with the moderate Democrat, Howell Cobb, to beg their state to accept this triumph for the Union. A convention had been summoned with power to take any action it chose, including secession; but because of the work of Toombs, Stephens, and Cobb the convention had a great majority of Union delegates. It accepted the Compromise, reserving the right to secede later in case Congress or the Northern states sought to weaken or to reinterpret the document. While winning this victory the three friends formed a new state organization, the Constitutional Union Party. The party sent Toombs to the Senate, but shortly thereafter collapsed. Both Toombs and Stephens returned to their former allegiance until the nomination of General Scott.

When these two Union patriots joined Cobb in the Democratic Party, Calhoun's plan had at last triumphed. Most of the leading cotton-state Whigs had finally become Democrats, giving to the South the intellectual and political control of the party for so long as she could hold the numerous Northern voters in line. This was not long. Within less than a decade of their break with the Whigs, Toombs was the Confederate Secretary of State and Stephens the Confederate Vice-President.

While the South was deserting the Whig Party on the ground that General Scott had free-soil tendencies, a number of Northerners were deserting it on the ground that he was a tool of the slave power. They joined a new group, under the leadership of Senator Charles Sumner of Massachusetts and Senator Salmon P. Chase of Ohio, which called itself the Free Democratic Party. In their 1852 platform they stated:

> That the Free Democratic party is not organized to aid either the Whig or Democratic wing of the great Slave Compromise party of the nation, but to defeat them both . . . ; That slavery is a sin against God and a crime against man . . . ; and that Christianity, humanity, and patriotism, alike demand its abolition. That the Fugitive Slave Act of 1850 is repugnant to the Constitution, to the principles of the common law, to the spirit of Christianity, and to the sentiments of the civilized world. We therefore deny its binding force upon the American People, and demand its immediate and total repeal.[10]

In the election the Democrats carried twenty-seven states for Franklin Pierce and the Whigs four for General Scott: Massachusetts, Vermont, Kentucky, and Tennessee. The popular vote was not so one-sided, for the Whigs were less than 300,000 behind in a total vote of about three million. Yet it was clear that the Whigs were perishing as a national party. In order to hold such Northern members as Seward and Thurlow Weed and Horace Greeley of the New York *Tribune,* who refused in any case to accept the Compromise with its Fugitive Slave Law, they had rejected "honest, commonplace Fillmore," and had thereby lost their best friends in the South. But the Whigs were the parents of the Compromise and they could not disown it. They could not make a deal with men who would rather break the Union than return one Negro to captivity—any more than with fire-eating Southerners who preferred secession to agreeing that there were limits to the slave empire.

No national party in America has room for men who hold one sacred belief to which all else must bow. When the issue arises (as it may always and honorably arise) on which men feel too deeply to compromise, they are obliged to put their own will first and the Union second. The "Conscience Whigs" preferred their conscience to the Whig unity, which was surely their privilege, but which consigned them to membership in a sectional group. They belonged where they were going—with Sumner and Chase and the Free Democrats into a new party which was to be purged of all friends of slavery. They had become unbending, not from self-righteousness, but because they felt they had made the last concession which their faith in man permitted. The Whig Party asked its Northern members to accept the ugly sight of fugitives chained and returned to slavery. As more and more Northerners found they could not do it, they were forced to abandon the party. And as the party leaders sought by worldly shifts and evasions to persuade them that they need not leave, that perhaps the Fugitive Slave Act did not mean quite what it said, the Southerners also became outraged and began to desert. The more the party strained for a formula which would satisfy both groups, the more it hastened its demise. By the time of President Pierce's inauguration in March, 1853, he and his Democratic Party were the one remaining hope of the Union.

The hope seemed by no means desperate. During the election even the fierce Southern-rights Democrats of Mississippi and South Carolina had quietly accepted the Compromise, the nomination of Pierce, and the party's promise to prevent further agitation of the slave question. The Free Democrats, meanwhile, had polled only 150,000 votes, and a secessionist candidate in the South only 3500. The country longed for harmony. In the midst of a gold boom and of a vast railway revolution, the country wanted to build and to grow rich, not to quarrel. A majority was in favor of enforcing the Compromise and saying no more about it. That act of assuagement had killed the Whigs because large numbers in the Northern and Western wings of the party resented it. They felt they had been overwhelmed by the august names of Clay and Webster. Some Democrats felt the same—but not the Democratic majority. They and the remaining faithful Whigs were grateful for the Compromise and would abide by it so long as no man dared reopen the fighting subject. But it is never as easy as it sounds to let sleeping dogs lie. It is a task for a political wizard to keep them asleep. The task was beyond the powers of poor vacillating Pierce, who not only woke them up but gave them insomnia.

Perhaps it was in any case too late. Perhaps the time had arrived when the wages of slavery must be paid. "For it must needs be that offenses come, but woe to the man by whom the offense cometh." Perhaps, as John Quincy Adams had written in 1820, "the seeds of the Declaration of Independence are yet maturing. The harvest will be what West, the painter, calls the terrible sublime." Yet the student of politics may reasonably ask whether a wiser and stronger President might have saved the day. The slave issue could not break the Union until it had broken the Democratic Party. If Pierce and his successor had been true leaders, they might have made such use of party loyalty as to preserve the peace.

Loyalty to an irrational party which lives by barter and by ignoring both logic and principles may be derided. Yet when men belong to an organization which has lasted a long time, to which they have given their hopes and their work, and from which they have won the gift of comradeship, of being members of one another, a sense of faithfulness arises, a fidelity with which it is vain to quarrel. Party loyalty is a refuge not only from the hurtful confusion of life but from the self-interest which turns man's hand against his friend. Within the magic circle of fealty men will compound their differences, or if that is impossible they will do their best to forget them. Loyalty may win concessions which would not be granted to logic. If a nation had to fight a civil war each time it faced an issue that could not be solved, the life of man would be more perilous than the jungle.

The parties in a free country depend for their health on those who understand the machine and use it with some detachment; but they depend for their lives on those who will vote as their fathers voted so long as the trust is not too grossly strained. Without the floating vote free politics would become corrupt; without the loyal vote free politics would dissolve in chaos.*

* In 1938, after thirty-five years in Washington and forty-five years in elective office, Vice-President John Nance Garner remarked that there are about fifteen million voters in each party "who will never scratch the party ticket and they serve a great purpose of stability. You have another fifteen million who swing often or occasionally, or go fishing or stay at home on election day, and these fifteen million

The American Union was an abstraction to many of the simpler citizens in 1852 and 1856, especially to the small farmers of the South and to the newest immigrants. But the Democratic Party was not an abstraction. In the big towns of the North, on the frontier, and in the upland country of the South, millions had lived in it, worked in it, triumphed and failed in it. To be sure, the party used different arguments in different states, but the name was honored everywhere, and the heroic (if unexamined) past of Jefferson and Jackson. For the sake of party unity and party victory these millions might have been persuaded to give the Compromise of 1850 a fair chance. But party loyalty was not invoked. Neither Pierce nor Buchanan could conjure that mighty spell. As we shall see in a later chapter, when the break came in 1860 Democratic "loyalty" was to the state or section—not to the national party which had won power in 1800 and which, under many forms and disguises, with many philosophies and systems, had ruled the nation during most of the intervening years.

---

serve a great purpose, too." (Cp. *Garner of Texas*, by Bascom Timmons, p. 236.) All the party combinations, all the desperate search for ideas which will please as many interests as possible and for candidates who will make as few enemies as possible, are directed toward these last fifteen million. Mr. Garner put the percentage of floating voters higher than many observers; but since he has hardly ever been wrong in predicting an election, his opinion has authority.

XVIII

The Fruits of Executive Weakness–I

1853–1857

"Of all presidents, I suppose none [was] more insignificant than Mr. Pierce, who was occupying the White House at the time of our visit." Such was the judgment of Laurence Oliphant,[1] who accompanied Lord Elgin in 1854 on his mission to make a treaty of reciprocity between the United States and Canada. The insignificance which the Englishman noted had been shown on the first day of the new President's Administration, when he made his undistinguished Inaugural Address and announced his distinguished but incompatible Cabinet.

The election of 1852 had shown that although the big majority was eager to give the Compromise a trial, strong-willed and bitter minorities did not intend that it should last. The best-loved leaders of New England thought the Fugitive Slave Act was immoral and that no good citizen should accept it. Ralph Waldo Emerson, for example, called it a law "which no man can obey or abet the obeying, without loss of self-respect and forfeiture of the name of a gentleman." And in the South the extremists were waiting for the first sign that Emerson's advice was to be followed, for the moderates would then be discredited. In the autumn of 1852 the governor of South Carolina told his legislature that recent Northern politeness to the South would not last. When the inevitable "aggression" occurred (such as a refusal to obey the Fugitive Slave Act), he hoped that the South would either compel respect for her rights or else insist on taking her place as a new nation. Two months before this disturbing message, Howell Cobb (the Union Democrat who had done so much to bring the state of Georgia to accept the Compromise) received a letter of foreboding from a friend:

> You well know that it has been my conviction for the last two or three years that nothing we could do, short of general emancipation, would satisfy the North. Your idea was that the measures of the Compromise would substantially effect that object, and you went for them for that reason chiefly, I think. Should it turn out that I am right and you are wrong it will not be long before it must be known. And it is, therefore, now time for you to be making up your mind for the new "crisis."[2]

The letter goes on to predict that Northern Whigs would soon join the Free Soilers, with the result that the anti-Southern party must control the North. And then? The writer makes a forecast which is remarkable for its pessimistic accuracy:

> The Democratic party there [in the North], in conjunction with pretty much the whole South, may be able to make one fight, say in 1856—a grand Union rally—but then the thing will be out. Is it not so? You must have thought of all this. Have you made up your mind as to what is to be done?

Presumably Howell Cobb had faced these chances, and had decided exactly what to do, for a few years later he was a major general in the Confederate armies.

With the country in such a mood, restless with such fears, the hope for the Compromise lay in strong leadership. The President should have said that the health of the nation depended on the great settlement, that it must be treated as irrevocable, that arguments about slavery must now cease since every acre of land under the American flag had been awarded either to the Northern or the Southern system, and that he would therefore give office to no man who did not promise to make the Compromise work. The Free-Soil Democrats in the North and the fire-eaters in the South would have protested; but the people had dismissed both groups in the election, and if no new hate-provoking deeds had been permitted the Union might have found time to heal its wounds, to diminish its rancors, and to seek an evolutionary cure for the race problem. The naming of Pierce's Cabinet put an end to such hopes.

Instead of insisting on men who upheld the Union and the election promises, Pierce put into his Cabinet able and forceful representatives of every diverse opinion. So his Administration was doomed to become a minor civil war within itself. And if one side conquered in the family quarrel, it would impose fresh disturbances at a time when the country craved and deserved a rest.*

Perhaps the wisest man in the new Administration was the Secretary of State, William L. Marcy. But unhappily he was not the most pushing. Marcy was an old Jacksonian and a lover of the Union, an old friend of Van Buren and a founder of the Albany Regency. We have seen him as the author of the political maxim that "to the victor belong the spoils of the enemy." He had been three times governor of New York, and Secretary of War in the Cabinet of Polk. He was efficient, companionable, amusing, and a lover of good literature. He belonged to the wing of the

* Pierce had followed normal practice in seeking to appease all party dissidents by his cabinet appointments. But Pierce was so weak that he could not control his own servants and the country was so shaken that it could not endure another uproar. So normal practice proved a disaster.

party from which the whole of the Cabinet should have been chosen. He could have worked creatively with the Union Democrats who had defeated the secessionists in Georgia, Mississippi, and South Carolina. But he was not a ruthless fighter, and when Jefferson Davis was made Secretary of War, Marcy could neither collaborate with him nor impose his own will against that of the domineering Southerner. He was a good Secretary of State, but he could not perform the President's proper task of bringing unity into the government. Neither could he stand against Caleb Cushing of Massachusetts, who allied himself with Davis to win the battle of the Cabinet and to destroy all hopes of appeasement.

Jefferson Davis was born in Kentucky in 1808, not far from where Lincoln was born a year later. His father had been an officer in the Revolutionary Army, his grandfather a Welsh immigrant. He was the tenth child in a very poor family and his prospects were small; but when he was still an infant the family moved to Mississippi and the eldest son began to prosper. Jefferson was given a good education at Transylvania University and at West Point, where he was a contemporary of Robert E. Lee. He then served for years as an officer at tiny Western posts, until his unhappy romance with the daughter of Colonel Zachary Taylor, which led him to resign from the army and return to Mississippi. During the next ten years (1835–45) he was a planter. With the help of his brother Joseph and of a small inheritance from his father, he bought and cleared new land and became one of the founders and leaders of a new state. He developed an intense local patriotism and a love for the easy life and patriarchal ways of the well-to-do in the Deep South. He worked hard during these years, both in the fields and in the library. His plantation prospered and he became learned in history and politics. His slaves were cared for with affection. They were lazy because of the climate, inefficient because of the slave system, and moderately content because Davis was a just man. If he and his beloved Mississippi and his regressive social system had been let alone, he might have become a mild and scholarly country gentleman; but he was stubborn as well as just, egotistical as well as affectionate, and when the abolitionists began to abuse the planters and their social system incontinently, Jefferson Davis responded with an equal scorn.

In 1845 he married Varina Howell (a famous beauty and a daughter of the ruling aristocracy) and the same year he began his political career in the House of Representatives. If Mississippi and her planters were to be attacked and traduced, Davis meant to see that the defense was not lacking. When the Mexican War broke out he resigned from Congress to command a regiment of volunteers from his own state. He became a minor national hero at the battle of Buena Vista and was sent back to Washington as Senator. In 1851 he left the Senate to seek the governorship of Mississippi. His opponent was a Compromise-man, whereas Davis was a

Southern "nationalist"; that is, he was opposed to the fire-eaters who were ready to secede when only two or three states would move, but he was prepared if tension grew worse to try to unite the entire South and take it out of the Union in a single *coup d'état*. Defeated by less than a thousand votes, Davis returned to his plantation until Pierce called him to Washington in 1853 to be Secretary of War. The appointment seemed providential in view of his longing to strengthen the South. At once he pushed for a Pacific railway along the Mexican border, tying the Gulf states to the coast of California and opening the trade of Asia to the slave society. To make the railway feasible he induced Pierce and Marcy to buy a tract of land from Mexico, known as the Gadsden Purchase. The treaty had a rough time in the Senate which objected to paying ten million dollars for a territory on which, according to Thomas Hart Benton, not even a Wolf could find a living.* But Davis and his Southern imperialistic friends were able to force ratification.

The other strong man of the Cabinet and defender of the Southern cause was the enigmatic Caleb Cushing of Essex County, Massachusetts— the county which had produced so many leaders of the once great Federalist Party. Secession was perhaps not a frightening word in that county, for in the days of Timothy Pickering the "Essex Junto" had toyed with taking New England out of the Union.

Cushing was a man of high talents who had made many enemies and was accused of many faults, but never of cowardice. He had a gift for finding and defending unpopular causes, and he seldom failed to bring them luster. He was born in 1800, was graduated from Harvard with high distinction in 1817, was admitted to the bar in 1821, and a few years later became a state senator. He supported John Quincy Adams against Jackson—the first and not the worst of his lost causes. In 1834 he went to Washington as a Whig member of the House of Representatives. Although he joined with Adams in defending the right of his constituents to petition Congress against slavery, he also joined with Webster and the "Cotton Whigs" in decrying all efforts to interfere with Southern rights and customs—thus insuring the maximum of unpopularity from all sides. As a protégé of Webster, however, he had a secure political future, and for a time he was the heir apparent. But when President Harrison died and President Tyler fought the Whigs who had elected him (destroying the program of their hero, Henry Clay), Cushing became a member of the hated "Corporal's Guard" and moved with Tyler toward the Democratic Party. The Senate refused to ratify his appointment as Secretary of the Treasury, so in 1843 Tyler sent him to China to make America's first com-

---

* The wolf would not have done badly, for the Purchase secured 45,535 square miles of land, much of which is today good cattle country. Tucson, Arizona, is in the Gadsden Purchase.

mercial treaty with that sprawling empire. He arranged for the opening
of five Chinese ports to the Americans and for the rights of "extra-terri-
toriality"—whereby American citizens in China became subject solely to
American laws and officials.

Needless to say, with the coming of the Mexican War Cushing was one
of the few important New Englanders to support President Polk. He raised
a regiment and led it to the Rio Grande. Before the war ended he was a
brigadier general, and the subject of one of James Russell Lowell's bitter-
est attacks in the *Biglow Papers:*

> Gineral C. is a dreffle smart man;
>> He's ben on all sides thet give places or pelf;
> But consistency still wuz a part of his plan—
>> He's ben true to *one* party and thet is himself. . . .
>
> Gineral C. he goes in fer the war;
>> He don't vally principle more'n an old cud;
> What did God make us raytional creeturs fer,
>> But glory and gunpowder, plunder and blood?

In 1852 Cushing was a delegate to the Democratic National Convention
and worked for the nomination of Pierce. He became Attorney General
in the new Cabinet, an ally of Jefferson Davis in defense of Southern
interests, a strong unshakable supporter of the act which was soon to destroy the Compromise of 1850. Until the day of South Carolina's secession he worked with the extreme wing of the Southern Democrats. He
then returned to Essex County, joined the Republican Party, and asked
permission to fight.

When compared with the benign Marcy and with these two powerful
and stubborn men, the rest of the Cabinet was of light weight. Its importance lay in the fact that it was disunited, and that the men who stood
by the Union were no match for the men who stood by the South. Benton said that the subsequent four years should not be known as the Pierce
Administration, since Pierce could never control his own followers. It was
"an Administration in which he was inoperative, and in which nullifiers,
disunionists, and renegades used his name and his power for their own
audacious and criminal purposes."

2

Into this precarious situation, already threatened by obstinate ambitious
men, a President who confused charm with statesmanship, and a Senator
who confused bravery with strength, dropped the most unsettling problem

which had yet bedeviled the republic. We have seen that Jefferson Davis meant to build his Pacific railway through Texas to El Paso, and then along the southern border of New Mexico and the valley of the Gila River to California. The chief advantage to the route was that it lay through country which was already organized under territorial government, whereas the rival routes of the Central West and the Northwest were controlled by Indians and had few white settlers and no government. It was widely believed that only one transcontinental railway would be built, so the Senators and Congressmen from the Middle West fought to keep the South from becoming the favored section. Not only were regional jealousies involved, but also the greed of land speculators, for it seemed likely that the city chosen for the eastern terminal of the railway would become a metropolis.

Beginning in 1850 bill after bill was introduced to create a territory of Nebraska. The Southern members of Congress blocked each attempt, both because they wished to save the railway for their own section and because the proposed territory lay north of the Missouri Compromise line and must one day increase the number of free states. The chairman of the Senate Committee on Territories was Stephen A. Douglas, the Democratic hope of Illinois, a bouncing, forceful Midwesterner—as stubborn as Jefferson Davis and even harder to pin down than Caleb Cushing. Douglas did not intend to see his section lose the golden railway prize. He set himself to lure the South into accepting a Nebraska bill. He was willing to pay a high price; but even Douglas would have flinched if he had known the price which destiny was to exact.

On January 4, 1854, Douglas reported a Nebraska bill which by implication repealed the Missouri Compromise, abolishing Henry Clay's greatest triumph, the nationally accepted trans-Mississippi frontier between freedom and slavery. The bill was based on the idea of "popular sovereignty"—or "squatter sovereignty"—whereby the people of the new territory were to settle the slavery question for themselves. Lewis Cass had suggested such a plan in 1847; and in the course of the Compromise measures of 1850 the territories of Utah and New Mexico were organized without the prohibition or the protection of slavery. In due time they were to be admitted as states, with or without slaves, according to the will of their citizens. This was the answer of Clay and Webster to the Wilmot Proviso, which would have excluded slavery from all the spoils of Mexico. Northerners were persuaded to swallow that part of the Compromise on the ground that slavery could not live in arid lands. But much of the proposed Nebraska territory lay east of the fateful ninety-eighth meridian, where the dry country begins. East of 98°, the rainfall is above twenty inches and slave agriculture might prosper. Douglas made a mistake when he thought the North would permit the introduction of slaves—or even the threat of such introduction—next door to Missouri or across the river from Iowa. It was a typical mistake, for it was grounded in moral obtuseness.*

Stephen Arnold Douglas was born in 1813 in Vermont. His father, a doctor, died when Douglas was an infant, and the boy was later apprenticed to a cabinetmaker. When his mother remarried he followed her to western New York, where he began to study law. At the age of twenty he went further west: to Ohio, Missouri, and finally Illinois. He was admitted to the bar before he was twenty-one and became a judge of the state supreme court at twenty-seven. Politics, however, was his true love, and law a mere convenience for forwarding that career. In his youth he had seen politics at its height of organized efficiency in the New York state machine of Van Buren and Marcy. He grew up with the Democratic machine of Illinois, and he was one of the first to urge the creation of county and state conventions. He was soon a member of the state legislature and at the age of thirty he went to the House of Representatives at Washington. He was an odd figure: five feet tall, with weak little legs, a big round head, a bull neck, and the chest and shoulders of a wrestler. He had a voice that beat upon the air like the deep notes of a tuba. He was known as "the Little Giant."

Douglas distinguished himself in the House as an expansionist and a defender of the Mexican War. In 1847 the legislature of Illinois transferred him to the Senate, where he was at once made chairman of the Committee on Territories. The following year, on the death of his father-in-law, his wife fell heir to property in North Carolina and Mississippi and to a hundred and fifty slaves. Douglas was accused of Southern sympathies as a result of the inheritance; but his willingness to tempt the South with the repeal of the Missouri Compromise came not from sympathy but from rivalry. In 1847 Douglas moved north to the little village of Chicago which had been founded fourteen years before at the portage between the St. Lawrence–Great Lakes waterway and the vast system of the Mississippi River. Jolliet and Marquette, exploring the wilderness for the King of France, had used this portage in 1673 and had urged the building of a canal. Their plan was accomplished in 1848, the year after Douglas moved to Chicago. It seemed clear to the ambitious Senator that if the village which presided over this superb water connection were also to become the terminus of the Pacific railway, the future would be secure and affluent. So he invested in Chicago real estate and bribed the South to support his Nebraska bill.

The South, however, was not satisfied with an implied repeal of the Missouri Compromise. The idea of "popular sovereignty," with its sugges-

* For the true dividing line between more and less than twenty inches of rain, see the map on page 272.

tion of democratic control, was displeasing to the fire-eaters and they would only accept it if combined with an explicit statement that the law of 1820 was dead. They could then make their final demand: that the federal government must protect slave property in the territories whether the inhabitants liked it or not. On January 22, 1854, a conference of Democratic leaders at the White House altered the bill to provide for open repeal and also to divide the land into two territories: one west of Missouri to be called Kansas and the other west of Iowa to be called Nebraska. Under pressure from Jefferson Davis and his friends President Pierce put the force of the Administration behind the Kansas-Nebraska Act. By so doing he assumed responsibility for the woe which followed.

The Southerners who took part in this conference did not care what trouble came, since if they could not get their way they would be glad of the excuse to secede. But it is strange that none of the Northerners knew they were stirring the ugliest forces in American life: deep hates and fears which the most careful statesmanship had coaxed into a fitful sleep but which were now never to rest until the nation had been torn apart and rebuilt by the sword. Pierce may have been too dull to understand, and Marcy may have been disregarded, and Cushing was on the side of the Southern cause; but how could Stephen A. Douglas have been fooled? He knew politics the way a skilled mechanic knows the engine in his charge. He could take the machine to pieces, and put it together, and he loved each smooth well-fitting part; but he did not sense that a political machine may have morals, and a soul, and even a heart.

> What remains mysterious, in even the most sympathetic view of his motives [writes Professor Nevins], is his attitude toward free soil opinion; an attitude curiously blind and callous, a mixture of incomprehension and indifference. For thirty-three years the Missouri Compromise had truly been enshrined in Northern hearts. Did he not realize that any sudden attempt to overthrow it would raise the greatest storm of the generation? . . . It was impossible for such a man to comprehend the fervent emotion with which millions of freedom-loving Northerners regarded the possibility that half the great West might become a land of slaves—for devote Kansas to slavery, and Colorado, New Mexico, and Arizona (to use present-day names) might all conceivably follow. When indignation welled up like the ocean lashed by a hurricane he was amazed. The fact that the irresistible tidal forces in history are moral forces always escapes a man of dim moral perceptions.[3]

The New England men of letters who molded and expressed the conscience of their region doubtless seemed silly to the proud Senator who knew all there was to know about handling Congress and bullying weak Presidents. Lowell and Melville and Whittier, Emerson and Thoreau—it was easy to dismiss them as sentimentalists when it came to framing a law;

yet Douglas was to find that such men spoke for more than half the country, and that their moralizings were backed in Congress by some of the most relentless fighters ever to perturb those contentious halls. Even before the Kansas-Nebraska Bill was presented to the Senate, six members of Congress issued an attack which, for timeliness, for bitterness, and for scornful insolence, has not been surpassed. This "Appeal of the Independent Democrats in Congress to the People of the United States" was chiefly the work of Senator Salmon P. Chase of Ohio—soon to become a member of Lincoln's Cabinet; but it was also signed by Senator Sumner of Massachusetts and by four members of the lower House. The "Appeal" was exaggerated in its wrath, unfair in its ascription of motives, and an ugly forecast of the wild words and wilder deeds to come. Yet Professor Binkley calls it "the most successful single piece of propaganda in American party history," and Senator Beveridge wrote that "its inflammable sentences fell like sprays of oil upon the fires which 'Uncle Tom's Cabin' had started in every northern community."[4] Douglas was burnt in effigy throughout the Northern and Northwestern states, and every day the village churches and the town halls were filled with anxious men and women forming anti-Nebraska groups under a variety of names. They were all soon to coalesce in the Republican Party.

Douglas had known, of course, that he would be attacked by the abolitionists; but he did not foresee that his Kansas-Nebraska Act would make abolitionism respectable. The men who signed the "Appeal" were extremists who had little hold on the nation until Douglas made them popular. Their document was reprinted in every important newspaper throughout the North. Clergymen read the "Appeal" from their pulpits. Men who had thought that the doctrines of abolition were almost treason began to wonder whether slavery was indeed a system which must grow and grow, corrupting the continent, if it were permitted to live at all. So instead of sweeping from his path a few wild and well-tried enemies whom he despised, and at whom the country laughed, Douglas found himself facing a conscience-troubled public which wondered whether it had laughed unwisely.

The extravagance of the "Appeal," however, and the inaccuracy of many of its statements, and the answering bitterness which it roused in Southerners who might not otherwise have come to Douglas's support, gave the Administration its chance to carry Congress. This was to prove a bitter and contaminated victory; but at the time Douglas only saw that Chase had called him a liar, a man who sold his honor for the hope of the presidency, so he leaped gladly into battle. All through the month of February, 1854, he defended his bill with superb address. If the moral issues and the resulting emotions were ignored, he had a strong case. His opponents had put themselves in the wrong and he hammered them without pity. Before he was through he had extracted an apology from Chase, and half an apology from Seward. Even Sumner was reduced to silence, the only form of politeness which he knew. And Douglas's power over the party machine was such that he could force Congress to forget the storms that were rising through the country. The Senate passed the bill on March 3, and the House on May 22 by 113 votes to 100. The President meekly signed. "Douglas," wrote Salmon P. Chase at the beginning of the struggle, ". . . has out-southernized the South; and has dragged the timid and irresolute administration along with him."[5]

3

In the course of defending his Act before the people of Illinois, Douglas had his first disquieting encounter with Abraham Lincoln. On October 4 in Springfield, and on October 16 in Peoria, Lincoln took the Douglas arguments to pieces and exposed them as callously unmoral. When a politician appeals to morals the public expects intolerance and over-statement, and perhaps a harsh demand for some reform which would involve setting the world on its head. So the public tends to be suspicious. As Big Tim Sullivan of Tammany Hall said in his gentle way, "God and the people hate a chesty man." But no one was ever less "chesty" than Lincoln, or less intolerant, or more cautiously conservative. He could use moral arguments humbly and simply (he could even use them unfairly at times), and because his soul was not swollen the people would listen.

> I think I have no prejudice against the southern people [said Lincoln in his reply to the well-polished defenses of Douglas]. They are just what we would be in their situation. If slavery did not now exist among them, they would not introduce it. If it did now exist among us, we should not instantly give it up. . . . If all earthly power were given me, I should not know what to do, as to the existing institution. . . . But all this, to my judgment, furnishes no more excuse for permitting slavery to go into our free territory, than it would for reviving the African slave trade by law. The law which forbids the bringing of slaves *from* Africa; and that which has so long forbid the taking of them *to* Nebraska, could hardly be distinguished on any moral principle; and the repeal of the former could find as plausible excuses as that of the latter. . . .
>
> But Nebraska is urged as a great Union-saving measure. Well, I too, go for saving the Union. Much as I hate slavery, I would consent to the extension of it rather than see the Union dissolved, just as I would consent to any *great* evil, to avoid a *greater* one. But when I go to Union saving, I must believe, at least, that the means I employ have some adaptation to the end. To my mind, Nebraska has no such adaptation.

"It hath no relish of salvation in it." It is an aggravation, rather, of the only one thing which ever endangers the Union. When it came upon us, all was peace and quiet. . . . In the whole range of possibility, there scarcely appears to me to have been any thing, out of which the slavery agitation could have been revived, except the very project of repealing the Missouri Compromise. . . . Repeal the Missouri Compromise—repeal all compromises—repeal the Declaration of Independence—repeal all past history, you still can not repeal human nature. It still will be the abundance of man's heart, that slavery extension is wrong; and out of the abundance of his heart, his mouth will continue to speak. . . .

In our greedy chase to make profit of the Negro, let us beware lest we "cancel and tear to pieces" even the white man's charter of freedom. . . . Let us turn slavery from its claim of "moral right" back upon its existing legal rights, and its arguments of necessity. Let us return it to the position our fathers gave it, and there let it rest in peace. . . . In his [Senator Douglas's] view, the question of whether a new country shall be slave or free is a matter of as utter indifference as it is whether his neighbor shall plant his farm with tobacco or stock it with horned cattle. Now, whether this view is right or wrong, it is certain that the great mass of mankind take a totally different view. They consider slavery a great moral wrong; and their feeling against it is not evanescent, but eternal. It lies at the very foundation of their sense of justice; and it cannot be trifled with.

It was to "the great mass of mankind" that Lincoln spoke. He seemed to muse aloud, arguing with himself, seeking firm ground in a slippery world. Yet he was a deadly opponent, for while putting the worst possible construction on the pro-Nebraska arguments, he tested them by the principles of the American Revolution, by the faith in natural law on which the nation rested. More than six years later, on his way to his first inauguration, after the Deep South had seceded and formed the Confederate States of America, Lincoln spoke at Independence Hall in Philadelphia.

All the political sentiments I entertain [he said] have been drawn, so far as I have been able to draw them, from the sentiments which originated and were given to the world from this hall. I have never had a feeling politically that did not spring from . . . the Declaration of Independence. . . . It was that which gave promise that in due time the weight would be lifted from the shoulders of all men. . . . I would rather be assassinated on the spot than surrender it.[6]

Here, indeed, was a new note, a relief from the logic-chopping about states' rights and property rights. Here was the combination of moral fervor and conservatism that Lincoln was to make his own. Slavery was wrong because the Declaration of Independence was right. Nothing, therefore, could justify a permission for slavery to extend. Yet slavery existed, and no man knew how to end it wisely, so nothing could justify the hate-provoking rant of the abolitionists. In the Peoria speech Lincoln said:

> Some men, mostly Whigs, who condemn the repeal of the Missouri Compromise, nevertheless hesitate to go for its restoration, lest they be thrown in company with the abolitionists. Will they allow me as an old Whig to tell them good humoredly that I think this is very silly? Stand with anybody that stands RIGHT. Stand with him while he is right and part with him when he goes wrong. Stand WITH the abolitionist in restoring the Missouri Compromise; and stand AGAINST him when he attempts the repeal of the fugitive slave law. . . . In both cases you are right. . . . In both you stand on middle ground and hold the ship level and steady. In both you are national and nothing less than national.

If the Presidents of the United States had taken this stand strongly, from 1853 onwards, the federal system might not have collapsed. But instead of morals and firm conservatism the Presidents tried expediency tempered by sudden deeds of rashness. The first fruit of this policy was "Bleeding Kansas."

4

As soon as Douglas's ill-fated bill became law the sectional struggle for the territory of Kansas began. Slaveholders from Missouri (and to a small extent from the whole South) sought to seize the new country for their own "peculiar institution," while free settlers poured in from the old Northwest. In New England emigrant-aid societies were formed to finance the anti-slavery migration—which for the most part went to the Kansas Valley, while the Missourians and other Southerners took their land along the Missouri River.* In November, 1854, there was an election for a territorial delegate to Congress, and the following spring for a territorial legislature. Much illegal voting took place on both sides; but the Missourians had the advantage of living next door, so the pro-slavery group won both elections. The results were not accepted by public opinion. "Squatter sovereignty" could not fraudulently settle a problem on which the passions of the nation were aroused.

Later, when the anti-slavery Northerners had attained a clear majority, they sought admission to the Union as a free state. This was blocked by Southern members of Congress, and the bitter feeling in that body led to Sumner's speech, "The Crime Against Kansas." Charles Sumner of Massachusetts had been in the Senate for five years. He was a learned man,

* See map, page 212.

handsome and cold and bitter. He was the hero of the abolitionists in New England, and his life was a picture of the wrong way to bring morals into politics. He was the opposite of Lincoln: intolerant, cocksure, humorless, and hate-ridden. High principles, for Sumner, were not an incentive to understand and pity his neighbor, but an excuse for calling those who disagreed with him bad names. In the Kansas speech he outdid himself. The Slave Power was accused of all the crimes which Sumner could remember from his classical and historical reading. This the Senators expected, and received with a minimum of resentment. But in his long rhetorical peroration he turned from the abuse of regions and institutions to the abuse of men—especially Douglas, and the much-loved Senator Butler of South Carolina, whom he accused of being a liar and a fool.

Three days later Senator Butler's nephew, Preston Brooks, a member of the House of Representatives from South Carolina, attacked Sumner at his desk, striking him many times on the head with a cane. Sumner was badly hurt and was unable to attend the Senate for several years. In his absence the Massachusetts legislature re-elected him, and the empty desk at Washington did more harm to the Southern cause than the loud self-satisfied words had ever done. Yet Brooks became a hero throughout the South. A Richmond newspaper referred to this "elegant and effectual caning," while in the North mass meetings described the deed as barbarism. The two regions could no longer comprehend each other.

Meanwhile, matters in Kansas grew rapidly worse. Douglas blamed the fraud and the fighting (the breakdown of his hopes for popular sovereignty) on the organizations in distant states which sought by promoting immigration to control the destiny of Kansas. He might have blamed his own folly for not knowing that when national passions were aroused the decision would never be left to temporary local majorities. For a short time the Missourians might flood across the border and falsify every election; but the real decision as to Kansas had been made years before by the population figures, and the North did not intend to see that decision challenged. In Nebraska, where there was no hope of Southern control, popular sovereignty worked smoothly, and, as Douglas pointed out, "the stream of immigration was permitted to flow in its usual and natural channels." But the unhappy first settlers in Kansas lived at the center of stresses which were nation-wide and which they could not hope to control. Pro-slavery men might burn and riot, and the mad John Brown might seek to promote God's vengeance by murdering five Southerners; but the decisions had been made elsewhere and were enforced by a majority which could not be slain. The battle for Kansas was really won in 1787 when the men who formed the Ohio Company petitioned the Congress of the Confederation for an ordinance which would forever forbid slavery in the old Northwest. As a result of that brave beginning there were too many free-soil states by 1855, and too many willing free-soil pioneers, for the South to capture Kansas by force.

Another factor in the battle for Kansas, and a decisive factor in the Civil War which that battle foreshadowed, was the development of the east-west railway lines. In 1852 the United States had less than 11,000 miles of railway; in 1860 it had more than 30,000. And most of the new lines were tying the Northwest and the Middle West to the East, contradicting the river system which had long tied the West to the South. By 1855 the eastern seaport towns of New York, Philadelphia, and Baltimore had built railways across the mountain barrier of the Alleghenies into the great central valley. These lines ran north of the Ohio River, and as soon as they had pierced the mountains they began reaching farther into the Middle West, the Northwest—and always at the end of the rainbow lay the Pacific. On Washington's Birthday in 1854, there was celebrated at Rock Island, Illinois, the opening of through traffic from the Mississippi River to the Atlantic Ocean. Here was a railroad to take Free-Soil settlers to Kansas. There was no similar road from the South.

The burst of railway-building which changed the habits of the nation during the eighteen-fifties was made possible by federal land grants and by abundant immigrant labor. In 1850 Senator Douglas and his Illinois delegation in Congress passed a law setting aside tracts of public land for the encouragement of railway expansion. The Illinois Central Railroad was given two and a half million acres, and within four years it had built a line from Chicago in the north of the state to Cairo at the junction of the Ohio and Mississippi Rivers. There was no bridge across the broad Ohio at that point, so the new line did not tie southern Illinois to Kentucky but to the fabulous city of Chicago. In 1850 Chicago was not on the railway at all; in 1855 it was the terminus of 2200 miles of new roads and had become one of the largest grain-exporting towns in the world. By 1856 five lines ran from Chicago to the Mississippi River, diverting the traffic of Iowa, Minnesota, Wisconsin, Missouri, Central Illinois—the whole northern valley—from the old north-south river route to the new west-east route of the railways. Situated at the southern tip of Lake Michigan, which bounds the prairies like a wall three hundred miles long, Chicago with her railways became a natural center for lake traffic as well. "The parallels," writes Allan Nevins, "had conquered the meridian lines of commerce. Had the South developed its manufactures, had New Orleans pushed its railroads to the northward energetically, had St. Louis flung a line into Iowa, the story might have been different. As it was, by 1860 the Northwest and Northeast marched arm in arm."[7]

The South had not been pushed aside without a struggle. By 1858 Memphis on the Mississippi had been joined to Charleston on the Atlantic, and also to Richmond. And as early as the eighteen-thirties a heroic effort

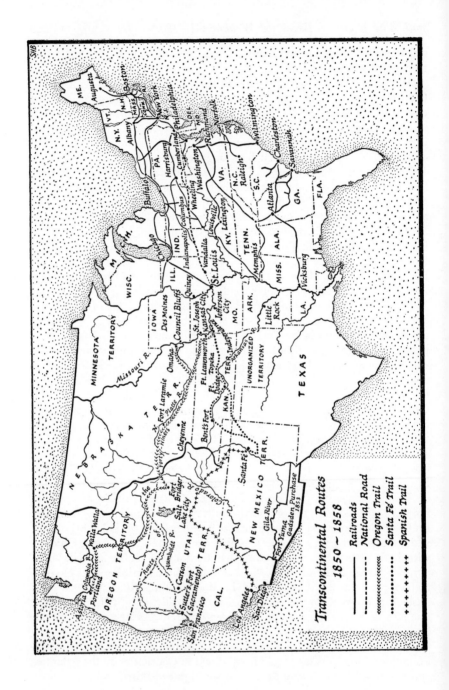

Transcontinental Routes
1850 ~ 1858

Railroads
National Road
Oregon Trail
Santa Fé Trail
Spanish Trail

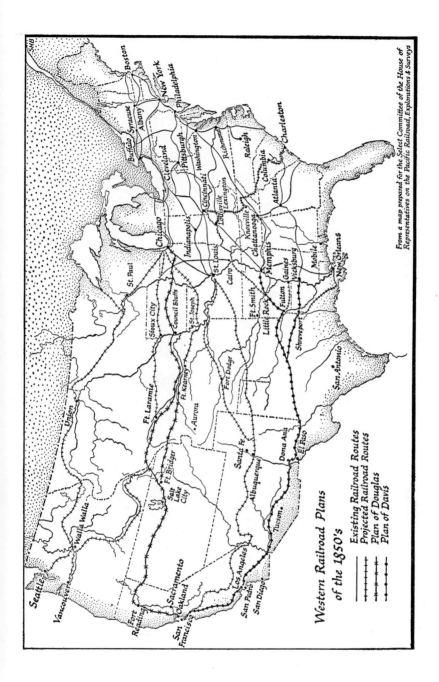

Western Railroad Plans
of the 1850's

	Existing Railroad Routes
	Projected Railroad Routes
	Plan of Douglas
	Plan of Davis

From a map prepared for the Select Committee of the House of
Representatives on the Pacific Railroad, Explorations & Surveys

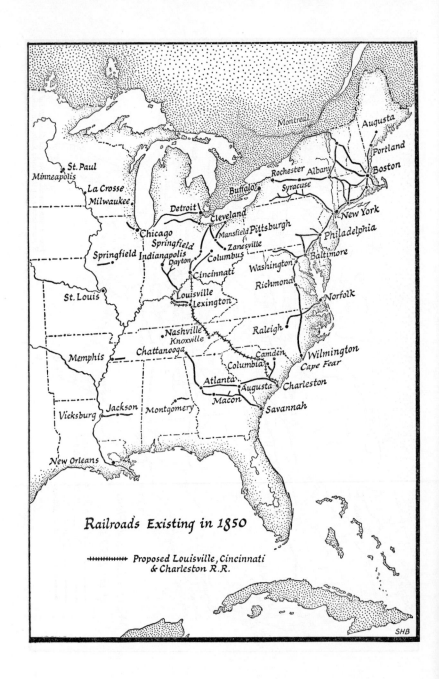

Railroads Existing in 1850

⊢⊢⊢⊢⊢⊢ Proposed Louisville, Cincinnati
& Charleston R.R.

SHB

had been made to build a road from Charleston to Louisville and to Cincinnati, thus tying the Deep South to the Middle West and eventually to the Northwest. But the panic of 1837 with the accompanying cotton slump, and the untimely death of Senator Hayne who was one of the chief promoters, frustrated the plan. This was a disaster for the Southeast. Hayne's Louisville, Cincinnati and Charleston Railway Company might have prevented the isolation of that section and kept alive its strong nationalist tradition. But the attempt was made before the era of federal land grants; Northern capital was not interested and Southern capital was not available in the needed quantities. The slave system was failing economically as well as in the moral sphere.*

5

An unforeseen result of the Kansas-Nebraska Act was the welding together of all who opposed the spread of slavery into a new Republican Party—a party "sectional in membership, national in politics," as Senator Beveridge called it, "a combination of moral and economic forces, of ancient partisanship and racial prejudice, of industrial philosophy and religious exaltation." We have already seen that the Whig Party was dying and that effective leadership in the Democratic Party had passed to the pro-Southern group—either real Southerners like Davis, or "northern men with southern principles" (popularly known as "doughfaces") like Caleb Cushing and President Pierce. The materials were at hand for a new alliance of interests and ambitions; but before the Republicans could seize the chance there arose from the general shifting and disintegrating of allegiances a brief but sinister party known as Native Americans, or Know-Nothings.

The immense increase in immigration which came in the forties and fifties led naturally to "nativist" movements. Most of the new immigrants were Germans or Irish, and most of the Germans and Irish were Catholics. To the fear of the foreigner was added the fear of a strange religion. The Irish, who were adroit politicians, settled mostly in the large

* The era of federal land grants, which began with Douglas's *coup* in 1850, continued until long after the Civil War and produced some of the thorniest problems in American history. The opportunities for corruption were among the grossest ever unfolded before man's dazzled eyes, yet the desire of each western state not to be left behind in the race for quick transport was so intense that men were willing to sell not only their souls but their earthly inheritance to the much-feared giant corporations rather than allow a neighbor state to gain a temporary lead. Between 1851 and 1858 the federal government gave twenty-one million acres of land to railway corporations in the Mississippi Valley. This, as we shall see, was but a small beginning.

The proposed Louisville, Cincinnati and Charleston Railway route is shown on the map on page 372. The route is now used by the Southern Railroad.

Eastern cities where the Democratic Party had long been the party of the poor; their political abilities thus became an affront to the Whigs, predisposing that moribund coalition to join with the nativists. The laxness with which immigration laws were administered in the seaport towns added sensible grievances to those of mere jealousy and meanness. New Orleans was even worse than New York in encouraging Europe, not only to

> Give me your tired, your poor,
> Your huddled masses yearning to breathe free,

but quite literally to send "the wretched refuse of your teeming shore" in the person of criminals, lunatics, and the incurably diseased.* So the first successful Native American Party started in Louisiana in 1841. The movement spread north under a variety of names—"Sons of '76," "Druids," "Foresters," and the like—electing a mayor in New York and a Congressman in Philadelphia in 1844. In 1852 and 1853 these quaintly named and pernicious bands came together into a national party, calling itself the Native Americans or the Order of the Star-Spangled Banner. The rest of the country called it the Know-Nothing Party, because it was said to be a secret order whose members were sworn to answer all questions with the words, "I know nothing about it." Know-Nothings were pledged to vote only for "natives," to demand that immigrants should spend twenty-one years in the country before they could become naturalized, and to work against the influence of the Catholic Church. For a few years it seemed as if they might draw a national majority into their strange and novel net.

Prohibitionists had a tendency to sympathize with the Know-Nothings because the Irish Catholics of the big cities, and the German Catholics who were filtering into the Middle West, regarded prohibition as a form of insanity. Anti-slavery men in the North had a weakness for Know-Nothings because the newest immigrants, being the poorest of the poor, could usually be stirred to oppose emancipation. The immigrants who moved West to the land became staunchly anti-slavery; but those who stayed in the slums of the big Eastern cities preferred to have some class of Americans whose lot was clearly inferior to their own. And the rich conservative Whigs, the class-conscious followers of Webster, the Lords of the Loom who had long been in alliance with the Lords of the Lash, and

* On the base of the Statue of Liberty in New York Harbor are the following lines by Emma Lazarus:

> "Keep, ancient lands, your storied pomp!" cries she
> With silent lips. "Give me your tired, your poor,
> Your huddled masses yearning to breathe free,
> The wretched refuse of your teeming shore.
> Send these, the homeless, the tempest-tost, to me!
> I lift my lamp beside the golden door."

in general all "sound" men of property, had a tendency to look with alarm at the unkempt foreigners who were flooding the land.*

Among their other shortcomings, many immigrants were suspected of "radical" ideas derived from the revolutionary fervor of Europe's 1848. So a temporary alliance was formed out of the anti-drink, anti-slave, anti-radical, and anti-immigrant enthusiasms. It was not a true basis for an American political party, because none of the groups had anything to offer in the way of bargains or concessions. Each wanted its own peculiar way, with the result that the party was far too rigid. As soon as this was proved in action, the Know-Nothings disintegrated; but meanwhile they astonished the nation with their success. In 1854 they won control of Massachusetts and Delaware, and in alliance with the Whigs carried Pennsylvania. About seventy-five Congressmen elected that year had Know-Nothing affiliations. In 1855 the Know-Nothings elected nine governors.** But the next year, meeting in convention in Philadelphia, they split on the question of slavery and the Nebraska Act. Southern delegates insisted on endorsing the Act, with the result that twelve Northern states seceded and demanded the restoration of the Missouri Compromise, thus moving toward the program of the infant Republican Party.

In 1856 poor harmless Millard Fillmore became the presidential candidate of the Southern Know-Nothings. He received 875,000 votes and carried only the state of Maryland. Thus ended the party of intolerance, the party described by one indignant Southern believer in freedom of religion as a "stupendous and far-reaching leprosy." The year 1856 also saw the end of the Whigs, whose dejected remnant had held a convention in Baltimore in September and had endorsed Fillmore as the candidate least likely to disturb the peace of the nation. In the election some of the Whigs voted for Fillmore, some for Buchanan (the Democratic candidate), and many for the new Republican Party. Fillmore's utter defeat meant that in the future such Whigs as wished to play a serious part in politics must join the Democrats or the Republicans.

6

The Republican Party was the chief beneficiary of the collapse of the Know-Nothings. The Republicans could make no place for the nativist or the pro-slavery elements of that abortive coalition; but they found room for all the others. Professor Binkley describes the party in its youth as "an aggregation of Free-Soilers, Independent Democrats, Conscience Whigs,

* Some of this latter group would soon be encouraging immigration in order to keep down the price of labor.

** They won the states of Rhode Island, New Hampshire, Massachusetts, Connecticut, New York, Pennsylvania, Maryland, Kentucky, California.

Know-Nothings, Barnburners, abolitionists, teetotalers."[8] We have seen each of these groups in action independently; we must now trace how they came together for victory, what bargains they made with one another, and what prizes they offered to the professional leaders without whom a lasting party is impossible.

In February, 1854, several months before the Kansas-Nebraska Bill was passed (but a month after it had been reported to the Senate), a group of Whigs, Free Soilers, and anti-slavery Democrats met at Ripon, Wisconsin, and resolved if this measure was pushed through the Congress "to throw old party organizations to the winds and organize a new party on the sole basis of the non-extension of slavery." They claimed to be the true descendants of Jefferson, who had backed the Northwest Ordinance of 1787 whereby slavery was banished from the land north of the Ohio River and east of the Mississippi. So they took the name of Jefferson's party and called themselves Republicans. Five months later, after the hated bill had become law, an anti-Nebraska state convention at Jackson, Michigan, chose the same name for the same reasons. And on July 13, the sixty-eighth anniversary of the Northwest Ordinance, state conventions in Indiana, Ohio, Vermont, and Wisconsin accepted the new name and demanded a party pledged to prevent the extension of slavery. Thus far the movement was merely one branch of the widespread agitation against the Nebraska Bill. Few would have predicted the birth of a new major party. Everyone knew the Whigs were dying but most people assumed the Know-Nothings would take their place.

One of the first to sense the true drift was Thurlow Weed of New York, the old political master. After the defeat of the Democrats in the midterm election of 1854, Weed guessed that in the victorious coalition the infant Republican Party would outlast the Know-Nothings, the Conscience Whigs, and the other anti-Nebraska groups. He began to maneuver his New York Whig machine toward the camp of the future conquerors. This was clever of Weed, for at the time it still seemed to most observers that the Republicans must fail for lack of a national leader. Salmon P. Chase of Ohio, whose "Appeal of the Independent Democrats" had lighted the raging anti-Nebraska fires, was not acceptable to Whig converts, for he had attacked them too often and too bitterly. Sumner of Massachusetts was so steeped in moral superiority that he could never head a popular movement. Seward of New York was disliked by the Know-Nothing converts, because under the expert guidance of Weed he had befriended the Catholics and the new immigrants in the hope of winning them from the Democratic Party. And Abraham Lincoln had not yet even joined the Republicans. His deep conservatism, and his distaste for the abolitionists, kept him among the dwindling Whig forces until 1856.

Another handicap for the Republicans was their taint of eccentricity and "reform." In this they were most unlike their predecessors, the worldly Whigs, who were never connected with anything socially odd. At first the more conservative Whigs turned their backs on these curious people who consorted with prohibitionists, and even abolitionists. Furthermore, with the help of Horace Greeley and his New York *Tribune* (whose European correspondent was Karl Marx), Northern labor began to join the Republican camp. And as the Democrats under Southern leadership became more conservative, the Republicans won converts from the radical wing of that party: the Locofocos, and the Barnburners, and the so-called "heirs of Jackson" under the leadership of Jackson's friend and party editor, Francis P. Blair. Blair was the permanent chairman of the first Republican National Convention, which met in Pittsburgh in February, 1856, and a member of the first Republican National Committee.

All this was not enough to make a victorious party, as the election of 1856 showed. The Republicans, so far, were scarcely more than a reshuffle of the Know-Nothing coalition, with labor taking the place of the fanatical "nativists." Since this was a Northern-and-Western sectional party, which could count on the united hostility of the South, it could not afford to lose the populous states in its own region. Yet it had nothing in its program or its membership to appeal to the business interests of New York, Pennsylvania, and Massachusetts (who were certain to be suspicious of the appeals to labor), and nothing to win the farmers in the southern fringe of Middle-western states, along the Ohio Valley, many of whom were Southern by blood and most of whom traded with the slave society. By 1860, a combination of good luck and superb political leadership had repaired this weakness; but in 1856 it seemed as if the party might disintegrate under defeat as quickly as the Know-Nothings.

7

The Democratic National Convention met at Cincinnati in June, 1856. The candidates for the nomination were President Pierce, James Buchanan, Lewis Cass, and Stephen A. Douglas. The two-thirds rule was maintained. Although at the end of his first term the President in office can normally control the convention, Pierce failed completely. He began with almost as many votes as Buchanan, but after a few ballots his Southern friends began to desert him for Douglas. The Kansas-Nebraska Bill which had brought such woe to the country had been intended to flatter the South, and the South now sought to repay its author. But Northern hostility to Douglas was too great. The North stood steadily for Buchanan, and since he was known to be another "doughface," another Northern man with Southern principles, the South was happy to take him as a compromise. Like Pierce, he was pliable; but unlike Pierce he was prudent, and it was thought he could be counted on to do nothing, rather than to make positive mistakes. "Nothing" was precisely the policy desired by the South and by the Northern conservative converts to the Democratic Party.

James Buchanan was a Pennsylvanian, born in 1791 of Scotch-Irish stock. He went to a local school and to a small college, and like most politicians in America he studied law. After serving an apprenticeship in local politics he was sent to Congress by the Federalists in 1820—one of the last victories of that once-formidable party. A few years later he joined the Jackson men, retaining his place in Congress and helping to elect Andrew Jackson in 1828. Thereafter he served as Minister to Russia, as United States Senator, and as Secretary of State to the dynamic James K. Polk during the years of expansion and of Manifest Destiny. When the Democrats returned to power in 1853, Buchanan (who had expected the presidency) was sent as Minister to England. There he showed himself a disciple of the imperialist Polk by joining with the American Ministers at Madrid and Paris in signing the "Ostend Manifesto" of 1854.

This was not in truth a manifesto. It was a confidential report to the Department of State, in which Buchanan and his fellow ministers argued that if Spain refused to sell Cuba (for which the Pierce Administration was willing to offer $130,000,000), the United States would be justified in "wresting" the island from its owners. When the "Manifesto" became public* the Administration was embarrassed; but the South, which had long coveted Cuba, was pleased to find in Buchanan another amiable "doughface" who might be counted on to take orders from the Southern Democrats at least as humbly as Pierce and perhaps more efficiently.

The feelings of Spain were ignored. These were the great days of the pax Britannica. Secure behind the British fleet, American politicians could forget politeness, convention, and all the normal usages of foreign relations, abusing or flattering the sovereign states or the revolutionary factions of Europe with no thought beyond the next election. Later, in a less safe world, the habit of a hundred years proved hard to break.

8

The Republican Convention met at Philadelphia, also in June. There was no "logical candidate," for the party had no national leader. Not a single delegate appeared from the Deep South, and only a small unrepresentative group from the border states of Delaware, Maryland, Virginia, and

* The press published so many garbled versions that Congress released the original in March, 1855.

Kentucky. Since they were a sectional party, the Republicans were not forced to make the usual concessions to unity. Their chief problem was to keep the abolitionists from spoiling the party's chances, even in the North. There was a tone to the meeting that the more professional and nationally representative conventions lacked.

> The Philadelphia scene had a pristine freshness, a bright hopefulness, an evangelistic verve which made it wonderfully refreshing. Its debates throbbed with feeling—its speeches struck fire. Here were qualities which went back, somehow, to the Declaration of Independence, to the old bill of rights, to the passion of the English-speaking folk in bygone centuries for adventures in justice and freedom.[9]

The platform showed that the party stood for little except opposition to the spread of slavery—although it did call for the immediate construction of a railway to the Pacific "by the most central and practical route," and it did attack the Ostend Manifesto as "the highwayman's plea that 'might makes right.' " This did not sound like a broad enough base for a national coalition. The Republicans still looked like the typical "third party," with one main excellent idea. They might have remained a third party, and have faded as such parties fade, except that the demise of the Whigs had left many experienced professionals without a job, organizers in search of something to organize. Before long they had shown the Republicans how to spread a wider net, and how to avoid losing old converts while gaining new and contradictory ones. Thereafter, the Republicans had less "pristine freshness" but more success.

The first Republican candidate was John Charles Frémont, the so-called "Pathfinder of the Rockies," the son-in-law of Senator Thomas Hart Benton. It is hard to do justice to Frémont's services and at the same time to his follies and extravagances. The first half of his life was mostly romance and success, the last half a long and sometimes sordid anticlimax. And 1856 was the dividing line.

Frémont was the illegitimate son of a Frenchman who taught school in Richmond, Virginia, and a Mrs. Pryor of that city. Brave, good-looking, and energetic, Frémont was an adventurer who followed his destiny into adventure's natural home: the unexplored West. A lieutenant in the United States topographical corps, he married Jessie Benton, who was almost as Byronic as himself. His powerful father-in-law, the Senator who had long wanted to seize the entire West, put him in charge of two exploring expeditions. Frémont's reports, written with his wife's masterly help, brought the Oregon Trail and the western mountains into splendid life for stay-at-home readers—and incidentally they made Frémont a national hero. He played a dubious but popular part in the conquest of California, from which he emerged with mining properties worth ten million dollars and a court-martial which in January, 1848, found him guilty of "mutiny, disobedience, and conduct prejudicial to order." The public was on his side (the public and Thomas Hart Benton), so he resigned from the Army without discredit and devoted himself to further explorations, to European travel, to his adoring Jessie, and to a brief term in the United States Senate. When the Kansas fight began, he declared himself a Free-Soiler and an enemy of the Fugitive Slave Law. Since these were his only known views on politics he was a good candidate for the new party.[10]

When the Republicans had made their choice, the Northerners who had left the Know-Nothings when the South insisted on a pro-slavery resolution met in convention, called themselves the North American Party, and endorsed Frémont. So there were three important candidates in 1856: Buchanan and the Democrats; Frémont and the Republican–North Americans; Fillmore and the Know-Nothings plus the remaining Whigs. We have already seen that Fillmore carried the state of Maryland, Buchanan carried nineteen states with 174 electoral votes, Frémont eleven states with 114 electoral votes. Buchanan received 1,838,169 popular votes, Frémont 1,341,364.* New England and New York and the northern Middle West had gone to the Republicans; but Pennsylvania, New Jersey and the southern counties of Indiana, and Illinois had stayed with Buchanan, and of course the entire South—and California, which had its own reasons for disliking Frémont and which Buchanan had wooed with the impossible promise of a Pacific railway at once. The victory was for conservatism, for dodging trouble, for the Union and for peace, even if peace meant appeasement.

The prediction made to Howell Cobb by his farsighted friend had come true: one more rally of all the forces of conservatism and compromise had produced one more victory for the Democrats. What would they do with this, their last chance?

* So Buchanan had 59 per cent of the vote in the electoral college but only 45 per cent of the popular vote. Frémont had 30 per cent of the popular vote and Fillmore 25 per cent.

XIX

The Fruits of Executive Weakness–II
1857–1861

ACCORDING TO THE STANDARDS of the twentieth century Buchanan's campaign was a simple affair; but at the time it seemed elaborate, costly, and perhaps corrupt. The candidate stayed at home in Lancaster, Pennsylvania, seeing visitors and answering letters. The Democratic National Committee appointed a sub-committee to raise money and a so-called "resident committee" in Washington to write pamphlets and send out speakers—and if necessary indulge in modest bribery. The Republicans, meanwhile, broke the painfully learned rules of federal politics by taking a positive stand. There were no compromises in their program, no vague words, no attempts to occupy several contradictory positions at the same time.

The Republicans could be brave because they were a sectional party and because they were young. The Democrats, who were neither, felt that such tactics were unfair. Also, the Democrats were fighting themselves. Their party had repudiated a first-term President. On the good and sensible grounds that he was incompetent, the machine had turned against its own boss. This did not make for harmony between the friends of Buchanan and the friends of Pierce. And it did not promise peace within the state organizations when the new Administration came to distributing jobs. In fact, the fierce quarrels which ensued consumed much of the attention and energy which might have been given to the problem of preserving the Union.

Buchanan saw himself, inaccurately, as a politician of rich experience and wisdom. He had been in public service for almost forty-two years and he mistakenly believed that he had been learning all that time. He was distressed at the planless discord of the Pierce Administration. He felt that as soon as his own trained hand took the helm there would be no more yawing and jibing. Added to this confidence in his political powers was a deeper and truer self-distrust which plagued Buchanan all his life. He never married and he never had an intimate friend of either sex. He took refuge from personal relations in a dignity which seemed put on, like a suit of armor, instead of being an expression of his spirit. Six feet tall, with abundant white hair, a high collar and broad white neckcloth, he was pompous rather than impressive, stubborn rather than resolute. And underneath the layers of protection he was timid. When hard-pressed his refuge was irresolution. It is a pity that at the age of sixty-six, after ten years of ill health, at a troublesome time in his country's history, he should have insisted upon pushing himself into the presidency.

Buchanan did not know it was a bad time. He thought a little sound management would bring peace and quiet—an opinion which alone was enough to convict him of overconfidence, obsolescence, and thorough misreading of the country's mood, North or South. As a first step toward sound management he sought to build a Cabinet which would have none of the faults of Pierce's mismated team. He wanted all the regions of the country represented, but not all the quarreling groups within the party. He rightly interpreted the election as a victory for conservatism, and he planned a strong conservative Administration. Unhappily, he and his friends did not seem to know many strong conservatives.

For Secretary of State Buchanan took the aging Lewis Cass of Michigan, who was about to leave the Senate. We have seen Cass as an extreme American imperialist and a hater of England. Buchanan did not like him or trust him; indeed, he made it a condition of the appointment that Cass should suppress his anti-British feelings and accept an assistant whom the President would name and who was to do all the work. Presumably, Cass took the appointment on such terms because he was too old to care for anything except employment. "At seventy-four," writes Professor Nichols, "senility was creeping up on the obese, indolent Lewis Cass. . . . He was a constant trial as an adviser, because he could not make up his mind and was glad to be made the mouthpiece of others."[1]

The Postmaster General, who controlled most of the patronage, was a Southerner with little national experience but a good knowledge of what the South wanted. The Secretary of the Navy was a careerist from Connecticut who was careful never to disagree with Buchanan and who did no noticeable harm. The Secretary of War was ex-Governor Floyd of Virginia, a bigoted states'-rights man of good family. "He was not particularly intelligent, energetic, efficient, or interested . . ." says Professor Nichols; " 'Careless' is the word that describes him. Buchanan was to have many anxious moments because of Floyd's unfitness for his position."[2] The Secretary of the Interior was a narrow-minded self-made Mississippian who had forced his way to success during the early unregulated youth of the state. The Attorney General was a Scotch-Irish Pennsylvanian—the one effective man in the Cabinet who was neither a Southerner nor a "doughface." And the Secretary of the Treasury was the charming Howell Cobb of Georgia, the baby of the Cabinet, only forty-one years old. He had many virtues and talents, but a knowledge of finance was not among them. A Union man from Georgia, a conservative who believed in the true spirit of federal compromise, he was a suitable member of the Administration; but Buchanan was perhaps wrong to give him the Treasury. Next to the Post Office, that was the department most concerned with patronage—and here Cobb must be a liability in his own region, for the fire-eaters hated him and whatever he did they would claim they were betrayed.

By and large, the Cabinet was a faithful mirror of the President. Most of it was old and unaware of the perilous mood of the country. None of it, with the exception of Cobb, was notably able. None of it could provide leadership at Cabinet meetings. If Buchanan went wrong there was no one to help. If he tried to evade decisions there was no one to compel action. It is pathetic to think of this tired, sick man, with his too dignified deportment masking the self-distrust which kept him from delegating power, working till late hours night after night in the White House, poring over a multitude of papers which he insisted on reading but which he failed to understand.

2

In his Inaugural Address Buchanan said that the country was on the verge of a long period of internal peace. Everything was working out well. There was no longer any reason for a sectional party, such as the Republicans. He intended to allay sectional strife and to make the Union secure forever. He also recommended economy, the payment of the public debt, and an increase in the Navy. On military grounds he recommended building a "road" to California (presumably the railroad of his campaign promise to that state), so that soldiers and supplies could move easily; but he gave no hint as to how to break the deadlock in Congress between the friends of Jefferson Davis's southern route and the friends of Douglas's Nebraska route. In general, the address proved Buchanan a strict-constructionist who refused to assume leadership even in such a vital political question as the tariff.* In foreign affairs, though he talked of peace and friendship, he managed to suggest that he still favored Southern expansion—presumably toward the Caribbean—from which the slave system might refresh itself.

The most important sentences in the Inaugural Address dealt with

* Buchanan went further than any President since Monroe in praise of strict construction and a weak government. In a letter written in 1852 he said that the "ancient principles of 1798" in Virginia could alone save the country from wasteful extravagance and from a loose interpretation of the central powers. This is Jefferson before he came to office; this is John Randolph and the "old Republicans." This is nostalgia for the innocent youth of the nation—charming, but inadequate for a chief executive during the fateful fifties.

Kansas, slavery, and the territories. The whole explosive question, said the President, was now "happily a matter of but little practical importance," because the Supreme Court would soon "speedily and finally" settle it. "To their decision, in common with all good citizens, I shall cheerfully submit." This was an odd statement from a follower of Andrew Jackson, who had denied the power of the Court to settle matters of public policy. It was an odd statement from anyone who had watched the dire effects of the Kansas-Nebraska Act, the rise of the Republican Party, and the clear repeated proof that the North would accept no decision, by President, Congress, or Court, which allowed slavery to spread beyond the Missouri Compromise line. On this issue Buchanan was as morally insensitive as Douglas—and as politically blind—if he thought a group of judges could calm the storm. And his statement was odd for still another reason. He said he would "cheerfully submit" to the decision of the Court, and he exhorted "all good citizens" to do the same. The implication was clear that he would obey the Court whatever it might rule in the pending Dred Scott case. He did not add that he had been told what the ruling would be.

3

Dred Scott was a Negro slave in Missouri who sued for his freedom on the ground that with the consent of his master he had lived for years in Illinois and in the unorganized territory across the Mississippi—lands where slavery was forbidden either by the Missouri Compromise or by the Northwest Ordinance. This was a familiar type of case. Between 1822 and 1837 eight similar cases had been decided in favor of slaves; but Dred Scott's suit for freedom began in 1846 when the approaching Mexican War had already sharpened and made bitter all questions touching slavery. The case was heard and appealed and re-appealed, with judgment sometimes in Scott's favor and sometimes against him, until at the end of six years it was carried to the federal courts. In 1854 the United States Circuit Court of Missouri ruled that since Scott was a Negro he was not a citizen of Missouri and not entitled to sue in federal courts. The case was then appealed to the United States Supreme Court. Six of the seven justices who formed the majority wrote individual opinions, coming on the whole to similar conclusions by a variety of routes. The opinion of Chief Justice Taney—the most outrageous of all from the Northern point of view—is commonly known as "the Dred Scott decision." It was delivered on March 6, 1857—two days after the inauguration. Taney's argument may be summarized under three headings:

First, no Negro could be a citizen, since citizenship derived from the federal government, and at the time when the Constitution was adopted

Negroes were regarded "as beings of an inferior order and altogether unfit to associate with the white race, either in social or political relations." At that time, he added, Negroes "had no rights or privileges but such as those who held the power and the government might choose to grant them."

Second, even if one dismissed the question as to whether a Negro could ever be a citizen, it was obvious that a slave could not be a citizen. Dred Scott was a slave. He had not become free by residence in territory covered by the Missouri Compromise, since the Missouri Compromise had been unconstitutional from the beginning. Congress had no power, while governing a territory, to interfere with the property of a slaveowner, any more than it could interfere with a man's peaceful enjoyment of his property in pigs. "An act of Congress," wrote Taney, "which deprives a citizen of the United States of his liberty or property, merely because he came himself or brought his property into a particular territory of the United States, and who had committed no offense against the laws, could hardly be dignified with the name of due process of law." Therefore, since Dred Scott was still a slave he was not a citizen, and could not sue in the federal courts. The interesting part of this argument was that it not only made the Missouri Compromise unconstitutional but the Republican Party as well—since that party was founded for the main purpose of preventing the spread of slavery into further territories.*

Third, even if one dismissed the question as to whether the Missouri Compromise could make Dred Scott free while he lived in territory north of 36° 30′, the fact remained that he had voluntarily returned to Missouri where his status was determined by Missouri law. The courts of Missouri had held that he was still a slave. Therefore he was not a citizen and could not sue in a federal court.

The Northern press—abolitionist and moderate Republican—fell upon the Dred Scott decision with a howl of fury. The New York *Tribune* called it "this wicked and false judgment" made by "five slave-holders and two doughfaces," and added that the decision was "entitled to just as

---

* In 1856 the Republican platform had anticipated Taney in his appeal to the "due process" clause of the Fifth Amendment. But Taney emphasized the property which should not be taken from the master, whereas the Republicans emphasized the liberty which should not be taken from the man. "As our Republican fathers . . ." said the platform, "ordained that no person shall be deprived of life, liberty, or property, without due process of law, it becomes our duty to maintain this provision of the Constitution against all attempts to violate it for the purpose of establishing slavery in the territories of the United States."

As we shall see in Chapter XXVIII, "due process of law" is one of the most ambiguous phrases in American history. When Professor Edward Corwin was a student he asked his teacher (the famous Andrew McLaughlin) what Taney meant by "due process" in the Dred Scott decision. "I don't know," said McLaughlin, and the young Corwin reflected that in that case nobody knew. He decided to try to find out. The results of his work appeared almost fifty years later in a fascinating book, *Liberty Against Government: The Rise, Flowering and Decline of a Famous Juridical Concept.*

much moral weight as would be the judgment of a majority of those congregated in any Washington Barroom." Taney was vilified throughout the North, and the six justices who agreed with him. It was accepted that they had made the Supreme Court an agent of Southern expansionism. No decision has ever done the Court more harm, or shown a more dangerous judicial ignorance of the mood of the day.

4

Buchanan and the politically naïve judges were disappointed in their hope that the most vexed of questions could be solved by a court decision. The Union was not saved but greatly endangered, for the rancorous discussion which followed made war more likely. Perhaps the only man who was clearly helped by the Dred Scott fiasco was Abraham Lincoln, whose combination of caution and simple inflexible morality was what the North wanted to hear. And the rough, insensitive Douglas soon gave Lincoln the ideal foil for his best qualities.

Senator Douglas was asked by his constituents what had become of popular sovereignty, in the light of Dred Scott. He replied that popular sovereignty was untouched. Of course a citizen had a right to take his slaves to a territory; but that was "a barren and worthless right unless sustained, protected, and enforced by appropriate police regulations and local legislation, prescribing adequate remedies for its violation."* Unwisely —perhaps lured by the pleasure of insisting that his Republican enemies were unconstitutional—Douglas went on to praise the decision and to insist that what the Court said must be accepted. "Whoever resists the final decision of the highest tribunal," he said, "aims a deadly blow at our whole republican system of government." This was the type of bombast that Lincoln enjoyed destroying. He quoted Andrew Jackson's message disregarding the Supreme Court's decision on the Bank, adding, "again and again have I heard Judge Douglas denounce that bank decision and applaud General Jackson for disregarding it." He pointed out that the Supreme Court had often overruled its own decisions, and said the Republicans would do what they could to have it overrule this. Then he turned to his favorite problem: how to reconcile slavery and the Declaration of Independence. There had been a time when the Declaration was sacred. "But now, to aid in making the bondage of the Negro universal and eternal, it is assailed and sneered at and construed, and hawked at and torn, till, if its framers could rise from their graves, they could not at all recognize it." What did the authors of the Declaration mean when they said all men were created equal?

* Speech at Springfield, Illinois. June 12, 1857.

They meant to set up a standard maxim for free society, which could be familiar to all, and revered by all. . . . The assertion that "all men are created equal" was of no practical use in effecting our separation from Great Britain; and it was placed in the Declaration, not for that, but for future use. Its authors meant it to be, thank God, it is now proving itself, a stumbling block to those who in after times might seek to turn a free people back into the hateful paths of despotism. They knew the proneness of prosperity to breed tyrants, and they meant when such should reappear in this fair land and commence their vocation they should find left for them at least one hard nut to crack.

The whole of this speech was printed in the New York *Times*. Lincoln was becoming a national figure. It was just a year since he had cautiously and with misgivings joined the Republican Party—pushed by William Herndon, his law partner. The first Republican state convention in Illinois was to meet at Bloomington in May, 1856. In April Herndon and a few friends called a county convention in Springfield to select local delegates. Although Lincoln was away attending court, Herndon signed his name to the call. Thus there came into the party the man who was to give it not only the most careful and expert political guidance, but also a soul.

5

Buchanan's luckless Administration, which had begun with the Dred Scott decision challenging Stephen A. Douglas on his favorite ground of popular sovereignty, soon found itself wholly at odds with that powerful and contentious Democrat. In the autumn of 1857 a convention at Lecompton, Kansas, attended solely by the pro-slavery minority in the territory, framed a constitution for a state government, to be submitted to the voters in a so-called referendum. The constitution contained an article declaring slave property inviolable. The voters might take the constitution with or without that article; but they could not reject the constitution as a whole, and even if they rejected the article there could be no interference with slave property already in Kansas, and no amendment before 1865. The free-state men in Kansas declined to vote, and on December 21 the constitution was approved, with slavery. In January, 1858, the legislature—in control of the Free Soil Party—arranged for a referendum on the whole constitution. This time the pro-slavery men refused to vote and the constitution was rejected. After this fraud and confusion, and in spite of the clear will of the majority in Kansas, Buchanan recommended to Congress that it accept the Lecompton Constitution and admit Kansas as a slave state. Douglas had stated in December that he thought the Lecompton Constitution a travesty on popular sovereignty. When the Administration backed it, Douglas turned against Buchanan with all his implacable force.

The President—who had once expected to heal the party breaches made by the amateurish Pierce—fought back. Douglas's friends were turned out of office. Douglas himself was denied all further patronage. The party press attacked him with vicious abuse—the Republicans watching with wide-eyed pleasure. The one pushing and popular Democratic leader in the North had broken with the dominant pro-slavery faction, and the party seemed to lie in ruins. The Democratic state convention in Illinois stood firmly behind Douglas, who had built a local machine so strong that the President could not break it. Buchanan forced the Senate to accept the Lecompton Constitution; but Douglas (with the help of the Republicans and a few Know-Nothings) contrived its defeat in the House. The torn, unhappy territory of Kansas did not become a state until January, 1861.

In the midst of this warfare Douglas sought re-election to the Senate. Eastern Republicans wished to widen the split in the Democratic Party by endorsing Douglas; but Illinois Republicans said it was "asking too much for human nature to bear, to now surrender to Judge Douglas . . . to quietly let him step foremost in our ranks and make us all take back seats."[3] So they put forward their own party candidate: Abraham Lincoln of Springfield. Douglas was in Washington when he heard the news. He said to his friends: "[Lincoln] is the strong man of his party—full of wit, facts, dates—and the best stump speaker, with his droll ways and dry jokes, in the West."

Magnanimously, since Lincoln could command no such audiences as the "Little Giant," Douglas accepted a challenge to debate in seven Congressional districts. As a result, Lincoln became a major national figure and a candidate for the presidency. In the debate at Freeport, Douglas was forced to restate his belief that in spite of the Dred Scott decision slavery could be kept out of the territories by police regulations. This set the Southern fire-eaters against him and led in 1860 to the break in the Democratic Party. For the rest, the debates are disappointing. They show the ability of both speakers to set traps and to avoid them. And they show that there was little difference between the candidates in regard to slavery. Both put the preservation of the Union above all other causes. Douglas believed that popular sovereignty would ensure freedom in all the territories north of the Compromise line. Lincoln believed that popular sovereignty might never be given an honest chance and that the deep perturbation of the people could only be met by a prohibition against new slave lands. Before the debates began, Kansas had been saved from slavery by Douglas's valiant fight against the Lecompton Constitution. Later, when the nation had broken, Douglas defended Lincoln in the

Senate and stood strongly behind him in upholding the Union. The chief difference between them was whether the opposition to slave-expansion should be put on moral or on legal grounds.

Perhaps the most remarkable feature of the debates was the number of problems which were ignored. The nation had just suffered a severe economic depression. Yet, as J. G. Randall points out, there was not a word about unemployment, the condition of factory workers, the tariff, immigration, railroads and federal land grants, homesteads and the protection of public lands against greedy plunder, agriculture, or banking, or any of the agrarian grievances which were soon to rend the nation.

Lincoln, of course, centered the debates on Kansas-Nebraska in order to hold the Illinois Republican Party together until other issues could be agreed upon, and until the loyalties arising from repeated campaigns could make themselves felt. He had to satisfy (and to keep in a loose precarious alliance) conservative Whigs like himself, abolitionists whom he regarded as a radical nuisance, Middlewestern Germans who distrusted Know-Nothings, and Know-Nothings who distrusted all immigrants. He divined that freedom in the territories was common ground, and from that he would not budge. Douglas was trapped and dared not introduce new issues, since Lincoln had already accused him of dodging and of inferior moral sense. In the election, Lincoln's tactics almost succeeded. The Republicans won a majority of the votes, but only a minority of seats in the next state legislature. So in January, 1859, when the two houses met in joint session, Douglas was elected Senator by fifty-four votes to forty-six.* He returned to Washington to find himself an outcast in his own party, which was now wholly in the hands of the Southerners. He was deposed from the chairmanship of the Committee on Territories. Under pressure from Jefferson Davis (who had returned to the Senate after the demise of the Pierce Administration) he was soon forced to meet the Southern attack and to declare himself opposed to any federal protection for slave property in the territories. The split in the party was complete. It only needed to be ratified by the next national convention.

6

While Lincoln had been talking cautiously in Illinois, seeking a position which might keep Whigs and abolitionists united, and which might satisfy the North's anxieties without provoking fear or rage among moderate Southerners, the Pennsylvanians had been making party policy with less

---

* The Senators, of course, were still chosen by the state legislatures under Article I, Section 3 of the Constitution. Lincoln and Douglas were canvassing for party, not personal, votes.

restraint. They were concerned with business and the depression, not with the Declaration of Independence. The iron industry of Pennsylvania had been heavily hit. Manufacturers blamed the "doughface" President from Pennsylvania who had allowed Secretary of the Treasury Cobb to recommend and secure the passage of the Tariff of 1857, which came close to making America a free-trade nation. The ironmakers won some support in Massachusetts, and from Greeley's *Tribune;* but Republicans on the whole still dodged protection as an election issue. So the high-tariff men in Pennsylvania gave money and leadership to a local "People's Party"—a coalition of Republicans and anti-Buchanan Democrats. Refreshed by the rain of cash, the People's Party, in 1858, elected eighteen of the state's twenty-five Congressmen. The Republicans were forced to pay heed, for they could not win in 1860 without Pennsylvania, and it was clear that they could not have Pennsylvania without protection. Reluctantly, they passed a tariff bill through the House of Representatives. It was defeated in the Senate; but the new party now had a new cause.*
And when, in the following year, President Buchanan vetoed a homestead bill on constitutional grounds, the long reluctance of Eastern business was overcome by this rich chance for vote-getting, and the Republicans declared themselves for free land. "Vote yourself a farm," and "Vote yourself a tariff," were campaign cries in 1860.

Lincoln, meanwhile, was trying to dissuade other party leaders from taking stands which might disrupt the Republicans before they had built a true national machine. His job, he said to a friend, was "to hedge against divisions in the Republican ranks generally and particularly for the contest of 1860." There were many such divisions which Lincoln, with his hard political sense, deplored. His worries during 1859 and 1860 are an index to the problems of party-building in America. Know-Nothing Republicans in one state, abolitionist Republicans in another, were an equal bother.

> Massachusetts Republicans [wrote Lincoln] should have looked beyond their noses, and then they could not have failed to see that tilting against foreigners would ruin us in the whole Northwest. New Hampshire and Ohio should forbear tilting against the Fugitive Slave law in such a way as to utterly overwhelm us in Illinois with the charges of enmity to the Constitution itself. Kansas, in her confidence that she can be saved to freedom on "squatter sovereignty," ought not to forget that to prevent the spread and nationalism of slavery is a national concern and must be attended to by the nation.[4]

* The Republicans in this back-handed fashion were committed to one of the few policies which in the period after the Civil War distinguished them sharply from the Democrats. Until the days of Franklin Roosevelt, for reasons which will become clear, the Democrats on the whole wished lower tariffs than the Republicans—although from 1865 onwards they were never again a free-trade party.

While Lincoln was struggling to prevent the destruction of the Republican Party from within, America's leading fanatic very nearly destroyed it from without. In the middle of October, 1859, the furious John Brown declared private war on the institution of slavery and invaded the South with a tiny army of liberation. He intended a series of raids along the line of the Allegheny Mountains, liberating slaves and endowing the conquered territory with a government which he and his friends had invented at a conference in Canada. Harper's Ferry in Virginia (now West Virginia) was selected for the first attack. It was the site of an armory and arsenal, and it was a gateway to the South. Brown's "army" consisted of seventeen white men and five Negroes. They may have hoped to stir a slave rebellion; but nobody lifted a helping hand. The raiders were driven into a fire-engine house and there killed or captured by United States Marines under the command of Colonel Robert E. Lee and Lieutenant "Jeb" Stuart. John Brown and six other survivers were hanged at the near-by county seat.*

The storm raised by this not very menacing foray was a sign of the tension under which the country lived. John Brown's chief crime was that he killed a most promising movement for conciliation and the union which had developed during 1858 and 1859 in the border states, led by such men as Crittenden of Kentucky and Rives of Virginia. After the raid their work was discredited. The South, which had long believed that the abolitionists meant to provoke a slave insurrection, enjoyed a shivering horror in recalling the bloody deeds of San Domingo. Northerners living in the South found themselves watched like enemy aliens. And in the North all the forces of conservatism threatened to turn against the Republican Party, which had reluctantly made room for the more conciliatory abolitionists, and some of whose national spokesmen (such as Seward and Greeley) might be blamed for inflaming the unbalanced mind of Brown. Many Northern writers and preachers were in favor of the raid; but the politicians drew back, sensing that praise of John Brown meant the loss of the next election. And if the Republican candidate in 1860 did less well than Frémont in 1856, the party would follow the Know-Nothings into oblivion.

* In his last speech John Brown denied that he had intended to incite slaves to murder. He said he only meant to set them free and take them away from Virginia. And he added: "This court acknowledges, as I suppose, the validity of the law of God. I see a book kissed here which I suppose to be the Bible, or at least the New Testament. That teaches me that all things whatsoever I would that men should do to me, I should do even so to them. It teaches me, further, to 'remember them that are in bonds, as bound with them.' I endeavored to act up to that instruction. . . . I am yet too young to understand that God is any respecter of persons. I believe that to have interfered as I have done—as I have always freely admitted I have done—in behalf of His despised poor, was not wrong, but right. . . . I feel no consciousness of guilt."

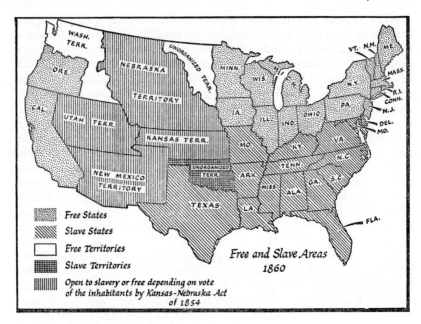

Free States
Slave States
Free Territories
Slave Territories
Open to slavery or free depending on vote
of the inhabitants by *Kansas-Nebraska Act*
of 1854

Free and Slave Areas
1860

Ralph Waldo Emerson called Brown "a new saint awaiting his martyr-
dom, and who, if he shall suffer, will make the gallows glorious like the
cross." Thoreau called him "an angel of light," and Wendell Phillips
declared that he carried "letters of marque from God." The politicians
were less lyrical. All the Republican leaders with hopes for the presidency
vied with each other in condemning the raid. They knew that John
Brown had brought war closer, and that the people of America, though
half-agreeing with the New England authors, did not choose to bleed in
the cause of the Negro. Even Seward, whose "irrepressible conflict" and
"higher law" had seemed to ask for violence, made a conciliatory speech
in the Senate and for once refrained from denouncing slavery. And in
February, 1860, Lincoln visited New York City and talked so conservatively at the Cooper Institute that he himself said the people of the West
were disappointed and he did not blame them. But an enthusiastic young
Republican from Wall Street wrote to Lincoln: "You and your western
friends, I think, underrate this speech. It has produced a greater effect
here than any other single speech. It is the real platform in the eastern
states, and must carry the conservative element in New York, New Jersey,
and Pennsylvania."[5]

The speech concentrated once more on the federal control of slavery
in the territories. There was no suggestion that the Republicans had been

so worldly as to consider a tariff for manufacturers, or the gift of free land to the settlers. And the control of slavery was discussed reassuringly, with an obvious lack of rashness or of radical bias. The audience must have felt that a man with such sound common sense would of course agree with themselves on all unmentioned matters. The capacity to remove anxieties and at the same time to flatter the conscience was one of Lincoln's leading assets. So far from being an angry and turbulent party, he said, friendly to disastrous follies such as John Brown's raid, the Republicans asked only that the people of America return to the attitude toward slavery which was expressed by the fathers of the Constitution in the eighteenth century:

> As those fathers marked it, so let it again be marked, as an evil not to to be extended, but to be tolerated and protected only because of and so far as its actual presence among us makes that toleration and protection a necessity. Let all the guarantees those fathers gave it, be, not grudgingly, but fully and fairly, maintained. For this Republicans contend, and with this, so far as I know or believe, they will be content.

Discussing the fears of the Southern people, he tried to be soothing and conciliatory.

> You say we [Republicans] have made the slavery question more prominent than it formerly was. We deny it. We admit that it is more prominent, but we deny that we made it so. It was not we, but you, who discarded the old policy of the fathers. We resisted, and still resist, your innovation; and thence comes the greater prominence of the question. Would you have that question reduced to its former proportions? Go back to that old policy. What has been will be again, under the same conditions. If you would have the peace of the old times, readopt the precepts and policy of the old times.

Finally, he made a strong plea for the Union—which to many of his hearers meant a plea for not interfering with the business relations between North and South.

> A few words now to Republicans [said Lincoln]. It is exceedingly desirable that all parts of this great Confederacy shall be at peace, and in harmony, one with another. Let us Republicans do our part to have it so. Even though much provoked, let us do nothing through passion and ill temper. Even though the southern people will not so much as listen to us, let us calmly consider their demands, and yield to them if, in our deliberate view of our duty, we possibly can. . . . Wrong as we think slavery is, we can yet afford to let it alone where it is, because that much is due to the necessity arising from its actual presence in the nation.

These calming words were believed by the audience because Lincoln had always opposed the abolitionists, defended the Fugitive Slave Law, and put the preservation of the Union ahead of any plans for dealing with slavery. He had made no inflammatory statements. His most disturbing speech, to the ears of the South, had been at the Republican State Convention of Illinois in 1858, when he quoted

> A house divided against itself cannot stand, [and went on to say:] Either the opponents of slavery will arrest the further spread of it, and place it where the public mind shall rest in the belief that it is in course of ultimate extinction; or its advocates will push it forward, till it shall become alike lawful in all the States, old as well as new—North as well as South.

Many Southerners interpreted this to mean that Lincoln was in favor of extinguishing slavery by force. All his deeds as well as all his words prove them wrong; yet the important fact is not that they were wrong but that they distrusted Lincoln. The wisest, most patient, most tolerant man in the North could no longer persuade them of his good faith. But he could persuade the conservatives in his own section, when Seward and Sumner and Chase and the other candidates could not, and by so doing he could save the party as well as forward his own cause. Once more his luck had held. In the midst of trouble he alone grew taller. Even Old John Brown had done Lincoln good.

7

When the Republican National Convention met at Chicago in May, 1860, the feud between Stephen A. Douglas and the Buchanan Administration had already led to a split in the Democratic Party. It seemed clear that there would be several candidates in the field, and the chief Democratic hope was that no one would get a majority in the electoral college. The House of Representatives would then choose the next President, and although the Republicans had a majority in the House they did not control a majority of the state delegations. The Constitution provides that when the election is thrown into the House "the votes shall be taken by states, the representatives from each state having one vote."[6] So the divided Democrats might still win, and there was an intense feeling at Chicago that nothing should be done which could alienate a single vote.

The platform was the first fruit of this feeling—perhaps the cleverest platform ever devised. "Here was that political maturity," writes Professor Craven, "which blends ideals and materialism without conscious effort."[7] It begins by asserting that the Republican Party is permanent.

The nation needs it, and the party will not dissolve like the evanescent Know-Nothings. The platform then quotes the "unalienable rights" from the Declaration of Independence, and pledges the party to maintain these principles, to defend the Union, to prevent the spread of slavery, to admit Kansas as a free state, and to treat the Dred Scott decision as "a dangerous political heresy . . . revolutionary in its tendency, and subversive of the peace and harmony of the country." Then the party turned to more practical matters: to luring the old "American Plan" Whigs, the westward expansionists, the rural settlers among the immigrants, the new manufacturers, while losing none of the free-soil enthusiasts and as few as possible of the abolitionists. No gentler words have ever been found for describing the high tariff so dear to Pennsylvania: "an adjustment of . . . imports," said the platform, and a ". . . policy of national exchanges, which secures to the workingmen liberal wages, to agriculture remunerative prices, to mechanics and manufacturers an adequate reward for their skill, labor, and enterprise, and to the nation commercial prosperity and independence." Who would guess that the happy dwellers in this Garden of Eden had ever heard of an iron manufacturer?

Finally, the platform asks for a homestead act, easy naturalization laws, river and harbor improvements at federal expense, and "immediate and efficient aid" by the federal government in the building of a railway to the Pacific—in other words, enormous land grants.

The South, by ruling itself out of Republican consideration, made possible this masterpiece of concessions and compliments between the Northeast, the Northwest, and the Middle West. Nobody was forgotten, and none of the plums conferred upon one group was likely to irritate another group unduly. Party managers from that day to this have dreamed in vain of another such platform. It had Hamilton's appeal to intelligent selfishness and good sense, combined with Jefferson's optimism and abstract moral excitement.

Lincoln was nominated for the presidency on the third ballot, for the reasons we have already seen. He was the only Republican who could win votes in the southern counties of Indiana and Illinois (where the settlers were mostly of Southern blood and still felt kindly toward their neighbors across the Ohio), thus ensuring victory in these two vital states. And he was the only Republican who might hope to win not only the old Jacksonian Democrats in the Northeast (who were disgusted at the "dough-face" Administration), but also a number of the old conservative Whigs, especially in rural areas. There was nothing about him to frighten a Pennsylvania manufacturer, or a New England factory hand, or an Indiana farmer whose grandfather came from the South. As for the abolitionists who disapproved of Lincoln's caution, they had to vote for him anyway, or stay at home. And the fact that he was not very well known did him as much good as harm, for the politicians knew that if he had made more fame and friends he must also have made more enemies. They knew that Lincoln was canny, and careful, and unlikely to put a foot wrong in the campaign; there is no sign that they knew he was wise, long-suffering, and illustrious in spirit.*

Neither Eastern conservatives [writes Professor Hesseltine], giving lip-service to homesteads and humanitarianism, nor Western radicals with their tongue-in-cheek endorsements of a protective tariff dominated the party. It was a situation in which each faction could claim a share of the victor's spoils and each could assume a mandate for its principles. Few of those who planned to claim the victory considered that Abraham Lincoln might have a mind of his own.[8]

8

When the Democratic Convention met at Charleston on April 23, the delegates knew that Stephen A. Douglas was their logical candidate and that if they nominated him they would win. They knew that if the Republicans were beaten again in 1860, the party might dissolve before it had time to build abiding loyalties. And in any case, with another Democratic Administration at Washington, no Southern state except fiery South Carolina would consider secession. So Douglas meant the salvation of the Union. Yet the stubborn, vindictive Buchanan Administration used all its strength against him—not for the sake of the President, who had said he did not want a second term, but in order to "punish" Douglas for opposing the Lecompton Constitution and for asserting that the Dred Scott decision did not make slavery safe in a territory if the inhabitants refused to support it with police power.

The fire-eaters and the "doughface" leaders did not choose to notice that in punishing Douglas they were punishing if not destroying the party and the nation. Buchanan and his advisers had at last been trapped by the extreme Southerners, who were glad to break the Democratic Party as a step toward breaking the Union, and who felt they had been duped by Douglas into accepting popular sovereignty and then duped again when Douglas insisted that the sovereign people had a right to make Kansas free.

Aside from the "doughfaces," Northern Democrats were as strong for rewarding Douglas as the Southerners were for punishing him. They still

---

* Writing to an Ohio delegate before the convention, Lincoln said: "My name is new in the field, and I suppose I am not the first choice of a very great many. . . . Our policy, then, is to give no offense to others—leave them in a mood to come to us if they shall be compelled to give up their first love."

thought in terms of an election, not of a revolution, and they felt it would be agreeable to win. They were a majority in the convention and they rejected the Southern demand for federal protection of slavery in every territory. Such a platform, they knew, meant handing the whole North to the Republicans. The spokesman for the South was William Lowndes Yancey of Alabama. He said all the trouble and the bitterness had come because Northern men refused to defend slavery. "If you had taken the position directly that slavery was right . . ." he cried, "you would have triumphed, and anti-slavery would now be dead in your midst." Thus Yancey justified Lincoln's remark in the Cooper Institute speech that every argument must in the end come back to the ethics of slavery: "Their thinking it right, and our thinking it wrong, is the precise fact upon which depends the whole controversy. Thinking it right, as they do, they are not to blame for desiring its full recognition, as being right; but thinking it wrong, as we do, can we yield to them? Can we cast our votes with their view, and against our own? In view of our moral, social, and political responsibilities can we do this?" At the Charleston Convention, Senator Pugh of Ohio gave Yancey the answer that Lincoln would have given. "Gentlemen of the South," he said, "you mistake us—you mistake us—we will not do it."

And the majority did not do it. They refused to commit the party to the protection of slavery in the territories, whereupon Yancey and the cotton-state delegates walked out. A few days later the convention adjourned with nothing done. "The great Democratic Party, one of the last truly national institutions in a dividing nation, had split. A sectional party for the South, comparable to the Republican Party at the North, was now possible."[9] "We are for principles," said a Mississippi delegate to a conciliatory Northerner; "damn the party." What he meant was, "damn the federal Union."

The convention adjourned to Baltimore, where on June 23, the Northern delegates made Douglas the official nominee of the Democratic Party with a platform promising that the party would stand by the Dred Scott decision or any future Supreme Court decision concerning the rights of property in the states and territories.* This was the typical noncommittal evasive plank upon which party promises must rest. The rejection of such compromise meant the rejection of federal politics in favor of logical, sectional, irreconcilable parties. A week later the seceding Southerners met at Richmond and nominated Buchanan's Vice-President, John C. Breckinridge of Kentucky, with Joseph Lane of Oregon for his running-mate. The platform affirmed the extreme Southern position put forward by Yancey.

---

* The convention did not nominate a vice-presidential candidate; but the Democratic National Committee later named Herschel V. Johnson of Georgia.

Meanwhile, on May 8, a last sad remnant of conservative Whigs and of Know-Nothings met at Baltimore and took the name of the Constitutional Union Party—the short-lived Georgian Party which had been founded by Stephens, Toombs, and Cobb in support of the great Compromise. The new Constitutional Unionists nominated John Bell of Tennessee for President and Edward Everett of Massachusetts for Vice-President. They stood on the vague platform: "The Constitution of the Country, the Union of the states, and the enforcement of the laws." These were the older men among the disciples of Clay and Webster: the enemies of nullification, the friends of compromise, the Whig planters who still found it impossible to join the Democrats.

Such were the fruits of eight years of weak, relaxed, irresponsible, leaderless politics, of "doughface" Administrations under Presidents who had been chosen because they were so unimportant that nobody disliked them, of rash and ill-advised and sudden raids against the public welfare by Senators and others who hoped to call attention to their strength: the Nebraska Bill, Bleeding Kansas, Sumner-Brooks, John Brown, and at last the rise of not one but three sectional parties. And the old order upheld by a few old and dying Whigs.

9

Stephen A. Douglas might be insensitive, but he was everlastingly brave. Against the custom of the day he campaigned actively, especially in the South, where he met every challenge boldly. He told the Southerners that if he were President he would put down secession by force, and he begged them to remember that the whole Northwest felt the same. In North Carolina he put the case bluntly: "Do you think that a citizen of Illinois will ever consent to pay duties at the custom house when he ships his corn down the Mississippi to supply the people there? Never on Earth! We shall say to the custom house gate keeper that we furnish the water that makes the great river, and that we will follow it throughout its whole course to the ocean, no matter who or what may stand before us."[10] His hearers may have remembered Henry Clay's somber warning, during the great debates of 1850, that the upper Mississippi Valley could never allow the lower valley to pass to foreign hands.

Yet Douglas received a light vote in the South. He was respected for his courage; but the real contest was between Breckinridge and Bell: between the fire-eaters and the conservatives who still believed in Union. These long-time foes did not stop to notice that while fighting each other (and distributing the Democratic vote among three men) they were helping Lincoln. "Not until the last few weeks of the campaign," writes

Professor Craven, "did it dawn upon them that, regardless of which group triumphed in the South, the Republican Party would triumph in the nation. Some even accused the radicals of fostering division in the interests of Lincoln's election and the opportunity to secure secession thereby."[11] Last-minute efforts to agree on one of the candidates—so that the South and the Northern conservatives might again defeat the Republicans—were a failure. The South walked stubbornly to her doom, lulled by boasts about the need of France and England for her cotton and the willingness of these Powers to bid for a Southern alliance.*

Lincoln took small part in the campaign. Even when rallies were held in his home town of Springfield, he usually did not attend. The Republican Party workers went back to the methods of the Harrison-Tyler campaign of 1840. They relied on bands and songs and torchlight parades by the young "Wide-Awakes," rather than discussions which might bring out the divisions within the party. For the party had as yet no true national organization, and no true national identity. Even more than is usual, the election depended on state campaigns.

> No political party had ever before been so largely a coalition of state parties [writes Professor Hesseltine]. The Republican victory in November could not be attributed to the national committee: it was weak, impoverished, and ineffective. Nor could it be credited to Abraham Lincoln: he was acceptable, but inarticulate—bound by tradition to hide his political skill and bide his days in almost monastic seclusion. . . . In the end the governors won their state campaigns, and their combined successes put Abraham Lincoln in the White House.[12]

Ironically, it seems that while the South ignored the coming Republican victory, Lincoln himself ignored the danger of secession. A politician from Ohio who visited Lincoln shortly after the election was disturbed by this seeming blindness.

> I soon discovered [he wrote] that this strange and strangely gifted man, while not at all cynical, was a skeptic. His view of human nature was low, but good-natured. I could not call it suspicious, but he believed only what he saw. This low estimate of humanity blinded him to the South. . . . Mr. Lincoln did not believe, could not be made to believe, that the South meant secession and war. When I told him, subsequently to this conversation, at a dinner table in Chicago . . . that the southern people were in dead earnest, meant war, and I doubted whether he would be inaugurated at Washington, he laughed

---

* Conservatives in the North made a last-minute effort to throw the election into the House of Representatives where the Republicans controlled a minority of states. In New York, New Jersey, Rhode Island, Connecticut, and Pennsylvania, the supporters of Douglas, Breckinridge, and Bell made fusion tickets of presidential electors, so that they could appeal to the merchants and the Cotton Whigs for money. They received a large sum; but it was not enough.

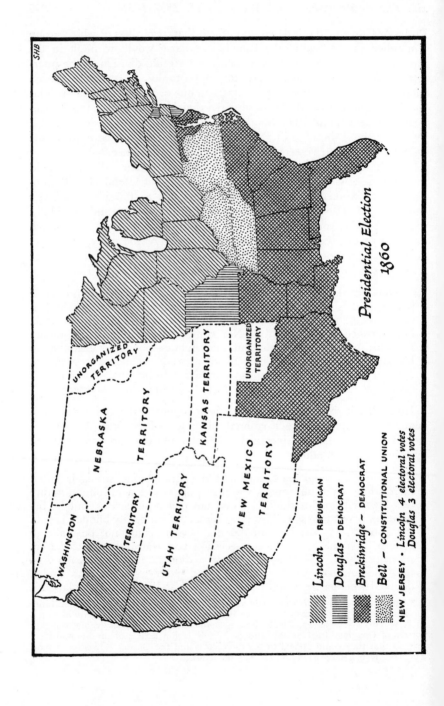

Presidential Election
1860

Lincoln ~ REPUBLICAN
Douglas ~ DEMOCRAT
Breckinridge ~ DEMOCRAT
Bell ~ CONSTITUTIONAL UNION

NEW JERSEY · Lincoln 4 electoral votes
Douglas 3 electoral votes

WASHINGTON TERRITORY

UNORGANIZED TERRITORY

NEBRASKA TERRITORY

UTAH TERRITORY

KANSAS TERRITORY

UNORGANIZED TERRITORY

NEW MEXICO TERRITORY

SHB

and said the fall of pork at Cincinnati had affected me. I became some-what irritated, and told him that in ninety days the land would be whitened with tents. He said in reply: "Well, we won't jump that ditch until we come to it," and then, after a pause, added, "I must run the machine as I find it."[13]

The map of the voting in 1860 is a portrait of a nation breaking in two. The whole tier of Northern states (including Oregon and California) voted for Lincoln; the whole tier of cotton states voted for Breckinridge; Douglas had the southern counties of the Middlewestern states and a few spots in the Far North and the Far South; Bell had the planters along the Mississippi, the tobacco-growers of Kentucky and Tennessee, the moun-taineers in western Virginia and North Carolina, and the state of Mary-land—all the Southerners who still preferred the Union. Lincoln had over 1,800,000 votes; Douglas almost 1,400,000; Breckinridge more than 800,000; and Bell a little less than 600,000. The three anti-Republican candidates combined received a million more votes than Lincoln, yet Lincoln would still have been elected if all those votes had gone to one man! Lincoln received 180 electoral votes; Douglas, 12; Breckinridge, 72; and Bell, 39. This is a sign of the electoral-college strength of the free states, where Lincoln won by moderate or narrow majorities, while his opponents received all the Southern votes. In ten Southern states not a single man voted for Lincoln.*

In his speech at the Cooper Institute early in 1860, Lincoln had said to the South:

> There is a judgment and a feeling against slavery in this nation, which cast at least a million and a half votes. You cannot destroy that judgment and feeling—that sentiment—by breaking up the political organization which rallies around it. You can scarcely scatter and dis-perse an army which has been formed into order in the face of your heaviest fire; but if you could, how much would you gain by forcing the sentiment which created it out of the peaceful channel of the ballot-box, into some other channel?

The answer must have seemed obvious to Lincoln, which may be why he could not believe in secession. But Lincoln, as his friend from Ohio said, "while not at all cynical, was a skeptic." He did not believe that enthusiasm and romance could overcome the mundane logic of numbers.

The youth and chivalry of the South in 1860 had been brought up on "Lara," "The Corsair," and "The Lay of the Last Minstrel." The spirit of those pleasing poems—the thought that bravery and love and adven-

---

* In South Carolina, one of the ten states, the electors were still appointed by the legislature. There was no popular vote.

ture can (or at any rate should) conquer—not only infused the leaders, but by some miracle of shared pride it extended to the led, to the great mass of yeoman farmers who were the strength of the South and of the Confederate armies. Lincoln could have told them, before they seceded, that life was not so gay and unaccountable, that war was a dreary, deadly balancing of accounts, and that the balance was against the South. It was against her physically, because she had kept her capital in slaves and cotton and so did not have the industrial plant or the railways for modern war. It was against her morally because she had abandoned the Jeffersonian view that slavery was an evil which must be brought to the earliest possible end, and had embraced the heresy that slavery was a good which must be everywhere protected. The moral weakness would discourage France and England from intervening to save the Confederacy and balk the power of the United States. The physical weakness would prevent the South's impetuous valor from triumphing over valor that was more calculating.

There was of course a chance that the North might defeat herself, if Lincoln failed to heal the deep divisions in his party, or if he behaved carefully and constitutionally when faced with a mortal threat. But if he could bring unity to his strange alliance of protectionists, abolitionists, homesteaders, railroad barons, and simple folk who knew that the Union was the guardian of democracy, and if he could seize power boldly and illegally in order to save a government which denied itself such power, then no amount of Southern suffering or bravery or military brains would suffice. Lincoln could save the Confederacy if he made a mistake; otherwise, the cause had been lost long before, when the decisions were taken which made the factories in the South so few, and slavery a growing rather than a waning system.*

* In 1860 the South turned out about eight per cent of the manufactured produce of the United States.

XX

"Preserve, Protect, and Defend"

THE MONTHS between the election in November and Lincoln's inauguration in March were a time of fear and anticlimax. Decisions had been made; yet the results were in abeyance while Buchanan lingered in the White House, fumbling and inconclusive. His temperament and his political opinions would not let him accept secession, or prevent it, or prepare to meet it after it had taken place. General Scott warned him in October that the election would be followed by an attempt to destroy the Union, and that he should strengthen the garrisons in Southern ports. Buchanan did nothing, and in his paradoxical message to Congress on December 1, he continued to do nothing, denying the right of secession and denying that the government could do anything about it. The Congress, he thought, should decide whether to change the laws so that the nation might save its life. But Congress preferred to leave the thorny trouble to the Executive. Since the last great federal compromise had been sacrificed by two soft Presidents, even Henry Clay might have had trouble in inventing a new one. "The Buchanan administration," writes Professor Swisher, "expired while engaged in futile speculation as to its own powers."[1]

It very nearly expired before its time, for members of the Cabinet began resigning within a few weeks of the election. Howell Cobb—for so long the faithful Unionist—went on December 2 because the President had denied the right of secession. The Secretary of State, Lewis Cass, resigned on December 12 because the President did not reinforce the forts in Charleston Harbor. Floyd of Virginia, the incompetent Secretary of War, resigned on December 29, ostensibly because his delicate spirit could no longer bear association with a dishonored régime, but really because he was about to be charged with fraud and treason—neither of which he probably planned, but both of which he permitted. Professor Nichols's description of the Secretary three days before his resignation suggests the murky atmosphere of the time:

> When Floyd presented himself at the White House . . . he had just been exposed as a careless, if not dishonest, administrator who was about to be indicted by the District grand jury for conspiracy to defraud and for malfeasance in office. He was to be accused of treason because of his

foolhardy gesture in trying to ship heavy guns into the South. The night before, Senator Wigfall and others had urged him to join a plot to kidnap Buchanan and make Breckenridge President; this he had refused to do. Also he had become suspicious of a large order for converted muskets which he had approved ostensibly for the Sardinian government; that order he would countermand.[2]

These were no days for the decrepit, like Cass, or the trivial, like Floyd and Buchanan. And Washington was no longer the place for Southern patriots like Cobb. A new cast was about to take that stage; the days of the "doughfaces" and their proud masters were done.

2

On December 20, 1860, a convention in South Carolina voted to secede. Within six weeks Mississippi, Florida, Alabama, Georgia, Louisiana, and Texas had followed. In all these states, with the possible exception of South Carolina, there was a strong Unionist minority—perhaps in some cases even a majority. This group urged that Lincoln's Administration be given a fair trial, asking what would be gained by breaking the Union until the North proved that it meant to attack and oppress the South. But there were many secessionists who had long felt the Union a burden—an economic threat as well as a moral reproach—and this time they did not mean to be balked. With stormy talk of "Black Republicans," of slave insurrections, and with many reminders of the insults abolitionists had thrown against the South, they stirred the people until Alexander Stephens admitted that "they are run mad." "They are wild with passion and frenzy," he added, "doing they know not what."*

The pity was that to the minds of many middle-of-the-road Southerners the fire-eaters now seemed justified. In 1860 the country was back again to the arguments of 1850, or of the Wilmot Proviso; but during the intervening years the great Compromise had been tried and had failed. The extremists who had said it must fail were therefore strengthened. In 1850 they had been silenced by the moderates; in 1860, at least in the cotton South, they were in control. Men like Cobb and Stephens and Toombs could no longer restrain them. These brave defenders of the Union were captured by the forces they had long fought, but which their local patriotism now bade them serve. On February 3, 1861, delegates from the seven seceded states met at Montgomery, Alabama. Five days later they formed the Confederate States of America, electing Jefferson Davis provisional President and Alexander Stephens Vice-President. Toombs, as we have

* Professor J. G. Randall believes a minority forced secession upon the South.

seen, entered the Cabinet, and Howell Cobb the army of the Confederacy.*

The arguments put forward by the seven state conventions to justify secession were arguments in defense of slavery and in denunciation of the North for acts inimical to the institution: "enticing" slaves, ignoring the Fugitive Slave Law, excluding slavery from the territories, plotting slave insurrections. South Carolina complained, candidly and simply, that the North had "denounced as sinful the institution of slavery . . . [and] united in the election of a man to the high office of President of the United States whose opinions and purposes are hostile to slavery." The long and bitter wrangle, in other words, had so frayed the nerves of the South Carolinians that they would no longer associate with men who thought slavery wrong. None of the conventions mentioned economic oppression as a cause for disunion. There was doubtless fear of such oppression, now that a Northern sectional party was about to take power; yet the South still had a tariff after her own heart, and she might long have continued to frustrate the hopes of Pennsylvania if she had not split the Union.

There was of course no question in the minds of Southern leaders about the "right" to secede. That "right," first proclaimed by John Taylor of Caroline County, later developed by the Federalists of New England, later still perfected in all its legal subtleties by John Caldwell Calhoun, had been accepted both as truth and as treason by each section of the country in turn, depending on whether its interests were temporarily served by affirming or by denying the sovereignty of the central government. History cannot compose the quarrel; but it can note that the binding test of sovereignty is power. If Buchanan had been President after 1861, the "right" to secede would doubtless have been established. Since Lincoln was President, and since enough people followed his lead in fighting for the Union, the "right" proved nonexistent. The question was too intricate for the lawyers; only soldiers could decide.

3

Meanwhile, federal property in the South was seized, with no finger lifted in defense. South Carolina took Fort Moultrie and Castle Pinckney in December. Georgia took Fort Pulaski at Savannah on January 3, and Alabama took Fort Morgan at Mobile on January 4. At Pensacola, in Florida, the Union held Fort Pickens; but the federal navy yard and Fort Barrancas were seized by Southern troops. Louisiana confiscated the mint

* Davis was inaugurated as provisional President on February 18. A regular election was held in accordance with the new Confederate Constitution in October, 1861. Davis was elected President for a term of six years. He was then inaugurated (or re-inaugurated) on February 22, 1862.

at New Orleans, and throughout the cotton states federal cutters, federal post offices and custom houses, were passing into rebel hands—thus creating the problem of Fort Sumter for Lincoln. By the time of the inauguration, Fort Sumter in Charleston Harbor was the most important post still held by the Union in the Deep South. Buchanan had agreed not to reinforce Fort Pickens at Pensacola so long as it was not attacked; but in a nervous moment of energy he had tried to reinforce Sumter. He had failed, because the Union ship, the *Star of the West,* had been fired on by the South Carolina batteries. So the nation, North and South, could not help but judge the intentions of the new Administration by what was done about Sumter.

Although Lincoln had said little during the campaign or after, anyone in touch with him must have known what he would recommend. But the decision to use or to abandon force was not truly his; it lay with the people of the North. No President could compel them to war with their fellow Americans, although a bolder, kinder man than Buchanan might have helped them face the tragic choice more rapidly. Leaderless, they groped for months through the mist, while Lincoln watched impotently, waiting to do what proved possible.

At first the Republican radicals (who cared nothing for economic or patriotic ties with the South) were confident the new Administration would be a Free-Soil, Barnburning, Old Jacksonian, secession-defying triumph. They formed a committee to urge abolitionists for the Cabinet. But powerful business interests, led by Pennsylvania and by Thurlow Weed of New York, thought the Republicans were merely the appeasing Whigs revived. On the eve of the election Andrew Gregg Curtin, the new Republican governor of Pennsylvania, spoke in Boston without mentioning slavery. For him the tariff was the issue, and he told his audience that to be good Republicans they must vote for men with sound Whig records.

Victory at the polls merely made sharper the conflict between the Republicans who would abolish slavery and the Republicans who would ignore it. Neither group gave heed to Lincoln's cautious and increasingly popular view that the task was to keep slavery from spreading and to save the Union; but both sent leaders to Springfield to tell the President-elect what he should think and do. Lincoln listened and said nothing.

In December the last-ditch compromisers tried to force the issue. Thurlow Weed called a meeting of the state governors to form a conciliatory policy and to impress it on the Congress and on Lincoln. And in the Senate Crittenden of Kentucky sought to revive the old assuaging magic of Henry Clay. He proposed several amendments to the Constitution; for example, a restored but weakened Missouri Compromise, whereby latitude 36° 30′ should divide freedom from slavery in all the territories, and whereby a territory on assuming statehood might decide for itself on

slavery; and a guarantee of slavery where it already existed for so long as
the people of each state might desire it. Lincoln roused himself to send
word to the governors and the Congress that he disapproved of extending
the Missouri line for the territories and that he would reject any form of
squatter sovereignty which might permit another slave state. "On that
point hold firm," he said, "as with a chain of steel."* For the rest, he
would commit himself to nothing except Jackson's old toast: "Our Federal
Union, it must be preserved."

The wisdom of Lincoln's caution, of his refusal to push the people
faster than they had yet prepared themselves to go, was shown by the
situation in New York City, which had heavy investments in the South
and in New England textile industries. New Yorkers were also annoyed
with the government at Albany for interfering in their local administration and for raising too much of the state's revenue at the expense of their
flourishing town. So in a message to the common council on January 7,
1861, the Democratic mayor of New York, Fernando Wood, calmly recommended that in case of Southern secession New York City should also
leave the Union, setting itself up as a free port and a taxless Paradise.

> With our aggrieved brethren of the slave states [he said] we have
> friendly relations and a common sympathy. We have not participated
> in the warfare upon their constitutional rights or their domestic institu-
> tions. . . . New York has a right to expect, and should endeavour to
> preserve, a continuance of uninterrupted intercourse with every sec-
> tion. . . . Why should not New York City, instead of supporting by her
> contributions two-thirds of the expenses of the United States, become
> also equally independent? As a free city, with but nominal duty on
> imports, her local Government could be supported without taxation
> upon her people. . . . When Disunion has become a fixed and certain
> fact, why may not New York disrupt the bands which bind her to a
> venal and corrupt master—to a people and a party that have plundered
> her revenues, attempted to ruin her commerce, taken away the power
> of self-government, and destroyed the Confederacy of which she was
> the proud Empire City?

Mayor Wood admitted that he did not see precisely how this was to be
done; but the fact that a vote-loving politician thought the message worth
delivering is a sign of the magnitude of Lincoln's task.

While waiting for the months to pass, helpless to intervene, Lincoln
began to build his Cabinet and thus to bind some factions of the restive
party to his own will, and to his support when a decision might at last
be made. He had early decided to offer the secretaryship of state to

---

* The words quoted were said on December 13, five days before the Crittenden
Resolutions were put forward; but they express Lincoln's view on every compromise

Seward, and he was half-bound by the promises of his managers at the nominating convention to make the conservative Caleb Smith of Indiana Secretary of the Interior, and the angry unscrupulous Senator Simon Cameron of Pennsylvania Secretary of War. He allowed the Vice-President-elect (Hannibal Hamlin of Maine) to choose a New Englander for Secretary of the Navy. Hamlin named Gideon Welles of Connecticut, famous for his enormous beard. Welles was a Democrat who broke with his party over slavery. He knew nothing of the sea, and has been described as "venerably insignificant." Yet he proved a good administrator and a vindictive diarist. The old-fashioned Whigs were awarded Edward Bates of Missouri as Attorney General, and the Jacksonian converts were given Montgomery Blair of Maryland, son of Francis Preston Blair of the "Kitchen Cabinet," as Postmaster General. The Free-Soilers won Salmon P. Chase of Ohio as Secretary of the Treasury.

The manysidedness and incongruity of the new party was mirrored in this group. The members did not like or trust each other, and most of them did not respect Lincoln. Each of them had bitter enemies among rival factions within his own state—which proved a help to Lincoln, for it enforced a semblance of loyalty, at least while the patronage was being distributed. These were the first federal plums ever awarded by a Republican President, and Lincoln strained to use them to build the nucleus of a national party. Boldly, he ordered that all applicants must be endorsed by their Congressmen—not by their governors or local leaders—thus helping the infant federal machine at the expense of the states.

The appointment of the tough unprincipled Cameron (which Lincoln regretted but could not evade) brought no peace to Pennsylvania. Cameron and the new governor Curtin had detested each other for years. Neither could control the state alone, yet either one might spoil the party's chances at the next election. But Cameron and Curtin were united on one point: greed for a high tariff. Their powerful state could be saved for the party of freedom by no other measure. So during the last days of Buchanan, when most of the Southern Democrats were gone from Congress, Cameron was encouraged to force the adoption of the Morrill Tariff by brusque and open blackmail. He made it plain that this was the price of loyalty in Pennsylvania. The Republicans in Congress passed the bill, and the inexplicable Buchanan, who had recently signed the lowest of tariffs, now meekly signed its antithesis.*

The anti-war governors, who had been vainly assembled by Thurlow Weed, were for the most part leaving office in January. By the middle of that month, when the newly elected group had been installed, there were

---

* The tariff—named after Representative Justin S. Morrill of Vermont—had been passed by the House in May, 1860. The Senate held it up until February, 1861. Buchanan signed it on March 2.

only three compromisers left among the Northern state executives. The rest of them were for coercion in one degree or another—for war if necessary, and in many cases for abolition. In default of national leadership the people began to rally round these positive, self-confident men. On February 11, when Lincoln set out on his long, roundabout trip to Washington, it was already probable that if he stood firm the citizens would back him in saving the Union. Yet he was still unwilling to declare a policy. "My friends . . ." he said to his neighbors from the rear platform of the train at Springfield, "to this place, and the kindness of these people, I owe everything. . . . I now leave, not knowing when or whether ever I may return, with a task before me greater than that which rested upon Washington. Without the assistance of that Divine Being who ever attended him, I cannot succeed. With that assistance, I cannot fail. . . ."

That was a charming good-bye; but it did not answer the anxious politicians who were waiting to hear what Lincoln intended. And on the trip—although he spoke at more than a dozen cities, and to the legislatures of Pennsylvania, New Jersey, New York, Ohio, and Indiana—he was no more informative. At his first stop, at Indianapolis, he told the people, "It is your business to rise up and preserve the Union and liberty for yourselves, and not for me." At every stop he said the same, in one form or another. He was seeking to learn from the people, not yet to guide them; but he seems to have been reassured by what he found.

Ten days before the inauguration he met at Washington with the so-called Peace Conference—delegates from twenty-one states who had gathered in a last hope to restore unity without resort to force. The Vermont delegate reports that William Dodge of New York told Lincoln, "It is for you, sir, to say whether the whole nation shall be plunged into bankruptcy; whether the grass shall grow in the streets of our commercial cities." The report continues:

A sad but stern expression swept over Mr. Lincoln's face. "I do not know that I understand your meaning, Mr. Dodge," he said, without raising his voice, "nor do I know what my acts or my opinions may be in the future, beyond this. If I shall ever come to the great office of President of the United States, I shall take an oath. I shall swear that I will . . . to the best of my ability, preserve, protect, and defend the Constitution of the United States. . . . It is not the Constitution as I would like to have it, but as it *is*, that is to be defended. The Constitution will not be preserved and defended unless it is enforced and obeyed in every part of every one of the United States. It must be so respected, obeyed, enforced, and defended, let the grass grow where it may."

4

The Washington in which Lincoln was inaugurated on March 4 was slightly improved over the distressing sea of mud to which poor John Adams had been forced to move in 1800; but it was still a wretched place. There were 61,000 inhabitants, 15,000 of whom were Negroes. An Ohio Congressman wrote that it was

> as unattractive, straggling, sodden a town, wandering up and down the left bank of the yellow Potomac, as the fancy can sketch. Pennsylvania Avenue . . . stretched drearily over the mile between the unfinished Capitol and the unfinished Treasury building on Fifteenth Street . . . where it turned north for a square and took its melancholy way to Georgetown. . . . It was the only paved street in the town. . . . As may be supposed the Capital of the Republic had more malodors than the poet Coleridge ascribed to ancient Cologne. There was then the open canal, a branch of the Chesapeake and Ohio, from Rock Creek to Anacosta, breeding malaria, tadpoles, and mosquitoes. . . .
>   Politically, the city—the fixed population—was intensely Southern, as much so as Richmond or Baltimore. Very few men of culture, and none below that grade, were Republicans at the advent of "Lincoln and his Northern myrmidons," as they were called in 1860–1861.[3]

In his Inaugural Address Lincoln said that legally and historically "the union is perpetual," since it is older than the Constitution, older than the states, older even than the Declaration of Independence. "It was formed," he claimed, "by the Articles of Association in 1774." This is dubious history, and in any case unimportant, since the problem of the permanence of the Union would be settled by the strength and the will of the North, not by research. Yet Lincoln's exegesis is interesting, for it is a tribute to the deep need of English-speaking peoples to feel that the law is on their side. The fathers of the Republic claimed they were defending the true British Constitution in their revolt; and when Parliament denied this, they appealed to natural law against a seemingly unnatural king. Similarly, both Jefferson Davis and Lincoln, taught respectively by Calhoun and John Marshall, were convinced that in making war upon one another they were backed by the Constitution of the United States and the obvious facts of history.*

The new President then disclaimed any intention of interfering with slavery in the states where it existed, and argued against the "right" of

---

* Davis, in truth, seems to have had the best of the barren argument in his message to the Confederate Congress of April 29, 1861.

secession. Toward the end of the address he rose to the serene simplicity which he alone could attain.

> Physically speaking, we cannot separate. We cannot remove our respective sections from each other, nor build an impassable wall between them. A husband and wife may be divorced, and go out of the presence and beyond the reach of each other; but the different parts of our country cannot do this. They cannot but remain face to face, and intercourse, either amicable or hostile, must continue between them. Is it possible, then, to make that intercourse more advantageous or more satisfactory after separation than before? Can aliens make treaties easier than friends can make laws? . . .
>
> This country, with its institutions, belongs to the people who inhabit it. Whenever they shall grow weary of the existing government, they can exercise their constitutional right of amending it, or their revolutionary right to dismember or overthrow it. . . . Why should there not be a patient confidence in the ultimate justice of the people? Is there any better or equal hope in the world?

Jefferson Davis would have answered that he and his people were merely seeking to exercise "their revolutionary right to dismember" the United States. Lincoln must have denied that right to a sectional majority, although he affirmed it for a national majority.

The Inaugural Address then asks for patience from the South, on the characteristically American ground that the government did not have sufficient power to do much harm:

> By the frame of government under which we live, this same people have wisely given their public servants but little power for mischief; and have, with equal wisdom, provided for the return of that little to their own hands at very short intervals. While the people retain their virtue and vigilance, no administration, by any extreme of wickedness or folly, can very seriously injure the government in the short space of four years.

The South would have answered that Lincoln's constituents had lost "their virtue and vigilance," and that nothing could now restrain the government from doing what it chose. Ironically, although the Southerners were wrong about the people of the North, they were right about the government, as Lincoln was about to prove. All the shoots of presidential power, large or small, which had been planted and nurtured by his predecessors, Lincoln was to bring to full growth. When he died the presidency was supreme above the states. "A new nation," writes Professor Hesseltine, "had been erected on the ruins of the old federal union."[4] So far did the change go that the people became uneasy, and the party system was called upon after the war to undo some of the centralization, and to rebuild some of the obstructive strength of sectional minorities—until a new crisis caused another President to revive the immense powers uncovered by Lincoln.*

In conclusion, the Inaugural Address puts the burden of choice upon the Southerners. "In your hands, my dissatisfied fellow countrymen, and not in mine, is the momentous issue of civil war. The government will not assail you. You can have no conflict without being yourselves the aggressors. You have no oath registered in heaven to destroy the government, while I shall have the most solemn one to 'preserve, protect, and defend' it."

In the course of preserving, protecting, and defending the Union, Lincoln decided that he must defend Fort Sumter. He has been accused of taking the offensive by this act; but it seems that he was trying to preserve the *status quo* as nearly as possible.[5] The purpose of the relief expedition under Captain Fox was to supply food to the garrison. Reinforcements were not to be landed unless the ships or the fort were attacked. There was no attempt at surprise. Notice of the expedition and a promise of its pacific purpose were sent to the governor of South Carolina. Yet, as Professor Randall says, "that purpose was not understood in the southern states and under these circumstances the decision to relieve Sumter was one of the most far-reaching and fateful acts in American history."**

At four-thirty on the morning of April 12, 1861, by authority of Brigadier General Beauregard of the Confederate Army, the batteries in Charleston Harbor opened fire on Fort Sumter. On April 14 Major Anderson of the Union Army surrendered the fort. The next day Lincoln issued a proclamation calling out 75,000 militia to suppress the rebellion, the North responding with an enthusiasm which showed he could have had many times the number. Stephen A. Douglas made a strong statement in support of the President, and shortly afterward offered to tour Illinois, where the southern counties were still disaffected, and sound the call of the Union. Lincoln accepted gratefully, and Douglas set out on his last

---

* The question of how much power a government needs and how that power can be reconciled with freedom—and the allied question, also posed in the Inaugural Address, of when a people may exercise their "revolutionary right"—bothered Lincoln steadily. In his message to the special session of Congress on July 4, 1861, he said that the war "presents the question whether discontented individuals, too few in number to control the administration according to organic laws in any case, can always, upon the pretences made in this case, or any other pretences . . . break up their government. . . . It forces us to ask: Is there in all republics this inherent and fatal weakness? Must a government, of necessity, be too strong for the liberties of its own people, or too weak to maintain its own existence?"

** It was made by Lincoln himself, against the advice of his Secretary of State who wished to hold Fort Pickens but to surrender Sumter. But the Secretary of State, as we shall see, was at this time in a whirl of crazy plans, including the interesting notion of bringing the South back to the Union by declaring war on France, Spain, and possibly England.

trip home. He spoke several times en route and on April 25 at Springfield, Illinois, he made a speech which has been called his greatest. A
few days later he broke down. He was said to have rheumatism, and developed a high fever, and on June 3 he died. He was forty-eight years old.
He left the Democratic Party without a national leader, and with only
fourteen members in the Senate (including Andrew Johnson of eastern
Tennessee who refused to secede with his state) and forty-four in the
House.

Two days after Lincoln's call for troops, Virginia seceded, followed
quickly by North Carolina, Arkansas, and Tennessee. Delaware and Maryland, Kentucky and Missouri, were split into bitter factions at home; but
none of these border states officially left the Union. If Kentucky had
gone, the war might have been lost before it started, for the frontier
would then have been the broad and turbulent Ohio all the way from
Cincinnati to the Mississippi River. Even as it was, with Virginia and
Tennessee seceding, the Confederacy was a formidable country to invade.

On May 15, 1861, a Virginian who had tried to help avoid the war
wrote to a friend: "My maxim has always been to choose among the evils
around me and do the best I can. I think the annals of the world furnish no instance of so groundless a war—but as our nation will have it
—if no peace can be made—let us fight like men for our own firesides."[6]
So groundless a war? Perhaps wiser guidance during the ten previous
years might have made it groundless indeed; perhaps the Compromise
of 1850 might have been enforced; but by the time Lincoln became
President the leaders of the Deep South were set to leave the Union.
He had no choice but to let them go in peace, to attack them as traitors,
or to attempt a policy of evasion and delay which might allow the conservatives to regain control and reverse the decision to secede. The
latter seems to have been Lincoln's purpose; but if he abandoned the
last federal forts he would defeat the purpose and encourage rebellion.
And if he held the forts he would give the Southern extremists a chance
to provoke war. He decided to hold the forts, and his intentions were mis-
construed, and the war began.

5

As all the world knows, the President to whom this calamity came had
been born and raised in the utmost poverty. We have seen that his Kentucky birthplace was a few miles from that of Jefferson Davis, whose
more prosperous family went south to Mississippi while the Lincolns, who
were destitute, moved across the Ohio River into Indiana. Lincoln's father
(whose people had come to Massachusetts from Norfolk in 1637) was a

typical shiftless frontier failure. He left Kentucky in 1816, when the boy was seven. And he left Indiana for Illinois in the year Lincoln came of age. He was not the man to urge a child toward self-improvement. "I suppose Abe is still fooling hisself with eddication," he said years later when Abe had left home to make his own way. "I tried to stop it, but he had got that fool idea in his head, and it can't be got out."

Perhaps the "fool idea" came from his mother, Nancy Hanks, the illegitimate daughter of a Virginian. Little is known about Nancy (not even the name of her father) except that she was illiterate, that she had two children (Abraham and Sarah) and that she died in 1818 when the boy was nine years old. The father soon married again, and his second wife seems to have been in every way his better. Lincoln was fond of his stepmother, who backed him in his strange addiction to books. Although he had less than twelve months of schooling, his little, typical frontier library was a good basis for straight thinking and a clear prose style: The Bible, *Pilgrim's Progress, Robinson Crusoe, Aesop's Fables,* and Parson Weems's *Life of Washington.*

The hard work of farming—and of clearing fresh land, fencing it, building new cabins—turned Lincoln into a physical giant: over six feet four in height and with a strength that became legendary even in the rough West. But he never lost his desire to learn. He would walk miles to borrow a book—and what was far more unusual, having borrowed it, and read it, he would actually think about it. He was one of the very few people who could go on thinking after he had stopped reading or talking. He never learned to turn his back, except briefly, on the great defeating questions of life and death and destiny. This may be why he was unhappy, and why he was great. He was oppressed by the mystery but never frightened; so in his long days alone—as a boy on the frontier or on a river-boat, as a man driving his buggy across the empty prairies from one county courthouse to another—he did not close or distract his mind or his spirit. He continued his rapt, sometimes morbid, search for understanding—and one day (although he never knew it) he became the wisest man in America. A fellow lawyer described Lincoln in court when he was lost in thinking: "He seemed to be pursuing in his mind some specific painful subject, regularly and systematically through various sinuosities; and his sad face would assume, at times, deeper phases of grief. No relief came till he was roused by the adjournment of court, when he emerged from his cage of gloom, like one awakened from sleep."

During such hours of abstraction, which came upon him from the time he was a child, Lincoln was not pursuing a mystic trance: he was trying to think. This is perhaps the most difficult of undertakings, and the rarest. Lincoln's addiction to it may explain why all his life he grew in mercy and in understanding. At forty he was a leading Western lawyer and an unsuccessful Congressman; at fifty he was not only a national figure, but in his own section he was an important moral force; at fifty-six, when he was murdered, he was one of the masters of his age. He was mourned in Europe and Asia by men who knew nothing about him, or about America, except that someone good had gone from the earth. The accidents of politics may make a man world-famous; but only richness of spirit can make him world-respected. In Lincoln the richness came from thought, from his painful prolonged brooding, "wrapped in abstraction and gloom." He had no clear religious faith. He believed in God, but seemingly in an unconsoling God. He said it was his destiny to live in twilight, feeling and reasoning his way through life. He said he was like the man in St. Mark: "Lord, I believe; help Thou mine unbelief."

If Lincoln's "feeling and reasoning" made him wise, pious, and subtle, it also made him irreverent, bawdy, impudent, ribald, and cruelly funny. He was the best storyteller in the West and the best mimic. He found it seductively easy to make an opponent look absurd; but he seldom used this power in court against a witness. He saved it to torment his political foes. His broad and racy laughter was probably his salvation. "Lincoln's humour," wrote Francis Grierson, "was the balance-pole of his genius that enabled him to cross the most giddy heights without losing his head."*

Flatboatman on the long trip to New Orleans; clerk in a country store, and later joint owner of a store that failed and left him burdened; captain of a local band in the Black Hawk Indian War; unsuccessful Whig candidate for the state legislature, and then successful candidate for four terms on end—Lincoln tried all these jobs. In 1836, in the middle of his term in the state legislature, he began the practice of law. Here was work suited to his tastes and talents. He rose to the front rank in the Illinois bar—yet his true love was politics. Although surrounded by fierce Jacksonian Democrats, Lincoln remained a Whig—perhaps because his political passions were first fired by Henry Clay, or perhaps because of his cautious, conservative bent. On the frontier, a man could honor the leveling doctrines of the Declaration of Independence and still be a conservative, an enemy of all sudden or extreme change. This was becoming difficult, if not impossible, among the Eastern banks and factories. The Republican Party might have been riven to its foundations if Lincoln had lived to fight for his Western brand of conservatism after the war. In 1859, for example, when he was unable to speak at a festival in Boston, he sent a letter in which he put his egalitarian faith briefly: "The principles of Jefferson are the definitions and axioms of a free society.

---

* *The Valley of Shadows,* 1948 ed., p. 196. Grierson's long-ignored classic, consisting of "recollections of scenes and episodes of my early life in Illinois and Missouri," was published in 1909. It gives far the best picture of the Western men to whom Lincoln first became a hero.

And yet they are denied and evaded with no small show of success. One dashingly calls them 'glittering generalities'; another bluntly calls them 'self-evident lies'; and still others insidiously argue that they apply only to 'superior races.' . . . We must repulse them, or they will subjugate us." This was carrying the fight home to his friends, for the man who had called the Declaration of Independence "glittering generalities" was Rufus Choate, the famous Whig lawyer of Boston.

In 1842 Lincoln married Mary Todd of Kentucky. Much dubious legend surrounds the marriage. It is true that Mrs. Lincoln's temperament was difficult; and so was her husband's; but there is small ground for believing that life in the Lincoln home was as unhappy or as odd as it has been pictured. There were four sons, only one of whom grew to maturity.

Between 1847 and 1849 Lincoln served a term in Congress, where he was the only Whig from Illinois. A loyal party worker, he opposed the Mexican War. On January 12, 1848, he made an anti-war speech which could well have been revived by any Southerner to justify secession. "Any people anywhere," he stated, "being inclined and having the power, have the *right* to rise up and shake off the existing government, and form a new one that suits them better. This is a most valuable, a most sacred right. . . . Nor is this right confined to cases in which the whole people of an existing government may choose to exercise it. Any portion of such people that can, may revolutionize." This is strong doctrine, though natural for a child of 1776. It seems that the young Lincoln, like Jefferson and Jackson and most Americans, approved resistance to the state when the state was "wrong"—that is, when it was opposed to his views. Or perhaps he was simply toeing the Whig Party line. In any case, his opposition to the Mexican War was so unpopular at home that he was accused of pleading the enemy's cause and denied re-election. He returned to his successful law practice at Springfield, and for five years was inactive in politics, though not in thought.

He was forever turning over and puzzling the entangled problems of slavery and Union. There was nothing impractical or softly emotional about Lincoln's distaste for slavery. He was not so foolish as to think that because a course was good it was therefore possible. He was never moved to ignore or deny the dangers in the path of emancipation—so he was not an abolitionist, and in no hurry to free any of the existing slaves. For this he was abused and called heartless; but in fact he was one of the few Northerners to think honestly about the plight of the Negro. He knew that a huge effort and a huge sum of money were needed if the Negro was to be freed without imposing upon him another miserable lot. The black man had been the victim of greed, and Lincoln did not choose to cure that wrong by making him the victim of sentimentality. Hence his statement in 1854: "When southern people tell us they are no more responsible for the origin of slavery than we are, I acknowledge the fact. When it is said that the institution exists, and that it is very difficult to get rid of it in any satisfactory way, I can understand and appreciate the saying. I surely will not blame them for not doing what I should not know how to do myself."

While in Congress he introduced an unsuccessful bill for gradual emancipation in the District of Columbia—the only slave territory which the federal government controlled. Children born of slave mothers after 1850 were to be free, although during their minority they were to be apprenticed to their mothers' owners. And owners who might wish to emancipate their slaves were to receive "full value" from the United States Treasury. The act was to be submitted to the free white citizens of the District in a referendum. As Professor Randall says, this was typical of Lincoln's "conservatism, his patience in letting a process work itself out over the years, his lack of antagonism toward the South, his regard for the rights of slaveholders, his attention to legal details, and his valuing of popular and democratic processes."[7] But for all his caution and his patience, there was one step Lincoln could never permit: the infection of new lands with the curse which was so hard to cure. On this he was confident and unrelenting. The more clearly he saw the problems of emancipation, the more bluntly he must oppose the planting of such problems on the territories. "We must give them a clean bed," he said, "with no snakes in it."

On one other point Lincoln was positive: whatever he might have said or written about man's "right" to revolution, he knew that no such right existed unless it could be enforced. The only sanction of a revolution, as of a legitimate government, is power. And Lincoln had slowly, painfully, made up his mind that the North ought to use power, if necessary, to save the Union. In this he was a true son of the West—like Henry Clay, like Stephen A. Douglas, like Vinton of Ohio, the Whig Congressman who proclaimed, "Massachusetts and South Carolina might, for all I know, find a dividing line that would be mutually satisfactory to them, but, sir, they can find no such line to which the western country can assent." This was not only because the West refused to give the mouth of its great river into foreign hands; but also because the whole vast region was the Valley of Democracy, almost the only place on earth where the new creed was lived as well as talked. If the Union fell, democracy might be discredited, and for the West that was a deplorable thought.

When the Missouri Compromise was repealed, therefore, and the resulting uproar led to new demands for secession, every political belief on which Lincoln had built his life was challenged. When he returned to politics after his five years in the wilderness he became the perfect spokesman of his region. When he joined the new party in 1856 he gave it strength and sanity. In his hands it would never be weakened by radicalism, or stray far from the simple and popular issue of preventing slavery in the territories. We have seen how he pinned Douglas to this issue, forcing him to discuss it in lieu of all else during the famous debates of 1858.

Grierson gives us a first-hand picture of Lincoln in the last of these debates:

> And now Abraham Lincoln, the man who in 1830 undertook to split for Mrs. Nancy Miller four hundred rails for every yard of brown jean dyed with walnut bark that would be required to make him a pair of trousers, the flatboatman, local stump-speaker and country lawyer, rose from his seat, stretched his long bony limbs upward as if to get them into working order, and stood like some solitary pine on a lonely summit, very tall, very dark, very gaunt, and very rugged, his swarthy features stamped with a sad serenity. . . . Every movement of his long, muscular frame denoted inflexible earnestness, and a something issued forth, elemental and mystical, that told what the man had been, what he was, and what he would do in the future. . . . Douglas had been theatrical and scholarly, but this tall, homely man was creating by his very looks what the brilliant lawyer and experienced Senator had failed to make people see and feel.[8]

XXI

Lincoln and the "War Powers"

"THE ROAR of the batteries beside Charleston Harbor . . . [writes Professor Ralph Henry Gabriel] announced the defeat of American political democracy. If political democracy be defined as government by consent of the governed, the shells over Sumter made clear that a large minority among the American people had withdrawn their consent from the existing federal institutions. If the definition be that democracy is government by discussion among free men, the arguments of statesmen were silenced by those of the cannon. If democracy is merely government by the majority, the American majority in 1861 was seeking to enforce, at the point of the bayonet, its will upon a recalcitrant and determined minority. By any definition, political democracy had, for the time being, lapsed."[1]

In 1860, the federal government which was to preside over this temporary lapse was by modern standards a very simple affair. Its methods and its problems were similar to those of Washington's day, although the nation which it served had grown enormously. The population had increased from about 4,000,000 to about 31,000,000,* the area from 820,000 square miles to 3,000,000, and the states from 13 to 33. As a result, the Senate had 66 members in 1860 and the House 237; yet this inflated Congress still dealt almost exclusively with the problems which had harassed it from the beginning: the tariff, slavery, the disposition of public lands, and internal improvements at federal expense. Although on these perennial subjects the negative policies long favored by the South were about to be abandoned, the government was still innocent of plans for social or economic legislation, and its tax program suggested the Arcadian youth of the world rather than harsh modernity.

Jackson and Polk had long since shown the latent powers of the Executive and Lincoln was about to transform the office wholly; but before 1861 no President had in the modern sense imposed strong leadership upon Congress, and the Executive departments which served the President would scarcely be adequate to staff a modern bank. The Department of State, for example, consisted of the Secretary of State with a salary of $8000, an assistant secretary with a salary of $3000, a chief clerk with

---

* Nine million in what was to become the Confederate South, 22,000,000 in the North.

a salary of $2200, and two minor aids with salaries of $2000. The War Department had no Assistant Secretary; but it had one aid with a salary of $2200 and eight other employees who received $1800 apiece. The Post Office Department was more regal. It had three Assistant Postmasters General who received $3000 each, and three other officers whose salaries averaged $2500. Today, as Professor Swisher points out, "the annual expenditure on the New York Police Department alone approaches the amount of the entire annual expenditure on the government of the United States in 1860."[2]

The most arresting sign of simplicity in the federal government of Civil War days was the absence of the so-called "fourth branch." Government still consisted of an Executive, a Legislature, and a Judiciary, as originally planned. There was as yet no federal regulation of private enterprise, so there were no independent regulatory commissions, no ambiguous agencies with part-administrative, part-legislative, and part-judicial powers. The American people had not yet lost their fight to maintain a government with strictly limited powers. They were about to dismember their country because to a large minority even the small powers which existed had come to seem oppressive; but in their worst nightmares they could not yet imagine the national state which the Industrial Revolution and the Civil War were to bring to birth. Lincoln, who began by pointing out that the public servants had "but little power for mischief," was soon compelled to extend that power—for good or evil—until the old America could scarcely recognize the new.

> For a third time in a hundred years [writes Professor Dunning] the conviction of a fact beat down the obstacles of established forms. The revolution of 1776 secured liberty; that of 1789 secured federal union; and that of 1861–67 secured national unity. In each case traditional principles were felt to be incompatible with existing facts, and the old gave way to the new. The question presented to the administration by the commencement of hostilities was: Has this government the power to preserve its authority over all its territory? The answer of the old school of constitutional lawyers was: "Yes, so far as it is conferred by the constitution and the laws"; but the answer we derive from the actual conduct of the war is "Yes" without qualification.[3]

Here lay the difference between Lincoln and Buchanan. Following correctly the precedents of seventy years, Buchanan decided that a state had no right to secede and that the federal government had no right to keep it from seceding. The relative strength of federal and state sovereignty had been left vague in the Constitution—wisely, for it could only be defined by force. In 1832, during the nullification crisis, Calhoun raised the question in all its perilous logic; but Henry Clay sidestepped it so skillfully that no one could say which side had won or what had been agreed. The nation returned to its healthy habit of evasion.

> The only constitutional course [writes Dunning] in case of a conflict of the "sovereignties" was to deny that such a thing was possible, eulogize the constitution as the greatest extant production of the human intellect, point out the dreadful consequences that would follow the recognition of supremacy in either claimant, and end by compromising the difficulty in such a way as to furnish precedents for both sides in the future. It would be erroneous to maintain that this method of action was as unprofitable as it was illogical. On the contrary, it was probably the only course that could have brought the United States intact through to the year eighteen hundred and sixty. But more than one of the nation's true statesmen foresaw that it was only a question of time when "dodging the issue" would cease to give satisfaction as a principle of constitutional construction.[4]

When that time came, Buchanan clung to the old ambiguities even though they threatened the life of the Union. But in Lincoln's mind "the conviction of a fact beat down the obstacles of established forms." When the people of the North had made clear that they would follow him, he announced that the federal government was sovereign and that the states were not. "What is 'sovereignty' in the political sense of the term?" he asked in his message to the special session of Congress on July 4, 1861. "Would it be far wrong to define it as 'a political community without a political superior'?" Since the Union was sovereign in this sense, the states could not be sovereign. By seceding they had forced a final clarification. When they lost the war they lost the ancient argument. Thenceforth they would have certain powers conferred upon them by the Constitution; but the federal government would be supreme.

The American political democracy whose temporary defeat was announced by the shells over Fort Sumter would one day be restored—but never in the form which it had known for the previous seventy years. A precious equivocation, a freedom-giving obscurity, was gone.

2

Lincoln's insistence that the North was fighting to save the Union, and thus to save the world's faith in democracy, did not please the radicals in his own party.* They were fighting to destroy slavery—some of them

---

* During the war and the Reconstruction, the so-called "radicals" were those who wished to uproot the historic South and plant in its place something nearer to their own desires. They believed in a policy of "thorough." Their motives were various and their political abilities noteworthy.

because they saw it as the greatest of evils, and others because they saw it as the keystone of the Southern economy. Good men who only wished to help the Negro worked closely with men who only wished to break the South financially, so as to break her politically and ensure a long rule for the Republicans. Both the selfless and the selfish radicals found Lincoln a steady and a wily foe—which was fortunate for their own cause, because if they had imposed their way at any time before the summer of 1863 the war would have been lost. Few Northern states would have voted for an abolitionist war, and the whole Border would have joined the Confederacy if such a war had been proclaimed. Yet there were many who sought to proclaim it.

In July, 1861, John C. Frémont was appointed to command in Missouri. Frémont's great days were done, but his ambitions were as pushing as ever, and his jealousy of Lincoln (who had replaced him at the head of the Republican Party) was cruel. When Frémont's shady friends were charged with corruption, and the powerful Blair family pressed for his removal, he tried to win favor with the radicals by declaring that all slaves of Southern sympathizers in Missouri were free. Lincoln, with his eye on the border states, asked Frémont to recall his order. Frémont refused, so Lincoln recalled the order and the general at the same time. The radicals now had an abolitionist hero, a victim of Lincoln's conservatism. Thenceforth, the more foolish of them hoped to replace Lincoln with the "Pathfinder" at the next election.

In December, 1861, the radicals in Congress set up a joint Committee on the Conduct of the War, ostensibly to inquire into the management of hostilities, but really to harry generals who were not sufficiently pro-Negro, to give leadership to the drive for abolition, and to prepare men's minds for a ruthless post-war policy toward the South. Although the radicals were still a small minority, in a few years they were to inherit the fruits of Lincoln's caution. They could not have won the war; but they proved competent to stain the peace.

Had radicals like John Andrew* [writes Professor Hesseltine] taken the pains to analyze the political situation in 1861, they would have discovered that, outside New England, only the Iowa Republicans had proved strong enough to win without Democratic support. Such an analysis might have indicated that Lincoln's cautious policy, his conciliation of border-state unionists, and his support of War Democrats met the approval of the Northern voters. But cautious analysis was not the forte of the radicals; their strength lay in their determination to crush slavery and subjugate the South. The party, the army, and the national government were but tools for their purpose, and Lincoln's moderate program only an obstacle before their goal.[5]

* The governor of Massachusetts.

Yet the situation in Kentucky alone should have been enough to make them pause.

Lincoln had truly said that "to lose Kentucky is nearly . . . to lose the whole game. Kentucky gone, we cannot hold Missouri, nor, as I think, Maryland. These all against us, and the job on our hands is too large for us. We would as well consent to separation at once, including the surrender of this capital." Heedless of these facts, the radicals would have driven Kentucky into the Confederacy. The governor's sympathies were with the South, the legislature's with the North. The people were sharply divided, except on two points: they did not wish to see their slaves confiscated, and they did not wish their farms and villages to become the battleground for the nation. So long as the war was for the Union, and not for abolition or the subjugation of the South, and so long as Lincoln promised to send no troops through Kentucky, that state would remain "neutral"; that is, she would not leave the Union, and she would compel her Confederate sympathizers to do their fighting elsewhere. This would suffice to ensure a Northern victory; but this the radicals would have prevented.

In May, 1862, in spite of Lincoln's treatment of Frémont the previous year, General David Hunter, commanding the Department of the South, issued an order freeing all the slaves in South Carolina, Georgia, and Florida. Lincoln again declared that the general had exceeded his authority and that the order was void; and the abolitionists again attacked the President for moral cowardice. In the following month the New England governors met at Providence, Rhode Island, to devise means for forcing the President's hand. They wanted a change of generals, a change in the Cabinet, and a change in Lincoln's policy toward slavery. The war had been going badly and discontent was inevitable. Lincoln would have to yield somewhere. He had already gladly rid himself of the undesirable Cameron, sending him as Minister to Russia. Edwin McMasters Stanton of Ohio became Secretary of War—a lifelong Democrat who was approved by the radicals. Stanton had served as Attorney General during Buchanan's last months, and was one of the ablest lawyers in the country. He had a rough harsh manner and a parade of efficiency. Unhappily, he was as bad an administrator as Cameron, and far more self-satisfied; but at least he was honest, so one source of scandal was eliminated.*

The Providence meeting was followed in September by a meeting of the Union governors at Altoona, Pennsylvania. Under pressure from the radical New Englanders there might have come a demand for far-

---

* Even as temperate a critic as Hamilton Fish, who agreed with Lincoln's war aims and his mild policy of Reconstruction, felt the Administration was lax in its handling of the huge war appropriations. He saw waste and thievery, speculation and special privilege, corroding the nation's character. "Some people are making lots of money," he wrote disgustedly, "and they are some *other* people's friends."

reaching changes in war aims. There might even have come a demand for putting Frémont in charge of the Northern armies—a ready and easy device for losing the war.[6] But Lincoln outmaneuvered the governors. The day before the Altoona meeting, the preliminary Emancipation Proclamation was announced in the press. This conceded very little, yet it deprived the radicals of their most useful complaint.

Lincoln had done all in his power to avoid emancipation by federal fiat. He had labored, as his latest biographer[7] says, with "pathetic earnestness" to have the slaves set free by state action, with federal compensation to their owners. But when the war dragged on miserably and unsuccessfully, foreign opinion alone required that something be done to prove that Northern victory meant the end of the disgrace of human bondage. As fatal as the loss of Kentucky might have been the loss of English working-class support, for at least until 1863 the rulers of England were playing with the thought of announcing that Jefferson Davis had built a nation. Such recognition would have broken the Northern blockade, and would either have lost or dismally prolonged the war. In July, 1862, therefore, Lincoln decided that after the next victory in the field he would declare freedom for the slaves of all who persisted in rebellion. He could not do more, for he had no power over private property in the loyal slave states.* And he could scarcely do less, for his proclamation had no effect in the states where it was alleged to apply. Yet it seized men's minds, and to this day the world thinks of Lincoln, not as the savior of the United States, but as the Great Emancipator.

On September 17, 1862, the battle of Antietam (which nobody won) was followed by General Lee's withdrawal from Maryland. This seemed the best Lincoln could expect for the time being, by way of a victory; so while the dissatisfied governors were assembling in Pennsylvania the President bewildered them by announcing that "persons held as slaves" within areas "in rebellion against the United States" would be free on and after January 1, 1863. He repeated that Union was the sole war aim, and that he still hoped and wished for compensated emancipation. He dodged the constitutional problem by treating his Proclamation as a war measure, a penalty for rebellion which anyone could avoid by ceasing to rebel during the hundred days between September and January. The document was wholly in keeping with his famous letter to Horace Greeley of August, 1862, in which Lincoln wrote:

> My paramount object in this struggle is to save the Union, and is not either to save or destroy slavery. If I could save the Union without freeing any slave, I would do it; and if I could save it by freeing all the

* Delaware, Maryland, Kentucky, Missouri—and West Virginia after June, 1863, when the mountain counties of the Old Dominion formed themselves into a new and loyal slaveholding state.

slaves, I would do it; and if I could save it by freeing some and leaving others alone, I would also do that. What I do about slavery, and the coloured race, I do because I believe it helps to save the Union; and what I forbear, I forbear because I do not believe it would help to save the Union. I shall do less whenever I shall believe what I am doing hurts the cause, and I shall do more whenever I shall believe doing more will help the cause.

If, as seems clear, Lincoln believed that to help the cause he must keep the impetuous governors quiet and keep the workingmen of England friendly, his preliminary Proclamation (which was followed by the final deed on January 1) succeeded. The governors, instead of blasting his Administration and his generals, sent him a humble message of thanks and of "most loyal and cordial support." And the workingmen of Manchester, assembled at the Free-Trade Hall, sent him the noble Address in which they welcomed the hardships they endured because of the blockade on Southern cotton, and only implored Lincoln,

> for your own honor and welfare, not to faint in your providential mission. While your enthusiasm is aflame, and the tide of events runs high, let the work be finished effectually. . . . Our interests . . . are identified with yours. We are truly one people, though locally separate. And if you have any ill-wishers here, be assured they are chiefly those who oppose liberty at home, and that they will be powerless to stir up quarrels between us, from the very day in which your country becomes, undeniably and without exception, the home of the free.

Lincoln in his answer said he knew the South had counted on a demand from Manchester that the blockade be broken in order that the textile mills should reopen.

> I know and deeply deplore [he wrote] the sufferings which the working-men at Manchester, and in all Europe, are called to endure in this crisis . . . Under the circumstances I cannot but regard your decisive utterances upon the question as an instance of sublime Christian heroism which has not been surpassed in any age or in any country.

The Proclamation, though timely and useful, roused bitter feeling at home. Northern Democrats who had supported the war felt betrayed. They would fight for the Union, they said angrily, but not for the destruction of other men's property. The legislature of Lincoln's own state resolved that the Proclamation was

> a gigantic usurpation, at once converting the war, professedly commenced by the administration for the vindication of the authority of the Constitution, into a crusade for the sudden, unconditional and violent liberation of 3,000,000 Negro slaves; a result which would not only be a total subversion of the federal Union but a revolution in the social or-

ganization of the southern states, the immediate and remote, the present and far-reaching consequences of which to both races cannot be contemplated without the most dismal foreboding of horror and dismay.

3

The wide acceptance of this conservative view, and thus the folly of the radicals in urging a war for abolition, was shown in the mid-term elections of 1862. The Emancipation Proclamation (in spite of its mildness), war weariness and the continued Northern defeats, difficulties in raising troops and the knowledge that the Administration would soon adopt the hated draft—all this made for Republican weakness. Ohio and Indiana and Pennsylvania held Congressional elections in October. The Democrats won heavily in the first two states, and in the last they elected half the new Congressmen. In November, therefore, troops were sent home from the field to vote Republican in the critical states; but still the Democrats won Illinois and Wisconsin. They might have won control of Congress, they might even have compelled a negotiated peace, had not the border states, soothed by Lincoln and patrolled by troops, and diligently combed of anti-war voters under Lincoln's suspension of the Habeas Corpus Act, returned enough Republicans to ensure a small majority. "The lesson was clear enough," writes Professor Hesseltine. "The governors had lost the power to control their states; they could neither deliver men to the armies nor voters at the polls. Only the President could preserve the party—and he could save it only through the methods that had been tested in Missouri, Kentucky, Maryland and Delaware."[8] Since those methods combined the maximum of concession and of emphasis on the Union with the maximum of repression against those who could not be wooed or wheedled, and since the Republicans barely succeeded even so, it is plain why Lincoln grew impatient when the radicals insisted upon a different and an impossible war.

The elections of 1864 were an even clearer proof of the wisdom of the middle-of-the-road policy, and of the fact that no one but Lincoln could hold together the confused, war-weary North. Before the end of 1863 the long tide of military defeat had turned, with the result that the weakness and quarrels within the Administration, which had been based upon failure, were replaced by larger weakness and bitterer quarrels based upon the expectation of success. The radicals became far more intractable when they felt victory in the air. So in December of '63, as a preliminary to what he knew would be a stern struggle for control when the conventions and the campaign drew near, Lincoln announced his post-war program for the Reconstruction and readmission of the rebel states. The program fitted the temper of the war which Lincoln had fought and defended. But it did not fit the war of Charles Sumner, who was prepared to postpone the rebuilding of the Union until the Negro was everywhere acknowledged as the social and legal equal of the white man. And it did not fit the war of Thaddeus Stevens, the lame, vindictive invalid from Pennsylvania, who was ready to poison the future rather than permit the Democratic Party to rise again to power.

Stevens was one of the most forceful men ever to sit in Congress. James G. Blaine called him "the natural leader, who assumed his place by common consent."[9] Yet as he grew older he grew steadily more bitter, and by the eighteen-sixties he could only harm whatever he touched. His wish to help the Negro brought fresh woe to that betrayed race.

Stevens was born in Vermont, in 1792, of very poor parents. He was educated at Dartmouth College and then moved to Pennsylvania where he became a lawyer and a partner in an iron business. He was first a Federalist, then an Anti-Mason, then a Whig—being drawn to protection and the National Bank by his business interests. Always he fought with bitterness and wrath for the unprivileged, and in his youth his tongue was not yet so noxious as to undo his good intentions. In 1834 and 1835, for instance, he helped to win a free-school system for Pennsylvania. In 1848 he went to Congress, where his true passion for the oppressed led him into the anti-slavery fight. He was so skillfully offensive that every time he spoke he brought war nearer. Later, he helped found the Republican Party in Pennsylvania. He hoped for Cameron's post in Lincoln's Cabinet, but had to be content with the chairmanship of the Ways and Means Committee in the House, where he was useful in pushing the wartime revenue bills. This was the sole field in which he helped the Administration, for his views on the war were the reverse of Lincoln's. He wanted to arm the slaves, expropriate the whites, reduce the South to "hopeless feebleness," desolate the region, exterminate the rebels, erase the state lines, and re-colonize the entire district.[10]

Stevens had no compassion, no understanding of man's divided heart. He could only hate, and persecute, and use his wide learning as a quarry for unrivaled abuse. He hated the sinner more than the sin, the slaveowner more than slavery, and his hate extended to all Southerners and thence to all Democrats. Inevitably, he stirred a resistance more implacable than his own dark soul. "Yes," wrote a Georgian to Stevens in 1866, "I *am* disloyal to any damned Government ruled by such men as you, and 'glory that I still live to hate you.' "[11] The Negro was, and is, the chief sufferer from the curse that Thaddeus Stevens laid upon the South.

The first question which the President had to face in his plan for Reconstruction was whether the states which had seceded were still states under the original compact, or whether (as Sumner was to contend) they had committed suicide and were to be considered territories, subject to the rule of Congress. Lincoln's answer was clear. In his Inaugural Address he had said that the Union could not be broken by a pretended act of secession. In a proclamation of August, 1861, he had said that the people of the Confederacy were in rebellion, not the states of the Confederation. In all his deeds and speeches, Lincoln held to this view. The rebellion* was blamed upon groups of conspirators, not upon states—with the result that Southerners who would rebuild the Union could be treated, not as members of a hostile nation, but as so many steadfast Abdiels, loyal in spite of the wiles of Lucifer:

> Among the faithless, faithful only he;
> Among innumerable false, unmoved,
> Unshaken, unseduced, unterrified.

This was gratifying for Lincoln, who liked his fellow men; but for Sumner, who merely wished to improve them, it would not do at all. Sumner knew that the Abdiels of the South did not mean to make the freedmen members of their clubs. So he did not admit a distinction between those Southerners who would be loyal to the Union and those who hated it. "He would shed tears," writes Professor Dunning, "at the bare thought of refusing to freedmen rights of which they had no comprehension, but would filibuster to the end of the session to prevent the restoration to the southern whites of rights which were essential to their whole concept of life."[12] Yet Sumner was something of a humanitarian and something of a gentleman. Thaddeus Stevens, who was neither, had still less thought of admitting that the South contained even a single "flaming Seraph, fearless though alone."

On December 8, 1863, when Lincoln issued his proclamation, he assumed that certain state governments had been subverted by persons in rebellion and that some of these persons now wished to restore loyal governments "within their respective states." So he announced that with the exception of important civil and military officers of the Confederacy anyone would be granted an amnesty who took an oath of allegiance to the United States. And when ten per cent of the people of any state had taken the oath, they might hold elections and establish a state government. The radicals, of course, deplored this act, for such a prompt amnesty meant the restoration of confiscated property (other than slaves), and it meant that there could be no vengeance. If the states had committed suicide, as Sumner believed, or if they were conquered provinces, as Stevens contended, the Congress could do as it pleased both with Southern property and Southern people. But if the states were still alive, with their local

---

* The words "rebel" and "rebellion" are used throughout, not invidiously, but because the South lost the war. The difference between a rebel and a father of his people is a matter of success.

powers of government intact, Congress would have to keep its hands off the Southerners who returned to an honest loyalty, and off their goods, and would even have to allow them the dangerous right of voting for the Democratic Party if they so chose.

The extreme radicals were not yet in charge of Congress; but they were able to pass a bill which made the conditions of pardon far more stringent, and which declared that Congress, not the Executive, must decide the time and the manner of Reconstruction. This was the Wade-Davis Bill, named after the coarse, noisy Senator Benjamin Franklin Wade of Ohio and the polished but hate-ridden Representative Henry Winter Davis of Maryland. Davis was the author of the bill. Like Thaddeus Stevens, he was a disappointed candidate for the Cabinet. He also hated Lincoln for seizing so much power and for brushing aside the Constitution on the plea of necessity—as in the suspension of habeas corpus and the imprisoning of thousands without trial.

Congress adjourned within ten days of passing the Wade-Davis Bill, so under the Constitution the President could kill the bill merely by withholding his signature.[13] This he did. And when he issued another proclamation renewing his promise of recognition to seceding states if loyal citizens would quickly reform their governments, the helpless radicals raged.* Even before the "pocket veto" some of them had been looking for a candidate to replace Lincoln in the campaign. Their choice had been the Secretary of the Treasury, Salmon P. Chase of Ohio; but Lincoln had eliminated this rival with little trouble. At the Baltimore Convention in June, where the party had been careful to conceal the name "Republican" and to refer to itself only as the Union Party, the delegates had renominated Lincoln without discussion and had obeyed his wish to drop Vice-President Hamlin and to substitute Andrew Johnson of Tennessee—thus making the party seem less sectional, and paying tribute to Southern friends of the Union. A few weeks later Chase had been removed from the Cabinet and Senator William P. Fessenden of Maine took his place.**

Foreseeing the defeat of Chase, another group of radicals had combined with Western war Democrats and nominated General Frémont. Since the election looked close Lincoln decided to get rid of Frémont. He made a bargain of some sort with the radicals—perhaps promising to remove the ultra-conservative Montgomery Blair from the Cabinet in return for Frémont's retirement. This was the end of the "Pathfinder," who on September 22 withdrew ungracefully into a private life which was thence-

---

* Characteristically, Lincoln also declared that the Wade-Davis plan was a "proper" one, and that he would welcome back any states which wished to return to the Union by that plan. He must have been trying, as usual, to soften antagonisms; but in this case his enemies would not be softened.

** In October, when Roger Taney died, Lincoln made Chase Chief Justice of the United States.

forth only redeemed by the affection and support of the ever-faithful, ever-competent, and ever-romantic Jessie.*

A third effort to rid themselves of Lincoln was made by the radicals in August, 1864. Although the election was hard upon them, and defeat more than possible, Wade and Davis were so angry when their bill was allowed to die without even the dignity of a veto message that they issued a manifesto attacking the President's "executive usurpation," which they said was "a studied outrage on the legislative authority." With the support of Horace Greeley, whose political judgment was the worst available, they suggested to the Republican politicians that a new convention be held to reconsider Lincoln's candidacy. This final revolt against the President's conservative leadership broke against the hard unwelcome truth that the very men who led the revolt might lose their jobs unless Lincoln led the ticket. So with ill grace, but with sufficient energy to save their party standing, the radicals (including Wade and Davis) at last accepted Lincoln and closed ranks for victory.

Victory seemed far from certain in the late summer of 1864. In spite of his hold over the army (where the men in the ranks knew him for a natural democrat), in spite of Sherman's capture of Atlanta on September 1 (and the seeming certainty of Northern victory), in spite of steady hard work by all the receivers of patronage and all the beneficiaries of the Republican tariff, the Republican Homestead Act, and the new Republican National Bank, Lincoln still felt in danger. And indeed without the soldier vote he might have lost.[14] Certainly, if the party had been so foolish as to repudiate Lincoln, it would have been ruined. In 1860, as Professor Hesseltine points out, the governors and the state organizations elected Lincoln; but in 1864 Lincoln elected them.

The Democrats had met at Chicago in August and nominated General George B. McClellan for the presidency. McClellan was certainly the most learned, and was in many ways the most expert, of the Union commanders with whom Lincoln struggled and suffered until he found Grant. Robert E. Lee thought McClellan the best of the Northern generals. Yet he seemed temperamentally averse to action. The question which shadowed his reputation at the time, and which has not been answered yet, was put to him by Lincoln in October, 1863: "Are you not overcautious when you assume that you cannot do what the enemy is constantly doing?" After many heartbreaking delays, demotions, and reinstatements, Lincoln retired him for good in November, 1863. The troops liked McClellan, and

---

* The radical Senator Zachariah Chandler of Michigan, in his letters to his wife, claimed to have arranged the Blair-Frémont bargain. Burton J. Hendrick (*Lincoln's War Cabinet,* pp. 457–59) is inclined to dispute the claim, and to explain Blair's resignation on the ground that it had been requested by the Union National Convention. In any case, Frémont did give up his candidacy the day before Blair gave up his Cabinet post.

he gave a high tone and competence to his army; yet Lincoln may be excused for wondering whether, by McClellan's methods, the war could ever end.

The Democratic Party which nominated McClellan in 1864 was held together by nothing but hope for office. It had lost most of its trained political brains when the Southern states seceded, and the rest of them when Stephen A. Douglas died. When Congress met in special session in July, 1861, the Democrats did not even hold a caucus and name a candidate for Speaker. They joined with the Republicans to form a new party of the Union, and there they might have remained throughout the war except that Lincoln did not have enough important jobs to go round. Before long, therefore, some of the Democratic leaders reminded themselves that it is the duty of an Opposition to oppose. Yet Lincoln held many of the "War Democrats" to the end. Some of them stayed with the Republican Party in the post-war period, after it emerged from its Union phase. Others drifted back to the Democrats during the fight over Reconstruction. And a fair number left Lincoln while the war was in progress, and joined the "Peace Democrats" in opposing the unconstitutional acts of the President. Thus the party of Andrew Jackson found itself attacking an Old Whig for his use of dictatorial powers!

The peace Democrats—known as "Copperheads," and sometimes as "Butternuts"—did not favor secession; they merely opposed war. They hated the abolitionists, whom they blamed for all the woe. They believed that the South could never be conquered, which was a possibility. And they believed that the Union could be restored by negotiation, which was absurd. A partial explanation for this faith may be found in the economic interests of the Copperheads. Fernando Wood of New York, for example, was mayor of a city whose merchants were owed a hundred and sixty-nine million dollars by Southern customers. It would not be reasonable to expect him to join with Thaddeus Stevens in demanding the ruin of the South. Similarly, the most famous of the Copperheads, Clement L. Vallandigham of Ohio, represented a section which would be equally hurt by secession or by armed opposition to secession. In Vallandigham's words, they wanted "the Constitution as it is and the Union as it was"—and they wanted it so badly that they persuaded themselves they could have it, if only Lincoln would stop fighting.

We have seen many times that the southern counties of Ohio, Indiana and Illinois tended to vote in sympathy with the South. The early settlers had been of Southern stock, with Southern prejudices about slavery; but more important, the district was tied to the South by trade.

> Wheat, flour, beef, pork, lard, whisky, and manufactured products [writes Professor Binkley], particularly from Cincinnati, the Wabash and

Illinois valleys, had passed down the Mississippi River and were, in no small degree, paid for by the counter traffic in molasses, sugar, and cotton. The loss of their bacon market alone in the South because of the war was estimated at $6,000,000. Only a few days before Lincoln's inauguration the *Cincinnati Enquirer* was insisting that the prosperity of the entire lower West depended on the Southern trade and the continued culture of cotton in the South through slave labour.[15]

These were Vallandigham's people, to whom he was a true and fearless friend. No wonder he had a large following. And since, in addition to being fearless, he was wholly without judgment, and without restraint in his use of invective, no wonder he landed in jail, exile, and conspiracy.

When the Democrats nominated McClellan they did not choose to attack the Republican (or Union) tariff, although by the time the war ended the average rates were forty-seven per cent—more than double the average for 1857. And they did not choose to attack the Republican (or Union) banking system set up by the Acts of 1863 and 1864, although the party of Andrew Jackson might have found something to say about the concentration of money in the Eastern cities, especially in New York. And they did not choose to attack the Homestead Act,* or even the Acts of 1862 and 1864 which donated more than thirty million acres of public lands to the Western railroads. In all this they were wise. The war was the issue, not yet the domestic economy. The Democrats must stand or fall by what they said about the war. It is instructive to study what they did say, and astonishing to remember that until the last month of the campaign they looked very strong.

The platform attacked the Administration for the suspension of habeas corpus and for all the other violations of civil liberties, for the use of troops to police and influence border-state elections, and for the vast increase of federal powers (especially of Executive powers) which Lincoln had brought to pass in the name of the emergency. These were true grievances against the war. The platform then stated, in all its pathetic absurdity, the Vallandigham peace policy:

Resolved, That this convention does explicitly declare . . . that after four years of failure to restore the Union by the experiment of war, during which, under the pretense of a military necessity of war-

---

* Signed by Lincoln on May 20, 1862. The hope of westward-moving pioneers throughout two centuries was thus finally attained. The Act gave to the head of a family (or to anyone who was of age and a citizen, or about to become a citizen) the right to obtain a hundred and sixty acres of land free of charge, by living on it for five years and meeting reasonable conditions of cultivation. This was a size of farm suitable to the regions of good rainfall, whereas most of the lands which were still free after 1862 lay west of the ninety-eighth meridian. The frontier line was leaving the timber for the open country, leaving the humid lands of agriculture for the arid lands of grazing and the stock farm.

power higher than the Constitution, the Constitution itself has been disregarded in every part . . . justice, humanity, liberty, and the public welfare demand that immediate efforts be made for the cessation of hostilities, with a view of an ultimate convention of the states, or other peaceable means, to the end that, at the earliest practicable moment, peace may be restored on the basis of the Federal Union of the states.

This was the triumph of hope over truth. The South had seceded; the North had fought during bitter bloody years to restore the Union; the Democrats then proclaimed that if the North stopped fighting the Union would restore itself. Such was not the view of Jefferson Davis, who on August 29 sent word to Lincoln: "I shall at any time be pleased to receive proposals for peace on the basis of our Independence. It will be useless to approach me with any other." And it was not the view of the Democratic candidate, George McClellan. He asked for votes on his record as a general—which meant that if he were elected he would seek victory in the field, not in the realm of dreams.

Yet the politicians were merely following their normal course. They needed the votes of the people who thought the war was a failure, so the platform called it a failure. They needed the votes of the people who thought the war was a sacred cause, so the candidate was a leading Union general. And above all they needed the votes of the people who were tired and lazy and who wanted the fruits of victory—a "federal Union of the states"—with no further strain; so they announced that the Union could be restored simply by stopping the fighting and calling a convention. One might have thought this was carrying cynicism too far. Yet the Democrats received 1,802,000 votes. Lincoln received 2,213,000 votes. In the electoral college Lincoln had 212 votes and McClellan 21. The figures sound overwhelming; yet, as late as September the Republicans feared that if the army were not sent home to vote where needed, and if fraud were not practiced where all else failed, McClellan might win.

In retrospect, we can see that the frauds and intimidations practiced by the Union Party in 1864 were unnecessary. Lincoln would have won anyway, even if no "steps" had been taken. Yet it is interesting that Lincoln did not choose to run the risk. He allowed the small frauds, as he had allowed the steady unconstitutional pressure on the border states throughout the war, not because he felt superior to the people, but because he felt he knew their needs and must safeguard their future. This is a perilous decision for the head of a free state. Lincoln made it in silence and on his own responsibility, as he made all the basic decisions of the war: to reinforce Sumter; to suspend habeas corpus and pay no heed to the protests of the Chief Justice; to ask for troops without authority; to start the fighting before he called Congress in 1861, so that he could present that body with a war which was already under way and which must be won; to build for the first time in American history a national army serving the national state, instead of depending on local forces which had long been thought the safeguard of republican freedom.

President Madison very nearly lost the War of 1812 rather than override the prejudice against a draft and a national army. He would have lost if the British had been more alert—and the Union would then have perished, if the Hartford Convention had its way. But when Lincoln decided to fight he decided to win. As Alexander Stephens, his admiring enemy, said: "The Union with him, in sentiment, rose to the sublimity of religious mysticism." Yet the Union might have perished because of the eccentric workings of the electoral college. This was more than Lincoln would permit.

New York—one of the six crucial states—allowed its soldiers to vote in the field. Each party sent three commissioners to supervise the voting; but the Democratic commissioners were put in jail in Washington, and McClellan votes were switched when necessary. Lincoln won New York by 368,000 votes to 362,000. In Connecticut, where Lincoln won by 2400 votes, and in Maryland where he won by 7000, there seems little doubt that fraud and the army helped to carry the day. In Ohio—whose soldiers also voted in the field and might have voted for Ohio's General McClellan, the methods used to insure acceptable results remind one of the twentieth century.[16]

Assuming that they were necessary for victory, were these thefts wrong? Assuming that Lincoln had lost all the states where frauds were permitted, he would then have lost the electoral college, and thus the election; but he would still have had a majority of the votes. His own followers plus the War Democrats made a huge majority for victory; but the war would still have been lost. The Democrats were pledged to a peace conference, and once the war stopped no one could start it again. Hundreds of thousands of young men had died, in the armies which Lincoln had assembled, for the cause which Lincoln had defined. They had almost won their war. Should Lincoln now give it away for an eighteenth-century plan of choosing presidents—a plan which had been abandoned in spirit before that century was out? How could he do the least harm—by cheating, or by allowing accidental circumstances to cheat? All these questions—like that of the morality of seizing "unconstitutional" powers—are implicit in the very idea of civil war.

We have no record of what Lincoln thought, only of what he did. He built a temporary dictatorship, brushing the Constitution aside when he thought necessary, and custom and legality as well. He changed the balance of powers within the government. Thenceforth, on a plea of emergency, a popular President could rule more authoritatively than Andrew Jackson had dared to dream. And the world was presently to move into a phase of almost permanent emergency. Before those days came, Lincoln had given his country not only a renewed Union but a federal government which was admittedly supreme over the states, and a presidency which had been made (and could again be made) supreme over the Congress. We do not know whether he approved the latter change, or whether, like doctoring the soldiers' votes from New York, he merely did it to win.

4

In April, 1865, the Confederate Government was at last driven from Richmond. Within a week General Lee had surrendered to General Grant at Appomattox, and on April 26 General Johnston surrendered the last important Southern army to General Sherman.* The war was over. It had accomplished its purpose; but like all wars it had raised more questions than it settled. The Union was saved; but it was not the federal Union of old. It was a national state wherein the central government alone had sovereignty. Yet the citizens of America were by no means reconciled to such a change, and were soon found devising methods for creating unofficially the system of concurrent majorities which Calhoun had wished to write into the Constitution. And slavery was abolished; but what of the freedmen? And what of the broken South? What of the balance of power at Washington, where the agrarian statesmen had long held aggressive capitalism at bay? Since the agrarian leaders were dead or banished, was the simplicity and idealism of the young republic to be swamped in millionaires? And above all, what of the strife between the men who wanted punishment and plunder, and the men who followed Lincoln in seeking justice? Was America to go forward, as Lincoln asked in the second Inaugural Address, "with malice toward none, with charity for all . . . to bind up the nation's wounds"? Or was she to be subjected for a time to an alliance of moral prigs, vindictive politicians, and greedy businessmen?

The problem was exacerbated by John Wilkes Booth, who killed Lincoln on the evening of April 14, 1865, at Ford's Theater in Washington. Booth was an actor who had played Brutus once too often. Born and raised in Maryland, he saw the war neatly and simply as a strife between the wicked North and the chivalrous South. He and some friends had planned to kidnap Lincoln and deliver him to Jefferson Davis at Richmond; but their

---

* Jefferson Davis, hoping to escape to the Southwest and carry on the war by sheer will power, was captured on May 10. The last Confederate force surrendered on May 26. Davis was sent to prison at Fortress Monroe, and released after two years on the grounds that the federal lawyers had failed to find a charge on which they thought it safe to try him. He lived for another twenty-two years—farming, writing *The Rise and Fall of the Confederate Government*, and refusing to ask for the federal pardon which would have allowed his state to send him back to Washington as Senator.

first attempt fell through and the war ended before they could prepare a second. So they decided to murder the President, the Vice-President, and the Secretary of State all on the same evening. Booth did his work tragically well, but his assistants bungled theirs.

The radicals of course claimed that the mad crime was a plot by the South, promoted by Jefferson Davis. They staged a "trial" that will forever disgrace them, wherein the defense was bullied and the prosecution suppressed Booth's diary because it proved that the charges against Davis and the South were monstrous nonsense. They did their best to stir the North to the most barren and hurtful of passions: revenge. They did their best to make Lincoln's life vain and his death dishonored.

5

At his last Cabinet meeting, on the day he died, Lincoln showed that he knew the dangers which came with long-desired peace, and that he hoped to surmount some of them. According to the Secretary of the Navy, who was present, Lincoln said that "he thought it providential that this great rebellion was crushed just as Congress had adjourned, and there were none of the disturbing elements of that body to hinder and embarrass us. If we were wise and discreet, we should reanimate the States and get their governments in successful operation, with order prevailing and the Union reestablished, before Congress came together in December."* These were strange words from the defender of American democracy. "So long as the people's representatives are absent," he seemed to be saying, "there is reasonable hope of doing what is right. If we work quickly and present Congress with a peace that cannot be poisoned—just as we presented it, in 1861, with a war that could not be stopped—all may yet be well."

Had Lincoln been so long accustomed to a dictator's power that he feared returning to the slow process of persuasion? Or was it merely the "disturbing elements of that body" which he had in mind when he spoke of Congress—the malignant, the mean of spirit and black of heart? He had fought and mastered those elements when they would have prevented the victory. Was he afraid that he could no longer control them now that they sought only to destroy the peace? We do not know; but at the same Cabinet meeting he said he hoped there would be no persecution, no bloody work after the war was over. Such hopes died with Lincoln, and

---

* Gideon Welles, "Lincoln and Johnson," in *The Galaxy*, April, 1872, p. 526. In his *Diary* for April 14, 1865, Welles also noted that Lincoln "was glad Congress was not in session." (Vol. II, p. 281.) And Nicolay and Hay describe the last Cabinet meeting in language similar to that of Welles in his *Galaxy* article. (Vol. X, p. 283.) There seems no doubt that Welles gave an accurate description of Lincoln's remarks.

so did the hopes for an honorable solution to the racial problem, whereby the Negro could quickly become a first-class citizen. Lincoln was gone but Thaddeus Stevens lived.

It was an enigmatic spirit which was taken from America in the hour of her great need. Lincoln never sought to explain or excuse himself, only to make lucid the cause for which he lived. Grierson describes a pioneer woman of Illinois, a contemporary of Lincoln's, in these words:

> Moulded and subdued by the lonely days, the monotonous weeks, the haunting hush of the silent nights, and the same thoughts and images returning again and again, she appeared as one who had conquered the world of silence. . . . Hers was a freedom which was not attained in a single battle—the conflict was begun by her ancestors when they landed at Plymouth Rock. In the tribulations that followed the successive generations were stripped of the superfluities of life. One by one vanities and illusions fell from the fighters like shattered muskets and tattered garments. Each generation, stripped of the tinsel, became acquainted with the folly of plaints and the futility of protests. Little by little the pioneers began to understand, and in the last generation of all there resulted a knowledge too deep for discussion and a wisdom too great for idle misgivings.[17]

Lincoln belonged to this "last generation of all"; he too "had conquered the world of silence." He knew that he must stand alone, decide alone, suffer and be blamed alone. He was gentle, unyielding, devious. Free from vanities and illusions, he had time to think. He saw so many levels deep into the motives and meanings of life that only his broad humor kept him from cynicism or despair. He knew far too much for comfort. He was a melancholy skeptic who seems to have understood that the world cannot be saved on its own terms and that to resist one wrong in the realm of politics, by the use of force, is but to substitute another. "Each looked for an easier triumph," he said, referring to the North and South in his second Inaugural Address, "and a result less fundamental and astounding. . . . The prayers of both could not be answered. That of neither has been answered fully. The Almighty has His own purposes." Nevertheless, Lincoln admitted that political parties must be organized, elections won, malefactors opposed, and sometimes wars fought, not because the results would be what anybody wanted or intended, but because man was not created to bow before iniquity. He must resist, although in the end he will be conquered—if not by the evil he is fighting, then by the evil which rises from the fight itself.

Jefferson, in spite of his magician's power in politics, was too bland, too enlightened, too thoroughly eighteenth-century, for such stormy truth to reach the surface of his mind. Jefferson lived contentedly with the most worldly myth that has ever lulled man's intelligence, hiding the disappointment of the next step, of any next step on the material plane: the myth of humanism, of culture without religion, morality without a moral sanction, peace based on reason and freedom on utility. Lincoln lived in the world which had taken that particular step. He knew the glad tidings of the Deists were false; but what was true? His sad eyes watched and his heart shared the troubles of man adrift, generous and selfish, magnanimous and venal, but adrift, with no compass, a forgotten port, and a strong cold wind. He saw so much so quietly, accepting it without complaint or pretense, and still relishing the strife of the presidency. Like all the important Presidents he expanded the office; but he expanded himself still more. Most men rattle about inside the job; but Lincoln transcended it. Sometimes he seemed about to break its earthly bonds and seize the truth toward which he was groping. But he could not. He knew the vanity of this world. He knew that every secular victory must be soiled. So he could not fulfill himself in politics. And he could find nothing beyond. This is the burden of modern man at his wisest, which may explain why Lincoln was sorrowful.

XXII

Congress versus the President

WHEN THE WAR ENDED, the South was ruined physically but by no means deprived of hope. Two hundred and sixty thousand men had died in the Confederate armies, out of a white population of about six million.[1] A quarter of the white men of productive age were either dead or incapacitated. The long blockade, the fact that most of the fighting was on Southern soil, the careful destruction of towns, roads, bridges, and railways by the Northern armies, the loss of almost two thirds of the livestock and of slave property worth $2,000,000,000, the repudiation (imposed by the North) of the entire Confederate debt—all this meant an equality of poverty and a return to the simplest survival-standard of life. Yet the land was still there, and the rivers, and the sun and rain—and the Negro, although he had lost his cash value. The South was mostly a rural economy which could not be scared or starved by a breakdown of industry or of communications. If Northern politicians had kept their hands off, the South might have recovered quickly and with little bitterness. Indeed, her worst non-political disasters made for a renewed sense of kinship with the North, for when famine conditions threatened in some of the towns, Northern charity was quick with relief, and also when a yellow-fever epidemic began in the lower Mississippi Valley. The two chief Northern generals, Grant and Sherman, had been chivalrous in their terms of surrender—in fact, the terms that the latter arranged had been repudiated by Congress on the ground that they were overfriendly.

The South, during the war, had been too concerned with her own problems to notice the changes in the Northern government. She did not understand that the Union to which Lincoln invited her to return differed sharply from the Union she had deserted. Power, which had been concentrating in Washington, remained widely diffused in the South. The preamble to the Confederate Constitution proclaimed the sovereignty of the states. The "Old Republicans" of 1798 would have signed it joyfully, whereas ever since Jefferson and Hamilton first disputed with each other in Washington's Cabinet, the preamble to the Federal Constitution had been a source of discord. "We the people of the United States," it begins, "in order to form a more perfect union . . . do ordain and establish this Constitution for the United States of America." Did this mean that all

439

the people joined together in one political body to form a nation? Or did it mean that the people, meeting in their several sovereign states, and acting through the representatives of their states, ordained the new government? Nobody knew. Possibly, nobody was intended to know. The fathers of the Constitution were not so foolish as to make clear troublesome statements when they might remain soothingly obscure.

There was no obscurity, however, in the Confederate document. "We, the people of the Confederate states," it says, "each state acting in its sovereign and independent character, in order to form a permanent federal government . . . do ordain and establish this Constitution. . . ." The South was handicapped throughout the war by her decentralized government; but she accepted the handicap rather than permit that concentration of power against which Southern leaders had so long fought.* She was by no means prepared, therefore, to discover that while her back was turned the old federal Union had abandoned even the polite fiction of divided sovereignty and had made the states little more than administrative units, possessed of many important powers of government but clearly subject to the nation. An administrative unit cannot set its will against the central power and say that the Constitution has been misinterpreted by that power and that it will therefore disobey the law. In the future, regional and economic interests wishing to obstruct a distant majority would be forced to find subtler means than nullification.**

The South did not at first know this; but her ignorance need have been no bar to Reconstruction. She would have accepted (soon instead of slowly) the war-born changes in the living Constitution, and she would have set herself (at once, instead of after barren resentful years) to devise new methods for warding off outside interference with her daily life, even if her economic fate must now be subject to faraway control. But the price of such creative reconstruction was that Abraham Lincoln's views and methods should prevail. And so far as the South knew, during the first

* Robert E. Lee, for example, was not appointed General-in-Chief of the Confederate armies until February, 1865. Up to that time the governors insisted on having final word as to the use of troops raised in their states. And the central government at Richmond did not get authority to control the railroads for military purposes until February, 1865.

** Aside from making explicit the sovereignty of the states, the Confederate Constitution closely follows the Constitution of the United States. Three features of the Southern document, however, were intended as improvements based on the experience of seventy years; first, the President was allowed to veto individual items in an appropriation bill, instead of having to accept or to reject the entire lump; second, each bill passed by Congress was to deal with only one subject, and the subject was to be clearly defined in the title; third, Congress was authorized to permit by statute the heads of the executive departments to sit in Congress and take part in the discussion of measures affecting their work. As we have seen, this was Alexander Hamilton's view of the proper relation between the executive departments and the legislature. Unfortunately, the Confederate Congress never passed the authorizing act.

strange hushed weeks after surrender, the spirit of Lincoln survived.

Returning to Washington after Appomattox, and finding the city gay with celebration, Lincoln had made his last public speech. It was a simple, urgent plea that men begin to think at once and magnanimously about Reconstruction. He begged his hearers not to bother their minds with theories as to whether the seceding states had committed suicide or had merely been absent for a time. The point was to get them back into the Union comfortably and quickly. "Finding themselves safely at home," he said, "it would be utterly immaterial whether they had ever been abroad. Let us all join in doing the acts necessary to restoring the proper practical relations between these states and the Union; and each forever after innocently indulge his own opinion whether, in doing the acts, he brought the states from without into the Union, or only gave them proper assistance, they never having been out of it."

We need not speculate whether the nation would have followed such leadership, since it was not given the chance. But the South chose to believe as long as possible that what Lincoln said would prevail, and during those hopeful deluded days she showed that her own internal divisions had survived the war and that if she were allowed to return to the Union without bitterness she would return with a two-party system. The first postwar elections in the South showed the revived strength of the Whigs who had opposed secession, but had supported the war out of patriotism. The Republicans were wrong in assuming that the South would vote solidly Democratic. The South as a whole felt no debt to the Democratic Party of the North. Southern Whigs would have joined a moderate Union Party, such as Lincoln desired, and the region would have been saved from the seventy-year-long curse of a one-party system. But the radical Republicans drove all respectable white Southerners into the Democratic Party by identifying Republicanism with a policy that only the outcasts of the white world could support—only the deserters, and the disaffected "poor whites," and carpetbaggers, and those who thought to better themselves by betraying their neighbors.[2]

Unquestionably, among those evil-doing radicals were men of rigid principle, like Sumner, who thought that whatever the cost in hatred or in pain their methods were right because they would help the Negro. Only a subtle and humble mind can combine rigid principle with politics. The self-satisfied, the priggish, the morally superior, are more dangerous than the men who treat politics simply as a livelihood. The latter at least understand that politics is the pursuit of the possible, not of the ideal. They at least refrain from doing needless harm in the name of perfection. But the Sumners, the credulous, high-minded Sumners, are not only the victims of political vandals like Thaddeus Stevens, but of pride, the first of the deadly sins. The greater the ruin that surrounds them, the more they preen themselves as members of a dwindling band that "sticks to principles."

If the South had been revived with its old two-party system, normal political rivalry and search for votes might have enfranchised the Negro within a decade. Sumner preferred to enfranchise him at once—which meant depriving him of his vote for two generations and debauching Southern politics by preventing the growth of an Opposition.

2

When the war ended, the North was tired and overprosperous—hence morally slack. Her losses had been heavy—about three hundred and sixty thousand dead, out of a white population three and a half times that of the South. But the war had proved an economic stimulus. Government contracts and the high tariff were more than a substitute in most cases for the loss of Southern trade. Meat-packers of the Middle West and the shoe manufacturers of New England could not keep pace with army orders; and although cotton textiles declined because of the shortage of raw materials, the manufacture of woolens increased inordinately. The infant oil industry was stimulated. Bankers did well out of war bonds, and the new national banking system promised to end the paper-money fantasies of the state banks. Farmers were helped both by the insatiable hunger of the armies and by several years of bad wheat crops in Europe.

There was of course another side to the picture. The federal debt was more than $2,600,000,000. Labor had shared little in the new prosperity, suffering from high prices, high taxes, military service (since the poor could not take advantage of the clause in the draft law which allowed a man to be released on payment of $300), and after 1864 from the system of "contract labor." By an act of that year, alien labor contracts were made enforceable in the courts. This meant that American employers could hire foreigners abroad for next to nothing, bring them to America, and make them work for the derisory terms which they had accepted. The American workman was threatened by cheap foreign competition, whereas the American manufacturer was protected more thoroughly each year. This was one of the jokers which sometimes made the system of "free enterprise" less benign than it sounded in the textbooks.*

Also, the new banking system was scarcely a boon to the people in the back-country. "Though it had some merit," writes Professor J. G. Randall, "it created an inelastic currency, tended toward the concentration of bank resources in New York [and] opened the way for serious abuses in the

* The law was repealed in 1868; but the practice continued until forbidden by the new law of 1885. It was not wholly abandoned until 1907.

speculative exploitation of bank funds. . . ."[3] Yet the system was a blessing compared to that which preceded it. From the days when Jackson and Van Buren destroyed the National Bank, but failed to find a substitute, the country had been at the mercy of state banks. Sometimes the state was the sole owner, sometimes a part owner; but more often the banks were chartered by states and privately owned. In South Carolina, Missouri, and Indiana the system worked admirably. In Massachusetts the private banks supervised themselves—extra-legally, and with fair success. But for the most part the state-chartered private banks were not supervised at all and were a danger to the economic and political stability of the country. The worst of them, mostly in the West, were known as "wildcat banks," because in order to make the presentation of their notes for redemption as hard as possible they settled in the most inaccessible spots—out among the wildcats. With little specie, with capital based on promissory notes, with loans based on land speculation, they nevertheless issued "money," and many people were so unfortunate as to have their wages or their bills paid in such "money."

In 1863 and 1864, under pressure from the exasperated business community, Congress passed acts "to provide a national currency, secured by a pledge of United States stocks, and to provide for the circulation and redemption thereof." Banks which were organized under the safeguards of these acts were subject to federal supervision. They might issue notes secured by federal bonds and engage in commercial banking. At last the nation would have a circulating medium with some stability. In 1865, Congress imposed a tax of ten per cent on the circulation of state bank notes, thus driving the majority of sound banks to take national charters and subject themselves to federal control. By 1913, when the Federal Reserve Act superseded the Act of 1864, 7509 national banks carried on most of America's commercial banking business.

The national banking system, however, had one serious flaw which remained uncorrected—perhaps because the new masters at Washington profited thereby. The system was supposed to distribute bank-note circulation with reference to need; yet a few years after the war

Woonsocket, Rhode Island, had more national circulation than North and South Carolina, Mississippi and Arkansas; Waterville, Maine, had nearly as much as Alabama. . . . The per capita figures are just as astonishing. Rhode Island had $77.16 for each inhabitant, Arkansas had 13 cents. . . . Not a single southern state had obtained, by October, 1869, its legal share of the $150,000,000 which was to have been apportioned according to existing banking capital, wealth, and resources. Louisiana was entitled to $7,200,000 on this basis, and received $1,094,-589; Georgia was entitled to $4,470,000 and received $1,234,100; South Carolina was entitled to $4,185,000 and received $192,500.[4]

These figures are a forecast of the chief domestic issue in America from the Civil War to the time of Franklin Roosevelt: the issue of economic colonialism. How can the provinces—especially the South and West— save themselves from what is popularly known as "Wall Street"? Reconstruction is but a phase of this issue; Populism springs from it, and Bryanism, and the trust-busting talk of Theodore Roosevelt, and such distortions of the American dream as Huey Long and Senator Bilbo, and such applications of it as the New Freedom of Woodrow Wilson. The problem was stated clearly by John Taylor of Caroline in the eighteenth century; but it did not develop its full potential danger until the Civil War had left the capitalists unchallenged at Washington.

Yet in spite of the national debt, and the unfair distribution of benefits both among the classes and the sections, the wealth and productive power of the North had increased immensely. The Industrial Revolution had been somewhat delayed in America, partly by lack of capital, partly by the nation's preoccupation with the troubles that led to war; but now it was to come with a rush. Ten years after the surrender at Appomattox the North was a great industrial power and the old America of small-scale production was gone forever. The growth of the Northern munitions industry during the war had been a presage of what was about to happen.

When the fighting began there were two national armories, one at Harper's Ferry, Virginia, the other at Springfield, Massachusetts. The armory in Virginia was quickly destroyed to prevent its capture by Confederate troops; so the Union began the war with a single armory, able to turn out about eight hundred muskets a month. During the first year, therefore, most of the Northern munitions were bought in Europe. For a time the federal and state governments were bidding against each other, until the War Department persuaded the state purchasing commissions to withdraw. By August, 1861, every munitions factory in Birmingham and London, with one exception, was working to fill orders from Ohio, Massachusetts, and Connecticut. Yet by the end of that year American production had been so expanded that it could meet all the needs of the Union armies.

Small-arms production at Springfield had increased from 800 a month to 10,000, and during the second year of the war the armory produced 200,000 muskets while private contractors produced half a million. Most of this production was in the Northeast—for example, Colt's Armory and Sharps' Rifle Works were at Hartford, Connecticut; Remington was at Ilion, New York, and the Burnside Factory was at Providence, Rhode Island. At Bridesburg, Pennsylvania, the Alfred Jenks Company converted a plant for making textile machinery to the manufacture of rifles. After the first year there was never a problem of quantity in armaments; but quality was another matter. The superiority of breechloading carbines had been clearly proved; yet the Army refused to give up the old muzzle-loading muskets. Not until the war was in its final stages did the North begin to make breechloaders, and then only in small numbers.

The war was chiefly a battle between infantrymen. More than four million muskets were issued to the Union armies, and only 7892 cannon. The largest supplier of heavy ordnance was the Fort Pitt Foundry at Pittsburgh. Inevitably the production of iron was greatly increased, Cleveland and Buffalo being the chief manufacturing centers. And while the North was discovering its industrial strength and learning to produce on a giant scale, the South had to depend largely on captured arms and on foreign purchases run through the blockade. The Confederacy began the war with one foundry that could cast cannon and one small powder mill, and although it built new arsenals and mills it was never able to come measurably close to supplying its own needs. At the end of the war its small industrial plant was in ruins, whereas the North was getting ready to challenge England as the workshop of the world.

3

When the war ended, the ancient rivalry between the Congress and the Executive was acute. For four years the President had gone his own way, appealing to Congress from time to time to validate his acts. Reluctantly, and often very slowly, the Congress had done what it was told. In the case of the suspension of the writ of habeas corpus, the President or the officials acting under his order might have been subject to heavy damage suits if the courts had ultimately decided that the suspension was illegal. Yet it was March, 1863, before Congress could bring itself to agree on a bill which protected the Executive and gave him permission to continue what he had so long been doing.*

Lincoln, as we have seen, was glad that the Confederacy collapsed at a time when Congress was in recess; but his pleasure was not shared by the Congressmen. They felt they had been unimportant long enough. To be sure, the Committee on the Conduct of the War had been able by enormous effort to do minor damage—to destroy the reputations of a few good generals, and to upset a few useful plans. But for the rest Congress had been powerless to make policy during four years. It had no intention of remaining powerless. Furthermore, the discordant groups which composed

---

* Lincoln derived what he called his "war power" from two clauses in the Constitution: that which made him Commander-in-Chief of the armed forces, and that which declared it was his duty "to take care that the laws be faithfully executed." (Cp. Article II, Sections 2 and 3.) Putting these two clauses together, it seemed to him he had the power to do whatever was necessary to win a civil war.

the Union Party had no intention of remaining peacefully under the same roof.

The temporary chairman at the convention that renominated Lincoln had said in his introductory speech, "As a Union party I will follow you to the ends of the earth and to the gates of death; but as an Abolitionist party, as a Republican party, as a Whig party, as a Democratic party, as an American party I will not follow you one foot." This was a popular statement in 1864; but in 1865 the war was ended and Lincoln was dead, and the Union Party was dead with him. After Appomattox, no threat from the outside held radicals and conservatives together. And after the fatal night of April 14 there was no leader for the conservative cause. Within a few hours of Lincoln's death the Congressional radicals held a caucus. They agreed to work for an entire change of Cabinet, and for an entire change of policy toward the South. They thought President Andrew Johnson would be their man, because he had once belonged to the Committee on the Conduct of the War. Coarse Ben Wade spoke to the new President for the Committee in these words: "Johnson, we have faith in you. By the gods, there will be no trouble now in running the government." As usual, Senator Wade was wrong.

Fate had brought to the White House a Southerner, a Democrat, a states'-rights enthusiast and one of the stubbornest men ever seen in Washington. Andrew Johnson, although very able, was also sadly stupid when it came to dealing with the cantankerous and touchy men of Congress. "Your President," he dared to say, "is now the Tribune of the people, and thank God I am, and intend to assert the power which the people have placed in me."[5] This is not the mood in which a wise President would approach Congress—especially a President who had come to power by accident, who could not claim to be the people's choice, and who had inherited a long-contained but deeply burning quarrel. At the beginning of a first term, or in the midst of a well-recognized danger to the nation, a vastly popular President should act like a tribune of the people, but he should never admit it. Johnson was really serving another man's second term; and instead of being in the midst of danger, he was in the midst of a carefree celebration because danger had passed. It was a time to tread softly and to attack his enemies with gentle stealth, as Jefferson would have done. Yet Johnson seemed to prolong in his own mind the mood of war, acting as if the fate of the nation still depended on strong Executive measures which were to be obeyed without question.

In defending his temporary dictatorship Lincoln had said:

> My oath to preserve the Constitution imposed on me the duty of preserving by every indispensable means the . . . nation of which the Constitution was the organic law. . . . I felt that measures, otherwise

unconstitutional, might become lawful by becoming indispensable to the preservation of the Constitution through the preservation of the nation. Right or wrong, I assumed this ground and now avow it.[6]

This was bold talk. Lincoln was upheld because most people believed the nation might die if he was opposed. But when Johnson came to the White House people believed the nation was safe, and that the time had come when Executive acts should once more be subject to criticism by Congress. Lincoln had set an example which would be followed by other Presidents in other emergencies; but he had not established an irresponsible government in which a "tribune of the people" decides what is good for the people and then goes his way.

And there was another reason why Johnson—if politically wise—might have chosen to move quietly and with conciliation. Congress was itself the scene of a relentless struggle for power, and a prudent President might have won to his support all members who were opposed to extreme measures. He would have had to give ground; he would have had to pretend to be converted by the wisdom of his advisers in Congress; he would have had to help rebuild the impaired dignity of that sensitive body. All this Jefferson could have done in his sleep; but Jefferson cared only for the substance of power and preferred to have other men enjoy the trappings.

The radicals did not yet control Congress; in fact, they were frightened that they never would. They had a clear, militant program. They believed (wrongly) that they had won the war. They were prepared to use all their formidable talents to impose their will. And they were strengthened by having no scruples, and by the fact that their policy was directed against men whom they despised or hated and whom they proposed to deprive of the vote. Yet they were still in a minority, and an adroit President might have marshaled against them all the leaderless conservatives: the ex-Whigs, most of the ex-Know-Nothings, the war Democrats who had joined the Union Party under Lincoln's persuasion, and even a scattering of the early Republicans, such as the powerful Seward and his friend Thurlow Weed. If these men had stood together on a merciful program they might have won public support in the mid-term elections of 1866. And America would have been saved much sorrow.

The radicals intended to keep the South a conquered province as long as possible. Some of them hoped thereby to help the Negro, by giving him control of what was left of the South and allowing him time to become at home in his political liberty, while the Southern whites were kept down. Some of them hoped to acquire Southern property for themselves, and to set up absentee ownership of a revived industrial and financial system. But most of them hoped only to protect and prolong the rule of their own party. They did not wish a Union Party. They did not wish a party which was the heir to the conciliatory and careful Whigs. And especially they did not wish a strong Democratic Party with Southern membership in Congress increased by the freeing of the Negroes.* What they wanted was a party of aggressive capitalism which could promise that no regional or class interest would be allowed to interfere with the free use of the nation's resources by the new brood of Northern and Middlewestern millionaires. And they intended that this party of aggressive capitalism should also be a party of aggressive cruelty toward Southern rebels—ostensibly for the sake of the Negro and for the punishment of past misdeeds, but really to make certain that the Democratic Party did not soon revive.

In spite of the high political abilities of many radicals, and in spite of their formidable double argument of humanity to the Negro and of punishment to the rebels who had made the war, and in spite of the appeal to the most forceful and ruthless economic group in the country, it is doubtful whether this program could have received the support of the unvindictive and unrapacious American people if it had been opposed quietly and persuasively and with the moral insight which Lincoln could have brought to the task. But President Johnson defended the good cause with many mistakes in taste and judgment, hardening the moderate men in Congress against him, and finally alienating the public. Each mistake was used by his enemies with expert skill.

4

Andrew Johnson was born in Raleigh, North Carolina, in 1808. His father, a bank porter, died three years later, leaving Johnson in a state of extreme poverty. At the age of ten he was apprenticed to a tailor, and at sixteen he moved to Greeneville in eastern Tennessee. When he was eighteen he married the charming and superior Eliza McCardle, daughter of a Scottish shoemaker. They had not a penny between them; but Johnson set up a tailor shop, and his wife undertook to widen his knowledge of books. This was not hard, for he had hitherto barely learned to read and write. At Greeneville there was a little college which allowed Johnson to attend debating classes, and thus he began to prepare for politics. Meanwhile his shop prospered and he acquired a small farm and several slaves. His leisure was given to the Democratic Party, which was then being shaped and organized by the master politicians who served Andrew Jackson.

* Under Article I, Section 2 of the Constitution, five slaves counted as three persons in apportioning representation in the lower House. But in December, 1865, with the ratification of the Thirteenth Amendment, slavery was abolished everywhere within the United States. Thereafter five southern Negroes counted as five persons, so if the South were allowed to return to normal political life it would have more representatives than before the war.

After a few years as alderman, and a term as mayor, Johnson was sent to the Tennessee legislature in 1835. In 1841 he moved to the state senate, and in 1843 to the House of Representatives at Washington, where he served for ten years on end. He then had two terms as governor of Tennessee and in 1857 was chosen for the United States Senate. This remarkable and steady rise puzzled observers at the time, and has puzzled biographers, because Johnson had a talent for making important enemies. Although he was a steady party man in his voting, he could not abide most of the Democratic leaders and they could not abide him. He quarreled, not only with anyone who put on airs, but with anyone who had the manners and graces of privilege. He was class-conscious in an aggressive, hostile sense, resenting the rich planters of western Tennessee, and indeed the well-to-do everywhere. In part, this may have been because of untrue rumors that he was illegitimate, and in part because a poor farmer in a slave-owning state had none of the rewarding and warming experience of democracy which Lincoln found in Illinois.

Yet Johnson was a notable vote-winner. He came from a poor man's district where his blunt democracy won favor—to say nothing of his attacks on the rich. He wished to amend the Constitution to provide for direct election of senators and federal judges, and to abolish the electoral college; but his great cause throughout the years in House and Senate was the Homestead Act, providing free land in small holdings for actual settlers. Twice he saw his favorite measure defeated by his own party—in the Senate in 1853 and by presidential veto in 1860. When at last the Republican-Union Party passed the bill in 1862, and Lincoln signed it, Johnson had a right to feel that the long-delayed victory was in good part his.

Although an extreme democrat and a dangerous leveler in the eyes of most Southern politicians, Johnson never favored the freeing of the slaves and was a strong foe of the abolitionists. He was in no sense a demagogue. He merely lacked judgment and charity, so that his remarks about the rich and the socially pretentious sounded unbalanced. They probably would have been more extreme, and more hurtful to his career, if his wise and gentle wife had not been always at his side. But what endeared Johnson to his own constituents, in spite of roughness and seeming coldness, was his clear pure faith that America could be made a land of boundless opportunity for all. His own life gave substance to the faith, and he insisted steadily that the remaining barriers to true democracy must be removed—except the barrier of slavery, which as a Southerner he did not notice.

In the campaign of 1860 Johnson deplored the schism in the Democratic Party but supported the Southern candidate, Breckinridge. Nevertheless, during the interval before Lincoln's inauguration he sought to avoid secession by compromise, aligning himself with Senator Crittenden of Kentucky. And in December, when South Carolina was seceding, he made a strong speech for the Union. Southerners called him a traitor, and he answered with eloquent violence in speeches that made him famous throughout the North. He had taken his stand, like Lincoln, because he believed the Union was the safeguard of democracy. Defeat of the Union, he thought, would mean defeat for the democratic movement everywhere. He did not know, as perhaps Lincoln did not know, that victory for the Union would raise up a new threat to democracy in the form of a greedy and ravenous capitalism. He hated privilege; yet it was his fate to see the party of Union victory conquered and enslaved by the abounding privilege of corporate industry. "Twenty years after the attack on Fort Sumter the railroads alone represented a greater investment and concentration of power than had ever the slave interest, and their influence in politics and in the economic activities of men were scarcely less far-reaching."[7] As Henry Nevinson said, "the battle of freedom is never done, and the field never quiet."

During the special session of Congress in July, 1861, the Senate adopted Johnson's resolution that the war was not for conquest, or for interference with the rights or institutions of seceding states, but for the defense of the Union and the Constitution. That was what Lincoln believed until he died, and what Johnson believed when he became President. That was what many soldiers believed, especially the men from the Middle West. But it was not what the politicians who were to rule Congress believed, so it was not true.

In March, 1862, just before his belated triumph with the Homestead Act, Johnson was appointed military governor of Tennessee. His views on the war were so close to Lincoln's that he had often been consulted on the handling of the border states. Thus, when the North had conquered a sufficient section of Tennessee so that a government might be installed, Lincoln sent Johnson to take charge. The post was dangerous for a Southerner; but Johnson was as brave as he was quarrelsome. His own eastern Tennessee, Unionist in sympathy, was held by the Confederates. Johnson had to set up his government in hostile, secessionist Nashville, where he was despised as a traitor. He ruled firmly, at times harshly; but he succeeded in building a civil government. Before the war ended, Tennessee—which had been omitted from the Emancipation Proclamation of January 1, 1863, because it was no longer officially in revolt—held a constitutional convention, abolished slavery, and was ready to re-enter the Union as a loyal state.

We have seen that Lincoln chose Johnson for the vice-presidency in 1864 because he wanted a Union Democrat who would broaden the base of the party. On Inauguration Day, March 4, 1865, Johnson was ill and wished to postpone taking the oath. Lincoln was opposed to delay so Johnson hurried to Washington. On a doctor's advice he took whisky to fortify himself against the weather and against exhaustion. He was not used to drinking and he took too much, with the result that he talked boastfully and cheaply, giving his enemies a rich theme for future slander.

5

Although Johnson angered the radicals by keeping Lincoln's Cabinet intact, he also gave them hope during his first days by some very wild talk. "Treason is a crime and must be punished," he is reported to have said, ". . . and traitors must be impoverished."[8] But he quickly abandoned this attitude and turned to carrying out Lincoln's plans.* By April, 1865, provisional governments had already been established in Tennessee, Louisiana, Arkansas, and Virginia. On May 29 Johnson issued a new amnesty proclamation which was almost the same as Lincoln's proclamation of December 8, 1863—except that Johnson included among those who needed special and separate pardon all the ex-rebels who had a taxable property of more than $20,000. The new President's distaste for the rich was undying.

On the day of his proclamation Johnson set up a provisional government for North Carolina, and by the end of July all the ex-Confederate states had been given temporary governors. These governors called state conventions which were elected by the white men who had been allowed to take the oath of allegiance. The conventions amended the old state constitutions, abolished slavery, repudiated the Confederate war debts, and undid the acts of secession. Elections were then held, and by the autumn of 1865 new governments were at work in all the rebel states except Texas. It was these summer elections, incidentally, which first showed that the South might have returned to the Union with her two-party political life intact.

By December the Southern states had ratified the Thirteenth Amendment, which made slavery contrary to the federal Constitution. Unfortunately, they had also passed a series of black codes, defining new rights and restrictions for the freedmen. These varied in harshness; but in no case were the freedmen allowed the vote or made eligible for juries. In some states the penalties for vagrancy, and the apprenticeship laws, were so framed that they could have led to a form of peonage. Northern friends of the Negro were outraged, and the radical enemies of Johnson's program were strengthened. "We tell the white men of Mississippi," said the

---

* Blaine, who regretted Johnson's conversion from vengeance to forbearance, puts the blame for this outbreak of humanity on Secretary of State Seward. Cp. *Twenty Years of Congress,* vol. II, pp. 80–86.

Chicago *Tribune,* "that the men of the North will convert the state of Mississippi into a frog pond before they will allow any such laws to disgrace one foot of soil in which the bones of our soldiers sleep and over which the flag of freedom waves."

The South would have benefited herself and the nation if she had followed Johnson's advice and given the vote to a few educated Negroes. Yet the testimony is clear, from black man and white man alike, that what the Negro first wanted was not the vote but land and education. While serving as an officer in the Union Army, the grandson of John Quincy Adams wrote: "My impression from what I see, is that emancipation as a government measure would be a terrible calamity to the blacks as a race. . . . The blacks must be cared for or they will perish, and who is to care for them when they cease to be of value?" And the same point was made by Frederick Douglass, one of the bravest Negro leaders and most fiery abolitionists, who wrote after the war that the Negro was "free from the individual master but a slave of society. He had neither money, property, nor friends. He was free from the old plantation, but he had nothing but the dusty road under his feet. . . . He was turned loose naked, hungry, and destitute to the open sky."

Land could have saved him, now that he had "ceased to be of value" —land and education. He longed for both, and begged for both. The Freedmen's Bureau established hundreds of schools, and Northern charity helped, and free state education (such as it was in the impoverished South) was made available for Negroes as well as whites; but nothing was done on a scale commensurate with the problem. And in regard to land nothing was done at all. All over the South the ruined planters were selling their great holdings at bargain prices. The small yeoman farmers and even the poor whites were buying. Congress had a chance to create economic democracy between the races. If the Negro had been made a property-owner, and if his thirst for learning had been slaked at federal expense, he would have become a truly free man. As Professors Morison and Commager say, "a government which found it possible to give forty million acres of public land to a single railroad might well have purchased ten million acres for the freedmen."[*9] But neither the Northern capitalist nor the Republican politician would be helped by making the Negro free and independent. So they left him "a slave of society," with "nothing but the dusty road under his feet." And for comfort they gave him the vote, and sent swarms of "friends" to make sure that he used it the right way.

Troubled by the outcry against the black codes and knowing he would have a fight when Congress met, President Johnson sent various agents to study the South in the autumn of 1865 and to tell him what they found.

* From *The Growth of the American Republic* by Samuel E. Morison and Henry Steele Commager. Copyright, 1930, 1937, 1942 by Oxford University Press, Inc.

With one exception the reports bear out the wisdom of the Lincoln-Johnson policy. General Grant, for example, wrote as follows:

> I am satisfied that the mass of thinking men of the South accept the present situation of affairs in good faith. The questions which have heretofore divided the sentiment of the people of the two sections— slavery and state rights, or the right of a state to secede from the Union —they regard as having been settled forever by the highest tribunal— arms—that man can resort to. I was pleased to learn from the leading men whom I met that they not only accept the decision arrived at as final, but, now that the smoke of battle has cleared away and time has been given for reflection, that this decision has been a fortunate one for the whole country. . . . The citizens of the southern states are anxious to return to self-government, within the Union, as soon as possible. . . . They are in earnest in wishing to do what is required by the government, not humiliating to them as citizens, and . . . if such a course were pointed out they would pursue it in good faith.

We know today that General Grant was right. The South had accepted defeat, with no thought of revenge or further war. All she wanted was "self-government, within the Union, as soon as possible." She was not a Poland, or an Ireland, harboring eternal wrath, eternal purpose to be free. In 1865 no Southerner would sing a reborn Confederacy with the implacable hate which burns in the Irish ode to "Dark Rosaleen":

> Oh! the Erne shall run red
> With redundance of blood,
> The earth shall rock beneath our tread,
> And flames wrap hill and wood,
> And gun-peal and slogan cry,
> Wake many a glen serene
> Ere you shall fade, ere you shall die,
> My dark Rosaleen!
> My own Rosaleen!
> The Judgment Hour must first be nigh,
> Ere you shall fade, ere you can die,
> My dark Rosaleen!

The South was prepared to let the Confederacy die, and was even prepared (as Grant said) to admit that her defeat may have been "fortunate for the whole country"—until the North imposed a peace more bitter than war. The radicals are responsible for the legend of the Lost Cause.

When Congress reassembled on December 4, 1865—by which time Lincoln had hoped to have rebuilt the Union so solidly that not even the legislators could undo it—Johnson seemed almost to have succeeded in his great conciliatory task. Reconstruction appeared to be complete. With one exception, the South had done what was expected of her, and the North seemed pleased, and the radicals seemed on the defensive. The black codes were the exception; but if the Congress had been interested in the Negro the codes could have been countered by land and education. "Power follows property." The family which owns its farm, and lives off it, is free. And the free man who knows more than his neighbor is strong. A two-party South would quickly have been bidding for the votes of property-owning and instructed Negroes. But Congress provided a South wherein ignorant and destitute freedmen were supported by Northern troops in their "right" to vote the Republican ticket.

6

The first decision of the new Congress was to refuse to hear even the names of the members-elect from the ex-rebel states. A Joint Committee of both Houses was then appointed to deal with Reconstruction. It was dominated by Thaddeus Stevens, who for the next two years imposed his will upon the nation. He was very old, very near the grave, and was about to earn the epitaph that his days of power were the most disgraceful in his country's history.

The Joint Committee gave proof of its sharp wits by inventing a theory of Reconstruction which allowed it to deny representation to the Southern states while proclaiming the ratification of the Thirteenth Amendment by the governments of those states. Others had thought that the states must either be in the Union or out of it. If in, they should be represented; if out, they should not lend their names to an amendment. But the Joint Committee put forward the "forfeited rights theory," according to which no state had ever left the Union, but the people of the rebel states had lost their political rights—just as an individual may lose his civil rights by committing a crime. This left the Congress supreme, and the Southerners at the mercy of that erratic body. Congress could confer upon the citizens of Georgia the "right" to ratify an amendment and deny them the "right" to be represented. As for the states, they were not dead, yet they did not seem to be alive. Strangely, uncannily, they lived in a Miltonic limbo, where

> The unaccomplished works of nature's hand,
> Abortive, monstrous, or unkindly mixed,
> Dissolved on earth, fleet hither, and in vain,
> Till final dissolution wander here.

Yet Johnson might still have snatched control from the Joint Committee if he had possessed the guile of Jefferson or the common touch of Lincoln.

The first test came on a bill to extend the Freedmen's Bureau—which had been set up by Congress, under the War Department, on March 3, 1865. The Bureau had been authorized for only a year, and although it had been staffed hastily and often unworthily it had done some useful work. The freedmen should obviously not be left to their own devices or to the mercy of the black codes. Until Congress was prepared to plan something genuinely helpful for the Negro, the Bureau was better than nothing, even though it was degenerating into a machine to get out the Republican vote. Johnson was ill-advised to veto the bill, in spite of the fact that the conservatives in Congress sustained him. And shortly thereafter he made a stupid speech abusing the Congressional radicals and alienating his friends —for after four years of humbly serving Lincoln, all members of Congress would stand together against Executive arrogance.

In March, 1866, Congress passed a Civil Rights Act to protect the Negro against the black codes and to secure him the vote. The act was perhaps unconstitutional, since it asserted that the civil rights of the citizen were to be protected by the federal courts against the laws of the state in which he lived. Johnson, with his states'-rights views, was forced to veto the bill; but Congress, with more than a two-thirds majority, overruled him. In July, a second Freedmen's Bureau Bill was also passed over his veto; and the Fourteenth Amendment (which in effect would put the Civil Rights Bill into the Constitution) was drafted by the Joint Committee. The Southern states—whose representatives elected under the President's Reconstruction plan were still waiting at the doors of Congress—were told that the ratification of this amendment was the price of readmission. Tennessee ratified at once and was grudgingly allowed back into the Union on July 24, 1866. But the rest of the South rejected the amendment, and it was rumored that this was on the advice of President Johnson.* If so, the advice was bad, for the problem of Reconstruction was about to be put to the people in the dramatic mid-term Congressional elections of 1866. The radicals took the Fourteenth Amendment for their platform. They should not have been allowed so good a cause.

The Fourteenth Amendment is the most momentous in the history of the Constitution, not only because it was the excuse for the defeat of the Lincoln-Johnson plans for Reconstruction, but because it was later used by the Supreme Court as a bulwark for corporate property against the people's efforts to control the new forms of capitalism. Yet the amendment, which was in four sections, sounded innocent and was intended to be helpful. The first section states that anyone born or naturalized in the United States is a citizen, and that "no state shall make or enforce

* Cp. the letter from Wager Swayne to Chief Justice Salmon P. Chase, which says that ratification failed in Alabama because the people were told the President was against it. *Diary and Correspondence of S. P. Chase*, pp. 516–17.

any law which shall abridge the privileges or immunities of citizens of
the United States; nor shall any state deprive any person of life, liberty,
or property without due process of law; nor deny to any person within
its jurisdiction the equal protection of the laws." This was an honest
effort to confer civil rights upon the freedmen, under the protection of
the federal government. It was intended to be revolutionary, to change
the legal relation between the federal government and the states. It was
unsuccessful because it failed to protect the freedmen, and before long
we shall find the Supreme Court returning the enforcement of civil rights
to the states. There they can be enforced only in accordance with the will
of the community, and the radicals had by that time done all in their
power to harden the will of the South against the long-betrayed Negro.
Yet this revolutionary, inefficient section of the amendment, which did
the Negro no good, became an inverted Bill of Rights for monopoly capitalism. It was interpreted to mean, not that the federal government should
protect the freedmen, but that it should protect corporations whose
property rights were threatened by state laws. We shall discuss later
whether this was intended by the men who framed the amendment. It
was certainly not intended by most of the men who urged the amendment
upon the public.

The second section says that if a state denies the right to vote at an
election "to any of the male inhabitants of such state, being twenty-one
years of age, and citizens of the United States . . . the basis of representation therein shall be reduced in the proportion which the number of
such male citizens shall bear to the whole number of male citizens twenty-
one years of age in such state." Nothing could be clearer. The radicals
intended that if the South should disfranchise the Negro (that is, the
Republican voter) the Democratic Party would be penalized by a reduction of Southern membership in the House of Representatives. Yet in
large parts of the South the Negro has been disfranchised for two generations, and nowhere has Southern representation been diminished.

The third section of the amendment disqualifies from office, federal or
state, anyone who had held office before the Civil War and who nevertheless helped the rebellion. This was meant to put the governments of the
Southern states in the hands of the Negroes, the carpetbaggers, and the
few white natives who opposed the Confederacy. For a short time, with
the help of federal troops, it succeeded. Section Four makes illegal the
payment of any part of the Confederate debt, and adds (perhaps unnecessarily) that the public debt of the United States "shall not be questioned." This is the only part of the amendment which has had the intended results.

7

In preparation for the autumn elections of 1866, the friends of conservative Reconstruction held a meeting at Philadelphia on August 14. It was called the National Union Convention. It had been planned by Secretary of State Seward and Boss Thurlow Weed, and the call went out under the name of the national chairman of Lincoln's Union Party. Under such auspices the gathering should have been smoothly professional; but it was muddled and amateurish. Famous and discredited "peace Democrats," or "Copperheads" (like Fernando Wood and Vallandigham), were first allowed to attend and were later sent away because the publicity had become damaging—thus ensuring the worst of both worlds. Also, there were too many "war Democrats" present, in proportion to famous Republicans like Seward and Weed. Although the convention used the name which had been chosen in 1862 by Lincoln's party, and endorsed the Reconstruction program of Lincoln and Johnson, the radicals in Congress were able to persuade their capitalist friends that a victory for the National Union Party was really a victory for the Democrats, for the old alliance of rural South and rural West. Such an alliance might give the public lands to the people instead of to the railroads; it might resist a quick return to the gold standard and a quick deflation of the war-swollen currency; it might lower the tariff wall which now surrounded the country; it might refuse to give federal protection to the Northerners who were buying the South.

Thurlow Weed should have known better than to allow his enemies to create a confusion of issues. He should have stuck to the one question which was embodied in the name of the party: was the nation to restore the Union in dignity and friendship? The currency and the public land and the tariff could be dealt with later, when America was herself again; but Reconstruction, and thus the Negro question, would go wrong for a long time if they went wrong that year. Yet the National Union Convention was so foolish as to frighten the more aggressive capitalists into the radical camp. The people were not given a chance to vote for the simple decency they would perhaps have chosen.

Even more remarkable for so experienced a group, the National Unionists made no attempt to capture the local party machines—to oust the radicals from control of the Republican machines wherever possible, and to oust the Copperheads from control of the Democratic machines. The voters therefore were faced, in far too many districts, with the choice between a radical Republican who had fought for the Union and a "peace Democrat" who called himself a Unionist. The handicap was in any case too great; but the President made it greater by a campaign trip in which he repeatedly abused his opponents, argued with hecklers, and boasted of the poverty from which he had risen. The realignment of parties, which had seemed imminent, was halted. Republicans voted for the radicals, and Democrats for the Unionists. Since Southern Democrats were not allowed to vote, the radicals in Congress won the two-thirds majority which enabled them to deprive the President of power, even the power of the veto.

After the election—when all was lost—Thurlow Weed tried to use the federal patronage to build a Union Party machine. For a time the President co-operated; but it was much too late. A year later, in a letter to Seward, Weed put the full blame for failure on Johnson. "I followed the President into the Ditch," he wrote. "I destroyed the consistency of a long political life. The President for the first month or two of his administration had the people warmly with him. He could have overwhelmed the Radicals. But he has thrown it all away."[10] This was true but incomplete. The President made every possible mistake; but so did his friends. If Andrew Johnson had been served as was Andrew Jackson—if a Van Buren and a Blair and a Kendall had been at hand, to organize and to advise and to write speeches—the radicals would have had to meet not only courage and goodness (which are seldom enough in politics) but a skill as careful as their own.

8

The rest of the tale can be briefly told. Thaddeus Stevens ruled Congress as an unofficial prime minister. There was in effect no President, since Johnson could be disregarded. The radicals undid the whole of his Reconstruction and started afresh as if the war had just ended. In March, 1867, they passed an act which said there was no legal government in the South outside of Tennessee. The land was divided into five military districts, each under a major general who was responsible for life and property. Any state would be readmitted to the Union when it set up a government based on universal male suffrage and ratified the Fourteenth Amendment. Since the amendment disqualified from officeholding the whole of the old political class in the South, voters were to have the privilege of choosing Negroes, Northerners, or white men who had taken no part in public life.

At once, military rule replaced the governments which had been elected in the summer of 1865. Office holders who would be disqualified under the Fourteenth Amendment were removed by the generals to make room for Negroes or carpetbaggers. Civil courts gave way to military courts, and the laws of the states were remade by military fiat.

In Washington, meanwhile, a revolution at least as daring was attempted. In spite of the Constitution, the President was deprived of control of the Army. It was decreed that all military orders must be issued through a general who could not be removed or suspended by the President. And by means of the Tenure of Office Act, the President was denied the right to remove civil officials, including the members of his own Cabinet, without the consent of the Senate. If these laws were to prevail, the President could not control his own Administration, since he would have no patronage at his disposal, and was no longer Commander-in-Chief of the Army. Congress was king. And to make the point clear, when Johnson tried to remove his Secretary of War in defiance of the Tenure of Office Act the House of Representatives voted to impeach him.

Under Article II, Section 4, of the Constitution, the President can be impeached for treason, bribery, or other high crimes and misdemeanors. And under Article I, Section 3, "the Senate shall have the sole power to try all impeachments. . . . When the President of the United States is tried, the Chief Justice shall preside: and no person shall be convicted without the concurrence of two thirds of the members present." Eleven charges were drawn up, ten of them referring in one way or another to the Tenure of Office Act, and the eleventh accusing the President of attacking Congress in his speeches!

The trial began on March 13, with one of the most able and conservative corporation lawyers of the day, William Evarts, among the counsel defending the President. The radicals had at last overplayed their hand. They had gone too far for their associates in the world of big business. If Johnson was removed, he would be succeeded under the statute then in force by Ben Wade, the president pro tempore of the Senate. Senator Wade, for all his unpleasant manners, was an honest radical. He had not joined that camp merely to seize power or to betray the South. He wanted free land for the Negroes, and women's suffrage, and a money policy which would help the farmer rather than the capitalist. Even Thaddeus Stevens had disappointed his more rapacious and inexperienced business friends by intervening to slow down deflation lest the rural Republicans be driven into Johnson's camp. So the business world began to wonder whether it wished to destroy the presidency and to set Congress free. Presumably, no one really thought Johnson was guilty. The Supreme Court has since upheld him not only on the Tenure of Office Act but on the reasoning in his strong, much-hated veto messages. The question was not whether Johnson had committed "high crimes and misdemeanors," but whether the Senate would dare to break him.

On May 16 a vote was taken on the eleventh charge, and ten days later on the second and third. Each time the radicals had one vote too few for conviction. Seven Republicans voted with the twelve Democrats in support of Johnson, and nineteen votes was enough. The attempt to undo the presidential form of government, and to establish Congress as the sole policy-maker, had failed. In view of the policy which Congress was then busily making, the failure may be considered a blessing. The representatives of geographic regions and of class interests, meeting together to barter with one another, can prevent policies which are harmful to their constituents and can resist mere numerical majorities; but there has never been a sign in American history that they are capable of making, and administering, and maintaining over a sufficient time, a truly national policy. For those who believe in Congressional rule, the record of the post-Civil War Congress is even more discouraging than the record of the Congress which seized power from the weak hands of Madison and made (and almost lost) the War of 1812. The nation then suffered a long period of Congressional government while Presidents Madison and Monroe watched benignly; but nothing occurred to recommend the system. And in the years after the Civil War America was to undergo another such period, beginning with the ignoble rule of Thaddeus Stevens. Once again, there was nothing reassuring in the experience.

9

Secretary of State Seward played a wise and dignified part in the melodrama of these years. Perhaps he was responsible for converting Johnson to Lincoln's policy, as Blaine charged; in any case, he backed that policy steadily. And he wrote some of Johnson's best veto messages. And he made many public speeches supporting the President during the critical campaign of 1866—meanwhile earning his country's gratitude by adroit handling of the French invasion of Mexico.

Yet Seward, as we have seen, began his secretaryship eccentrically on April Fool's Day, 1861, by recommending that Lincoln restore the Union through the unusual device of making war on most of the Great Powers simultaneously. He urged that the United States demand immediate explanations (on matters which were nowhere critical) from France, Spain, Russia, and Great Britain. And if the explanations of France and Spain were not satisfactory he would at once declare war. He seemed to feel that the Confederacy would not be able to refuse so pleasing a suicide and would at once rejoin the family.

Even after Lincoln had calmed him down from this delirium, Seward could not resist a minor brush with Spain. On May 19, 1861, five weeks after the firing on Fort Sumter, Spain suddenly reannexed the Republic of San Domingo from which she had been expelled in 1821. Seward protested with a clear and able statement of the Monroe Doctrine. But he was overemphatic at the end.

With profound regret at this unhappy state of affairs [his note concluded], the undersigned has now to fulfill the duty imposed upon him by the President, and in the name of the government of the United States of America solemnly protests against the assumption or exercise of Spanish authority in the island of San Domingo; and this protest the United States in every case will expect to maintain.

These were stirring words. Since the armies of the two portions of the once United States were at that time assembling for the first battles of a mighty war, Spain was not impressed. Furthermore, because of the Mexican War and all the subsequent talk of further expansion, and in the light of the *Ostend Manifesto,* Europe was not inclined to listen gracefully to the combination of moralism and bluster with which America chose to conduct her foreign affairs. Spain therefore replied to Seward that the people of San Domingo had consented to rejoin the Spanish Empire—which was true, but irrelevant, since the voting had been a farce—and that as for the so-called Monroe Doctrine, this was the first that the Spanish Government had officially heard of it.

The Government of the Queen neither accepts nor declines this policy; it limits itself to saying that it does not think this an opportune time to discuss it, because it does not see the usefulness or convenience of entering at present into such an examination.[11]

Seward was to blame for this rebuff and could do nothing but accept it. The armies of his own government were learning, at the first battle of Bull Run, that they could not yet coerce the Confederacy, let alone the empire of Spain. As had happened once before, however, the black men and mulattoes of San Domingo now rescued the United States from a difficult position. Rising in revolt and fighting a savage guerilla warfare, they destroyed the armies of Spain as they had once destroyed those of the first Napoleon. By the time the Civil War was ending in America, Spain was withdrawing from San Domingo.

Seward learned from this experience. In later and far more dangerous encounters his truculence was suppressed; and there came a steady growth in the dignity and strength with which America's views were stated. In November, 1861, when an enthusiastic Union captain seized two Southern diplomats and their secretaries from an English ship at sea, Seward surrendered them to the British Government, although if he were still yearning for another and larger war this was his chance. And he was skillful in warding off French and English intervention on the side of the South, especially in making use of the Emancipation Proclamation to help the Northern cause in Europe. But his real triumph came after the war was ended, when he gave to the tormented Johnson Administration its one clear victory. No one could have prevented the French invasion of Mexico; but it took patience and tact and quiet firmness to get Napoleon III to withdraw peacefully. If Seward had treated that capricious emperor the way he treated Spain, he might have provoked a useless war in 1866.

One reason for Napoleon's adventure was the belief throughout most of Europe that if someone did not bring order and strength to Mexico the United States would annex it. As early as 1855 the French Minister in Mexico was writing that Russia and the United States were the two threats to peace. "Russia," he said in a dispatch on May 15, "aspires to dominate in Europe in the name of despotism, and the United States to dominate in America in the name of liberty. The principle of monarchy, imposed with all its exaggerations and abuses by the sabre of the Tsar and the lance of the Cossacks, and the democratic principle, imposed by the rifle of Yankee adventurers, end in the same results, absolutism and tyranny." It seemed to many foreign statesmen that the Americans were as strong as they had any need to be, that further expansion would endanger the world, and that the way to prevent such expansion was to block America from taking Mexico.

This was clearly the view of Napoleon III. As early as 1859, urged by ill-informed Mexican exiles, he was dreaming of establishing a monarchy next door to the United States, under the protection of French arms. He could take no steps while France was deep in the war of Italian liberation; but the longer he waited the better the excuses which Mexico offered for intervention. Soon she could pay neither her foreign debts nor the indemnities for outrages against foreign citizens.

In the autumn of 1861, France, England, and Spain decided to intervene and collect their money. England insisted that the United States be asked to join; but the United States refused. Early in 1862, when the magnitude of French ambitions became clear, the Spanish troops and the seven hundred English marines were withdrawn. Napoleon—alone at last with his dream—still seemed to believe that a monarchy would be popular in Mexico. He reinforced his armies, and in the summer of 1863 captured Mexico City. He then offered the crown and the title of Emperor to the unfortunate Maximilian, younger brother of Francis Joseph of Austria.

After much thought, and the rejection of much good advice, Maximilian accepted the throne. In May, 1864, he landed at Vera Cruz on a daring, improbable adventure. He was dependent on the support of French arms; but the French people deplored their Mexican policy. The United States was biding its time to make trouble. Sooner or later Napoleon must withdraw; and the Mexicans, who took an unrivaled pleasure in killing their own rulers, could scarcely be expected to refrain from killing foreign ones.

In the summer of 1865—with the Civil War won—General Grant suggested sending an army against Maximilian. Seward restrained him, knowing that the French who opposed Napoleon's policy might turn to his support if their pride was roused. Steady diplomatic pressure, he said, combined with growing discontent at home, must force Napoleon out. All through the summer he kept reminding the French Government that "the sympathies of the American people for the Republic of Mexico are very lively, and that they are disposed to regard with impatience the continued intervention of France in that country."[12] In January, 1866, the matter was settled. The French troops were on their way home in the autumn of that year. Maximilian refused to leave with them, so he was captured and executed by the armies of the Mexican Republic.

Thus ended two challenges to the Monroe Doctrine. The Civil War was clearly the time for European intervention in the Americas. France and Spain took advantage of their opportunity, but only half-heartedly. By the time they had both returned home, no foreign office could usefully pretend that the Monroe Doctrine was unknown. The world had heard of it, and understood that the Americans meant it, and that they had the power with which to support it. The doctrine no longer depended entirely on the British fleet, for although the United States soon reduced her armies to the size of a small police force, the world did not forget what those armies had been or what they had accomplished.

XXIII

Grant Obeys the Senators

BEFORE THE PRESIDENTIAL ELECTION of 1868, the Republicans wanted as many Southern states as possible to be reconstructed under the new plan—with the maximum of whites disqualified and with all the blacks voting. During the summer of 1867, therefore, the generals in charge of the "conquered territory" hurried to enroll new electorates, which could choose new constitutional conventions, which in turn could set up new governments. In five states there were more Negro voters than white on the lists; in one the numbers were even; and in four the whites had a majority.* The Negroes had been slaves less than three years before. The whites divided into several groups: Northerners who had moved south since the surrender; Southern Unionists from the poor districts (like Andrew Johnson's eastern Tennessee) who had no happy memories of the old order; and Southern Unionists of the professional and business classes, who had withdrawn from politics when their Whig Party disappeared and who were the only substantial, experienced, and well-thought-of citizens who were now allowed to vote. The same groups were represented at the conventions, to which only South Carolina sent a majority of Negroes.

By the summer of 1868 all but three states had been readmitted, and were presumed to be ready, under the eyes of Northern troops, to give large Republican majorities. (Texas, Mississippi, and Virginia were still in limbo. And Georgia was soon to be cast out once more, when she refused to allow the Negro members of her legislature to take their seats.) Each of the restored states had to vote in favor of the Fourteenth Amendment, which was declared ratified on July 28.

The new constitutions, written by the "black-and-tan" conventions, were on the whole good. In most cases they provided for a more democratic government than of old, for free-school systems, property rights for women, tax reforms, state charitable institutions, and the abolition of imprisonment for debt. A high tribute to these constitutions is the fact that they were not abolished when the last Northern troops were withdrawn in 1877 and Southern whites were once more in undisputed control.

---

* There were eleven states in the Confederacy; but Tennessee is omitted from the present discussion because Tennessee was allowed back in the Union—after ratifying the Fourteenth Amendment—in 1866.

The same is true of many laws passed during the years of so-called "black Reconstruction."

Even the extravagance of the Negro governments had its useful side. Reconstruction would in any case have been expensive, and state bonds would in any case have had to be floated in the North at ruinous discounts. But the spending was so wild, and fraud so open, that when Southern white men regained control they felt justified in repudiating most of the obligations. More than a hundred and twenty-five million dollars of debt was shrugged off in this fashion.

It is not the deeds or plans of the "black Reconstruction" which should be deplored, but the aftermath. And this is less the fault of the men who sat in the conventions and legislatures than of the members of Congress who put them there. The American political system has not yet recovered from that act of malicious folly. If we would understand some of the system's eccentricities, we must remember how the Congressional radicals forced the South into that one-party mold which is only now beginning to show the first faint signs of breaking.

Under the Lincoln-Johnson Reconstruction, party lines in the South followed their pre-war pattern. Old-fashioned Unionists—mostly Whigs who had voted for Bell and Everett in 1860—formed the most important group of white men whose loyalty was accepted by the two Presidents. In 1866 a "Conservative Union Party" was emerging, and would undoubtedly have joined with the party of Lincoln if Lincoln had lived. Deprived of most of their old leaders, blamed for secession, war, and failure, the Democrats were by no means the dominant party. Yet the strong efforts of the Republicans to build a Southern organization in 1865 and 1866 failed—chiefly because of the threats and abuse poured forth by the radicals in Congress. No Southern white man who did not hate his neighbors could be expected to ally himself with a group which gave power to Thaddeus Stevens. There was, however, a fair number of "radicals" in the South, in 1866, who wished to move quickly toward Negro suffrage and toward true economic freedom for the ex-slaves. These might have been the wisest, most helpful friends of the Negro. They were a minority, but they were respected. They were not yet associated with the Northern radicals.

After the Reconstruction Acts of March, 1867, and the complete destruction of the President's power and prestige, all this changed. Agents of the Freedmen's Bureau and the Union Leagues took charge of the enfranchised Negroes and hurried them into the Republican Party, which at once became thoroughly organized throughout the South. Many Southern radicals followed the freedmen, thus destroying their influence for good among their white neighbors. A Southern organization for bringing the Negro to full citizenship was permissible, and respectable, and might have done much good. But white Southerners in the party of Stevens and Ben Butler could only add to the bitterness of life. So long as the Butlers set the tone of Reconstruction, affiliation with Republicans was taken as proof that the purpose was not to raise the Negro but to degrade the white.

In any case, after the Congressional elections of 1866—after the triumph of the radicals and the quick destruction of Johnson—there was no national Union Party which the Conservative Unionists of the South could join. There were only the Republicans, who were preparing to rule the South by means of the Negro, and the Democrats, who naturally became more friendly each time the radicals became more ferocious. So the remaining Southern Whigs, who had withdrawn from public life rather than join the Democratic Party, were left with nowhere else to go. By the end of the Reconstruction era the whole South had been forced into that party—except the Negroes, the carpetbaggers (good and bad), a few poor whites who had been too much oppressed, a few rascals who hoped to hold office long enough to profit from plunder, and some of the pro-Negro Southern radicals who ought to have been helping the freedman instead of ruining him. Not only had the entire respectable white South been forced into a single party, but that party had been forced into a mood of strong reaction. Many years were to pass before an idea which might be described as "radical" would receive fair treatment in the South, or before the white electorate was ready to distinguish between treating the Negro like a citizen and insisting that the Negro dominate.

The more one understands that on the whole the Negro in his sudden brief responsibility did well, and that among the discredited whites who worked with him were honest humanitarians who might have helped him if wisely guided, the more heartbreaking becomes the treatment of the Negro by the radicals. He was never given a chance. Innocent, ignorant, propertyless and hence subject to economic blackmail, abandoned by the best men North and South and corrupted by the worst, an ugly future was ensured for him by the Congressmen who took orders from Thaddeus Stevens, and after the death of Stevens in 1868 from Benjamin Butler of Massachusetts, who according to Lincoln was "as full of poisoned gas as a dead dog."

It was wicked to force the Negro to rule the disfranchised white man, when everyone knew the positions would be reversed as soon as Northerners grew sick of governing their fellow Americans with the sword. It was wicked to turn the Negro free without property, without security, without education, without a thought for his future except that he must be bought or bullied into voting Republican. It was extra wicked to commit both these cruelties at the same time. No one who wishes to understand politics should be easily alarmed at human iniquity; but there is a limit beyond which only mad moralists and the truly corrupt will go. It was the fate of the Negro, at the hour of his deliverance, to be sacrificed to an alliance between those two. He didn't want to run the South. He wanted to learn how to read, so that the long-forbidden magic of books might be open to him—especially the Bible, whose store of lamentations had already inspired him to a new literature of song.* And he wanted a few acres of land, with laws to protect his ownership until he had learned to look after himself. But his Northern friends wanted to prove their political theories, or they simply wanted his vote. The moralists thought he could eat freedom, and live in it, and cover himself with it against the cold, and against unkindness. And the others didn't think at all, beyond the next election. But of course he gave them his vote, since they asked for it. And the white South has not forgiven him in eighty years. He still remains the freedman who was never set free. His own hymns are the best words to do justice to such misfortune:

> Nobody knows the trouble I've seen;

or,

> Go down, Moses,
> Way down in Egypt land.
> Tell old Pharaoh
> To let my people go;

or the simple cry for deliverance,

> Swing low, sweet chariot,
> Coming for to carry me home.

2

Republicans and Democrats would have been equally glad to appropriate Grant in 1868. In so far as he had been anything during his curious past, he seems to have been a Democrat. He had voted against the Republicans in 1856 on the excellent grounds that he knew Frémont. In 1860 he did not vote, and in 1864 he supported the Union Party of Lincoln and Johnson. The fact that McClellan's platform condemned the war was probably enough to turn Grant against the Democratic Party. In January, 1868, he had an unpleasant public disagreement with President Johnson, and immediately the radical Republicans courted him and flattered him. They

---

* Booker T. Washington, who had been a slave, wrote (*Up From Slavery*, pp. 29–30): "Few people who were not right in the midst of the scenes can form any exact idea of the intense desire which the people of my race showed for an education. . . . It was a whole race trying to go to school. Few were too young, and none too old, to make the attempt to learn. . . . The great ambition of the older people was to try to learn to read the Bible before they died."

soon had him lobbying for them, seeking to persuade Senators to vote for Johnson's guilt. So when the Republican Convention met at Chicago in May, Grant was nominated on the first ballot. Ben Wade, who was to be deprived of the interim presidency by the Senate's refusal to convict Johnson, was denied the vice-presidential nomination. He led for four ballots; but the prize was then given to Schuyler Colfax of Indiana, Speaker of the House of Representatives. The extreme radicals were still powerful in Congress and were still allowed to torment the South; but the new rich Eastern lords of the party viewed them with some alarm. The men of business naturally preferred Colfax, whose only shortcoming was a tendency to acquire money in unusual ways.

The platform showed how thoroughly the party was being remade to meet the issues of a new day. There was little continuity either in doctrine or in members. Professor Binkley points out that among thirty-four Republican leaders in the House and Senate at this time, nineteen had once been Democrats and only fifteen were former Whigs.[1] The post-war party was to be radical in Reconstruction, generous in favors to industry, and conservative in matters of finance. Nothing was said in the platform about the tariff, for fear of annoying the farmers who did not need protection; but the silence meant that there would at least be no lowering of the rates. Reconstruction was to go forward on extreme radical lines; immigration was to be encouraged so that the price of labor might not too quickly rise to meet the price of protected commodities; and the party pledged itself to "hard money," and against the plan to pay off government bonds in irredeemable notes. Yet this plan, known as the "Ohio Idea," was so popular in the Middle West that Republicans throughout that region ignored the platform.

Here was the first sign since the war of the cheap-money problem which was to trouble the country for fifty years. Rural America—especially western and southern America—had not the capital to finance the vast expansion and the vast reconstruction which engrossed the post-war generation. The money came largely from the East, or from Europe. And the debtors —burdened at best, and crippled in bad times—did not want to pay their debts in money which was more valuable than the money they had borrowed. All nations face this problem; but very large nations face it in an acute form. For if an entire region becomes a debtor, it will probably become a colonial economy as well—especially if the lending region is the chief industrial center and has the power to impose tariffs, subsidies, and a money-system favorable to its own interests. From the days of John Taylor and the "Old Republicans," this is what the South feared. And this is what came to pass with overwhelming finality during the Civil War and the Reconstruction. In fact, Reconstruction was only a new type of war in which the South faced heavier odds than in the war of blood and iron. The stakes of Reconstruction were the economic rules and devices which Northern business and finance had fixed upon the country while other men were fighting.

If conservative support was withdrawn from the radicals, and the Democratic Party allowed back to power, tariffs would be lowered, land grants to railways diminished or abolished, and the policy of deflation reversed. The South must have known that she was abandoning Washington to the capitalists when she went to war and withdrew her agrarian Senators and Representatives. Those that take the sword have often perished by the sword, so perhaps the white South had no just ground for complaint. But the black South might complain at having its future debauched for the sake of an economic system pleasing to Northern business. And the West (still largely rural), which had helped to win the war, might complain at being subjected to the same colonial status as the South. In fact, the West did complain. Its loud reproaches are a major note in politics from Grant to Franklin Roosevelt.

Before turning to the cheap-money problem in the form it assumed in 1868, we should remind ourselves that the troubles of the South and West were genuine. They varied from the annoying to the desperate—the former in times of relative well-being, the latter in times of crisis. In 1938, describing the entire period from the Civil War to President Hoover, Professor Donald Davidson wrote:

> Does the northeasterner exclaim in horror at the spectacle of southern lands eroded and worn-out, at the devilish one-crop system and the tenant system, at the burned and cut-over mountain slopes, the illiterate and diseased population, the fierce despair or the terrifying apathy of large districts, rural and urban? Let him never think that these sins against good order were always wilfully committed or arose from human sloth and malignity alone. The ravaged lands of the South are, rather, a mute testimony, indeed a fearful accusation, against a distant tyranny of money—which the South did not have and was forced to try to gain. . . . The southern planter or farmer (and not the southern one only!) gullied and exhausted his lands, sold his timber, held his tenants pinned with a dollar mark, not because he was a limb of Satan but because money had to be forthcoming. . . . The old outcry against Wall Street is an outcry against a regional foe symbolized by a single institution. It means that the towers of New York are built upon southern and western backs.[2]

The facts to support this indictment have been collected by Professor Walter Prescott Webb. He points out that at the end of the Civil War the South was kept quiet by force, the West was kept quiet by free land, and the North reveled in the privileges it had long desired: a high tariff, internal improvements (that is, railroads) at national expense, abundant immigrant labor, and a banking system which helped to centralize the money power.* Quoting Charles Sumner, Professor Webb says that in Reconstruction days the South was *tabula rasa,* a clean slate whereon a Congress of Northern men might write what it chose.

> At the end of the War [he adds] the West was also *tabula rasa,* not because it had been conquered, but because it had not been developed. It remained primitive, occupied by wild Indians, buffalo and a few traders; for not yet had the cowboys come swinging their ropes on their "paint" horses from Texas. The West was still *territory,* and as such was subject to Congress, composed of and controlled by men from the North. Like the South, it, too, was a clean slate.[3]

These "clean slates" were a prize worth seizing. Between them they contained the most valuable natural resources that mankind had yet uncovered. To develop the resources fast, outside capital was needed. America was in a mood for speed and sudden wealth, so it is doubtful whether the natives of the South and West would have protested at being financed from "Wall Street" even if they had been given the chance. But in any case the West had too few people to protest, and the South was held down by Reconstruction; so absentee capital and ownership became the rule. In the lively image of a modern writer, the natives of these areas resemble the runt pig in the litter, which gets only the hind tit.

There was a post-war recession, or small depression, in 1868, which led as usual to an agrarian demand for inflation. Since the Republican Convention said "No," the Democrats who met six weeks later in New York felt they should say "Yes," at least in their platform. Undismayed by their long championship of "hard money" (since the days of Jackson, Benton, and the Locofocos), they turned to the "Ohio idea" which had been popularized by "Gentleman George" Pendleton of Cincinnati. The idea was a simple one. During the war the federal government had printed about $450,000,000 of fiat money, known as "greenbacks." It also issued a number of United States bonds which were redeemable after five, and payable after twenty, years. These bonds carried no specific promise of redemption in gold, so Pendleton and his friends urged that they be redeemed at once with new greenbacks. Like the original greenbacks, these should be legal tender for all debts public and private within the United States except import duties. The proposal had a double charm to its backers: it was inflationary, and it would retire a tax-free investment on which the "money power" was receiving interest in gold. And behind this plan lay the more widespread "greenback movement," which long outlived the

* The North, as Professor Webb uses the word, means the war-time Union north of the Ohio River and excluding the West coast; the South means the Confederacy, including eastern Texas; the West means the region from the Great Plains to the Pacific.

"Ohio idea." This movement welcomed the fact that depreciated green-backs had been the standard of value since they were first issued in 1862, and opposed all plans either to reduce them in number or to appreciate them by resuming specie payments for all paper money.

The Democratic Convention, meeting at Tammany Hall in New York, adopted the "Ohio idea" and attacked the Republicans for their conduct of Reconstruction.

> After the most solemn and unanimous pledge of both Houses of Congress [said the platform] to prosecute the war exclusively for the maintenance of the government and the preservation of the Union under the Constitution, it has repeatedly violated that most sacred pledge, under which alone was rallied that noble volunteer army which carried our flag to victory.
> Instead of restoring the Union, it has, so far as in its power, dissolved it, and subjected ten states, in time of profound peace, to military despotism and Negro supremacy.

Something might have been made of the Reconstruction issue, but only under the leadership of a man willing to campaign on the charge that the Republicans, who claimed to have saved the Union, were in fact dividing it. This was risky doctrine, and the more cautious leaders were probably wise in thinking that the less said about the war and its results the better. In that case cheap money would seem to be their chance, with "Gentleman George" playing the rôle of an early and uninflammatory Bryan. But the money question, as we shall see again and again, was so sectional in its appeal that it divided the parties against themselves rather than against each other. The Republican platform, for example, favored sound money; yet the Republican state machines in the Northwest and Middle West let it be known that they were really for the "Ohio idea." Similarly, the Democratic platform favored inflation; yet in order not to throw away the votes of the populous Northeast the Democrats nominated for the presidency ex-Governor Horatio Seymour of New York, who not only opposed the "idea" but repudiated that part of the platform.

In spite of this battle among themselves the Democrats might have done well if they had not given the Republicans too many excuses for "waving the bloody shirt."* First, the convention at New York City was attended by two of the Confederacy's most famous cavalry generals (Nathan Bedford Forrest and Wade Hampton) and by Robert Barnwell Rhett, "the father of secession." This may have shown a Christian spirit; but it did not show political brains, especially since the convention was to condemn Negro suffrage. Second, the candidate for the vice-presidency was Francis Preston Blair, Jr., the youngest son of Andrew Jackson's Blair, who had

* This phrase, which appears to have been imported from Scotland, refers to all furious oratory designed to revive the hatreds and bitterness of the Civil War.

served brilliantly both as a Congressman and as a Union major general with Sherman's armies. In a famous letter to a friend who had helped him save Missouri for the Union, Blair attacked the program of the radicals as both disastrous and wicked, adding that the people must elect a President who would declare the acts of the Congress null and void, "compel the army to undo its usurpations at the South, disperse the carpetbag state governments, allow the white people to reorganize their own governments and elect senators and representatives." But the presidential nominee did not care to press this issue, and such strong views from a mere vice-presidential candidate allowed the Republicans to suggest conspiracy. "If you want another Civil War," wrote the New York *Tribune,* "vote the Blair ticket."

With Blair, Forrest, Wade Hampton, and Barnwell Rhett to shoot at, and with a lively desire to avoid stressing the money question for fear of losing the Middle West and Northwest, the Republicans concentrated on appeals to war-born hatreds, to patriotism, to gratitude toward "the party that saved the Union," and to the fear of losing not only office but all the recent bonanzas such as tariffs and land grants in case "black Reconstruction" was undone. They had a very strong case—so strong that it is surprising how nearly they lost.

There was nothing about Horatio Seymour to excite the country or add to Republican fears. He was a conservative lawyer who lived at Utica, New York, and had long refused to take part in federal politics because he thought both the opponents and the defenders of slavery were too extreme. Under the expert guidance of William L. Marcy, however, he learned the methods of the Albany Regency and became a useful compromiser and appeaser in the Democratic feuds which wracked the state. In 1852 he was elected governor of New York, serving only one term; but in the midst of the Civil War he was elected again. He became the leader of the opposition to Lincoln's assumption of emergency powers, and to the Emancipation Proclamation. In 1868 he did not want the nomination, and his campaign suggests that he did not particularly want the presidency. Yet he was very nearly given it.

The vote was 3,012,833 for Grant, 2,709,249 for Seymour. In the electoral college the vote was 214 for Grant, 80 for Seymour. Grant received 700,000 Negro votes; yet his popular majority was only 300,000. Forty-one of his 214 electoral votes came from states in the late Confederacy. Six of those states were controlled by troops and by oppressive laws: few Democrats could vote, but all Republicans. Three other Southern states (where radical rule was not yet established) were still excluded from the Union. So Seymour might have come close to a popular majority (although he would have lost the election in any case) if the South had been running its own affairs.[4] In view of the confused, self-contradicting Democratic campaign, and the emotional and economic appeal of the Republican arguments, this disappointing result suggests that the Grand Old Party, "the party of patriotism," was not yet firmly founded. With the use of force, intimidation, and every available Negro, the Republicans had elected Grant, a conquering hero. What would happen when they lost their black allies? They could not keep troops in the South forever; and even in the North, Republican states were relapsing from the strict radical creed on race relations. Absurdly, at the height of the "black Reconstruction," Ohio, Michigan, Minnesota, and Kansas had refused to extend the suffrage to the Negro. If this trend continued, where were the votes of gratitude to be garnered in the future?

Such thoughts led to the Fifteenth Amendment, which was proposed by Congress to the state legislatures in February, 1869. "The rights of citizens of the United States to vote," says the amendment, "shall not be denied or abridged by any state on account of race, color, or previous condition of servitude." This was not what the radicals would have chosen, for it did not confer the vote finally and forever on the Negro; but it was the best they could get. Even the Northern states objected to federal interference with suffrage laws, and the Constitution did not provide for amendments which would only affect the South. In this negative form the amendment was useless. Like the other devices for securing the black man's rights, it was soon nullified.

3

On the day Grant became President, the American people watched and waited almost with a sense of awe. After Lincoln, here was the greatest man the North had discovered during the war: strong, stubborn, quiet, and of pure integrity. The country believed that the wrangles of the Johnson régime would be succeeded by order and firmness within the Republican Party, by order and firmness and kindness in dealing with the South, by smoothness and speed in cleaning up the débris of long years of fighting, and above all by "reform." The nation was in a mood for more seemly government, aware that the public finances were chaotic, the tariff a scandal of special privilege, and the civil service inefficient even by the modest standards of American politics. All this, men thought, would be put right by an honest President who could not be frightened and who knew how to insist on his own way. Seldom has there been such a "tidal wave of expectation," as Henry Adams described it, and never has a wave withdrawn more rapidly, or left behind a sorrier detritus: *le souvenir cuisant de son limon amer.*

In a sense, the disappointment was the people's own fault. Grant possessed all the qualities that were ascribed to him, and upon which so many hopes were built; but the qualities were pathetically insufficient for his new job. Once and for all, in the harshest and most expensive school, the United States was to be taught that a good President must be a good politician, that politics is a subtle and difficult profession, and that one way to unfit a man for the profession is to train him to be a soldier. General Washington was not really an exception, for he had rather less military training than many civilians in the modern world. General Jackson was not really an exception, for he was a leader of frontier militia, which means simply a leader of men; and in the White House he surrounded himself with a band of sensitive politicians. They taught the aging autocrat what the people wanted, and he taught the "Kitchen Cabinet" how to use the presidency to accomplish the people's will. But poor muddled Grant did not even know what a President was intended to do, and if he had known he could not have done it. Both by training and temperament he was doomed to be the dupe of special interests, and of the trickiest men in Congress. He never could take advice. He never could regard even the smallest opposition from his supporters as anything but treason—as if an officer in the midst of battle had begun to query his orders. He never could understand the nature of political pressures. He never could believe that a corrupt and faithless man might meet him smilingly and betray him with praise. He suspected his real friends because they argued with him; he trusted his enemies because they told him he was right. Few men have been more easily disarmed by flattery.

The first decisive act of a new President is the choice of his Cabinet. As we have seen many times, this is a delicate task, requiring expert knowledge of the rivalries (and of the relative weight of opposing factions) in the state machines. Grant had no such knowledge; but he had a store of good will upon which he could have drawn if he had been willing to ask for help. He consulted nobody—in many cases not even the people he intended to name. The result was a list of appointments which at once told the Congress all it wished to know (and more than it had dared to hope) about Grant's incapacity to govern. No man who could select such a Cabinet could build a strong Administration, or uphold the national interest against the scuffling of class lobbies and local machines. Congress relaxed, happy in the knowledge that it would not have to conquer a popular President before continuing its own wayward rule.

There was nothing bad about Grant's selections, except that they did not compose a political Cabinet at all. They were merely a group of friends and benefactors whom he was pleased to reward. There were men of ability on the strange list, which was given to a startled country two days after the inauguration. And there were no downright rascals. Later, with more experience, Grant was to do much worse, and to appoint men who were both incompetent and deeply corrupt; but never again would he alarm his friends so thoroughly as with this first revealing deed.

The President's choice for Secretary of the Treasury, Alexander Stewart of New York, was a sample of his political folly. Stewart was a native of Northern Ireland who had settled in America at the age of twenty and become the owner of the largest retail store in the world. Very rich, very charitable, and very niggardly with his employees, Stewart had contributed heavily to Grant's campaign expenses and to a fund for buying Grant a house. There is no reason to think he would have been a good Secretary of the Treasury, and he could bring no political strength or experience to the Administration; but he would have been honest and able. Unfortunately, he was ineligible. The law of 1789 which created the Treasury Department forbade a man engaged in business from holding the post of Secretary.

When Grant was told of the law he asked Congress to repeal the section disqualifying Stewart. Congress refused, precipitating the first disaster of the Administration—for the low politicians wanted George S. Boutwell at the Treasury. An extreme radical, a bitter enemy of the South, and either dishonest or stupid to the point of disgrace, he could be counted on to forward their plans. While Grant was confused at the loss of Stewart, the spoilsmen closed on him and flattered him into appointing their man. Within a few months Boutwell of Massachusetts, who had taken a leading part in the impeachment of Andrew Johnson, allowed the Treasury and the dazed President to be caught in the "Black Friday" shame, of which Henry Adams wrote: "The worst scandals of the eighteenth century were relatively harmless by the side of this, which smirched executives, judiciary, banks, corporate systems, professions, and people, all the great active forces of society, in one dirty cesspool of vulgar corruption."[5]

Grant was more fortunate in his second thoughts on the Department of State. He began by nominating an old friend who had helped him to his first command in the Civil War, and who only wanted the appointment for a few days. Then, after some wavering and crossed purposes, he settled on Hamilton Fish of Garrison, New York, a man who revived in his own person the golden youth of the Republic. Learned, urbane, aristocratic, with a mind of excellent shrewdness, he remained as Secretary of State to the end of Grant's two terms. To a Cabinet which was forever changing, and usually for the worse, he gave continuity. To a party which seemed bent on throwing away the gratitude of a nation, he gave unfalteringly wise advice on domestic as well as foreign affairs, and the priceless asset of success in at least one field. He brought no political strength at the time of his appointment; but before his long term was out the weight of character and of disciplined mind had earned him authority to reach outside his own department, and sometimes to save the Administration from mistakes even more gross than those which were committed.

The question has been raised how such a man could endure such surroundings. The answer lies in the splendor of the hopes which inspired his foreign policy. The relations between the United States and England were dangerously bad when he came to office, and they were degenerating under the influence of plans for the acquisition of Canada, cherished by the chairman of the Foreign Relations Committee of the Senate, Charles Sumner. Eight years later the relations between the United States and England were based firmly on good sense and good deeds, cemented by the most successful and delicate arbitration of modern history.

> All men have their ideals [writes Allan Nevins] whereby we judge them. Zach Chandler had seen the vision of 200,000 American veterans marching into Montreal. To Sumner had come a vision of his statue rising above the St. Lawrence, the architect of Manifest Destiny and the grand reviser of international law. The simple, unimaginative gentleman from Garrison had formed a simple, unimaginative ideal, devoid of martial pomp, personal vanity, or nationalistic glory: the ideal of not two but three great kindred democracies at peace, their differences justly settled, their paths stretching side by side into the remotest future.[6]

In such a cause a good man could bring himself to breathe the air of Grant's Washington, and thus to purify it somewhat, for the influence of one such man passes understanding.

4

Long before the presence of Hamilton Fish could make itself felt, the worst of the Congressmen had begun to take over the Administration. Grant was just what they wanted: an incompetent popular hero. For a time at least, the magic of his name would disinfect their crimes, while the abundance of his ignorance would ensure that the crimes went unchallenged.

Even if Grant had known the forces which surrounded him, and the laws to which those forces moved, he would have been vulnerable to pressures from Congress for two reasons. First, he had been trapped by the radicals into lobbying for their cause against Andrew Johnson, thus weakening himself as a representative of the nation against their local greeds and fanaticisms. Second, in so far as he had any political ideas, he seems to have accepted the old Whig doctrine of the supremacy of the legislature in making policy. The moderate and sensible Senator John Sherman of Ohio, younger brother of the Union general, put the doctrine succinctly: "The executive department of a government like ours should be subordinate to the legislative department. The President should obey and enforce the laws, leaving to the people the duty of correcting any errors committed by their representatives in Congress."[7] This is as misleading as some of Jefferson's remarks on the same subject; but Sherman meant what he said, whereas Jefferson did not. Jefferson was never content to recommend a policy, and then to wait for Congress in its wisdom to decide. He knew that "the people" were helpless to correct "any errors committed by their representatives in Congress," unless they could speak with the voice of the President—or of the national party for which the President is spokesman. Otherwise they had no voice at all, as a nation. They had only the many voices of their local communities. And if the people of Kansas and Nebraska and Iowa were outraged by the dominating voice of Pennsylvania and New York, they had nowhere to turn except toward the White House, or toward a man whom they hoped to put in the White House.

When Victor Emmanuel opened the Piedmontese parliament on January 10, 1859, prepared at last to fight for a united nation, he said that he could no longer ignore *il grido di dolore*—the cry of pain—that came to him from all parts of Italy. This was the traditional use of monarchy. There was no one to hear that cry if the throne was unwilling. And in America there is no one to hear it when the White House is deaf. All great Presidents must carry through their four-year terms the burdens of a democratic minister and the burdens of a people's king as well. Jefferson knew this; but John Sherman and President Grant did not. They thought that out of goodness of heart Senator Cameron of Pennsylvania or Senator Conkling of New York would be moved to legislate, not in the interests of his own career or even of his own constituents, but in the interests of people who lived thousands of miles away. Or else they thought that the humble voters of the empty West or the impoverished South—the farmers and the country lawyers and the merchants at the crossroads stores—could bring as much pressure to bear upon Congress as could the lordly Senators of the Eastern plutocracy.

Representative George Frisbie Hoar of Massachusetts described the position in which Grant soon found himself.

> The most eminent senators [he wrote], Sumner, Conkling . . . Frelinghuysen, Simon Cameron . . . would have received as a personal affront a private message from the White House expressing a desire that they should adopt any course in the discharge of their legislative duties that they did not approve. If they visited the White House, it was to *give, not to receive advice.*[8]

Andrew Jackson would have ridden down these "eminent senators," to the applause of the large and decent majority who did not want a policy of ravage but who were helpless under a President incapable of "expressing a desire." Jefferson and Lincoln would have outcontrived them, destroying the few who stood to fight but bringing the rest amiably into their own camps. Washington would have been so surprised at their lack of moral accountability that he might have shocked them into grace, or at least into silence. But Grant became their false front and their tool. His best instincts, and many of his most high-minded servants, were sacrificed to these men. The tariff policy of his Administration was a sad example.

The conflict between the national interest and special local interests becomes clear in every tariff debate. Unless the President stands for the nation, no one with sufficient power will do so. When Grant became President he inherited an ill-planned, hurried, wartime tariff structure which everyone who understood the subject knew was excessive. The country was still accustomed to thinking in terms of a moderate tariff. The Middlewestern farmers, and consumers everywhere, and such important newspapers as the New York *Post* and the *Springfield Republican*, were asking for reductions. Furthermore, Grant had inherited from Lincoln's Administration the many-sided, expert and persuasive David A. Wells, Special Commissioner of Revenue. Wells's annual reports exposed with fresh lucidity the evil of the existing tariffs and their tendency to breed monopoly. Although his own views went further toward free trade than a Republican Administration could be expected to go, he was not making policy; he was exposing facts, and doing it with a combination of clarity, knowledge, and ardor which is seldom found in the field of taxation.

Grant could have earned the nation's gratitude by supporting a moderate downward revision. But Boutwell wanted an increased tariff for his friends in industry, and so did most of the "eminent senators." As a result, not only did the Act of 1870 increase many of the most indefensible rates, but the President abolished the office of Special Commissioner of Revenue, so that the intelligent and informed Wells could no longer harass the lobbyists with information. Grant thereby set the pattern for many distasteful tariffs which were to follow, not designed to meet the proper needs of industry, or to serve the national community, but to enrich small groups of men who could be counted on to repay the favor. One need not explore the merits of protection or of free trade in order to feel sure that this is no way to make laws. Yet this is the way which Congressmen choose unless a popular President, in control of the party machine, steadily insists that they lift their thoughts above the demands from the home district and consider the fate of the nation and of the world. It is not reasonable to criticize a Congressman, who is elected to represent his district, for representing it. Perhaps it is equally unwise to criticize a President, who is elected to represent the nation, for doing so. If he refuses, who else can attempt the task?

An even sorrier example of the betrayal of presidential duty was Grant's attitude toward the South. He had received many votes from the followers of Lincoln, who thought the war had been fought for the Union (and also, in the end, for the abolition of slavery), not for the animosities of Stevens and Wade and Sumner. These voters felt, like the Democrats, that they wanted peace with the South, and an end to the sordid buying of votes at the price of stored-up hatreds against the Negro. They expected Grant to be firm, and to accept no "black codes" that might restore a semi-slavery; but they also thought he meant what he said in his letter accepting the nomination for President: "Let us have peace." The big majority deplored the injection of poison into old wounds. In April, 1869, when Grant recommended to Congress that Virginia and Mississippi be allowed back into the Union on terms that would not discriminate against former rebels, the country was glad. Grant was praised, and Congress acted at once. For three months the mephitic atmosphere of Washington seemed cleaner, and the nation dreamed it could find its way back to the mood of Appomattox. Then Grant—the strong, the stubborn, the man who could do what he wanted and who held the hearts of the people—bowed to the radicals. The hopes of reconciliation and of goodness vanished.

On July 13, at a Cabinet meeting, the pressure began to descend upon the President. Cries of distress had come from the carpetbag governments which would be ousted if the South were allowed to go free, and more cries from the party machines in the North who knew the Republicans might soon lose a national election if the white South could vote. So at the meeting in July, Boutwell attacked the recent steps toward conciliation. Grant was strengthening the Democratic Party, he said, and Northern Republicans were angry. All through the summer the pressure on Grant increased. Professor Nevins points out that the good men in the Cabinet represented only themselves, with no backing from party machines, and that "the moderate press was asleep to the danger; the moderate voters were unorganized. But the Radicals attacked in battalions, and with the weight of the whole party mechanism behind them."[9]

By December, when the Congress met, the President had once more been conquered. He allowed the harshest conditions to be attached to the re-entry of Virginia, Mississippi, and Texas—and of Georgia, who had been to all intents admitted, and then expelled again when she expelled the Negro members of her legislature. Furthermore, a proclamation of general amnesty which Grant had been planning for months was now indefinitely shelved.

The national community and the national interest had been denied a voice. There was no cause for surprise that the little leaders of the state and city machines should put the success of their party before the moral health of the nation. They were busy with local jobs and local interests, neither of which seemed to require a national view. But the President was not "getting out the vote" for an alderman or a police-court magistrate; he was not seeing to it that the flow of small favors to families in the poorest districts was sufficient to engender gratitude. That useful work had to be done, and there were men to do it—ably and with enthusiasm. The President's work was also important, and there was no one else to carry it on. *Il grido di dolore*—the South cried for relief and the nation for magnanimity; but the "eminent senators" had persuaded Grant that he should leave policy to the Congress.

5

Grant was born in 1822 in an Ohio village. His father owned a tannery and a farm. During his ten years at school Grant spent his spare time working on the farm, chiefly in charge of the horses. By his own testimony he understood horses better than people, and it seems fair to add that he also liked them better. He had a distaste for killing or wounding horses which did not influence his relations with men.

When he was seventeen his father got him an appointment to the United States Military Academy, where he was undistinguished as a scholar but outstanding as an equestrian. Perhaps because of this he was assigned to an infantry regiment. Soon the Mexican War gave him a chance to practice his profession; but although he was an excellent officer he did not like the Army and he did not approve of the war. "I have never altogether forgiven myself for going into that," he wrote in his old age. "I do not think there was ever a more wicked war than that waged by the United States against Mexico. I thought so at the time, when I was a youngster, only I had not moral courage enough to resign."

The first rumors of Grant's heavy drinking date from the Mexican War. Lonely, shy, uncompanionable, moody, taking no pleasure in the work which he did well, he seemed fated to become a hard drinker. Marriage might have saved him. At the end of the war he did marry the girl to whom he had been engaged for four years; but they were soon parted once more by the demands of army life. Julia Grant gave birth to a son, and when Grant was ordered to the Pacific coast via the plague-infested Isthmus of Panama the trip seemed too dangerous for her to take. So Grant found himself in a series of desolate posts, still lonely and bored, and without even hard work to keep him busy. In 1854, having been promoted to a captaincy, he drank himself out of the Army. He borrowed money for his passage East from his classmate, Simon Buckner, whose troops he was to capture in his first great battle of the Civil War.

The next seven years were the strangest even in Grant's astonishing life. He joined his family at St. Louis, where he gave every sign of being a broken man. He tried to farm, but couldn't. He tried to sell real estate, but couldn't. He was finally given a job by his two brothers who kept a leather store in a small town in Illinois. Even as a clerk he was no good. Yet when the war came, this half-alive failure, whose mind and soul had seemed asleep for thirty-nine years, woke like the prince in a fairy tale from whom an old enchantment has been struck. Nobody knows what woke him. He did not like war. He hated armies. Years later he was to astonish Bismarck at a military review by saying, "I never went into the army without regret and never retired without pleasure." He had no political opinions, even about slavery. His wife owned two slaves, and in 1862 he wrote to his father: "I have no hobby of my own in regard to the Negro, either to effect his freedom or to continue his bondage." Perhaps it was the attack on the Union that brought Grant to life.

At first it seemed as if he had awakened too late. His request to the adjutant-general at Washington for command of a regiment went unanswered. But his friend Elihu Washburne—Republican Congressman, and a leading citizen of the town where Grant worked as a clerk—took him to the state capital and induced the governor to make him a colonel. Two months later Washburne persuaded Lincoln to make Grant a brigadier general. This is the man whom Grant in 1869 appointed Secretary of State "for a few days." If Washburne had wanted the job for a few years he would doubtless have had it; but he preferred to be Minister to France.

From the day Grant rejoined the Army his fortunes improved, though if it had not been for Lincoln this second chance would also have ended badly. In February, 1862, Grant captured Fort Henry on the Tennessee River and Fort Donelson on the Cumberland—the keys to the line guarding the enemy's supply depot at Nashville. In April he moved south through Tennessee to fight the battle of Shiloh, which almost ruined him. He knew that a large, well-led Confederate army was near, yet he allowed himself to be surprised. He was saved by lucky reinforcements and by the death in the midst of the battle of Albert Sidney Johnston, one of the great men and great generals of the South.

The losses at Shiloh were severe. The press and the politicians turned against Grant, revived the story of his heavy drinking, and raised a clamor for his removal, or for his summary dismissal from the Army. In Congress the lone voice of Washburne supported him. Alexander McClure (the Pennsylvania politician who had helped effect Lincoln's nomination in 1860 and who was a wise and cautious influence in the party) called at the White House to add his voice to the general censure. He found the President worn out, but ready as always to listen.

I appealed to Lincoln for his own sake [wrote McClure years later] to remove Grant at once, and, in giving my reasons for it, I simply voiced the admittedly overwhelming protest from the loyal people of the land against Grant's continuance in command. I could form no judgment during the conversation as to what effect my arguments had upon him beyond the fact that he was greatly distressed at this new complication. When I had said everything that could be said from my standpoint, we lapsed into silence. Lincoln remained silent for what seemed a very long time. He then gathered himself up in his chair and said in a tone of earnestness that I shall never forget: *"I can't spare this man; he fights."*[10]

Lincoln was accustomed to generals who did not fight, but who talked. "I don't know what to make of Grant," he said on another occasion; "he's such a quiet little fellow." Grant was five feet eight, and slightly stooped. He had cold blue eyes and a big jaw hidden behind a scrubby, messy, light-brown beard which went well with his scrubby, messy uniform. Lean and tough, he weighed only a hundred and forty pounds.

No wonder Lincoln found Grant inscrutable. As in his youth, he was still unsocial and retiring, uncommunicative, an enigma in mind and soul. The most devoted members of his staff did not know what he was thinking, or whether he was thinking. Years later, in Washington, Henry Adams wrote:

A single word with Grant satisfied him that, for his own good, the fewer words he risked, the better. Thus far in life he had met with but one man of the same intellectual or unintellectual type—Garibaldi. Of the two, Garibaldi seemed to him a trifle the more intellectual, but, in both, the intellect counted for nothing; only the energy counted. The type was pre-intellectual, archaic, and would have seemed so even to the cave-dwellers. Adam, according to legend, was such a man.[11]

The emphasis on energy was doubtless correct; yet if Grant's mind was primitive, it was also clear as ice when it dealt with military problems.

When the armies were struggling and dying at Shiloh, in April, 1862, Admiral Farragut was forcing the river defenses of the lower Mississippi. On May 1 New Orleans fell to the Union troops which Farragut had transported. The unhappy town was occupied and governed by Ben Butler, who for the time being was a general. This left Vicksburg—a hundred and fifty miles to the north—the last rebel stronghold on the Mississippi River. If Vicksburg were conquered the Confederacy would be cut in two. For twelve months Grant tried plan after plan against the strong defenses, but was always thrown back. Finally, with grim daring, he crossed the river, moved his army south of the town, and recrossed into enemy territory with inferior forces and no communications. Rear Ad-

miral Porter, meanwhile, had run the batteries of Vicksburg with his gunboats and transports—or Grant would have been marooned on the west
bank.

The great gamble succeeded. On July 4, 1863, Vicksburg surrendered;
"the Father of Waters again went unvexed to the sea"; Grant became a
national hero, a major general in the Regular Army, and shortly thereafter the commander of the Northern forces from the Allegheny Mountains to the Mississippi. One of the armies he inherited was being starved
into submission at Chattanooga. Grant not only freed the army, but on
November 25, at near-by Missionary Ridge and Lookout Mountain, his
troops won a victory which opened the road for Sherman toward Atlanta.

Grant was now commissioned a lieutenant general and put in command
of the armies of the United States. He made a single plan for the scattered
Union armies, and at last the war was fought with co-ordination. In May,
1864, the Army of the Potomac attacked General Lee, the Army of the
James attacked Lee's communications, and the Army of Tennessee set out
for Atlanta. Thenceforth the hammering was steady and increasingly
harsh. Slowly, Grant cut the Confederacy into pieces and kept its armies
so busy that they could not reinforce each other but were destroyed one
by one. Lee frequently outmaneuvered him and sometimes outfought him;
but after the spring of 1864 Lee never had the initiative.

When the end came, in April, 1865, Grant was at his splendid best:
chivalrous and soldierly. He had already shown, at the fall of Vicksburg,
his good temper and his pride in protecting the feelings of beaten men.
His conduct at Appomattox has become one of the legends which gives
the country strength. "He went as to his own surrender," writes Lloyd
Lewis, "dust and ashes over his mussy uniform, a private's stained overcoat
upon his back, looking, as he entered, like a Missouri farmer who had by
mistake crawled into a blouse that carried, unnoticed, three little silver
stars on its shoulders."[12] Finding Lee in full-dress uniform with shining
sword, Grant explained (not sarcastically, but simply) that he had been
too hurried to dress properly. Then he wrote out his terms: the officers to
keep their arms, the men to surrender them; all to give their paroles and
to go home, not to be disturbed so long as they honored their word. Lee
asked if the cavalrymen and artillerymen—who owned their horses—
might keep them. Grant said he would "let all the men who claim to own
a horse or mule take the animals home with them." "This will have the
best possible effect upon the men," said Lee. The Union rations were then
shared with the Confederate troops and the brave part of the war was
ended.

6

It is good to recall at least these outlines of the years of Grant's greatness, lest too much injustice be done by concentrating on the years of his failure. After Appomattox the fire which had burned so bright, so briefly, began smoldering again. The enchanted prince went back to sleep. He was replaced by the man who had been unable, before the war, to hold the humblest job except by nepotism. The Grant of the Civil War did not reappear until as an old man he sat down to write his *Memoirs* while dying of cancer. His son had become involved with a scoundrel and had started a banking and brokerage firm to which he had persuaded the General to lend his name. The firm failed for sixteen and a half million dollars. Ferdinand Ward, the partner, was sent to prison for ten years. Grant lost everything he owned, and everything his family owned, and the savings of many old soldiers who had invested in the glory of his legend. "I have made it the rule of my life," he said pathetically, "to trust a man long after other people gave him up; but I don't see how I can trust any human being again."

Destitute in his old age as he had been in his youth, Grant was told to his surprise that he could make money for his family by writing an autobiography. Tormented by pain from cancer in the throat, miserable in his disillusion, he suddenly revived the old magic of energy and of clear thought. Almost five sixths of the *Memoirs* are devoted to the Civil War. Nobody, reading them, can believe there was anything accidental about Grant's success. The accident, the inexplicable accident, is the magnitude of his many failures. To some of these we must now return.

XXIV

"Grantism" and Congressional Policy-Making

THE FRAUDS and thefts of the Grant era have been described so often
that there is no need to review the details. Yet the major scandals must be
mentioned, for they help us to understand a breakdown in government
which came close to discrediting American institutions.

We have already mentioned "Black Friday," a disaster which Boutwell
permitted to smirch the Administration in the autumn of its first year.
The Friday was the twenty-fourth of September, 1869; it marked the
climax of an effort by Jay Gould and James Fisk, Jr.—the most unseemly
of the New York money-men—to corner the ready supply of gold in the
United States. Gold, as a currency, had been almost driven out of circulation by the depreciated greenbacks; but there was trade in gold on the
New York Exchange, since it was needed by businessmen for their dealings
abroad. The New York banks held only $14,000,000 in gold. A corner in
the commodity seemed easy, if the United States Treasury would refrain
from interfering. So Grant's brother-in-law, who was part of the plot, introduced the New York gamblers to the President.

Perhaps because of his unhappy past, the mere sight of a very rich man
was a pleasant experience for Grant. Gould and Fisk were intolerable,
even to the unexacting society of New York; but Grant enjoyed their
company. In June, 1869, he was entertained by these rococo knaves on
one of Fisk's steamboats. He showed no resentment—although he did not
answer—when they tried to learn from him the future gold policy of the
United States Government. In the same month, Gould persuaded the
President to appoint Daniel Butterfield—an old friend of the financier's,
but a man with no qualifications whatever—to the assistant-treasuryship,
in charge of the New York sub-treasury. Confident that Butterfield would
stay with them to the end, reassured by the President's mildness when they
sought to extract government secrets, and doubtless still more reassured by
the wide incompetence of Boutwell, the conspirators went ahead. It seems
incredible that they should have tried to corner gold without definite as-
surances from the Treasury, which could of course break them at an hour's
notice. It is now clear that the only government official they had bought
was the unhappy Butterfield, who could not make policy, though he might
briefly delay its execution. They must have assumed that the President

485

and the Secretary of the Treasury were too fuddled or too stupid to understand what was happening. To the alarm of the nation, they were very
nearly right.

On September 2, Gould began buying gold. On the fifteenth Fisk joined
in with heavy purchases. By the twenty-third they had lifted the price
from 134 to 144.

> Bankers' bills . . . were offered without takers at 105½; merchants'
> bills were unsaleable at any price. This meant that the foreign trade of
> the nation had come to a dead stop; that commodities offered for ex-
> port could not be sold; that goods ready for shipment could not be
> shipped; that vessels half-laden received no more cargo; that clerks,
> warehousemen, stevedores, sailors, and the rest of the great army em-
> ployed in our export trade were being thrown into idleness.[1]

Meanwhile, ten days before matters had reached this stage, Greeley's
New York *Tribune* foretold the plan and called on Boutwell to intervene,
adding that it was the duty of the Treasury to sell gold and break the plot.
Boutwell visited New York and discovered that the *Tribune* was right in
its facts. He felt, however, that it was the "duty" of the Treasury to keep
hands off; so he went back to Washington, leaving the nation at the
mercy of the two millionaires. By Friday, the twenty-fourth, they had
driven gold to 160. Hundreds were ruined, thousands grievously hurt, and
in every trading community across the world the livelihood and security
of harmless men was damaged.

At last Grant and Boutwell acted. The Treasury telegraphed an order
to sell four million dollars of gold, and within a few minutes the price was
back to 135. Butterfield may have warned Gould, who sold in time. Fisk
was caught, but repudiated his contracts. Nothing could lower his reputation or that of his friends; but the renown of the President of the United
States was grievously hurt.

The next scandal concerned the greatest engineering feat in American
history: the building of the first transcontinental railroad. Work had
begun in 1864, under two companies: the Central Pacific working east
from Sacramento and the Union Pacific working west from Omaha. In
1869 the roads met at Promontory Point, 53 miles west of Ogden. The
Union Pacific had built 1086 miles of track—hastily graded and ill-bal-
lasted as compared with the Central Pacific, but still workable. The continent had been bound together with steel and the nation was proud—until
it discovered how the Union Pacific had been financed.

The federal government had given the railroad 13,900,000 acres of land
along its right of way (an area more than two and a half times the size of
Massachusetts), and had loaned it $27,000,000 in addition. This loan, plus
the sale of first-mortgage bonds, provided the company with more than

enough to pay for the whole construction; but men were avid gamblers in those days and such conventional financing did not satisfy them. The promoters of the Union Pacific bought a Pennsylvania corporation which had a charter permitting it to do almost anything, changed its name to the Crédit Mobilier, and made a contract with themselves to build the Union Pacific at a price that allowed them a notable profit. This might have caused no comment, and no investigations, except that a government loan was involved. Even so, the company felt safe, for one of its chief officers was Oakes Ames of Massachusetts, a member of the House of Representatives. When Congress began to criticize, Ames took 343 shares of Crédit Mobilier stock and sought to divide them among Senators and Representatives. He sold the stock at par value, although it was worth twice as much. If a favored Congressman was short of money, he was told he could pay out of dividends—an accurate statement, since in the year 1868 the dividends came to 805 per cent. Only 60 per cent was in cash, the rest in Union Pacific stock and first-mortgage bonds.

In January, 1868, Ames wrote to his associates, "I don't fear any investigation here. I have used this [the shares] where it will produce most good to us, I think." And later he added, "I have found there is no difficulty in inducing men to look after their own property." He was probably right. Congress would probably have remained quiet. But a quarrel among the promoters, and an attempt at blackmail, ended in a leak to the press. By that time the company had wound up its affairs, with a profit of $23,000,-000 on an investment of about a million. The results of the belated investigations by Congress were summed up in the *Nation* in January, 1873: "Total loss, one senator; badly damaged and not serviceable to future political use, two vice-presidents and eight congressmen. The condition of Ames's reputation language is inadequate to describe." The Vice-Presidents were Schuyler Colfax, who served during Grant's first term, and Henry Wilson, who served during his second.* Colfax was the more serious casualty, for he had not only accepted the bribe, and then lied about it, but in the course of the investigation it turned out that years before, when he was Speaker of the House, he had sold his influence to a manufacturer of envelopes for the United States Post Office. The ruined Senator was unimportant; but among the damaged members of the lower House was James A. Garfield, soon to become President. The *Nation,* as often happens to the high-minded, had overestimated either the length or the severity of public censure. Yet in all conscience the damage was sufficient, for the building of one single-track railway.

The public, of course, was the final and the chief loser, for what really happened was that "the managers stripped the Union Pacific of what Congress had intended should be a permanent endowment, and placed it

* Wilson died of a stroke in 1875.

in their own pockets."[2] The public land was the basis of this endowment: the land which John Quincy Adams had thought should be used to endow education and science; the land which Jefferson and a host of followers (including the ill-fated Andrew Johnson) had thought should be used to endow democracy, by providing a basis of small property-holders on which America's freedom might rest secure. All told, between 1850 when Stephen A. Douglas's friends got the first grant for the Illinois Central and 1871 when the system was brought to an end, 131,000,000 acres of public land were given to the railways. This is an area almost the size of France.* It is not surprising that some men made money out of the railroads, or that the settlers in the Western states and territories did not regard these men as benefactors. William Allen White, who was a baby in Kansas when the Union Pacific was finished, describes the so-called years of empire-building as follows: "The West was going under the plow, but just behind the plow were flocks of evil birds of plunder—railroad promoters, political shysters, real-estate swindlers, fattening on the farmers' seed and on the worms and slugs in the new furrows."[3]

By 1874 Grant had a Secretary of the Treasury called W. A. Richardson. He proved even more bothersome than Boutwell. Congress discovered that Richardson had given a friend contracts to collect overdue internal revenue taxes at a commission of fifty per cent. The Treasury had virtually told its own collectors to leave as many taxes as possible in arrears, so that the friend might have a restful and profitable life. Worst of all, Congress proved that Richardson was acting in collusion with Benjamin Butler of Massachusetts, once a general in charge of New Orleans, now a member of the House of Representatives. The Secretary of the Treasury resigned; the Congressman was defeated for re-election; the Administration sank a little farther into the mire.

The next Secretary of the Treasury, Benjamin Bristow of Kentucky, proved disconcertingly honest, for he unearthed a long-standing scandal which involved Grant's private secretary, Brigadier General Babcock, and a number of Treasury officials. Early in Grant's first term there had developed (out of small beginnings in Johnson's days) a conspiracy between whisky-distillers and officials of the Internal Revenue Department to divide illegal abatements of taxes. By 1874 St. Louis alone was defrauding the government of $1,200,000 in revenue, and the "Ring" had spread to Milwaukee, Chicago, Indianapolis, and many other towns. This was thievery on a scale to attract important people. Unhappily, when Bristow broke the "Ring," Grant refused to believe Babcock guilty, testified in writing to that effect at Babcock's trial, and treated Bristow so coldly that he too soon resigned.** The result was to give enemies of the Administra-

---

* France contains 136,151,680 acres.

** Although the grand jury at St. Louis returned a true bill against Babcock

tion the false impression that Grant himself might have been involved.

No sooner had Brigadier General Babcock escaped jail than Grant was called upon to help Brigadier General Belknap, Secretary of War, in a similar predicament. Belknap was exposed as having accepted payments of some $6000 a year in return for an appointment to a post-tradership in Indian Territory—a total of $24,450. Hearing he was about to be impeached, Belknap rushed to the White House with his resignation—which Grant accepted! This was fortunate for the accused, because at the impeachment trial twenty-two Senators took the view that the resignation put Belknap outside their jurisdiction. The matter was dropped, Belknap pleading that his wife had done the buying and selling, although he had continued to receive the inexplicable income after her death.

The Belknap trouble had barely subsided when the President's own brother became similarly involved. Orvil Grant testified to a Congressional committee that he had asked the President for a license as an Indian trader and had been told that four traderships would soon be available. He had applied for the four separate licenses and somewhat to his surprise had received them all. He had not really wanted to trade himself, so he had placed a "partner" in each post and had appropriated a large share of the profits. He gave no time or labor to the business, and almost no money. In fact, he was receiving a good income simply because of his influence with the President. According to the *Nation,* the difference between the President and the ex-Secretary of War was "that while Belknap allowed his wife to sell traderships and apply the money to his household expenses, the President allowed his brother to sell them and keep the money himself."

"What a nasty crew to have about one!" wrote Hamilton Fish in November, 1873. "Drunken, stupid, lying, venal, brainless. Oh! that 'Somebody' were rid of such surroundings!"[4] Yet the President liked his crew, and as its nastiness was exposed he seemed chiefly annoyed at the people who dragged the facts into the light. Life would be easier to understand if men like Grant, who attract and enjoy thieves, were themselves always thievish. But it is not true. Fish, who saw the worst of Grant, and suffered him the longest, never doubted that the President was wholly honest. Years later he wrote, "I think he [Grant] was the most scrupulously truthful man I ever met."

The interesting question was how someone who was not corrupt could bear to have such people near him. But the question applies to the American public as sharply as to the President. The nation was largely to blame, even for events in Washington, because the nation gave every sign of

---

"for conspiracy to defraud the revenue," Grant's deposition at his trial secured his acquittal—but not his rehabilitation, either in the public mind or in the White House. Babcock soon retired permanently from view.

viewing the spectacle with an indulgent disgust. "Rich and poor," wrote Henry Adams, "joined in throwing contempt on their own representatives. Society laughed a vacant and meaningless derision over its own failure."[5]

Why should the sudden plague of rascality have cursed America? One answer is suggested by the fact that the plague receded after 1873, with the coming of a long and bitter depression. Some of the scandals were unearthed in later years; but most of the stealing had been done during the post-war boom. May not the explanation lie in the simple truth, mentioned long ago, that it is hard for a camel to squeeze through the eye of a needle? The nation was too much tempted by easy wealth. For the first time in American history it was possible for a great many men to make a great deal of money with very little trouble—provided they abolished all rules for the time being. Delicious incitements to greed were offered to every man who would take a vacation from morality: the joy of plundering a recent enemy in the South, the joy of stealing a virgin empire in the West, the joy of grabbing the vast quick profits of new industry in the East. As Milton remarked of the delicacies spread before the Saviour in His desert trial:

> Alas how simple, to these Cates compared,
> Was that Crude Apple that diverted Eve!

Perhaps we should not be surprised that the Americans proved frail when Satan led them to the mountaintop and repeated:

> Money brings Honour, Friends, Conquest, and Realms . . .
> Riches are mine, Fortune is in my hand;
> They whom I favour thrive in wealth amain,
> While Virtue, Valour, Wisdom sit in want.

2

As the presidential campaign of 1872 drew near, politicians agreed that in spite of the absurd Cabinet, the emerging scandals, and the growing unpopularity of his policy toward the South, Grant was the only regular Republican who could be elected. The party had not done too well even in 1868, with everything in its favor. After four years of "Grantism" the one hope was to close ranks and to pray for the Opposition to commit some vast folly. The Negro vote was for Grant, and the business and banking interests, and all the machine leaders whom he had served well and who would now return the favor. The Republican rank and file would follow the leaders, barring some unimaginably shocking exposure at the last minute.

Grant's Opposition was not merely the Democratic Party. His first term had been so squalid that many of the best Republicans had turned from him—the men who remembered the party in its early ardent days. Grant's abuse of the civil service lost him some of these party heroes, his cowardice on the tariff lost him others, his betrayal of his own generosity toward the South lost him still more. The list of the disillusioned reads like a blue book of the party founders. When they seceded, and met in convention at Cincinnati (under the name of Liberal Republicans), they were embarrassed by the numbers of their candidates for the presidency. Since the Democrats were ready to endorse whomever the Liberal Republicans chose, it is a pity that their embarrassment drove them to the most unsuitable man in the field.

The Cincinnati Convention was heterogeneous even for an American party meeting. The delegates had nothing in common except a large distaste for Grant. The platform, for example, had to please high protectionists like Horace Greeley and free traders like the discharged David A. Wells. In the end, the convention agreed on demanding civil service reform, the resumption of specie payment for all paper money, a universal amnesty for ex-Confederates, and a withdrawal of troops from the South. This was harmless if unexciting. Nobody could say the same for the choice of candidate.

The delegates passed over Charles Francis Adams, son of the sixth President and grandson of the second, a man of brains, character, and high service to the Republic. They passed over Salmon P. Chase, Chief Justice of the Supreme Court; and David Davis, Associate Justice. They passed over many others who longed for the nomination and who might have had some chance of being elected with the help of the Democrats. They chose one of the few famous Americans who must certainly lose: Horace Greeley of the New York *Tribune,* "impulsive and unpredictable, ambitious and intriguing, vain and vindictive."[6] Hamilton Fish wrote that there was no other intelligent and honest man who could make so bad a President as Greeley. Eastern business at once rallied to Grant, for in addition to his other handicaps Greeley had been a supporter of Fourier "communism," vegetarianism, spiritualism, and prohibition. He was not the man to make Wall Street feel at ease.

The Democrats were even less pleased than the men of money at the thought of Horace Greeley, who for thirty years had been the sharpest-tongued abuser of the South and of the Democratic Party. Yet they had to take him. Their chance (their duty, as many thought) was to tie themselves to the Republican revolt and build that clean, moderate Union Party which Lincoln had dreamed. So they accepted the candidate of the Liberals, and were heavily defeated. The figures were 2,834,125 votes to 3,597,132; 66 electoral votes to 286. Although Grant had been saved chiefly by the folly of the Opposition, he took the result as a vindication.

The campaign had been bitter, even for American politics. Three weeks after his defeat Greeley died, heart-broken; so not only was an election lost, and a chance to build a better party, but a good editor and a useful citizen was destroyed. No one knows why the convention made its fatal choice; for this was no dark horse: ambiguous, unknown, suave, and supposedly harmless. Greeley was one of the nation's leading characters: cranky and able and cantankerous, and no more capable of politics than of handling a clipper ship in a typhoon. The professionals knew this, and so did most of the amateurs. Yet in a burst of shared madness they combined to choose him. It was not even a gay gesture of revolt against expediency, because within half an hour the delegates were sorry. Perhaps there are no lessons to be learned from 1872, except that in politics all things are unpredictable, and that we should beware of the folklore which says that free people will find the right man in an emergency. Grant was an emergency if America ever saw one—and the people knew it, or there would have been no coalition between the Democrats and the Republican purists. Yet all the people found was Horace Greeley.

3

Six months after the election of 1872 Chief Justice Chase died. The last of the dominating figures of Lincoln's Cabinet, he had done his best work in the Supreme Court. As Chief Justice his intense ambition was almost satisfied, though even in his last years he was never free from a nagging desire to become President. He had been a Democrat, an Independent Democrat, a Republican, a Democrat again in 1868, and a Liberal Republican in 1872. Every four years since 1856 he had sought the nomination, in vain. "It seems to me," he once wrote, "that if the most cherished wish of the people could prevail, I would be nominated."[7] He never deviated from this faith.

Chief Justice Chase had succeeded Taney, who had succeeded John Marshall, who had been appointed by John Adams, the second President of the United States. The whole life of the Republic was symbolized by these three men. Where would Grant find a fourth who could be matched with them? As we have seen many times, the appointment of a Supreme Court Justice is a fateful task, for the President molds and often remakes the living Constitution through the men he appoints. All forceful Presidents, if they have been lucky enough to find vacancies, have used this power aggressively and for their own ends. Even weak Presidents like Grant have used it to meet a political demand for revising the ancient text. Any theory of American history which denies the President's duty to exert political influence upon the Supreme Court is unworthy of its majestic theme. The Opposition will describe such influence as impious and the Administration will insist it is unthinkable; but it is nevertheless essential to good government in the United States.

Fortunately for Lincoln, five vacancies occurred during his four years in office. The constitutional revolution which Lincoln brought about—in the powers of the presidency and of the central government—might have been frustrated if he had not appointed a majority of his own Court. He chose only strong nationalists, strong anti-slavery men, and (he thought) strong believers in the power of Congress to issue fiat money and to make it legal tender. If the matter came before the Court he expected his judges to support the greenbacks, to support the Emancipation Proclamation, and even more important, to support the use of emergency powers to win the war, whether strictly constitutional or not.

The Prize Cases of 1863, argued after Lincoln had made his first three appointments, showed his need for a Court which would put "the logic of facts" above the written document. As we have seen, Lincoln raised troops and began fighting without authority from Congress. And he imposed a blockade upon part of his own country—an act which presupposes war, although Lincoln insisted that no war was taking place, merely an insurrection. When Congress met in special session in July, 1861, it passed laws which were intended to legalize the state of affairs, retroactively. But what of the merchant vessels which had been captured as prizes by the Union Navy before Congress acted? The position of the government would become untenable if the Court took a narrow view of this and similar cases. There seems little doubt that the previous Court would have been hostile, since even with the help of his three new justices Lincoln won the Prize Cases by a mere five-to-four decision.

When Chief Justice Taney died Lincoln had a choice between three members of his Cabinet: Chase, Stanton, and the faithful Montgomery Blair. Blair was eliminated by the unwritten law that a President must always be kinder to his enemies than to his friends—since the former may upset the precarious balance of power by which he rules, whereas the latter can be relied upon, at least for grudging help, no matter what happens. According to George Boutwell's *Reminiscences,* Lincoln was refreshingly frank in discussing the appointment. "We wish for a Chief Justice who will sustain what has been done in regard to emancipation and the legal tenders," Boutwell quotes Lincoln as saying; "we cannot ask a man what he will do, and if we should, and he should answer us, we should despise him for it. Therefore, we must take a man whose opinions are known."[8] Whether the President said exactly this or not, he probably thought it. And if he did, Chase was clearly his man. For Chase was so firm on emancipation that long before the war he had been known as "the attorney-general of the fugitive slaves." And Chase was the Secretary of the Treasury who had issued the legal tender notes. In any case, he was appointed.

The most careful presidential foresight, however, cannot assure that a Supreme Court Justice will preserve his opinions unchanged—as Theodore Roosevelt was to learn on a famous occasion. Lincoln had done his best to choose "a man whose opinions are known"; yet they proved unknown. In 1870 Chief Justice Chase wrote the majority opinion which declared the legal-tender legislation unconstitutional! He did not question the power of the government to issue greenbacks, but only its power to make them legal tender for the payment of debts, especially for the payment of debts contracted before the fiat money was printed. The Court decided against the greenbacks by five to three; but one of the five (who was senile) resigned before the opinion was announced, leaving the alignment four to three. The opinion was politically untenable because of the West, where the demand was for more inflation, not less.

The most that could be hoped by financial conservatives was to prevent the issuance of further greenbacks, until such time as the country could resume specie payment. No Middlewestern or Northwestern politician would care to defend the thesis that the old greenbacks must be deprived of their legal-tender status. Yet Chief Justice Chase was doubtless right in saying that the Constitutional Convention had discussed the matter carefully, and that "the power to make notes a legal tender" was "absolutely excluded from the Constitution."* Here was a clear conflict between the written document of 1787 and the political necessities of 1870. The speed with which the conflict was resolved and the text reviewed in the light of *Realpolitik* is a proof of the flexibility of a seemingly rigid system.

Congress had diminished the Supreme Court from nine members to eight during the fight with Andrew Johnson, so that the unhappy President would not be allowed to nominate even one friend. It now quickly restored the earlier number, which meant that with the resignation of the ancient Justice Grier, Grant had two vacancies to fill. Since the decision against the greenbacks was four to three, two vacancies should suffice. On the very day when the adverse decision was announced, Grant sent the names of the new members to the Senate. This time there was no mistake. One of the new justices had given a decision in favor of the Legal Tender Act while on the bench in Pennsylvania, and the other had defended the Act at the bar. Over the protest of the four members who had made the majority in 1870, the Court reopened the question of constitutionality the following year, reversing the decision of Chief Justice Chase and finding that the Congress could after all make greenbacks legal tender.

When the names of Grant's new justices had gone to the Senate, the

---

* The quotations are from his dissenting opinion of 1871, not from his majority opinion of 1870.

Washington correspondent of Greeley's *Tribune* wrote that they were being carefully studied with an eye to the legal-tender decision, since the Republican radicals "demand that the President appoint to the Supreme Court none but men about whom there is not the shadow of doubt." And when Hamilton Fish, some years later, urged Grant to declare that he had not "packed" the Court, Grant said "it would be difficult for him to make a statement; that although he required no declaration from Judges Strong and Bradley on the constitutionality of the Legal Tender Act, he knew Judge Strong had on the bench in Pennsylvania given a decision sustaining its constitutionality, and he had reason to believe Judge Bradley's opinion tended in the same direction; that . . . while he would do nothing to exact anything like a pledge or expression of opinion from the parties he might appoint to the bench, he had desired that the constitutionality should be sustained by the Supreme Court. . . ."[9]

In the light of this calm avowal it seems a waste for historians to argue that the Court reversed itself by accident, not by design. And the argument does less than justice to the strength of a political system which can bend without breaking, in spite of a written document which seems to make bending impossible. The Constitution is what the Supreme Court says it is, and the Supreme Court is what the Presidents make it.

The legal-tender justices were so successful politically, and did what was expected of them so smoothly, that Grant may have thought the finding and appointing of judges an easy task. If so he was soon disillusioned. The tale of his nine months' efforts to find a successor for Chief Justice Chase is at once a parable and a satire on politics in those disordered days. The first man to whom Grant offered the appointment was Senator Roscoe Conkling of New York: a pure spoilsman, a man who knew nothing of the philosophy of law or politics, nothing of the fierce economic upheavals which accompanied the march of industry and the mechanization of agriculture. His spirit was bounded by the New York Custom House on the south and by the state capitol at Albany on the north. He was a chief of the arrogant Senate oligarchy which had seized the powers of the President from Johnson and had discovered delightedly that Grant did not want them back. As we shall see, Conkling attained such capacity for mischief that he had to be broken before the American Government could work smoothly again; but positive abilities he neither possessed nor desired. He was good-looking, and unlike most Senators took pride in his athletic figure. His torso and his control over the New York state patronage were his major interests. James G. Blaine once referred to Conkling's "haughty disdain, his grandiloquent swell, his majestic, super-eminent, overpowering, turkey-gobbler strut." He had won his leadership in the New York Republican Party by becoming an extreme radical, a blind follower of Thaddeus Stevens, when Seward defended the policies of Johnson and Lincoln. He had confirmed his leadership with spoils. Perhaps the wisest and most gracious act of his life was the refusal of the chief justiceship on the ground that he did not have the temperament of a judge.

Grant then asked Fish to take the job; but Fish also refused. Next, at a Cabinet meeting, the President suggested Caleb Cushing: the learned and brilliant fighter, the defender of lost causes, the man of many enemies. The Cabinet insisted that Cushing could not be confirmed. Without further consultation Grant appointed a man as unsuitable as Conkling though not as unpleasant: Attorney-General George Henry Williams of Oregon, who was so incompetent a lawyer that he could not even win the government's case against the Crédit Mobilier and who in any case was about to be charged with fraud by the Senate. Williams was compelled to withdraw his own name, and Grant then insisted on nominating Cushing. As the Cabinet had predicted, Cushing was not acceptable to the Senate. He had fought on almost all sides of almost all subjects and his abilities were so formidable that whomever he fought he hurt. His long-accumulating enemies now had their revenge.

Nine months had passed, and still no Chief Justice. "It has been a hard parturition," said Hamilton Fish. At last Grant consulted his friends in the Senate and nominated a harmless man whom they suggested and who was at once confirmed: Morrison Waite of Ohio. As compared with his predecessors he was not reassuring; but as compared with Conkling or Williams he was indeed a Daniel.

The whole silly story was pure Grant. No harm was intended: the President suggested as many good men as bad. No intelligence was used: the President did not know what political intelligence was. The result was mediocre; but it might just as well have been a catastrophe, or (if Fish had accepted) a blessing. Politics under Grant was a lottery in which the bad prizes were more frequent than the good. The innocent President blandly drew the numbers and was shocked at the hatred with which some of them were greeted. No wonder Henry Adams found that "Grant's simplicity was more disconcerting than the complexity of a Talleyrand."[10]

4

Meanwhile, both before and after the election of 1872, life grew steadily darker in the South. As Professor Randall writes, "the worst abominations of reconstruction came after the readmission of the states to representation in the Federal Congress, a process mainly achieved in 1868 and completed in 1871."[11] The moment of greatest danger was when the white South lost hope of rescue by politics, or by due process of law.

In December, 1869, when Grant was for the second time subdued by the radicals, after his brief flurry of magnanimity, the hope of restoring free politics to the South seemed indefinitely postponed. And the courts had been a frail protection since 1867, when the Supreme Court welcomed an Act of Congress curtailing its jurisdiction, in order that it should not have to pass upon the most dubious of the Reconstruction laws.

In 1869 the lower House showed the length it was prepared to go in terrorizing, or if necessary destroying, the Supreme Court in order to maintain Republican rule in the South. By a vote of 99 to 50 the House passed an amendment to a judiciary bill, providing that any judge might retire on full pay at seventy, if he had served ten years, and that if he refused to retire the President might appoint an additional judge with the same powers and duties. In other words, if the old men became troublesome they could either be pensioned off or outvoted by new men who would do the will of Congress. The amendment was later dropped from the bill; but it had done its work in warning the Court not to interfere with Reconstruction—much as a similar proposal by Franklin Roosevelt in 1937 was to help bring a change in the Court's attitude toward the New Deal.

As despair spread through the South the appeal to force and fear spread also. The Ku Klux Klan and similar organizations were born and flourished. At their best they were vigilante committees, at their worst terror gangs. Their purpose was to restore white rule by the only means permitted. Although the Klan had been formally disbanded in the spring of 1869, its organization and its methods survived and its underground membership grew. For some years the North sought to meet force with force, which is easy for an occupying Power in wartime but not easy in days of so-called peace. Between 1870 and 1875 Congress passed four laws to compel recognition of the Negro's civil and political rights. If these could be enforced, and if the disfranchisement of many white men under the Fourteenth Amendment could be prolonged, the Republican Party should continue to win elections. The laws permitted the use of federal courts, marshals, district attorneys, and troops to enforce penalties on states or individuals; and they provided for election supervisors appointed by the federal government, and for the reimposition (if necessary) of martial law in the South. The last of these "Force Acts," passed on March 1, 1875,* as a memorial to Charles Sumner, conferred social equality upon the Negro and declared he must be treated exactly like a white man in theaters, public conveyances, hotels, restaurants, and other places of amusement.

---

* This was the dying Act of the House of Representatives which had been elected in 1872. The new Congress, elected in the autumn of 1874, would have a Democratic lower House.

The issue was now joined. The South had been driven into open revolt, based on violence, and the North had passed laws to suppress the violence. There could be only one end. A large Northern army would be needed to patrol the South; and since the policy of the radicals was at last becoming unpopular even in the North, no such army could be raised. Having done everything possible to poison the Negro's freedom, having failed to provide him with land or with education, having ruined his relations with his neighbors and used him for eleven years as the tool of political corruption, there was now nothing for the radicals to do except abandon the black man to his fate. The wretched retreat began in 1876, and was completed in 1894.

As early as 1874 most reasonable men knew that the Republican policy toward the South had failed. Yet as the mid-term Congressional elections approached, the party wished to evade the money question (which merely divided Republicans against themselves) and to distract the country from the contemplation of scandals. The conduct of foreign affairs by Hamilton Fish was the only constructive achievement which might have been discussed; but it was not thought sufficiently interesting to win votes. So the attempt was made to squeeze one more victory out of "rebel outrages," "southern lawlessness," "the oppression of the Negro," and the other stereotypes dear to the orators of the bloody shirt. The attempt failed. The North was waking to the fact that the scandals in Washington under Grant were nothing compared to the scandals of federal control in the South. The strange and daring experiment of compelling racial equality by the use of arms might have won Northern support for a few years longer if the federal officials imposed upon the South had been the wisest and the ablest men available. As the news spread that they were rogues, knaves, thieves, and incompetents, the voters lost heart. They did not demand a better enforcement of the policy. They merely wanted to forget the whole thing—to get out of the South no matter what festering troubles they left behind them.*

So the Republicans lost control of the House of Representatives in 1874. They also lost several senatorships, and the governorship of New York. The only comfort their leaders could find was that Representative Benjamin Butler—a Republican, but hated equally by all parties—was defeated in Massachusetts. "Butler defeated, everything else lost," telegraphed one Republican on the night of the election.

The Supreme Court, meanwhile, had also begun to undermine the work of the radicals. The essence of radical Reconstruction (not the purpose, which was to keep the Republicans in power, but the means) was the

---

* There were also economic interests in the North which were impatient for an end to radical Reconstruction—textile-mill owners, for example, and investors who wanted to put money in the South.

insistence that the federal government should control race relations. This was the meaning of the Fourteenth and Fifteenth Amendments and of the punitive enforcement laws. Yet between 1876 and 1883 the Supreme Court declared the severest of those laws unconstitutional, reverting to Calhoun's position that the racial problem must be left to the local community. It does not seem likely that the decisions were compelled by law or abstract logic. The Constitution could presumably have been stretched to cover the Reconstruction Acts if the national will had demanded it; but then the national will must also have demanded large and permanent armies to rule the South. Since there was no such will, the Court, as a matter of common sense, admitted that Washington did not possess the power to enforce a code of conduct in a Florida theater, or in a Texas bar.*

The vital decision, which set the white South free and was the prelude to a new oppression for the Negro, was given on October 15, 1883, in the Civil Rights cases. This disposed of the "Sumner memorial law"— which decreed equal privileges for the two races in inns, public conveyances, and theaters—by ruling that the Constitution did not give Congress the power to legislate on such matters. The Fourteenth Amendment, to be sure, prohibited a state from denying equal privileges; but the amendment did not apply to individuals. If innkeepers or theater managers in the South treated the Negro unjustly, that was a matter for the local authorities, not for the Congress or the federal marshals.

By this decision, writes Professor Gabriel,

> the Court, in effect, turned over to local Southern communities the solution of the all-important race problem, subject to the limitation that chattel slavery should not be re-established. . . . The mass of the Northern people acquiesced. The reason for this approval was to be found in the fact that, as early as 1883, Northern folkways in the matter of race relations were developing similar, though not identical, patterns to those of the post-war South. In both regions a caste system had crystallized. The Court's decision was a tacit recognition of this system.[12]

The political as opposed to the legal retreat from Reconstruction had begun in 1877, when for reasons which we shall discuss in the next chapter the last federal troops were withdrawn from the South. At once there began the sad process of building a new set of codes, unwritten laws, and disciplines to enforce the subordination of the Negro. All hopes of a happy evolution from slavery to true freedom had been ruined by 1877. The Negro was now to be made politically impotent and economically unprivileged to an extent that would have broken the hope of any less hardy people. And the American idea was incidentally to be betrayed

* Cp. below the influence upon radical Reconstruction of the Supreme Court's decision in the Slaughter House Cases (1873).

to an extent which has at times almost destroyed its power in world affairs. By the eighteen-nineties, in North and South alike, although the Negro was legally free, he was socially, economically, and politically confined to a point little short of servitude. At the best, from that day forward, he might be described as a third-class citizen.

While all this was happening Republican leaders continued to talk as if the Negro was their daily care. And at every presidential election the Republican Party Platform promised a faithful enforcement of the Reconstruction Amendments. As late as 1904, for example, the platform says "we favor such congressional action as shall determine whether by special discrimination the elective franchise in any state has been unconstitutionally limited, and, if such is the case, we demand that representation in Congress and in the electoral college shall be proportionately reduced as directed by the Constitution of the United States."

This was nonsense. Everybody knew that the Negro had been denied the vote in the South. Everybody knew that Congress would not dare reduce Southern representation in accordance with the Fourteenth Amendment. Senator Benjamin Tillman—"Pitchfork Ben" of South Carolina, one of the first and worst of the new breed of Southern demagogues sired by Reconstruction out of scalawags—had put the truth brutally. "The brotherhood of man exists no longer," he said in the Senate, "because you shoot Negroes in Illinois when they come in competition with your labor, and we shoot them in South Carolina when they come in competition with us in the matter of elections."[13]

Here was the result of that vulgar use of morals for an electoral advantage which was the meaning of the Stevens-Wade-Butler radicalism. And sharing in the shame was the entire system of Congressional government, Congressional policy-making. For once, Congress imposed its will effectively and steadily, and this is what happened. The American form of government must take great blame for the betrayal of the people's good will by radical Reconstruction.

> The contrast between the social consequences of emancipation in the West Indies [wrote Professor Ford], as guided by British statesmanship, under conditions of meagre industrial opportunity, and the social consequences of emancipation in the United States, affords an instructive example of the complicated evils which a nation may experience through the sheer incapacity of its government.*[14]

The final effort to keep at least one promise to the Negro was made by Senator George Frisbie Hoar of Massachusetts. He prepared a bill which would empower the courts to appoint officers from both parties

* From *The Cleveland Era* by H. J. Ford, vol. 4, THE CHRONICLES OF AMERICA, copyright Yale University Press.

to supervise elections, and which in case of a disputed election would allow the federal circuit court to intervene and to award a certificate to one of the contestants. The bill was favorably reported in August, 1890, but was laid aside forever during the following session. This was the last of the Force Bills. In 1894 the remaining statutes for protecting the political privileges of the freedmen were repealed.

5

Another reason for Republican losses in the election of 1874 was the panic of '73, which was a prelude to the worst depression the nation had known. All economic depressions have their political influence. The one which began in 1819 was an aid to the rise of Jackson. The depression of 1837 prevented Van Buren's re-election three years later. The depression of 1857 turned much of the industrial East toward the young Republican Party, which could promise a high tariff, whereas the Democratic Party under Southern leadership could not.

Foreign as well as domestic dislocations were responsible for the collapse in 1873. The Prussian wars and the railway expansion in Europe paralleled the war and the railway boom in the United States; but currency and credit inflation was greater in America than elsewhere, and so was overinvestment. The blow fell in September, with a series of failures—notably the failure of Jay Cooke and Company, private investment bankers of Philadelphia and Washington, who had recently opened a house in New York. Jay Cooke had handled the controversial government war bonds, the "five-twenties" which the Greenback Party wanted to retire, and in the public mind the firm was closely associated with the Treasury. Heavy advances to railways, especially the Northern Pacific, brought the house down in '73. Before the storm receded, a majority of the nation's railroads had gone bankrupt and more than two thirds of the iron mills and furnaces were idle. Within a year the building of new railway lines fell to less than a third of the average of the five preceding years. Almost half a million men lost their jobs from this cause alone. And the trouble grew steadily worse. During the years 1876 and 1877 more than 18,000 businesses failed.

Next came the usual wage reductions which led to class bitterness, and the usual deflation which led to sectional bitterness. The coal and textile strikes of 1875 to 1878, and the fiercely violent railway strike of 1877, seemed to accomplish little at the time; yet they prepared the way for a new type of labor movement. Similarly, the Western demand for inflation was resisted in 1874; but the demand was a prelude to Populism, and thus to the great Bryan campaign which was to rend the country in

1896. And behind the demands of labor, and the demands of the debtors, lay a new concept of the role of government. During the depression of 1857, responsible people in all classes and sections agreed that the federal government could do little except wait and suffer with the public. But now, because of the wartime legislation favored by the rich, Washington had direct control of the volume of currency. Furthermore, Washington had begun to subsidize private industry on a large scale—directly through the land grants to railways, and indirectly through the high Republican tariff. Obviously, if the currency could be contracted for the sake of creditors it could be expanded for the sake of debtors; and if the consumer could be made to pay higher prices for the benefit of the iron manufacturer, the farmer might also demand a bounty, and the factory worker. For the first time since Jackson won his war against Nicholas Biddle, the sectional pressure for cheap money which accompanies all depressions was directed at Congress, rather than at the state capitals or the banks. And for the first time in the history of the country Congress also felt a sustained class pressure for public works to offset unemployment and for such forms of relief as a moratorium on eviction for nonpayment of rent.

It had long been orthodox American doctrine that if government could be prevented from taking steps to help the rich (especially the manufacturers and bankers) at the expense of the rest of the community, all would be well. Whether right or wrong, that doctrine was now irrelevant. Since the destruction of the planter interest, government was becoming a welfare agency for capitalists. And once the politicians were embarked on large-scale positive interferences with the economy, it was not easy to argue that they could only interfere on the side of the privileged. The end of an era and the start of a strange new world was foreshadowed when respectable Americans admitted that the federal government might have to take positive steps to protect the poor—and that it might even have to protect them against the results of its own tariffs and subsidies for business. The day was coming when politicians would heed Lord Acton's statement that "Laws should be adapted to those who have the heaviest stake in the country, for whom misgovernment means not mortified pride or stinted luxuries but want and pain, and degradation and risk to their own lives and to their children's souls."

That day, however, was still in the future. It would not dawn until the new monopoly capitalism made the old arguments against interference with the economy seem foolish, and until labor unions became strong enough to weather bad times. In the seventies and eighties, Rockefeller was building the first giant Trust, and the unions were local organizations with no resources to meet long unemployment—or else they were part of the "one big union," the Noble Order of the Knights of Labor. The

Knights included farmers and intellectuals, white men and Negroes, males and females, skilled and unskilled workers. This was brotherly; but it made for diffusion of interests and power, looseness of organization, vagueness of demands.

The best unions of trained craftsmen held aloof from the Knights of Labor. These unions were moving toward national federations in each trade, with policy-making powers vested in the federal headquarters, and with membership dues high enough to build a large reserve fund. And in addition they were moving toward a super-federation of all the separate federated craft unions—a holding company for labor's élite. When this finally came into being, in 1886, as the American Federation of Labor, it held itself strictly to collective bargaining on wages, hours, and working conditions, and refused to become involved with a political party, or with large programs for social or moral or economic reform. Samuel Gompers of the cigar makers' union—for years the chief figure in the A.F. of L.—held that whereas a specific demand for a wage increase might succeed, a vague demand for a good society could produce nothing but words.

So out of the desperate and unsuccessful strikes of 1873–77 came the American Federation of Labor: practical, exclusive, and for its own skilled members effective. But for the most part workers in the new huge factories, and in the mines, remained unorganized and helpless.

While labor struck, and suffered, and prepared for the future, the West fought vainly for inflation. Some Western Senators demanded the reissue of the $44,000,000 of greenbacks which had been retired between 1865 and 1868, bringing the total back to $400,000,000. Others wanted to go beyond $400,000,000. Still others asked that the national banks be exempted from all reserve requirements, so that they might expand credit indefinitely. Finally, in April, 1874, Congress passed an act to raise the greenbacks to $400,000,000 and to issue an extra $46,000,000 of national bank notes. Grant vetoed the Act on the ground that the party had promised to resume specie payments as soon as possible, and that the promise was incompatible with such inflation. Congress not only accepted the veto, but in January, 1875—emboldened by the fact that the Republicans were about to lose control of the House and wanted credit for keeping at least one promise—it passed the long-delayed bill for resumption. The greenbacks were to be reduced gradually to $300,000,-000, and to become redeemable in specie on January 1, 1879.*

Meanwhile, by accident, the inflationists had acquired another grievance and another fiery cause. From the time of Hamilton's Coinage Act

---

* In 1878 Congress halted the retirement of the greenbacks when there were still more than $346,000,000; but resumption took place promptly at the appointed time.

in 1792 until 1873, the American money system had in theory been bi-metallic. But in practice the ratio between gold and silver had never been accurately fixed. Until 1834 silver was overvalued, for the mint ratio between the two metals was fixed at 1 to 15, whereas in fact gold was worth almost sixteen times as much as silver. So it paid to take silver to the mint to be coined, whereas gold was more valuable if used as a metal or if shipped to foreign countries. The United States was thus on a silver standard in fact until a law of 1834 altered the ratio to 16 to 1. Gold, instead of silver, was now slightly overvalued at the mint, with the result that by the late forties silver had almost disappeared from circulation.

This was inconvenient; so the next step was the Coinage Act of 1853, creating short-weight silver coins for small change of less than a dollar. In effect (though not in theory) the country was now on a gold standard, for the gold coins were the only full-weight currency in use, although the law still allowed the free coinage of silver dollars. If silver should suddenly drop in price, so that it was worth more at the mint than it was in the market, silver would once again be coined.

The fiat money of the Civil-War period drove gold coins, and the little short-weight coins, into hiding. The country was on a paper, or greenback, standard until January 1, 1879. Yet in 1873, as a step in preparation for returning to a metal standard, the coinage laws were revised. Because bimetallism had never worked, and had been a bother ever since the eighteenth century, it was abolished by the Act of February 12, 1873. The silver dollar was removed from the list of coins which could be freely struck at the mint. At the time, nobody paid any heed. The fight for inflation was still concerned with paper. The new coinage act had been considered in five sessions of Congress and had been read and debated repeatedly. Nobody saw sinister implications. Yet within three years this innocent bill became known in the West as "the crime of '73," the inflationists charging that it was a plot by English and American financiers to put the country surreptitiously on the gold standard. The reason for the excitement was that rich new silver mines had been discovered in the mountain states. The price of silver had dropped. The Westerners woke to the fact that silver might be a more practical form of inflation than paper, if the full-weight silver dollar could be restored to the list of coins which might be freely struck. And those inflationists who understood politics saw a still more interesting fact: namely, that for the first time the debtors had a group of rich men on their side. In 1874, thirty-six million dollars' worth of silver was taken from a single mine in Nevada. The return to bimetallism, to "the free coinage of silver," might raise the price of this metal by as much as ten per cent.

The advocates of "sound" money had won two important battles in two years; but the cheap money forces had just begun to fight.

6

While the Grant Administration guttered out, while the party sought re-election on the promise that it would be as unlike its recent past as possible, one good deed partially redeemed the eight years from ignominy. Hamilton Fish had made peace with England—sensible, permanent peace —in spite of the chairman of the Foreign Relations Committee of the Senate, who seemed to insist on war.

The quarrel with England concerned the damage done by the Confederate cruisers which had been built, or equipped, in British ports. The most famous of the cruisers, the *Alabama*, had been launched at Liverpool on May 15, 1862. Belatedly, the British Government sent orders that she should not sail; but she escaped, and in the next two years she destroyed more than sixty Union ships. John Bright in the House of Commons applied to her the lines from *Lycidas:*

> It was that fatal and perfidious Bark,
> Built in the eclipse, and rigg'd with curses dark,
> That sunk so low that sacred head of thine.

She caused so much trouble that all the American grievances were finally known as the "Alabama claims." In the minds of the self-righteous —of whom Sumner was as usual the king—these claims went far beyond the money value of the destroyed commerce. They included the belief that the Queen's proclamation of neutrality, which conferred belligerent rights upon the South, was in itself a deadly wrong and had greatly prolonged the war. Adding to this injury the harm done by the cruisers, and by the other moral and material support which England had given the Confederacy, Sumner decided that the United States was owed $2,125,000,000—or half the cost of the war. This vast damage, he claimed, could only be atoned if England ceded Canada to the United States. And for a time the puzzled President seemed to agree.

If Sumner and Grant wanted war, this was the way to begin. If they thought they could take Canada without a fight, they were mad. And in any case they were serving their country shabbily, for the precedent they sought to establish might one day prove fatal to America. Pugnacious, moralistic America, whose diplomatic aggressiveness was deplored by every foreign office, might find herself a neutral in a European war. And then, if Sumner's method of reckoning were applied, America's habit of doing and saying exactly what she chose, confident that her lightest whim represented the will of God, might lay her open to damages which could only be repaid with the entire Western Hemisphere. If the

Queen of England had sinned by recognizing that the South was a
belligerent, what might not follow from the cheerful fecklessness with
which the American Congress welcomed and encouraged revolutions
in Europe?

All this was unpleasantly clear to Hamilton Fish. Yet Sumner was
chairman of the Foreign Relations Committee in the Senate. And for
twenty years, except for a brief period after Preston Brooks had beaten
him into silence, Sumner had been proclaiming that Truth was simple,
and single, and that he was its prophet. Luckily, his intolerance was at
last to cause his downfall. Having blustered and abused his way through
every obstacle for decades, Sumner was now to quarrel with the President.
As Henry Adams wrote:

> A quarrel with General Grant was lunacy. Grant might be what-
> ever one liked, as far as morals or temper or intellect were concerned,
> but he was not a man whom a lightweight cared to challenge for a
> fight; and Sumner, whether he knew it or not, was a very light weight
> in the Republican party, if separated from his Committee of Foreign
> Relations. As a party manager he had not the weight of half-a-dozen
> men whose very names were unknown to him.[15]

The break came over San Domingo, which Grant wished to annex.
Sumner quite properly opposed the annexation, and was able to thwart
it. But when speaking on the subject he could not refrain from attacking
Grant—as he had attacked so many enemies throughout his bitter life—
as a man depraved beyond belief, stupid beyond describing. This time,
instead of being chastised with a cane, Sumner was deposed.

Grant's military mind did not take kindly to opposition from those he
considered his subordinates. And Grant's friends in the Senate were the
men whose names, according to Henry Adams, Sumner did not even know,
but who were the real party managers. So the last of the old Free Soil
founders of the Republican Party was brushed aside by the new group of
"stalwarts," the clique of spoilsmen whose power rested on patronage,
money, and well-run state machines. Grant asked the stalwarts to get rid
of Sumner, so they deposed him from his chairmanship. And Grant probably did not know enough politics to understand what a prodigious deed
he had accomplished. It is not often that Senators turn upon each other,
least of all at the bidding of a President. But Sumner had no friends. Yet
with all his faults he was a better man than the Senators who pushed him
out.

Henry Adams was right in saying that alongside the Department of
State, over which Hamilton Fish presided, "there had risen a department
of foreign relations over which Senator Sumner ruled with a high hand at
the Capitol." The creation of such a department is always a possibility

under the American system. And if the man who presides over it hates the Administration and is popular with some of his fellow Senators—as in the case of Henry Cabot Lodge—he may help to destroy the world. He has power without responsibility or knowledge. He does not study the reports which come to the Department of State from every country. He does not talk officially with the representatives of foreign governments, or negotiate treaties. But he can rouse fear and hatred, at home and abroad. And he can make sure that no treaty is ratified.

When Sumner was deposed, Disraeli rejoiced that at last the Senator had gone "from his seat of ceaseless mischief and malice." The whole world might appropriately have joined in the rejoicing.

Fish could now proceed to make a settlement with England. In addition to the Alabama claims, there was an unsettled northwestern boundary, and also the recurring problem of the Canadian fisheries. The Oregon Treaty of 1846 had defined the water boundary between the United States and British Columbia as the channel separating the continent from Vancouver Island. Later, two channels were discovered. If the line ran through the western channel, or Haro Strait, the island of San Juan belonged to the United States—but not if the line ran through the eastern channel. This was important, because a fort built on the island would command the shipping routes.

The fisheries dispute was more serious. Ever since 1783, the "liberty" of American citizens to fish within the territorial waters of British North America had been argued, contested, sometimes enlarged, sometimes diminished, but never accurately and finally settled. Since the livelihood of hard-bitten sailors was involved, the dispute was fruitful of local fights. Whenever Anglo-American relations worsened, the fisheries question became critical—never more so than at the time of Sumner's departure from his chairmanship.

Hamilton Fish and Lord Granville, the British Foreign Minister, agreed to lay all three disputes before a joint commission. As a result, the Treaty of Washington was concluded on May 8, 1871. First, the fisheries question was put before a mixed commission which succeeded in quieting the dispute until 1885, when it again became a nuisance. It was finally settled, precisely and accurately, in 1910, by the Permanent Court of Arbitration at The Hague. Second, the northwest boundary dispute was submitted to the German Emperor, who found in favor of the United States in October, 1872. The line was to pass through the Haro Strait, and the island of San Juan was to be American. Third, and far the most important, the Alabama claims were referred to a board of five arbitrators: Italian, Swiss, Brazilian, British, and American. They met at Geneva, and in September, 1872, agreed that England had failed in her duties as a neutral and that she should pay the United States fifteen and a half million dollars in gold, to compensate for the direct damages. The indirect claims were forever laid to rest.

Like all great triumphs, the Treaty of Washington, and the resulting arbitrations, seemed easy once they had succeeded; but they were threatened with failure at every step in the long, tortuous way. Negotiations between touchy national states were hard enough at best; but when they were complicated by men like Sumner, and by the legacy of Manifest Destiny which made many Americans feel that they had a duty to take whatever they wanted, negotiations became almost impossible. Only a man with the firmness, the patience, and the moral authority of Fish could have made the English admit that they were wrong and the Americans admit that there was a limit to what they might demand.

> By a happy stroke of fate [writes Professor Nevins], at the moment when the American Government sank to the very nadir of disrepute, when greed and corruption seemed to sway most departments of American activity, there was reincarnated in the second officer of the republic the high integrity, the selfless patriotism, the regard for principle, the far-sighted judgment, which recalled the days when Fish's idols, Hamilton and Jay, walked the earth.[16]

XXV

The Powers of the Presidency Revive

THE CAMPAIGN OF 1876 was the most important since 1864 and the most fraudulent. Since the country was sick of Republican scandals and Republican Reconstruction, it seemed likely that the Democrats would win. This had a good effect upon the nominations, but a bad effect on the election itself.

The Republican Convention met on June 14 at Cincinnati. The favorite candidate during the early ballots was James G. Blaine—once of Pennsylvania, but now a resident of the state of Maine. Gay and impulsive and much-admired, Blaine had been in the House of Representatives since 1863, and was about to move to the Senate. He had been Speaker from 1869 until the Democrats took over the House in 1875, when he became leader of the Opposition. He was a bitter foe of Roscoe Conkling. The rivalry between these men had divided the Congressional Republicans into "stalwarts" (the supporters of Grant and of the Senators who controlled Grant) and "half-breeds," of whom Blaine was the natural leader. The struggle was merely for power, not for policy; eight years of Grant, Conkling, and dishonorable chaos, had put the half-breeds in control of the convention, and they would certainly have chosen their hero—their "plumed knight," as Blaine was called in the nominating speech—except for the unhappy incident of the "Mulligan letters" which had occurred a fortnight before.

The letters concerned Blaine's relations, while Speaker of the House, with the Little Rock and Fort Smith Railroad. Blaine had made a ruling which saved a land grant for the railroad, and had subsequently been given the privilege of selling the road's bonds. The commission must have been generous, for Blaine quickly became rich. Nevertheless, he seems always to have thought himself strictly, indeed quixotically, honest, on the ground that he conferred a favor upon the railway before receiving anything in return. This was not the view of the reform element in the Republican Party, which had bolted in 1872, and which would do so again unless the candidate was clearly unsullied by the recent grimy years.

Blaine got possession of the Mulligan letters on the promise to return them. He did not return them; but he read extracts to the House of Representatives in the course of a brilliant but defensive speech which aroused more suspicions than it allayed. So the convention, reluctantly, had to face the fact that if it nominated its favorite, the man to whom its heart was given, the party would once more be split.

Senator Morton of Indiana was the candidate of the stalwarts. Characteristically, he had rounded up the carpetbag delegates from the Republican provinces in the South. He therefore came next to Blaine during the first few ballots. But if the half-breeds had to abandon their "plumed knight" for the sake of party unity, they could not be expected to support a stalwart. And the liberal Republicans, who had bolted in 1872, would not take anyone too closely identified with Grantism. The convention needed a man more honest than Blaine, less smirched than the friends of Grant, yet not so ardently a reformer that the stalwarts would refuse to work for him. Strangely and luckily, they had a man who fitted the prescription exactly: Rutherford B. Hayes of Ohio.

Hayes was born in 1822, the posthumous son of a farmer. A generous uncle paid for his education. He went to Kenyon College in Ohio, and then to Harvard law school. He was a Whig who had turned Republican after the Kansas-Nebraska Bill and had supported Frémont. He first attracted attention during the war, rising to the rank of brigadier general and serving with distinction under Sheridan in the Shenandoah Valley. In 1864 he was elected to the House of Representatives, but refused to take his seat until the war ended. In 1867 he became governor of Ohio, serving for two terms and then voluntarily retiring. In 1875, a bad year for the Republicans, he was persuaded to try for a third term, and was elected—thus becoming a national figure. Although honest, and a sincere reformer, he had stayed with the party and worked for Grant in 1872. He was therefore acceptable to the stalwarts. He was so clearly "available" that his nomination had often been predicted. He was in no sense a dark horse.

The Democratic Convention met at St. Louis on June 27, and on the second ballot nominated Samuel Jones Tilden of New York. Eighteen seventy-six was expected to be the year of Democratic triumph and vindication; yet the convention turned (wisely, almost without dissent) to a little, nervous, unimpressive corporation lawyer. This was a triumph of intellect and of "reform" over the qualities which are supposed to bring political success. The people had made plain their distaste for the rowdy antics of the past few years.

Tilden was the son of a village postmaster in New York State. His childhood was itself a political education, for Van Buren, Silas Wright, and William L. Marcy—the great men of the Albany Regency—were friends of his father and frequent visitors. The boy's health was bad and he was educated mostly at home; but he went to New York City to study law. He was admitted to the bar in 1841. He made a brilliant success, and within a few years had most of the great railway companies for his clients. He became a friend and adviser of the Democratic chieftains in the state; so during Polk's Administration he had to face the harsh choice which rent the party in New York. His father's friend, William Marcy, became a "Hunker" who favored the Mexican War and the annexation of new slave territory; but his father's other friends, Van Buren and Silas Wright, became "Barnburners," Free-Soilers, enemies of the expansion which was so dear to the South. Tilden went with Van Buren. He did not later become a Republican like many Free-Soilers and ex-Barnburners; but the split in his own state party kept him from national prominence for many years.

After the war, in which he took no part, Tilden became chairman of the Democratic State Committee and quickly gained fame by opposing and breaking the unspeakable Tweed Ring in New York City. William Tweed, head of Tammany Hall, not only owned the government of the city, but in 1869 elected one of his servants governor of the state. The four chief members of the ring had for years been content to steal one dollar for each dollar spent on genuine contracts or salaries. In spite of this self-denying ordinance they made more than forty-five millions in three and a half years. The money must have gone to their heads, because they began inventing not only imaginary employees and contractors, on whom to lavish the city's funds, but imaginary hospitals and charitable institutions. They owned three judges and many Albany legislators, as well as the governor, and they felt so safe that they challenged Tilden for control of the state party. To the amazement and pleasure of the country, and especially of the New York City taxpayers, Tilden destroyed them. The three judges were impeached, and Tweed died in jail. Tilden was elected governor of New York.

The state capital provided him with another large, useful fraud which he was able to expose and to abolish with much publicity. So in a year when "reform" was in the air Tilden's nomination was almost unopposed. However, since Tilden was known as a "hard-money" man who wished an early return to specie payments, the convention selected Thomas A. Hendricks of Indiana as vice-presidential candidate. Hendricks was a "soft-money" man, or inflationist.

The campaign, in which neither Tilden nor Hayes took much part, was unpleasant. The Republicans waved the bloody shirt and the Democrats waved the abundant dirty linen of the Grant régime. The Republicans called on the Grand Army of the Republic—an organization of Union veterans to promote philanthropy and pensions—for "patriotic" riots and the stirring of sectional hatred. The Democrats called on the various terror organizations throughout the South to use any methods, including murder, to prevent the Negroes from voting.

The morning after election day, it was clear that Tilden had a popular majority of 250,000 votes. In the electoral college, where 185 made a majority, Tilden had 184 undisputed votes and Hayes 165. Twenty electoral votes were disputed—one in Oregon, and 19 in the states of Louisiana, South Carolina, and Florida. Obviously, if Southern white men had been in control of these states, if they had all been allowed to vote and to prevent their black neighbors from voting, Tilden would have won. And if the Reconstruction laws had been enforced, if the Negroes had been protected in their civil rights, Hayes would have won. But out of the chaos of blackmail, bribery, murder, martial law, and competitive fraud, which was a Southern election under Reconstruction, nobody knew at the time, and nobody knows now, what really happened. One historian suggests that the Democrats stole the election in the first place and that the Republicans then stole it back again. In any case, the Republicans ended in full possession.

An electoral commission was appointed with five members from the House of Representatives, five from the Senate, and five from the Supreme Court. The decision was given on March 2, two days before the new President must be inaugurated. Eight members of the commission were Republicans, seven were Democrats. By an eight to seven majority, each of the twenty disputed electoral votes was awarded to Hayes. Feeling ran high; but the South did not want another war and Northern Democrats were not in a position to fight. Henry Watterson of the Louisville *Courier-Journal* announced that a hundred thousand Kentuckians would see justice done to Tilden; but luckily he was wrong. Tilden remained calm and conciliatory, earning the gratitude of his country for all time. And Hayes allowed his friends to promise that the last troops of Occupation would be withdrawn from the South if he were permitted to assume the presidency in peace. This was decisive. A Republican President could end the immoral farce of Reconstruction more cleanly and more quickly than a Democrat. The Negro had no hope anyway. The question was whether he should be betrayed quickly or slowly, and there was much to be said for speed.

> The southerners saw their chance and seized it [writes the latest biographer of Hayes], the disputed election was their golden opportunity. They got more from Hayes than they could have obtained from Tilden, for the latter could have withdrawn the troops from the three states only with the greatest difficulty. . . . Indeed, here, as a dozen times before and after, northern and southern Democrats pursued different purposes. The northern Democrats, in 1876, were bent on obtaining control of the national administration. . . . The southerners . . . were concerned in having the troops removed from South Carolina, Florida, and Louisiana; and if this were done they did not greatly

care who was President, since they expected little federal patronage in any event.[1]

More important to the white South than the withdrawal of the troops was the acknowledgment of states' rights which was forced upon the electoral commission. In order to make sure of Hayes votes in Florida and Louisiana, the Republican majority on the commission had to refuse to go behind the returns of the state canvassing boards. Those boards were the servants of the carpetbag governments, and with their help Hayes was elected. But they were soon to become the servants of white, Democratic governments. And no matter how much the Republicans in Congress might wish to question the returns in the future, they could not, because of the precedent of the electoral commission. The white Southerners had made a good bargain. In return for allowing one more Republican President to be elected with the help of Southern Negro votes, they not only got rid of the troops but they won a victory for state control of elections.

Incidentally, the nation had also made a good bargain, for Hayes at once proved himself an able President. Such a man was overdue in the White House.

2

The Cabinet appointments were as revealing in the case of Hayes as in the case of Grant; but this time the revelation was cheerful. It was also infuriating to the Congressional oligarchy which had broken Johnson and ruled Grant, and which expected to find Hayes easy to control. Another weak President would have been ruinous at this time, for the Congress was once more demonstrating that without Executive leadership it becomes a rabble which is run by a few cynics for party, regional, or class interests.* At the end of the first Congressional session of Grant's Administration, Henry Adams described the chaos accurately.

In both houses all trace of responsibility is lost [he wrote], and while the Executive fumes with impatience or resigns himself with the significant consolation that this is the people's government, and the people may accept the responsibility, the members of the lower house are equally ready with the excuse that they are not responsible for the actions of the senators, and the senators, being responsible to no power under Heaven except their party organizations, which they control,

---

* Congressional leadership, to be sure, produced the excellent Compromise of 1850; but within four years Congress destroyed its own handiwork, in order that one region should benefit by a railway.

are able to obtain precisely what legislation answers their personal
objects or their individual conception of the public good.[2]

By the time Hayes became President many observers thought the Senate
wished to upset the system of checks and balances and to substitute a
parliamentary form with the Chief Executive as a figurehead.[3] If so, they
would have destroyed their country. A legislature representing the fierce
regional rivalries which then disturbed America could not make national
policy under a parliamentary system. Furthermore, a legislature dominated by the men who ran the Senate in the seventies and eighties could
not make policy at any time or place. William Allen White described the
initiation to the Senate of Benjamin Harrison who was soon to become
President of the United States.

> Judge David Davis of Illinois [writes White], an honest man with a
> sense of humor, a statesman who had left the United States Supreme
> Court to enter the senate, sat with Harrison the day he came into the
> chamber to take his seat, and as the senators filed by, Davis called them
> off as Adam named the animals in the morning of the world: There
> came the jackal, the vulture, the sheep-killing dog, the gorilla, the
> crocodile, the buzzard, the old clucking hen, the dove, the turkey-
> gobbler. Then, as the big hulk of a greedy westerner—coarse, devious,
> insolent—came swinging in heavily, Judge Davis pointed his stubby
> forefinger at the creature and exclaimed: "A wolf, sir; a damned,
> hungry, skulking, cowardly wolf!"[4]

These were the men who had gained power during the years when
America was too much tempted, the years of post-war boom and easy
money and cheap immigrant labor and imperial land grants and a prostrate South and a whole new technology for spoiling the untouched West.
Sobered by the long depression, America would gladly have dismissed
some of this menagerie; but Senators are not easy to oust once they have
seized firm hold on their state machines. There is often a lag of ten years
between a change of public opinion and a change in the temper of the
upper House. In 1877, President Hayes represented the new will for a
cleaner public service; but the Senate represented the roaring days of
Grant's first term. Conkling expected to see his man, Tom Platt, made
Postmaster General and lord of the federal patronage. Cameron wanted
his son continued in the Cabinet; and Blaine (who moved from the
lower House to the Senate after losing the nomination) had a candidate
whom he expected to foist on Hayes without argument. Between them
they would have given the new Administration a Cabinet to serve the
Congress, not the President. But Hayes had other plans.

For Secretary of State, Hayes chose William Maxwell Evarts of New
York, one of the nation's greatest lawyers who had twice been considered

for the chief justiceship of the Supreme Court—and one of Conkling's enemies. For Secretary of the Treasury, at a time when the silver problem was acute, he chose Senator John Sherman of Ohio, brother of the general and the most learned of American politicians in the theory of money. For Secretary of the Interior he chose ex-Senator Carl Schurz of Missouri: civil-service reformer, leader of the Liberal Republican revolt in 1872, detested by the oligarchs. For Postmaster General, instead of a New York spoilsman, he first intended to nominate Joseph E. Johnston of Virginia, the most important of surviving Confederate generals. This would have been a magnificent gesture of conciliation, and as a bonus it might have killed Conkling; but the President was persuaded that the appointment would stir too much trouble, so he chose a lesser Confederate for the Post Office: David M. Key of Tennessee. Key was a Democrat and a valiant soldier of the South. He had also served for two years as United States Senator from Tennessee.

The rest of the Cabinet was good, except for the Secretary of the Navy, who was a concession to the powerful Senator Morton of Indiana, defeated rival for the nomination and oligarch from Hayes's neighbor state. Since there was virtually no navy, the Secretary could do little harm.

When the Cabinet nominations came from the White House the oligarchy did not know whether to laugh or be angry, since they did not know whether the President meant to fight for this strange list of competent men or whether it was a political gesture in view of the campaign promises for reform. In any case, they intended to refuse confirmation. They sent the whole list—including the name of John Sherman, their fellow Senator—to the appropriate committees for examination and report. The names were not expected to emerge from committee.

The power of the presidency was never shown more clearly than during the next three days, when little Rutherford Hayes with his tarnished title and his small fame conquered the ruthless, cynical, self-assured men who dominated the Senate. The nominations for the Cabinet were good, and the disdain with which the Senate buried them was insulting, so the people rose to support *their* representative, the President, the only man who stood for something larger than silver in the West, or tobacco in the South, or steel in Pennsylvania, or lobsters in Maine. Telegrams and letters, mass meetings, churches, newspapers, insisted on confirmation. The startled Senate surrendered. If the Democrats had stood with Conkling's crew in opposing the President, Hayes would have been beaten; but the Democrats had been promised the withdrawal of the troops, and were temporarily grateful.[5]

How does a President win the backing of the people? Andrew Johnson toured the country in a great cause, unselfishly, yet he annoyed his audiences with rancor and cheap talk. And his friends, who sought to

organize a Union Party to support him, made every silly mistake, while
his enemies made none. So Johnson was beaten. Grant was beaten before
he began, because he knew nothing about government and little about
civilian America. He was a great man in the wrong place, which is an
awkward sight. Hayes was not a great man, but he was in the right place.
He had dignity, which the people desire in their Chief Executive. He had
a clear, simple case, which the haughty Senators helped him to dramatize.
And for the moment the Democratic Opposition was friendly. He was
certain to win, if he dared to fight. Since he was trained in politics, he
knew exactly when to fight—just as Grant, who was trained at West
Point, knew when to fight on the battlefield, but not at Washington.

3

Hayes was soon in need of his political acumen, and of the strength which
came to him from having renounced a second term. When accepting the
nomination in 1876 he had said flatly that he would only serve for four
years. Since he meant what he said, none of the party oligarchs could
threaten him with reprisals at the next convention. This was fortunate,
for the beasts were soon closing on him: Judge Davis's jackals and wolves
and sheep-killing dogs. The President was to find that removing the
federal troops from the South was a far more ticklish process than ordering them there in the first place.

There were two governments in South Carolina, and two in Louisiana:
the government which had been declared elected by the Republican
canvassing board, and the one elected by the white men whose votes the
board had disallowed. The minute the Northern troops withdrew, the
carpetbag governments would be thrown out and the rival governments
installed. This was embarrassing to Hayes, for it was the carpetbag canvassing boards which had made him President. Seemliness required that
they be kept in power for at least a few weeks; yet delay was impossible,
for the local courts controlled by the Democrats had forbidden the banks
to pay state funds except on court orders, and the carpetbag governments
were therefore starving. Hayes either had to send more troops, and money
with them, or he had to live up to his promise and get out quickly. On
April 10 the last federal soldiers left South Carolina. General Wade
Hampton's government took over the state for the white men.

There was further delay in Louisiana, where the situation might have
been created by an unkind satirist to make Hayes ridiculous. The carpetbag governor, whose name was Packard, had done much better than
Hayes in the election. Yet Hayes officially won, and it was now necessary
that Packard should officially lose. In order to withdraw the troops,

Hayes had to certify that "domestic violence" did not exist; yet Louisiana would be nothing but domestic violence if the soldiers left and the carpetbag governor remained. Packard must leave with the troops. But he did not want to leave. He felt he had done the Republicans a great service—which was true—and that the least the party could do in return was to spare him a few regiments so he could go on being governor. He kept pointing out, rudely, that if he was not the duly elected governor then Hayes was not the President of the United States.

In the end, Hayes appointed another commission—like the commission which had made him President, only this one was to unmake Packard. Perhaps it was a humorless device; but it worked. The commission reached Louisiana on April 5. Within less than three weeks the Packard government was out and the troops had left New Orleans: that much-tormented town which had known the cruel and unusual fate of being governed by Ben Butler.

Florida had been "liberated" some time before, so the whole South was now restored to white rule. Hayes had done what Grant should have done, and what would never have needed doing if Lincoln had lived or if Johnson had made the people understand what was happening in their name. Symbolically, as if to remind the country how the long disgrace had started, Hayes's policy of conciliation was attacked by the following men: Blaine of the bloody shirt, old Ben Wade who would have become President if the impeachment of Johnson had succeeded, Ben Butler (who to the alarm of both parties had returned to the lower House), Boutwell of "Black Friday" fame, and the two abolitionists, Wendell Phillips and William Lloyd Garrison. Allies to the last, the moralists and the morally infirm cried out against the ugly end of their ugly policy. Yet Hayes had not only saved whatever could be saved in the South (nothing but long and bitter years could revive the lost opportunities for the Negro), but he had saved the Republican Party. The bad conscience of the North would probably have defeated the Republicans by 1880 if federal troops had still been involved in the unholy struggles of Reconstruction.

Hayes saved the Republicans by abandoning radical Reconstruction just in time; but he could not save the party in the South. It was one of his dearest hopes to create an honorable Republicanism in the old Confederacy and thus to protect that region from one-party corruption and from the local tyrannies of one-party demagogues. This he could not do. It was a noble plan. Lincoln might have carried it out, but Hayes came too late. "In 1865," writes H. J. Eckenrode, "the South was singularly lacking in ill feeling; in 1876, the land was consumed with hatred."[6] Generations had to be born, "and till the soil, and lie beneath," before the name Republican could be anything but detestable to the Confederacy.

4

In his Inaugural Address Hayes promised civil-service reform—"thorough, radical, and complete." He promised appointments on the ground of ability alone; security of tenure; and exemption of the civil servants from the need to do party work. Hayes knew better than to think this was possible. But he knew it was desirable and he intended to do the best he could.

One reason why nothing "thorough" could be done was the number of people who had to be paid off for procuring Hayes's election. Twenty electoral votes, in four states, cannot be transplanted from the Democratic to the Republican column merely by kindness.

> Numberless promises had been made [writes Eckenrode] and the President now proceeded to keep them. All the members of the Louisiana canvassing board or relatives were granted federal jobs. Forty-seven members of the disrupted Negro legislature of Louisiana were taken care of, mostly in the treasury, which Sherman made a house of refuge for discarded Republican politicians.[7]

On a higher level there were men like ex-Governor Packard, whose services had been invaluable and who was made consul at Liverpool, where his fees (to say nothing of his freedom from the nightly threat of murder) made up for his lost grandeur. On a still higher level were the men who had persuaded the state canvassing boards that they had better elect Hayes, or heaven protect them. Three of these "visiting statesmen" were made ministers to Great Powers, and a fourth was given John Sherman's place in the Senate. It was not the moment for anything "radical and complete" in civil-service reform.

In any case, even if Hayes had not come to office under odd circumstances, he could not have founded an uncontaminated merit system. A President who abolished all Executive patronage would do more harm than good, for he would reduce the power of his office dangerously. As we have seen, the President has two weapons when dealing with the state machines: public opinion and the patronage. Public opinion cannot be mobilized for every minor issue, or every appointment. The appeal to the people must be saved for great occasions. And during the incessant little conflicts between the national interest and the wishes of regional Representatives, the President must have some favors to offer in return for the favors he asks. If a Senator who has been sent to Washington to get a higher tariff on wool, and whose re-election depends upon his success, is merely told to stop asking for the tariff because it interferes with national policy, he may join with other disappointed Senators in polite blackmail: refusing to confirm appointments except at a price, refusing to ratify treaties, etc. But if the President can offer him good jobs for some of his constituents, thus helping him to remain a power in his own state, the Senator's future becomes more secure and he may think less about wool and more about world trade.

In 1877, however, after eleven years of the Congressional oligarchy, most of the federal patronage had been seized by the Senators and was used to strengthen the willfulness and selfishness of the state machines, instead of being used to wheedle them into serving the national interest. Also, Hayes faced a condition in the public service which was luckily unique, which was nobody's fault, but which had to be changed if the nation was to prosper. Throughout the Civil War the Republican Party had ruled by whatever means seemed necessary. For the sake of victory and the Union, the Constitution had been warped and disregarded; border-state elections had been bought, or coerced by troops; thousands of "Peace Democrats" had been jailed and habeas corpus had been suspended to keep them immured as long as was desired; the federal elections of 1864 had been "controlled" (unnecessarily, to be sure), so that the voice of the people would speak correctly. These were rough deeds, and rough men were needed to see them through; so in addition to the financial dishonesty which wartime spending normally breeds, there spread a new slackness and dishonesty in many public services. The institutions on which the people's liberties depended were being perverted in what seemed a good cause, and the men who did the more unpleasant acts of perversion were promised safe jobs in return. Government offices became a dumping ground for some very strange characters, and there was a feeling that the worst of these men had earned their rest and should not be expelled—at least not by a Republican Administration.

By the time Hayes became President, however, these particular debts had been abundantly paid. There could be no more excuses, based on the Civil War, for degraded services, and the voters were showing that they would not much longer be patient. Both parties had promised reform. And although the Congressional oligarchy regarded the promise as a joke, Hayes did not. The first step he took was to make his Cabinet Ministers responsible for appointments in their departments. He asked Carl Schurz and William Evarts to draft rules to guide the Ministers. Since this was the passion of Schurz's life, the regulations were drawn up quickly and well. And on the whole they were followed, except in Sherman's Treasury Department, which as we have seen was needed for other purposes.

Under the heroic Schurz, in the Department of the Interior, was lodged the Indian Bureau: one of the most disgraceful government agencies in the long history of man's corruption. Schurz appointed an investigating board in 1877, and the report stated that the six million dollars a year which the government spent on the Bureau was mostly stolen. The Indian agencies were described as "simply a license to cheat and swindle the Indians in the name of the United States of America." Schurz cleaned house, and for the first time introduced the concept of honor into the nation's treatment of its wards; but he had no authority to make a permanent reform. Much of his work had later to be done again.

In trying to protect the Indian, Schurz found himself face to face with the lumber pirates: the men who took their impious sawmills into the great forests, destroying Indian reservations and the public domain alike, with no license, no property rights, no permission, nothing but impudence and a zest for imperial thievery. Schurz tried, says Eckenrode, "to check the suicidal policy of denuding the forest areas of the West for no better purpose than to make fortunes for scoundrels."[8] Needless to say, he failed. In the end the scoundrels drove him from public life. But here too his work was not wasted. Forest conservation and an honest Indian Bureau were both to come, and so long as they endure they will be monuments to a German immigrant who served his new country well.

While Schurz faced the large and little bandits of the empty West, Hayes calmly undertook to clean out the New York Custom House, a more than Herculean task. The Custom House was the center of Senator Conkling's machine, the fortress in which his political workers took refuge, the spoilsman's paradise. An investigating committee discovered two hundred little politicians on the Custom House pay roll who were doing nothing at all, except party work for Conkling. It also revealed that goods landed in New York were habitually undervalued, so that importers might be tempted to use that harbor. And of course it found that the salaries of all employees were assessed for the party funds.

Hayes began the war by ordering that there should be no more political assessments on salaries and no more political work by employees. Chester Arthur, the honest but lazy collector of the port, and Alonzo Cornell, the naval officer, defied the orders. Hayes asked for their resignations. When they paid no heed, Hayes appointed their successors, one of whom was the father of the future President Theodore Roosevelt. The Senate referred the names contemptuously to the Committee on Commerce, of which Conkling was chairman. When the session ended, the committee had taken no action. Imperturbably, Hayes sent the names back to the next session, and finally Conkling's committee reported on them unfavorably. After a bitter debate, in which some Democrats supported the Republican President, confirmation was refused. Hayes wrote in his diary: "In the language of the press, 'Senator Conkling has won a great victory over the administration.' . . . But the end is not yet. I am right and I shall not give up the contest." He waited until Congress adjourned, when the stalwart Senators were temporarily helpless; then in July, 1878, he dismissed Arthur and Cornell and appointed their successors.* So the fight was revived at the next session, which opened December 2, when the names of the new appointments came before the Senate.

The committee once more reported adversely; but during the full debate Hayes sent a message attacking Arthur and Cornell as pure spoilsmen. Conkling then overplayed his indignation and his attacks on the President, and the nominations were confirmed. As Eckenrode writes, "It is hardly possible for a congressman to win over a determined President . . . The long domination of the executive by the Congress was at an end; the issue was settled that the appointive power rests in the President."9

As a matter of fact, the battle against Conkling and the stalwarts had to be fought and won a second time, by Hayes's successor. Then it was ended forever.

5

While restoring home rule to the South and beating the proud leader of the stalwarts, Hayes was also faced with the remaining major problem of the day: cheap money. The depression which began in 1873 was still severe when Hayes became President, and the demand for cheap money from the West and South grew stronger as each successive season found farm prices still low and the farmer's need for cash still desperate. Meanwhile, the East remained confident that the economy would never be healthy until deflation had run its course, and that specie payments must be resumed on January 1, 1879, so that American credit would rise in Europe and capital might once more be attracted. This was a sectional and not a party question. Republicans and Democrats from the West and South wanted cheap money; Republicans and Democrats from the East wanted gold. Hayes was a convinced "sound-money" man. He took the unpopular side, the side of the rich Eastern "gold-bugs," at a time of furious passions.

Agriculture was undergoing a revolution during these days, and the farmer was bearing even more than his accustomed burdens. His trouble was not that his money was "sound" or "unsound," but that he had no money at all. Until that could be rectified he was sure to support any program which would raise the value of his commodities and lower the value of his debt.

The revolution which was ruining the farmer was commonly described

* The elder Roosevelt had died in the meantime.

by the city-dweller as modern progress. It took two forms: first, the opening of vast new territory to the west, so that more land was brought under cultivation between 1860 and 1890 than in the entire previous history of the United States; and second, the introduction of expensive labor-saving machinery, such as the reaper, the automatic self-binder, the corn-planter, the tractor, and the railways and steamships to carry farm produce to the ends of the earth. Once the overexpansion into virgin soils took place, the older farms of the Middle West and East were driven toward bankruptcy. And once the new machinery was invented, the growers of staple crops had to buy it, since the price of such crops on the world market was set by production-costs on mechanized farms. And progress in transport was making the market for unprotected staples a world market.

Doubtless the new machinery saved much labor. But it also lost many farms; for when the landowner goes bankrupt he comes out with nothing —unlike the businessman, who often seems refreshed by the experience.

The revolution meant, as Professors Morison and Commager point out, that "the average farm ceased to be a self-sufficient economic unit, where a man and his family raised most of what they ate, wore, and used, and provided their own amusement in neighborhood groups. It became, like West Indian sugar plantations, a cog in an industrial system, devoted to the raising of a staple crop, mechanized, and tied up with banking, railroading, and manufacturing."[10] The trouble with being "tied up with banking, railroading, and manufacturing" is that in a time of long depression the farmer is helpless. He cannot, as of old, reduce his cash purchases and live off his own, for he is deep in a money economy. His crops have become almost valueless, but his debts have not. He must pay them (in cash which has a higher purchasing power every day) or he must lose his farm. Hence the appeal of cheap money. We shall see the cause of free silver inspire a dedication, a feeling of glory and of despair, which would be absurd if men were merely discussing the relative virtues of two kinds of coin. But in the words of the Declaration of Independence, they were discussing "their lives, their fortunes, and their sacred honor." If we miss that point we shall underestimate the hopes and the hatreds of American politics between Hayes and McKinley.

We have seen the rise and defeat of the "Ohio idea," and the prolonged effort of the Greenback Party to maintain the paper-money standard. When Hayes was inaugurated, the Resumption Act of 1875 was on the statute books; but nobody knew whether it would be put into effect in 1879. And the demand for paper money was beginning to give way to the demand for a return to the free coinage of silver. "After all," thought the Westerner, "silver at 16 to 1 is worth ninety cents on the dollar. Even if the eastern 'gold-bugs' boggle at a paper coinage which is worth nothing, they should be happy to compromise on silver which is worth 90 per cent." The refusal of so mild a demand seemed to most of the farmers to be sheer hard-heartedness.

The first problem for Hayes was the Resumption Act. "The way to resume is to resume," said Secretary of the Treasury Sherman. Hayes told him to go ahead, promising to veto all attempts to repeal the Act. Sherman sold bonds for gold until he had a reserve of 40 per cent against the greenbacks, and confidently waited for January 1. As he expected, since the gold was available nobody wanted it. In New York, $135,000 of notes were presented for gold, and $400,000 of gold were presented for notes.

The next problem was silver. The success of resumption was fatal to the greenback movement; but it had no effect on the cry for free silver. The Congressional leaders of the silver movement were Representative Richard Bland of Missouri, a Democrat, and Senator William Allison of Iowa, a Republican. "Silver Dick" Bland was the more extreme. During the summer before Hayes was elected, Bland had introduced a bill for the free coinage of all silver brought to the mint, just as gold was freely coined. In November, 1877, the bill passed the House by 165 to 34. But the heart of the bill was removed in the Senate. Instead of the free coinage of all silver brought to the mint, the Senate provided that the Secretary of the Treasury should buy between two million and four million dollars' worth of silver bullion each month and should then coin it at approximately 16 to 1. The superior worldliness of the Senate is suggested by the fact that the bill, as amended, helped the silver kings of Nevada and Montana and California, but did nothing for the farmers. It would not bring down the price of money; but it might help to keep up the price of silver.

In February, 1878, Bland attacked the amended bill in the House. "I do not like this bill," he said; "it is not what the country expects." Yet he urged that it should be passed, as a prelude to a bill for free silver. The temper of the West is shown by his statement that if they could not get a genuine free-silver bill soon, "I am in favor of issuing paper money enough to stuff down the bond-holders until they are sick." So the Bland-Allison Bill passed, and went to President Hayes. On February 28, he returned it to the Congress with his veto. He pointed out that the market value of the silver dollars for which the bill provided would be ninety or ninety-two cents.

> Thus the silver dollar authorized by this bill [he wrote] is worth eight to ten per cent less than it purports to be worth, and is made a legal tender for debts contracted when the law did not recognize such coins as lawful money. . . . The standard of value should not be changed without the consent of both parties to the contract. . . . There is no power to compel a nation to pay its debts. Its credit depends on its honor.

The South and West would have answered that the standard of value was constantly changing without the consent of both parties to the contract. For six years every penny they had borrowed had grown more valuable before the day came to pay it back. Congress passed the Bland-Allison Bill over the President's veto on the very day that he returned it. Hayes was savagely attacked; but he had frustrated the inflationists at least for the time. Bland might have persuaded a small majority in the Senate to accept a bill for the unlimited coinage of silver; but he could not persuade the two-thirds majority which was needed to override a veto. Furthermore, business improved during 1878, and the following year prosperity at last returned. So the final battle over silver, the most passionate political fight in American history, was postponed until the next period of depression in the nineties.

6

As the problems of the Civil War receded, the problems of class conflict took their place. The Hayes Administration saw the last sorrows of Reconstruction and the first premonitory strikes—and also the series of murder trials which ended the "Molly Maguires" in Pennsylvania. Life in the anthracite country was bad, and bitterness unending. Most of the miners were Irish, and thus not docile. When the depression of the seventies drove starving men to take any jobs that were offered, the owners tried to bring in cheap labor, and the miners changed their secret society of "Molly Maguires" into a brotherhood for murder, sabotage, and indiscriminate terror. Private war raged in the coal valleys. Strike-breakers, owners, and superintendents were killed and maimed, and the companies were not slow to retaliate. At last a Pinkerton detective contrived to join the "Mollies" and to rise to a position of power. The murder trials for which he gave evidence destroyed the secret band; but they did not bring peace to the coal fields.* As we shall see, one reason for the change of immigration—from northern and western, to southern and eastern, Europe—which began in the eighties, was the hope of the anthracite owners to replace the Irish with cheaper and less quarrelsome workers.

In the same year, just after Hayes took office, the nation was stirred by its first big railway strikes, which crippled most of the lines east of the Mississippi. The depression had brought repeated wage reductions, and when a final cut of ten per cent was imposed in July, 1877, trainmen on the Baltimore and Ohio stopped work. The movement spread fast, with

---

* In order to ingratiate himself the detective posed as a murderer, a counterfeiter, and the holder of a war pension to which he had no right—unusual credentials, but they worked.

rioting and arson in the big towns. Then the bystanders grew bitter, for the strikes interfered with business and with many people's convenience. Class hatreds were probably stronger in the summer and autumn of 1877 than they had ever been in lucky America.

In West Virginia the governor called on the militia to break the strike; but the militia refused. So the governor turned to President Hayes, who perhaps unfortunately did not refuse. He sent a general and two hundred federal troops, and was soon asked for similar aid by the governors of Pennsylvania and Maryland.

Neither Hayes nor anyone else had faced the stormy problems involved in the use of federal power during industrial disputes. The day had come when industries not only spread across state borders, but sometimes grew richer and more powerful than the states in which they resided. Their minor class wars could not be controlled by the local police. Yet the immense, distant, impersonal power of the federal community was not likely to be used with sympathy or restraint if invoked in the midst of a strike. It was a new aspect of the old federal problem: to what extent can power be wisely used by a group of men who may never have come within hundreds (or thousands) of miles of the community which is affected? The militia of West Virginia probably understood their own B. and O. trainmen, whose strike they refused to break; but General Hancock saw nothing but a problem of "law and order."

Hayes felt he was right to "show firmness" and to send the troops. Although the precedent proved unfortunate there is no doubt the people backed Hayes at the time; for the first big strikes frightened America and the natural response of frightened people is to call for soldiers. Much sophistication is needed, and much experience with the strange world of mechanical progress, before strikes are taken stoically by the public as part of the inconvenient climate of modern life. America was a long way from such sophistication in the eighteen-seventies. The railway strikes bred a dangerous reaction. Courts, and in some cases state legislatures, sought to retreat into old doctrines of conspiracy. Labor for the first time began to listen attentively to new doctrines of socialism. A few more outbreaks as badly handled as the strikes of '77, and America might follow the pattern of class struggles on the Continent of Europe.

7

Before Hayes had successfully ended his war with the Senate he began a similar battle with the House of Representatives. The Democrats had control of the lower House in 1878 and they undertook to force the repeal of the remaining Reconstruction Acts—the laws allowing federal supervision of state elections. They attached the repeal as a series of riders to appropriation bills. The Republican Senate refused approval; but in the next Congress the Democrats had a majority in both houses. The money bills, with riders attached, were passed and sent to the President, who recorded in his diary on March 9, 1879: "They [Congress] will stop the wheels—block the wheels of government if I do not yield my convictions. . . . It will be severe, perhaps a long contest. I do not fear it. . . . The people will not allow this revolutionary cause to triumph."

The Democrats in the lower House excused their use of the riders on appropriation bills by quoting "grievance before supply," that famous phrase in the history of the English House of Commons. They said that the lower House in America, also, was the popular agency of government, and that its grievances must therefore be satisfied before it would vote supply. Hayes, who had studied constitutional law at Harvard under Justice Joseph Story, wrote in his diary on March 23: "With the doctrine established that the House may legitimately refuse to act unless the other branches of the Government obey its commands, the House of Representatives becomes a despotism." Hayes stood firm, and in the end the House surrendered.

"The people of this country," said Hayes, "are unwilling to see the supremacy of the Constitution replaced by the omnipotence of any department of the Government." In his view that applied to the Executive as well as to the Congress. Woodrow Wilson's remark that "the President is at liberty both in law and conscience to be as big a man as he can" would have seemed to Hayes as unconstitutional as the behavior of his own Congress. He would have agreed with Lord Bryce, who wrote that the President "does not sway the councils and guide the policy of those members of Congress who belong to his own side. The expression of his wishes conveyed in a message has not necessarily any more effect on Congress than an article in a prominent party newspaper. No duty lies on Congress to take up a subject to which he has called attention as needing legislation."[11]

This is a far cry from Wilson's words, and Wilson's practice; yet it is an accurate description of the office, until a popular President chooses to use its powers aggressively. Lincoln might have been the last strong President if Congress had been able to bully Hayes after ruining Johnson and making a dupe of Grant. Since Hayes stood firm Congress waited grimly for his successor. Conkling and the stalwarts showed what they **had in** mind when they decided on General Grant for a third term.

XXVI

Civil Service versus the Stalwarts

Toward the end of Hayes's term the position of the Republican Party was slightly improved. The business revival helped; but more important was the four-year-long proof that the party leadership did not consist solely of political babes, like Grant, or of stalwart ruffians. Hayes was a sensible and effective politician, but also an honest man. His Cabinet would do honor to any political group at any time. The Democrats, meanwhile, had been in control of the lower House for six years and of the Senate for two years. They appeared to have no policy, and their factional spirit has been described as "violent and depraved." Although they had long demanded home rule for the South and honest appointments in the civil service, they did little to help President Hayes when he fought for these reforms. So the record of Congress hurt the Democrats, while the record of the Executive helped people to forget the years of Republican shame.

The Republican National Convention met in Chicago on June 2, 1880. There Blaine and Conkling fought each other in a battle so furious that it is hard to remember they were fighting about nothing. Neither man had an idea or a principle; but each was consumed with malevolence toward the other. The ill will had been building since 1866, when both were in the House of Representatives and Blaine answered Conkling's arrogance by laughing at his "turkey-gobbler strut." The votes of the New York machine had helped to nominate Hayes in 1876; but the true purpose was to defeat Blaine. And for the same reason, in 1880, Conkling proposed a third term for Grant.

General Grant had recently returned from a two-year tour around the world. His fame in foreign countries had pleased the American people who found it easy to forget the black days of his presidency in the glory of the war years. Grant was only fifty-eight. He wanted the nomination, and he would probably have won it if Conkling had been a wiser man. The tradition against a third term did not seem to hurt Grant. As Professor Ford wrote, "it may be questioned whether this tradition does not owe its strength more to the ambition of politicians than to sincere conviction on the part of the people. . . . The reasoning of *The Federalist* in favor of continued re-eligibility is cogent in itself and is supported by the experience of other countries. . . ."*[1]

Aside from Blaine and Grant (who was really Conkling in disguise), the chief candidate was Hayes's Secretary of the Treasury, John Sherman. James A. Garfield, a popular party man with a good war record, and a career in the lower House which had been slightly stained by Crédit Mobilier, was floor manager for Sherman. Conkling, sarcastic and overbearing as ever, was floor manager for Grant. He had set the stage for the last stand of the Old Guard, the final triumph of the men who had saved the Union. The galleries were full of old soldiers; the delegations were stiff with major generals; and the bands played all the Northern songs of the war. If Conkling had confined himself to martial nostalgia and romance he might have won; but he could not resist the pleasure of insulting his neighbors. He fought every preliminary point—on the seating of delegates, on the rules for the convention—with such arrogance and rudeness that he had lost many votes for Grant before the nominations began. Then he almost repaired the harm with one of the famous nominating speeches of American politics.

He began by quoting in his rich voice:

> If asked what state he hails from
> Our sole reply shall be
> He hails from Appomattox
> And its famous apple tree!

This was good; but it almost exhausted the subject. What more was there to say about Grant? "His name is the most illustrious borne by living man," added Conkling. "Take the tried and true old hero—with the Old Guard behind him. . . . Nobody now is really disquieted about a third term except those who are longing for a first time." Doubtless very few people were disquieted by a third term; but a great many were disquieted by the Old Guard, which was all too literally behind Grant, and would troop back into power with him. Not even the noble battle music could lift men's hearts once they began thinking about Boutwell, and Babcock, and Belknap, and similar characters from the unlamented past.

Garfield made a good speech for his candidate, John Sherman. Then the voting began. The real fight was between Blaine and Conkling, the half-breeds and the stalwarts. The convention soon saw that neither could win, because the hatred was so great that there could be no shifting of votes between the two camps. For thirty-four ballots Grant's vote varied between 302 and 313, Blaine's between 282 and 285. There were 756 delegates, 379 being a majority.

* From *The Cleveland Era* by H. J. Ford, vol. 4, THE CHRONICLES OF AMERICA, copyright Yale University Press.

Sherman had expected to benefit when the break came; but Sherman was cold and unpopular, though everyone praised his ability. Garfield, on the other hand, was one of the best-liked men in the party; so when the delegates felt they had been faithful long enough they turned to him. The stalwarts never broke; Grant had 309 votes at the end. Years later Sherman came to feel that his floor manager had been disloyal to him; but there is no evidence that Garfield had planned or expected the nomination, or that he did anything but accept a wholly unexpected accident.

Knowing Conkling's vengeful temper, the convention sought to placate him by naming his henchman, Chester A. Arthur, for the vice-presidency. This was a wasted effort. The followers of Blaine and of Sherman worked faithfully in the campaign; but the stalwarts sulked until September, when Grant, Cameron, and Conkling made their famous trip to Ohio to see Garfield and repair the breach. Garfield wrote in his diary, "I had no private conversation with the party." This was not the view of the others, who insisted they received promises which were never fulfilled. So the good-will visit ended by adding to a bitterness which was already wicked.

The Democratic Party, meanwhile, met in convention at Cincinnati and nominated General Winfield Scott Hancock who had been a Union commander at the battle of Gettysburg. Tilden refused to be a candidate because of his age and health; and the party turned to Hancock (who knew and cared nothing about politics) in order to prove that it was loyal and that it, too, had generals.

The campaign was listless so far as the public was concerned, but furious on the part of the politicians, who abused each other with more than normal folly. The Democrats published (in a magazine humorously called *Truth*) a forged letter from Garfield which endorsed the importation of cheap Oriental labor. The lie was successful, for Hancock won five electoral votes in California. The Republicans retaliated with simple and extensive bribery. Garfield won by only 10,000 votes in a total of more than nine million.*

2

The new President, with a nice regard for American tradition, had been born in a log cabin. His father, a pioneer farmer in Ohio, died when Garfield was two years old, so the boy knew hard poverty in his childhood. Yet by 1856, when he was twenty-five, he had worked his way through Williams College and had gained a capacity for studying which was to be

---

* Garfield had 4,454,416 votes, Hancock 4,444,952. Garfield had 214 electoral votes, Hancock 155.

his strength throughout life. Unlike many politicians, he acquired knowledge through books rather than people.

He married when he was twenty-seven, and the next year was elected as a Republican to the state senate of Ohio. In the summer of 1861 he raised a regiment of volunteers and became its colonel. He learned military theory exhaustively and well from his books; the practice was soon provided by the enemy. Garfield was a brigadier general of volunteers when he fought at Shiloh, the most deadly battle in the West. At Chickamauga he was chief of staff to Rosecrans, and although the commanding general's reputation suffered from that battle Garfield's was enhanced. He was made a major general, but soon left the army for the House of Representatives, where he served for the next eighteen years. He and Blaine were the dominant figures after Thaddeus Stevens died, and when Blaine went to the Senate Garfield ruled alone. The House was by that time Democratic, so he became leader of the Opposition.

Garfield's name was on the list of those to whom Oakes Ames distributed Crédit Mobilier stock. Garfield denied receiving it; but he could not deny having taken a fee from a paving-block company which was seeking favors from the government. His constituents, however, re-elected him in spite of these disclosures, and in spite of the fact that he was a "sound-money" man at a time when Ohio was for inflation. They were proud of his record as a parliamentarian; and as for his irregularities, they doubtless took the view of the Milwaukee *Sentinel* which wrote in 1880 that Garfield's name "is exceptionally clean for a man who has been engaged for twenty years in active politics."

In 1880 the Ohio legislature promoted Garfield to the United States Senate. His comment in his diary on January 28 would not have endeared him to his new associates. "I have this premonition," he wrote, "that the Senate is composed of old men whose ideas and opinions are crystallized into fixed and well-nigh unchangeable forms. A decided majority of all my associates who have gone from the House to the Senate have been measurably lost in its silences. . . . I enter the Senate with great doubt." In fact he never entered it at all. He became President instead, and John Sherman returned to the Senate.

3

As usual the appointment of the Cabinet was the first sign of the new Administration's purpose. This time it was a sign of war—literally to the death. Garfield chose Blaine as Secretary of State, showing that he was prepared to finish the battle against Conkling and the stalwarts which Hayes had begun. The rest of the appointments are not important, since

Garfield was to be President so short a time; but they included a "sound-money" Westerner as Secretary of the Treasury, and Robert Lincoln (eldest and only surviving son of Abraham) as Secretary of War.

On March 23, less than three weeks after his inauguration, Garfield sent to the Senate a list of appointments which included William Robertson as collector of the port of New York. Robertson was an anti-Conkling New Yorker, a "half-breed." The challenge was as sharp as when Hayes sought to oust Chester Arthur. Garfield wrote:

> This [nomination] brings on the contest at once and will settle the question whether the President is registering clerk of the Senate or the Executive of the United States. Summed up in a single sentence this is the question: shall the principal port of entry in which more than ninety per cent of all our customs duties are collected be under the control of the administration or under the local control of the factional senator.[2]

As Professor Binkley points out, this letter is an adequate reply to those who think that Garfield challenged Conkling by accident.

Conkling was not one to dodge a fight. He announced that the President had made a declaration of war and had violated the promises given when Grant and Conkling visited Ohio during the campaign. He asked for the rejection of William Robertson on the grounds of "senatorial courtesy," declaring once again that federal appointments in New York must be personally acceptable to the Senators from that state. Since the other Senator from New York was known as "Me-too" Platt, this meant that appointments must be acceptable to Conkling.*

While taking this stand, Conkling persuaded many leading Republicans to advise the President to compromise, so as to save the party. Garfield's comment is interesting: "If it were a difference between individuals there could be some sense in such advice. But the one represents a whole independent function of the government. The other is 1/76 of 1/2 of another independent branch of the government with which compound vulgar fractions the President is asked to compromise."[3] Clearly, the office would lose none of its prerogatives while Garfield was at the White House. According to John Hay, the President said, "They may take Robertson out of the Senate head first or feet first. I will never withdraw him."

What Conkling and his friends planned to do was neither to accept Robertson nor to reject him: not to carry him out head first or feet first, but to leave him to die of old age. When this became obvious, Garfield withdrew all the nominations except those for the Custom House. There would be no appointments of any sort until the question of the President's independence from "compound vulgar fractions" was settled.

---

* Thomas Platt was a hardened stalwart. He had been elected to the Senate by the New York legislature the previous January.

Meanwhile, the "star route" frauds had been revealed to a public which thought the days of such surprises were past. A ring of criminals in Washington had received contracts for delivering the mails on routes where neither railways nor steamboats ran. They had hired local carriers to do the work for a small sum, and received a large sum from the Post Office for themselves. An ex-Senator and the Second Assistant Postmaster General were heavily involved. Although the evil centered in the Executive Department, and the Assistant Postmaster General in question had been active during the recent campaign, the tale smacked so of "Grantism" and the Old Guard that it helped to turn the public against the stalwarts. When Garfield insisted on vigorous prosecution he strengthened his position in the country and the Senate saw that it would have to confirm the appointments.

Conkling had one last hope. He resigned his seat in May, after Robertson was accepted, and induced Platt (who had scarcely unpacked) to resign also. The two of them then appealed to the New York State legislature for vindication and re-election. "If they had been returned," wrote John Sherman, "the President would have been powerless to appoint anyone in New York without consulting the senators, practically transferring to them his constitutional power."[4]

The struggle at Albany for rehabilitation became intense and furious. But Conkling had been losing strength at home ever since his first defeat by President Hayes. In spite of all that Vice-President Arthur could do the once pliant legislature of New York rebelled and neither of the Senators was returned. The country was startled but amused. Conkling disappeared from politics.

Platt had still a long career ahead of him as Republican boss of New York—perhaps the strongest and certainly the most smooth and silent manipulator of patronage the state has known. "He organised . . . the alliance between politics and business," writes William Allen White, "a necessary function in the clash between agriculture and industry that the times were staging. . . . American capital had been struggling for three decades for just the privileges which in New York State Platt's leadership was giving to capital."* The ex-Senator was far happier in this secret work

---

* William Allen White, *Masks in a Pageant,* p. 56. On pages 46 and 47 of the same book White gives a classic description of one type of state boss. "As a rule," he writes, "a man running for the legislature has no money to spend on his campaign. Platt furnished the candidate with money for election expenses through the agency of the State Central Committee. . . . Certain things in politics are changeless. For instance, when the legislature is elected a legislator is inclined to abide by the decision of the party caucus on questions that require his vote. If he bolts the caucus, a new man often appears from his district the next session. If a corporation, or an interested citizen or business concern has a bill pending before the legislature, it is evident that the person to see about that bill is the man who controls the party caucus. That man is he who sends the campaign expenses to the

than in playing "Me-too" to Conkling on the national stage. Nothing disturbed him in his darkness until the end of the century when he had the misfortune to collide with the rising young Theodore Roosevelt.

Garfield did not have time to enjoy the fall of Conkling. The vicious personal bitterness which had stained American politics ever since the murder of Lincoln, the degradation of great causes (indeed, of the Union victory itself) for the sake of party triumphs and of spoils, finally bred a deed of madness which marked symbolically the end of a bad era. On July 2, 1881, while Conkling and Platt were fighting for their jobs at Albany, Garfield was shot by a disappointed office-seeker, a lawyer named Charles Guiteau. The assassin gave himself up to the police, who found the following statement on his person: "The President's tragic death was a sad necessity, but it will unite the Republican party and save the Republic. . . . I had no illwill toward the President. His death was a political necessity. . . . I am a Stalwart of the Stalwarts."[5] In other words, the mad crime was done to put Chester Arthur in the presidency, because Arthur was the henchman of Conkling. Presumably Arthur would not interfere with the spoils system perfected by his master—that man of noble presence and commanding voice who had inherited all the evil of the Vindictives (the radicals of Andrew Johnson's day) without even their thin pretense of a principle. Guiteau had only carried into crazed, logical action the language and the manners which had been made fashionable by Conkling.

Garfield died after eleven weeks of pain. If he had served for two terms he could not have done more for his cherished purpose of breaking the hold of the spoilsmen. The stalwarts could no longer hope, as when Hayes was President, to sit through one honest Administration and then gaily return to the pigsty. The public at last was ready for civil-service reform. When Conkling was asked if he would remain in public life he answered: "How can I battle with a shroud? How can I speak into an open grave? Silence is a duty and a doom."[6]

---

candidates for the legislature. . . . From 1882 until 1902 that particular man to see about New York legislation was Thomas Collier Platt."

The state boss is likely to rule by being helpful to business or to strong pressure groups. The city boss is likely to rule by giving private social services to families who would otherwise be destitute, and who become properly grateful. In either case the boss may be a blessing or a nuisance. The distinction between a good and a bad machine is likely to depend upon the origin of the money which makes the services possible. But good or bad, city or state, these are the machines with which every President must deal. If he fights with too many of them his Administration will fail, for the machines are likely to own (or to be owned by) members of Congress. And even when he fights successfully, and gets rid of a Conkling, the next stage is likely to be a Platt—an improvement certainly, but still short of perfection.

4

Chester Arthur could scarcely have become President under more distressing circumstances. Guiteau had murdered Garfield in order to put an old-fashioned spoilsman in the White House. Although there was no connection between the criminal and the Vice-President, vague, unpleasant talk was inevitable. The country did not welcome Arthur. Also, the Senate was so evenly divided that neither party could rule, and the small Republican majority in the House was lost in 1882. Yet in spite of these handicaps, Arthur was a good President. He could not impose his own policies, since he lacked both the public and the party support which are essential; but he maintained the dignity which Hayes had restored to the White House, and falsified the hopes of his Custom-House cronies as well as the expectations of the demented Guiteau.

Arthur was born in 1830, in Vermont, the son of a Scotch-Irish Baptist clergyman. He was educated at Union College, and soon moved to New York City, where he became a successful lawyer. Shortly before the Civil War he married a charming wife, the daughter of a naval officer. New York State had a Republican government during the first two years of the war, and Arthur became inspector general and quartermaster general— exacting and troublesome posts because of the system of recruiting. Volunteers were enlisted in their local communities, and were received and equipped by their own state government. They were then turned over to the federal authorities and the state was repaid for their equipment and maintenance. No system could be more cumbersome or more conducive to fraud. As always, Arthur was efficient in administration and accurate in accounts. In 1863, when Horatio Seymour became governor, Arthur was replaced. He retired with a vast accumulation, not of public funds, but of knowledge about the politics and politicians in every district of the state. This was to be his hobby: the handling of these devious characters, the sorting and balancing and juggling of their strange rivalries and greeds. While imposing the most rigid financial honesty upon himself, he seems never (in his New York State days) to have cared how his companions behaved.

Silently, and perhaps with the interest a botanist might feel in some monstrous distortion of a flower, he watched the Tweed Ring at work, and even held office under it. Slowly, he became one of the trusted and important figures in the state machine of Roscoe Conkling. In 1871 Grant made him collector of the Port of New York, where again he saw to it that no money was stolen, and also that none of the thousand employees wasted too much time on the public business.* As we have seen, he and Alonzo Cornell (the naval officer of the Port who was also state chairman of the Republican Party) thought Hayes must be joking when he told the civil servants to take no part in politics. When the Senate backed Hayes against Conkling, Arthur and Cornell were out of jobs. The latter became governor of New York State, and the former Vice-President. When Conkling and Platt resigned their seats, Arthur went with them to Albany to work for their re-election, or "vindication." No wonder Guiteau thought he was putting a reliable "stalwart" in the White House. Yet from the moment he became President Arthur was a disappointment to his political friends.

Whether he was shocked by the melodramatic end of Conkling's battle with two Presidents, or whether he felt that the amused detachment with which he had taken part in state politics was inappropriate to the Washington scene, he turned against the spoils system, against the Custom House habit of padding the rolls, and against his Custom House friends. Most daring of all, he attacked that monument of corruption and special privilege, the Republican tariff. The public backed him on civil-service reform; but on the tariff he could only help to prepare for a far distant day.

5

In 1879, "Gentleman George" Pendleton of Ohio was elected to the United States Senate. We last saw him at the Democratic National Convention of 1868, when he and his "Ohio idea" were candidates for the nomination and for the platform respectively. The "idea" was put into the platform; but the man was rejected in favor of Seymour. After years of retirement, Pendleton returned to Washington resolute to improve the tone of government. He believed—as Alexander Hamilton and Justice Joseph Story had fervently held—that the needlessly sharp separation between Congress and the Executive was a chief cause of inefficiency. The separation, as we have seen, was not made by the Constitution, but by the will (or the jealousy) of Congress. Pendleton proposed a law to allow Cabinet members to defend and debate the Administration's measures on the floor of Congress.

This system [said the Congressional committee which reported the bill] will require the selection of the strongest men to be heads of depart-

* There seems to have been an accepted difference, in the code of those days, between putting money in one's own pocket and bribing business men to use the Port of New York by undervaluing their imports.

ments, and will require them to be well equipped with the knowledge of their offices. It will also require the strongest men to be the leaders of Congress and participate in the debate. It will bring those strong men in contact, perhaps into conflict, to advance the public weal, and thus stimulate their abilities and their efforts, and will thus assuredly result to the good of the country.[7]

Blaine, who was about to become Secretary of State, and the Republican Senators Allison of Iowa and Ingalls of Kansas, and the Democratic Senator Voorhees of Indiana, backed Pendleton in this proposal, agreeing it would be "the first step toward a sound civil service reform, which will secure a larger wisdom in the adoption of policies." Nothing happened. This is a plan which seems destined to be put forward in each generation, to be treated with respect, and then to be ushered back to the limbo from which it briefly emerged.

While pressing for his major reform, Pendleton had also introduced a bill for the merit system in the civil service. This was neglected during the last days of the Hayes Administration, for Congress still hoped to revive the worst excesses of "Grantism" as soon as Hayes retired to his farm. The bill continued to be neglected while Garfield and Conkling fought each other to extinction. But when Arthur became President he astounded his friends and enemies alike by supporting the Pendleton Act. It became law on January 16, 1883. Although supplemented by many presidential rules and orders, and by later Acts of Congress, it remains the basic statute to this day.

There were three main points to the Pendleton Act. First, it forbade political assessments on federal officeholders. There is so close a bond between the spoils system and political assessments that the one will not flourish without the other. To the true spoilsman, public offices are part of the assets of the machine. Officeholders, therefore, have a direct financial interest in the success of the machine. They must contribute according to a set scale: usually from two to five per cent of their salary. If the thousands, or tens of thousands, of appointees cannot help to fill the party chest, and are not even allowed to do political work in their spare time, what is the use of giving them jobs?*

Many years were to pass, of course, before the prohibitions in the Pendleton Act became wholly effective. And it was not until the Hatch Act that every form of political work was forbidden to all federal employees except policy-making officials. Then at last the civil servants, no matter how they may have acquired their jobs, were compelled to be neutral, and thus useless to the machine.

---

* Under the Hatch Act (1939), as interpreted by the Civil Service Commission in 1940, federal employees may contribute to political parties—but no one may contribute more than $5000.

Second, the Pendleton Act provided for a Civil Service Commission* to build and to administer a new type of service, on the merit system. At first, only thirteen per cent of the federal jobs were affected; but the President could expand the classified service at his discretion. Most Presidents have done so: especially Cleveland, Theodore Roosevelt, Wilson, and Franklin Roosevelt. During the last year of President Hoover's term eighty per cent of the federal civil service was under the merit system. Four years later, in 1936, because the emergency New Deal agencies were not under civil-service regulations, the percentage had dropped to sixty; but by 1948 it had risen again to eighty-three.

Third, the Act provided that all appointments to jobs in the "classified" services—that is, those coming under the merit system—should be made as a result of open competitive examinations. Appointments, however, were to be apportioned among the states according to population: an inevitable arrangement in a federal system, although reformers complained. An impoverished state such as Mississippi, with an impoverished educational system, could not be asked to support a civil service from which her own citizens were virtually excluded.

In 1883, the spoils system was put on the defensive in Washington and it has remained there ever since. Yet it has not been abolished, and is not likely to be abolished, for two main reasons: first, the usefulness of Executive patronage in a government of divided powers; and second, the slightly disappointing results of civil-service reform. Security of tenure, regularity of salary increases, promotion according to merit, and guarantee of pensions, have not always attracted the ablest types of men from business and the professions. Presidents with vast new federal agencies to staff sometimes find they can do better on the patronage than on the "merit" system. Men will work for the political cause, the party, or the President himself, who would not want a permanent place in a bureaucracy.**

In the states, meanwhile, there has been no rush toward civil-service reform. In the year of the Pendleton Act, New York passed a civil-service law of its own, and about fifteen other states have since done the same. The Acts are not everywhere well administered;*** and in the counties, where the political machines have their true roots, the spoils system is almost uncontaminated. There are 3056 counties in America, and forty of them have adopted the merit system. In 1939 the forty-eight states con-

* This is the first of the new Executive agencies under the President—under the President but not connected with a regular department.

** The federal civil service had about 3000 employees in 1800, and 2,090,732 in 1948.

*** In Louisiana, for example, the civil-service system was recently wrecked by a statute placing it practically in the hands of the governor and destroying the independence of the state commission.

tained 175,000 local units of government, which employ more than 900,-
000 people altogether. So the machine still has jobs at its disposal.

6

President Arthur succeeded with the Pendleton Act because the public
was behind him; but he had no similar support in his other attempts at
reform. When he sought an appropriation to improve the Mississippi
waterways, Congress allowed him $4,000,000, but at the same time ap-
propriated another $14,000,000 for river and harbor schemes which he
did not want and which had no national value. This is a type of legislation which always threatens a large federal society, wherein the legislators
think of their own districts first and of the nation afterwards.* Arthur
wanted four million dollars to repair the waterway which served the vast
central valley of America. Congressmen from other regions said, in effect,
"Yes, you can have your money for your useful cause, so long as we get
something extra to fritter away at home. Our people would not like to pay
taxes to improve the Mississippi, unless they got a commission for themselves." By the time every member had added his bit, three and a half
times as much money was to be wasted as was to be used in the common
interest. "Thus," said the President in his veto message, "as the bill becomes more objectionable it secures more support." The excellence of the
epigram did Arthur no good, for he lacked a national following to which
he could appeal over the heads of the parochial representatives. The bill
was passed in spite of his veto.

Nobody wanted to waste fourteen million dollars. But once the game of
exchanging favors began, most Congressmen were willing to raise the
stakes, and raise them again, in order that they themselves might have a
share. When the crazy total was reached, nobody but the President could
even try to intervene. But the President's veto failed—for the strength of
his office depends upon influence rather than authority, and the influence
depends upon circumstances, which were all unpropitious for Arthur. He
had cut himself off from his political friends by supporting the Pendleton
Act, so he had no normal channels for reaching the local machines, for
promising favors and asking favors in return. And the public as a whole
was worried about him—not hostile, but certainly not friendly—because
of his lighthearted past, and because of the unhappy way he came to
power. He was useless to the Congressmen in fighting their district battles:
the support of Chester Arthur did not bring votes. With no party to impose

* "A Congressional district is sometimes a hard taskmaster," said Vice-President
Garner after forty-six years in public life. "None of them ever reach a point where
they say: 'Just let our interests rock along and go be a national statesman.' " (Cp.
Bascom Timmons, *Garner of Texas,* p. 286.)

discipline, and no public backing to inspire hope or fear, Arthur was helpless. Fourteen million dollars was thrown away.

Yet the story has a happy ending. The clarity and intelligence of the President's veto was more effective than the Congressmen thought. The voters noticed that their tribune had tried to protect them, and had been thrust aside. Senator Hoar, who favored the bill, says that "a large number of the members of the House who voted for it lost their seats," and that it "cost the Republican Party its majority in the House of Representatives."[8] This only meant that future vetoes by Arthur might be given more weight, since he had proved that he could command a public hearing. It did not mean that Congress would refrain from similar bills in the future. It is in the nature of a Congress representing localities to pass such bills. Except in foreign affairs—in times of recognized danger—most Senators represent their states, or the great economic interests of their region, and most members of the lower House represent their city wards, their small towns, their rural counties, their trade unions. America would suffer if this were not so. But America also suffers when the President's influence declines so far that he cannot sustain his veto. In a huge federal society, the secret of good government is often to prevent things from happening.

7

Having failed over rivers and harbors, Arthur boldly turned to the most vexed issue of all: the tariff. Here was the easy, long-unchallenged field for the lobbying and jockeying and log-rolling which produces the type of bill that gets more support as it becomes more objectionable. We have seen how Grant feared to use his prestige for tariff revision when the country had but recently abandoned free trade—just as he had feared to support the first faint efforts toward civil-service reform in 1871. By the time Arthur faced the problem, vested interests had been accumulating behind the tariff wall for twenty years, and if a single brick blew down there came a cry for help. Yet Arthur had one point in his favor: the government was burdened with too much money. The annual surplus was more than $145,000,000. In his message to Congress on December 4, 1882, the President said: "Either the surplus must lie idle in the treasury or the government will be forced to buy at market rates its bonds, not then redeemable, and which under such circumstances cannot fail to command an enormous premium, or the swollen revenues will be devoted to extravagant expenditures, which, as experience has taught, is ever the bane of an overflowing treasury."

Hoping to evade all talk of reducing the tariff—which was even more regional and contentious in its benefits than the Mississippi River—the House passed a bill reducing internal revenue taxes, so that the surplus might become less tempting and embarrassing. But the Senate, under its power to amend money bills, added onto this simple bill a complete revision of most of the tariff schedules. The two houses appointed a joint committee which reported forty-eight hours before the close of the session. The members of the committee had abandoned themselves to bartering one favor for another. The statute on which they agreed was one of the silliest in the history of the American tariff; yet both houses passed it without delay. There was no time for thought, and if action were postponed until the next session the President might marshal public opinion behind the wise recommendations of his tariff commission, which gave no special favors to districts with powerful or wily Congressmen.

> Thus pressed for time [writes Professor Ford], Congress passed a bill containing features obnoxious to a majority in both Houses and offensive to public opinion. Senator Sherman in his *Recollections* expressed regret that he had voted for the bill and declared that, had the recommendations of the . . . commission been adopted, "the tariff would have been settled for many years," but "many persons wishing to advance their particular interests appeared before the committee and succeeded in having their views adopted."*[9]

Here are some examples of how they succeeded:

> The office and duty of a conference committee [wrote a member of the House of Representatives in 1884] is to adjust the difference between two disagreeing houses. This House had decided that bar-iron of the middle class should pay $20 a ton; the Senate that it was to pay $20.16 a ton. The gentlemen of the conference committee reconciled this difference—how? By raising bar-iron (of this class) above both House and Senate to $22.40. The Tariff Commission reported that the tariff on iron ore should be 50 cents a ton. The Senate said it should be 50 cents a ton. The House said it should be fifty cents a ton. Gentlemen of the conference committee reconciled the agreement of the House, Senate and Tariff Commission into a disagreement, and made the duty on iron ore 75 cents a ton. The gentlemen of the conference did a similar service for the great corporation of corporations, the Iron and Steel Association, by giving it a tax of $17 on steel rails, which the House had fixed at $15 and the Senate at $15.68 per ton.[10]

The President accepted this inane bill, admitting that he thought it bad, but seeing no reason to believe the public cared. And without the public he could do nothing, because the Congress and the political parties only wanted to dodge responsibility.

* From *The Cleveland Era* by H. J. Ford, vol. 4, THE CHRONICLES OF AMERICA, copyright Yale University Press.

XXVII

Cleveland, Reform, and Laissez-Faire

Early in June, 1884, the Republican National Convention met in Chicago. Chester Arthur hoped for the nomination and felt he deserved it; but his only support came from the waning faction of stalwarts, and even they were not enthusiastic since they rightly felt that Arthur had betrayed them by supporting the Pendleton Act. The friends of reform, who should have been grateful to Arthur, had never trusted him. Men like Senator Hoar, and the charming George William Curtis of *Harper's Weekly,* and the young Theodore Roosevelt and Henry Cabot Lodge, gave their support to Senator Edmunds of Vermont, who had been in the upper House since 1866 and who was a merciless, bitter foe of every type of jobbery. But Edmunds never had more than ninety-three votes. Blaine was once more the favorite of the convention, and this time he could not be stopped. The Mulligan letters had undone him in 1876; Conkling, with the help of Grant, had blocked him in 1880. But now Conkling was ruined, and Grant was dying, and Garfield who had snatched the prize so unexpectedly was dead. The first ballot showed that neither George Edmunds nor Chester Arthur had a serious following. On the fourth ballot Blaine was chosen.

Before long the delegates were sorry for what they had done. Thousands of Republicans were in no mood for Blaine. They wanted to forget the bloody shirt, the feuds of stalwarts and half-breeds, the long disgrace of the spoilsmen. But Blaine, with his Little Rock and Fort Smith Railroad, would not help them forget. If the Democrats should find a man with a fresh, clean name, he might attract Republican votes. Strangely, they possessed such a man in Governor Cleveland of New York. And even more strangely, they had the wisdom to nominate him.

Stephen Grover Cleveland, son of a Presbyterian clergyman, was born in a parsonage at Caldwell, New Jersey. He became a national figure not because of brilliance but because of strong conscience and unbending character, so it is interesting to notice that during four generations his family had bred ministers of the church.

> So much has been made of the humble circumstances in which Grover made his start in life [wrote Professor Ford] that the unwary reader might easily imagine the future President was almost a waif. Nothing

could be farther from the truth. He really belonged to the most authentic aristocracy that any state of society can produce—that which maintains its standards and principles from generation to generation by the integrity of the stock without any endowment of wealth.*[1]

Cleveland's father died when the boy was sixteen, leaving the mother with nine children on her hands, so Grover did not have the education which was intended for him. After a few years of earning his living planlessly, he went to stay with his uncle at Buffalo, where he studied law and was admitted to the bar in 1859.

He was already a Democrat, although his uncle and patron was a Whig who had become a Republican, and although the Republicans were the strongest party in upper New York. Years later he said he chose to be a Democrat because that was the party of solidity and conservatism, and because he disapproved of Frémont as presidential candidate. This was typical of Cleveland, the most guarded of men, bound to take offense at the Byronic qualities of Frémont and to resent the abolitionist wing of the Republican Party. Yet as Allan Nevins says, there were two Clevelands, and it is easy to lose sight of the cheerful, amusing companion in the wary, austere figure of the public man.

> He was a hard-working young lawyer, spending incredibly long hours at his desk and seeming to those who knew him but slightly to be growing into a stiff, heavy, and stern man. Many hasty observers spoke of his impassivity and dignity. But he was also a roystering blade, who knew the inside of dozens of saloons, led the chorus in lusty drinking songs, and prided himself on feats of conviviality which sometimes, as he puts it later, caused him to "lose a day." The picture of Cleveland at 2 A.M. laboring over his law books is strictly accurate; and so is the picture of Cleveland at 2 A.M. in the back room of Diebold's, or Schwabl's, or Louis Goetz's . . . cafés, chanting "There's a hole in the bottom of the sea" with cronies as intent as himself on filling it up. . . .[2]

At the age of twenty Cleveland began attending Democratic city conventions and at twenty-five his party elected him ward supervisor. A few months later he was appointed assistant district attorney, an office which taught him all that a man should know about the unpleasant side of local government. During the same year, 1863, his name was called under the Conscription Act. He had the choice of serving in the army, or furnishing a substitute, or paying a commutation of $300. Since he was without military ambition and was helping to support his mother, he found a substitute, to whom he paid $150.

In 1865 he was nominated for district attorney, but was beaten in the

---

* From *The Cleveland Era* by H. J. Ford, vol. 4, THE CHRONICLES OF AMERICA, copyright Yale University Press.

election. Except for purely party work, such as serving as delegate to the state convention at Albany, he then refrained from politics until 1870, when he accepted election as sheriff of Erie County. This was an office which brought rich fees, and which again put Cleveland in touch with the most unsavory aspects of government. Buffalo at the time was said to have more saloons, brothels, and gambling houses than any other American town of its size. The office of sheriff was not a sinecure. He served for three years and then returned to the law until 1881, when he began the most sudden and spectacular rise to high office in the history of American politics.

Cleveland was forty-four in 1881, an unknown, middle-aged bachelor of small means, with a respectable law practice. Three years later he was elected President of the United States. His first chance came because of his careful and painful knowledge of the Buffalo underworld, both criminal and political. There was a sudden demand by citizens of both parties for a mayor who would reform the local government. The Democrats, caring only for victory, nominated Cleveland, who was known to be honest and who inspired trust on sight. He was elected, and at once set to work to do precisely what he had promised. Unlike most reform mayors he understood the secret ways of city government. The politicians were soon eager for his term to end; but the taxpayers were pleased and his reputation spread. Then came the astonishing accident, which not only made Cleveland a national figure but which allowed Roscoe Conkling (without knowing what he did) once more to frustrate Blaine.

When Conkling and Platt resigned from the Senate in 1881, and returned to Albany for "vindication" and re-election, the governor was Alonzo Cornell of Custom House fame. Like Arthur, he had turned a new leaf, and he was making an excellent governor. He saw no reason why he should stir himself to strengthen the Conkling machine; so he did nothing for the Senators who thereupon failed of re-election. Although Conkling was ruined as a leader, he still had enough strength to destroy Cornell, whom he described as "that lizard on the hill." With the help of President Arthur, of all possible pressure from the Administration, and of considerable fraud, Cornell was defeated for renomination in 1882. The Republican state convention chose Charles James Folger, Arthur's Secretary of the Treasury, and thereby opened the governorship to Cleveland. Folger had been a good Secretary of the Treasury. There was nothing against him except his patrons; but that was too much. The ousting of Cornell revived all the bitter memories of all the "stalwart" fights, and the public was disgusted. George Curtis wrote in *Harper's Weekly* that Folger's nomination "was procured by the combined power of fraud and patronage, and to support it would be to acquiesce in them as legitimate forces in a convention."

The Democrats needed only an honest candidate. Their man did not have to be famous; but he did have to be clean and upright. Wisely, they chose Grover Cleveland, and he was elected by 534,318 votes to 342,464. At that moment his special qualities were exactly what was wanted for the job. Ever since the days of Aaron Burr and the Clinton family, New York State politics had been dark and complicated; but never more than when Cleveland went to Albany in 1883.

Perhaps the largest swindles at the state capital were committed on behalf of business, but the most numerous were committed at the expense of business, and were known as "strike" bills—that is, bills which were introduced for the purpose of being withdrawn after the payment of blackmail. With his strength and good sense, with the help of reformers in both parties, and with an abundant use of the veto, Cleveland found his way through the fog of corruption and gave the people renewed hope that they could understand and control the political machinery which surrounded them. Incidentally, Cleveland won the hatred of John Kelly, boss of Tammany Hall. And this, too, was to stand him in good stead.

The Democratic National Convention of 1884 met at Chicago, a month after Blaine had been nominated. Because of the disgruntled Republicans who were prepared to desert their "Plumed Knight" for a man of unquestioned strength and honor, Cleveland was the obvious choice. Tilden once more refused to be considered, and though Senator Bayard of Delaware and ex-Senator Thurman of Ohio had strong claims on the party, Cleveland was nominated on the second ballot. The enmity of Tammany had helped him greatly, for the party outside New York City was tired of Tammany, with its endless, devious jealousies and feuds. And at this time Tammany made itself more than usually hateful by conspiring with Benjamin Butler! Having failed as a Republican, Butler had joined the Greenback Party. Then he made overtures to the unhappy Democrats, with whom he had begun his political life in 1853. In Massachusetts the Democrats accepted him; but the thought that the most detested of the Republican radicals and the ex-military governor of New Orleans should seek favors from a Democratic National Convention would have made anyone but Butler and Tammany Hall cringe. "We may be willing to eat crow," said a Georgia delegate, looking disgustedly at Butler and perhaps remembering 1872 and Horace Greeley; "but we'll be damned if we'll eat turkey buzzard." General Edward Bragg of Wisconsin put the sense of the convention when he told Tammany that the young men from his part of the country "love Cleveland for his character, but they love him also for the enemies he has made." Three times in four years—in town, state, and nation—Cleveland was chosen because the spoilsmen hated him.

2

The nomination of Cleveland gave the anti-Blaine Republicans a cause and a leader. What little they knew about Cleveland was good, and best of all was the fact that his rise to fame had been fast, and his record was therefore short. He was uncontaminated by the stale hatreds of the previous twenty years. Blaine was steeped in those hatreds, and according to Godkin had "wallowed in spoils like a rhinoceros in an African pool"; yet Blaine was widely popular. He could stir a mass enthusiasm which was beyond the reach of the stolid Cleveland. And the Republicans who deserted him were more remarkable for their names than for their numbers. Carl Schurz had turned against his party, and Benjamin Bristow (the Secretary of the Treasury whom Grant had elbowed out because of his inconvenient honesty), and Charles Francis Adams, Jr., and Leverett Saltonstall, and Thomas Wentworth Higginson, and President Eliot of Harvard, and a whole list of papers including *Harper's Weekly,* the *Nation,* the Boston *Transcript,* and the New York *Times.* Significantly and sensibly, ambitious young politicians like Roosevelt and Lodge, who had fought against Blaine at the convention, did not join the "Mugwumps," as the seceders were called.*

There were no real issues between the parties. Both platforms avoided saying anything sensible on either the tariff or the currency, and Blaine was forced to go at least as far as Cleveland in promises for civil-service reform. The Republican statement on the vexed question of money was a masterpiece of evasion. "We have always recommended," said the platform, "the best money known to the civilized world; and we urge that efforts should be made to unite all commercial nations in the establishment of an international standard which shall fix for all the relative value of gold and silver coinage." The Democratic platform when referring to the other major issue, the tariff, is almost as vague:

> Knowing full well, however, that legislation affecting the operations of the people should be cautious and conservative in method, not in advance of public opinion, but responsive to its demands, the Democratic party is pledged to revise the tariff in a spirit of fairness to all interests. . . . Many industries have come to rely upon legislation for successful continuance, so that any change of law must be at every step regardful of the labor and capital thus involved.

This is not the stuff of which flaming speeches are made.

* "Mugwump" was taken from Eliot's translation of the Bible into Algonkian Indian, which was printed on a hand press in 1663. The word was applied to the Independent Republicans of 1872, but was first made popular by Dana of the New York *Sun* in 1884. In Algonkian, "mugquomp" means chief.

The platforms were more sprightly when they turned to abusing the enemy. "The Republican party," said the Democrats, "during its legal, its stolen, and its bought tenure of power, has steadily decayed in moral character and in political capacity." "We denounce the fraud and violence," said the Republicans, "practised by the Democracy in southern states, by which the will of a voter is defeated . . . and we solemnly arraign the Democratic party as being the guilty recipients of fruits of such fraud and violence." These were the comprehensible statements, and the only ones which were demonstrably true. But they did not lead to a high level of debate. Emotion and personal attacks were clearly to be the staples of the campaign; yet nobody realized, in the innocent days of June, 1884, just how far the emotions or the attacks were to go.

The Mugwumps of New York sent a lawyer to Mr. Mulligan in Boston, to see if he had any more incriminating letters from Blaine. Much to everyone's surprise, he uncovered a whole new bundle. Mulligan had been bookkeeper for James Fisher, Jr., a Boston businessman and an official of the Little Rock Railway. It was to Fisher that Blaine wrote the unfortunate letters which Mulligan preserved. Among the new batch—published in the middle of September—were several that proved Blaine had lied in his famous speech to Congress eight years before when he defended himself against the implications of the first Mulligan letters. At that time he said, "My whole connection with the road has been as open as the day." Yet only a week before, he had written to his friend Fisher, at a false address, and had telegraphed Fisher where to call for the letter. "I want you to send me a letter such as this enclosed draft," Blaine had urged. And the "enclosed draft" would have exonerated him completely. "Regard this letter as strictly confidential," he added; "Do not show it to anyone." And on the back he had written: "Burn this letter."*

If Blaine had made no explanations in the first place, he would have been better off; his efforts to extricate himself were what hurt him, rather than the fact that he had received some relatively harmless favors from a railroad. He behaved like a man who had something to hide, so the public assumed that he probably knew his own past and had reasons for his behavior. He should have remembered that few men admire self-righteousness in politics, and that the Mugwumps had therefore no popular following. They succeeded in proving that Blaine was what everybody had always assumed him to be, a man of somewhat lax principle. But nobody thought he would be dishonest in the White House, and one may doubt whether all the roaring of the Mugwumps lost Blaine many votes. What it

---

* Blaine's tribute to Blaine, which Fisher was asked to copy out and sign, said in part: "Your action was as open and fair as the day. . . . Your conduct was in the highest degree honorable and straightforward." Apparently Fisher did not agree. In any case, the heartfelt praise was never returned to its author.

did accomplish, however, was to drive the Republicans to seek some unpleasant stories about Cleveland with which to retaliate. They did not
have to seek far.

Even before the publication of the second set of Mulligan letters the
Republicans had found, and revealed, what they smugly called "a terrible
tale"; namely, that Cleveland had an illegitimate son by a Mrs. Halpin,
and that the boy had been brought up in an orphan asylum. In fact, there
was some doubt about Cleveland's responsibility, for Mrs. Halpin had
been the mistress of several men at the time the child was conceived. But
she claimed that Cleveland was the father, and he accepted financial
responsibility. The mother became a drunkard, and was committed to an
institution, and the boy was sent to an orphanage at Cleveland's expense.
He was later adopted into a good family and had a distinguished career.[3]

When this tale was given to the press there was woe among the right-
eous. But Cleveland was wiser than Blaine. Asked what the Democratic
Party should say in reply, he answered "Tell the truth." When the facts
were admitted, and simply stated, the vast and delicious fancies which
were gathering about the story disappeared. It is not likely that the incident did Cleveland harm. If the Mugwumps had been uninterrupted in
their campaign of moral superiority, they might have made him sound so
good as to be unsupportable. From that, at least, he was saved by Maria
Halpin.

More important than Blaine's bonds or Cleveland's babies was the influence of the Pensions Bureau, which almost won the election for the Republicans, and of Parson Burchard, who finally contrived to lose it. Since
the Republicans had been in office ever since pensions for the Civil War
began, the Bureau had become little more than an adjunct to their national machine. Every four years the agents of the Bureau promised more
pensions if the Republicans were returned and threatened the decrease of
pensions if the Democrats won. In 1884 the head of the Bureau spent the
last two months of the campaign touring the Middle West asking the old
soldiers to vote for the Grand Old Party and pouring (according to the
report of his successor) "a tide of men and money" into the districts which
seemed doubtful. During the same two months the field expenses for
"special pensions examiners" rose from about $28,000 a month to $46,000.
This was a hard system to beat, especially when the work of the Pensions
Bureau was ably backed by the Grand Army of the Republic, the well-
organized association of Union veterans whose members were the recipients of the pensions. The G.A.R. was officially non-partisan; but its
chief aim was to ask for higher pensions, and it may have felt it would
receive better treatment from the party which glorified the war than from
the party which had viewed it askance.

By the last week of the campaign everyone believed the vote would be close, and on the whole the Republicans felt confident. It now seems that they were right, and that Blaine would have won if it had not been for Burchard. On October 29 Blaine reached New York City, tired and bored. He found he had to receive a delegation of second-string clergymen and he can perhaps be excused for not listening too closely while their spokesman, the Reverend S. D. Burchard, droned through an address. But Blaine should have had an assistant whose business it was to stay awake during such affairs, for Parson Burchard remarked, "We are Republicans, and don't propose to leave our party and identify ourselves with the party whose antecedents are Rum, Romanism, and Rebellion." Blaine, since he did not hear it, said nothing to disassociate himself from the apt alliteration. This was unfortunate, because his chance for the election depended on the Roman Catholic vote of New York. Blaine's mother was a Catholic, and Tammany Hall still hated Cleveland, and the two facts were expected to help the Republicans in the Democratic city. Some of the Tammany braves, who could not go so far as to vote for Blaine, were helping Ben Butler's Greenback Party in New York State in the hope that it might win enough votes to ruin Cleveland. All such hopes were sunk forever by Burchard. Although Blaine was not listening to the speech, the Democrats were, for they had sent a shorthand reporter to take it down. Within a few hours New York and all the Eastern cities were placarded with "Rum, Romanism, and Rebellion."

Cleveland won New York State by 1049 votes out of a total of 1,125,159. Without New York he would have lost the election. With 525 fewer votes he would have lost New York. Throughout the nation, Cleveland had a tiny lead, with 4,874,986 to 4,851,981 for Blaine. In the electoral college Cleveland had 219 votes, Blaine 182. It had been the most abusive campaign in American history, but not the most enlightening. Hardly anything had been discussed except personalities; yet this was proper enough, since the parties did not differ on tariffs, or currency, or labor, or land use, or civil service, or on any other matter of public policy.

> The only difference, after all their rout,
> Is, that the one is in, the other out.

This was a more important difference than it sounds, if the two men are taken as symbols. Blaine symbolized "Grantism," and Cleveland "reform." And it may be just as well that Cleveland went to the White House with no clear policies to enforce, for he had a divided Congress, the Republicans being in a majority in the Senate, the Democrats in the House. Under such conditions a President with a policy can only make trouble.

3

The first and most frightening problem before Cleveland was that of appointments. The last Democratic President had been Buchanan, whose major appointments were made in 1857. Although Cleveland had promised to continue civil-service reform, he could not simply ignore the hungry hordes of Democrats infesting Washington. In particular, he could not ignore those who were recommended to him by Congressmen. But neither could he disappoint the pushful Mugwumps, who believed they had put him in power and who now felt it their duty to keep watch over his political acts. Indeed, the unhappy Cleveland could not even wait until he took office before facing his most painful problems: spoils, and cheap money.

In 1885 the federal government had about 126,000 employees, of whom 16,000 were in the classified civil service. The remaining 110,000 were appointed by the President or his aides, and traditionally they were appointed on political grounds. Within a month of his election, and three months before taking office, Cleveland was half distracted by the clamor of the men who wanted those 110,000 jobs for themselves or for their friends.

> I am sick at heart and perplexed in brain [he wrote to a friend on Christmas Day, 1884] during most of my working hours. I almost think that the profession of most of my pretended friends are but the means they employ to accomplish personal and selfish ends. It's so hard to discover their springs of action and it seems so distressing to feel that in the question of who shall be trusted, I should be so much at sea.[4]

Partly to protect himself from the greedy hordes and from the pretended friends whose motives he dared not trust, Cleveland arranged to receive a letter from the National Civil Service Reform League in which Carl Schurz, George Curtis and others pointed out that the triumph of a party which had not controlled the Executive for a quarter of a century raised the question of spoils in an acute form. Cleveland answered that he believed in the Pendleton Act and that he would enforce it. Furthermore, he would follow the spirit of the law in appointments outside the classified service, and would not remove able men on partisan grounds if their work had nothing to do with the policy of the Administration. On the other hand he would of course remove all who used their federal jobs to forward the interest of the opposition party. He had the post offices chiefly in mind when he made this reservation.

In numerous instances [he wrote years later] the post-offices were made headquarters for local party committees and organizations and the centers of partizan scheming. Party literature favorable to the post-masters' party, that never passed regularly through the mails, was distributed through the post-offices as an item of party service, and matter of a political character, passing through the mails in the usual course and addressed to patrons belonging to the opposite party, was withheld; disgusting and irritating placards were prominently displayed in many post-offices, and the attention of Democratic enquirers for mail matter was tauntingly directed to them by the post-masters. . . . In some quarters official incumbents neglected public duty to do political work.[5]

In a sense, this was lucky for Cleveland. It gave him a proper reason for discharging a great many employees, especially fourth-class postmasters. Without these vacancies he would have had little to give the faithful party-workers, and would have become the most-hated President in history.

The suave and popular Adlai Stevenson, who had left Congress in 1881 and returned to his law practice at Bloomington, Illinois, was appointed first assistant postmaster general, with the task of making the necessary removals. About 40,000 postmasters were retired as gently and politely as possible; yet a certain uproar could not be avoided. The abuse heaped on Cleveland for dismissing these men was small, however, compared to the abuse he received from his own party for not dismissing a great many more.

The civil-service letter was not the only unpopular move which Cleveland felt forced to make before he was inaugurated. The currency problem, which was to leave him a party outcast in the end, became acute in the month before he took office. We have seen that under the Bland-Allison Act of 1878 the Treasury was to buy between two and four million dollars' worth of silver monthly. This was to be coined, and the Act declared sixteen ounces of silver worth one ounce of gold. As a result, by 1885, the government had minted about 200,000,000 silver dollars. Their proper market value was about eighty-five cents apiece. Naturally, since these dollars were legal tender, debtors were inclined to pay the government in silver while creditors were inclined to ask for payment in gold. Yet a gold reserve of about $100,000,000 was needed to protect the resumption of the greenbacks. This reserve was threatened so long as the Treasury had to take in mostly silver and pay out mostly gold.

Cleveland's advisers, who were all "sound-money" men from the East, told him that he should announce at once (in a letter) that he was opposed to silver coinage and that he wished to see the Bland-Allison Act repealed. The "cheap-money" Democrats in Congress warned him that if he followed this advice he would split the party. Yet Cleveland followed it. As a result he was the first President to be overridden by Congress even before he took office. On February 26, two days after the appearance of Cleveland's letter and six days before his inauguration, the House turned down a bill to stop the coining of silver. Fifty-two Republicans joined 118 Democrats to save silver, whereas 64 Republicans and 54 Democrats voted as Cleveland wished.

In the course of an interesting defense of Cleveland's anti-silver letter of 1885, Allan Nevins writes, "By its very vigor it put heart into frightened bankers." This is precisely what the South and the West resented. They preferred to keep their bankers frightened, in the hope that fear might lead to thought. They themselves were frightened most of the time, frightened of the grinding deflation that was taking away their land. If a cheap dollar was not the proper answer, they said, let the bankers find something better; but do not let them sleep the long night through, dreaming cheerfully of the rising price of money.

4

Cleveland's Cabinet was a credit to the party, but also a revelation of the President's extreme conservatism. Cleveland was an enemy of the social-service state, the paternal state. He believed that the government should never interfere except for a negative end. He would not help to overcome the woes of the farmer, but he would resist inflation. He would do nothing to save the worker's wages in a depression; but he would use the Army to break a strike. In this he represented the temper of the age—the point of view which has been described by Professor Hofstadter as "social Darwinism": a confusion of evolution with mechanical progress and of "the survival of the fittest" with the economic theories of laissez-faire.[6] The high priest of this cult was Herbert Spencer, who for a number of years was the chief influence on American political thinking. Whatever Spencer's true faith may have been (and he seems to have been none too clear in his own mind), it was transformed in America into a travesty of conservatism. As Professor Hofstadter writes:

> His [Spencer's] categorical repudiation of state interference with the "natural" unimpeded growth of society led him to oppose all state aid to the poor. They were unfit, he said, and should be eliminated. "The whole effort of nature is to get rid of such, to clear the world of them, and make room for better." Nature is as insistent upon fitness of mental character as she is upon physical character, "and radical defects are as much causes of death in the one case as in the other." He who loses his life because of his stupidity, vice, or idleness is in the same class as the victims of weak viscera or malformed limbs. Under nature's laws all

alike are put on trial. "If they are sufficiently complete to live, they *do* live, and it is well they should live. If they are not sufficiently complete to live, they die, and it is best they should die."

Thus Spencer deplored not only poor laws but also state supported education, sanitary supervision other than the suppression of nuisances, regulation of housing conditions, and even state protection of the ignorant from medical quacks. He likewise opposed tariffs, state banking, and government postal systems.[7]

Here, with a little deft selection, was the perfect creed for soothing the consciences of millionaires, and it was widely used for that humane purpose. With the help of Spencer, we find John D. Rockefeller comparing his oil trust to a rose.

> The growth of a large business is merely a survival of the fittest . . . [he said in a Sunday-school address]. The American Beauty rose can be produced in the splendor and fragrance which bring cheer to its beholder only by sacrificing the early buds which grow up around it. This is not an evil tendency in business. It is merely the working out of a law of nature and a law of God.[8]

And Andrew Carnegie in his *Autobiography* tells how Darwin and Spencer rescued him from doubt. "Light came as in a flood," he wrote, "and all was clear. Not only had I got rid of theology and the supernatural, but I had found the truth of evolution. 'All is well since all grows better,' became my motto, my true source of comfort." And in 1889, in the *North American Review*, he brushed aside the critics of the law of competition. "It is here," he wrote; "we cannot evade it; no substitutes for it have been found; and while the law may sometimes be hard for the individual, it is best for the race, because it insures the survival of the fittest in every department." All must indeed be well when the same "law" which makes the rich richer insures that the poor grow steadily more fit, more worthy to survive.

The world in which this "social Darwinism" was taken for granted was the world from which Cleveland chose his Cabinet. The Secretary of State was Senator Thomas Francis Bayard of Delaware. The Bayards were one of the great political families of America. They were Federalists who had joined the Democratic Party. Thomas Francis belonged to the fourth generation of Bayards to represent his state in the Senate. He was Jeffersonian in his fear of government and intensely conservative.

The Secretary of the Treasury was Daniel Manning of Albany, who had risen from newsboy to proprietor of his own paper, and who had succeeded Tilden as leader of the Democratic Party in New York State. His appointment pleased the friends of Tilden, and also the friends of gold, for he was a strong conservative on money matters.

The Secretary of War was William Crowninshield Endicott of Massachusetts: a Whig who had become a Democrat when his party disintegrated, a rich man, a New England patrician and scholar.

The Secretary of the Navy was William Collins Whitney, a very rich and successful lawyer who had moved to New York City after graduating from Harvard Law School and had married the sister of Oliver Payne, one of John D. Rockefeller's partners in Standard Oil who was charged with buying a legislature in order to put his father into the United States Senate. Whitney was a Tilden Democrat who had helped in the battle against the "Tweed Ring," and who had just allied himself with Thomas Fortune Ryan to acquire the Broadway Street Railway franchise by whatever means might prove necessary. Although the appointment was criticized by reformers, Whitney became a first-class Secretary of the Navy. Indeed, he was in large part responsible for the fact that the United States began once more to possess a navy.

Criticisms of Whitney were slight, however, compared to those lavished on the new Secretary of the Interior, Senator Lucius Quintus Cincinnatus Lamar of Mississippi. Lamar was a scholar, a lawyer, an ex-professor of metaphysics at the University of Mississippi, and a conservative on money matters who had ignored the instructions of his own state legislature during the free-silver debates of 1878. He was also the author of the secession ordinance of Mississippi, and a Confederate lieutenant colonel and diplomat. In 1888 he was to become a Justice of the United States Supreme Court.

When Bryan rose to leadership a few years later, the character of the Democratic Party changed sharply. It is interesting, therefore, to remember these men who gathered about Cleveland, and to remember that he himself had first joined the party because he thought it more conservative than the new group which named Frémont for President. This helps to explain the tone of his Administrations.

> When Cleveland departed as a leader of his party [wrote William Allen White], with him went a host of gentlemen of the old school; rich, respectable gentlemen, high-minded and courteous; men of family and social distinction; the silk-stockinged men who placed principle far above preferment . . . men who in a changing era made the Democratic party in the United States the last stronghold of a political aristocracy.[9]

Cleveland, of course, was by no means "a silk-stockinged man," nor rich, nor a scholar. But he was at home in the world represented by his Cabinet, and wholly lost in the world which was about to conquer his party: the world of men who expected government to redress their wrongs, rather than to protect their natural rights. William Allen White describes Cleveland's appeal perfectly, in the last days of the old Democracy:

> He was plain-spoken. If he thought a proposition was a steal he said so, and he used the short word. A robber, a thief, a sneak, a liar, and a cheat wore no perfunctory titles in the bright lexicon of Cleveland's veto messages. Naturally the people were pleased. Nothing wearies the flesh of the taxpayers so quickly as to find their servants putting in valuable time arranging rhetorical feather-beds with which to break the fall of scoundrels. Also, the people were tired of statesmen eternally saving the country with their vote-getting plans for salvation. What the people desired just then with a furious passion was a vigorous, uncompromising man without any plans, who would save the State from its statesmen. The times crying out for an obstructionist to stem corruption found young Grover Cleveland.[10]

As we have seen, the twenty years from 1865 to 1885 explain this "furious passion" adequately. For better or worse, however, it was a short-lived passion. Cleveland's two terms of brave obstruction marked the end, not only of the bad old world of spoilsmen and unabashed graft, but also of what many regarded as the good old world of non-interference by government. Until the strange, brief days of Calvin Coolidge, Cleveland was the last purely negative President, who felt his duty was to prevent bad things from happening, but not to make good things happen. There came to be less and less room for the Jeffersonian, negative view, in that world which was being remodeled by the friends and relatives of Cleveland's Secretary of the Navy.

XXVIII

The Old Order Changes

"WHAT SHALL WE DO with our great cities," wrote the Reverend Lyman Abbott in 1891; "What will our great cities do with us? These are the two problems which confront every thoughtful American." Yet only ten years before, the cities had been no problem at all. According to the census of 1880, there were fifty million people in America and nearly forty million of them lived on the open land or in villages of less than four thousand inhabitants.[1] Within the next decade the lure of the city became the dominant note in the nation's life. In 1880 one out of every five Middlewesterners lived in an urban community, and in 1890 one out of every three. Chicago increased from half a million to almost a million and a quarter; Minneapolis and St. Paul trebled in population; Detroit, Milwaukee and Cleveland increased from 60 to 80 per cent.[2]

The new immigration into the Middle West was so heavy that the cities could grow without draining the countryside; but in the Northeast the flight from the land was frightening.

> In this great seaboard section [writes Professor Schlesinger], stretching from the Potomac to the St. Croix, the city had completed its conquest. Already in 1880 about half the people—seven and a half millions—lived in towns or cities of four thousand or more inhabitants; within a decade the proportion grew to nearly three fifths or eleven million. In 1890 about two out of every three persons in New York and Connecticut were townsfolk, four out of every five in Massachusetts and nine out of every ten in Rhode Island. . . . The eclipse of the Eastern countryside had, of course, been long in process, indeed ever since the old farming districts of the Atlantic states first felt the competition of the virgin lands of the interior.[3]

The concentration of wealth that accompanied this concentration of people was one reason for the agrarian discontent. According to the census of 1880, the farms of the country were worth about ten billion dollars, and urban real estate was worth the same. In 1890, farms were worth thirteen billion dollars and urban real estate about twenty-six billion. "If personalty were included," adds Professor Schlesinger, "the contrast between city and country became even sharper, particularly since the tangible personalty on the farms was in a considerable degree offset by mortgages held in the towns and cities."[4]

This was not merely the town-versus-country problem which is so familiar to the politics of Europe; for in the American Federal Union even the rise of the cities became a struggle between regions. By the eighteen-nineties, in the East and in the older Middle West, the discontented farmers could no longer sway the majority of Congressmen from their own states. The cities had grown so fast that the Senators from these regions represented the new industrial kingdoms, and most members of the House represented urban needs and wishes. This was shown dramatically in '93, when Ohio, Indiana, Illinois, Michigan, Wisconsin, Minnesota—the old "corn belt" states where the new towns were multiplying—voted in both houses of Congress against cheap money and in favor of repealing a Silver-Purchase Act. Cleveland, as we have seen, had failed to get such a repeal in 1885. And in 1868 Republicans in the Middle West had insisted that their party's "sound-money" platform meant nothing, and that they really favored greenbacks. But by 1893 the cities had imposed financial conservatism upon these states. The solid regional votes for cheap money now came from the Old South and from the New West beyond the Mississippi—beyond even Iowa and Minnesota—where the prairies began to merge with the high plains, where the spring wheat or the corn or the cotton began to give way to sheep and cattle, to silver and gold and copper. This was Bryan's West, known to itself as the Great West. Easterners complained that nobody could tell the truth about this region without lying. Here the population doubled or tripled between 1880 and 1890. Here the old cattle kingdom rose and fell, to be replaced (after the coming of barbed wire and the cheap metal windmill for the timberless plains) by the stock farm and the fenced ranch with fewer but better-bred cattle. And here the fabulous mines were discovered, opened, emptied, and in a few years abandoned. Here also, in Kansas and Nebraska, in North and South Dakota, where the lands of adequate rainfall bordered on the lands of drought and grass, farmers would prosper during a wet cycle, and borrow money, and then face ruin during the dry years, and detest the money-lenders.

Except for the Mormon capital in Utah there were no real cities in all this immense, self-confident country to spread the creditor's doctrine of "sound money." And there were very few cities in the South, where industries at first grew slowly. The South was still the country of small farmers who had acquired land at the break-up of the great plantations. Some of them had done tolerably well; but most had either lost their farms to an absentee owner or lost themselves in a helpless debt-peonage to local merchants or bankers. In either case the need for cash pinned them to the one-crop system which not only deteriorated the soil but left the farmer

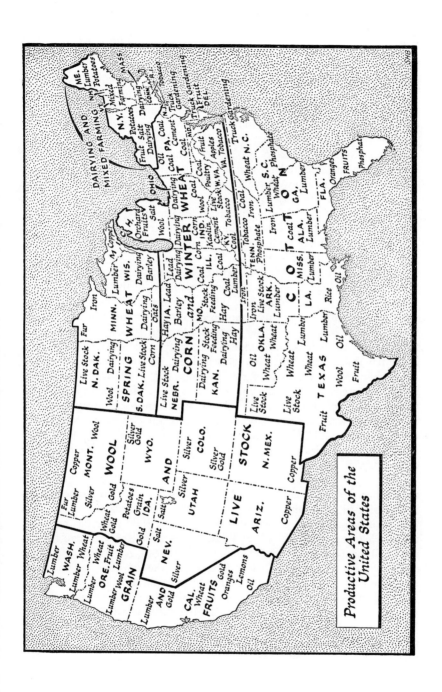

Productive Areas of the United States

resourceless in bad times, with none of the normal rural self-sufficiency.

Here, then, was the solid sectional backing for the Populist-Bryan uprising of the nineties: here in the dejected South and in the booming, borrowing, Great West. When times were bad the ferment (and thus the Congressional votes) would move eastward across the Mississippi and encroach upon the urbanizing Middle West. When times were better the discontent and the demand for money remedies were confined to two regions: the old Confederacy and the newest (and last) of the many American Wests which we have followed from the Piedmont of the eastern coastal range all the way to the Pacific Ocean. If these regions, during the depression of the nineties, had been able to bring Eastern labor into their alliance, they would have ruled the country.

Meanwhile, "What shall we do with our great cities? What will our great cities do with us?"—remained the major questions in America and throughout much of the Western world. No country today, and no civilization in the past, has found an answer. This flight to the cities is the road from which there is no returning. When it opens before man's astonished eyes, he may complain, he may moralize, he may deplore the trend of the times; but he moves down the road, if not with pleasure, at least with fascination. All civilizations come to the many-millioned city in the end. None has resisted the lure. "No wretchedness, no compulsion, not even a clear vision of the madness of this development, avails to neutralize the attractive force of these daemonic creations. . . . Here there is only forward, never back. Long, long ago the country bore the country town and nourished it with her best blood. Now the giant city sucks the country dry, insatiably and incessantly demanding and devouring fresh streams of men, till it wearies and dies in the midst of an almost uninhabited waste of country."[5]

The very words, "provincial" and "cosmopolitan," are a sign that a nation has entered a new stage of history. There were no cosmopolitans in America in 1850, and thus no provincials. The words are meaningless in a land of farmers and country towns. But by 1900 their meaning was all too clear, except in the Great West. There, as on the sea, man's works were still dwarfed by nature. There, in her last West, America made a rich mythology out of the brief "cattle kingdom"—the cowboys and the open range and the longhorn drives. In fact, the cattle kingdom was born in 1865, when the Civil War ended, and died of barbed wire and the railways within thirty years. But the myth was woven and cherished because the West was a refuge from the most discouraging of class divisions: big city and farm, the New Yorker and the hayseed. "All other contrasts pale before this one, which dominates all events, all habits of life, all views of the world."[6] A New Yorker may settle comfortably in Paris, France—but never in Paris, Kentucky.

This uprooting change, like so many others, had come to America in a hurry: this fateful change from the market town which serves the countryside to the steel or stone colossus which drains and despises the surrounding land and which seeks to be its own world, its own law. "Thy wisdom and thy knowledge, it hath perverted thee," said the prophet Isaiah to Babylon; "and thou hast said in thine heart, I *am,* and none else beside me." And he added a strangely modern note: "Desolation shall come upon thee suddenly, which thou shalt not know. . . . Thou art wearied in the multitude of thy counsels. Let now the astrologers, the star-gazers, the monthly prognosticators, stand up, and save thee from these things."

In America, it was not "long, long ago" that the country bore the country town. America had charged headlong, in a hundred and fifty years, through the whole cycle from primitive agriculture to Cosmopolis. In discussing the mistakes of the eighteen-fifties we pointed out that "the United States had never known a time of rest, of calm self-possession." This was even more true in 1900. America had done everything by 1900, except compose her soul: an act which she omitted by necessity, not by choice. In Jefferson's Arcadian plans, America was given a thousand years to reach the Mississippi. In fact, she had fifty years to reach the Pacific Ocean and another fifty years to reach the great stone deserts of mass-industry and finance. That was as far as any nation had ever gone. There were no more precedents, and all the warnings were bad. The future must be decline or innovation: the old Caesarian wars which have marked the end of many civilizations, or a step into a new world, with new methods, illusions, hopes.

2

Creating and accompanying the vast cities were the vast industries and monopolies. Standard Oil was founded in 1870. By 1878 it controlled ninety-five per cent of the refining in the United States and virtually all the transportation of oil.

One of the conditions which made monopoly certain lay in the railway practices of the period. The grant of special rates to those shippers who, by superiority of capital or enterprise, promised to supply the most freight was general, and the great lumbermen, the meat packers and others profited only less than Rockefeller. A measure of justification existed for such favors since the large companies served as "eveners" of traffic. In the oil industry the fluctuation of production and prices, the uncertainty of the outlook three months in advance and the wastefulness of small companies, all militated in favor of a large-scale business. Monopoly was economical and efficient.[7]

The argument might not have pleased the victims of monopoly; but it was accepted at first by the country, or at least by the Congress, which for a few years rejected all bills aimed at controlling such practices.

While one group of railways helped Standard Oil, another group helped to monopolize anthracite coal. And all over the country railway pools were forming, to share the business of an area, and to maintain high rates. The most ambitious of these pools was composed of the Erie Railroad, the New York Central Railroad, the Pennsylvania Railroad, and the Baltimore and Ohio. The four "competitors" agreed that on westbound traffic from New York the Erie and the New York Central should each have thirty-three per cent of the whole, the Pennsylvania twenty-five per cent, and the Baltimore and Ohio nine per cent.

Meanwhile the age of iron was giving way to the age of steel. The Bessemer process of making steel from iron was invented in England in 1856 and brought to the United States after the Civil War. In 1868 the open-hearth (or Siemens-Martin) process was also imported from Europe. In 1875 American production of steel was about 380,000 tons; in 1900 it was 10,000,000 tons; in 1929, 56,000,000. Before the turn of the century huge combinations controlled the entire process from the mining and transportation of the ore to the production of finished materials. In 1901, a gigantic consolidation—encouraged by Andrew Carnegie who wished to retire, and organized by J. Pierpont Morgan—merged ten major companies to form the United States Steel Corporation. The authorized capital was $1,404,000,000.* The corporation owned 149 steel plants, 250,000 acres of coal lands, 112 ships on the Great Lakes, and more than 1000 miles of railroad. It could have financed the United States Government of Alexander Hamilton's days out of its petty cash.

Along with the turbulent new towns and industries came a third change, equally fateful for the nation: a change in the volume and the source of immigration. For this there were four main reasons. First, the mines and factories, growing by geometrical progression, desperately searched for cheap labor. Second, the transcontinental railways needed customers for their enormous holdings of land. Unless the population increased with quite abnormal speed, many of the railways would be bankrupt. Third, the steamship companies were eager for steerage passengers. Their advertisements, appealing to the poorer and more persecuted peoples of Europe, reinforced those of the railways. According to testimony before the Immigration Commission, two of the steamship lines had between five and six

---

* At the time, this may have been almost half water; but the assets of the corporation were soon built up to beyond a billion and a half.

thousand ticket agents in Galicia in the year 1911.[8] Fourth, the anthracite mine-owners of Pennsylvania wished to rid themselves of the recalcitrant Irishmen who gave them such trouble at the time of the "Molly Maguires."

As a result of these forces—and of the overpopulation and the racial intolerance in southern and eastern Europe—not only the number but the nature of the American people was suddenly changed. The figures are impressive. In the decade before the Civil War, the United States received two and a half million immigrants. In the decade 1871 to 1880, the figure had scarcely risen; but in the next ten years it was five and a quarter millions. Then there came a drop, because of the long depression of the nineties; but between 1901 and 1910 almost nine million immigrants entered the United States, and between 1911 and 1920, almost six million.*

Even more interesting than the rise in numbers was the change in source. Until 1880, the large majority of immigrants came from northern and western Europe. The American racial stock was still chiefly English, Irish, Scotch, German and Scandinavian. But the change came with the rise of the cities and of the new industry. Between 1881 and 1890, southern and eastern Europe sent a million immigrants; between 1891 and 1900, two million; between 1901 and 1910, six million—or seventy per cent of the total immigration for the decade.

During the twenty years from 1891 to 1910, twelve and a half million foreigners settled in America, and more than eight million of them were the so-called "new immigration" from Italy, Poland, Hungary, Bohemia, Slovakia, Croatia, Greece. The total population of the United States, meanwhile, increased from about 63,000,000 to about 92,000,000; so the immigrants alone, without considering their many American-born children, accounted for more than three sevenths of the population growth. The map on page 562, showing the percentage of foreign-born in America in 1910, makes the figures look even more astounding. Here was a new many-tongued nation, called into being overnight in order to nourish the new industry and the new towns.

Most of the old immigration from northern Europe moved West and took up land, although many Germans settled in the Middlewestern towns. The Irish were the exception; they tended to stay in the East and to earn their living by unskilled labor and by politics. From the former occupation—but not from the latter—they were ousted by the new immigrants, who were mostly unskilled workers and who were too poor in any case to buy farms or farm equipment. They quickly sank to the bottom of the labor market, in mines, factories, railway-construction camps, and lumber camps. They were a formidable problem for organized labor,

---

* The total population of the United States was about 23,000,000 in 1850, 31,000,000 in 1860, 39,000,000 in 1870, 50,000,000 in 1880, 63,000,000 in 1890, 76,000,000 in 1900, 92,000,000 in 1910, and 106,000,000 in 1920.

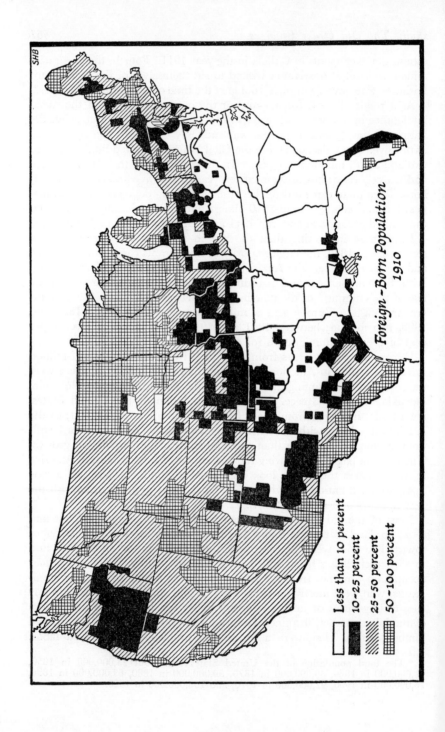

Foreign–Born Population
1910

☐ Less than 10 percent
■ 10–25 percent
▨ 25–50 percent
▦ 50–100 percent

SHB

which was struggling to build strong unions. Since they were separated from the native Americans by language, customs, and religion, they tended to stay together in colonies in the big cities. They had come from the land, and most of them had seen enough of it, preferring even the most dejected urban slums. In 1930, three quarters of the foreign-born were gathered in towns and cities.

The one region where the new immigrants did not encroach upon the lowest-paid jobs was the South. There the Negro maintained his melancholy right to the harshest forms of labor. The map shows the South as almost untouched territory, except where the Mexicans streamed into Texas, New Mexico, and Arizona, and where the Cuban and Puerto Rican cigarmakers settled in Florida. A glance at the map will also suggest the political intricacies that followed the new immigration, and some of the reasons why national politicians do not offer simple, lucid platforms, with no hedging.

During the first hundred years of American independence the federal government had left the control of immigration almost wholly to the states at whose ports the immigrants landed. Then in 1882, Congress prohibited Chinese immigration—only for ten years, but the exclusion was later made permanent. There were 150,000 Chinese in California when this law was passed, and under the Fourteenth Amendment all of their native-born descendants became American citizens.* President Theodore Roosevelt sought to control Japanese immigration without such brusque exclusion, by means of a "gentleman's agreement" between the two governments; but the Pacific states were not satisfied until the Japanese were kept out by law, under the Immigration Act of 1924.

While Asia was denied entry, the principle of selection was applied to European immigrants. After 1882 the door was closed to more and more groups which were considered undesirable: prostitutes, polygamists, drunkards, anarchists, and the incurably diseased. In 1917 Congress went still further, and in spite of Woodrow Wilson's veto passed an Act excluding all illiterate immigrants over sixteen years of age. And a few years later, at the end of the First World War, the American people at last decided on serious restriction. The Act of 1921 limited immigration from any country in Europe, Africa, Australasia, or the Near East, to three per cent of the number of people from that country residing in the United States in 1910. In 1924 a more drastic law was passed: the annual quota was reduced from three to two per cent, and 1890 was taken as the basic

---

*The amendment declares that "all persons born or naturalized in the United States and subject to the jurisdiction thereof, are citizens of the United States and of the state wherein they reside." In 1898 the Supreme Court confirmed this in the case of a Chinese laborer, born in San Francisco, whose parents were ineligible to Citizenship. Cp. *United States* v. *Wong Kim Ark,* 169 U.S. 649 (1898).

year instead of 1910.* This was to favor the English, Irish, Germans, and Scandinavians over the people of southern and eastern Europe.

In 1929 the total number to be admitted in any one year was reduced to 153,541. The quotas from each country were to be in proportion to the "national origins" of the American people in 1920. This gave Great Britain and Northern Ireland about 66,000; Eire about 18,000; Germany 26,000; Sweden, Norway, Denmark, and Holland combined 10,025, Poland 6524; Italy 5802; and the rest were nowhere.**

As Professor Wittke points out, we customarily speak of the year 1890, when the Census Bureau announced that there was no longer a "frontier," as closing an epoch in American history. But "it is just as true to say that the enactment of drastic, restrictive legislation against immigrants, following the close of the [first] World War, brought to a close an equally important epoch in American and, perhaps, in world history." And he adds that during the depression decade, following the Immigration Act of 1929, more people left the United States than entered it.[9]

One of the most rewarding experiences in the history of any land was clearly at an end. For a hundred years no control over immigration had been needed or wanted—except here and there when harbor authorities sought to impose a fifty-cent head tax to pay for the expense of handling the traffic.*** Then the rise of the cities and of the giant corporations made such a demand for labor that the immigrant stream became a river, and the river a roaring waterfall. Then came control, under pressure from union labor and from the world-malaise of racial theories. And then the gate swung shut. "I lift my lamp beside the golden door," proclaims the Statue of Liberty, still; but the golden door is closed.

3

During these same years the Supreme Court of the United States had played a decisive part in encouraging that "rise of the cities and of the giant corporations" which made the booming days of immigration. By an ingenious use of the Fourteenth Amendment the Court set business free to develop its new forms.

As we have already seen, the first section of the Amendment reads in part: "No state shall make or enforce any law which shall abridge the

* India, Siam, Indo-China, China, Japan, and some other parts of Asia, were now a barred zone.
** France, 3086; Czechoslovakia, 2874; Russia, 2712; Switzerland, 1707; Austria, 1413; Belgium, 1304; Yugoslavia, 845; Hungary, 869; Finland, 569; Greece, 307; Spain, 252; etc.
*** The Supreme Court ruled the tax unconstitutional.

privileges or immunitites of citizens of the United States; nor shall any state deprive any person of life, liberty or property, without due process of law; nor deny to any person within its jurisdiction the equal protection of the laws." The Fifth Amendment to the Constitution had long ago declared that the federal government might not deprive a "person" of "life, liberty or property without due process of law." The words sound simple; yet they proved to be among the most complicated ever used by man. The chief problems of interpretation were: first, what is a "person"; second, what is meant by "due process"; and third, what are the "privileges and immunities" of a citizen of the United States?

The Supreme Court first began to deal with these problems in the famous Slaughter House Cases in 1873.[10] The carpetbag government of Louisiana had given a monopoly of the New Orleans slaughtering business to a single corporation. The monopoly was challenged in the courts as a violation of the Fourteenth Amendment, the other butchers complaining that when their businesses were taken from them they were deprived of their "privileges and immunities," and also deprived of property without due process of law. Justice Miller, delivering the majority opinion, said in regard to all three of the Civil War amendments (Thirteenth, Fourteenth, and Fifteenth): "On the most casual examination of the language of these amendments, no one can fail to be impressed with the one pervading purpose found in them all . . . and without which none of them would have been even suggested; we mean the freedom of the slave race, the security and firm establishment of that freedom, and the protection of the newly made freeman and citizen. . . ." It seemed to follow that the amendments were not passed to protect the owners of slaughterhouses from invidious laws.

Justice Miller spoke for a Court which was divided, five to four. The majority believed it was their duty to save the "federal equilibrium" from the rough hands of the radical Republicans. As we have seen, the Fourteenth Amendment was the heart of the radical program. "The debates in Congress on the amendment," writes Professor Corwin, "leave one in little doubt of the intention of its framers to nationalize civil liberty in the United States, primarily for the benefit of the freedmen, to be sure, but incidentally for the benefit of all. This would be done, it was calculated, by converting state citizenship and its privileges and immunities into privileges and immunities of national citizenship."[11] The Court resisted such far-reaching change by its doctrine that the "one pervading purpose" of the amendment was "the freedom of the slave race." As for the "privileges or immunities of citizens of the United States," the Court decided that they were few in number: the right to protection abroad, the right to visit the seat of the government, the right to engage in interstate or foreign trade. But the important rights and immunities of the citizen, the "civil rights" for which men had so long struggled, were conferred by state citizenship alone. Professor Corwin points out that Justice Miller, whose interpretation "stands substantially unimpaired today" (1948), really obliterated the privileges and immunities clause from the amendment. "The Court felt that its duty lay in endeavoring to assimilate the amendment to the constitutional system as a whole, as it had come down from the past, and particularly to the principle of dual federalism."[12] Once this "duty" was done, the Court was prepared to consider a definition of the word "persons" which would make the amendment a protection to corporate business.

In 1882 Roscoe Conkling—who, after his comic failure to return to the Senate, had taken up the practice of law in New York City—argued strongly before the Supreme Court that the men who framed the Fourteenth Amendment intended it to protect the property of corporations from the folly of legislatures.[13] This contention has not been proved true; and in any case there is no doubt that the Northern public thought the amendment protected the freedmen, and not the clients of Senator Conkling.[14] Soon, however, the Court came round to the Senator's point of view. In 1886 Chief Justice Waite stated: "The Court does not wish to hear argument on the question whether the provision in the Fourteenth Amendment to the Constitution, which forbids a state to deny to any person within its jurisdiction the equal protection of the laws, applies to these corporations. We are all of the opinion that it does."[15] This unanimous opinion was contradicted by Supreme Court Justice Black as recently as 1938. Mr. Justice Black argued that the Court had long been wrong in holding that corporations were among the persons protected by the Fourteenth Amendment. Yet as Professor Swisher points out,

> even if corporations had not been accepted as persons within the meaning of the amendment, the courts could take jurisdiction over the subject matter through suits brought in the name, not of the corporation, but of stockholders and bond-holders. Furthermore, the social philosophy of the judges of the period, and their concern for the preservation and promotion of economic enterprise which could be carried on only through corporations, were such as to lead to the conclusion that, if one channel was closed, another would be found through which the courts could give protection to corporate interests.[16]

This is unquestionably true. The courts were probably interpreting the dominant public mood when they gradually developed a new Fourteenth Amendment which would protect corporations against the acts of the representatives of the people. Incidentally this was typical American practice: instead of making the legislators responsible, and replacing them with better men in case they behaved badly, the public condoned a set of interpretations which left the Supreme Court in the position of a quasi-upper chamber, intervening occasionally and erratically with a resounding "No." Yet the desired end was attained, since the power of government to act was sharply diminished.

Having made the corporations into "persons," the Court had next to decide exactly what protections the Fifth and Fourteenth Amendments conferred upon the property of these persons: in other words, what was the meaning of "due process of law"? What was it that the legislators might not do to such a "person" as Standard Oil, or United States Steel?

The phrase, "due process of law," has a venerable history. Again and again the Supreme Court has said it was identical with "law of the land," as used in Magna Charta. "No freeman shall be taken," says that ancient text, "or imprisoned, or disseized, or outlawed, or exiled, or in any way harmed—nor will we go upon or send upon him—save by the lawful judgment of his peers or by the law of the land." And a statute of Edward III, confirming Magna Charta, reads: "No man shall be put out of land or tenement, nor taken, nor imprisoned, nor disherited, nor put to death without being brought to answer by due process of law."

In England, and for a long time in America, the words were taken as a restriction upon procedure. An act of government which affected the rights or liberties of a freeman must be in keeping with the customs and the legal machinery which have been accepted as the "law of the land." The limitation fell chiefly upon the executive and judiciary, rather than upon the legislature. Just before the Civil War there were two instances where American courts held that "due process" implied a curb upon the type of law that a legislature might enact. This did not become the prevailing view, however, until a generation later. Justice Curtis in his dissenting opinion in the *Dred Scott Case* (1857) adhered to tradition when he said "that the necessity of any law is necessarily a legislative question."[17]

The new gigantic corporate persons of the 1880s could not accept this view. How could property be protected from the people, if the necessity of any law is a legislative question? The state legislatures, and the lower House of the federal Congress with its two-year term, were dangerously susceptible to the opinions of the people. And those opinions were not in all cases friendly to big business. Yet the dominant opinion (not necessarily the majority opinion) was markedly friendly from the Civil War until the turn of the century. Under the influence of "social Darwinism," it was felt that government should not interfere with business, that competition was the only effective regulator of enterprise, and that the consumer must learn to protect himself instead of running to the government for help. This view was taught in the colleges, mirrored in the press, and widely regarded as plain common sense. Yet the people—the consumers of the new monopoly goods and services who felt the squeeze and who had not read the textbooks—kept asking awkward questions. What about railway rates when there was only one railroad, and no possibility of competition? What about railway pools, which by agreement abolished competition? What about the monopolies in oil and anthracite, which appeared to have repealed the law of supply and demand? If government confined itself to watching benignly and administering the police laws, one of these vast new consolidations might buy it, and suppress it, like an inconvenient patent.

The next step was for the states to begin regulating railway rates and grain elevator rates. Almost all the grain from the West which was to be sold in Europe or in the Eastern states passed through Chicago, where it was usually unloaded and reloaded. Nine companies controlled the warehouses and elevators, and they of course made a "gentleman's agreement" with each other and set their own prices. So the Illinois legislature passed a law fixing maximum charges. The question of its constitutionality was brought to the Supreme Court, where in 1877 it was settled along with the so-called Granger cases, involving railway rates. The fundamental doctrine of the grain elevator case, *Munn* v. *Illinois,* applied to them all.

Chief Justice Waite, for the majority, found the laws constitutional on the ground that they applied to property which was "affected with a public interest."

> It has been customary in England [said the Chief Justice], from time immemorial, and in this country from its first colonization, to regulate ferries, common carriers, hackmen, bakers, millers, wharfingers, innkeepers, etc., and in so doing to fix a maximum of charge. . . . We think it has never yet been successfully contended that such legislation came within any of the constitutional prohibitions against interference with private property. . . . It is apparent that down to the time of the adoption of the fourteenth amendment it was not supposed that statutes regulating the use, or even the price of the use, of private property necessarily deprived an owner of his property without due process of law. Under some circumstances they may, but not under all. The amendment does not change the law in this particular.

According to the majority of the Court, therefore, there was still a field of private enterprise in which government might control prices without depriving "persons" of their constitutional rights. "We know that this is a power which may be abused," said the Chief Justice; "but that is no argument against its existence. For protection against abuses by legislatures the people must resort to the polls, not to the courts." Nothing could sound more reasonable; yet the position was soon abandoned. The future belonged to the dissenting opinion of Justice Field, who was not content to allow abuses to be rectified at the polls, who insisted that the lawmakers should have no power to do wrong in the first place, and that it was the business of the Supreme Court to detect "wrong" and to declare it unconstitutional. Justice Field dissented strongly in *Munn* v. *Illinois,* and even more strongly in the railway cases, where Chief Justice Waite applied the same principles with the same results.

Of what avail [asked Field] is the constitutional prohibition that no state shall deprive any person of his property except by due process of law if the state can, by fixing the compensation which he may receive for its use, take from him all that is valuable in the property? To what purpose can the constitutional prohibition upon the state against impairing the obligation of contracts be invoked, if the state can, in the face of a charter authorizing a company to charge reasonable rates, prescribe what rates shall be deemed reasonable for services rendered? That decision will justify the legislature in fixing the price of all articles and the compensation for all services. It sanctions intermeddling with all business and pursuits and property in the community, leaving the use and enjoyment of property and the compensation for its use to the discretion of the legislature.[18]

Chief Justice Waite spoke good English doctrine when he said, "for protection against abuses by legislatures the people must resort to the polls, not to the courts." But Justice Field had a deep American prejudice on his side when he assumed that if Congress and the state legislatures were allowed to make decisions affecting business, all "pursuits and property" would soon be destroyed. "If this be sound law," he said in his dissenting opinion on *Munn* v. *Illinois,* "if there be no protection, either in the principles upon which our republican government is founded, or in the prohibitions of the Constitution against such invasion of private rights, all property and all business in the state are held at the mercy of a majority of the Legislature."

Within a very brief period the majority of the Supreme Court came to agree with Justice Field. In so doing they worked a constitutional revolution, which may have been for the best, and which was probably inevitable, but which surely deserves more notice than it is usually accorded.

The revolution made overt what may always have been covert; namely, that the Supreme Court may declare a law unconstitutional, not only on the ground that the Congress had no power to legislate in a particular field, but also on the ground that the legislation was unreasonable or unjust. The earlier view, which prevailed for eighty years, was laid down by John Marshall in *Marbury* v. *Madison.* And in *Fletcher* v. *Peck,* Marshall declared that the Supreme Court had no right to inquire whether a legislature acted from good motives or corrupt. This was the famous case of the Yazoo land frauds which had almost driven John Randolph daft. There was no doubt that most of the Georgia legislators had been bought; yet Marshall ruled that since they had the power to authorize the land grants, the contract stood, and the Supreme Court had no say in the matter. But the followers of Justice Field took the view that if a legislature did something of which they deeply disapproved, or which they felt to be subversive of property rights, there must be some way of declaring it unconstitutional—or if not, the Constitution should be amended.

In 1889 the New York Court of Appeals, following Chief Justice Waite's reasoning in *Munn* v. *Illinois,* held that a state law fixing the maximum charges of grain elevators was constitutional, and gave the same answer as the Supreme Court had given to the argument that such powers, if permitted, might be abused: "There is a remedy at the polls, and it is an efficient remedy." This led to a sense of despair on the part of those who believed that such interference with private property was little better than communism, and that legislatures, if allowed to fix the price of grain elevators, would soon be interfering in every detail, public and private, of every citizen's life. "The paternal theory of government is to me odious," said Justice Brewer, dissenting in the Budd case; and he went on to predict that if this was indeed the law of the land America would soon find herself socialized according to the dreams of Edward Bellamy. And in the following year a prominent New York lawyer published a most revealing article in the *American Law Review,* demanding a new constitutional amendment for the protection of property.[19]

> A learned ex-Judge of one of the federal courts [says the article] remarked on reading the opinions in Munn against Illinois: "If this government is to endure, the views expressed in the dissenting opinion of Mr. Justice Field must be adopted as the law of the land." . . . But perhaps the subsequent decision . . . by the New York Court of Appeals will strengthen the opinion that the law is so clear both in judicial expression and precedent that the courts have but little discretion in the matter. . . . An amendment to the federal and the state constitutions is now necessary. . . .
>
> It is perhaps in the natural course of things that the first great question in American political history should have been the question of personal liberty and that the second great question is that now before the American people, the question of private property. In the latter there are elements which "could furnish forth" a history surpassing in importance that of the slavery question. The latter was a struggle between sections. The property question must be a struggle between classes. In the one, America as the civilized nation last to abolish her slaves closed an epoch in history. In the other there is much to show that she will open an epoch. . . . Years ago the Supreme Court introduced the

slavery struggle with the *Dred Scott* decision. Today it may be that it has introduced the property struggle with the decision of *Munn* v. *Illinois.*

Times have changed since the appearance of this article, and the reader may have difficulty in remembering that the cause of the author's excitement—indeed, of his declaration of class war—was the regulation of railway rates and of the prices charged at grain elevators. In any case, he need not have excited himself, because the "learned ex-judge of the federal courts" was about to have his way, and "the views expressed in the dissenting opinion of Justice Field" were to become the law of the land.

Already there had been signs of retreat from the position of *Munn* v. *Illinois.* In 1886, Chief Justice Waite admitted there were sharp limits to the regulatory power of the state, and he significantly did not repeat his earlier advice that the victims of legislative abuse should seek redress at the polls, not from the courts. On the contrary, he said: "This power to regulate is not a power to destroy, and limitation is not the equivalent of confiscation. Under pretense of regulating fares and freights, the state cannot require a railroad corporation to carry persons or property without reward; neither can it do that which amounts in law to a taking of private property for public use without just compensation, or without due process of law."[20] So Chief Justice Marshall seems to have been wrong when he said it was not the business of the Court to inquire into the wisdom or propriety of legislation. "It was now apparent," writes Professor Swisher, "that the Supreme Court would keep a watchful eye over abuses which it had previously threatened to ignore, and would give protection if necessary."[21]

In 1890 the Supreme Court went much farther, holding unconstitutional a Minnesota law which provided that a state commission could rule finally as to the reasonableness of railway rates. "It deprives the company of its right to a judicial investigation, by due process of law," said the Court, ". . . and substitutes therefor, as an absolute finality, the action of a railway commission which, in view of the powers conceded to it by the state court, cannot be regarded as clothed with judicial functions."[22] In a vigorous dissent on the part of three justices, it was argued that this overruled *Munn* v. *Illinois* and the Granger cases, which had stated flatly that the regulation of railway rates and similar charges was a power of the legislature, not of the judiciary. The reasonableness of a charge, said the dissenting justices, was a problem for the legislature, not for the courts. But the majority ruled otherwise. Professor Swisher comments:

> In arrogating to the judiciary the final determination of reasonableness in government price-fixing, the Supreme Court transferred tremendous powers to that branch of the government. The next logical step

was the holding that in order to be reasonable the rates fixed must be such as to yield to owners a fair return on a fair value of the property involved. The word "fair" and the word "value" like the word "reasonableness," were terms of extremely indefinite content. The content was left to be determined by the courts in each case.[23]

Meanwhile, the state courts had been busily taking the next step: invalidating laws which protected labor. In 1885 the New York Court of Appeals overthrew a statute which forbade the making of cigars in tenements. According to the unanimous court, not only was the cigarmaker's liberty infringed, and the tenement-owner's property impaired, but the institution of the home was threatened. "It cannot be perceived," said this decision, "how the cigarmaker is to be improved in his health or his morals by forcing him from his home and its hallowed associations and beneficent influences to ply his trade elsewhere."[24]

The decision had a result unforeseen by the learned judges, but not unimportant in American history. One of the ardent champions of the statute, the man who had persuaded Governor Cleveland to sign it in 1884, although it was poorly drawn, was young Theodore Roosevelt. He had been appointed to a committee of three to investigate conditions in the tenement houses of New York City, and he took the work seriously. He had expected to oppose the law concerning cigarmakers, until he visited the tenements.

> In the overwhelming majority of cases [he writes] . . . these were one-, two- or three-room apartments, and the work of manufacturing the tobacco by men, women, and children went on day and night in the eating, living, and sleeping rooms—sometimes in one room. I have always remembered one room in which two families were living. On my inquiry as to who the third adult male was I was told he was a boarder with one of the families. There were several children, three men, and two women in this room. The tobacco was stowed about everywhere, alongside the foul bedding, and in a corner where there were scraps of food. The men, women, and children in this room worked by day and far on into the evening, and they slept and ate there. They were Bohemians, unable to speak English, except that one of the children knew enough to act as interpreter.[25]

So Theodore Roosevelt was surprised when the Court of Appeals spoke of the "beneficent influences" of those homes, and the folly of forcing a man "to ply his trade elsewhere."

> It was this case [he mildly remarks] which first waked me to a dim and partial understanding of the fact that the courts were not necessarily the best judges of what should be done to better social and indus-

trial conditions. I grew to realise that all that Abraham Lincoln had said about the *Dred Scott* decision could be said with equal truth and justice about the numerous decisions which in our own day were erected as bars across the path of social reform.[26]

During the next few years after the Jacobs case, the courts of Pennsylvania, West Virginia, Illinois, Missouri, and Kansas all declared void laws which forbade mine owners and other employers from paying their men in scrip instead of in currency. The scrip, except by special arrangement with merchants, was payable only at company stores, where the company might charge what it pleased. For years the unions had struggled against this system; but when they obtained the laws for which they pleaded, the courts held that such statutes infringed the right of contract. The Pennsylvania court found that the law was "an insulting attempt to put the laborer under a legislative tutelage, which is not only degrading to his manhood, but subversive of his rights as a citizen of the United States." The Missouri court held that the statute said to the employee: "Though of full age and competent to contract, still you shall not have the power to sell your labor for meat and clothing alone, as others may." And the Kansas court added that the law classified the workman "with the idiot, the lunatic, or the felon in the penitentiary." "What right had the legislature," the court continued, "to assume that one class has need of protection against another. . . . No class distinctions exist in this country."[27]

In two of the above cases the state courts quote Chief Justice Marshall's words in *Brown* v. *Maryland* (1827): "Questions of power do not depend upon the degree to which it may be exercised. If it may be exercised at all it must be exercised at the will of those in whose hands it is placed." This would seem to mean that no labor legislation whatever must be permitted, since otherwise the legislatures would be free to pass any labor laws they chose. And indeed, the West Virginia court underlined the point, saying that if "the legislature, without any public necessity, has the power to prohibit or restrict the right of contract between private persons in respect to one lawful trade or business, then it may prevent the prosecution of all trades, and regulate all contracts." Therefore the legislature must have no power, for fear it might have too much. For eighty years the courts had followed John Marshall in saying that if the power to legislate on a subject existed at all there could be no further question as to the constitutionality of the statute. Now the state courts appeared to be saying that *since* there could be no further question, *therefore* the power to legislate must not exist, and did not exist. Again they were giving expression to the dominant mood, and it was not long before the Supreme Court itself followed the states in their attitude toward labor laws. In 1905 Justice Peckham wrote the famous majority decision in *Lochner* v. *New York*.

The Supreme Court had recently upheld a Utah statute regulating the hours of labor for men in dangerous industries. Emboldened by this precedent the New York legislature passed a law providing for a maximum sixty-hour week and ten-hour day in the baking trade. The Utah decision seemed to settle the question of power to legislate, so the attorneys for the defendant in the Lochner case argued that while laws for maximum hours might be constitutional in a dangerous industry, they were unnecessary (and thus unconstitutional) in a trade where cleanliness and sanitation were imposed by the nature of the job. The Supreme Court accepted this reasoning, holding that the act did not come under the police power of the state, as a proper regulation of the health, safety or morals of the people, and that it was therefore a violation of the freedom of contract, and of the liberty of the individual under the Fourteenth Amendment.

Statutes [said Justice Peckham] of the nature of that under review, limiting the hours in which grown and intelligent men may labor to earn their living, are mere meddlesome interferences with the right of the individual, and they are not saved from condemnation by the claim that they are passed in the exercise of the police power and upon the subject of the health of the individual whose rights are interfered with, unless there be some fair ground, reasonable in and of itself, to say that there is material danger to the public health, or to the health of the employees, if the hours of labor are not curtailed. If this be not clearly the case, the individuals whose rights are thus made the subject of legislative interference are under the protection of the Federal Constitution regarding their liberty of contract as well as of person; and the legislature of the state has no power to limit their right as proposed in this statute.

Justice Holmes, in his dissenting opinion, said in part:

This case is decided upon an economic theory which a large part of the country does not entertain. If it were a question whether I agreed with that theory, I should desire to study it further and long before making up my mind. But I do not conceive that to be my duty, because I strongly believe that my agreement or disagreement has nothing to do with the right of a majority to embody their opinions in law. . . . The fourteenth amendment does not enact Mr. Herbert Spencer's Social Statics.

This was a view which Justice Holmes was to express for many years in many famous dissents. In 1921, for example, when the Supreme Court decided that no state could prevent its own judges from granting injunctions in labor disputes, Holmes again protested:

There is nothing that I more deprecate than the use of the fourteenth amendment beyond the absolute compulsion of its words to prevent the making of social experiments that an important part of the community desires.

Yet this is precisely the way the Fourteenth Amendment was used during most of Justice Holmes's life upon the Court: as a substitute for that "new amendment" to protect property which some hasty people felt was needed when the new giant corporations rose to power about 1890. As we have seen, instead of a new amendment the Court provided a new theory; namely, that questions of constitutionality are not solely questions of power to legislate but of the reasonableness of the legislation. Thus the Court acquired veto powers not easily distinguishable from those of the President, and like the President it became, in some of its functions, a part of the legislature. More than ever, the Constitution was what the Supreme Court said it was. More than ever, therefore, the President must now pray that a sufficient number of justices die or retire during his term of office, so that there may be reasonable agreement as to the nature of the government he is administering. When a Court with these new powers comes face to face with a popular President, intent on enforcing his own policies, the results are bound to be interesting—unless the President himself has the good fortune to appoint the Court. And even then he may have some sharp surprises.

4

When Cleveland first came to the White House, all these tremendous changes were just beginning. When he left in 1897, after his non-consecutive second term, the vast monopolies and the vast cities dominated the land, and the new immigration was flooding in to serve the one and to fill the other. And the Supreme Court had taken unto itself its new powers, which for the time being it chose to use in the defense of corporate property—but which, like all powers, might one day be used for any purpose whatever. Industry and commerce and finance had never been more dynamic than during the Cleveland years, and labor never more discontented. America had never been changing more rapidly. And the federal government—inventing new forms of veto and delay to add to the old— had seldom been more negative, more faithful to the theory that a government should do as little as possible. Yet the time was coming when the continent-wide combinations of power would either take over government and make it the servant of a single class, or government must find for itself immense new powers—not to say *No,* like the Supreme Court; but to say *Yes,* like Theodore Roosevelt and Woodrow Wilson. But first the greatest No-sayer of them all, Grover Cleveland, was to stand rock-like against spoilsmen, against pension-hunters, against cheap money, against labor, against the Senate, and against the prevailing wicked system of making tariffs.

America was not to look upon his like again. By the time Cleveland left Washington, the power to do great good merely by negation was gone with the quiet horse-and-buggy days.

XXIX

Both Parties Sowing the Wind

CLEVELAND'S INSISTENCE on doing what he thought right, rather than what the politicians thought possible, was brave but not always wise. He could obstruct his enemies; but he could not accomplish his own aims. He destroyed the machinery of his party. "If it is the function of an American statesman to search for the integrating ideas that make party combinations tolerable," writes Professor Binkley, "then Cleveland does not answer the description. One does not find him, like Lincoln, searching with superb intelligence to discover the point of equilibrium among the conflicting social forces of the nation and tolerant of all sorts and conditions of men."[1] Cleveland opposed not only the old abuses in government, which had been growing since Lincoln's day, but also the new demands for help to the unfortunate. Whether these were sectional demands sweeping from the West, or class demands rising from the trade unions, Cleveland set himself to break them. And for a time he was successful.

The first fight of the new President was waged against the Senate. It was the old fight which Grant had refused, but which Hayes and Garfield and Arthur had accepted to their honor. At last, under Cleveland, the Senate was shorn of the powers which it had taken during the war on Andrew Johnson and which it had used unchallenged during the years when Grant was the willing captive of the Stalwarts.

The Republicans had a majority in the Senate when Cleveland became President. They meant to invoke the Tenure of Office Act to hamper the Administration and to turn the presidency "into an office much like that of the doge of Venice, one of ceremonial dignity without real power."[2] But they faced a man on whom they could not practice their subterfuges and their frustrating tricks. Cleveland did not like to be balked. He could break out of any traps devised by politicians, not because he was ingenious but because he was impervious—and because (as William Allen White discovered) he could summon "such virile hate, such courageous scorn, such blustering bull-roaring indignation as would have made Washington or Jackson in their profanest moments lift reverent hats in humble awe."[3]

On the whole, these attributes are of small value to the leader of a political party, who should usually be conciliatory, tolerant of selfishness, patient before the immodesty of little men. Rage and stubbornness delight the onlooker but fill the party worker with dread. This may explain why Calvin Brice, chairman of the Democratic National Committee, said that with all regard for Cleveland's lofty nature and noble character "in future I prefer to look on at his proceedings from the safe summit of some neighboring hill."[4] But if the President's temperament made compromise difficult it also made senatorial dictatorship impossible.

The Senate Republicans planned to approve Cleveland's nominations whenever the previous dismissal was satisfactory. Otherwise, they would demand information upon the man who was discharged as well as upon the man who was appointed—hoping that they could then use a careful selection of the facts to show that the President was dismissing officers for political or personal or purely spiteful reasons. Cleveland's nominations, therefore, were referred to the appropriate Senate committees, and the committees called on the Executive departments for the information with which to do their damage. Sternly the President told the members of his Cabinet to refuse all information about dismissals, and to send only strictly official papers dealing with appointments. The distinction was vital: the Senate had a right to official data on all appointments in which the Senate, under the Constitution, must concur; but it had no right to letters or memoranda in which facts or gossip about candidates had been given to the President in confidence. If such matters were made public the flow of private news would be stopped forever. And as for information about dismissals, the Constitution gave the Senate no power over dismissals.

The Senate then chose a test case (in which the Attorney General had refused to send documents about a suspension) and passed a resolution ordering that copies of all the relevant documents be transmitted at once. The Attorney General declined to obey. The Republicans in the Senate moved to censure the Attorney General and resolved that they would no longer confirm anybody nominated to succeed a dismissed officer unless the reasons for dismissal were given. Seeking public support, the Senators announced that the question was "whether it is within the constitutional competence of either House of Congress to have access to the official papers and documents in the various public offices of the United States, created by laws enacted by themselves."

Cleveland met these efforts at obstruction the way a fighting bull meets a horse. On March 1, 1886, he published a message to the Senate which the Republican members of that body would have preferred to ignore. He ridiculed their statement as to the nature of the contest, pointing out that while the Executive departments had been created *by* the Congress they were not created *for* the Senate, which had no authority over them beyond what was implied in the Constitution. . . . And he pointed out the absurdity of saying that every irrelevant and unsolicited letter dealing with an appointment was an "official document" simply because it was kept for the time being in official files.

There is no mysterious power of transmutation in departmental custody [he said]. . . . If the presence of these papers in the public offices is a stumbling block in the way of performance of senatorial duty it can easily be removed. . . . I consider them in no proper sense as upon the files of the department but as deposited there for my convenience, remaining still completely under my control. I suppose if I desired to take them into my custody I might do so with entire propriety, and if I saw fit to destroy them no one could complain.

Having shown his disregard for the Senators' arguments with heavy but wounding sarcasm, Cleveland briefly rejected their demands.

My oath to support and defend the Constitution [he wrote], my duty to the people who have chosen me to execute the powers of their great office and not relinquish them, and my duty to the chief magistracy which I must preserve unimpaired in all its dignity and vigor, compel me to refuse compliance with these demands.

The people backed the President. Once again they showed that they expected him to assert the national interest, just as they expected their Congressmen to make sure that the home town gets its fair share of federal spending. In 1886 they were more than usually likely to feel that the President, rather than the Senate, had the interests of the whole country at heart, for the era of railroad-building, land-grabbing and trust-begetting did not show the Senate at its best.

A United States senator . . . [writes William Allen White of those roaring days] with few exceptions, represented something more than a state, more even than a region. He represented principalities and powers in business. One senator, for instance, represented the Union Pacific Railway System, another the New York Central, still another the insurance interests of New York and New Jersey. Here, out of the West, came not one but a group representing the Southern Pacific. The Santa Fé divided, with the Gould system, an interest in another. Coal and iron owned a coterie from the Middle and Eastern seaport states. Cotton had half a dozen senators. And so it went. These senators either had campaign contributions directly from the great business interests which they openly championed; or the attorneys for these interests, controlling state conventions and legislatures, named these senators, and so owned them. It was a plutocratic feudalism, not rigidly organised, but eminently respectable. The collar of any great financial interest was worn in pride. No one wore his more proudly than he who represented the New York Central, and Jim Hill's senators from the Northwest flaunted their golden chains. They were faithful. No one charged them with duplicity or dishonor. Their status grew out of the manner, customs, needs, ideals of the times.[5]

The President's message went to the country on March 1, and before the month was out the Senate had capitulated. As a last protest, by a majority of one, the motion to censure the Attorney General was adopted; but leading Republican Senators then told the newspapers there would be no more calls for information.

An ironic aspect of the story is that Cleveland, during his first years of office, was the least inclined of all Presidents to quarrel with Congress over a matter of power. Inexperienced in government, he came to the presidency with the strictest views on the constitutional division of powers. He made much trouble for himself by these views and in the end he had to abandon them; but at the time the Senate challenged him and roused him to a fight he was feeling as unaggressive as a man may be. Indeed his unwillingness to interfere with Congress was the despair of his friends.

In his first annual message Cleveland said, "I recommend the suspension of the compulsory coinage of silver dollars, directed by the law passed in February, 1878." Since this was a major issue on which he had declared himself even before his inauguration, the country expected him to use the full power of the new Administration, party pressure and patronage alike, to insist on repeal. But he did nothing. In fact, when the New York *Herald* predicted that he would take a firm line he announced publicly that he intended to do nothing. On January 4, 1886, he said to the press:

> I believe the most important benefit that I can confer on the country by my presidency is to insist upon the entire independence of the executive and legislative branches of the government, and compel the members of the legislative branch to see that they have responsibilities of their own. . . . I believe that this is an executive office, and I deem it important that the country should be reminded of it. I have certain executive duties to perform; when that is done my responsibility ends.

He was asked whether Congress would carry out his recommendations on the tariff and on silver. He said he did not know. The matter was out of his hands. He did not wish to influence Congress any further.

Cleveland meant exactly what he said. The party was therefore without a leader. The President's enemies within his own camp were safe in their obstruction; his friends were powerless and dejected. One Congressman lamented:

> If only Mr. Cleveland had been content to say nothing, he had the game in his own hands. The opposition to his policy was melting away like snow in a thaw. He need not have done anything, if only he had

said nothing. We should presently have had a united party, confident and happy, with the President as our natural and proper leader. It makes me sad—for what he so needlessly said is a direct invitation to confusion and discord.[6]

The invitation was accepted. Confusion and discord reigned unhampered until the President changed his mind and his methods and began using the powers of his office to compel action. Ignorant of federal government as it is actually conducted, Cleveland had made the mistake of reading the Constitution and it had confused his mind—just as the Harvard professor whom we quoted earlier feared that it might confuse the minds of his students. The harm the President had done to his party was at once made clear. His wishes in regard to silver were brushed aside, and even on the tariff issue he was treated with small respect.

Nobody in either party was so rash as to defend the existing tariff schedules, which were unfair to the consumer, a nuisance to large sections of industry, and productive of a Treasury surplus which was an invitation to waste. Both parties had admitted that something must be done; but the Democratic Party held the presidency and would thus take the sole blame for inaction. On April 12, 1886, the Ways and Means Committee of the House of Representatives reported a moderate and useful measure. When nothing had happened by June, the President abandoned his hands-off policy and sought to put pressure on wavering Congressmen. He was too late. On June 17, by 157 to 140, the House voted not to consider the measure. One of the members was quoted in the New York *Herald* as saying:

It is a black eye for the President, and I for my part am not sorry for him. If he had not declared in January that he took no interest in the silver suspension question he could have carried that. He chose to go back on his policy in that matter, and he ought to have kept out of this tariff business. He fancied he had some influence, and he brought pressure to bear on some of us . . . and got snubbed, as he deserved. A President of the United States ought to have great influence with his party, but Mr. Cleveland deliberately threw his away, and he can't now pick it up again.

After this rebuff Cleveland never again said, or thought, "I have certain executive duties to perform; when that is done my responsibility ends." He now knew what happens when a President refuses to do more than state his preferences. Characteristically, and to the alarm of his friends, he began to assume forceful leadership on the tariff toward the end of his first term, just at the time when wilier politicians are content to coast along, praying for a minimum of discord until after the campaign.

2

Whenever Cleveland turned from positive projects (such as a new tariff or a new law for the currency) to some purely negative deed he was at home, and strong, and successful. One of the bravest of his acts of negation was his attack on the pensions frauds.

By a law of 1862 all soldiers and sailors who had suffered any physical disability as a result of their service were entitled to pensions, and so were their widows, orphans, and other dependents. When Cleveland became President the pensions cost more than sixty million dollars a year. And the cost was mounting rapidly, because in 1879 President Hayes had approved a law by which every claimant (no matter when his claim was made or approved) might recover the full amount owed to him from the day he was mustered out. As a result claim agents traveled the country looking for ex-soldiers who had something the matter with them and persuading them to blame it on the war. By 1885, 325,000 pensioners were on the roll. The pension authorities were lax and the list was growing rapidly; but the authorities were not lax enough to satisfy the more sentimental or the more vote-hungry Congressmen.

A veteran whose claim was too silly to be considered by the Pensions Bureau would take it to his Senator or Representative, who would introduce a special pension bill. Such bills were sure to pass both Houses as a matter of courtesy. On April 21, 1886, for example, the Senate passed four hundred of them. It is safe to assume that three hundred were fraudulent. Yet a Democratic President needed great courage to veto bills rewarding men who had fought in the Civil War. During every campaign the Republicans warned the members of the G.A.R. that if they allowed a Democrat in the White House they would lose their pensions.

This was the type of challenge before which Cleveland never faltered. If he believed something was wrong he would oppose it. And if everyone he liked and respected told him it was right, he would still oppose it. So he began sending back the worst of the pension bills with short and scornful messages. Many of the claims were so absurd that it was only necessary to state them in order to destroy them. And always Cleveland harped on the simple theme that Congress should either trust the Pensions Bureau or reform it. There was no excuse, he reiterated, for a lawmaking body to waste its time behaving like a court of appeals. Thus he called the nation's attention to a senseless inefficiency, and strengthened himself for his stand against the last and most dishonorable stage of the pensions fraud.

This stage was reached in 1887 with the Blair Bill, the darling of the Grand Army of the Republic. The bill provided that anyone with three months' honorable service during the war, and who supported himself, might have a pension if he suffered from any form of disability, no matter how or when acquired, including the disability of old age. The bill also pensioned the dependent parents of soldiers who had died in the war. One Republican Senator with a gallant war record claimed that every Union soldier should be pensioned, on the ground that every soldier came out of the war weaker (or at any rate older) than he went into it. Cleveland vetoed the Blair Bill, and his message received such support from the country that the matter was dropped until he left the White House.*

3

By the autumn of 1887 Cleveland seemed safe for renomination and re-election the following year. He had already made up his mind, however, to hazard his reputation on a renewed attack against the tariff. He believed that the heavy Treasury surpluses endangered the nation, and he knew it was not fair to collect unwanted revenue by a tax upon the necessities of the poor. On December 6 he devoted the whole of his annual message to this subject.

The surplus revenue in the fiscal year 1886–87 was about $103,000,000. Customs duties for the year had been more than $217,000,000 and internal taxes had been about $118,000,000. Since all agreed that the surplus was a nuisance the easy vote-getting plan would have been to cut taxes on whisky and tobacco at home, and to cut tariffs on such luxuries as wine and silk, leaving the duties that protected American industry alone. Cleveland did the reverse. He would not touch internal taxes or luxury tariffs; he demanded a heavy cut in the tariffs on necessities. These bore cruelly, he said, upon the workman and the farmer. He ridiculed the "infant industry" theory in a nation whose major economic problem was the giant trusts, and he showed that many of the tariffs merely gave these trusts immoderate profits for which they did not even have to compete. "Our progress toward a wise conclusion," he said, "will not be improved by dwelling upon theories of protection and free trade. It is a condition which confronts us, not a theory."

* In 1890, under President Harrison, a bill was passed giving pensions to Civil War veterans incapacitated from any cause. In 1904 an administrative order made the mere fact of being more than sixty-two a pensionable disability. By 1893 the cost of Civil War pensions had risen to $159,000,000; by 1912, to $180,000,000; and by 1923 (fifty-eight years after the close of the war) to $238,924,872. About eight billion dollars were paid in Civil War pensions, and this vast redistribution of income inevitably had a sectional bias. As Professor Walter Prescott Webb points out, although the money was raised by taxation throughout the country, "about seven billion dollars went to the North and about one billion dollars has been distributed to the South and West combined."

To a friend who urged him not to deliver this message Cleveland answered: "What is the use of being elected or re-elected, unless you stand for something?" And even after the harm had been done, and he and his party had been defeated in the election of 1888, Cleveland was unrepentant.

> They told me it would hurt the party [he said]; that without it I was sure to be re-elected, but that if I sent in that message to Congress it would, in all probability, defeat me; that I could wait until after election and then raise the tariff question. The situation as it existed was, to my mind, intolerable, and immediate action was necessary. Besides, I did not wish to be re-elected without having the people understand just where I stood on the tariff question and then spring the question on them after my re-election. Perhaps I made a mistake from the party standpoint; but damn it, I was right.[7]

This is a statement which has often been applauded as an example of firmness in public life. Yet if the situation was in fact "intolerable" and if "immediate action was necessary," Cleveland did the nation a disservice. If he had produced his message a year sooner or a year later he might have won the fight. By disregarding all political advice, by assuming that boldness and stubbornness and the possession of a good cause would suffice, he insured a Republican Congress at the next election and a tariff even more obnoxious than the one he attacked. The type of reform for which he pled so inopportunely was postponed for twenty-six years.

In July, 1888, the bill which Congressman Mills introduced as a result of Cleveland's message passed the House of Representatives and was sent to the Senate, which quietly consigned it to limbo. The long debates on this Mills Bill had served one purpose: they had committed the Democratic Party to the theory of tariff reform, and the Republican Party to the theory of higher and ever higher protection. From the end of Cleveland's first Administration to the end of Woodrow Wilson's second, those who believed that the two major parties should be sharply distinguished from one another could at least point to this one difference. As soon as the debates began in the House, Cleveland deprived the high-tariff Democrats of patronage, so that all but the most stubborn recanted; and in order to make the most of the issue in the campaign of 1888 the Republicans either silenced or exiled their Northwestern low-tariff wing. This unaccustomed uniformity was possible because the issue was on the whole vague. It was not a question of free trade versus protection, but of a somewhat lower tariff versus a somewhat higher tariff.

Early in June, in the midst of the House debate on the Mills Bill, the Democratic National Convention at St. Louis quietly renominated Cleveland. Although Tammany's old hatred still smoldered and led to some futile plots, there was no serious opposition. Ex-Senator Allen Thurman of Ohio was chosen for the vice-presidency, probably because he disagreed with Cleveland sharply on the money question and slightly on the tariff. He was beloved by the party workers who knew him; but he was seventy-five years old and in bad health and could do nothing to strengthen the ticket nationally. The convention's platform committee, after an all-night argument, repeated the tariff statements of 1884 but added significantly that the convention "indorses the views expressed by President Cleveland in his last annual message to Congress."

On June 19 the Republican Convention met at Chicago. The big majority of the delegates once more wanted Blaine, who was in Europe at the time and who had affirmed and reaffirmed that he would not take the nomination. When the convention opened, therefore, the leading candidate was John Sherman, whose managers were William McKinley and Mark Hanna. In spite of such backing Sherman's coldness and remoteness stood in his way. For a romantic moment there was thought of turning to the brilliant, dangerous Chauncey Depew of New York; but Republican conventions are seldom swept by romance, so the decision was reached to compromise on a man from the prosaic state of Indiana, whom William Allen White described as "this rather circumspect, erudite, self-willed, dainty little aristocrat, Benjamin Harrison." Harrison was an ex-Senator, an ex-brigadier general with a good war record, and a high-tariff man who had no marked talents, no bad habits, no taint of corruption. He was also the grandson of William Henry Harrison, who had been President of the United States for a month in 1841.

Since an attack on Cleveland's tariff message seemed the only hopeful campaign strategy, the Republican Convention ignored its Northwestern dissenters and demanded the utmost in protection.

> We are uncompromisingly in favor of the American system of protection [said the platform]; we protest against its destruction as proposed by the President and his party. They serve the interests of Europe; we will support the interests of America. . . . The Republican party would effect all needed reduction of the national revenue by repealing the taxes upon tobacco. . . . If there shall remain a larger revenue than is requisite for the wants of the government we favor the entire repeal of internal taxes rather than the surrender of any part of our protective system.

The *Nation* said this platform was so at variance "with the report of the Republican tariff commission only five years ago, and with the recommendations of successive Republican Presidents and secretaries of the treasury, that the party can only be likened to the man who made a monster of which he became the unhappy victim." Protection, however, proved a docile and friendly monster for a long time. It put the Republican Party in power and kept it there for thirty-two out of the next forty-four years. The high-tariff program, and the campaign of 1888, completed the transformation of the party of Abraham Lincoln into the party of big business. The program was not chosen deliberately. It was thrust upon the party by Cleveland's belated message which offered a sudden chance for victory where there had previously been no hope.* The program was not even maintained deliberately. In September, 1901, President McKinley announced in a speech that he had doubts about the high tariff with which his name was associated; but the next day he was murdered by an anarchist. The Republican Party has never since asked for a downward revision of duties.

4

The campaign of 1888 proved once more the weakness of the American form of government in dealing with foreign affairs. The old problem of the Canadian fisheries had again become acute in 1885, when Congress allowed the fishery article of the Treaty of Washington (1871) to lapse. Thus the Americans lost valuable rights of inshore fishing in Canadian waters, bait-buying, and transshipment of cargoes. In spite of bitter opposition from the Republican majority in the Senate, President Cleveland arranged with Great Britain for a joint commission to make a new treaty. After three months of negotiation a draft was agreed to in February, 1888. This was a fair and wise settlement of a dispute which threatened the livelihood of 15,000 New England seamen and which since 1885 had repeatedly provoked bloodshed and dangerous border "incidents." The Americans were awarded free navigation of the strait which flows between Cape Breton Island and Nova Scotia, the right to buy supplies on homeward voyages, and in case the United States removed the duties on fish the right to buy bait and fishing tackle and to transship their catches.

---

* Even during the campaign which was to commit them irrevocably, the Republicans played both sides of the tariff question. In August, 1888, Senator William Boyd Allison of Iowa offered a substitute for the Mills Bill which was far more moderate than the Republican platform. The farmers of Iowa and Nebraska, of Minnesota and Illinois, feared the high protectionist stand of Harrison and of the platform; but they liked the Allison Bill. And they wanted to be reassured that the Republican Party would not simply defeat the Mills Bill and then go home and do nothing, leaving the Treasury surplus as it was. So Congress remained in session until two weeks before the election, pretending to be busy with the Allison Tariff. In the Northwest it represented Republican policy, while in the manufacturing East it was ignored and the platform was put forward as the party promise. As soon as the election was over the Allison Bill was shelved.

This excellent treaty was sent to the Senate on the eve of the political campaign. There was no pretense of considering it on its merits. A Republican Senator told one of the British commissioners, "we cannot allow the Democrats to take credit for settling so important a dispute." In August, at the height of the campaign, the treaty was rejected: partly to deprive the Democrats of credit and partly to please the Irish-American voters who preferred to have the United States and Great Britain angry at each other. As we have already seen, the vexed problem of the fisheries was not settled until it was referred to the Permanent Court of Arbitration at The Hague in 1909.

Toward the end of the campaign Harrison received some unexpected help from the dim-witted British Minister at Washington, Sir Lionel Sackville-West. A California Republican, who posed as a naturalized Englishman by the name of Murchison, wrote to the Minister to ask how he should vote in order best to serve the mother country. Sackville-West walked blindly into the trap and answered that it would be best to vote for the Democrats. The letter, which was made public on October 24, lost both Cleveland and Sackville-West their jobs. Harrison received 100,000 fewer votes than his rival; but the combination of Sir Lionel and the Canadian treaty and the enmity of Tammany lost Cleveland the state of New York, which was once more the decisive factor. Harrison received 233 electoral votes and Cleveland 168.

"The principles of tariff reform will surely win in the end," said the outgoing President. In the very long run he was right; but in spite of Woodrow Wilson's brief success there was no lasting tariff reform until Franklin Roosevelt devised a system for depriving Congress (temporarily) of its power to set rates.

5

Benjamin Harrison was born in Ohio in 1833. His ancestors had been wealthy planters in Virginia. One of his great-grandfathers—a governor of Virginia and a signer of the Declaration of Independence—was described by John Adams as "an indolent, luxurious, heavy gentleman, of no use in Congress or committee, but a great embarrassment to both." Like most of Adams's judgments this was doubtless too harsh. In any case, the governor's son and Benjamin's grandfather moved to Ohio and became the ninth President of the United States. President William Henry Harrison's eldest son served for a time in the House of Representatives and was the father of Benjamin, the twenty-third President. The boy was educated at Miami University in Ohio, was admitted to the bar, and settled in the neighboring state of Indiana. He was among the first to join the new Republican Party, because of the slave issue, and he soon gained a local reputation as a political speaker.

In 1862 Harrison helped raise an Indiana regiment and was appointed colonel. After two years of hard work he and his surviving troops had become disciplined veterans, fit for the fierce battles of Sherman's Atlanta campaign. He ended the war as a brevet brigadier and at once returned to his law practice. In 1876 he was defeated for the governorship of Indiana but in 1880 the state legislature chose him for the United States Senate. There he had a quiet career, favoring civil-service reform and a liberal waste of the public funds on Civil War pensions. In 1886 the Democrats controlled the legislature of Indiana, so Harrison failed of re-election. Had Blaine felt strong enough to accept the nomination in 1888, this failure would have marked the end of a harmless little career suitable to a harmless little man.

Honest and informed and hard-working, icy and haughty in his dealings with most men, Harrison neither understood the forces that surrounded him nor made any perceptible effort to master them. He seemed to feel that so long as he kept himself clean and untouchable, preserving the dignity of his great office, he should not be held responsible for the behavior of the astonishing men about him. No administration has ever been more responsive to pressure from the spoils-hungry machines, from the pensions-hungry soldiers, or from the greedy rich. But Harrison ignored the existence of such vulgarities. He had a touching quality of gentleness and goodness which in an earlier, simpler, cleaner day might have made him a useful President. William Allen White has described him with charming sympathy:

> Benjamin Harrison was physically a little man, five feet six or less, bearded, soft-voiced, small boned . . . meticulous of dress and in manners, in speech, in thought. . . . His desk was cleared at night, not as the desk of a captain of industry, for there was nothing brusque, vigorous or overwhelming about him. His desk was cleared as a gentleman's desk is cleared, with a certain deference to tomorrow. Personally he was shy, most diffident and unassertive. . . . All the altruism in our politics was diffused in the heroic adventure that came when men poured pell mell, helter-skelter over the Alleghenies into the Mississippi Valley and up the slopes of the Rockies, dragging railroads, cities, colleges, factories, farm houses and equipment . . . behind them. Harrison rose when that adventure was over, and for a moment glowed, a cold, thin, white little flame of aristocracy in a sordid day.[8]

He glowed for his friends, like William Allen White, but not for his lamentable party associates. Not for James G. Blaine, his Secretary of State, who imposed a rough chauvinism upon American foreign policy; not for John Wanamaker, his Postmaster General, who made a joke of the platform promises of civil-service reform, removing thirty thousand postmasters in a year and inducing the President to suspend the civil-service rules for the railway mail workers; not for James Tanner, the ex-corporal who had been badly wounded at the second battle of Bull Run and who was now made Commissioner of Pensions. "God help the surplus," said Corporal Tanner as he waded in to raise as many disability ratings as possible and to give "an appropriation to every old comrade that needs it." Tanner could scarcely be blamed, since the President himself had said during the campaign that "it was no time to be weighing the claims of old soldiers with apothecary's scales."

The Executive Department, however, was seemly compared to the new Congress which first met in December, 1889. We have already mentioned the Disability Pension Act of 1890 which gave pensions to all Union veterans who were incapacitated for any cause whatever. In the same year came the Sherman Anti-Trust Act, one of the most ambiguous laws ever framed. Perhaps because nobody could tell what it meant the Act passed Congress by an almost unanimous vote.

We have seen that the Supreme Court, after a little wavering, decided that corporations are "persons," and are thus entitled to the protections extended to "persons" under the Fifth and Fourteenth Amendments. And we have traced the early stages of the growth of trusts. These trusts were hated by labor for their size and impersonality, by small businessmen for their piratical methods, by economic theorists for their tendency to destroy the system of competition and enterprise, and by consumers who had to accept monopoly prices. A number of Southern and Western states had passed anti-trust laws and Cleveland had announced in 1888 that "corporations which should be carefully restrained creatures of the law and servants of the people are fast becoming the people's masters." Both parties in the campaign of that year promised relief from the burden of trusts and monopolies. The result was the Sherman Act, which declared: "Every contract, combination in the form of trust or otherwise, or conspiracy, in restraint of trade or commerce among the several states, or with foreign nations, is hereby declared to be illegal. . . ." The Act contained no definition of "trust," or "conspiracy," or of the unusual expression "trust or otherwise." The second section was directed against monopolies; but that word also was left undefined. Some people thought the purpose was to give to the federal courts common law jurisdiction over monopolies and acts in restraint of trade; yet according to the common law only "unreasonable" restraints were illegal. Did the Sherman Act go further than the common law?

In 1897 Supreme Court Justice Peckham took the view that the Act must mean what it says, and that Congress intended to outlaw all contracts in restraint of trade and not merely those which were unreasonable.

Little by little, however, the Court began to apply the "rule of reason" and to soften the Act until it became almost meaningless as applied to trusts. It remained hard and clear, however, as applied to trade unions, which were brought under its control by the mysterious words "trust or otherwise." By 1900 the Sherman Act had failed either to stop the growth of trusts and monopolies or to impede their "unreasonable" restraints of trade. Matthew Josephson writes:

> After the panic of 1893, a strong movement of consolidation, mainly led by J. Pierpont Morgan . . . steadily eliminated the quarrelsome "robber barons" in both the railroad and the industrial field. Judging, after November 3, 1896,* that all signs were propitious, Morgan boldly extended his operations beyond the railroad world that had been his special province hitherto. In one great industry after another he brought about "community of interests" by throwing together the leading corporations into great, centralized holding companies or trusts. McKinley's inauguration marked the beginning of the greatest movement of consolidation in American business.[9]

In the busy year of 1890 Harrison's Congress also passed the McKinley Tariff, which showed the Northwesterners what babies they had been to take comfort from the Allison Bill, put forward to distract them during the campaign. The heavy popular vote for Cleveland suggested that the country might not want a higher tariff; but the industrial and financial interests demanded quick payment for their campaign contributions and for their votes. To make sure of a Congressional majority for the McKinley Tariff the Administration had to promise a new silver law to the Western Republicans. They then forced through the highest rates the country had yet seen, designed not only to protect old industries but to create new ones. Professor Taussig comments:

> This measure may fairly be said to be the direct result of Mr. Cleveland's tariff message of 1887. The Republicans, in resisting the doctrine of that message, were led by logical necessity to the opposite doctrine of higher duties. . . . Notwithstanding grave misgivings on the part of some of their leaders, especially those from the northwest, the . . . bill was pushed through after long and wearisome debates.[10]

The "grave misgivings" were justified, for this rich man's tariff added strength to the storm that was gathering in the West. Sensing the ominous drop in the barometer, Cleveland had spoken of the Two Nations in his last message to Congress.

> The gulf between employers and the employed is constantly widening, and classes are rapidly forming, one comprising the very rich and

---

* The day on which McKinley was first elected President.

powerful, while in another are found the toiling poor. . . . The communism of combined wealth and capital, the outgrowth of overweening cupidity and selfishness, which insidiously undermines the justice and integrity of free institutions, is not less dangerous than the communism of oppressed poverty and toil.

Congress hoped for the time being to distract the "oppressed poverty and toil" of the Western farmer with the Sherman Silver Purchase Act of 1890, which was the price of Western votes for the McKinley Tariff. It provided that the Treasury should buy four and a half million ounces of silver each month, at the market price, and pay for it with Treasury notes which were redeemable in either gold or silver, "it being the established policy of the United States to maintain the two metals on a parity with each other upon the present legal ratio or such ratio as may be established by law." Here was a triumph of Congressional policy-making and Executive abnegation. The Eastern Republicans voted for a silver bill which they feared would ruin the country, and in return the Western Republicans voted for a tariff bill which they feared would ruin themselves.

The maneuver was too boldly absurd. In the mid-term elections of 1890 the country turned from the Administration, reducing the Republican majority in the Senate and electing 235 Democrats and 88 Republicans to the House of Representatives. Congressman William McKinley was retired briefly to private life.

The last year of the Harrison Administration was appropriately illuminated by the baleful fires of the Homestead Strike, when the Amalgamated Association of Iron, Steel and Tin Workers were denied further recognition of their union by the Carnegie Company at Homestead, Pennsylvania. A small war resulted, involving workers, 270 Pinkerton detectives hired by Henry Frick, and finally the state militia. The strike was broken, with the result that many bitter destructive years were to pass before unions could establish themselves in the new mass industries. The little aristocrat in the White House could not understand such issues, and the crass tradesmen who dominated the Congress did not choose to do so.

By the time the campaign of 1892 was well under way the West was preparing for the great Populist uprising, while Eastern labor was feeling beaten and vengeful. The next four years were to be the wildest in American history.

XXX

Agrarian versus Capitalist

THE REPUBLICAN CONVENTION met at Minneapolis on June 7, 1892, and renominated Harrison on the first ballot. Tom Platt and other Eastern bosses were sorry, for they did not like the little man who looked at them as if they were sub-human; but Harrison had been as good a President as the party would permit and he could not be repudiated after only one term.

The Democratic Convention met at Chicago later in the month and renominated Cleveland on the first ballot, in spite of the fact that the New York delegation was once more against him. Adlai Stevenson of Illinois was nominated for Vice-President.

The unpopularity of the McKinley Tariff helped Cleveland to win the nomination. Also, after four years of big-business Republicanism the reformers and the enemies of "boss rule" were enthusiastic for his return. And finally, the more intelligent conservatives of Wall Street were behind him—not the men who looked to Washington for special favors but the men who looked for protection from the silver-heretics of the West. In 1891 Cleveland had issued another blast against the free-silver elements in the party, and ever since leaving the White House in 1889 he had been practicing corporation law in New York City and learning to feel at home with the very rich. It was not by accident that William C. Whitney, the partner of Thomas Fortune Ryan and the brother-in-law of Standard Oil, guided and controlled the Chicago convention. Professor Binkley comments:

> Four years in the peculiar climate of opinion of the mighty metropolis had given Cleveland a more pronounced capitalistic ideology than any Republican President from the corn-belt except Grant. His, indeed, was now a strange pattern of thought for a leader of the historic party of the agrarians and the urban masses just at the moment when the ferment of populism was turning the South and West into a madhouse of radical discontent. No doubt the new Cleveland was as honest, conscientious and courageous as ever, but he looked out upon the tumultuous American scene through spectacles he had not worn before.[1]

Before the convention opened, Henry Watterson of Louisville had warned against a New York candidate. "If we go there for a nominee," he said, "we shall walk through a slaughter-house into an open grave." By 1896 it almost seemed he had been right.

Much to Cleveland's displeasure, Watterson contrived to put a strong and bitter anti-tariff statement into the platform. "We denounce Republican protection as a fraud," it said, "a robbery of the great majority of the American people for the benefit of the few. . . . We denounce the McKinley tariff law enacted by the Fifty-First Congress as the culminating atrocity of class legislation . . . and we promise its repeal as one of the beneficent results that will follow the action of the people in intrusting power to the Democratic party." Cleveland wanted a moderate tariff plank. He was afraid these rash words would lose him the election. He and Watterson quarreled and were never again on speaking terms.

The money plank in the platform was as meaningless as possible. It favored bimetallism on condition that "the dollar unit of coinage of both metals must be of equal intrinsic and exchangeable value, or be adjusted through international agreement or by such safeguards of legislation as shall insure the maintenance of the parity of the two metals and the equal power of every dollar at all times in the markets and in the payment of debts." The West was expected to accept this gibberish as favorable to silver, and the East as an incantation for warding off bimetallism by naming prerequisites which could never possibly be met.

The election was expected to be close, but in fact it was a heavy defeat for Harrison. His own party leaders were indifferent; labor tended to blame the Republicans for Henry Frick and his hired gunmen; and the Westerners who had been fooled and decoyed by the Allison Bill during the previous campaign, and who were then fobbed off with the McKinley Tariff, now turned against the party. Some of them voted for Cleveland; but more than a million joined the Populists, thus defeating the Harrison ticket in states which the Democrats could never hope to win. In Colorado, Idaho, Kansas, North Dakota, and Wyoming, for example, the Democrats did not even nominate electors. They voted with the Populists in order to take those states from the Republican column. The Populist candidate, James Baird Weaver of Iowa, won 22 electoral votes: all the votes from Kansas, Colorado, Idaho and Nevada, and one each from North Dakota and Oregon. Cleveland won 277 electoral votes, including those of New York, Indiana, Illinois, Wisconsin and California. Harrison won 145 votes.

2

As we have seen repeatedly the anger and the political programs of the Western farmer were related to the steady fall of agricultural prices and to the steady suppression of competition by monopolistic agreements among railways, warehousers, the makers of farm equipment, and the owners of grain elevators. The price-raising tariffs of 1883 and 1890 added to the burdens and to the discontent. The farmers of the trans-Mississippi were almost wholly dependent upon outside markets. During the Civil War food prices were high, and for a short time thereafter the German wars in Europe prevented too fast a fall; yet for thirty years the fall was continual, relentless. To pay off a mortgage in the eighteen-nineties, a man needed three times as many bushels of wheat as he had needed in 1865. No wonder he asked for cheap money, and anti-trust laws, and lower freight rates, and warehouse and elevator rates made by state authority and not by the agents of monopolies.

In Minnesota in the late sixties farmers began to form themselves into Granges, to study and discuss their troubles. Quickly the study groups changed into political action groups, to fight monopolies at the state capitals and to experiment with co-operative buying and selling. When they could get nothing from the Republican or the Democratic machines, they set up "Independent" or "Anti-Monopoly" parties of their own. In the eighteen-seventies, in Illinois, Iowa, Wisconsin, and Minnesota they achieved a series of "Granger laws" regulating railways and warehouses. In 1877, as we have seen, the Supreme Court of the United States decreed that these laws were constitutional.

During the eighteen-eighties two National Farmers Alliances were formed. One alliance, centered in Kansas, Nebraska, the Dakotas, and Minnesota, becoming a loose federation of state machines to fight the unfair railway rates. The other began in Texas and spread through the South. Because of the one-party system in the old Confederacy the Southern Alliance had to work solely through the Democratic Party, which it controlled in several states. Among the successful candidates in the elections of 1890, four Senators and about fifty Representatives were either Alliance-Independents or Alliance-sponsored Democrats. Cheered by this success the agrarian leaders undertook to build their own political party.

In 1892 the Grangers and the two Alliances and the remnants of the Greenbackers and the Western free-silver men united to form the People's Party, or Populist Party, which in spite of its short life proved the most influential "third party" in American history.* The Populists held their first national convention at Omaha in July, 1892. The platform put forward by that convention gives a picture of the farmer-labor grievances of the time and a forecast of federal legislation from the days of Theodore Roosevelt to the days of his distant cousin's New Deal. Indeed a young Nebraska Populist of 1892 by the name of Arthur F. Mullen was

---

* Not counting the Republican Party, which immediately established itself as one of the two main groups and which never after 1856 had the characteristics of a "third party."

floor manager for Franklin Roosevelt at the convention which first named him for the presidency. In his autobiography Mr. Mullen calls the Populist platform "a document that was the real beginning of the Roosevelt campaign of 1932. . . . For those issues of 1892 which were not already settled by fate or by incorporation into other party platforms remained the issues of 1932."²

"We meet in the midst of a nation brought to the verge of moral, political and material ruin," said the People's Platform. "Corruption dominates the ballot-box, the Legislatures, the Congress, and touches even the ermine of the bench. . . . The newspapers are largely subsidized or muzzled, public opinion silenced . . . homes covered with mortgages, labor impoverished, and the land concentrating in the hands of capitalists. . . . From the same prolific womb of governmental injustice we breed the two great classes—tramps and millionaires." Arthur Mullen's memories of his youth in Nebraska make these hard words seem scarcely exaggerated. "Nominally," he writes, "Nebraska was owned by its settlers, most of them Civil War veterans who had taken advantage of the Homestead Act. . . . Actually, Nebraska was owned by the big insurance companies of the East and by the railroads that traversed the country between Kansas and South Dakota." These railroads "owned the executive, judicial and legislative branches of the state government lock, stock and barrel. Entrenched in the security given them by this stranglehold, they raised rates, dodged damages for their negligence, and generally strangled the people."³ He points out that the Union Pacific Railroad alone had been given by the federal government 4,845,977 acres of the best land in Nebraska; every other section along its right of way for twenty-four miles on each side of the track.*

After the angry Preamble came the far-seeing Populist program: "the free and unlimited coinage of silver and gold at the present legal ratio of 16 to 1"; a flexible currency controlled by the government and not by the private banks, with the circulating medium "speedily increased to not less than $50 per capita" (it had been $31 per capita in 1865, the highest for thirty years); a graduated income tax; postal savings banks; the restriction of immigration in order to raise the price of labor; the eight-hour day; the direct election of Senators instead of election by state legislatures; the Australian ballot (that is, compulsory secrecy in

* This is a tenth of the land in Nebraska, which contains 49,331,680 acres. The insurance companies to which Mullen refers were the holders of mortgages. Not only was the entire trans-Mississippi a "debtor land," as William Allen White calls it, with every town bonded for its public improvements and almost every business mortgaged, but enthusiastic settlers had pushed too far into the arid lands of western Kansas, Nebraska, and the Dakotas, where the tall prairie grass gave way ominously to the short grass of the plains. Here the farmers were at the mercy of the ever-returning cycle of dry years. Such a cycle began in 1887. Between 1889 and 1893 eleven thousand farm mortgages were foreclosed in Kansas.

the marking and polling of the ballot); the initiative and referendum (that is, the process whereby legislation may be proposed by a vote of the people, and whereby measures passed by the legislature may be referred to the people for approval or rejection); the return to the government, to be held for "actual settlers," of all land owned by aliens or "by railroads and other corporations in excess of their actual needs"; public ownership and operation of railroads, telegraph, and telephone, since the latter are "a necessity for the transmission of news," and since "the time has come when the railroad corporations will either own the people or the people must own the railroads."

Except for free silver and the socialization of railroads and communications there is little in this program which has not been incorporated either into federal law or into the law of many states.* Sometimes the Republican Party has been the agent and sometimes the Democratic Party. The function of the Populist Party, as of all "third parties," was to bring forward the new ideas and to argue them up and down the country so that the people could know them and judge them. When an idea which is thus proposed by a "third party" (or by a citizens' committee, a trade union, a church, or any other group) makes sufficient headway, it will be adopted by one, or more often by both, of the major parties. But it will not be adopted until all (or nearly all) of the regions and the economic interests favor it. The "third parties" and the citizens' groups play the part of enthusiastic youth promoting panaceas; the two major parties, with their vast organizations extending into every district of the land, are the bored and cynical elders who have seen everything and heard everything and do not believe that the troubles of life can be cured. No one can persuade them of an idea, for they do not deal in ideas; yet they will move with a certain stiff and elephantine alacrity as soon as they are shown that a program has become so popular that section by section it will win more votes than it loses. It is the task of the enthusiasts to preach the program until it reaches that stage; then the professionals take over.

A President of the United States can of course do more than anyone to hurry a program from the stage when only amateurs dare touch it to the stage when the two party machines will make it their own. In the case of the Populist program, for example, Theodore Roosevelt adopted some of it, and so did Taft, and so did Woodrow Wilson. Yet when Franklin Roosevelt came to office in the midst of the great depression he still found those "two great classes—tramps and millionaires." And he spoke to the people in the spirit of the Preamble of 1892.

* By 1940, for example, twenty states had adopted the initiative and twenty-two the referendum. South Dakota led the way by adopting both in 1898.

3

The first result of Populist ardor and impatience was to put back into the White House the most negative and conservative man in politics. Cleveland's obliviousness to the excitements of Omaha was shown by his new Cabinet. The Secretary of State, Walter Q. Gresham, who was not a success in dealing with Congress or in strengthening the Administration before the country, was chosen from the reform wing of the Republican Party; the Secretary of the Treasury was a Kentuckian, John Carlisle, one of the most brilliant and able men in Congress, although slightly addicted to the bottle. He was a recent convert from silver to the gold standard and was therefore feared by the Westerners. When someone accused Carlisle of being too pliable, Cleveland defended him charmingly: "We are just right for each other. He knows all that I ought to know, and I can bear all that he needs to bear." The other influential member of the second Cabinet was the Attorney General, Richard Olney of Massachusetts. He was an ominous choice in a day when trusts and organized labor were both on the warpath: a learned, stubborn, fighting, Yankee conservative, who had already shown in private practice that he had a contempt for the Sherman Anti-Trust Law except as it could be used against trade unions.

When Cleveland was inaugurated President on March 4, 1893, the Democrats had at last achieved a working majority in both houses of Congress. There was no excuse for not keeping their promises except for the fact that they differed among themselves as to what the promises were. Everybody knew that Cleveland stood for reforming the tariff and the civil service, for preserving the value of the currency and for economy in government. But many of the Democratic Senators were pleased with the McKinley Tariff, most of them thought civil-service reform a cranky nuisance, and those from across the Mississippi were almost unanimous for cheap money. It only needed the advent of hard times to expose the hollowness of this alliance, and within two months of Cleveland's inauguration the hard times came. The first big failures were among the railroads, which were hurt by the agricultural depression in the West, especially since 1887. The Reading, the Erie, the Northern Pacific, the Union Pacific, the Santa Fé—all went down. Then the banks felt the strain and responded by calling in their loans and in many cases closing their doors. In the South and West, during 1893, a hundred and fifty-three national banks failed. Within a year there were four million industrial unemployed, out of a population of about sixty-five million.

The causes of the panic were doubtless multiform and world-wide, though Cleveland put the blame almost wholly on the Sherman Silver Purchase Act. Huge British investments in the Argentine, and the subsequent default of the Argentine Government, had led to the "Baring Panic" of 1890–91, which halted the flow of foreign capital into American business. Most of America's westward expansion since the Civil War had been too fast and too flimsily financed. The heavy expenditures of the Harrison Administration ("God help the surplus") added to the drain on the gold reserve caused by the redemption of the Sherman Act notes. Rumors began to circulate abroad as well as at home that the United States would be forced off the gold standard.* The rumors led to a further sale of American securities held in Europe, to a further export of gold, and to a partial market collapse in New York. Within a month of Cleveland's return to the White House the Treasury's gold reserve had, for the first time since its establishment, fallen below the accepted minimum of $100,000,000. Meanwhile labor troubles, and the over-speculation which accompanied the building of dozens of trusts and combines, added to the insecurity.

Cleveland clearly oversimplified when he blamed the depression on the Silver Purchase Act; but in one sense he was right. That fugitive and shy commodity known as "business confidence" was in danger of going underground. Bankers and manufacturers had been frightening each other with grisly tales of revolution coming from the West. When Cleveland promised resoundingly that gold payments would be maintained whatever happened, Andrew Carnegie wrote him that he had "saved this country from panic and entire confusion in its industrial interests." In the light of recent history it seems improbable that the silver experiments would have been as harmful as men feared; but the mere fact of their fears might have worked havoc upon the American economy. In any case, right or wrong, Cleveland agreed with the men of business. He called a special session of Congress in August, 1893, to repeal the Sherman law.

Throughout the East the press of both parties applauded Cleveland, and he won support in the older Middle West. But in the South and across the Mississippi the farmers were united to defend the Sherman Act unless they were offered the free coinage of silver in its place. Their case was argued in Congress by William Jennings Bryan of Nebraska and "Silver Dick" Bland of Missouri. This was a sectional fight and a class fight also—agrarian against capitalist. It roused the passions of a religious war.

On the one side, said Bryan, stood "the moneyed interest, aggregated

---

* Legally, of course, the Treasury could redeem the Sherman Act notes in either gold or silver; but if they were redeemed in silver the world would consider America a soft-currency country and a bad place for investments.

wealth and capital, imperious, arrogant, compassionless. . . . On the other side stand the unnumbered throng. . . . Work-worn and dust-begrimed, they make their mute appeal, and too often find their cry for help beat in vain against the outer walls." This was the oversimplified faith of the agrarians to match the President's oversimplified belief in gold. Bryan's followers thought themselves the victims of an international plot to demonetize silver and to drive up the price of gold for the sake of the "arrogant, compassionless" rich. They pointed out that Germany turned to the gold standard in 1871 and that the Latin Union (France, Belgium, Switzerland, Italy and Greece) followed at once, and that two years later the United States demonetized silver by the so-called "Crime of '73." Later, Austria-Hungary and India stopped the free coinage of silver. During all these years the Sherman Act was the chief concession to the "unnumbered throng" of sufferers. If that too were abandoned, the agrarians predicted that commodity prices would fall until the American farmer reached an Asiatic standard of life. And in the end mankind would starve upon the altars of gold.

In August the Repeal Bill passed the House of Representatives. During the debate Cleveland had been absent because of an operation for cancer in the roof of his mouth. According to American custom the Vice-President was as strongly pro-silver as Cleveland was pro-gold, so if the President had died the repeal would never have gone through the Senate; but on September 1 he was declared out of danger. A few days later he was back in Washington with normal looks and normal speech, but doubtless feeling a little strange with his artificial jaw of vulcanized rubber.* By ruthless use of the patronage and by the force of his character Cleveland won the votes of a majority of the Senate after two months' debate. Unhappily the repeal did not restore prosperity, or have any perceptible effect on the depression, although conditions might have grown even worse had not the timorous men of business been reassured.

4

When Congress met in regular session, in December, 1893, Cleveland tried to carry out the party promise of tariff reduction; but the bitterness roused by the fight on silver made agreement impossible. Dick Bland had warned the President that the Western and Eastern Democrats had come to "a parting of the ways." Discipline and loyalty no longer prevailed, and under those conditions the American form of government simply ceases to func-

---

* Although there were rumors at the time, the full story of Cleveland's operation did not become known for almost twenty-five years.

tion. The House passed a reasonably good bill which the Senate tore to pieces. Many of the Eastern Democratic Senators were high protectionists, and so were the Southern Senators from the sugar states. The latter now took pleasure in frustrating Cleveland, who accepted a number of bad amendments in the hope that the conference committee of the two houses would remove them. But the Senate refused to back down even in committee, and after eight months of bitterness and futility the House accepted the bill with more than six hundred Senate amendments—most of them bad.

Cleveland, meanwhile, had allowed the publication of his letter to a member of the House, in which he said: "Every true Democrat and every sincere reformer knows that the bill in its present form . . . falls far short of the consummation for which we have long labored. . . . Our abandonment of the cause or the principle upon which it rests means party perfidy and party dishonor." For this he was savagely attacked by Senators in his own party. In the end he refused to sign the wretched tariff act; yet he felt it was probably better than the McKinley Act, so he also refused to veto it. In accordance with the Constitution the bill became law without his signature after the lapse of ten days.

The new tariff had started its stormy life as a bill for downward revision, which would reduce the federal revenues, so it contained a provision for a two per cent tax on all incomes above $4000. As we have seen, the demand for an income tax was part of the Populist revolt against the concentration of wealth and power in the hands of capitalists. During the Civil War, when Congress had imposed high tariffs it had also added an income tax to reassure the West that the Easterners were paying their share of the cost of battle. The tax had since been repealed; yet in 1880 the Supreme Court had unanimously declared it constitutional. Undeterred by this fact, a group of rich Easterners quickly brought a test case against the new income tax and in May, 1895, by a five to four decision, the Supreme Court found it unconstitutional.

This proved one of the most unpopular decisions in the history of the Court. Not only Western agrarians but the Eastern poor believed it to be an act of bitter class discrimination. The New York *World* wrote that "the overthrow of the income tax is the triumph of selfishness over patriotism. Great and rich corporations, by hiring the ablest lawyers in the land and fighting against a petty tax upon superfluity as other men have fought for their liberties and their lives, have secured the exemption of wealth from paying its just share toward the support of the government that protects it." The agitation against this decision never subsided until the Supreme Court was overruled by the Sixteenth Amendment to the Constitution, in 1913. It is interesting to note, however, that the majority of the Court which was attacked for class discrimination believed that it was resisting such discrimination and that an income tax is in itself a form of class warfare.

> The legislation [says Mr. Justice Field in his concurring opinion], in the discrimination it makes, is *class legislation*. Whenever a distinction is made in the burdens a law imposes or in the benefits it confers on any citizens by reason of their birth, or wealth, or religion, it is class legislation, and leads inevitably to oppression and abuses, and to general unrest and disturbance in society. . . . The present assault upon capital is but the beginning. It will be but the stepping-stone to others, larger and more sweeping, till our political contests will become a war of the poor against the rich; a war constantly growing in intensity and bitterness.

5

The gold reserve, meanwhile, was still threatened in spite of the repeal of the Silver Purchase Act. Holders of the large number of silver certificates which had been issued while the Act was in force began presenting them to the Treasury and asking for gold. Cleveland and Carlisle felt they must meet the demands or ruin the credit of the government. They began to sell United States Government bonds for gold, and when the public was apathetic they turned to the house of Morgan, which formed a banking syndicate to absorb three bond issues: in January and November, 1894, and in February, 1895. It was not until 1896 that the Treasury could float an issue by popular subscription. And it was not until the bad European harvest of 1897, which stimulated the export of American farm products and the importation of gold, that the long depression was really past and the Treasury crisis ended. By that time the unlucky Grover Cleveland was out of the White House. Of all the actions forced upon him by his faith in his rich Eastern friends, the most unpopular with the agrarians was the selling of bonds to the New York bankers with the help of J. Pierpont Morgan. And the most unpopular with labor was his intervention in the Pullman strike.

The Pullman Company, like the railroads which used its cars, made heavy wage cuts during the depression. By the spring of 1894 the cuts came to twenty-five per cent; but there was no reduction in the rentals for houses and rooms in the "model town" of Pullman, which was completely owned by the company. One witness testified that after paying the rent the workers had about seventy-six cents a day for food and clothing for an entire family. Yet the Pullman Company had just paid more than $2,500,-000 in dividends on a capital of $36,000,000, and held undivided surplus profits of about $25,000,000. When George Pullman was asked by federal investigators whether he thought it would have been wiser, under these circumstances, to pay his workmen a living wage, he answered: "I do not. It would have amounted to a gift of money to these men; it was simply a matter of business."

In May, 1894, the men asked for lower rents or higher wages. They were refused, and their spokesmen were discharged, so 2500 employees stopped work and the shops were closed. The American Railway Union, with which some of the men were affiliated, tried to arbitrate the differences; but the company said there was nothing to discuss. The Railway Union, a strong group led by Eugene Debs, then voted to boycott all Pullman cars. When Pullman was supported by the newly formed General Managers' Association of Railroads, the strike spread rapidly from Chicago throughout the West and then to the whole country. At this point Cleveland's Attorney General intervened with the vast powers of the federal government.

Richard Olney was not only anti-labor by temperament, he was pro-railway by profession. He had been attorney for the New York Central, the Santa Fé, the Chicago, Burlington and Quincy, and the Boston and Maine. As recently as 1889 he had been a director of the Burlington and a member of the General Managers' Association which had sprung to the defense of Pullman. The President might have taken this into account when Olney urged him to intervene; but the case was presented as a matter of supporting the federal courts, and protecting the movement of the mails, so Cleveland agreed to act.

Using a device which he had perfected in private practice, Olney arranged for the federal circuit court at Chicago to serve a "blanket injunction" on the officers of the American Railway Union against obstructing the railways or interfering with the mails. This was based in part on the Sherman Anti-Trust Act. If the injunction were obeyed the strike would be broken. If the injunction were ignored (as in fact happened) Olney could tell the President that the courts were being flouted and that federal troops must go to the rescue. All happened according to plan, and on July 4 Cleveland walked into the trap. With unaccustomed bombast he said, "If it takes the entire army and navy of the United States to deliver a post card in Chicago, that card will be delivered." He ordered a regiment of regulars to the city to "restore law and order." The result, as Professors Morison and Commager observe, "was like that of sending British regulars to Boston in 1768." The troops stimulated the violence which they were intended to stop, and which was nonexistent until they arrived. On July 7 seven men were killed and many injured. On July 10 Eugene Debs was arrested for obstructing the mails, and the strike quickly collapsed.

The governor of Illinois, John P. Altgeld, had protested throughout that he was ready and able to preserve order with the state militia. He sent troops wherever they were called for, and kept a large force to put into Chicago in case of riots. He objected to interference from Washington and demanded vainly that the federal troops be withdrawn, pointing out that they created disorder instead of quelling it. The Altgeld-Cleveland wrangle strengthened labor's belief that the regulars were sent to break the strike and not to keep the peace. If this was so the fault lay with the Attorney General who had misinformed the President. The Pullman strike came while Cleveland was absorbed in the fate of his tariff bill and was writing his famous letter about "party perfidy." Some of his just but stifled indignation against the Congress may have found expression in his rant about the army and the post card.

1894–95 was a bad year for Cleveland and for America. The depression was at its worst, but the thought that the nation might have a duty to the unemployed had not yet crossed the minds of America's rulers. Armies of hungry men ranged the country, foraging or begging, living in hobo camps, some of them marching on Washington to ask for help from a government which was itself helpless. And behind the industrial unemployed were the despairing farmers, with wheat at forty-nine cents a bushel and cotton at five cents a pound. And beyond the breakdown of the economic system lay the breakdown of politics. The great federal government could frustrate the Pullman strike but it could not feed one starving man. It passed an Anti-Trust Act, yet when the law was invoked against the Whiskey Trust, and against the Sugar Trust which controlled ninety-eight per cent of the refining of the country, the Supreme Court ruled that no restraint of trade had been proved and Attorney General Olney wrote: "You will observe that the Government has been defeated in the Supreme Court on the trust question. I always supposed it would be, and have taken the responsibility of not prosecuting under a law I believed to be no good." Yet the law was good enough when turned against the American Railway Union.* And the farce of the Sherman Act was repeated in the farce of tariff reform, from which nothing resulted except an income-tax law which was voided by the Supreme Court. The only positive deeds which were carried out and which meant what they said were the repeal of the Silver Purchase Act and the sale of bonds to Mr. Morgan to preserve the security of gold. No wonder the Republicans won back their majority in the House, in the mid-term elections of 1894, while the Populists increased their vote to a million and a half. And no wonder 1896 saw the most fateful presidential election since 1860.

* In 1908 the Supreme Court held unanimously that the Anti-Trust Act applied to labor combinations.

6

Toward the end of May, 1895, the Secretary of State died. This was a personal misfortune to Cleveland, who lost a friend. It became a misfortune to the country as well when Richard Olney was given the vacant post, for the United States was involved in a delicate negotiation with England which the impatient Olney very nearly turned into a war. Ever since the eighteen-forties Great Britain and Venezuela had differed as to the boundary between the latter country and British Guiana. Neither nation was greatly concerned, and in 1850 both agreed not to encroach upon the disputed territory. There the matter might have rested but for the discovery of gold in this tranquil no-man's-land. At once both nations extended their claims far into the other's country. In 1886 relations were broken off and the following year Lord Salisbury refused an American offer to arbitrate.

The American offer was renewed in 1894, and was again refused. During the next six months, partly through the efforts of a special agent of the Venezuelan Government, the matter began to attract popular attention in America and to be related to the defense of the Monroe Doctrine. When Olney became Secretary of State his combativeness was roused and he drafted instructions to the American Minister in London which may be described as unusual. Years later he defended himself on the ground that "in English eyes the United States was then so completely a negligible quantity that it was believed only words the equivalent of blows would be really effective." If any Englishman did think the United States negligible, his opinion was perhaps not changed by this revelation that the American Secretary of State was ignorant of history and geography, and was prepared to insult not only Great Britain but all his country's neighbors to the north and to the south.

"Today the United States is practically sovereign on this continent," wrote Olney, "and its fiat is law upon the subjects to which it confines its interposition." The statement seemed ridiculous to the Canadians and arrogant to the jealous Latin Americans. "Distance and three thousand miles of intervening ocean," said Olney, "make any permanent political union between a European and an American state unnatural and inexpedient." This, too, was a surprise to the Canadians, and a surprise to Lord Salisbury who called attention to the large number of American territories who found their union with Great Britain notably expedient and natural. The Latin-American Republics, said Olney, were "by geographical proximity, by natural sympathy, by similarity of governmental institutions," the "friends and allies" of the United States. Since the United States is farther from a large part of Latin America than from Europe, since the natural sympathy of Latin America turns toward the Mediterranean and Catholic world, and since the chief similarity in governmental institutions, between the United States and her southern neighbors, is the use of the word "republic" to cover a multitude of institutions, nobody in the British Foreign Office found this sentence "the equivalent of blows."

Behind the bad history, bad geography, and bad manners was a simple and sensible request for arbitration. If it had been made without adornment, and if the question as to whether the Monroe Doctrine applied had been omitted, Lord Salisbury might have given a soft answer. As it was, after waiting rather too long he produced a masterpiece of condescension. The worst faults of the American diplomacy had again been matched by the worst faults of the British, and the result might have been another needless and reprehensible War of 1812. The dispute, said Lord Salisbury, did not in fact concern the United States. It was "simply the determination of the frontier of a British possession which belonged to the Throne of England long before the Republic of Venezuela came into existence." And as for the famous Monroe Doctrine:

> I have argued on the theory that the Monroe Doctrine itself is sound. I must not, however, be understood as expressing any acceptance of it on the part of Her Majesty's Government. It must always be mentioned with respect, on account of the distinguished statesman to whom it is due, and the great nation who have generally adopted it. But . . . no statesman, however eminent, and no nation, however powerful, are competent to insert into the code of international law a novel principle which was never recognised before, and which has not been since accepted by the Government of any other country.

We are reminded of the days of Canning and Madison, except that Madison was not hot-headed like Cleveland. On December 17, 1895, the President sent to Congress a message which made public Olney's instructions to the American Minister in London and which would have led to war had Great Britain been in a mood to fight. In that case history might have had some difficulty in explaining what the war was about. Cleveland's message stated that if England continued to refuse to arbitrate the United States would send a commission to judge the dispute independently and to report as quickly as possible.

> When such report is made and accepted [the President said], it will, in my opinion, be the duty of the United States to resist by every means in its power, as a wilful aggression upon its rights and interests, the appropriation by Great Britain of any lands or the exercise of governmental jurisdiction over any territory which after investigation we have determined of right belongs to Venezuela. . . . In making these recom-

mendations I am fully alive to the responsibility incurred and realize all the consequences that may follow.

Carl Schurz referred to this message as "a grievous break in Mr. Cleveland's otherwise so dignified and statesmanlike foreign policy." Perhaps an even heavier condemnation is the fact that Senator Henry Cabot Lodge, when asked how he liked the message, said that he was "bubbling over with delight." Cleveland later excused himself on the ground that if England and Venezuela had drifted into armed conflict Congress would have intervened and forced a war. His own aim, he said, was by one sharp stroke to compel arbitration and prevent Congress from intervening. This is doubtless the exact truth; but it convicts Cleveland of a grave lack of imagination and an unwise contempt for the usages of diplomacy. In seeking peace he issued a threat of war—unaware, apparently, of the passions which such a threat would rouse throughout America.

Perhaps the long, bitter depression made people more than normally willing to "let slip the dogs of war." In any case, the whole nation rose to support Cleveland and to demand action, action, as if anything must be better than their present plight. The Irish National Alliance offered 100,-000 troops. The Washington *Post* cried joyously, "It is the call to arms!" And one foolish Senator announced that "war would be a good thing even if we get whipped." As Cleveland should have known, these winds of madness never blow themselves out harmlessly. Having tasted the guilty excitement of a war scare, the American people remained more truculent than ever before, more willing to find threats or insults behind harmless gestures, more friendly to the thought of armed expansion. And within three years they were at war.

Fortunately, the British in 1896 were not inclined to a similar excitement. Lord Salisbury, as Professor Dexter Perkins writes, was "as little prone to nervous agitation as any man in British public life." Seeing the sad results of his exercise in sarcasm, and finding that public opinion agreed with Joseph Chamberlain, the Colonial Secretary, who said that war between the English-speaking nations would be an absurdity as well as a crime, Salisbury prepared to back down as quietly as possible. Just at that moment came the Jameson raid into the Transvaal, and the telegram from Kaiser Wilhelm II congratulating President Kruger on the repulse of the British raiders. The press and public could thus vent their indignation on Germany while their government made peace with America. A treaty was concluded with Venezuela appointing an arbitration committee and setting a period of fifty years' occupation as making a good title. The commission included the Chief Justices of Great Britain and the United States. In 1899 a unanimous decision awarded England substantially her original claim.

One useful result of the crisis was the beginning of the rehabilitation of the United States Navy. In 1895 that navy possessed one modern battleship, which might have found difficulty in holding the seas against "the meteor flag of England." Congress quickly voted funds for three battleships and ten torpedo boats, and thereafter the public never wholly forgot that the defense of the Monroe Doctrine must rest upon sea power. In the past that power had been supplied by England; but in the future the United States was to share the rule of the seas. These were the years when America was taught the meaning of sea power by Rear Admiral Mahan. The readiness to learn and the superb teacher coincided. Suddenly newspapers, politicians, and lecturers all over the country were telling each other how Cornwallis off Brest, Collingwood off Rochefort, Pellew off Ferrol, and Nelson before Toulon saved Europe from Napoleon: "those far distant, storm-beaten ships, upon which the Grand Army never looked, stood between it and the dominion of the world." Alfred Thayer Mahan played a notable part in America's coming of age in world politics.

The Venezuela crisis was also the last dangerous conflict between Great Britain and the United States. From the time McKinley became President, as we shall see, the two nations moved steadily closer in their world interests and their foreign enterprises. No one in either country, except local politicians seeking Irish or German votes, ever again tried to disturb this movement. Even Richard Olney repented and wrote in 1900 that America must have England for a friend, since England alone could help or harm the United States.[4] And Henry Adams, commenting on Olney's article, wrote:

> My preference has always been for the alliance with France and the Latin races. . . . Still I admit that we have never succeeded in carrying on the French alliance. We drift inevitably back to the British. Economical and social interests are too strong. Our administration, whether Olney or Hay run it, must be British; Bayard or Frelinghuysen or Fish or Seward—it is all the same. Even I who hate England and love everything un-English, should have to do the same.[5]

And a few years later, in 1905, Adams gave one of the reasons for this steady drift:

> We have got to support France against Germany, and fortify an Atlantic system beyond attack; for if Germany breaks down England or France, she becomes the center of a military world, and we are lost.[6]

The moment when twentieth century Americans could first admit to themselves that a war in Europe might cause them to be "lost" was the beginning of the end of irresponsibility in foreign affairs. Yet the old mood lingered in men like Senator Lodge to plague another generation.

7

The Congressional elections of 1894 showed that Cleveland's opposition to silver had split the party. If the friends of gold controlled the next convention and wrote the platform and chose the candidate, the South and the West would join the Populists, and the Democrats might wither away as the Whigs had withered in the eighteen-fifties. The fierce hardships of the depression had turned the silver faith into a pure fanaticism. Men no longer discussed trusts and tariffs and money policy and taxation as the several parts of a much-needed reform. The battle between silver and gold had become the one issue for the impoverished farmers. Silver was a magic cure and gold the symbol of their suffering. A West Virginia Congressman, after trying to argue with his constituents, said: "I have never seen the masses of the people so wild over a question they know little or nothing about. To reason with them is as impossible as to talk down an angry cyclone."[7] Senator Tillman of South Carolina called Cleveland "a besotted tyrant," and the Secretary of the Treasury "this Judas from Kentucky," adding that "millions are on the march" and may "come to Washington with rifles in their hands to regain the liberties stolen from them."

In the spring of 1895 Bryan and Dick Bland issued an "Appeal to the Silver Democrats," charging that the Easterners would reduce the people to bondage. "We believe that it is the duty of the majority, and within their power, to take charge of the party organization." At once the advice was heeded; in every state the friends of silver united to seize the party machinery. There were forty-four states in 1895, and within a year the silver Democrats had captured thirty of them. The whole of New England stood with Cleveland and the gold standard, plus New York, New Jersey, Pennsylvania, Delaware, and Maryland. When the National Convention met at Chicago in July, 1896, the silver delegates controlled the all-important credentials committee and resolutions committee; they could write their own platform and name their own candidate. So if anyone was to secede it would be the little group of Eastern "goldbugs." And if there was to be a fusion with the Populists, the new party would have to merge itself with the old.

When the delegates reached Chicago the Easterners still had hopes of a compromise. Within six hours they were disillusioned. The implacable mood of the back-country was revealed when the resolutions committee reported. The proposed platform attacked with bitterness most of the policies of the Cleveland Administration. Senator Tillman saluted the platform and abused the Administration as "undemocratic and tyrannical." "You ask us to endorse Cleveland's fidelity," he said. "In reply, I say he has been faithful unto death—the death of the Democratic Party!" New York and Massachusetts answered South Carolina ably, defending Cleveland and proposing a declaration in favor of gold. Thus far, the speeches by the new masters of the party had been disappointing. The agrarians had the votes and the loud indignation; but the East had the best arguments. Then William Jennings Bryan made his way down the aisle to close the debate: a tall, strong, young man with a handsome actor's head and the most beautiful voice in America. Without rant, with perfect courtesy, with audacity and with moral passion, he said at last what the bewildered victims of falling prices and rigged markets and absentee ownership had been longing to hear. "As he confronted the 20,000 yelling, cursing, shouting men before him," wrote Professor Harry Thurston Peck, "they felt at once the indescribable magnetic thrill which beasts and men alike experience in the presence of a master. Serene and self-possessed and with a smile upon his lips, he faced the roaring multitude with a splendid consciousness of power."[8]

"I come to speak to you," said Bryan, "in defense of a cause as holy as the cause of liberty—the cause of humanity." He told how he and his friends had fought in every state and county of the nation to get control of the Democratic Party. "With a zeal approaching the zeal which inspired the Crusaders who followed Peter the Hermit," he said, "our silver Democrats went forth from victory unto victory until they are now assembled, not to discuss, not to debate, but to enter up the judgment already rendered by the plain people of this country." He turned to the Eastern delegates:

> When you come before us and tell us that we are about to disturb your business interests, we reply that you have disturbed our business interests by your course.
>
> We say to you that you have made the definition of a business man too limited in its application. The man who is employed for wages is as much a business man as his employer; the attorney in a country town is as much a business man as the corporation counsel in a great metropolis; the merchant at the cross-roads store is as much a business man as the merchant of New York; the farmer who goes forth in the morning and toils all day . . . and who by the application of brain and muscle to the natural resources of the country creates wealth, is as much a business man as the man who goes upon the Board of Trade and bets upon the price of grain. . . .
>
> We do not come as aggressors. Our war is not a war of conquest; we are fighting in defense of our homes, our families, and posterity. We have petitioned, and our petitions have been scorned; we have entreated, and our entreaties have been disregarded; we have begged,

and they have mocked when our calamity came. We beg no longer; we entreat no more; we petition no more. We defy them!

By that time each sentence was punctuated by a crash of applause, followed by a deathly stillness so that no word would be missed. Bryan then gave a long defense of the platform, criticizing the Supreme Court for the income tax decision, and appealing to Andrew Jackson, Thomas Hart Benton and Jefferson in support of his money theories.

If they ask us why it is that we say more on the money question than we say upon the tariff question [he concluded], I reply that, if protection has slain its thousands, the gold standard has slain its tens of thousands. If they ask us why we do not embody in our platform all the things that we believe in, we reply that when we have restored the money of the Constitution, all other necessary reform will be possible; but that until this is done, there is no other reform that can be accomplished. . . .

You come to us and tell us that the great cities are in favor of the gold standard; we reply that the great cities rest upon our broad and fertile prairies. Burn down your cities and leave our farms, and your cities will spring up again as if by magic; but destroy our farms and the grass will grow in the streets of every city in the country. . . .

If they dare to come out in the open field and defend the gold standard as a good thing, we will fight them to the uttermost. Having behind us the producing masses of this nation and the world, supported by the commercial interests, the laboring interests and the toilers everywhere, we will answer their demand for a gold standard by saying to them: You shall not press down upon the brow of labor this crown of thorns, you shall not crucify mankind upon a cross of gold.

The platform which Bryan thus defended asked for "the free and unlimited coinage of both gold and silver at the present legal ratio of 16 to 1"; it opposed "the issuance of notes intended to circulate as money by National banks," since "Congress alone has the power to coin and issue money"; it promised a tariff for revenue only and a stricter control of trusts and pools; it denounced "government by injunction," the income tax decision, the bond issues of the Cleveland Administration, and "the importation of foreign pauper labor." The convention gave this platform a large majority, and the following day it nominated the thirty-six-year-old Bryan for the presidency.

The Eastern press talked as if the Democrats had chosen a man from Mars, thus showing its ignorance of the rest of the country. For two years Bryan had been touring the West and South, speaking to excited crowds, building an organization, planning to seize the leadership of the anti-Cleveland forces from the aging Dick Bland. His triumph at Chicago was neither sudden nor accidental. He was the natural leader for a middle-class revolt, representing every virtue and aspiration of the small farmer, the crossroads merchant, the lawyer or doctor in the little country town. He had been born in such a town in southern Illinois, of Scotch-Irish and English stock. He was educated in a rural college, joined the Presbyterian Church, studied law, married an able young woman who also became a lawyer in order to help him with his work, and moved West to the frontier. He believed and practiced with utter sincerity the simple, strict moral code of his time and class and section. He never doubted that morals and politics were one and the same, and that the judgment of the unsophisticated majority would always be right. He had immense vitality, a moderate store of information, and a friendly though sedate nature. "Bryan's strength," wrote William Allen White, "was in his deadly seriousness. From the caverns of his inexperience came no cackle of mirth at his own presumption, such as invariably comes to a man of ripe philosophy."⁹

The Populist Party held their convention at St. Louis, endorsing Bryan and his money policy and reaffirming their belief in government ownership of the railways and telegraph system. The Eastern gold-standard Democrats repudiated Bryan and his platform, and nominated a candidate of their own. And a group of silver Republicans, led by Senator Teller of Colorado, organized the National Silver Party in support of Bryan.

The Republican Convention had met at St. Louis, three weeks before the excitements at Chicago. Through the skillful work of Marcus Alonzo Hanna, a rich Ohio businessman who had taken to political management in order to ensure that the country should be run by its business interests, William McKinley was nominated for the presidency. Although the name, McKinley, contained the promise of a high tariff, the Republicans accepted the currency as a major issue and declared in their platform: "We are opposed to the free coinage of silver, except by international agreement with the leading commercial nations of the earth . . . and until such agreement can be obtained the existing gold standard must be maintained. All of our silver and paper currency must be maintained at parity with gold." The true issue—the first clean-cut issue since the Civil War—was symbolized by Mark Hanna and William Jennings Bryan: Should the government be run by Eastern business or by the agrarians of the West and South? The answer would depend upon whether Bryan, like Andrew Jackson before him, could combine the agrarian vote with the vote of industrial labor.

Bryan had a farmer-labor platform in the true Jacksonian tradition, and he worked tirelessly to build a farmer-labor alliance. The negative philosophy of Cleveland was repudiated. The party was pledged to action

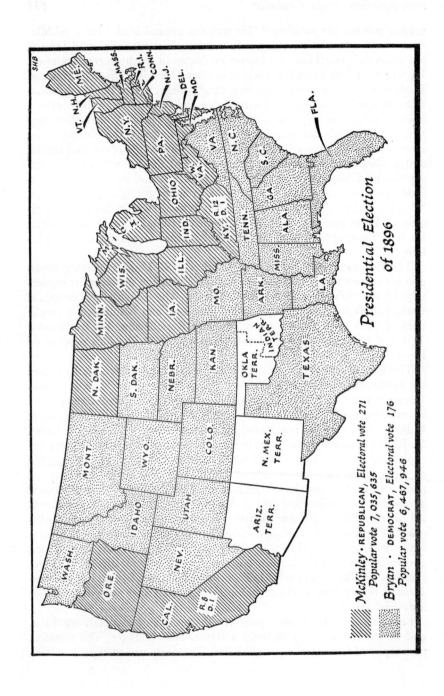

Presidential Election of 1896

McKinley · REPUBLICAN, Electoral vote 271
    Popular vote 7,035,635

Bryan · DEMOCRAT, Electoral vote 176
    Popular vote 6,467,946

in the cause of social justice. The plutocracy was to be curbed in the interest of the farmer and the factory hand. But somehow Bryan failed to win many labor votes. Perhaps some of the workers were intimidated, for many businesses gave notice not to return to work on the day after election in case Bryan won. The experienced Senator Teller was frightened by this new type of campaign. "Boys," he said, "I am afraid it beats us. If I were a workingman and had nothing but my job, I am afraid when I came to vote I would think of Mollie and the babies." But in most cases labor appears to have distrusted the agrarians, and to have accepted the Republican argument that free trade and free silver meant unemployment. Bryan lost every county in New England. He lost every Northern state east of the Mississippi, in addition to the agrarian states of Iowa, North Dakota, and Minnesota, where party loyalty must have outweighed economic interest. He carried the late Confederacy and most of the West, receiving six and a half million votes to McKinley's seven, 176 electoral votes to McKinley's 271.

> For a hundred years [wrote Henry Adams, who had annoyed his friends by supporting silver] the American people had hesitated, vacillated, swayed forward and back, between two forces, one simply industrial, the other capitalistic, centralizing, and mechanical. . . . The issue came on the single gold standard, and the majority at last declared itself, once and for all, in favor of a capitalistic system with all its necessary machinery. All one's friends, all one's best citizens, reformers, churches, colleges, educated classes, had joined the banks to force submission to capitalism; a submission long foreseen by the mere law of mass.[10]

From this decision there could be no quick returning. For many years to come the old agrarian order had lost its fight against the centralizing power of money. Reformers would now turn their hopes toward the social-service state.

XXXI

Hanna, McKinley, and the Transition

THE STRUGGLE between agrarians and capitalists in 1896 was in one sense a by-product of the Homestead Act of 1862. When the Civil War ended, hundreds of thousands of young veterans took their families across the Mississippi, beyond the first tier of states, into the country which became known as the Great West. As we have seen, if a man settled where there was enough rainfall, his hundred and sixty acres of free land might provide a living; but if he pushed west of the ninety-eighth meridian, to the edge of the Great Plains, ruin was almost certain with the next cycle of dry years. In either case the first step was to borrow money, for scarcely a homesteader possessed capital beyond his courage and his character and the skill of his hands.

They all mortgaged their farms as soon as they acquired them, in order to fence the land and plant it and stock it with animals. State after state was built on borrowed money. The Great West was the least self-sufficient rural community in the world. Just as the one-crop system—that dark legacy of slavery—pinned the Southern farmer to world markets and falling world prices, so did mortgages pin the homesteader of the trans-Mississippi to his ever-appreciating dollar payments. Greenbackers and silver men, Grangers and Farmers' Alliances, Populists and Bryan Democrats, they all stemmed from the rising price of cash, from which they thought a friendly government could save them. We have seen their three main demands, none of which had been met by 1896: more democracy (such as the secret ballot, the initiative, and the referendum); more state control (such as regulation of freight and elevator rates, or outright public ownership); and more money (paper, silver, anything to lower the cost of a dollar in terms of wheat or cotton).

When the pitiful revolt failed, some timorous Easterners predicted violence, repudiation, even threats of secession. But America was spared such trouble—partly by good luck and partly by the leadership of two capable politicians. The good luck was the discovery of large new gold deposits—in Alaska, South Africa, Colorado. Within a few years the demand for cheaper money had been met. When the McKinley Administration passed the Gold Standard Act of 1900 (which remained in force until 1933), there was no outcry, for there was no grievance. During the presidential campaign of 1900 Bryan remained faithful to silver; but the public was apathetic.

Yet the demands for more democracy and for more control over business were still strong in 1900, and still unmet. Indeed, when they were no longer associated with the demands for cheap money, they won a broader backing than in 1896. They required respectful treatment, although the country was clearly not ready for new theories when McKinley first became President, or even when he was re-elected. A few more years of argument and pain were needed before the majority could shift from the old concern for production and private freedom to the new concern for distribution and social justice, for saving national resources and spreading economic democracy. The last days of the old order and the transition to the new might have been a time of discord, in fact the transition might have been thwarted and the country might have taken the road toward dull plutocracy, if Mark Hanna and William McKinley had not lifted politics to a high level of competence.

The most famous cartoon of Hanna shows him in a suit covered with dollar marks. This was true but unfair, like most good cartoons. Hanna did, of course, confirm the alliance between business and politics. And he did use a great deal of money, when necessary, to get his way.

> His scheme was simplicity incarnate [wrote William Allen White]: high tariffs keep foreign goods made by cheap labor out of American markets. Politics controls Congress and Congress makes high tariffs. . . . Those who benefit by high tariffs should contribute the money which influences elections and controls politics. . . . So Hanna's idea was not particularly Utopian. He was not tinkering at the abolition of poverty, for instance. His was simply a device to provide for more work, more sweat, more business, more dividends.[1]

The last sentence is the clue to Hanna, and explains why he was not just another rich man buying his way to power. As Herbert Croly pointed out, "Mr. Hanna did embody the most vital social and economic tradition in American history—the tradition, that is, of the pioneer." The statement was not meant as a paradox. "The keen, hardy frontiersman" who began the pioneer tradition and "the affluent Cleveland merchant" who may be said to have ended it had a similar view of the relation between politics and business. The chief task of the pioneers was to take and develop the land and resources of the continent. "From the beginning," wrote Herbert Croly, "they recognized and acted on the theory that the individual and social profits were indistinguishable. They conceived it to be the business of their government, as the agent of social betterment, to assist them in attaining their personal ends." After the Civil War, "Washington became the headquarters from which was directed a comprehensive scheme of state-aided business." As we have seen, the farmers got their homesteads and the manufacturers their high tariff; the prospectors and the lumber kings and the railways got their free mines, timber, and land grants; corporate property got its Supreme Court decisions plus its lax terms of incorporation. "In return for all these privileges the various special interests were required only to make use of them. . . . Public and private interests were still conceived to be substantially identical, and the national economic interest a comprehensive collection of special interests." The election returns of 1896 suggest that even after a cruel depression this was the majority view.

The pioneer system contained its own doom, however.

> Even in a country as richly endowed as the United States [wrote Croly], natural resources had a limit. As soon as the process of their appropriation had reached a certain stage and had given their proprietors a certain advantage over their future competitors, the machinery began to creak. Under such conditions the state encouragement of private enterprise assumed a different appearance and began to look less like a system of social and more like a system of individual benefits. . . . The balance of the whole system was upset as soon as natural resources became even a little scarce and as soon as the corresponding artificial opportunities, created by state law, became even comparatively inaccessible.[2]

That day had arrived when Mark Hanna put McKinley into the White House; but most of the country was not yet aware of it, not ready for a wholly new relation between politics and business.

Herbert Croly's analysis, in fact, explains the trouble America still encounters in sloughing off the old pattern. Even after Bryan and Theodore Roosevelt and Woodrow Wilson had finished their work, the country half-returned under Harding to a debased form of the system which, "dangerous as it is for both business and politics, lies deep . . . in the American democratic tradition." The nation was lucky that when the system first began to break down, and before there was time to devise something better, the "scheme of state-aided business" was in the hands of men who believed in it unselfishly, who did not see it merely as an excuse to make their friends rich. Hanna and McKinley, of course, served the system uncritically. Their views would soon have seemed hopelessly old-fashioned; but they were the right men to preside over the transition. Without them the "progressive era" might have been strangled in its cradle, to the pleasure of the socialists and of the belated pioneers, the Left and the extreme Right.

The proof that Hanna was sincere in thinking the old system could be made to help everybody was his treatment of labor. Here he was so far ahead of his time—and of his friends—that his record is often ignored as if it were impossible. It was not ignored by labor in 1896, which is one of the reasons McKinley was elected. Twenty years before this campaign Hanna had a strike in one of his coal mines. The use of strikebreakers led to violence, to the calling of the militia, and to the killing of at least one striker. Hanna never forgot the bitter lesson. It taught him the need for arbitration, for labor unions, and for a personal relation between employers and workers which would make such hatred impossible. He never had another strike; but all his life, in speeches and articles, he referred to this early failure and to his chagrin at having allowed what should have been a negotiation to become a fight. The secretary of the Miners' National Association in the year of that strike testified that Hanna "was the first mining operator in the bituminous fields of the United States to recognize the cardinal principle of arbitration in the settlement of wages disputes, and the first to recognize the Miners' National Association."[3] Incidentally, the rioting miners were defended by young William McKinley in the face of bitter community prejudice. Only one man out of twenty-four was convicted, and he was sent to jail for three years. Long afterward Hanna said this was when he first saw McKinley's ability and courage.

Hanna has been accused of favoring labor unions because he found he could get what he wanted from a few leaders more easily than from the mass of workmen. Herbert Croly admits this may have been true, but adds that it was irrelevant.

> Economic radicals [he writes], who believe in the inevitability and righteousness of class warfare, like to read into the mind of every representative of wealth a "class consciousness" similar to their own, and they insist upon interpreting every action of such a man as the result of a more or less conscious purpose of exploitation. But "class consciousness" of any kind was precisely the kind of consciousness which an American like Mark Hanna did not have. There welled up in him a spring of the old instinctive homogeneity of feeling characteristic of the pioneer American. . . .
>
> He had always been sincere in his belief that business expansion and prosperity would be of as much benefit to the wage-earners as to the capitalists. But he was obliged to recognize that the former were not satisfied with the share of the product which they received under competitive conditions; and he came to realize that they were right in not being satisfied.[4]

It was this feeling about labor that led Hanna to make a scene in the Cleveland Union Club at the time of the Pullman strike, cursing George Pullman for refusing to arbitrate. Someone suggested that Pullman deserved credit for his "model town." "Oh hell!" said Hanna; "Model——! Go and live in Pullman and find out how much Pullman gets selling city water and gas ten per cent higher to those poor fools!" Hanna never deviated from his contempt for anyone "who won't meet his men half-way." He was convinced of "the essential harmony between the interests of business and that of the whole community." He feared that men like George Pullman, denying or perverting that harmony, would end by discrediting the entire system of production which for Hanna was the rock on which the United States was built.

McKinley shared Hanna's views on business and labor, and Hanna's tolerance; but he had a subtler knowledge of the prejudices and interests which moved the people in all regions and classes. He had held elective office for thirty years and was perhaps the most experienced and careful politician ever to live in the White House. He thought so steadily in terms of politics, writes William Allen White, that

> he lost his private life and his private view. . . . He played politics with Congress. . . . He played politics with the people—always deferring to them when he could not persuade them, using them with craft rather than with force. He played politics with his Cabinet. . . .[5]

After two terms of Cleveland and one of Benjamin Harrison, it was well for the country to have a President who could get his way with politicians. "One is compelled to go back almost a century to President Jefferson," writes Professor Binkley, "to find the prototype of President McKinley as the gentle but undoubted leader of Congress. . . ."[6]

> Lincoln had held the rank and file of his party while losing the politicians. Cleveland's obstinate independence alienated, in the end, both those elements in the Democratic Party. It was McKinley's unique achievement to have captivated both. . . . "We who know him regard him as a man of extraordinary ability, integrity and force of character," wrote his intimate friend, John Hay, who had been Lincoln's private secretary. And two weeks before McKinley's first election Hay added: "There are idiots who think Mark Hanna will run him."[7]

The "idiots" must soon have been disabused. McKinley was too impersonal for anyone to run him, whereas Hanna was sentimental and hot-blooded.

> He wore on his bones the clay of the inexplicable old Adam—rich in weakness and strength, graces and foibles.[8]

Hanna loved McKinley and McKinley loved politics. And both served the loved one well.

2

William McKinley was born in Ohio—that prolific mother of Presidents —in 1843. He was the son of an iron manufacturer of Scotch-Irish descent. Eighteen years old when the Civil War began, he enlisted as a private in a local regiment. He ended the war as a brevet major—the last of the Union veterans to become President of the United States. After leaving the army he studied law in the East, then returned to his native state to practice, and to enter politics. In 1871 he married; but his wife soon became an invalid and played no part in his impersonal public life.

He was sent to the House of Representatives at Washington in 1876, where he rose to be chairman of the powerful Ways and Means Committee, Republican leader of the lower House, the sponsor of high tariffs, and a half-hearted bimetallist: half-hearted because his constituents lived halfway between Grover Cleveland's New York and Bryan's Nebraska. At the convention which first named McKinley for the presidency Hanna amused himself by arranging for the Eastern delegates to "force" a gold standard plank upon him. He knew there must be such a plank, and he favored it; but he hoped to please the Easterners by letting them think they had coerced him and to please the Westerners by letting them think the McKinley-Hanna partnership might not be too immovably for gold. Later, he remarked that "the whole affair was managed in order to succeed in getting *what we got.*"

Hanna and McKinley would have preferred to treat the money question gently, and to concentrate on the tariff and "the full dinner pail"; but this was made impossible by events at the Democratic Convention. The result of the Democratic platform and the Bryan nomination was "to set up against a rich man's cure for the business depression a poor man's cure, and thereby to convert a controversy over a technical economic question into a sectional and class conflict."[9] McKinley (and Hanna, who was made chairman of the Republican National Committee) had to accept the challenge; but they did their best to underline the *sectional* interest in the demand for cheap money and to deny the *class* interest. If Bryan could turn the campaign into a contest between the poor and the rich, the poor would win. So the Republicans under Hanna's and McKinley's guidance sought to turn it into a conflict between the national interest (represented by wage-earners and employers and farmers throughout most of the country) and the local interest of the old Confederacy plus the new homestead states.

This was sensible, and successful; yet it seems meager beside the exalta-

tion of the Bryan Democrats, which we can recapture in Vachel Lindsay's
lament over the defeat:

> There were real lines drawn
> Not the silver and the gold,
> But Nebraska's cry went eastward, against the dour and old,
> The mean and cold
>
> .   .   .   .
>
> Prairie avenger, mountain lion,
> Bryan, Bryan, Bryan, Bryan,
> Gigantic troubadour, speaking like a siege gun,
> Smashing Plymouth Rock with his boulders from the West,
>
> .   .   .   .
>
> Election night at midnight:
> Boy Bryan's defeat.
> Defeat of western silver.
> Defeat of the wheat.
>
> .   .   .   .
>
> Defeat of the Pacific and the long Mississippi.
> Defeat of the young by the old and the silly.
> Defeat of tornadoes by the poison vats supreme.
> Defeat of my boyhood, defeat of my dream.
>
> Where is McKinley, that respectable McKinley,
> The man without an angle or a tangle,
> Who soothed down the city man and soothed down the farmer,
> Who climbed every greasy pole, and slipped through every crack;
>
> .   .   .   .
>
> Where is that boy, that Heaven-born Bryan,
> That Homer Bryan, who sang from the West?
> Gone to join the shadows with Altgeld, the Eagle,
> Where the kings and the slaves and the troubadours rest.[10]

There was a lot of nonsense talked and written during 1896—the worst
of it by some of the most respectable newspapers, and by men like Theodore Roosevelt who should have known better.* But Hanna had no part

---

* "Messrs. Bryan, Altgeld, Tillman, Debs . . . and the rest," said Roosevelt in
a campaign speech, "have not the power to rival the deeds of Marat, Barrère,
and Robespierre, but they are strikingly like the leaders of the Terror of France
in mental and moral attitude." And after McKinley's victory, the New York
Tribune wrote that Bryan "was only a puppet in the blood-imbued hands of Altgeld, the anarchist, and Debs, the revolutionist, and the other desperadoes of that

in the nonsense and no sympathy for his frightened friends who chattered of "revolution." "You're just a lot of damn fools," he told the shivering members of the Cleveland Union Club. The speakers who covered the country for the Republican National Committee were asked to talk sense and to assume that the public was capable of thinking. The campaign literature from headquarters was as reasonable as most literature dealing with the emotional subject of money. Perhaps a number of voters were convinced. Certainly the good harvest hurt Bryan, whose campaign depended largely upon discontent. Hanna believed that if the election had been in August or September the Democrats would have won. He believed that if his "damn fool" friends had made the campaign an orgy of class hatred, the Democrats would have won. He and McKinley thought they had saved the day by keeping calm, by arguing as if the people had brains, and by insisting that the Republican Party stood for no class or region, but for America. Since they believed that startling statement, they probably convinced a number of voters. And at least they were not handicapped by lack of cash. The National Committee raised about $3,500,000 —three million from New York and the rest from Chicago. The Republicans may have been working devotedly for the nation; but one group took a special pride in their efforts.

3

Mark Hanna refused a Cabinet appointment. He wanted to be a Senator, so a place was made for him by naming the aged John Sherman as Secretary of State. This provoked an outburst from Henry Adams. "John Sherman," he wrote, "otherwise admirably fitted for the place, was notoriously feeble and quite senile, so that the intrigue seemed to Adams the betrayal of an old friend as well as of the state department. . . . John Sherman must inevitably and tragically break down. The prospect for once was not less vile than the men."[11] Sherman was indeed ill fitted for the direction of foreign affairs while the country was drifting toward war. He soon resigned. In fact most of McKinley's first Cabinet gave way, under the pressure of events, to abler men. By the time John Hay had become Secretary of State, Elihu Root Secretary of War, and Philander Knox Attorney General, the Administration could feel proud.

The new Congress passed the high tariff which businessmen expected,

---

type. . . . He goes down with the cause and must abide with it in the history of infamy." The reason ex-Governor Altgeld of Illinois was so hated by the Republicans, and so loved by Vachel Lindsay, was that he had pardoned three men, victims of the "malicious ferocity" of a Chicago judge, and that he had protested against Grover Cleveland's use of federal troops during the Pullman strike. It was easy to become an "anarchist" in those days.

and established the gold standard as soon as the recently discovered mines had eased the pressure for cheap money. But aside from these promised laws, the President and the Congress alike intended to let the country alone, to let business create prosperity and prosperity create the proper gratitude toward the Republican Party. McKinley, who represented a vanishing world in so many respects, was the last of the great leaders who truly thought that the Grand Old Party and the United States were one and the same, and that whatever helped either of those institutions must equally help the other. Since he also identified the party with business enterprise he had no objection to the renewed vigor with which the Morgan interests turned to the building of trusts. He agreed with his friend Mark Hanna that labor should organize and demand a fair share of the profits; but he was confident that the larger the profits the better for everyone, since there would thus be more money to seep down from the top and fill the nation's dinner pails. If he had been asked how the farmer could profit from the granting of favors to the new giant industries McKinley would have answered that high tariffs added more to the riches of the country by stimulating production than they took from consumers in terms of prices. Yet his enigmatic last speech, which he did not live to explain, shows that he had begun to wonder whether trade, instead of production, might not soon need government help. "The period of exclusiveness is past," he said. "The expansion of our trade and commerce is the pressing problem. Commercial wars are unprofitable. . . . Reciprocity treaties are in harmony with the spirit of the times. . . . If perchance some of our tariffs are no longer needed for revenue or to encourage and protect our industries at home, why should they not be employed to extend and promote our markets abroad?" This was strange doctrine from the high priest of protection.

4

On one important policy the Administration, which otherwise moved so smoothly, met sharp resistance. In spite of the appalling chaos in Cuba McKinley wanted peace with Spain, and so did Mark Hanna, and so did many responsible leaders throughout the country; but a noisy public wanted war. It consisted mostly of people who had not yet calmed down from the excitements of Cleveland's quarrel with England. Whipped on by the new cheap press they wanted to fight somebody, and they wanted America to start expanding again. And too many politicians aped the language of the Hearst and the Pulitzer newspapers. Senator Cullom of Illinois announced: "It is time someone woke up and realized the necessity of annexing some property. We want all this northern hemisphere."

And Senator Henry Cabot Lodge was ready to back any baleful foreign policy. "From the Rio Grande to the Arctic Ocean," he wrote, "there should be but one flag and one country." These people did not care which nation was nominated for the enemy, so long as America fought somebody and stole some land. At the time of the Venezuela crisis Theodore Roosevelt wrote to Lodge: "The clamor of the peace faction has convinced me that this country needs a war." And later, when he had become Assistant Secretary of the Navy in McKinley's Cabinet, Roosevelt called the President a "white-livered cur" for thinking twice before attacking the Spaniards.

With such a public clamor to depend upon, the friends of violence could always find "incidents" and prolong the uproar.* It was hard for a gentle and politically sensitive President like McKinley to hold back. He sought to ease his conscience by handing the decision to Congress, and in April, 1898, Congress chose war. Ex-President Cleveland wrote gloomily:

> With all allowances I can make . . . I cannot avoid a feeling of shame and humiliation. . . . My only relief from the sick feeling which these thoughts induce consists . . . in the hope, almost amounting to expectation, that we shall find Spain so weak and inefficient that the war will be short and that the result may not be much worse than a depreciation of national standing before the world abroad, and, at home, a demoralization of our people's character, much demagogy and humbug, great additions to our public burdens and the exposure of scandalous operations.

With exception of the "great additions to our public burdens," every troubled word came true.

The Cuban uprising against Spanish rule had begun in 1895. The war was fought cruelly on both sides and the civil population suffered almost as much as the military. American lives were endangered, and American capital. More than fifty million dollars were invested in Cuba, and the annual trade between the island and the United States was more than a hundred millions. It was proper that the Americans should wish the war

---

* The most gory incident was the explosion of the United States battleship *Maine* in Havana Harbor, in February, 1898. Two hundred and sixty lives were lost. The Spaniards argued that the tragedy was caused by an internal explosion, and the Americans that the explosions within the ship were started by an external explosion, presumably by a mine. The mystery has never been solved; but it was no mystery to Mr. William Randolph Hearst, or to Joseph Pulitzer. As Godkin of the *Nation* complained, referring to Hearst, "a blackguard boy with several million dollars at his disposal has more influence on the use a great nation may make of its credit, of its army and navy, of its name and traditions, than all the statesmen and philosophers and professors in the country." Pulitzer later confessed that he "had rather liked the idea of a war—not a big one—but one that would arouse interest." Yet according to his biographer the war was a disappointment. "Dealers failed to cut their orders between battles and the paper was swamped with returns. Mr. Pulitzer lost interest in war and turned to urging an earlier peace."

to cease, and it was natural that their sympathies should be with the Cuban rebels. But there was nothing in the situation that need lead to a Spanish-American war. The demands made by McKinley upon Spain were reasonable, and were receiving reasonable treatment. The President asked that the rebels should be granted an armistice, that the hideous concentration camps for Cuban civilians should be broken up, and that Spain should accept American mediation to settle the quarrel.

Spain was slow in giving way; but McKinley kept up a steady and polite pressure, and in April, 1898, the government at Madrid capitulated. The American Minister cabled McKinley that if he would continue to treat Spain with courtesy he could obtain Cuban autonomy, or independence, or even annexation to the United States. Two days later McKinley sent his message to Congress. He did not advocate war; but he wrote nine pages of angry comment on Spain's behavior, and said "I have exhausted every effort to relieve the intolerable condition of affairs which is at our doors." At the end of the message, as if adding an unimportant footnote, he remarked that Spain had lately yielded on every point. "This fact," he wrote, "with every other pertinent consideration, will, I am sure, have your just and careful attention in the solemn deliberations upon which you are about to enter." Congress, which was feeling neither solemn nor deliberate, at once chose war. McKinley had in fact given in to public pressure, for fear of disrupting his party and losing the autumn elections. The pressure was very great. Congress might have insisted upon war no matter what the President said. But McKinley would stand higher in history if he had refrained from the Pontius Pilate gesture of refusing responsibility.

Spain proved weak and inefficient, as Cleveland hoped. And there was much "demagogy and humbug . . . and the exposure of scandalous operations," as Cleveland feared. The War Department and the organization of the army proved incompetent beyond anything which even Cleveland could put into words; but the navy was less shocking, partly because if a ship can put to sea at all it must be more adequate than a regiment sans arms or equipment, and partly because of the foresight and energy of Theodore Roosevelt. As Assistant Secretary he had prepared to attack Spain in the Far East as well as the Caribbean, with the result that McKinley soon faced another unpleasant decision: Should the United States annex the Philippines with their eight million inhabitants? He toured the Middle West to see what the Republican voters felt, and they seemed to feel that expansion was part of America's destiny. Then he examined his own conscience, which on the whole agreed with the voters.

> Late one night [he wrote] it came to me this way . . . (1) That we could not give them [the Philippines] back to Spain—that would be

cowardly and dishonorable; (2) that we could not turn them over to France or Germany—our commercial rivals in the Orient—that would be bad business and discreditable; (3) that we could not leave them to themselves—they were unfit for self-government—and they would have anarchy and misrule worse than Spain's war; (4) that there was nothing left for us to do but take them all, and to educate and uplift and civilize and christianize them.

After this very practical communication from his better nature McKinley telegraphed the commissioners of peace at Paris to hold the islands. Spain was given twenty million dollars in compensation.

The Filipinos, however, had received a different guidance from that of McKinley. They did not agree that "there was nothing left to do but take them all." Several years of hard fighting—far more savage than the ten weeks' war against Spain—had still to be spent in persuading them. Meanwhile the Hawaiian Islands were annexed, partly because they would be needed to defend the Philippines. Puerto Rico was also taken in the peace treaty with Spain. And Cuba, which had been promised political freedom, was given it conditionally after two years, and completely in 1934. Economically, however, she became the colony of a few New York banks, who soon had investments in the island of more than $1,500,000,000.

Thus the Americans who wanted to annex some property were satisfied. And so were the people who merely wanted to fight. "It has been a splendid little war," wrote John Hay to Theodore Roosevelt.

This was not the view of the whole country. In 1900, when news of the fierce battling against the Filipinos reached the United States, a protest against imperialism grew strong. Republicans like Senator Hoar and Senator Edmunds joined with Democrats like Grover Cleveland and Bryan. The attack was moral, economic, strategic, and constitutional. On all these grounds the anti-imperialists argued that the annexation of the Philippines would prove an evil deed—the constitutional case being that there was no authority in the sacred text for taking and governing alien peoples without their consent. The Supreme Court found ways of rejecting this argument, but not until after the elections had shown that the anti-imperialists were a minority.

5

Bryan, who was renominated by the Democrats without opposition, made imperialism the main issue in his campaign of 1900. The Republicans answered with a slogan: "Don't haul down the flag." And they pointed with pride, not only to the war and its stirring results, but to the many signs of

America's new place in the world. During the Boxer Rebellion of 1900, United States troops had been sent to the relief of the legations at Peking. In the previous year Secretary of State Hay, with the support of the British Foreign Office, had urged the "Open Door" policy in China upon the Great Powers. Hay accepted the "spheres of influence" which had lately been established; but he asked that there be no discrimination in the treatment of trade. In the midst of the Boxer trouble he went further, announcing that "the policy of the Government of the United States is to seek a solution which may bring about permanent safety and peace to China, preserve China's territorial and administrative entity, protect all rights granted to friendly powers by treaty and international law, and safeguard for the world the principle of equal and impartial trade with all parts of the Chinese Empire." The Powers reluctantly gave verbal assent; but neither Russia nor Japan paid any practical heed, and within fifteen years the policy was abandoned. Yet it had a lasting effect upon world affairs, because in return for John Hay's support of the Open Door in the East, Great Britain gave America a free hand in the Western Hemisphere, and especially in the Caribbean.

At once the United States set about establishing the largest "sphere of influence" ever attempted—though reserving the right to criticize all spheres of influence as immoral. And England, which had long been the only great power with major interests in every continent, accepted a markedly secondary position in the American Hemisphere. The world had expected, and some of the world had hoped, that America's coming-of-age would be accompanied by an Anglo-American war. Instead, the years from McKinley's first inauguration until 1903 saw a series of peaceful accommodations between the two countries.

> The withdrawal of the British Caribbean squadron to waters nearer home [writes Professor William T. R. Fox], the dismantling of fortifications in the Caribbean and in Canada, the renegotiation of the Isthmian Canal question to permit the United States to build and operate the Panama Canal alone, and finally the sacrifice of the Canadian claim in the Alaskan boundary dispute, all were evidences of British retreat. Henceforth, the way was open for Anglo-American collaboration, especially since the United States did not challenge British interests in Europe or other parts of the world.[12]

Few people, of course, were aware in 1900 that this history-making change was afoot, although the German Foreign Office sadly suspected it. But the majority of Americans knew they were enthusiastic about the policy their country was pursuing. There was more to this enthusiasm than can be explained by the expanding economic interests of the nation. For better or worse, after years of tranquillity and self-absorption, the

Americans were waking to a deep desire to play a part on the world-stage. This desire was a help to the Republicans and a handicap to Bryan in the campaign of 1900.

The real Republican argument in 1900, however, was McKinley. He had never before been so popular. The war which he did not want had been a delightful and easy success. The people were dazzled with victory and with prosperity. The harmony between the President and the Congress was complete. The only problem facing the Republican Convention was how to replace the Vice-President, who had died. Theodore Roosevelt, who had returned from the war a hero and become governor of New York State, was disliked by Boss Platt, for reasons which we shall see. Platt conspired with his fellow boss Quay of Pennsylvania to force Roosevelt upon the convention as Vice-President, although neither McKinley nor Hanna wanted him. Hanna might have induced McKinley to intervene; but he made the mistake of thinking that Roosevelt was merely a blusterer, and not the voice of a new spirit which would undo the world of Mark Hanna.*

The two deluded bosses, Platt and Quay, had a few months of peace, enjoying the discomfiture of Hanna and thinking they had buried Theodore Roosevelt in the vice-presidency and need nevermore be troubled by his brash commotion. Then McKinley was murdered, and the new generation came to power. The men of the Civil War were gone forever: the Union generals, the Vindictives, the Stalwarts and Half-breeds, the robber barons and the first trust-builders. On the whole they were a graceless lot. Yet among the many gaudy knaves were also many patriots and unsung pioneers. The last of their leaders were the wisest and the best. Their naïve but not always harmful view of how a nation should dispose of its natural resources was made to seem almost sensible by McKinley and Mark Hanna.

* In 1899 Hanna had blocked Matt Quay's admission to the Senate, so Quay helped in forcing Roosevelt on the convention to annoy Hanna. When the deed was done Hanna remarked, "Don't any of you realize that there's only one life between this madman and the White House?" (Cp. Henry Pringle, *Theodore Roosevelt*, pp. 221–23.)

XXXII

"I Did Greatly Broaden the . . .
Executive Power"

D URING THE YEARS from Grant to McKinley, Republican Presidents had on the whole refrained from open and avowed policy-making. The one Democratic President had fought a dogged drawn battle against Congress. And it was the exception for either party to have control both of the presidency and of the two houses of Congress. Under the circumstances the Speaker of the House of Representatives became an officer of great importance; indeed, during much of this time, the Speaker supplied what little leadership existed in the federal government. The result might have been a constitutional revolution. If there had not come a return toward Executive leadership during the "progressive era" from Theodore Roosevelt to Woodrow Wilson, the Speaker might have become an unofficial and inefficient prime minister—inefficient because he could not act as the political head of the government, using every party device to impose his will, and at the same time maintain even the small shadow of impartiality which is required of the Speaker under the American system. Yet in keeping with the Hamiltonian thesis that by one means or another, no matter what the Constitution provides, the public business must and will go forward, the absence of leadership elsewhere compelled the Speaker to assume wide powers.

These were the years which Lord Bryce had in mind when he wrote that "it is no exaggeration to call him [the Speaker] the second, if not the first political figure in the United States, with an influence upon the fortunes of men and the course of domestic events superior, in ordinary times, to the President's, although shorter in its duration and less patent to the world."[1] The promotion of the Speaker to such power was the work of one remarkable man.

Until Speaker Thomas Brackett Reed ("Czar Reed") undertook in 1889 to enforce order and authority, the situation in the lower House was distressing. On the theory that Congress had the sole responsibility for lawmaking, recommendations from any quarter were received without discrimination. A measure proposed by the President and his Cabinet was treated on a par with a measure proposed by a citizens' study-group in a Nebraska village: each was sent to the appropriate committee, and in each case the committee had the power to report in favor or disfavor, or not to report at all. Party membership on a committee was in proportion to party membership in the whole House. "Although the system was originally introduced with the idea that it would give the House of Representatives control over legislative business, the actual result has been to reduce this body to an impotence unparalleled among national representative assemblies in countries having constitutional government."[*2]

The reason for the impotence was described by a Congressman from Delaware in 1884.

> The committees were formed [he wrote]; they met in their respective committee rooms day after day, week after week, working up the business which was committed to them by this House, and they reported to this House 8290 bills. They came from the respective committees, and they were consigned to the calendars of this House, which became for them the tomb of the Capulets; most of them were never heard of afterward. From the Senate there were 2700 bills.[**]

Under such conditions (when it would have taken more than sixty-six years to go through the calendars of one session if each member debated each bill for a minute) the House had to give to some group the right to decide which bills must die unheard. Inevitably, the Committee on Appropriations received this power, since the appropriations had to pass whatever else failed. A motion to go into Committee of the Whole to consider appropriation bills was thus always in order, and took precedence over other similar motions. "For the last three Congresses," Thomas Reed complained in 1885, "the representatives of the people of the United States have been in irons. They have been allowed to transact no public business except at the dictation and by the permission of a small coterie of gentlemen. . . . " And on another occasion Reed declared that the House was trying "to run Niagara through a quill."

From 1882 onwards Reed fought for a reform of the rules. For six years nothing was accomplished except the scattering of the power of the Committee on Appropriations among eight committees. This made the confusion considerably worse. Protesting against the change a Kansas Representative said: "You do not propose to remedy any of those things

* From *The Cleveland Era* by H. J. Ford, vol. 4, THE CHRONICLES OF AMERICA, copyright Yale University Press.

** In the British Parliamentary session of 1885, 202 public bills were brought in and 279 private bills. One hundred and forty-four of the public bills passed the House of Commons, and 203 of the private bills. Fortunately, less than one thirtieth of the bills introduced in the American Congress in those years survived.

of which you complain by any of the rules you have brought forward. You propose to clothe eight committees with the same power, with the same temptation and capacity to abuse it. You multiply eightfold the very evils of which you complain." The comment is so obvious and so true that it forces consideration of a further question: Why did the Congress prefer to remain "in irons"? Why, for example, was there no discussion of one easy way in which the House could regain freedom of action—"namely, by having the Administration submit its budget demands and its legislative proposals directly to the committee of the whole House. . . . Congress would thus save the months of time that are now consumed in committee incubation and would almost certainly be assured of opportunity of considering the public business. Discrimination in legislative privilege among members of the House would then be abolished, for every member would belong to the committee on appropriations."*³ This very suggestion was put forward in the Senate Report of February 4, 1881, as a cure for the paralysis of Congress.

There are two reasons why the House gave no heed. In the first place, the change would strengthen the President by requiring that his suggestions be debated responsibly and in the open. In the second place, it would make for a speed and efficiency in legislation which were contrary to the whole American plan. The Constitution had decreed a division of powers in order that the government should be weak, not strong. During the long debates on the new rules proposed by Tom Reed, a Representative from Pennsylvania said it was a good thing that the rules did hamper action, and "that the country which is least governed is the best governed." And Reed himself pointed out that "all the rules of the House were bent for the obstruction of action on the part of Congress." Thus, since the House would not reform itself, and since all of the public business could not be neglected all of the time, there only remained one recourse: a strong Speaker must impose new rules by the power of his will. This was done after the newly elected Republican House had met on December 2, 1889, and had chosen Tom Reed for Speaker.

2

"Reed is too clever, too strong-willed, and too cynical, for a bankers' party," wrote Henry Adams in 1896 when Reed sought the presidential nomination. The description was apt. Reed had for years been the dominant Republican in the House; but not even to win the presidency

* From *The Cleveland Era* by H. J. Ford, vol. 4, THE CHRONICLES OF AMERICA, copyright Yale University Press.

could he conceal his low opinion of most men. Pope's comment on Sir Robert Walpole was applicable to Reed:

> Would he oblige me? let me only find
> He does not think me what he thinks mankind.

Yet he mastered the House of Representatives as it was never mastered before. A scholar, a mordant wit, a brave, unbending character, he made his way by strength and not by diplomacy. He was six feet three, and weighed more than two hundred and fifty pounds. He had a smooth round face that suggested good nature until he opened his mouth for one of the brief, drawling, sardonic speeches that made him feared and followed. In 1876, at the age of thirty-seven, he was sent to the lower House to represent his native district of Portland, Maine. Within six years he had become his party's leader in the House, retaining the position until he resigned from politics. In 1889, when he won the speakership, the Republicans has just captured the presidency and both houses of Congress. Harrison made no effort to impose his will, but gladly accepted the Whig doctrine of Congressional sovereignty. So if the party was not to be disgraced the House of Representatives must be disciplined.

A quorum in the House was a majority of the whole membership. According to precedent if a member did not answer his name on the roll call he could not be counted present. Since the Republicans in 1889 had only three votes more than the necessary quorum, the Democrats could often stop all action merely by remaining quiet. Reed put an end to this by directing the clerk to record the necessary number of Democrats as present even though they did not answer. For three days the House was in an uproar; but Reed stood firm. He pointed out that the Constitution authorized Congress to take steps to compel the attendance of members. "Inasmuch as the Constitution only provides for their attendance," he said, "that attendance is enough. If more was needed the Constitution would have provided more."

This was an attack on the dearest possession of the House: its facilities for obstruction. Yet Reed held fast and won his way. He also imposed another fateful rule, that "no dilatory motion shall be entertained by the Speaker." The preceding Congress had been blocked and bedeviled by such motions. And a few years later, when a Democratic majority repealed his rules, Reed made such use of the "silent quorums" that for weeks the House could do no business. Then the Democrats reimposed the "Czar's" system which they had abused so bitterly.

Under the new rules the Congress which assembled in 1889 had no trouble in passing laws. In fact, it soon legislated its own majority party out of power. This was the famous "billion dollar Congress" which (with the help of Corporal Tanner) quickly disposed of the Treasury surplus.

This was the Congress which passed the inscrutable Sherman Anti-Trust Act. And this was the Congress which, in order to get Northwestern votes for the McKinley Tariff, promised Eastern votes for the Sherman Silver Purchase Act: thus ensuring that most Republicans should vote for at least one important law which they believed would injure the country. There was something to be said, apparently, for legislatures which could not legislate.

Reed remained Speaker until the end of the century, supporting McKinley (his successful rival for the presidency) until the Spanish-American War. He opposed that war, and the annexation of the Hawaiian Islands, on the ground that the governing of subject peoples was alien to American character. "Tom Reed is playing the devil," wrote Henry Adams in February, 1899. "In the next Congress, if he is Speaker, the Administration will be at his mercy."[4] But the next Congress had to do without Tom Reed. After twenty-three years in the House he resigned in disgust and turned to the practice of law in New York City.* He was soon succeeded by "Uncle Joe" Cannon, a Speaker in the Reed tradition, who controlled the House with firm autocracy, but who could work (at least for the first years) with Theodore Roosevelt—a task which the sardonic Reed would have found difficult. Reed and Roosevelt were friends; but they were too strong-willed for team-mates. And Roosevelt was worried by people who made fun of the verities. "Theodore," said Reed, "if there is one thing for which I admire you, it is your original discovery of the ten commandments."

3

Theodore Roosevelt was born in New York in 1858. His father was descended from one of the early Dutch settlers in what was then New Amsterdam; his mother was a Georgian with Scotch-Irish and Huguenot blood. He was a sickly child; but he set his mind on growing strong and by the time he went to Harvard College he had repaired most of his bodily weaknesses—except the faulty eyesight which troubled him throughout life. The year of his graduation he married Alice Lee of Boston. He began the study of law, then dropped it to enter the New York State legislature. This was an eccentric decision in the eighties for a well-to-do youth of good family. His friends warned him that his associates would be grooms, liquor dealers, and low politicians. "In that case," he

---

* William Allen White, and others, claim that Reed knew McKinley and Hanna were too strong for him, and that instead of the Administration being at his mercy it was prepared to force him out. In any case, Reed resigned. (Cp. William Allen White, *Autobiography*, p. 336.)

answered, "they belong to the governing class, and you do not. I mean, if I can, to be one of the governing class."

Roosevelt was a success in the legislature. In 1884, as we have seen, he was a delegate to the Republican National Convention which nominated Blaine. He opposed the nomination vigorously. When he decided to support Blaine in the campaign, in spite of his personal distaste, he may be said to have crossed the line which separates a professional in politics from an amiable amateur. "A man cannot act both within and without the party," he announced. "It is impossible to combine the functions of a guerrilla chief with those of a colonel in the regular army." The decision to be "regular" was relatively easy for Roosevelt because by nature he was a strong partisan. Unlike Tom Reed ("that fat, sarcastic man," as Spring Rice called him), to whom even the Grand Old Party was a joke, Roosevelt could not help feeling that God intended Republicans to be better than Democrats. At the end of one of his mocking letters, Reed said to Roosevelt, "I know that this frivolity will grieve you, but I love you in spite of your seriousness."[5] The seriousness was a lifelong blessing. It liberated Roosevelt from the doubts that bedevil most men, leaving him free to spend his vast energies in action.

> The thing which the gods gave Roosevelt in excess was energy [wrote his friend William Allen White]. He was Gargantuan in his capacity for work. It was one of those utterly unthinkable coincidences . . . that a man of Roosevelt's enormous energy should come to the Presidency of exactly that country which at exactly that time was going through a transitional period—critical, dangerous, and but for him terrible—between an old, rural, individual order and a new highly socialized industrial order.

And Henry Adams made the same comment in his less enthusiastic way:

> Power when wielded by abnormal energy is the most serious of facts, and all Roosevelt's friends know that his restless and combative energy was more than abnormal. Roosevelt, more than any other man living within the range of notoriety, showed the singular primitive quality that belongs to ultimate matter—the quality that mediaeval theology assigned to God—he was pure act.[6]

In the summer of 1884, before taking to the stump for Blaine, Roosevelt went West to the Dakota Territory where he had bought two cattle ranches. He wanted to think over his political future and to escape as far as possible from his domestic past. His wife had died in February, 1884, after giving birth to a daughter. And on the same day his mother died. Even Roosevelt's burning joy in life was for a time quenched. He spent most of the next two years on his ranching ventures, losing almost fifty thousand dollars, which he could ill afford, but gaining a knowledge of the West which was an asset both to him and to his country. Roosevelt was the first President to know the Great Plains from intimate experience, and there is perhaps no other way in which that dry land, so strange to men who know only Europe or eastern America, can be understood.

In 1886 Roosevelt was married to Edith Kermit Carew, whom he had known since early childhood. Ever since leaving Harvard he had been giving his spare time to the writing of history, and by 1889 had published seven books, including *The Naval War of 1812, Thomas Hart Benton, Gouverneur Morris,* and the first two volumes of *The Winning of the West.* Then, after five years away from his true and inevitable work, he returned to politics.

When Benjamin Harrison became President he made Roosevelt a civil-service commissioner, an appointment which had not amounted to anything during the six years since the job was created. But Roosevelt brought to this inconspicuous office a blaze of publicity and a continuous bustle. He managed to get 20,000 federal employees transferred from the spoils system to the civil service, and also to make the work of the commissioners seem interesting to the public. Meanwhile he and his wife were gathered into the social life of Washington, which was in one of its happier phases during those years. John Hay and Henry Adams formed the intellectual center, with the Cabot Lodges, the Roosevelts, and Cecil Spring Rice of the British Embassy in constant attendance.

In 1895 Roosevelt returned to New York City to be president of the Board of Police Commissioners. Even in this unpromising job his bubbling, noisy, strenuous administration brought wide publicity. Every strife in which Roosevelt engaged became to him a battle in a glorious war between right and wrong. If he dismissed a thieving policeman, he somehow made it sound like a chapter in *Pilgrim's Progress.* With such capacity for moral excitement he naturally flung himself into the campaign of 1896, making (as we have seen) speeches which were more flamboyant than logical. Neither McKinley nor Hanna was impressed. Roosevelt's friends had to push and wheedle, and promise he would be quiet, before he was offered the position of Assistant Secretary of the Navy.

During the year of his return to Washington, before he went off to war, he first met the Kansas editor who was to serve him and love him till he died.

> I met Roosevelt [wrote William Allen White years later]. I went hurrying home from our first casual meeting . . . to tell Sallie of the marvel. . . . I had never known such a man as he, and never shall again. He overcame me. And in the hour or two we spent that day at lunch, and in a walk down F Street, he poured into my heart such

visions, such ideals, such hopes, such a new attitude toward life and patriotism and the meaning of things, as I had never dreamed men had. . . . It was youth and the new order calling youth away from the old order.[7]

For those who felt his spell, Roosevelt ever roused such hopes and dreams. For those on whom his magic was lost he was simply a rather pugnacious adolescent. At the time he was filling William Allen White with rapture, a Congressman from Pennsylvania noted sourly: "Roosevelt came down here looking for war. He did not care whom we fought as long as there was a scrap." His biographer puts the two impressions into one charming sentence: "Theodore Roosevelt's life was the ultimate dream of every typical American boy: he fought in a war, killed lions, became President, and quarreled with the Pope."[*8]

In May, 1898, Roosevelt left Washington to raise a regiment of volunteer cavalry, the "Rough Riders": cowboys, ranchmen, college athletes, and New York policemen, a summary of Roosevelt's life. Brave and impetuous in war as in peace, Roosevelt the colonel was a daily front-page story. He ended the war not only a hero but the people's delight. He was promptly elected governor of New York after promising Tom Platt that he would co-operate with the state machine so far as his conscience permitted. He proved a good administrator and a mild reformer, whose cautious deeds were sometimes thought to be radical because of the furor which accompanied them. The most modest reform, however, was too much for Platt. When the governor contrived to put through a tax on corporation franchises Platt decided to move him as far as possible from Albany and from political power. Roosevelt himself said he had been "entirely good humored . . . [and] cool" in his dealings with Platt, and then added: "I have always been fond of the West African proverb: 'Speak softly and carry a big stick, you will go far.' " On this occasion he went farther than Platt had planned.

4

Roosevelt became President on September 14, 1901. He knew that Hanna had thought him a "madman" and that Wall Street suspected him of liberalism. Hoping to calm all fears he asked McKinley's Cabinet to stay with him and pledged himself "to continue, absolutely unbroken, the policy of President McKinley for the peace, the prosperity, and the honor of our beloved country." In his first message to Congress, which he had

---

* The quarrel, in 1910, was really with the Papal Secretary of State, Merry del Val, over an audience with the Holy Father which never took place.

submitted to Mark Hanna and other Senate conservatives, he was as soothing as McKinley, making clear that he expected the new Administration
to stand in the exact political center, not so reactionary as to annoy
labor nor so liberal as to bring sorrow to J. Pierpont Morgan. Corporations, he said, should be cautiously controlled, but not to the point of
discouraging business confidence; labor must know that its rights entailed
heavy obligations; the tariff might be too high, but also it might not; and
as for McKinley's suggestion of lowering the tariff by means of reciprocity
agreements, the idea should be commended, but "reciprocity must be
treated as the handmaiden of protection." Mr. Dooley summed up the
message sardonically: " 'Th' trusts,' says he, 'are heejoous monsthers
built up be th' enlightened intherprise iv th' men that have done so much
to advance progress in our beloved country,' he says. 'On wan hand I wud
stamp thim undher fut; on th' other hand not so fast.' "

Yet in spite of his sincere, soothing words, men whose hearts were still
with the Civil War generation had good reason for distrusting Roosevelt.
A new age was struggling to be born; the people were giving their
allegiance to strange new creeds; and Roosevelt, even if he had tried,
could not help divining the people's mood. This was his third outstanding
gift, in addition to an energy surpassing mortal bounds and a sense of
publicity surpassing P. T. Barnum. The winds of doctrine were stirring
in 1901, and Roosevelt half-consciously sensed the breeze. The plans of
the Populists and of Bryan were becoming respectable, after ten years of
repetition and of reassuring proof that neither the Populists nor Bryan
would themselves gain power. The state of South Dakota had adopted the
initiative and the referendum. The state of Wisconsin had chosen Robert
La Follette for governor, that "strong, determined, indomitable man,"
to whom "reform" did not mean moral abstractions, but statistics,
economics, railway rates, and a concept of government's relations to business which Mark Hanna could not be expected to enjoy. In other words,
the "progressive era" was being born. And Roosevelt, who did not yet
know what it meant or why it had come to pass, recorded the changing
climate as a seismograph records a quake under the farthest seas.

This is the virtuosity of the politician at its best. This is what White
meant when he said that Roosevelt saved America from "terrible" danger
during the transition from the old rural order of individualism to the
"new highly socialized industrial order." If men had known too clearly
what was happening they might have tried too strenuously to prevent it.
This could only have led to class or sectional war, for the decisive deeds
had been committed long before and society must move in the new
direction or perish. What the people needed was to be reassured, and
given a sense of continuity, while the ground changed under their feet.

If Roosevelt had known what Henry Adams knew he would have

scared the nation out of its wits. But luckily Roosevelt did not peer into the future. He could catch men's thoughts clairvoyantly, but he was spared Adams' knowledge of the woes to come. He believed (and made others believe) that every trouble could be banished by optimism and the ten commandments and a lot of exercise. After a few simple reforms, he implied, the old America would be reborn—miraculous, shining, virginal. Meanwhile, with insatiable gusto and six young children, he lived his private life in a whirl of publicity. The whole nation felt that it took part in the uproarious fun at the White House.

5

During his seven years in office Roosevelt came to believe confidently in more power for the central government as compared with the states, in more power for the President as compared with the Congress, and in less power for Wall Street as compared with Washington. He explained his views on the latter point in 1905. "The great development of industrialism," he said, "means that there must be an increase in the supervision exercised by the Government over business enterprise." Government, he explained, must make sure that the power of wealth is "used for and not against the interests of the people as a whole. . . . We do not intend that the Republic shall ever fail as those Republics of olden times failed, in which there finally came to be a government by classes, which resulted either in the poor plundering the rich or in the rich . . . exploiting the poor."

This was the faith of the entire "progressive era": business should be policed by government and compelled to work for the general welfare; government should be made subject to popular control so that it could not be corrupted by what Roosevelt called "the dull, purblind folly of the very rich men, their greed and arrogance." Thus, thought the Progressives and the Populists before them, the benefits of a reformed and socially directed big business would accrue to the whole of society; work would become less burdensome; wages would increase; monopolies and the "money-power" would at last be humbled by a government responsive to the people; economic democracy (which had been preached for a hundred years by the followers of Fourier and the Utopians, and which had been attempted at Brook Farm, New Harmony, and similar settlements) would be achieved.

In keeping with this creed, Roosevelt twice strengthened the Interstate Commerce Commission, which had been created by Congress in 1887,*

---

* Article I, Section 8 of the Constitution gives Congress power to regulate commerce among the states.

but which did not have sufficient powers over the railroads to produce the desired results. Roosevelt's laws gave the Commission control over rate-cutting and rebates, and allowed it to set maximum rates and to establish through routes. The Commission's orders were made binding without court action. The second of these laws (the Hepburn Act of 1906) met sharp resistance from Congress. The President then declared himself a convert to McKinley's last speech, wherein tariff reduction had been hinted. He wrote, printed, and circulated among his advisers, a message to Congress asking for a lower tariff. Speaker Cannon was so alarmed that he offered to back the Hepburn Act if the President would withdraw the message. This the President did, and the Act promptly passed with only seven dissenting votes. In the Senate it was saved because the Democrats (urged by Tillman) helped the Roosevelt Republicans against some of the most powerful leaders of the party.

Late in his second term Roosevelt's relations with Congress became unhappy, probably because he had a view of the powers of the presidency which no Congress can welcome. "I have a definite philosophy about the presidency," he wrote to George Trevelyan, the historian. "I think it should be a very powerful office, and I think the President should be a very strong man who uses without hesitation every power that the position yields." And in his *Autobiography* he wrote:

> The most important factor in getting the right spirit in my administration . . . was my insistence upon the theory that the executive power was limited only by specific restrictions and prohibitions appearing in the Constitution or imposed by Congress under its constitutional powers. . . . Under this interpretation of executive power I did and caused to be done many things not previously done by the President and the heads of the departments. I did not usurp power but I did greatly broaden the use of executive power.

No President with such views can expect a long peace with Congress. In his last days Roosevelt received rebukes unknown since the times of Andrew Johnson or of Andrew Jackson. Yet first he accomplished a great deal—a fact which tends to be forgotten because he asked for much more than he got. He was always willing, as with the Hepburn Act, to make a bargain, whether real or fictitious. And ever since 1903, when the autocratic but mild-mannered "Uncle Joe" Cannon became Speaker, Roosevelt had maintained with him one of the most successful relations between Executive and Congressional leader that America has seen. The two men often disagreed, and when that was the case the President was usually frustrated. But when they agreed, or when they could strike a bargain, or when Roosevelt persuaded Cannon that the people could be roused to back the President, there was a channel for Executive leadership which most Republican Presidents have failed to find. "Uncle Joe" (who made full use of "Czar" Reed's rules) explained it as follows:

> The chairmen of committees conferred with the Speaker as to legislation before their committees . . . and the Speaker could intelligently present the majority opinion to the President. . . . I think Mr. Roosevelt talked over with me virtually every serious recommendation to Congress before he made it and requested me to sound out the leaders in the House, for he did not want to recommend legislation simply to write messages. . . . He wanted to know how to secure results with the least friction.[9]

Like all efforts to heal the division of powers, this finally broke down. Under the presidency of Taft, in 1910, the House revolted against the Cannon-Reed rules. A combination of Democrats and angry Republicans enlarged the Committee on Rules, excluded the Speaker from membership, and provided for the election of the committee by the House. This did not make for efficiency.

> Prior to 1910 the Speaker controlled the House in collaboration with a coterie of trusted party lieutenants. Since 1910 the leadership of the House has been in commission. The chief difference between the old oligarchy and the new is that control of the House was formerly open, centralized, and responsible, whereas today it is invisible, dispersed, and irresponsible. Formerly the country could see the wheels go round, but now it could not.[10]

And after 1910 there was no one man with whom a President could deal.

Toward the end of his second term, as he admits in his *Autobiography,* Roosevelt could no longer work with the heads of Congress. "I was forced to abandon the effort to persuade them to come my way," he writes, "and I achieved results only by appealing over the heads of the Senate and House leaders to the people, who were the masters of both of us." As a matter of fact he accomplished little (in the way of legislation) at the very end; but so long as the Roosevelt-Cannon alliance held he went forward steadily with his middle-of-the-road, middle-class program of mild reform. Only those who would have preferred revolution or bleak reaction should feel that Roosevelt did very little. In addition to his interstate-commerce laws, he secured an Employers Liability Act (annulled by the Supreme Court in 1908), a Pure Food and Drugs Act, and a new approach to the vital problem of conserving the nation's resources. And in 1903 he persuaded Congress to create a Department of Commerce and Labor, headed by an officer of Cabinet rank and with certain powers of supervision over corporations with interstate business.* And lastly, he

---

* Later, under Woodrow Wilson, this was split into the Department of Commerce and the Department of Labor, each with a Cabinet officer at its head.

succeeded in making known to the whole country a series of further reforms which he himself could not procure from Congress, but which his successors procured, and which had been regarded as dangerous Bryanite radicalism until Roosevelt took them up. Commenting on the last angry months of recriminations between the President and Congress, Henry Pringle writes: "On the one hand, Roosevelt had defeated himself. On the other, the very recklessness of his language advanced the day when workmen's compensation, the inheritance tax, valuation of railroad properties, and the rest of the reforms were adopted. He made these heresies familiar."[11]

6

Meanwhile, as early as 1902, Roosevelt had begun to move against the trusts. In February of that year Attorney General Philander Knox announced that the government would seek the dissolution of the Northern Securities Company on the ground that it transgressed the Sherman Act. This was a daring move because the Northern Securities Company (the first of the great holding companies in America) could be defended as reasonable and economical and in the public interest. Furthermore, ever since the Supreme Court had decided in 1894 that the American Sugar Refining Company was not a combination in restraint of trade, both Cleveland's and McKinley's attorney generals had taken the view that the Sherman Act could scarcely be made effective against trusts.* During McKinley's years in office there was not one indictment under this Act.

In 1900, J. Pierpont Morgan, James J. Hill, and their associates controlled the Northern Pacific, the Chicago, Burlington and Quincy, and the Great Northern Railways, while E. H. Harriman controlled the Union Pacific. Seeking an entrance into Chicago, Harriman began a battle with the Hill-Morgan interests. In 1901, after bidding the stock to $1000 a share and causing the "Northern Pacific Panic" he got control of the majority of the voting rights of that railway. Morgan threatened retaliation, but also offered a friendly settlement, from which came the Northern Securities Company—a merger of the three men's holdings in Great Northern, Northern Pacific, and Burlington. The capital of the holding company was put at $400,000,000. It would establish a railroad monopoly in the Northwest, with peace and unification and sound finance instead of the wars and the overexpansions of the robber barons. The hurried construction of the Northern Pacific had dragged down Jay Cooke and

---

* When Olney became Secretary of State, in 1895, his successor as Attorney General secured several convictions under the Sherman Act; but such efforts ceased with McKinley.

set off the Panic of 1873. Morgan was shocked by such instability and waste. He felt he was doing a public service by substituting order for the old anarchy.

The Northern Securities group also had thoughts of linking the productive centers of the Middle West with America's emerging imperial markets in the Far East. After a transcontinental railway-monopoly, why not steamships on the Pacific? Yet as Frederick Lewis Allen points out, it it is an exaggeration to say that Morgan planned a railway or a steamship "empire." So far as we know he merely wanted enough power so that he could prevent inefficiency, and so that he could insist on being consulted.

> At the most, it amounted to a veto power over anything that he and his colleagues regarded as hurtfully competitive or financially reckless; at the least, it amounted to little more than an opportunity to keep informed as to what was going on. In any case, it was sufficient to assure that no new Jay Goulds or Daniel Drews could run amuck, and that the management of American railroads would be more respectably and responsibly conducted than in earlier years. . . . He believed in order, believed in reducing competition to a minimum, believed in protecting the solvency of properties which he had backed.[12]

All this seemed so reasonable to Morgan (and to many others) that he could not understand a sane man attacking "his" companies, or even his judgment. He realized that when he and Harriman had bid Northern Pacific all the way up to 1000, they had in fact bought more common shares than there were in the market, and that the brokers (who suddenly saw they could not deliver the shares they had sold) had then dumped their other stocks to raise cash for the day of reckoning. Hence the "Northern Pacific Panic." But Morgan and Harriman had promptly dispelled the panic by making an agreement to save the short-sellers, to stop fighting each other, to build a peaceful holding company. What could be wrong with that? When Morgan received word that the government planned to prosecute his company he turned from the telephone, writes Mark Sullivan, "showing appalled dismay but little anger. In telling the news to his guests he dwelt on what he felt was the unfairness of Roosevelt's action. Roosevelt, he said, ought to have told him, ought to have given him the chance to make over the Northern Securities Company, if necessary, so as to conform to whatever Roosevelt thought was right. . . . He had regarded Roosevelt as a gentleman."[13]

Morgan hurried to Washington. "If we have done anything wrong," he said to Roosevelt, "send your man [meaning the Attorney General] to my man [meaning one of his lawyers] and they can fix it up." To which Roosevelt's "man," Philander Knox, answered: "We don't want to fix it up; we want to stop it." Then Morgan asked whether the President meant to "attack my other interests." "Certainly not," said Roosevelt, "unless we find out . . . they have done something we regard as wrong." After Morgan had left Roosevelt said to Knox: "That is a most illuminating illustration of the Wall Street point of view. Mr. Morgan could not help regarding me as a big rival operator, who either intended to ruin all his interests or else could be induced to come to an agreement to ruin none." Morgan, on the other hand, doubtless thought the President was an "illuminating illustration" of the political point of view, which thought nothing of insulting a man of honor and upsetting an enterprise of promise just to please the public.

In his *Autobiography,* written some years later, when he had become more accustomed to the language of progressivism, Roosevelt tells in detail why the Northern Securities Case seemed to him so important. He first describes the state of the nation when he became President:

> The total absence of governmental control had led to a portentous growth in the financial and industrial world both of natural and of artificial individuals—that is, corporations. In no other country in the world had such enormous fortunes been gained. In no other country in the world was such power held by the men who had gained these fortunes. . . . The courts, not unnaturally, but most regrettably . . . had for a quarter of a century been on the whole the agents of reaction, and by conflicting decisions which, however, in their sum were hostile to the interests of the people, had left both the nation and the several states well-nigh impotent to deal with the great business combinations. . . . Of all forms of tyranny the least attractive and the most vulgar is the tyranny of mere wealth, the tyranny of a plutocracy.
>
> When I became President, the question as to the method by which the United States Government was to control the corporations was not yet important. The absolutely vital question was whether the government had power to control them at all. This question had not yet been decided in favor of the United States Government. . . . A decision of the Supreme Court had, with seeming definiteness, settled that the national government had not that power.* This decision I caused to be annulled by the court that had rendered it. . . . The representatives of privilege intimated, and sometimes asserted outright, that in directing the action to be brought I had shown a lack of respect for the Supreme Court, which had already decided the question at issue by a vote of eight to one. . . . It was necessary to reverse the Knight case in the interests of the people against monopoly and privilege just as it had been necessary to reverse the Dred Scott decision in the interest of the people against slavery and privilege. . . .

By a five to four vote the Supreme Court reversed its decision in the

---

* The Sugar Trust decision, known as "the Knight case." (*U.S.* v. *E.C. Knight,* 1895.)

Knight case, and in the Northern Securities case sustained the Government. . . . After this latter decision . . . suits were brought by my direction against the American Tobacco Company and the Standard Oil Company. Both were adjudged criminal conspiracies and their dissolution ordered.*[14]

The Sherman Act had been brought back to life. Before he left the White House Roosevelt started twenty-five proceedings which led to indictments under this Act. His successor, President Taft, began forty-five; and in 1914 Woodrow Wilson secured the passage of the Clayton Act and the Federal Trade Commission Act, which greatly strengthened the government in its fight against monopoly. The Clayton Act forbade practices which "substantially tended to lessen competition," such as discrimination in prices, the acquisition of stock in one company by another, interlocking directorates. It also prohibited the use of injunctions "unless necessary to prevent irreparable injury to property, or to a property right . . . for which injury there is no adequate remedy at law." At the same time the Federal Trade Commission was set up to investigate businesses engaged in interstate commerce, to determine whether there had been violations of the anti-trust laws, and when necessary to issue orders to "cease and desist."

7

Again and again in the *Autobiography* we learn that Theodore Roosevelt had no great respect for the Supreme Court. At times he seemed to feel it was his personal enemy. Naturally, therefore, he was even more blunt than Lincoln and Grant in admitting that he hoped to put upon the Court men who shared his views. And since an appointment was pending at the time of the Northern Securities case, he took great pains to find a judge with "correct" ideas.

"The President and the Congress are all very well in their way," he said in 1906. "They can say what they think they think, but it rests with the Supreme Court to decide what they have really thought." This was scarcely tolerable to so strong-willed a man. "He was . . . shaken to the depths of his sometimes too vigorous nature," writes Henry Pringle, "by the extent to which the courts nullified Rooseveltian conceptions of what was right."[15]

In 1902 Justice Horace Grey of Massachusetts retired from the Supreme Court. Roosevelt thought of Oliver Wendell Holmes for the vacant place.

---

* The decree for the "dissolution" of the Standard Oil Company of New Jersey, issued by a circuit court in 1909, was upheld by the Supreme Court in 1911, while Taft was President.

Holmes was another Massachusetts man. His good record in the Civil War attracted Roosevelt, and so did the breadth of his mind, for Holmes was known not only as a legal scholar but as a student of literature, philosophy, history. Yet the President had no intention of promoting him if he was "wrong" on the Northern Securities case. He believed that four of the justices were against the Administration, and that victory in the fight for a stronger federal government might depend on who took Judge Grey's place. Roosevelt was soon to write that the nation possessed "an inherent power . . . outside of the enumerated powers conferred upon it by the Constitution, in all cases where the object involved was beyond the power of the several states." Hamilton and Marshall, he said, had shown by their deeds that they shared this view. If the Court were now to construe the Constitution narrowly, America would be "at a great disadvantage in the battle for industrial order."[16]

The previous year, on the one hundredth anniversary of the day John Marshall took his seat as Chief Justice, Holmes had made a speech which bothered Roosevelt because it did not seem to show sufficient reverence for Marshall's centralizing work. So the President wrote to Henry Cabot Lodge for more information about Judge Holmes.

> In the ordinary and low sense which we attach to the words "partisan" and "politician" [wrote Roosevelt], a judge of the Supreme Court should be neither. But in the higher sense . . . he is not in my judgment fitted for the position unless he is a party man, a constructive statesman, constantly keeping in mind . . . his relations with his fellow statesmen who in other branches of the government are striving . . . to advance the ends of government. . . . Now I should like to know that Judge Holmes was in entire sympathy with our views, that is with your views and mine and Judge Grey's, for instance. . . . I should hold myself as guilty of an irreparable wrong to the nation if I should put in his place any man who was not absolutely sane and sound on the great national policies for which we stand in public life.

The President told Lodge to show this remarkable letter to Holmes "if it became necessary." In this, Roosevelt went further than any of his predecessors in acknowledging that Supreme Court appointments are politics. From the day when John Adams appointed Marshall, most Presidents have of course put their own partisans on the Court. Lincoln and Grant, as we have seen, said openly that they looked for men who would agree with them on specific issues; but they both added that they would not ask the men to promise agreement in advance. When Roosevelt told Lodge that he might show the letter of inquiry to Holmes, he seemed to be hinting that it would be well to get positive pledges. If so, he was right. Lodge, presumably without showing the letter, reassured Roosevelt. Oliver Wendell Holmes was appointed, and on March 14, 1904, joined the minority who dissented from the Supreme Court's decision on the Northern Securities case.* Roosevelt won the case but lost the edge of his pleasure in Justice Holmes's company.**

8

Professor Binkley points out that between 1900 and 1912 Roosevelt experienced a "personal conversion" in social philosophy. He started as a deeper conservative than McKinley or Mark Hanna, the former having defended striking miners against angry local opinion as far back as the eighteen-seventies, and the latter being the first leader in American business to encourage trade unions. In those days Roosevelt was praising Cleveland for sending federal troops against the strikers, and opposing labor legislation with dogmas from John Stuart Mill. By the end of his "conversion" he was asking for a high degree of paternalism in government, and was endorsing not only the initiative and the referendum, but the recall of elective officers by popular vote and even—as a last resort against obstruction—the recall of state judicial decisions on constitutional questions, and if necessary of state judges. This was farther to the left than his old enemy Bryan. "We advocate . . ." said Roosevelt, "all governmental devices which will make the representatives of the people more easily and certainly responsible to the people's will."[17]

Shortly before the Republican National Convention of 1904 (when Roosevelt was renominated without opposition, since Hanna, his only possible rival, had died four months before), the New York *Sun* wrote:

Why should people wonder that Mr. Bryan clings to silver? Has not Mr. Roosevelt absorbed and sequestered every vestige of the Kansas City platform [that is, the Democratic platform in 1900] that had a thread of practical value? Suppose that Mr. Bryan had been elected President. . . . A regiment of Bryans could not compete with Mr. Roosevelt in harrying the trusts, in bringing wealth to its knees, and in converting into the palpable actualities of action the wildest dreams of Bryan's campaign orators.

* A lower court in St. Paul had ruled for the government in 1903, and the case was then appealed.

** In 1921, two years after Roosevelt's death, Holmes wrote to Sir Frederick Pollock, recalling that a Senator had told him, "What the boys like about Roosevelt is that he doesn't care a damn for the law." "It broke up our incipient friendship . . ." said Holmes, "as he looked on my dissent to the Northern Securities case as a political departure (or, I suspect, more truly, couldn't forgive anyone who stood in his way). We talked freely later, but it was never the same after that. . . . He was very likeable, a big figure, a rather ordinary intellect, with extraordinary gifts, a shrewd and I think pretty unscrupulous politician. He played all his cards—if not more. *R. i. p.*"

This was apparently what the Democratic Party thought, for in the campaign of 1904 they opposed Roosevelt, not with the fiery Bryan, but with the conservative Judge Alton Brooks Parker of New York. The result was total defeat. Roosevelt received more than seven and a half million votes, Parker five million. Roosevelt won 336 electoral votes, Parker 140.

One reason for the steady leftward shift in Roosevelt's opinion was his sense of the public mood. He knew that the world was changing, not so much because of what he saw or studied, but because he knew the wants of the people were changing. Another reason for his new and more radical views may have been his fight against the forces of inertia within the government. These had thwarted many Presidents, but never before a President so impetuous. It was Roosevelt's nature to run faster when Congress sought to clog his feet. And the more radical he became, the more impatient; and the more impatient, the less successful in his mediatory task. For not only did he have to conciliate Speaker Joseph Cannon of the House of Representatives (into whose mind no hint of a changing world would ever stray), and Republican leaders in the Senate to whom even Mark Hanna seemed rashly modern, but throughout the country, while the din of industrial strife grew louder, he had to make the "square deal" (the moderate reforms which he hoped would not frighten any major group) acceptable to a solid majority.

So long as the United States is a federal nation, this will be a main task for all Presidents. No President has done it better than Theodore Roosevelt, or been more abused for his success—with the possible exception, in both cases, of his distant cousin. The classic attack on the first Roosevelt was made by Robert M. La Follette, in his *Autobiography:*

> Roosevelt's most savage assault upon special interests was invariably offset with an equally drastic attack upon those who were seeking to reform abuses . . . demagogues and dangerous persons. In this way he sought to win approval both from the radicals and the conservatives. This cannonading, first in one direction, then in another, filled the air with noise and smoke, which confused and obscured the line of action, but when the battle cloud drifted by and quiet was restored, it was always a matter of surprise that so little had been accomplished.

The description is exact. This is how Roosevelt held together his extraordinary personal following and gave his country rest from too great anxiety during a time of transition. "When the battle cloud drifted by" one thing at least had been "accomplished": the nation was not divided into irreconcilable classes or regions.

A third reason for Roosevelt's change in social philosophy was his experience with the immobility of the more backward business mind, which made the immobility of Congress seem frisky. This experience began with the coal strike of 1902—in the anthracite fields of Pennsylvania, which ever since the days of the "Molly Maguires" had contributed so much blood and bitterness to American life.

Between 1897 and 1900 the United Mine Workers, led by John Mitchell, had organized the anthracite miners. In the latter year, after a brief strike, they won a ten per cent wage increase—largely because of political pressure by Mark Hanna upon the recalcitrant owners. But the union was still outlawed, so in 1902 the miners struck again, both for better wages and for union recognition. The average wage was a little more than five hundred dollars a year. The accident rate was terrifying. And there was no workmen's compensation. The case for the owners was so bad that J. Pierpont Morgan, Charles Schwab, and John D. Rockefeller, Jr., were on the side of Roosevelt when he finally intervened. The most talkative of the mine operators was George F. Baer of the Philadelphia and Reading Coal and Iron Company. "Mining," he said, "was a business . . . not a religious, sentimental, or academic proposition." The interests of the miners, he said, would be safe in the hands of "the Christian men to whom God in His infinite wisdom has given the control of the property interests of this country."

Six months before the strike began Mark Hanna tried to head it off, asking Morgan to put pressure on the railroads which controlled the coal fields. Railroads and their affiliated companies would have listened to Morgan; but George Baer persuaded him that Hanna was wrong and that nothing should be done. The men, he said, had no grievances. The United Mine Workers were destroying the discipline essential to business. He would not meet Mitchell. So the strike began in May, 1902. By the end of the summer, with the mid-term elections and the cold weather scheduled for November, the mines were still closed.

In October, Roosevelt called representatives of both sides to a conference. Baer stormed at the President for not sending federal troops, like Cleveland, and for not prosecuting the miners' union under the Sherman Anti-Trust Act. Mitchell said he would submit the case to an impartial commission appointed by the President. Roosevelt said of Baer: "If it wasn't for the high office I hold I would have taken him by the seat of his breeches and the nape of his neck and chucked him out of the window." And Roosevelt said of Mitchell: "There was only one man in the conference who behaved like a gentleman and that was not I."[18] An arbitration commission, for whatever it might be worth to the workers, was made certain by Baer's treatment of the President.

Morgan now realized that Baer was a menace to sensible business men, who did not wish to precipitate government ownership. He told the operators to accept arbitration, which they promptly did. Then at the last minute, when the commission was being set up, Baer insisted that no laboring man would be acceptable, though he might be willing to pass a "sociologist." Furthermore, and this must have surprised even Roosevelt, the operators refused to accept Grover Cleveland on the commission. Somehow they must have sensed the troubling truth that the old President, like the new one, was disgusted with their bad manners and their stupidity.

Suddenly, as he later wrote to Henry Cabot Lodge, it came to Roosevelt that these odd people would "submit to anarchy rather than have Tweedledum, yet if I would call it Tweedledee they would accept with rapture. . . . It gave me an illuminating glimpse into one corner of the mighty brains of those 'captains of industry.'" So Roosevelt appointed a well-known labor leader to the commission under the title of "sociologist," and the man was accepted by the coal owners with no more trouble.

The commission gave the miners a ten per cent wage increase, dealt fairly with a few of the abuses in work practices, but denied recognition to the United Mine Workers. If this seemed a small reward for all their sacrifices, the workers could congratulate themselves that Theodore Roosevelt would thenceforth look with disillusioned eyes upon the representatives of industry. "The last, lingering suspicions of the sapience of the American industrialist must have vanished during those hours on the night of October 15, 1902. Political expediency might, in the future, dictate caution, but the nation's business leaders were not, after all, dangerous foes."[19]

9

When Roosevelt left the presidency in 1909 Robert La Follette paid the following tribute to one part of his work:

> There is the great and statesman-like movement for the conservation of our National resources, into which Roosevelt so energetically threw himself at a time when the Nation as a whole knew not that we are ruining and bankrupting ourselves as fast as we can. . . . This globe is the capital stock of the race. It is just so much coal and oil and gas. This may be economized or wasted. The same thing is true of phosphates and other mineral resources. . . . This immense idea Roosevelt, with high statesmanship, dinned into the ears of the Nation until the Nation heeded. He held it so high that it attracted the attention of the neighboring nations of the continent, and will so spread and intensify that we will soon see the world's conferences devoted to it. Nothing can be greater or finer than this.

La Follette grudged praise, and on the whole disliked Roosevelt. But he saw that the whole human race was in danger because of man's newfound ability to waste the earth with giant machines instead of with simple hand tools. So he gave thanks that a man with Roosevelt's ability to create drama and loud excitement had seen the danger also. Yet Roosevelt might have been as blind as previous Presidents except for his years of cattle-ranching in the dry West.

We have already seen that the federal government gave 137,000,000 acres of the public domain to the railways, or to the states for railway building. Under the Homestead Act another 226,000,000 acres of land passed to private ownership, much of it ending in the hands of large corporations.* Land which was so easily acquired was naturally thought to be "endless," and a large part of it was plundered. By 1890 wise men had begun to understand that in the Mississippi Valley, with its harsh "continental" type of climate, land must be even more carefully used than in Europe or the whole top soil will wash into the rivers. Yet the standard American practice had been to plow steep hillsides recklessly, and to tear off the forests or grass as fast as possible, on the assumption that there would always be more land. Then at last, in 1891, Congress passed an Act allowing the President to set aside certain public lands as forest reserves, withdrawing them from sale or any other form of private use. Under the influence of his friend, Gifford Pinchot, head of the Forest Service and a student of forestry in France, Germany, and Switzerland, Roosevelt began to make large use of this Act. By 1909 he had increased the forest reserves from 43,000,000 to 194,000,000 acres; in other words, he had saved from rapid exploitation an area considerably larger than the whole of France. And he had used his influence with Speaker Cannon to aid the passage of a bill (introduced by the Democratic Senator Newlands of Nevada) for irrigation in the West. And he had set up a public lands commission and an inland waterways commission. Railways, utility companies, mining companies, and other private groups using the public lands, were now regulated on the novel ground that the property of the people should accrue to the benefit of the people. Finally, in 1906, the Forest Service was enlarged and given new authority.

These acts did not go unopposed by the men who had learned to think of the public domain as their own private plunder. But on a case containing so much drama Roosevelt was hard to beat. He roused the public with his tale of scandal and his warnings of a diminished future. Although no such fight can be won permanently, although much of Roosevelt's work has had to be done over and over again, the cause has never been wholly neglected since his day. It might never have been popularized in time if Theodore Roosevelt had not been President.

Under pressure from local interests, Congress undertook to block this

---

* The combined area of England, Scotland, Wales, and Northern Ireland is 59,728,640 acres. The area of France is 136,151,680 acres.

new national policy. A bill was passed (or was added as a "rider" to
a Department of Agriculture appropriation bill) forbidding the President
to reserve any more forest lands in six Northwestern states. Roosevelt sent
for a report on every foot of soil throughout these states that could possibly
grow a tree during the wettest cycle of years. He put the whole lot into
the reserve, and then signed the bill which denied him such powers for
the future. "When the friends of the special interests in the Senate . . .
woke up," wrote Roosevelt, "they discovered that sixteen million acres
of timberland had been saved for the people . . . before the land-grab-
bers could get at them. The opponents of the Forest Service turned hand-
springs in their wrath; and dire were their threats against the Executive."[20]

10

The other field in which Roosevelt could act happily, and with small heed
for Congress, was foreign affairs. When he came to the presidency, Secretary of State Hay was completing a treaty with Great Britain which superseded the Treaty of 1850 and allowed the United States a free hand to
build, maintain, and defend an isthmian canal between the Atlantic and
the Pacific. The Senate approved the treaty within a month, and the
following year Congress authorized a canal on the Panama route, rather
than the Nicaraguan, if Colombia would agree within "a reasonable
time." Roosevelt and Hay then drafted a treaty with Colombia which
was ratified by the American Senate but rejected by the government at
Bogotá.

A French company already had rights in the canal, and the United
States proposed to buy these rights for a fair sum. But the Colombians—
whom Roosevelt impatiently dismissed as "inefficient bandits"—wanted
some of the money for themselves. This was as frustrating to the French
company as to Roosevelt. In November, 1903, after a little judicious
prodding by the company's representatives, Panama suffered what Roosevelt called "a most just and proper revolution." American warships were
on hand to see that the justice and the proprieties were not hampered by
Colombian troops. The new state of Panama was recognized an hour and
sixteen minutes after it was born, and eleven days later signed the treaty
which "the contemptible little creatures in Bogotá" had refused. Congress
was none too happy at this display of American realism; but the President did not care. "I took the canal zone," he later remarked, "and let
Congress debate, and while the debate goes on the canal does also."*

* When Woodrow Wilson was President he made a treaty offering Colombia
twenty-five million dollars and an apology. Henry Cabot Lodge prevented ratification in the Senate. But in 1921, under President Harding, Colombia received her
money though not her apology. Oil had been discovered in the little Republic.

In 1902, meanwhile, there occurred another Venezuela incident, when European Powers began a "pacific blockade" in order to collect their debts. There is still doubt as to what threats, if any, Roosevelt made to Germany at this time, for his own memory appears to have played him false. In any case, the foreign claims were compromised or sent to arbitration, and the blockade was lifted. But a problem remained which Roosevelt states succinctly: "If we are willing to let Germany or England act as the policeman of the Caribbean, then we can afford not to interfere when gross wrong-doing occurs. But if we intend to say 'hands off' to the powers of Europe, sooner or later we must keep order ourselves." The time had come, in other words, when the Monroe Doctrine must either shrink or expand, and with Roosevelt there could be only one answer. In 1904 the Dominican Republic, in financial trouble, was threatened with intervention from Europe. After a little pressure from Washington, Roosevelt was invited to set up a financial receivership, with an American to collect and spend the revenues of the Republic. The anti-imperialists in the United States Senate were again displeased but helpless.

And once more they were helpless when Roosevelt, as a proof to the Japanese of American power, sent the whole fleet into the Pacific, and then round the world on a "practice cruise." Congress had to pay the bills or allow the ships to rot quietly in some foreign port. The fourteen months' tour was well organized and perfectly timed. One of Roosevelt's happiest moments was when he welcomed the fleet home three weeks before he left office. Well might he write: "I did and caused to be done many things not previously done by the President and the heads of the departments."

11

Henry Adams and John Hay had built themselves houses across Lafayette Square from the White House, where the Hay-Adams Hotel now stands. Roosevelt asked Adams to dinner on March 2, 1909, two days before the inauguration of William Howard Taft. "After this spring," wrote Adams in reply, "Andrew Jackson and I will be the solitary monuments of the Square, and he will have to drop in to cheer me up.* I don't find the prospect amusing. Andrew may be as handsome as you, but he is not as good company at dinner. I feel no disposition to celebrate the occasion in crowds, and still less to see others do it, so, if you please, I will play cheerful as well as I can, on the 2nd. at dinner." Yet the misanthropic Adams was drawn back on the last day (March 4) to shake hands again with the President and tell him "I shall miss you very much." He had already written to Sir Ronald Lindsay: "My last vision of fun and gaiety

* An equestrian statue of Jackson is in the center of the Square.

will vanish when my Theodore goes . . . *Tout passe! tout casse!* and now that Theodore has broken everything, *tout lasse!* Never can we replace him."[21]

For once Henry Adams expressed the sentiment of the people. Anybody who has traveled America widely, especially rural America, even thirty years after Theodore Roosevelt's death, will have met scores of elderly men and women whose greatest political excitement in all their lives was once to have seen or heard "T.R." on the back platform of one of his campaign trains. The woeful intervening years are forgotten when they recall that figure of abounding strength and hope. Some of the old faith in the future, and in the American dream, is revived at the thought of the boy who enjoyed life so much that he grew up to lead a cavalry charge, kill lions, become President, and quarrel with the Pope.

CONCLUSION

XXXIII

Some Modern Instances: I

WHEN THEODORE ROOSEVELT left the White House in 1909 the uses
of the American Constitution seemed to be set. At every crisis power
tended to consolidate, and the people seemed to welcome authority and
leadership from the President, while with the return of quiet times power
tended to become decentralized, and the people seemed content with the
delays, evasions, and compromises of Congressional policy. The system
suited the national preference for weak government and the need for
action in emergency. It had successfully met three emergencies: the surge
of democracy at the time of Andrew Jackson, the Civil War, and the
transition from laissez-faire to the beginnings of social control over industry
and finance. And the system had failed once, during the years between
the Mexican conquest and the fall of Fort Sumter. We cannot prove that
the failure was avoidable; but we may note that it took place when a time
of great strain coincided with a time of weak Presidents.

"Our system," writes Professor Herring, "can respond quickly to
emergency conditions once the public is convinced of the need. Presidential leadership sustained by a united people has power for any crisis."[1]
This is true; and we may add that if the people do not see the need, in
spite of warnings, they must pay the heavy cost of freedom. "The world
will never be safe for democracy," said Chesterton; "it is a dangerous
trade." And we should also add that if the people do see the need, or are
capable of seeing it, but receive no presidential leadership, the system itself
has failed. Such a failure may occur at any time. Another crisis may be
met by another Pierce and Buchanan, since the method of selecting
Presidents favors men who are not too strong and whose ideas are not too
positive. Lincoln, who presided over one time of danger, was chosen
because he had the fewest enemies of any man available. And Theodore
Roosevelt, who presided over another, had been banished to the vice-
presidency and was only rescued by murder. Yet it is doubtful whether
any system of choice could discover, except by accident, the combination
of qualities that makes a good President. Political genius is needed (or the
highest political talent), and there is no school in which that can be
taught. Jefferson, Lincoln, the two Roosevelts—where did they learn to
cast spells over their fellow men?

Theodore Roosevelt, for example, was the last of the Republican Presidents to understand the nature of the job. He was a master of that "group diplomacy" with which a President builds and maintains his inharmonious party. He gathered behind him classes, races, economic interests which had never before co-operated. He did it mostly by the methods which La Follette condemned: by flattering and appeasing both the Left and the Right, by making an immense commotion so that a great deal seemed to be happening, and by preaching a simple "uplift" which reassured the voters. As he said himself, there was nothing in his speeches "except a certain sincerity and a kind of commonplace morality which put him *en rapport* with the people."

The "commonplace morality" amused the more worldly members of his Cabinet. "Knox," wrote John Hay, "says that the question of what is to become of Roosevelt after 1908 is easily answered. He should be made a bishop." Yet the "bishop" left behind him a smooth party machine which had controlled the presidency and both Houses of Congress for twelve years and which had just been triumphantly re-elected for a new term. Within two years of his departure the machine had stalled. The Republicans had not only lost the House of Representatives, but they had begun the quarrels which were to divide them, and to allow their enemies to label them (unfairly but effectively) the party of mere wealth.

2

William Howard Taft, under whom this ruinous change began, was not the choice of a venal or stupid convention. He was the choice of Theodore Roosevelt. He had been Roosevelt's Secretary of War, and was hand-picked as the man best fitted to carry on the Square Deal. The genial, intelligent, unassertive, rotund Taft—a scholar in law and an experienced administrator—seemed just the man to soothe and please the public and to win co-operation from Congress. But politics was not in his blood and bones, as with Roosevelt. In spite of his learning in constitutional law he knew nothing of the unwritten constitution or of the true powers of the presidency. In 1916 he wrote:

> The President can exercise no power which cannot be reasonably and fairly traced to some specific grant of power, or justly implied or included within such express grant as necessary and proper to its exercise. Such specific grant must be either in the Constitution or in an act of Congress passed in pursuance thereof. There is no undefined residuum of power which he can exercise because it seems to him to be in the public interest.

If he had said this while serving Roosevelt he would not have become President. The boisterous "T.R." would never have chosen as his heir a man who spurned an "undefined residuum of power."

Taft suffered at once the fate of Presidents who treat Congress meekly. The platform on which he was elected had promised a revision of the tariff. For seven years Roosevelt had sidestepped this issue, lest it divide the farm Republicans from the factory. But Taft bluntly asked in his Inaugural Address for a new and lower set of duties which would merely make up the difference between the cost of production at home and abroad.* The House passed a tolerable bill and sent it to the Senate, where the representatives of industry slaughtered it. Even Henry Cabot Lodge, an expert in such matters, was surprised at what he called the "ruthless selfishness" of the amendments. The Senate made 847 changes. The Progressive Republicans of the Middle West, whom Roosevelt had kept closely bound to the party, fought this tariff item by item in one of the Senate's most venomous debates. Taft urged them on, and added his protests to theirs. Yet when they were beaten, he humbly signed the bill. The split between the Progressives and the "Standpatters" had begun.** It was soon made more bitter by the Ballinger incident.

Roosevelt's great drive for conservation had been made possible by the zeal and skill of two men: James R. Garfield, his Secretary of the Interior, and Gifford Pinchot, Chief of the Forest Service. Roosevelt thought Garfield would remain in the Cabinet; but Richard Ballinger was appointed in his place. Ballinger was more cautious than his predecessor and less inclined to act without clear legal authority. The Progressives were soon charging that Roosevelt's work was undone, and that the party was returning to its old habit of giving away the national domain. The crisis came when Pinchot and a young assistant charged Ballinger with letting the Guggenheim interests appropriate public coal lands and power sites in Alaska. The President asked for a Congressional investigation, which

---

* This harmless-sounding phrase may justify any lengths of folly in tariff-making. Professor Taussig (*Tariff History of the United States,* p. 364) comments: "In a familiar passage of *The Wealth of Nations,* Adam Smith remarked that 'by means of glasses, hot-beds, and hot walls very good grapes can be raised in Scotland, and very good wine can be made of them at about thirty times the expense for which at least equally good wine can be brought from foreign countries.' In the same vein, it may be said that very good pineapples can be grown in Maine, if only a duty be imposed sufficient to equalize cost of production between the growers in Maine and those in more favored climes."

** This unfortunate bill was known as the Payne-Aldrich Tariff. Taft, who knew better, was soon defending it as "the best tariff bill." Mr. Dooley commented: "Th' Republican party has been thru to its promises. Look at th' free list if you don't believe it. Practically ivrything nicessary to existence comes in free. Here it is. Curling stones, teeth, sea moss, newspapers, nux vomica, Pulu, canary bird seed, divvy-divvy, spunk, hog bristles, marshmallows, silk worm eggs, stilts, skeletons an' leeches. Th' new tariff bill puts these familyar commodyties within th' reach iv all."

found Ballinger guiltless. Pinchot was dismissed, and the Progressives raged. So the party approached the Congressional elections of 1910 in a self-destructive mood—and only because the President could neither impose his wishes nor explain his motives. Taft had wanted a lower tariff, which would have satisfied the Westerners. And he was not opposed to conservation; in fact, he did much to carry forward Roosevelt's work. But he allowed the extreme conservatives to claim him and to seem to speak for him, and this offended powerful sections of the party. "Taft," said the Progressive Senator Dolliver of Iowa, "is an amiable island entirely surrounded by men who know exactly what they want."

In the election of 1910 the Republicans lost to the Democrats and the "Standpatter" Republicans lost to the Progressives.* Thereafter, the Administration was a small civil war against itself. In the new Congress the Progressive Republicans held the balance of power. If they united with Bryan's followers among the Democrats they could make a majority against the conservative Republicans. It was just such a coalition in 1910 which had removed the Speaker from the Rules Committee of the House, and stripped him of his power to appoint the Standing Committees and their chairmen.** This was greeted as a Progressive gain; but in fact it was a gain for disorder and inefficiency.

The Progressive balance of power, however, was often used wisely. While Taft through his ineptitude was winning a reputation for extreme reaction, the Congress was passing (and he was signing) a long series of useful bills. The Interstate Commerce Commission was strengthened; a postal savings bank and a parcel post were created; publicity for campaign expenditures was imposed by statute; the territories of New Mexico and Arizona were admitted as the forty-seventh and forty-eighth states of the Union; the Sixteenth Amendment to the Constitution (permitting a federal income tax), and the Seventeenth Amendment (providing that Senators should be elected by the people, and no longer by the state legislatures), were adopted by Congress. Both amendments were ratified by the states in 1913.[2]

Yet all this did the fumbling President no good. Instead of receiving credit for the excellent laws, he quite unjustly got the reputation of being opposed to them. And when he sought to repair the worst harm of the Payne-Aldrich Tariff by making a reciprocity treaty with Canada, the Progressive Republicans from the grain-growing states accused him of selling the farmers to the trusts. Canadian food, they said, would destroy the home market while American manufactures moved profitably into Canada. With the help of the Southern Democrats the President pushed

* For example, in Kansas (a Republican state) the Progressives won almost every party contest for a nomination.
** The power was given to a committee on committees.

his agreement through Congress, but there had been such insulting talk during the debates that the Canadian Parliament rejected it. The only result was to make deeper the division between the Eastern and Western wings of Taft's party: the manufacturers and wage-earners on the one hand, and the corn-and-wheat farmers on the other. This is the alliance which Hanna and McKinley and Roosevelt had so skillfully nursed, the loss of which must bring Republican defeat.

> The party was caught in the 1910–11 crisis [writes Professor Bink-ley], without one of the specialists in group diplomacy such as Jefferson, Jackson, Clay, Lincoln, McKinley, Hanna, or the Roosevelts. Taft had a confessed distaste for party politics. Not one of the leaders just men-tioned would have ignored the interests of the grain-growers, without whom no party since the disappearance of the Federalists has remained in power.[3]

As a result of Taft's political folly, the National Republican Progressive League was formed in January, 1911, at Senator La Follette's house in Washington, and the Senator was put forward as the Progressive candidate for the Republican presidential nomination. The split within the party was thus made official.

3

Theodore Roosevelt, meanwhile, had returned from hunting game in Africa and making speeches in Europe. While traveling he had read Herbert Croly's *The Promise of American Life,* a book which recom-mended a Hamiltonian centralization of power, not for the benefit of an élite, but to give "democratic meaning and purpose" to the nation's life. This was the "New Nationalism" which Roosevelt thenceforth preached, and which lured some of the more adventurous men of Wall Street into the Progressive camp. For according to the New Nationalism the great trusts and corporations need not be outlawed; they could be made to serve the emerging social and economic democracy. In his *Autobiography* Roosevelt explained the difference between the old view and the new:

> They [the advocates of the Sherman Act] tried to bolster up an individualism already proved to be both futile and mischievous; to remedy by more individualism the concentration that was the inevitable result of the already existing individualism. They saw the evil done by the big combinations, and sought to remedy it by destroying them and restoring the country to the economic conditions of the middle of the

nineteenth century. This was a hopeless effort, and those who went into it . . . really represented a form of sincere rural toryism. . . .

On the other hand a few men recognized that corporations and combinations had become indispensable in the business world, that it was folly to try to prohibit them, but that it was also folly to leave them without thoroughgoing control. . . . Government must now interfere to protect labor, to subordinate the big corporations to the public welfare, and to shackle cunning and fraud. . . .

Here was a program more friendly to big business than anything preached by Bryan—one of the "sincere rural tories." It could be made acceptable to labor, and also to the Progressives (when combined with the "commonplace morality" of which Roosevelt was master). But it made no appeal to President Taft, or to Senator Aldrich, or to "Uncle Joe" Cannon. These men and their cronies were in charge of the Republican machine. Roosevelt with his clairvoyance had found a unifying idea, with which the party could win the next election. But the men who controlled the party preferred defeat to the New Nationalism, and to its unpredictable inventor.

Shortly after his return from Europe, Roosevelt had said, "I stand for the square deal. . . . I mean not merely that I stand for fair play under the present rules of the game, but that I stand for having those rules changed so as to work for a more substantial equality of opportunity and of reward for equally good service." "Changing the rules" was red revolution to Senator Aldrich and the Standpatters. And when Roosevelt had handed the party leadership to Taft he had in fact handed it to the Standpatters. This knowledge probably did not improve his temper.

In any case, although he had promised repeatedly to stay out of politics, Roosevelt was soon drawn into the leadership of the Progressives. In February, 1912, he arranged to receive an open letter from seven Republican governors, asking him to become a candidate for the presidential nomination. The Progressives gladly deserted La Follette for the magic of the Roosevelt name. Before the end of the month he announced his candidacy, pledging himself to the New Nationalism and to such radical plans as the initiative, the referendum, and the recall of judicial decisions. He quickly proved that the mass of the Republican voters was behind him. In the thirteen states which chose delegates to the convention at primary elections, Roosevelt won 278 delegates and Taft 46. But the party bosses and the local machines were with the President. They gave him most of the delegates not chosen by the people. And they controlled the National Convention, its chairman, and its major committees, and thus were able to award almost all the disputed seats to Taft delegates. Seeing that Taft was sure to be nominated, Roosevelt claimed that victory had been stolen from him. He and his followers seceded from the convention. On August 5 they formed the Progressive Party, which at once nominated Roosevelt for the presidency.

Describing the Progressive (or Bull Moose*) Convention William Allen White wrote:

> I have seen many a protest convention. As a boy I had watched the Greenbackers. As a young man I had reported many a Populist convention. Those agrarian movements too often appealed to the ne'er-do-wells, the misfits—farmers who had failed, lawyers and doctors who were not orthodox, teachers who could not make the grade, and neurotics full of hates. . . . I knew that crowd well. But . . . here was another crowd.
>
> Here were the successful middle-class country-town citizens, the farmer whose barn was painted, the well-paid railroad engineer, and the country editor. . . . Proletarian and plutocrat were absent, except George Perkins, who was too conspicuous.** He and his satellites and sycophants from Wall Street and lower Broadway, who had known Roosevelt in Harvard, loved him and misunderstood him; but they had their influence.[4]

The master craftsman had collected a winning combination once again —if only it had been backed by the national machine of a major party. As it was, this helter-skelter party of middle-class enthusiasts from every section of the country except the South did better than the regular machine and ensured the victory of the Democrat, Woodrow Wilson. Roosevelt received a little more than 4,000,000 votes, Taft a little less than 3,500,000, and Wilson 6,296,574. In the electoral college Wilson had 435 votes, Roosevelt 88, and Taft 8.*** Many of the Progressives thought they had helped in the founding of a new major party, and that the Republicans would now disappear like the Federalists and the Whigs. When someone spoke thus hopefully to Roosevelt, he was answered coldly: "I thought you were a better politician. The fight is over. We are beaten. There is only one thing to do and that is to go back to the Republican party. You can't hold a party like the Progressive party together . . . there are no loaves and fishes."[5] What Roosevelt understood instinctively was that in 1854 the Republican Party had been created in (and by) the states, and had a proper foundation in local organizations, and could therefore survive the defeat of 1856. But the

---

* When Roosevelt was a vice-presidential candidate in 1900 he told Mark Hanna he felt "as strong as a bull moose." The phrase became his trade-mark ever after.
** Perkins had been a partner in the House of Morgan.
*** Utah and Vermont were faithful to Taft.

Progressive Party was born at a national convention. It had no roots. It could only live on victory. If the Progressives had won, they could have taken over most of the local Republican machines; but since they lost there was nothing to do but go back to the old party and wait to be forgiven.*

4

The history of Woodrow Wilson's nomination is an irony and a warning. Although as a child Wilson had planned to become the American Gladstone and although he had studied law (presumably with an eye to politics), he changed his mind in his middle twenties and decided to be a scholar and teacher of government rather than a practitioner. In 1890 he became professor of jurisprudence and political economy at Princeton, and in 1902 he was chosen president of the university. Because of his struggles to make that privileged institution more democratic he won a national reputation. He was also known as a severe critic of Congressional government and an advocate of stronger powers for the President. His politics during the Princeton years seemed to be those of a conservative Southern Democrat. He opposed Bryan in 1896, and did nothing to help him in 1900 or 1908. In fact he had written in 1907, "Would that we could do something, at once dignified and effective, to knock Mr. Bryan once and for all into a cocked hat!" And in the summer of that year, in a speech on "The Authors and Signers of the Declaration of Independence," he attacked government controls and defended the Jeffersonian thesis "that free men had a much more trustworthy capacity in taking care of themselves than any government had ever shown or was ever likely to show in taking care of them."[6]

It is no wonder, therefore, that the conservatives of New York thought Wilson might be the man to break Bryan's hold on the Democratic Party. In 1906, when Roosevelt was "trust-busting" and talking about "malefactors of great wealth," and when it was feared he would seek a third term, George Harvey in an after-dinner speech proposed Wilson for

---

* Roosevelt's eldest daughter, Alice Roosevelt Longworth, explains in her reminiscences (*Crowded Hours*, p. 224) why the Progressive Party could not establish itself: "It had a program, policies, ample financial backing, and a leader who inspired his followers. But it did not have the organization—the plodding organization in precinct, ward and county—that is on the job in season and out, and that seems to be essential to the existence of a political party. Without organization, no party has a survival value." The Roosevelt revolt was a struggle between the conservative and progressive Republicans for control of the organization. And the conservatives remained in possession. They have not been ousted to this day, whereas if Roosevelt had continued his fight within the party, instead of bolting, he would doubtless soon have triumphed.

President. Harvey was editor of *Harper's Weekly* and friend of the great men of Wall Street. He claims that in "discovering" Wilson he had the backing of Thomas Fortune Ryan and August Belmont. But Roosevelt refused another nomination, and the conservatives turned happily to Taft. In 1909 and 1910, however, it seemed that Taft was doing so badly with his first term that a Democrat might win in 1912. So the conservatives renewed their search for a man to displace Bryan. George Harvey announced, "We now expect to see Woodrow Wilson elected governor of the state of New Jersey in 1910 and nominated for President in 1912 upon a platform demanding tariff revision downward."

The politics of New Jersey were as unseemly in 1910 as the politics of New York had been in 1882, when Grover Cleveland was given his first chance. In each case the state had been governed by a bi-partisan machine. The bosses of the two parties were in secret alliance; they exchanged the more valuable offices and divided spoils and patronage as they chose. This is the most discouraging of all systems for the voter; but in New Jersey the long corruption had at last bred a revolt. The time had clearly come for an interlude of honesty. George Harvey explained this to ex-Senator Jim Smith, the Democratic boss of New Jersey. Smith agreed, and undertook to explain to the astonished delegates at the next state convention that they would have to nominate Wilson, of whom many had never heard. Smith described Wilson as "a Presbyterian priest," but admitted that only such a man could be elected in that distasteful year of "reform."

Wilson was not only elected but he proved to have a natural political genius and "to catch public opinion as by wireless."[7] He broke the power of Boss Smith, broke with George Harvey and his Wall Street friends, broke with his own Jeffersonian notions of laissez-faire, forced through a series of progressive laws, and emerged as the favorite of the Western, Bryan wing of the party—the very group which his discoverers had intended him to defeat.

At the Democratic National Convention of 1912 it seemed that the conservative Eastern Democrats and their allies were in a majority, and would force the nomination of Champ Clark of Missouri. But Bryan waged the greatest of his many convention fights. His language and his audacity were so dramatic that he managed to get rank-and-file Democrats from all over the country to telegraph their support. Slowly this took effect on the assembled delegates. On the forty-sixth ballot Wilson won. The platform denounced the tariff, denounced the existing currency and banking laws, and promised strong measures in dealing with trusts and monopolies. In his campaign Wilson made clear his conversion from laissez-faire to a program of government control; but unlike Roosevelt he did not plan to regulate monopolies and make them serve the public good; he planned to abolish them, and then see that government enforced the rules of competition. This was the chief difference between Roosevelt's "New Nationalism" and Wilson's "New Freedom."

"Essentially," writes Professor Hofstadter, "the New Freedom was an attempt of the middle class, with agrarian and labor support, to arrest the exploitation of the community, the concentration of wealth, and the growing control of politics by insiders, and to restore, as far as possible, competitive opportunities in business."[8] And William Allen White (a delegate at the "middle class, agrarian and labor" convention of the Progressives) described the Roosevelt platform as follows:

> The national income must be shifted so that the blessings of our civilization should be more widely enjoyed than they were. To make that shift, what Colonel Roosevelt called "predatory wealth" or "aggrandized capital" should have its claws pared, its greed checked, its rapacity quenched so far as humanly possible. And the shift or redistribution of national income should be achieved by using government where necessary as an agency of human welfare. Lord, how we did like that phrase, "using government as an agency of human welfare!" That was the slogan, that was the Bull Moose platform boiled down to a phrase.[9]

In other words (and as usual in American politics) Roosevelt and Wilson were offering slight variations on the same theme to meet the same shift in public opinion. Both the great leaders sensed that the vast middle class (which was most of America) had moved slightly to the left—to about the position of the Populists in 1892. As recently as the days of Cleveland and McKinley, most Americans would have agreed with John Stuart Mill's statement in the *Principles of Political Economy:* "The great majority of things are worse done by the intervention of government than the individuals interested in the matter would do them, or cause them to be done, if left to themselves. . . . *Laisser Faire,* in short, should be the general practice: every departure from it, unless required by some great good, is a definite evil." And as recently as the days of Cleveland and McKinley most Americans would have felt that the government should help the private citizen to appropriate and exploit the national resources. Both those opinions had changed. The majority now favored regulation and conservation, and as a result so did the leaders of *both* parties.

The unconventional (and unfortunate) feature of 1912 was the split in the Republican Party. The conservative wing controlled the machine—but only because Roosevelt had handed it to them by mistake when he backed Taft in 1908. If Roosevelt had been patient, had been "regular" in 1912 (as he was in 1884, when he campaigned for Blaine), he would have controlled the party again by 1916. But when he bolted he ensured that for a long time the party would be run by its extreme conservatives—among whom were those clumsy vulgarians who nominated Warren Harding in 1920.*

5

Wilson's following resembled the Democratic Party of Andrew Jackson, except that it was not so strong in the West and Middle West, but stronger in the South. The South had of course become solidly Democratic since Jackson's day, as a result of Reconstruction, whereas the prosperous farmers of the grain-growing states (at least as far west as the first tier beyond the Mississippi) tended to vote Republican. Bryan's West (the "Great West") was large, but relatively empty of votes. In the East the chief Democratic strength was still the Irish and the newer immigrants in the industrial areas. Because the party received virtually all the votes in the South (and most of them in the new Southwest—that is, Oklahoma, New Mexico, and Arizona), it did far better in the popular vote than in the electoral college. If Wilson, a minority President, was to be re-elected in 1916, when the Republican Party would be itself again, he would need an astonishing advance in popularity. In fact, he made an advance of almost three million votes.

In character Wilson resembled Jefferson rather than Jackson. His well-trained but rigid intellect did not fit him for rough-and-tumble politics, and his cool aloof nature made it impossible for him to mingle with the people, whom he loved in the abstract and served well. Jefferson, who never appeared in public, who preferred to deal even with his friends by letter, could nevertheless build and lead a party; but it was a small and simple affair compared to the party which Wilson inherited. In Jefferson's day most people were content to be guided unobtrusively by the gentry; but by Wilson's time the very word would have been a vote-loser. "High-minded and cold-blooded," was the description of Wilson by one member of his Cabinet. And the gregarious William Allen White called him "a cold fish," adding that "the hand he gave me to shake felt like a ten-cent pickled mackerel in brown paper—irresponsive and lifeless." Yet White danced on his reporter's table and cheered when Wilson won the nomination.[10]

Wilson's conception of the presidency was clear and unconventional. He believed that a modern state could only discharge its immense and increasing responsibilities with strong Executive leadership. He believed that the American Constitution, especially after it had been stretched to bursting-point by Lincoln, permitted a strong President to take every power that

* Even after his bolt Roosevelt would probably have prevented this last disaster if he had not died in 1919.

was needed. He believed that he himself was such a President, and he planned to make himself master of the government. His success and his failure were both beyond precedent.

In his Inaugural Address Wilson made clear that he intended a change in the relations between the government and the world of business.

> No one can mistake the purpose for which the nation now seeks to use the Democratic party [he said]. It seeks to use it to interpret a change in its own plans and point of view. . . . We have been refreshed by a new insight into our own life. . . . We have made up our minds to square every process of our national life again with the standards we so proudly set up at the beginning and have always carried in our hearts. [Then he listed some of the things that ought to be altered.] A tariff which cuts us off from our proper part in the commerce of the world . . . and makes the government a facile instrument in the hands of private interests; a banking and currency system based upon the necessity of the government to sell its bonds fifty years ago and perfectly adapted to concentrating cash and restricting credits; an industrial system which . . . holds capital in leading strings, restricts the liberties and limits the opportunities of labor, and exploits without renewing or conserving the natural resources of the country; a body of agricultural activities never yet . . . served as it should be through the instrumentality of science taken directly to the farm, or afforded the facilities of credit best suited to its practical needs. . . .

The new President meant these words exactly. And he meant what he had been preaching about Executive leadership. He delivered his messages in person before the two houses of Congress—something which had not been done since the days of John Adams. He spent hours in the President's room at the Capitol, pressing for action on his administration bills. He learned rapidly from his Postmaster General the uses of the vast federal patronage, and abandoned his early plans for making appointments without consulting the Congressmen concerned. And when all else failed, at exactly the right moment he appealed to the public over the head of Congress.

On May 26, 1913, when the Senate showed signs of mutilating his tariff bill, Wilson gave this statement to the press:

> I think that the public ought to know the extraordinary exertions being made by the lobby in Washington to gain recognition for certain alterations in the tariff bill. Washington has seldom seen so numerous, so industrious or so insidious a lobby. . . . There is every evidence that money without limit is being spent to sustain this lobby and to create an appearance of a pressure of public opinion. . . . It is of serious interest to the country that the people at large should have no lobby and be

voiceless in these matters, while great bodies of astute men seek to create an artificial opinion and to overcome the interests of the public for their private profit. . . .

The public responded, and the Senate passed the Underwood Tariff, reducing average duties to about twenty-seven per cent, greatly increasing the free list, and providing for a tax on incomes of three thousand dollars and over. The tax ranged from one to six per cent.

While the tariff was still under debate Wilson presented his plan for banking and currency reform. "The great monopoly in this country is the money monopoly," he had said in 1911. "So long as that exists our old variety and freedom and individual energy of development are out of the question." The Federal Reserve Act, which was promptly passed, divided the country into twelve districts, each with a Federal Reserve Bank. These were bankers' banks, to receive deposits, make rediscounts, and hold reserves for member banks. All national banks were compelled to become members and state banks were permitted. A Federal Reserve Board supervised the regional banks. The board consisted of the Secretary of the Treasury, the Comptroller of the Currency, and five others nominated by the President. The twelve Reserve Banks were authorized to issue to the member banks Federal Reserve notes secured by short-term commercial paper and backed by a forty per cent gold reserve.

In 1908 Andrew Carnegie had called the American banking system "the worst in the civilized world." The new Federal Reserve System was an improvement wherever it prevailed, bringing greater elasticity of credit, and a far wider distribution of banking facilities. But the federal government could not compel membership in its system, and too many little banks still went their own strange ways. Between 1921 and the great collapse in 1933, there was never a year with less than 367 bank failures, and the largest number was 4004. Fourteen thousand eight hundred and twenty banks failed during the thirteen years.

Everything that Wilson asked from Congress he received, usually on his own terms, during these first magic years. We have already discussed the Clayton Anti-Trust Act and the act creating the Federal Trade Commission. Congress also passed a Federal Farm Loan Act, a Workmen's Compensation Act for the federal civil service, a Rural Credits Act, an act providing for an eight-hour day on interstate railways, an act providing millions of dollars for farm demonstration work in rural counties—and all under the direct, steady, forceful guidance of the Executive.

Perhaps the President's most surprising victory was in the matter of the Panama Canal tolls. By treaty with England the Canal was "to be open to British and American vessels on equal terms." But in 1912 Congress passed a law exempting coastwise vessels of the United States from payments. England protested, and when Wilson found he could win English co-operation with his Mexican policy in return for the repeal of this law he went before Congress and said frankly: "I ask this of you in support of the foreign policy of this Administration. I shall not know how to deal with other matters of even greater delicacy and nearer consequence, if you do not grant it to me." This is the type of request which Congress enjoys refusing. To humiliate a President and complicate a foreign policy at the same time, seems almost irresistible. Yet the repeal was passed within two and a half months of Wilson's request.*

6

In the midst of the President's domestic triumphs the war began in Europe and history entered a new phase. Even in the United States there were many who knew that this was a fateful moment and who were "concerned with what they believed to be a deliberate intention by Germany to wage war at a moment so favorable that it might ensure German hegemony not only in Europe but in the world. . . . Far removed from the scene of conflict, the English-speaking peoples oversea believed that the triumph of imperial Germany would have involved a fatal and irretrievable step on a road that led to human bondage."[11] It was of course only the Dominions among "the English-speaking peoples oversea" who believed this at once; yet a surprising number of American leaders (including the President) suspected that it might be true.

Colonel House, Wilson's closest friend and adviser, wrote him on August 22, 1914, that if Germany should win "we will have to abandon the path which you are blazing as a standard for future generations . . . and build up a military machine of vast proportions." And the Colonel said in his diary that Wilson agreed. In July, 1915, he wrote again to the President: "I feel we are taking a terrible gamble ourselves in permitting our safety to rest almost wholly upon the success of the Allies." And two months later Wilson told House that "he had never been sure that we ought not to take part in the conflict and, if it seemed evident that Germany and her militaristic ideas were to win, the obligation upon us was greater than ever."[12] As we have seen, there had been support for such views among students of foreign relations ever since the eighteen-nineties, when men like Henry Adams and John Hay began saying that America's safety depended on an Atlantic community strong enough to keep Germany from dominating France and England.

No matter what Wilson felt, however, there was no possibility at first of his taking the American people into war. Aggressive isolationism, which

* The Canal had not been completed, so no tolls had yet been charged.

had been diminishing, was still an important force; and throughout the Middle West not only the German-Americans but the Scandinavian-Americans denied that the Central Powers were a menace. Nevertheless, in view of his opinions on Germany and his fears for America, it is odd that Wilson issued the proclamation of August, 1914, urging the people to be neutral in thought as well as in deed. Such a plea could only make sense if there was no moral difference between the combatants and if America's national interest was not involved. If Wilson had educated his public from the beginning in simple geopolitics, he might not have had to present the war later in language so emotional and moralistic that it returned to haunt him. Most Americans thought that they finally entered the war for the purpose of improving mankind, rather than of saving themselves from the disaster of German victory. They were disillusioned, therefore, when mankind remained obdurately unimproved, and they did not even know they had avoided a disaster.

In the midst of Wilson's vacillations on war and peace came the election of 1916. Wilson won many new labor votes, and many new votes from the prosperous farmers; but the two wings of the Republican Party had reunited and the election was so close that the results were in doubt for days. In the electoral college Wilson had 277 votes and Charles Evans Hughes, the Republican, had 254. The Senate was held safely; but the House was lost. With the help of nine independent members, however, the House could still be controlled by the Democrats. Yet the Republican candidates for Congress had received several hundred thousand more votes than the Democratic candidates—a warning for 1918.

If Wilson had been as wary as Franklin Roosevelt, when the war came he would have drawn the Republicans into the closest non-partisan responsibility, so that they could not make politics out of the peace. Unhappily he did just the reverse. Throughout the seventeen months of America's participation in the war Wilson had received complete support from both parties in Congress; nevertheless, a fortnight before the midterm elections of 1918 he issued the most unwise appeal in American history.

> My Fellow Countrymen [he said]. . . . If you have approved of my leadership and wish me to continue to be your unembarrassed spokesman in affairs at home and abroad, I earnestly beg that you will express yourselves unmistakably to that effect by returning a Democratic majority to both the Senate and the House of Representatives. . . . My power to administer the great trust assigned to me by the Constitution would be seriously impaired should your judgment be adverse. . . . I mean only that the difficulties and delicacies of our present task are of a sort that makes it imperatively necessary that the nation should give its undivided support to the Government under a unified leadership, and

that a Republican Congress would divide the leadership. . . . If the control of the House and the Senate should be taken away from the party now in power an opposing majority could assume control of legislation and oblige all action to be taken amid contest and obstruction. . . .

They certainly could. And they certainly did. But no one has ever explained how the man who had been such a brilliant politician in 1913 could have made this blunder five years later. What had become of his power "to catch public opinion as by wireless"? The 1916 election suggests that Wilson would probably have lost the House in any case; but after this appeal he lost both the House and the Senate. The public did not want the war to belong to one party. And not only did Wilson lose, but the new Republican majorities felt they had been insulted and their patriotism impugned. They returned to Washington ready for the maximum of "contest and obstruction." And finally, because of this foolish plea the mid-term elections (which might otherwise have reflected local issues) could be interpreted as a direct rejection of Wilson. The Republicans were not slow to take this advantage. When Wilson sailed for France on December 13, to attend the Peace Conference, Theodore Roosevelt announced to "our allies, our enemies, and Mr. Wilson himself" that "Mr. Wilson has no authority whatever to speak for the American people at this time. His leadership has just been emphatically repudiated by them. Mr. Wilson and his fourteen points and his four supplementary points and all his utterances every which way have ceased to have any shadow of right to be accepted as expressive of the will of the American people."

The good days were over for the President. He had lost his political touch and his enemies were gathering to destroy him. His appointments to the peace delegation were another sign of his declining tact: Robert Lansing, the Secretary of State, an expert on foreign relations with no political weight or knowledge; General Tasker Bliss, Chief of Staff, a good soldier and a wise man with no political weight or knowledge; Henry White, an experienced diplomat whom Theodore Roosevelt described as "the most useful man in the diplomatic service during my presidency and for many years before." White was vaguely a Republican, but he too had no political weight or knowledge. These men would have been useful as expert advisers; but their appointment to the delegation ensured a political fight over the treaty. The last chance to undo the harm of his pre-election message was to name at least two leading Republicans for the peace delegation: one from the Senate and one a national figure like Elihu Root or ex-President Taft. When Wilson missed this chance, the treaty, and the League of Nations, and the promises which Wilson had made in America's name, became a matter of party politics. The Senators who were piqued at

Wilson's autocratic manners, and the few who were genuine isolationists, and the many who merely wished to weaken a Democratic Administration, combined to confuse the public. They roused the Italian-Americans against the treaty because of Fiume, and the Irish-Americans because the Commonwealth of Nations had five votes in the Assembly of the League, and the German-Americans because the Fatherland was treated harshly, and the anti-German-Americans because it was treated well. And even more dangerous, they roused the Presbyterian stubbornness in Wilson, who refused to accept moderate amendments to his handiwork. From October, 1918, when he made his appeal for a Democratic Congress, until September, 1919, when he suffered a stroke while defending the treaty on a nation-wide speaking tour, Woodrow Wilson gave a long demonstration of how a President of the United States should not behave. He seemed to have forgotten that he was just a Democratic politician, and not a prophet. Peremptory when he should have been persuasive, messianic when he should have been offering worldly bargains, angry when he should have been reconciling his foes, he met total defeat although there was never a moment when a majority of the people and three quarters of the Senate would not have accepted a League with minor amendments.[13]

Before this sudden decline in his intelligence and thus in his power, Wilson had ruled as a constitutional dictator. He not only took the full "war power" of the President as developed by Lincoln; but he added immense further authority which he persuaded Congress to delegate to him. Whereas Lincoln preferred to meet his emergencies by lonely Executive action, Wilson preferred to ask Congress for specific laws to stretch his authority. In this way he gained a control over the nation's economy which would have caused a second civil war if Lincoln had attempted it. Lindsay Rogers described Wilson as a combination of King, Prime Minister in control of legislation, Commander-in-Chief, party leader, economic dictator, and Secretary of State for Foreign Affairs.[14] The Lever Act of August, 1917, is an example of how Congress gave him his head.

> Under the terms of this statute the President . . . could regulate the importation, manufacture, storage, mining and distribution of any necessaries; could requisition foods, fuels, and other supplies . . . could purchase, store, and sell certain foods; could fix a reasonable and guaranteed price for wheat . . . could take over and operate factories, mines, packing houses, pipe lines . . . could fix the price of coal and coke and regulate their production, sale, shipment, distribution. . . .[15]

7

While still on the eve of war, after breaking diplomatic relations with Germany but before the declaration of hostilities, Wilson came hard against that formidable institution, the Senate filibuster. Even here he won a partial victory. He had asked the Congress for permission to arm American merchant vessels. On March 1, 1917, the House passed the bill by 403 votes to 14; but the session was to end on March 4, so a small group of Senators decided to talk the bill to death, preventing it from coming to a vote. On the last morning of the session seventy-five Senators announced that they favored the bill and would pass it if they were allowed to vote. This was more than three fourths of the Senate membership; yet the filibuster continued to the end.

The President armed the merchantmen anyway. But he also issued the following statement to the public:

> In the immediate presence of a crisis fraught with more subtle and far-reaching possibilities of national danger than any the Government has known within the whole history of its international relations, the Congress has been unable to act either to safeguard the country or to vindicate the elementary rights of its citizens. . . . The Senate of the United States is the only legislative body in the world which cannot act when its majority is ready for action. A little group of wilful men, representing no opinion but their own, have rendered the great government of the United States helpless and contemptible. . . .
>
> The only remedy is that the rules of the Senate shall be so altered that it can act. The country can be relied on to draw the moral. I believe that the Senate can be relied on to supply the means of action and save the country from disaster.

This brusque statement may explain some of the troubles of the President over the Versailles Treaty. The Senators have been a touchy and unforgiving race (although highly privileged) ever since the days when they suspected George Washington of seeking to override them. And of all their privileges the one they have liked best (and with good reason) has been the privilege of talking as much as they chose. Throughout American history this undemocratic veto, in a chamber which was undemocratic by constitution, has been the last resort of threatened minorities. In 1789, when the Senate had been organized for less than six months, one of its members wrote: "I gave my opinion in plain language that the confidence of the people was departing from us, owing to our unreasonable delays. The design of the Virginians and of the South Carolina gentlemen was to talk away the time, so that we could not get the bill passed."[16] And in 1841, when Henry Clay sought to impose a check on Senate debates for the benefit of the Whig majority, Thomas Hart Benton said that he and his friends in the minority would resort to "any possible extremity" to resist such action.[17] The same view was expressed by Senator La Follette on March 8, 1917, in answer to Wilson's demand for a change in the rules:

> . . . I shall stand while I am a member of this body against any cloture that denies free and unlimited debate. Sir, the moment that the majority imposes the restriction contained in the impending rule, that moment you will have dealt a blow to liberty, you will have broken down one of the greatest weapons against wrong and oppression that the members of this body possess.

La Follette was an advanced liberal and a devoted servant of the people. Such words from such a source show how rooted in American practice is the fear of unchecked majorities. On this occasion, however, because of the dangers of impending war, the Senate did accept a partial cloture rule, which has been in force ever since. Under the rule sixteen Senators can insist that there be presented for an aye-and-nay vote the question: "Is it the sense of the Senate that the debate (upon any pending measure) shall be brought to a close?" And if there is a quorum, and if the question is decided in the affirmative by two thirds of those voting, "then the measure shall be the unfinished business to the exclusion of all other business until disposed of." And thereafter no Senator shall be entitled to speak for more than one hour on the pending measure.

This is not a very strict cloture, since one third of the Senators present can keep it from being invoked, and since in any case ninety-six hours, or sixteen legislative days, may still be given to the debate. Yet if the Senate were to accept cloture by a majority vote it would lose one of its chief functions. It would no longer be a bulwark against the tyranny of mere numbers. And in America it is not the powerful or the rich alone who fear such tyranny. When Coolidge's Vice-President, Charles G. Dawes, attacked the dilatory Senate rules and demanded a change, the national convention of the American Federation of Labor unanimously condemned this "campaign to abolish free speech in the United States Senate . . . the Dawes scheme which does not come from the people but emanates from the secret chambers of the predatory interests." The statement continued: "For several months the Vice-President of the United States has conducted an agitation for the purpose of abolishing free speech in the United States Senate, the only forum in the world where cloture does not exist and where members can prevent the passage of reactionary legislation. . . . It is a vicious idea, a vicious purpose. . . ."[18]

8

One important and harmful precedent from the Civil War was rejected by Woodrow Wilson. The Congressional Committee on the Conduct of the War had been a minor nuisance to Lincoln for three and a half years—and a major nuisance to several generals whom it pestered with ignorant questions.* Several attempts were made by Congressmen to set up a similar committee in the First World War. Wilson protested strongly and the plan was dropped.[19] Then in January, 1918, Senator Chamberlain of Oregon announced that government had broken down through inefficiency and that a war Cabinet composed of "three distinguished citizens of demonstrated ability" should be established. Theodore Roosevelt was to be one of the "distinguished citizens," and the Cabinet was to take over the direction of the war. Since Roosevelt and Wilson disliked each other and underestimated each other's abilities, and since neither was of a humble nature, this might have meant German victory. But Wilson boldly asked Congress to give to the President himself all the powers which had been suggested for the war Cabinet. Congress obeyed, and on May 30, 1918, authorized Wilson to reorganize the government and the administrative agencies as he saw fit. Thenceforth, until his lamentable appeal for a Democratic victory, his powers seemed absolute. Yet the suddenness with which they fell from him when he began to lose public confidence proved once more that the true strength of the office lies in its influence, not its legal authority.

Throughout the summer of 1918 Wilson acted as King, Prime Minister, Commander-in-Chief, and Foreign Secretary rolled into one. Yet in December of 1918 Theodore Roosevelt warned the world that Wilson—still the President, and with his emergency powers unrepealed—had "no authority whatever." No wonder the world was confused.

---

* This was a joint committee of the two houses formed in December, 1861, and dissolved in June, 1865. Most of the members were Republican radicals who became steadily more critical of Lincoln as the war progressed.

XXXIV

Some Modern Instances: II

"Isolationist sentiment [in 1919–20] was a product of the fight to prevent American participation in world affairs," wrote Alan Cranston; "it was not the cause of it."[1] This is largely true. The old isolationism had been weakening ever since the imperial excitements of the nineties. Most people in 1919 probably wanted a Wilsonian policy; but they were tired of Wilson and his prim didactic ways. Foolishly, they let themselves be trapped by tawdry politicians into accepting an unworthy deed. Then they sought to justify the deed by overpersuading themselves that the United States could (and should) go her own way in safety and in honor. Specious arguments could be found for the safety; but the honor was more difficult. Only on the most material grounds could a nation so fortunate and so rich refuse to associate with her neighbors in the hope of peace. The most material grounds were therefore adopted, and the result was not attractive, either morally or physically. The era was personified in President Harding—simple and warmhearted, stupid and sensual, ignorant as a pre-Columbian savage. And the era ended in the depression of 1929.

There is no need to linger over this horrid interlude, except to note that as usual a period of strong Presidents relapsed into a period of Congressional rule. Harding was slipped into the White House by a little clique of Senators who were tired of living under the shadow of a great man. The cynicism of the choice astonished the New York *Times* into putting its editorial comment on the front page. "The nomination of Harding," wrote the staid and soft-spoken *Times*, "for whose counterpart we must go back to Franklin Pierce if we would seek a President who measures down to his political stature, is the fine and perfect flower of the cowardice and imbecility of the Senatorial cabal that charged itself with the management of the Republican convention."

The cabal, in any case, got what it wanted: a very weak President who believed that "the party is bigger than any man," and who would never give orders. Even from their partisan point of view they were wrong to want such a President. Even if there had been no thievery, and no return to the old Republican policy of giving away the nation's resources, they were wrong (politically wrong) in trying to turn back the presidential office to the days of Pierce or Buchanan. Professor Binkley comments:

"So blind had Republican leadership become to the historical transformation of the presidency in the twentieth century, the fact that it had become as never before the focal point of a major party's strength, that they could not see how their emasculation of the great office was impairing if not even dooming their party."[2] That is the lesson of the days of Republican power after the First World War. Harding (except that he brought in his train the maximum of dishonor) was scarcely more inadequate than Coolidge, who brought rigid New England virtue—or than Mr. Hoover, who brought not only virtue but high intelligence and world-wide experience. They all had a conception of the President's office which did not fit the times, so they were all preparing their party to descend into the minority rôle to which it has condemned itself for twenty years.

Harding and Coolidge, in their provincialism, may have thought America would never again be in danger, and that government could therefore be weakened with impunity. But Mr. Hoover had seen beyond Ohio and Vermont. And he became President in 1929, the black year. He cannot have indulged such illusions. Yet he too behaved as if the presidency was what Benjamin Harrison had thought it, or James Madison, and as if the twentieth century had not seen the rise of the positive state. He thus did honor to a great American tradition; but he neglected another tradition, to the effect that while strong government is a nuisance it is sometimes a necessity, and that the powers of the presidency must therefore be left ambiguous so that they can be raised or lowered at will. There was nothing ambiguous about the abdication in the twenties.

In 1932, toward the end of his unhappy term, while accepting a renomination which did him no good, Mr. Hoover said: "It does not follow, because our difficulties are stupendous, because there are some souls timorous enough to doubt the validity and effectiveness of our ideals and our system, that we must turn to a State-controlled or State-directed social or economic system in order to cure our troubles. That is not liberalism; it is tyranny." And two years later, when his ideals and hopes for America had become the subject of unworthy gibes, he repeated his faith. "While I can make no claim for having introduced the term 'rugged individualism,'" he wrote, "I should be proud to have invented it. It has been used by American leaders for over a half-century in eulogy of those God-fearing men and women of honesty whose stamina and character and fearless assertion of rights led them to make their own way in life. It is they who have borne the burdens and given leadership in their communities."*

Obviously, with such views, Mr. Hoover could not do much to mitigate

* A recent volume of speeches suggests that Mr. Hoover has slightly modified his faith in "rugged individualism"; yet he would probably still wish to be known as a strong defender of the old view of government.

the depression by federal paternalism, by heavy taxation and redistribution of incomes. He believed that savings and self-denial were the road to security, and that if the state (instead of the individuals) did the saving and the denying, the end would be worse than the beginning. With the possible exception of Theodore Roosevelt and Taft and Wilson, this would have been the view of every previous President. But it was no longer the view of the people, and in this the people were probably closer than Mr. Hoover to the realities of modern life. During the forty years since Benjamin Harrison had entered the White House, manufacture, distribution, and finance had organized themselves on a continent-wide scale, with few concessions to laissez-faire. Labor had to some extent done the same, and intended at any cost to finish the job. The problems of production had largely been solved, by means which led to the problems of mass unemployment. Local government had entered the public-utilities field, accustoming people to think of government as something which can provide amenities and not merely policemen. The First World War had brought government into every family's life through the draft, and into the life of almost every business through the economic controls.

The draft, furthermore, had raised strange questions by showing that the federal and state governments, instead of being sacred circles of power revolving in isolation, could co-operate to impose their will on the citizen. State officers did most of the unpopular work for the federal government. The draft was administered by 192,000 people working under state supervisors and 429 people working under the federal provost marshal. If in spite of state rights and all the theories of federalism a man's freedom of choice could be taken from him by the two "separated" powers working in concert, perhaps (in a depression) his lost security might be similarly restored?

In 1929 the depression struck. "Everything nailed down is comin' loose," as the Angel Gabriel said in *Green Pastures*. The people were in no mood for lectures on individual responsibility—such as Van Buren administered during the depression of 1837, or Grover Cleveland when he vetoed a bill for sending seed-grain to drought victims in the Southwest.* The people had been shown the vast powers of their government in 1918, so they looked to Washington for help.

Mr. Hoover, in spite of his views, did more to fight the depression than many Presidents would have approved. Federal aid was given to drought victims and the farmer was helped to buy food for his cattle. Wheat was distributed through the Red Cross; but Hoover was opposed to the distribution of money. In January, 1932, the Reconstruction Finance Cor-

* "I do not believe that the power and duty of the federal government ought to be extended to the relief of individual suffering," wrote Cleveland in rejecting this modest appropriation of $10,000 in 1887. "Federal aid in such cases . . . weakens the sturdiness of our national character."

poration was created, with two billion dollars to lend to banks, insurance companies, building and loan associations, railroads, agricultural credit groups, and the like. This was a workable plan for bolstering the nation's credit and thus creating employment; but since the Administration still refused to provide money for the starving poor, the R.F.C. was named "the millionaires' dole." Finally, in the summer of 1932, the government undertook to lend $1,800,000,000 to states and cities for relief and public works. At last the principle of federal responsibility to the hopelessly poor was accepted. The road was open for the New Deal.

2

Franklin Roosevelt's theory of government and of the presidential office was the reverse of Herbert Hoover's. "History proves that dictatorships do not grow out of strong and successful governments," said Roosevelt, "but out of weak and helpless ones. If by democratic methods people get a government strong enough to protect them from fear and starvation, their democracy succeeds; but if they do not, they grow impatient. Therefore, the only sure bulwark of continuing liberty is a government strong enough to protect the interests of the people, and a people strong enough and well enough informed to maintain its sovereign control over its government."[3] From the moment of Roosevelt's unprecedented flight to the Chicago Convention to accept his nomination, there was to be no question whether a President has the necessary powers to fight a depression.

Six weeks before his nomination Roosevelt had spoken at Oglethorpe University, in Georgia. "The country needs and, unless I mistake its temper, the country demands bold, persistent experimentation. It is common sense to take a method and try it: If it fails, admit it frankly and try another. But above all, try something. The millions who are in want will not stand by silently forever while the things to satisfy their needs are within easy reach." This willingness to "try something" fitted the mood of the country. So did the willingness to admit grave faults in American life; for the masses were bored with hearing that fundamentally all was well. "While my elders were talking to me about the perfection of America," said Franklin Roosevelt, "I did not know then of the lack of opportunity, the lack of education, the lack of many of the essential needs of civilization which existed among millions of our people who lived not alone in the slums of the great cities and in the forgotten corners of rural America, but even under the very noses of those who had the advantages and the power of Government in those days."[4] And again, "If we do not allow a Democratic government to do the things which need to be done, and if we hand down to our children a deteriorated nation, their legacy will not be a legacy of abundance or even a legacy of poverty amidst plenty, but a legacy of poverty amidst poverty."[5]

The people enjoyed President Roosevelt's restlessness under delay—especially judicial delay. A federal system lives by delay, as we have seen, but it also lives by the power to break restraints when the public impatience rises. This was the point of Justice Holmes's quotation from a Senator: "What the boys like about [Theodore] Roosevelt is that he doesn't care a damn for the law." And the boys liked the same quality in the new Roosevelt—when he let it be seen, which was never by accident. He could wait imperturbably until his followers were maddened by the inaction; or he could express the plain man's conviction that the law in all its slow obscurity is an ass.

> It cost a civil war [he said] to gain recognition of the constitutional power of the Congress to legislate for the territories. It cost twenty years of taxation on those *least* able to pay to recognize the constitutional power of the states to pass minimum wage laws for their protection. . . . We know it takes time to adjust government to the needs of society. But modern history proves that reforms too long delayed or denied have jeopardized peace, undermined democracy and swept away civil and religious liberties. Yes, time more than ever before is vital in statesmanship and in government, in all three branches of it.
>
> We will no longer be permitted to sacrifice each generation in turn while the law catches up with life.[6]

"Many books will be written about Franklin Roosevelt," said his Secretary of Labor, Frances Perkins, "but no two will give the same picture. . . . He was the most complicated human being I ever knew."[7] The prophecy, which was made in 1946, has already been fulfilled. Recent books on Franklin Roosevelt seem to have been written about at least four different men, none of whom were on good terms with each other. We do not need to plunge into this discussion of the unknown, or into the question whether the measures of President Roosevelt were well conceived; but it is important to see the place of the New Deal in American history and to understand its effect upon the form of government.

> We can now see that the "Roosevelt revolution" was no revolution [wrote Professor Commager in 1945], but rather the culmination of half a century of historical development, and that Roosevelt himself, though indubitably a leader, was an instrument of the popular will rather than a creator of, or a dictator to, that will. Indeed, the two major issues of the Roosevelt administration—the domestic issue of the extension of government control for democratic purposes, and the international issue of the rôle of America as a world power—emerged in the 1890's, and a longer perspective will see the half century from the 1890's to the present as a historical unit.[8]

Many people found the Roosevelt years shocking because they were so unlike the tranquil, doomed period from Harding to Hoover. If the New Deal had followed at once on Wilson's New Freedom the continuity would have been clear. As we have seen, Roosevelt's floor manager at the national convention which gave him his first nomination was an ex-Populist from Nebraska who asserted that the platform of 1892 "was the real beginning of the Roosevelt campaign of 1932."

With a Wilsonian view of the powers of the presidency, with a Jeffersonian pliability of mind and taste for the politically devious, with a zest for responsibility which recalled his fifth cousin, Theodore, and above all with that complication of character which Frances Perkins remarked and behind which he could rest himself from the loud, demanding world, the new President was ready to meet the people's cry for action and for the positive state. Again the emergency had been matched with the man. And again the party system and the convention system do not seem to deserve much credit. Luck seems to have played the major part as usual—luck and Mr. James Farley, who showed himself during the year before the nomination to be the most tireless and ingratiating promoter of a candidate America had yet seen. But one may doubt whether Mr. Farley knew what he was promoting.

Although Roosevelt had served Wilson as Assistant Secretary of the Navy, and had received his party's nomination for the vice-presidency, and had been governor of New York State for two popular and successful terms, few people in 1932 seemed to suspect his resolution, his tireless strength, or his political magic. Perhaps the pain of the long fight against infantile paralysis had put the unknown iron in his nature; but the joyful talent for politics must always have been there. Nevertheless, until the Republicans began to see what he was doing to them towards the end of the campaign in 1932, most people appeared to agree with Mr. Walter Lippmann, who wrote that Roosevelt was "no tribune of the people . . . no enemy of entrenched privilege . . . a pleasant man who, without any important qualification for the office, would very much like to be President."[9] A few years later the majority would have laughed at such condescension, and the minority would have said it was far too kind.

By that time the nation's natural resources were being conserved and rehabilitated on a scale which Theodore Roosevelt would have envied; the federal government was committed not only to temporary work-relief for the unemployed, and to the promotion and protection of trade unionism, but to a permanent reform and social-security program: public works for "pump-priming" the economy, old-age pensions, public health, maximum hours and minimum wages, rural rehabilitation, and the future promise of federal aid to the burdened school systems of the states. By that time also, bank deposits had been insured; the sales of securities had been regulated; the dollar had been devalued and the country taken off the gold standard; the farmers had been paid from the federal Treasury not to grow crops which could not be marketed at satisfactory prices; the Tennessee Valley Authority had been created to develop the resources of an entire watershed of forty thousand square miles,* to control floods, to promote river navigation, to sell electric power in competition with private business, and to discover whether the federal government, by altering the economic climate, could lift a dejected region into ambition and hope, could foster local private enterprise in business and on the farm, and could thus build economic democracy. All things seemed to be changing during these years except the depression, which sometimes dwindled but never disappeared. Yet it had lost its terrors for the poor, since the government offered everybody a job.

Whether these laws and plans and promises were well or badly chosen, well or badly carried out, one thing seems sure: the New Deal shifted the balance of American government. It brought almost as sharp a concentration of power—from the state governments to the federal, and within the federal government from the Congress to the President—as did the Civil War. The change had long been preparing and maturing. Big government developed in America almost fifty years after big business, and for once it seems fair to say *post hoc ergo propter hoc*. Only if business (and labor unions, and farm blocs) grow little, will government become simple again, and decentralized, and unconcerned with economic problems. Franklin Roosevelt did the inevitable in allowing power to concentrate; yet after twelve years of deluded mooning it felt like a revolution.

"Nine crazy years at the ticker and three long years in the breadlines!" was Roosevelt's tribute to the post-war era during his 1936 campaign; "Nine mad years of mirage and three long years of despair!" And he added, "Powerful influences strive today to restore that kind of government with its doctrine that the Government is best which is most indifferent." The latter statement was just campaign talk; for the most striking proof of the need for the New Deal was that the Republican platform in 1936 promised virtually the same aids and benefits to the same discontented groups—only the Republicans would do it with less waste, less politics, fewer bureaucrats, less money, and less centralization. The people seemed to feel this might prove difficult, for they gave Roosevelt twenty-seven and a half million votes and the Republican candidate, Mr. Landon, a little more than sixteen and a half.**

The unlucky Mr. Landon in 1936, and Wendell Willkie in 1940, and Mr. Dewey in 1944, were blamed by some of their partisans (after losing the elections) for not attacking the Roosevelt policies hard enough. They

* The area of England is 50,870 square miles.
** Electoral votes for Roosevelt, 523; for Landon, 8.

were called "me-too" candidates, because they had concentrated on saying
how much better, and with how many fewer inconveniences, they could
carry America toward the social-service state. But they were right—and
they were in the main tradition of American politics—to offer a slightly
different version of the New Deal and to insist that the New Deal would
be more agreeable if entrusted to them. If they had done anything else
they would have taken their party, not merely to defeat, but to ruin. Mr.
Hoover (if the party had wanted a policy all its own) would gladly have
attacked the New Deal root and branch; but after 1932 the leaders were
careful not to nominate him.

The people had turned their backs on the old order, after the calamities
of 1929 to 1933, and politicians who wanted to be elected must do the
same. The depression had put an end to the America in which a majority
could be persuaded that government was the greatest of evils. A privileged
minority could still afford that conviction, and those who did afford it
naturally blamed the New Deal, feeling themselves "borne darkly, fearfully
afar." They were right in so feeling. The America of their schoolbooks
was gone. Professor Corwin, commenting on the New Deal, concludes:
"And that these developments spell a diminished importance for the conception of Constitutional liberty which we have heretofore stressed, which
is that of liberty *against* government, there can be no reasonable doubt."[10]
This was the conception on which the Republic was founded, and its defeat might well be mourned.

> Men are we, and must grieve when even the shade
> Of that which once was great, is passed away.

The pity was that the grief so often turned to hatred, a less dignified
memorial.

Mr. Roosevelt had not created the demand for the paternal state. The
proverbially wicked English had done that, by inventing the Industrial
Revolution. Yet one can understand the irritation of the Republicans.
Their party had kept a long lease on power (56 out of the previous 72
years) partly by giving the public domain to homesteaders, railway and
mining promoters, cattle men, sheepherders, and lumber barons. Then
came the strange new doctrine of conservation, also invented by a Republican, and also easy to translate into votes. Unhappily, however, instead of standing by the Square Deal and moving to new strength in a
new world, the party under Warren Harding allowed a few thieves to
revert to the old policy and to give the navy's oil reserves to millionaires.
This started the voters thinking that the Grand Old Party might be a little
out of date; so when Mr. Hoover faced the depression with talk of
"rugged individualism" they were discouraged, and turned to the Demo-

crats. And at once the Democrats found something to give away even more appealing than the public domain; namely, the federal taxes. As these poured out—to the farmers for not growing crops or for helping in demonstrations of better farming and of land repair; to the unemployed for building roads, bridges, post offices, housing projects; to the young men in the Conservation Corps for preserving and restoring forests and farm lands and national parks; to the South for the Tennessee Valley Authority with its attendant cheap power, cheap fertilizer, and cheap river transport—the old Jacksonian party rose from the grave, the farmer-labor alliance of Southern and Western agrarians with Eastern industrial workers. And the Democrats had enough taxes left over for pensions to the aged, for milk to the school children, and even for some honest slum clearance for the Negroes.

The whole of this vast redistribution of income was directed by one of the greatest opportunists and political strategists ever to reach the White House. And worst of all (from the Republican point of view) much of the redistribution was desirable—or in any case was clearly and ardently desired by a large majority. Under the circumstances, Landon's sixteen and a half million votes were impressive. And Willkie's twenty-two million three hundred thousand votes in 1940 were a triumph for the man, the party system, and the instinct of the American people not to divide on class lines.* The sudden coming of the New Deal, with its largesse for the poor instead of the rich, might have split the country in terms of income and killed the American system of politics. But although recent studies prove this has happened in a very small way, it has not happened enough to matter.[11] It can be reversed the next time fate gives the Republicans a master of "group diplomacy"—a Lincoln, a McKinley, a Roosevelt. It would never have happened in the first place if Theodore Roosevelt had stayed with the party in 1912, or if he had lived to fight for the nomination in 1920.** He would have picked up where Woodrow Wilson stopped—insisting, of course, that he was reversing the New Freedom while in fact he completed it and anticipated the New Deal by more than a decade.

3

How did the New Deal fit itself into the Constitution and escape destruction at the hands of the Supreme Court? The Court began, inevitably, by applying the restrictive view of federal powers which it had

* In 1940 President Roosevelt received 27,243,468 votes—about 230,000 less than in 1936.
** He died in 1919 at the age of sixty.

elaborated since the eighteen-nineties. Under the old theory of federalism, the national government and the states were seen as rivals who should be encouraged to frustrate each other. A chief duty of the Court was to see that neither of the rivals was weakened, so that the frustration might be as great as possible. And under the theory of the Separation of Powers, the Legislature and the Executive were also seen as rivals who should be helped to thwart each other. And liberty was defined chiefly as liberty *against* government. This was all good American doctrine—until the people began to ask for economic help from Washington.

So in 1935 the Supreme Court declared the National Industrial Recovery Act unconstitutional on the ground that it delegated too many legislative powers to the President.* And in 1936 the first Agricultural Adjustment Administration was declared unconstitutional on the ground that the regulation of agriculture belonged to the states, and that the payment of cash benefits to farmers was in fact coercive, since it attempted to do indirectly what would not be lawful if it were done directly.[12] And in the same year the Guffey Coal Act—which regulated wages, hours, working conditions, and prices in the coal industry—was found unconstitutional because the production of coal was not interstate commerce and because too many legislative powers were delegated by the act.[13]

This was pleasing to many Republicans, for they had a brief hope the whole New Deal might prove impossible—just as the Democrats in 1857 hoped that the Dred Scott decision might abolish the Republican Party. Already, however, there was a rift within the Court. The movement to alter the interpretations to fit political reality had begun. In the case of the AAA, Justice Stone wrote an angry dissent for himself and two others, which included these statements:

> Courts are not the only agency of government that must be assumed to have capacity to govern. Congress and the courts both unhappily may falter or be mistaken in the performance of their constitutional duty. But interpretation of our great charter of government which proceeds on any assumption that the responsibility for the preservation of our institutions is the exclusive concern of any one of the three branches of government, or that it alone can save them from destruction, is far more likely in the long run "to obliterate the constituent members" of "an indestructible union of indestructible states" than the frank recognition that language, even of a constitution, may mean what it says: that the power to tax and spend includes the power to relieve a nationwide economic maladjustment by conditional gifts of money.

* The act provided for the formulation of codes of fair competition in each industry, which would have the effect of laws when signed by the President. The Court declared the act null in the case of *U.S.* v. *Schechter,* 295 U.S. 495.

If the Court had been unanimous against paternalism, and if the people had rejected Franklin Roosevelt in 1936, the New Deal might have been postponed. But since the Court was usually divided, and since the people gave the President eleven million more votes than Mr. Landon, there was no doubt that the obstructive justices must give way. The President, however, would not wait for the capitulation. Cheered by his immense victory he undertook the task which Jefferson had twice attempted vainly. He tried to conquer the Court once and for all. In February, 1937, he proposed a bill providing that for every justice of the Supreme Court who failed to retire at seventy an additional justice should be appointed, up to a total of fifteen. The country was not pleased. There were few favors which Franklin Roosevelt would have been refused at that moment; but he had chosen one of them. The proposal seemed flippant and spiteful. After months of argument the Senate rejected the bill, which had meanwhile become irrelevant, for the Supreme Court had quietly and sensibly changed its own mind. Two justices who had usually voted against the New Deal measures now usually voted for them. The Constitution had been unofficially amended.

Later, because of deaths and resignations, President Roosevelt was to appoint seven out of the nine members of the Supreme Court; but when the great change came he had appointed none.

In April, 1937, the self-corrected Court found the National Labor Relations Act constitutional, thus giving the federal government powers over industry and over the relations between employer and employee.[14] And in May the Court accepted the federal old-age annuities plan. This meant national and state co-operation in social services. Jealous federalism had at last given way to co-operative federalism—which we first saw in the 1917 draft law. As the Supreme Court had always foreseen, when the federal and state governments began working together the central power was strengthened. Similarly, federal control over industry and labor relations meant that the Executive was strengthened. The President must thenceforth have more to say about legislation, and must be allowed to ask for greater delegations of power. What had previously been tolerated during the emergency of war was now to become normal practice in peace. And the "fourth branch" of government was to proliferate—the commissions and other regulatory agencies wherein legislative, executive, and judicial powers were mingled inextricably.*

Summing up this change Professor Corwin writes:

> The Court has discarded the idea that the *laissez-faire*, non-interventionist conception of governmental function offers a feasible ap-

---

* Franklin Roosevelt had nothing to add to the war powers developed by Wilson, which were well-nigh absolute. It was the peace powers which Roosevelt extended.

proach to the problem of adapting the Constitution to the needs of the Twentieth Century. Rendered into the idiom of American constitutional law, this means that *the National Government is entitled to employ any and all of its powers to forward any and all of the objectives of good government.* This fundamental point being established, however, the principal doctrines of American constitutional theory . . . have become largely otiose and superfluous. . . . The Court appears at the present moment to be bent upon minimizing its own rôle in favor of the political forces of the country and such wisdom, or unwisdom, as these can muster to the task. . . . So we emerge more and more upon a scene dominated by the political process and political forces—or more concretely—by electoral majorities, however contrived, however led; a scene in which either we save ourselves through said electoral process, in which as citizens and voters we all participate, or we go unsaved.[15]

This sounds like majority rule on the English model, with a strong Executive who is finally responsible only to the voters. Yet President Truman's troubles with Congress in 1949 suggest that the American Government has not yet become so simple.

We have traced the failure of many efforts to stem the double concentration of power, first within Washington, and second within the presidential office: the failure of states' rights, the failure of strict constitutional construction, the failure of Congressional government, the failure of senatorial oligarchies, and the failure of the Speaker of the House. Many Americans applauded each of the efforts; but history was on the other side—history in the form of big business, big finance, big wars, big depressions, and Manifest Destiny (which is a polite phrase for a big head). Until the New Deal, one formal defense remained: the Supreme Court. In 1937 even the Court half-abdicated; yet nothing fearful happened. Twelve years later, although neither federalism nor the separation of powers nor the once-magic "due process" could prevent government from making rules to guide much of the economy, an embattled minority in Congress could still prevent the President from imposing his majority plans.

How was this done, when every constitutional barrier had been weakened? Only by the unwritten barrier, the party system, which the Fathers feared as the enemy of balanced powers, but which has outlived all their balances and is the last refuge of federal compromise. For the parties are still true federations, with the maximum of home rule. Eastern Democrats must still move more conservatively than they like if they want to win national elections with the help of Southern votes. Eastern Republicans must still pretend a liberalism which they may not practice if they want to win with the help of Northwestern votes. The party ties are so weak that whole blocs will join the Opposition whenever they feel themselves badly treated. Sometimes they do this publicly; but just as often (and just as effectively) they do it in the Congressional committees. Yet when the nation knows it is in danger they stop obstructing and give strength to the President. This is indeed a flexible system, suitable to a very large nation whose people want their government vigorous when necessary but weak when possible. The American tends always to remember that

> The strongest poison ever known
> Came from Caesar's laurel crown.

XXXV

The Parties and the Union

Duration Grover Cleveland's first term in the White House, James Bryce published his remarkable book, *The American Commonwealth*. Surveying the party system from the English point of view, and with quiet surprise, he made the classic statement of the difference between the Republicans and the Democrats.

> What are their principles [he wrote], their distinctive tenets, their tendencies? Which of them is for free trade, for civil-service reform, for a spirited foreign policy . . . for changes in the currency, for any other of the twenty issues which one hears discussed in the country as seriously involving its welfare? This is what a European is always asking of intelligent Republicans and intelligent Democrats. He is always asking because he never gets an answer. The replies leave him in deeper perplexity. After some months the truth begins to dawn on him. Neither party has anything definite to say on these issues; neither party has any principles, any distinctive tenets. Both have traditions. Both claim to have tendencies. Both have certainly war cries, organizations, interests, enlisted in their support. But those interests are in the main the interests of getting or keeping the patronage of the government. Tenets and policies, points of political doctrine and points of political practice, have all but vanished. They have not been thrown away but have been stripped away by Time and the progress of events, fulfilling some policies, blotting out others. All has been lost, except office or the hope of it.[1]

This is a true description of the parties as they were, and as they still are; but Bryce's explanation of how they came to be that way is misleading. He assumes that if the American parties were healthy they would resemble the parties of Great Britain. They would have "principles" and "tenets," and would thus be forced to take sides on all "the twenty issues that one hears discussed." And he assumes that "Time and the progress of events" have deprived the parties of their principles, leaving them with nothing but "office or the hope of it." But this is too short a view; Lord Bryce was confused by the brief history of the Republican Party, which possessed principles in 1856 and none in 1886. He thought this

688

was a sign of failure and decay; but in fact it was a sign of health: 1856 had been the exception and the danger; 1886 was the reassuring norm.

The purpose—the important and healthy purpose—of an American party is to be exactly what Lord Bryce describes, and by implication deplores. The party is intended to be an organization for "getting or keeping the patronage of government." Instead of seeking "principles," or "distinctive tenets," which can only divide a federal union, the party is intended to seek bargains between the regions, the classes, and the other interest groups. It is intended to bring men and women of all beliefs, occupations, sections, racial backgrounds, into a combination for the pursuit of power. The combination is too various to possess firm convictions. The members may have nothing in common except a desire for office. Unless driven by a forceful President they tend to do as little as possible. They tend to provide some small favor for each noisy group, and to call that a policy. They tend to ignore any issue that rouses deep passion. And by so doing they strengthen the Union.

The decisive American experience—the warning against politics based on principles—took place between 1850 and 1860. A subtle and healing compromise had been effected in 1850; yet year by year, whether through fate or through human folly, it slowly disintegrated. The best men watched in anguish but could not halt the ruin. In the name of principles and distinctive tenets the Whig Party was ground to bits. A new party was born which met Lord Bryce's requirements. The Republicans knew exactly where they stood on the major issue and would not give an inch. Finally, the same "principles" broke the Democratic Party, and the Union of 1789 perished.

The lesson which America learned was useful: in a large federal nation, when a problem is passionately felt, and is discussed in terms of morals, each party may divide within itself, against itself. And if the parties divide, the nation may divide; for the parties, with their enjoyable pursuit of power, are a unifying influence. Wise men, therefore, may seek to dodge such problems as long as possible. And the easiest way to dodge them is for both parties to take both sides. This is normal American practice, whether the issue turns section against section, like "cheap money"; or town against country, like Prohibition; or class against class like the use of injunctions in labor disputes. It is a sign of health when the Democrats choose a "sound-money" candidate for the presidency and a "cheap-money" platform, as they did in 1868; or when they choose a "wet" Eastern candidate for the presidency and a "dry" Western candidate for the vice-presidency, as they did in 1924. It is a sign of health when the Republicans choose a "sound-money" platform but cheerfully repudiate it throughout the "cheap-money" states, as they did in 1868.

A federal nation is safe so long as the parties are undogmatic and contain members with many contradictory views. But when the people begin to divide according to reason, with all the voters in one party who believe one way, the federal structure is strained. We saw this in 1896, during the last great fight for "free silver." To be sure, there remained some "gold Democrats" and some "silver Republicans" in 1896; yet the campaign produced the sharpest alignment on principle since the Civil War. And the fierce sectional passions racked the nation. Luckily, the silver issue soon settled itself, and removed itself from politics, so the parties could relapse into their saving illogicality.*

The faults of such irrational parties are obvious. Brains and energy are lavished, not on the search for truth, but on the search for bargains, for concessions which will soothe well-organized minorities, for excuses to justify delay and denial. Unofficially, and in spite of any constitution, successful federal politics will tend to follow Calhoun's rule of concurrent majorities. Every interest which is strong enough to make trouble must usually be satisfied before anything can be done. This means great caution in attempting new policies, so that a whole ungainly continent may keep in step. Obstruction, evasion, well-nigh intolerable slowness—these are the costs of America's federal union. And the endless bartering of minor favors which we saw at its silliest in President Arthur's Congress is also part of the price. And so is the absence of a clear purpose whenever the President is weak or self-effacing, since the sum of sectional and class interests is not equal to the national interest, and the exchange of favors between blocs or pressure groups does not make a policy.

Yet no matter how high one puts the price of federal union, it is small compared to the price which other continents have paid for disunion, and for the little national states in which parties of principle can live (or more often die) for their clearly defined causes. And the price is small compared to what America paid for her own years of disunion. The United States, of course, may some day attain such uniformity (or have it thrust upon her) that she will abandon her federal structure; but until that happens she will be governed by concurrent majorities, by vetoes and filibusters, by parties which take both sides of every dangerous

---

* Vice-President Garner said in 1938: "This talk about dividing the country into two political camps—one progressive and the other conservative—is all so much stuff. . . . Each of the two parties is in a sense a coalition. Any party to serve the country must be a party of all sorts of views." To be sure, the people who talk most about dividing the country into logical parties—"one progressive and one conservative"—would regard Mr. Garner's distaste for their ideas as an endorsement. Yet few men have seen so much of American politics. When he retired in 1941, at the end of his second term as Vice-President, he had served at Washington, in elective office, for one quarter of the entire life of the Republic. He reviewed his length of service vividly when he said: "The cost of government the year I went to Washington was $486,439,407. Any appropriation item that small now is merely interim." (Cp. *Garner of Texas,* by Bascom Timmons, pp. 236 and 288.)

question, which are held together by the amusements and rewards of office-seeking, and which can only win an election by bringing many incompatible groups to accept a token triumph in the name of unity, instead of demanding their full "rights" at the cost of a fight.

The world today might do worse than study the curious methods by which such assuagements are effected.

THE END

THE CONSTITUTION

NOTES

BIBLIOGRAPHY

ACKNOWLEDGMENTS

INDEX

The Constitution

PREAMBLE

WE THE PEOPLE of the United States, in order to form a more perfect union, establish justice, insure domestic tranquillity, provide for the common defense, promote the general welfare, and secure the blessings of liberty to ourselves and our posterity, do ordain and establish this Constitution for the United States of America.

Article I

Legislative Department

SECTION 1. CONGRESS IN GENERAL

All legislative powers herein granted shall be vested in a Congress of the United States, which shall consist of a Senate and House of Representatives.

SECTION 2.

THE HOUSE OF REPRESENTATIVES

a. Election and term of members. The House of Representatives shall be composed of members chosen every second year by the people of the several States, and the electors in each State shall have the qualifications requisite for electors of the most numerous branch of the State Legislature.

b. Qualifications of members. No person shall be a Representative who shall not have attained to the age of twenty-five years, and been seven years a citizen of the United States, and who shall not, when elected, be an inhabitant of that State in which he shall be chosen.

c. Apportionment of representatives and of direct taxes. Representatives and direct taxes shall be apportioned among the several States which may be included within this Union, according to

their respective numbers, which shall be determined by adding to the whole number of free persons, including those bound to service for a term of years, and excluding Indians not taxed, three fifths of all other persons.[1] The actual enumeration shall be made within three years after the first meeting of the Congress of the United States, and within every subsequent term of ten years, in such manner as they shall by law direct. The number of Representatives shall not exceed one for every thirty thousand, but each state shall have at least one representative; and until such enumeration shall be made, the state of New Hampshire shall be entitled to choose three; Massachusetts, eight; Rhode Island and Providence Plantations, one; Connecticut, five; New York, six; New Jersey, four; Pennsylvania, eight; Delaware, one; Maryland, six; Virginia, ten; North Carolina, five; South Carolina, five; and Georgia, three.

d. Filling vacancies. When vacancies happen in the representation from any State, the Executive authority thereof shall issue writs of election to fill such vacancies.

e. Officers; impeachment. The House of Representatives shall choose their Speaker and other officers; and shall have the sole power of impeachment.

SECTION 3. THE SENATE

a. Number and election of members. The Senate of the United States shall be composed of two Senators from each state, chosen by the legislature thereof,[2] for six years, and each Senator shall have one vote.

b. Classification. Immediately after they shall be assembled in consequence

[1]Changed by Amendment XIV.

[2]This method of election has been changed by Amendment XVII.

of the first election, they shall be divided as equally as may be into three classes. The seats of the Senators of the first class shall be vacated at the expiration of the second year, of the second class at the expiration of the fourth year, and of the third class at the expiration of the sixth year, so that one third may be chosen every second year; and if vacancies happen by resignation, or otherwise, during the recess of the legislature of any State, the Executive thereof may make temporary appointments until the next meeting of the Legislature, which shall then fill such vacancies.

c. Qualifications of members. No person shall be a Senator who shall not have attained to the age of thirty years, and been nine years a citizen of the United States, and who shall not, when elected, be an inhabitant of that State for which he shall be chosen.

d. President of Senate. The Vice President of the United States shall be President of the Senate, but shall have no vote, unless they be equally divided.

e. Other officers. The Senate shall choose their own officers, and also a President *pro tempore,* in the absence of the Vice President, or when he shall exercise the office of President of the United States.

f. Trial of impeachment. The Senate shall have the sole power to try all impeachments. When sitting for that purpose, they shall be on oath or affirmation. When the President of the United States is tried, the Chief Justice shall preside; and no person shall be convicted without the concurrence of two thirds of the members present.

g. Judgment in case of conviction. Judgment in cases of impeachment shall not extend further than to removal from office, and disqualification to hold and enjoy any office of honor, trust or profit under the United States; but the party convicted shall nevertheless be liable and subject to indictment, trial, judgment and punishment, according to law.

SECTION 4. HOW SENATORS AND REPRESENTATIVES SHALL BE CHOSEN AND WHEN THEY ARE TO MEET

a. Method of holding elections. The times, places and manner of holding elections for Senators and Representa-

tives shall be prescribed in each State by the Legislature thereof; but the Congress may at any time by law make or alter such regulations, except as to the places of choosing Senators.

b. Meeting of Congress. The Congress shall assemble at least once in every year, and such meeting shall be on the first Monday in December, unless they shall by law appoint a different day.[3]

SECTION 5. RULES OF PROCEDURE

a. Organization. Each house shall be the judge of the elections, returns and qualifications of its own members, and a majority of each shall constitute a quorum to do business; but a smaller number may adjourn from day to day, and may be authorized to compel the attendance of absent members, in such manner, and under such penalties, as each house may provide.

b. Rules of proceedings. Each house may determine the rules of its proceedings, punish its members for disorderly behavior, and, with the concurrence of two thirds, expel a member.

c. Journal. Each house shall keep a journal of its proceedings, and from time to time publish the same, excepting such parts as may in their judgment require secrecy; and the yeas and nays of the members of either house on any question shall, at the desire of one fifth of those present, be entered on the journal.

d. Adjournment. Neither house, during the session of Congress, shall, without the consent of the other, adjourn for more than three days, nor to any other place than that in which the two houses shall be sitting.

SECTION 6. COMPENSATION, PRIVILEGES, AND RESTRICTIONS

a. Pay and privileges of members. The Senators and Representatives shall receive a compensation for their services, to be ascertained by law, and paid out of the Treasury of the United States. They shall in all cases except treason, felony and breach of the peace, be privileged from arrest during their attendance at the session of their respective houses, and in going to and returning

[3]The time of meeting was changed by Amendment XX.

from the same; and for any speech or debate in either house, they shall not be questioned in any other place.

b. Holding other offices prohibited. No Senator or Representative shall, during the time for which he was elected, be appointed to any civil office under the authority of the United States which shall have been created, or the emoluments whereof shall have been increased during such time; and no person holding any office under the United States shall be a member of either house during his continuance in office.

SECTION 7. MODE OF PASSING LAWS

a. Revenue bills. All bills for raising revenue shall originate in the House of Representatives; but the Senate may propose or concur with amendments as on other bills.

b. How bills become laws. Every bill which shall have passed the House of Representatives and the Senate shall, before it become a law, be presented to the President of the United States; if he approve he shall sign it, but if not he shall return it, with his objections to that house in which it shall have originated, who shall enter the objections at large on their journal, and proceed to reconsider it. If after such reconsideration two thirds of that house shall agree to pass the bill, it shall be sent, together with the objections, to the other house, by which it shall likewise be reconsidered, and if approved by two thirds of that house, it shall become a law. But in all such cases the votes of both houses shall be determined by yeas and nays, and the names of the persons voting for and against the bill shall be entered on the journal of each house respectively. If any bill shall not be returned by the President within ten days (Sundays excepted) after it shall have been presented to him, the same shall be a law, in like manner as if he had signed it, unless the Congress by their adjournment prevent its return, in which case it shall not be a law.

c. Approval or disapproval by the President. Every order, resolution, or vote to which the concurrence of the Senate and House of Representatives may be necessary (except on a question of adjournment) shall be presented to the President of the United States; and before the same shall take effect, shall be approved by him, or being disapproved by him, shall be repassed by two thirds of the Senate and House of Representatives, according to the rules and limitations prescribed in the case of a bill.

SECTION 8. POWERS GRANTED TO CONGRESS

The Congress shall have power

a. To lay and collect taxes, duties, imposts, and excises, to pay the debts and provide for the common defence and general welfare of the United States; but all duties, imposts and excises shall be uniform throughout the United States;

b. To borrow money on the credit of the United States;

c. To regulate commerce with foreign nations, and among the several States, and with the Indian tribes;

d. To establish an uniform rule of naturalization, and uniform laws on the subject of bankruptcies throughout the United States;

e. To coin money, regulate the value thereof, and of foreign coin, and fix the standard of weights and measures;

f. To provide for the punishment of counterfeiting the securities and current coin of the United States;

g. To establish post offices and post roads;

h. To promote the progress of science and useful arts by securing for limited times to authors and inventors the exclusive right to their respective writings and discoveries;

i. To constitute tribunals inferior to the Supreme Court;

j. To define and punish piracies and felonies committed on the high seas and offences against the law of nations;

k. To declare war, grant letters of marque and reprisal, and make rules concerning captures on land and water;

l. To raise and support armies, but no appropriation of money to that use shall be for a longer term than two years;

m. To provide and maintain a navy;

n. To make rules for the government and regulation of the land and naval forces;

o. To provide for calling forth the militia to execute the laws of the Union, suppress insurrections, and repel invasions;

p. To provide for organizing, arming and disciplining the militia, and for governing such part of them as may be employed in the service of the United States, reserving to the States respectively the appointment of the officers, and the authority of training the militia according to the discipline prescribed by Congress;

q. To exercise exclusive legislation in all cases whatsoever, over such district (not exceeding ten miles square) as may, by cession of particular States, and the acceptance of Congress, become the seat of the government of the United States, and to exercise like authority over all places purchased by the consent of the legislature of the State, in which the same shall be, for the erection of forts, magazines, arsenals, dock-yards, and other needful buildings;—and

r. To make all laws which shall be necessary and proper for carrying into execution the foregoing powers, and all other powers vested by this Constitution in the government of the United States, or in any department or officer thereof.

SECTION 9. POWERS DENIED TO THE FEDERAL GOVERNMENT

a. The migration or importation of such persons as any of the States now existing shall think proper to admit, shall not be prohibited by the Congress prior to the year one thousand eight hundred and eight, but a tax or duty may be imposed on such importation, not exceeding ten dollars for each person.

b. The privilege of the writ of habeas corpus shall not be suspended, unless when in cases of rebellion or invasion the public safety may require it.

c. No bill of attainder or ex post facto law shall be passed.

d. No capitation, or other direct, tax shall be laid, unless in proportion to the census or enumeration herein before directed to be taken.

e. No tax or duty shall be laid on articles exported from any State.

f. No preference shall be given by any regulation of commerce or revenue to the ports of one State over those of another: nor shall vessels bound to, or from, one State be obliged to enter, clear, or pay duties in another.

g. No money shall be drawn from the Treasury, but in consequence of appropriations made by law; and a regular statement and account of the receipts and expenditures of all public money shall be published from time to time.

h. No title of nobility shall be granted by the United States: and no person holding any office of profit or trust under them, shall, without the consent of the Congress, accept of any present, emolument, office, or title, of any kind whatever, from any king, prince, or foreign state.

SECTION 10. POWERS DENIED TO THE STATES

a. No State shall enter into any treaty, alliance, or confederation; grant letters of marque and reprisal; coin money; emit bills of credit; make any thing but gold and silver coin a tender in payment of debts; pass any bill of attainder; ex post facto law, or law impairing the obligation of contracts, or grant any title of nobility.

b. No State shall, without the consent of the Congress, lay any imposts or duties on imports or exports, except what may be absolutely necessary for executing its inspection laws; and the net produce of all duties and imposts, laid by any State on imports or exports, shall be for the use of the treasury of the United States; and all such laws shall be subject to the revision and control of the Congress.

c. No State shall, without the consent of Congress, lay any duty of tonnage, keep troops, or ships of war in time of peace, enter into any agreement or compact with another State, or with a foreign power, or engage in war, unless actually invaded, or in such imminent danger as will not admit of delay.

Article II

Executive Department

SECTION 1.
PRESIDENT AND VICE PRESIDENT

a. Term of office. The executive power shall be vested in a President of the United States of America. He shall hold his office during the term of four years, and together with the Vice

President, chosen for the same term, be elected as follows:

b. Electors. Each State shall appoint, in such manner as the legislature thereof may direct, a number of electors, equal to the whole number of Senators and Representatives to which the State may be entitled in the Congress; but no Senator or Representative, or person holding an office of trust or profit under the United States, shall be appointed an elector.

Method of electing President and Vice President. The electors shall meet in their respective States, and vote by ballot for two persons, of whom one at least shall not be an inhabitant of the same State with themselves. And they shall make a list of all the persons voted for, and of the number of votes for each; which list they shall sign and certify, and transmit sealed to the seat of government of the United States, directed to the President of the Senate. The President of the Senate shall, in the presence of the Senate and House of Representatives, open all the certificates, and the votes shall then be counted. The person having the greatest number of votes shall be the President, if such number be a majority of the whole number of electors appointed; and if there be more than one who have such majority, and have an equal number of votes, then the House of Representatives shall immediately choose by ballot one of them for President; and if no person have a majority, then from the five highest on the list the said house shall in like manner choose the President. But in choosing the President the votes shall be taken by States, the representation from each State having one vote; a quorum for this purpose shall consist of a member or members from two thirds of the States, and a majority of all the States shall be necessary to a choice. In every case, after the choice of the President, the person having the greatest number of votes of the electors shall be the Vice President. But if there should remain two or more who have equal votes, the Senate shall choose from them by ballot the Vice President.[4]

c. Time of elections. The Congress may determine the time of choosing the electors, and the day on which they shall give their votes; which day shall

[4]Changed by Amendment XII.

be the same throughout the United States.

d. Qualifications of the President. No person except a natural born citizen, or a citizen of the United States, at the time of the adoption of this Constitution, shall be eligible to the office of President; neither shall any person be eligible to that office who shall not have attained to the age of thirty-five years, and been fourteen years a resident within the United States.

e. Vacancy. In case of the removal of the President from office or of his death, resignation, or inability to discharge the powers and duties of the said office, the same shall devolve on the Vice President, and the Congress may by law provide for the case of removal, death, resignation, or inability, both of the President and Vice President, declaring what officer shall then act as President, and such officer shall act accordingly, until the disability be removed, or a President shall be elected.

f. The President's salary. The President shall, at stated times, receive for his services, a compensation, which shall neither be increased nor diminished during the period for which he shall have been elected, and he shall not receive within that period any other emolument from the United States, or any of them.

g. Oath of Office. Before he enter on the execution of his office, he shall take the following oath or affirmation:—"I do solemnly swear (or affirm) that I will faithfully execute the office of President of the United States, and will to the best of my ability, preserve, protect and defend the Constitution of the United States."

SECTION 2. POWERS OF THE PRESIDENT

a. Military powers; reprieves and pardons. The President shall be commander in chief of the army and navy of the United States, and of the militia of the several States, when called into the actual service of the United States; he may require the opinion, in writing, of the principal officer in each of the executive departments, upon any subject relating to the duties of their respective offices, and he shall have power to grant reprieves and pardons for offences against the United States, except in cases of impeachment.

b. Treaties; appointments. He shall have power, by and with the advice and consent of the Senate, to make treaties, provided two thirds of the Senators present concur; and he shall nominate, and by and with the advice and consent of the Senate, shall appoint ambassadors, other public ministers and consuls, judges of the Supreme Court, and all other officers of the United States, whose appointments are not herein otherwise provided for, and which shall be established by law; but the Congress may by law vest the appointment of such inferior officers as they think proper, in the President alone, in the courts of law, or in the heads of the departments.

c. Filling vacancies. The President shall have power to fill up all vacancies that may happen during the recess of the Senate, by granting commissions which shall expire at the end of their next session.

SECTION 3. DUTIES OF THE PRESIDENT

He shall from time to time give to the Congress information of the state of the Union, and recommend to their consideration such measures as he shall judge necessary and expedient; he may, on extraordinary occasions, convene both houses, or either of them, and in case of disagreement between them with respect to the time of adjournment, he may adjourn them to such time as he shall think proper; he shall receive ambassadors and other public ministers; he shall take care that the laws be faithfully executed, and shall commission all the officers of the United States.

SECTION 4. IMPEACHMENT

The President, Vice President and all civil officers of the United States shall be removed from office on impeachment for, and conviction of, treason, bribery, or other high crimes and misdemeanors.

Article III

Judicial Department

SECTION 1. THE FEDERAL COURTS

The judicial power of the United States shall be vested in one Supreme Court, and in such inferior courts as the

Congress may from time to time ordain and establish. The judges, both of the Supreme and inferior courts, shall hold their offices during good behavior, and shall, at stated times, receive for their services, a compensation, which shall not be diminished during their continuance in office.

SECTION 2. JURISDICTION OF THE FEDERAL COURTS

a. Federal courts in general. The judicial power shall extend to all cases, in law and equity, arising under this Constitution, the laws of the United States, and treaties made or which shall be made, under their authority;—to all cases affecting ambassadors, other public ministers and consuls;—to all cases of admiralty jurisdiction;—to controversies to which the United States shall be a party;—to controversies between two or more States;—between a State and citizens of another State;—between citizens of different States;—between citizens of the same State claiming lands under grants of different States, and between a State, or the citizens thereof, and foreign states, citizens or subjects.[5]

b. Supreme Court. In all cases affecting ambassadors, other public ministers and consuls, and those in which a State shall be a party, the Supreme Court shall have original jurisdiction. In all the other cases before mentioned, the Supreme Court shall have appellate jurisdiction, both as to law and fact, with such exceptions, and under such regulations as the Congress shall make.

c. Rules respecting trials. The trial of all crimes, except in cases of impeachment, shall be by jury; and such trial shall be held in the State where the said crimes shall have been committed; but when not committed within any State, the trial shall be at such place or places as the Congress may by law have directed.

SECTION 3. TREASON

a. Definition of treason. Treason against the United States shall consist only in levying war against them, or in adhering to their enemies, giving them aid and comfort. No person shall be convicted of treason unless on the testi-

[5]This clause has been modified by Amendment XI.

mony of two witnesses to the same overt act, or on confession in open court.

b. Punishment of treason. The Congress shall have power to declare the punishment of treason, but no attainder of treason shall work corruption of blood, or forfeiture except during the life of the person attained.

Article IV

The States and the Federal Government

SECTION 1. STATE RECORDS

Full faith and credit shall be given in each State to the public acts, records, and judicial proceedings of every other State. And the Congress may by general laws prescribe the manner in which such acts, records, and proceedings shall be proved, and the effect thereof.

SECTION 2. PRIVILEGES AND IMMUNITIES OF CITIZENS

a. Privileges. The citizens of each State shall be entitled to all privileges and immunities of citizens in the several States.

b. Extradition. A person charged in any State with treason, felony, or other crime, who shall flee from justice, and be found in another State, shall, on demand of the executive authority of the State from which he fled, be delivered up, to be removed to the State having jurisdiction of the crime.

c. Fugitive workers. No person held to service or labor in one State, under the laws thereof, escaping into another shall in consequence of any law or regulation therein, be discharged from such service or labor, but shall be delivered upon claim of the party to whom such service or labor may be due.

SECTION 3. NEW STATES AND TERRITORIES

a. Admission of new States. New States may be admitted by the Congress into this Union; but no new State shall be formed or erected within the jurisdiction of any other State; nor any State be formed by the junction of two or more States, or parts of States, without the consent of the legislatures of the States concerned, as well as of the Congress.

b. Power of Congress over territory and property. The Congress shall have power to dispose of and make all needful rules and regulations respecting the territory or other property belonging to the United States; and nothing in this Constitution shall be so construed as to prejudice any claims of the United States, or of any particular State.

SECTION 4. GUARANTEES TO THE STATES

The United States shall guarantee to every State in this Union a republican form of government, and shall protect each of them against invasion; and on application of the legislature, or of the executive (when the legislature cannot be convened) against domestic violence.

Article V

Method of Amendment

The Congress, whenever two thirds of both houses shall deem it necessary, shall propose amendments to this Constitution, or, on the application of the legislatures of two thirds of the several States, shall call a convention for proposing amendments, which, in either case shall be valid to all intents and purposes, as part of this Constitution, when ratified by the legislatures of three fourths of the several States, or by conventions in three fourths thereof, as the one or the other mode of ratification may be proposed by the Congress; provided that no amendments which may be made prior to the year one thousand eight hundred and eight shall in any manner affect the first and fourth clauses in the ninth section of the first article; and that no State, without its consent, shall be deprived of its equal suffrage in the Senate.

Article VI

General Provisions

a. Public debt. All debts contracted and engagements entered into, before the adoption of this Constitution, shall be as valid against the United States under this Constitution, as under the Confederation.

b. Supremacy of the Constitution. This Constitution, and the laws of the United States which shall be made in pursuance thereof; and all treaties made, or which shall be made, under the authority of the United States, shall be the supreme law of the land; and the judges in every State shall be bound thereby, anything in the Constitution or laws of any State to the contrary notwithstanding.

c. Oath of office; no religious test. The Senators and Representatives before mentioned, and the members of the several State legislatures, and all executive and judicial officers, both of the United States and of the several States, shall be bound by oath or affirmation, to support this Constitution; but no religious test shall ever be required as a qualification to any office or public trust under the United States.

Article VII

Ratification of the Constitution

The ratification of the conventions of nine States shall be sufficient for the establishment of this Constitution between the States so ratifying the same.

AMENDMENTS TO THE CONSTITUTION

Article I (adopted 1791)

Freedom of Religion, Speech, and the Press; Right of Assembly

Congress shall make no law respecting an establishment of religion, or prohibiting the free exercise thereof; or abridging the freedom of speech, or of the press; or the right of the people peaceably to assemble, and to petition the government for a redress of grievances.

Article II (adopted 1791)

Right to Keep and Bear Arms

A well-regulated militia, being necessary to the security of a free State, the right of the people to keep and bear arms, shall not be infringed.

Article III (adopted 1791)

Quartering of Troops

No soldier shall, in time of peace be quartered in any house, without the consent of the owner, nor in time of war, but in a manner to be prescribed by law.

Article IV (adopted 1791)

Limiting the Right of Search

The right of the people to be secure in their persons, houses, papers, and effects, against unreasonable searches and seizures, shall not be violated, and no warrants shall issue but upon probable cause, supported by oath or affirmation, and particularly describing the place to be searched, and the persons or things to be seized.

Article V (adopted 1791)

Guaranty of Trial by Jury; Private Property to be Respected

No person shall be held to answer for a capital, or otherwise infamous crime, unless on a presentment or indictment of a grand jury, except in cases arising in the land or naval forces, or in the militia, when in actual service in time of war and public danger; nor shall any person be subject for the same offense to be twice put in jeopardy of life or limb; nor shall be compelled in any criminal case to be a witness against himself, nor be deprived of life, liberty, or property, without due process of law; nor shall private property be taken for public use without just compensation.

Article VI (adopted 1791)

Rights of Accused Persons

In all criminal prosecutions, the accused shall enjoy the right to a speedy and public trial, by an impartial jury of the State and district wherein the crime shall have been committed, which districts shall have been previously ascertained by law, and to be informed of the nature and cause of the accusation; to be confronted with the witnesses against him; to have compulsory process for obtaining witnesses in his favor, and to have the assistance of counsel for his defense.

Article VII (adopted 1791)

Rules of the Common Law

In suits at common law, where the value in controversy shall exceed twenty dollars, the right of trial by jury shall be preserved, and no fact tried by a jury, shall be otherwise re-examined in any court of the United States than according to the rules of common law.

Article VIII (adopted 1791)

Excessive Bail, Fines, and Punishment Prohibited

Excessive bail shall not be required, nor excessive fines imposed, nor cruel and unusual punishments inflicted.

Article IX (adopted 1791)

Rights Retained by the People

The enumeration in the Constitution of certain rights, shall not be construed to deny or disparage others retained by the people.

Article X (adopted 1791)

Powers reserved to States and People

The powers not delegated to the United States by the Constitution, nor prohibited by it to the States, are reserved to the States respectively, or to the people.

Article XI (adopted 1798)

Limiting the Powers of Federal Courts

The judicial power of the United States shall not be construed to extend to any suit in law or equity, commenced or prosecuted against one of the United States by citizens of another State, or by citizens or subjects of any foreign state.

Article XII (adopted 1804)

Election of President and Vice President

The electors shall meet in their respective States, and vote by ballot for President and Vice President, one of whom, at least, shall not be an inhabitant of the same State with themselves; they shall name in their ballots the person voted for as President, and in distinct ballots the person voted for as Vice President, and they shall make distinct lists of all persons voted for as President, and of all persons voted for as Vice President, and of the number of votes for each, which lists they shall sign and certify, and transmit sealed to the seat of government of the United States, directed to the President of the Senate;— the President of the Senate shall, in the presence of the Senate and House of Representatives, open all the certificates and the votes shall then be counted;— the person having the greatest number of votes for President shall be the President, if such number be a majority of the whole number of electors appointed; and if no person have such majority, then from the persons having the highest numbers not exceeding three on the list of those voted for as President, the House of Representatives shall choose immediately, by ballot, the President. But in choosing the President, the votes shall be taken by States, the representation from each State having one vote; a quorum for this purpose shall consist of a member or members from two thirds of the States, and a majority of all the States shall be necessary to a choice. And if the House of Representatives shall not choose a President whenever the right of choice shall devolve upon them, before the fourth day of March next following, then the Vice President shall act as President, as in the case of the death or other constitutional disability of the President.—The person having the greatest number of votes as Vice President, shall be the Vice President, if such number be a majority of the whole number of electors appointed, and if no person have a majority, then from the two highest numbers on the list, the Senate shall choose the Vice President; a quorum for the purpose shall consist of two thirds of the whole number of Senators, and a majority of the whole number shall be necessary to a choice. But no person constitutionally ineligible to the office of President shall be eligible to that of Vice President of the United States.

Article XIII (adopted 1865)

Slavery Abolished

SECTION 1. ABOLITION OF SLAVERY

Neither slavery nor involuntary servitude, except as a punishment for crime whereof the party shall have been duly convicted, shall exist within the United States, or any place subject to their jurisdiction.

SECTION 2. ENFORCEMENT

Congress shall have power to enforce this article by appropriate legislation.

Article XIV (adopted 1868)

Citizenship Defined

SECTION 1. DEFINITION OF
CITIZENSHIP

All persons born or naturalized in the United States, and subject to the jurisdiction thereof, are citizens of the United States and of the State wherein they reside. No State shall make or enforce any law which shall abridge the privileges or immunities of citizens of the United States; nor shall any State deprive any person of life, liberty, or property, without due process of law; nor deny to any person within its jurisdiction the equal protection of the laws.

SECTION 2. APPORTIONMENT OF
REPRESENTATIVES

Representatives shall be apportioned among the several States according to their respective numbers, counting the whole number of persons in each State, excluding Indians not taxed. But when the right to vote at any election for the choice of electors for President and Vice President of the United States, Representatives in Congress, the executive and judicial officers of a State, or the members of the legislature thereof, is denied to any of the male inhabitants of such State, being twenty-one years of age, and citizens of the United States, or in any way abridged, except for participation in rebellion, or other crime, the basis of representation therein shall be reduced in the proportion which the number of such male citizens shall bear to the whole number of male citizens twenty-one years of age in such State.

SECTION 3. DISABILITY RESULTING
FROM INSURRECTION

No person shall be a Senator or Representative in Congress, or Elector of President and Vice President, or hold any office, civil or military, under the United States, or under any State, who, having previously taken an oath, as a member of Congress, or as an officer of the United States, or as a member of any State legislature, or as an executive or judicial officer of any State to support the Constitution of the United States, shall have engaged in insurrection or rebellion against the same, or given aid or comfort to the enemies thereof. But Congress may by vote of two thirds of each house, remove such disability.

SECTION 4. PUBLIC DEBT OF THE
UNITED STATES VALID; CONFED-
ERATE DEBT VOID

The validity of the Public debt of the United States, authorized by law, including debts incurred for payment of pensions and bounties for services in suppressing insurrection or rebellion, shall not be questioned. But neither the United States nor any State shall assume or pay any debt or obligation incurred in aid of insurrection or rebellion against the United States, or any claim for the loss or emancipation of any slave; but all such debts, obligations, and claims shall be held illegal and void.

SECTION 5. ENFORCEMENT

The Congress shall have power to enforce by appropriate legislation the provisions of this article.

Article XV (adopted 1870)

Right of Suffrage

SECTION 1. THE SUFFRAGE

The right of citizens of the United States to vote shall not be denied or abridged by the United States or any State on account of race, color, or previous condition of servitude.

SECTION 2. ENFORCEMENT

The Congress shall have power to enforce this article by appropriate legislation.

Article XVI (adopted 1913)

Income Tax

The Congress shall have power to lay and collect taxes on incomes, from whatever source derived, without apportionment among the several States, and without regard to any census or enumeration.

Article XVII (adopted 1913)

Direct Election of Senators

a. Election by the people. The Senate of the United States shall be composed of two Senators from each State, elected by the people thereof, for six years; and each Senator shall have one vote. The electors in each State shall have the qualification requisite for electors of the most numerous branch of the State legislatures.

b. Vacancies. When vacancies happen in the representation of any State in the Senate, the executive authority of such State shall issue writs of election to fill such vacancies: *Provided* that the legislature of any State may empower the executive thereof to make temporary appointments until the people fill the vacancies by election as the legislature may direct.

c. Not retroactive. This amendment shall not be so construed as to affect the election or term of any Senator chosen before it becomes valid as part of the Constitution.

Article XVIII (adopted 1919)

National Prohibition

SECTION 1. PROHIBITION OF INTOXICATING LIQUORS

After one year from the ratification of this article the manufacture, sale, or transportation of intoxicating liquors within, the importation thereof into, or the exportation thereof from the United States and all territory subject to the jurisdiction thereof for beverage purposes is hereby prohibited.

SECTION 2. ENFORCEMENT

The Congress and the several States shall have concurrent power to enforce this article by appropriate legislation.

SECTION 3. LIMITED TIME FOR RATIFICATION

This article shall be inoperative unless it shall have been ratified as an amendment to the Constitution by the legislatures of the several States, as provided by the Constitution, within seven years from the date of the submission hereof to the States by the Congress.

Article XIX (adopted 1920)

Extending the Vote to Women

SECTION 1. WOMAN SUFFRAGE

The right of citizens of the United States to vote shall not be denied or abridged by the United States or by any State on account of sex.

SECTION 2. ENFORCEMENT

The Congress shall have power to enforce this article by appropriate legislation.

Article XX (adopted 1933)

The "Lame Duck" Amendment

SECTION 1. TERMS OF PRESIDENT, VICE PESIDENT, AND CONGRESS

The terms of the President and Vice President shall end at noon on the 20th day of January, and the terms of Senators and Representatives at noon on the 3d day of January, of the years in which such terms would have ended if this article had not been ratified; and the terms of their successors shall then begin.

SECTION 2. SESSIONS OF CONGRESS

The Congress shall assemble at least once in every year, and such meeting shall begin at noon on the 3d day of January, unless they shall by law appoint a different day.

SECTION 3. PRESIDENTIAL SUCCESSION

If, at the time fixed for the beginning of the term of the President, the President elect shall have died, the Vice President elect shall become President. If a President shall not have been chosen before the time fixed for the beginning of his term, or if the President elect shall have failed to qualify, then the Vice President elect shall act as President until a President shall have qualified; and the Congress may by law provide for the case wherein neither a President elect nor a Vice President elect shall have qualified, declaring who shall then act as President, or the manner in which one who is to act shall be selected, and such person shall act accordingly until a President or a Vice President shall have qualified.

SECTION 4. CHOICE OF PRESIDENT BY THE HOUSE

The Congress may by law provide for the case of the death of any of the persons from whom the House of Representatives may choose a President, whenever the right of choice shall have devolved upon them, and for the case of the death of any of the persons from whom the senate may choose a Vice

President whenever the right or choice shall have devolved upon them.

SECTION 5. DATE EFFECTIVE

Sections 1 and 2 shall take effect on the fifteenth day of October following the ratification of this article.

SECTION 6. LIMITED TIME FOR RATIFICATION

This article shall be inoperative unless it shall have been ratified as an amendment to the Constitution by the legislatures of three fourths of the several States within seven years from the date of its submission.

Article XXI (adopted 1933)

Repeal of Prohibition

SECTION 1. REPEAL OF ARTICLE XVIII

The eighteenth article of amendment to the Constitution of the United States is hereby repealed.

SECTION 2. STATES PROTECTED

The transportation or importation into any State, territory or possession of the United States for delivery or use therein of intoxicating liquors in violation of the laws thereof, is hereby prohibited.

SECTION 3. LIMITED TIME FOR RATIFICATION

This article shall be inoperative unless it shall have been ratified as an amendment to the Constitution by conventions in the several States, as provided in the Constitution, within seven years from the date of the submission hereof to the States by the Congress.

Notes

CHAPTER ONE

1. Merrill Jensen, *The Articles of Confederation: An Interpretation of the Social-Constitutional History of the American Revolution, 1774–1781*, p. 11.
2. According to John Adams's notes taken at the time.
3. Andrew C. McLaughlin, *The Foundations of American Constitutionalism*, pp. 124–27. The whole of chapter five in this important book deals with the background for the American doctrine of judicial review.
4. F. S. Oliver, *Alexander Hamilton*, pp. 20–21.
5. Bernard Mayo, *Jefferson Himself*, pp. 50–51.
6. John Dickinson, *Letters from a Farmer in Pennsylvania to the Inhabitants of the British Colonies*.
7. Carl Becker, *The Declaration of Independence*, p. 95.
8. *Ibid.*, pp. 203–07.
9. Kentucky Resolutions.
10. Thomas Dawes, Jr., quoted by McLaughlin, *The Foundations of American Constitutionalism*, p. 77.

CHAPTER TWO

1. F. S. Oliver, *Alexander Hamilton*, p. 40.
2. Merrill Jensen, *The Articles of Confederation*, p. 176.
3. *Ibid.*, p. 243.
4. James Bryce, *The American Commonwealth*, 2d ed., revised, vol. I, p. 639.

CHAPTER THREE

1. Henry Jones Ford, *The Rise and Growth of American Politics*, p. 45. The quotations from the delegates' remarks at the convention are taken from Madison's Journal.
2. *The Federalist*, no. 79: "A power

over a man's subsistence amounts to a power over his will."
3. *Ibid.*, no. 10.
4. Allan Nevins, *The American States During and After the Revolution*, p. 110.
5. Merrill Jensen, *The Articles of Confederation*, pp. 3–4.
6. James Bryce, *The American Commonwealth*, 2d ed., revised, vol. I, p. 25.
7. *Ibid.*, p. 27.
8. Andrew C. McLaughlin, *The Foundations of American Constitutionalism*, p. 162.
9. Charles A. Beard, *The Economic Origins of Jeffersonian Democracy*, p. 105.
10. Henry Adams, *John Randolph*, pp. 33–34.
11. *The Federalist*, no. 6.
12. *Ibid.*, no. 78.
13. Edward S. Corwin, *Constitutional Revolution, Ltd.*, p. 130.

CHAPTER FOUR

1. S. E. Morison, *The Maritime History of Massachusetts*, p. 11.
2. Henry Adams, *History of the United States, 1801–1817*, vol. I, pp. 172–73.
3. S. E. Morison and H. S. Commager, *The Growth of the American Republic*, vol. I, p. 216.
4. William Roscoe Thayer, *The Life and Letters of John Hay*, vol. II, p. 170.
5. Cp. John Sloan Dickey, "Our Treaty Procedure Versus Our Foreign Policies," in *Foreign Affairs*, vol. 25, no. 3, pp. 357–77.
6. Henry Jones Ford, *The Rise and Growth of American Politics*, pp. 79–80.
7. Wilfred E. Binkley, *President and Congress*, p. 35.
8. James Bryce, *The American Commonwealth*, 2d ed., revised, vol. I, p. 160.

9. *Ibid.*, vol. I, p. 154.
10. *Ibid.*, vol. I, pp. 157 and 158.
11. *Hamilton's Works,* vol. VI, p. 201.
12. Henry Adams, *Albert Gallatin,*
    1943 edition, p. 159.

CHAPTER FIVE

1. Wilfred E. Binkley, *American Political Parties,* p. 27.
2. Henry Jones Ford, *The Rise and
   Growth of American Politics,* p.
   126.
3. *Ibid.*
4. Wilfred E. Binkley, *President and
   Congress,* p. 19.
5. Nathan Schachner, *Alexander
   Hamilton,* p. 299.
6. Henry Adams, *History of the
   United States, 1801–1817,* vol. I,
   pp. 113–14.
7. Wilfred E. Binkley, *President and
   Congress,* pp. 78–79.

CHAPTER SIX

1. Cp. manuscript letter of Uriah
   Tracy to Hamilton, quoted in
   Nathan Schachner, *Alexander
   Hamilton,* p. 363.
2. Alexander Hamilton, *The Public
   Conduct and Character of John
   Adams, Esq.*
3. Kentucky Resolutions.

CHAPTER SEVEN

1. W. E. Dodd, *Statesmen of the Old
   South,* p. 19.
2. *Novanglus* papers.
3. Henry Adams, *Albert Gallatin,* pp.
   236–37.
4. *Ibid.*, pp. 238–39.
5. Quoted in R. V. Harlow, *The History of Legislative Methods in the
   Period Before 1825,* p. 175.
6. W. E. Binkley, *President and Congress,* pp. 53–54.
7. Henry Adams, *Albert Gallatin,* pp.
   218–19.
8. *Ibid.*, p. 410.
9. Charles A. Beard, *The Economic
   Origins of Jeffersonian Democracy,*
   p. 467.

CHAPTER EIGHT

1. Henry Adams, *History of the
   United States, 1801–1817,* vol. I,
   pp. 378–79.

2. *Ibid.*, p. 391.
3. *Ibid.*, vol. II, p. 4.
4. *Ibid.*, vol. II, pp. 20–21.
5. *Ibid.*, vol. II, p. 90.
6. *Ibid.*, vol. II, p. 130.
7. Edward S. Corwin, "John Marshall," in *Dictionary of American
   Biography.*
8. *Blodgett* v. *Holden.*
9. A. J. Beveridge, *John Marshall,*
   vol. III, p. 104.
10. Edward S. Corwin, "John Mar-
    shall," in *Dictionary of American
    Biography.*
11. A. J. Beveridge, *John Marshall,* vol.
    III, p. 133.
12. Henry Adams, *History of the
    United States, 1801–1817,* vol. I, p.
    256.
13. *Ibid.*, vol. II, pp. 243–44.
14. *Ibid.*
15. Henry Adams, *John Randolph,* p.
    127.
16. Henry Adams, *Albert Gallatin,* p.
    356.
17. *Ibid.*, p. 356.
18. Henry Adams, *History of the
    United States, 1801–1817,* vol. IV,
    p. 98.
19. Henry Adams, *The Formative
    Years,* vol. I, p. 466.
20. *Ibid.*, vol. II, pp. 490–91.
21. Carl Becker, *The Declaration of
    Independence,* pp. 216–18, xiv–xv.

CHAPTER NINE

1. Quoted in Henry Adams, *Albert
   Gallatin,* pp. 390–91.
2. Henry Adams, *History of the
   United States, 1801–1817,* vol. I, p.
   236.
3. Quoted by Julius W. Pratt: "Madison," in *Dictionary of American
   Biography.*
4. Henry Adams, *Albert Gallatin,* p.
   392.
5. Henry Adams, *The Formative
   Years,* vol. II, p. 573.
6. Henry Adams, *Albert Gallatin,* p.
   416.
7. Gerald W. Johnson, *America's Silver Age,* p. 59.
8. Quoted by W. E. Binkley, *President
   and Congress,* pp. 59–60.
9. Henry Adams, *Albert Gallatin,* p.
   455.
10. Cp. W. E. Binkley, *President and
    Congress,* p. 58, for a recent version
    of the story; and compare Henry

Adams, *Albert Gallatin,* pp. 456–59, for a refutation.

CHAPTER TEN

1. James Bryce, *The American Commonwealth,* 2d ed., revised, vol. I, p. 261.
2. W. P. Cresson, *James Monroe,* pp. 226–27.
3. Henry Adams, *The Formative Years,* vol. I, pp. 417–58.
4. Cp. Henry Adams, *John Randolph,* pp. 242–48.
5. William Plumer, Jr., quoted by W. E. Binkley, *President and Congress,* p. 61.
6. *Ibid.,* p. 60.
7. W. P. Cresson, *James Monroe,* p. 351.
8. *Ibid.*
9. W. E. Binkley, *American Political Parties,* p. 99.
10. Henry Adams, *Albert Gallatin,* p. 562.
11. W. P. Cresson, *James Monroe,* p. 342.
12. J. Q. Adams, *Diary,* February 24, 1820.
13. Speech in the Senate, April 8, 1850.
14. Dexter Perkins, *Hands Off: A History of the Monroe Doctrine,* p. 50.
15. *Ibid.,* p. 58.

CHAPTER ELEVEN

1. W. E. Binkley, *American Political Parties,* p. 109.
2. *Ibid.,* p. 112. Cp. Glyndon G. Van Deusen, *Thurlow Weed,* pp. 42–49.
3. Henry Adams, *John Randolph,* p. 277.
4. Quoted in Brooks Adams's introduction to Henry Adams, *The Degradation of the Democratic Dogma,* pp. 24–25.
5. *Ibid.,* p. 35.
6. J. Q. Adams, *Diary,* November 6, 1830.

CHAPTER TWELVE

1. Cp. Marquis James, *Andrew Jackson: Portrait of a President,* pp. 429–32.
2. T. H. Benton, *Thirty Years' View,* vol. I, p. 735.
3. *The Autobiography of Martin Van Buren,* p. 198.
4. *Ibid.,* p. 449.

5. H. J. Ford, *Alexander Hamilton,* p. 364, and cp. p. 363.
6. Edward Stanwood, *A History of the Presidency,* vol. I, pp. 136, 148.
7. H. J. Ford, *The Rise and Growth of American Politics,* pp. 171–72.
8. T. H. Benton, *Thirty Years' View,* vol. I, p. 219.
9. *Ibid.,* vol. I, p. 218.
10. Quoted by H. J. Ford, *The Rise and Growth of American Politics,* p. 210.
11. *Ibid.,* p. 215.

CHAPTER THIRTEEN

1. Arthur M. Schlesinger, Jr., *The Age of Jackson,* p. 525.
2. *Ibid.,* p. 120.
3. July 10, 1832. Cp. *Documents of American History,* edited by Henry Steele Commager, vol. I, pp. 270–74.
4. A. M. Schlesinger, Jr., *The Age of Jackson,* p. 129.
5. *Ibid.*
6. *Ibid.,* p. 239.
7. *Ibid.,* p. 236.
8. *Ibid.,* pp. 247–48.
9. *Ibid.,* p. 209. On the other hand, William A. Sullivan has shown that Eastern labor was by no means wholeheartedly Jacksonian. Cp. *Political Science Quarterly,* vol. LXII, pp. 569–80.
10. S. E. Morison and H. S. Commager, *The Growth of the American Republic,* vol. I, p. 375.
11. Claude G. Bowers, *The Party Battles of the Jackson Period,* p. 199.
12. Walter Prescott Webb, *The Great Plains,* p. 405.
13. *Ibid.,* pp. 409–10.
14. Martin Van Buren, *Autobiography,* p. 320.
15. *Ibid.,* p. 323.
16. H. J. Ford, *The Rise and Growth of American Politics,* p. 182.
17. *Ibid.,* p. 193.

CHAPTER FOURTEEN

1. Carl Becker, *Freedom and Responsibility in the American Way of Life,* pp. 15–16.
2. S. E. Morison and H. S. Commager, *The Growth of the American Republic,* vol. I, p. 448.
3. A. M. Schlesinger, Jr., *The Age of Jackson,* p. 292.

4. Cp. Glyndon G. Van Deusen, *Thurlow Weed*, chapters 3 and 4, and W. E. Binkley, *American Political Parties*, pp. 158–59.

CHAPTER FIFTEEN

1. According to Carl Schurz, Clay also took part in the revising. Cp. Schurz, *Henry Clay*, vol. II, p. 194.
2. W. E. Binkley, *President and Congress*, p. 89, and cp. pp. 89–90 for quotations from the address.
3. Cp. S. E. Morison and H. S. Commager, *The Growth of the American Republic*, vol. I, pp. 462–63.
4. John C. Calhoun, *Works*, vol. I, pp. 55–56.

CHAPTER SIXTEEN

1. S. E. Morison and H. S. Commager, *The Growth of the American Republic*, vol. I, p. 458.
2. Avery Craven, *The Coming of the Civil War*, pp. 217–18; and cp. pp. 203–19, *passim*.
3. Bernard De Voto, *The Year of Decision, 1846*, pp. 7–8.
4. H. J. Ford, *The Rise and Growth of American Politics*, pp. 279–83.
5. *Ibid.*, p. 356.
6. Allan Nevins, *Ordeal of the Union*, vol. I, p. 334.
7. Gerald W. Johnson, *America's Silver Age*, p. 270.
8. Allan Nevins, *Ordeal of the Union*, vol. I, pp. 290–91.
9. S. E. Morison, *The Maritime History of Massachusetts*, p. 298.
10. *Ibid.*, p. 299.
11. W. E. Binkley, *President and Congress*, pp. 106–07.
12. Cp. the posthumous (1852) *Disquisition on Government*, *passim*.

CHAPTER SEVENTEEN

1. Among recent important books dealing with the problem, or with parts of it, are: Arthur Charles Cole, *The Irrepressible Conflict, 1850–1865*; Avery Craven, *The Coming of the Civil War*, and *The Repressible Conflict*; J. G. Randall, *The Civil War and Reconstruction*, and *Lincoln the President*, vol. I; Allan Nevins, *Ordeal of the Union*, two volumes; Roy Franklin Nichols, *The Disruption of American Democracy*; William B. Hesseltine, *Lincoln and the War Governors*; Ralph Henry Gabriel, *The Course of American Democratic Thought*; and Merle Curti, *The Growth of American Thought*.
2. Roy F. Nichols, *The Disruption of American Democracy*, pp. 20–21.
3. *Ibid.*, p. 40.
4. The best picture of the reality as opposed to the theory of party structure is found in Pendleton Herring, *The Politics of Democracy*.
5. Pendleton Herring, *The Politics of Democracy*, pp. 215–16.
6. Perry Patterson, *Presidential Government in the United States*, pp. 248–49, and cp. p. 96.
7. *The Public Papers of Woodrow Wilson*, vol. I, p. 342.
8. Pendleton Herring, *The Politics of Democracy*, p. 238.
9. Cp. Allan Nevins, *Ordeal of the Union*, vol. II, pp. 19–20.
10. Platform of the Free Democratic Party, Articles XX, V, VI, and VII.

CHAPTER EIGHTEEN

1. Laurence Oliphant, *Episodes in a Life of Adventure*, p. 51.
2. Quoted in Avery Craven, *The Coming of the Civil War*, pp. 270–71.
3. Allan Nevins, *Ordeal of the Union*, vol. II, pp. 107–08.
4. W. E. Binkley, *American Political Parties*, p. 192; A. J. Beveridge, *Abraham Lincoln*, vol. II, pp. 186–87.
5. *Diary and Correspondence of Salmon P. Chase*, pp. 255–56.
6. Both the speech in Independence Hall and the Peoria speech are preserved in varying versions. The quotations here used are from *Abraham Lincoln: His Speeches and Writings*, edited by Roy P. Basler, 1946.
7. Allan Nevins, *Ordeal of the Union*, vol. II, p. 227.
8. W. E. Binkley, *American Political Parties*, p. 206.
9. Allan Nevins, *Ordeal of the Union*, vol. II, p. 461.
10. For a somewhat less kindly account of Frémont in the West, see Bernard De Voto, *The Year of Decision, 1846*, *passim*. A friendly and

absorbing biography is Allan Nevins's *Frémont, the West's Greatest Adventurer,* 2 vols.

CHAPTER NINETEEN

1. Roy F. Nichols, *The Disruption of American Democracy,* p. 78.
2. *Ibid.,* p. 79.
3. Quoted by Avery Craven, *The Coming of the Civil War,* p. 390.
4. Nicolay and Hay (ed.), *Complete Works of Lincoln,* vol. V, p. 136. Quoted by W. E. Binkley, *President and Congress,* pp. 227–28.
5. Roy P. Basler, *Abraham Lincoln: His Speeches and Writings,* p. 538.
6. Cp. Constitution, Article II, Section I.
7. Avery Craven, *The Coming of the Civil War,* p. 417.
8. William B. Hesseltine, *Lincoln and the War Governors,* p. 92.
9. Avery Craven, *The Coming of the Civil War,* p. 416.
10. Quoted by W. E. Binkley, *President and Congress,* p. 205.
11. Avery Craven, *The Coming of the Civil War,* p. 427.
12. William B. Hesseltine, *Lincoln and the War Governors,* p. 74.
13. P. M. Angle (ed.), *The Lincoln Reader,* p. 299.

CHAPTER TWENTY

1. Carl B. Swisher, *American Constitutional Development,* p. 257.
2. Roy F. Nichols, *The Disruption of American Democracy,* p. 427.
3. P. M. Angle (ed.), *The Lincoln Reader,* pp. 318–19.
4. William B. Hesseltine, *Lincoln and the War Governors,* p. vi.
5. Cp. J. G. Randall, *The Civil War and Reconstruction,* pp. 233 ff.
6. Jonathan Worth to T. C. and B. G. Worth; quoted by Avery Craven, *The Coming of the Civil War,* p. 438.
7. J. G. Randall, *Lincoln the President,* vol. I, p. 17.
8. Francis Grierson, *The Valley of Shadows,* 1948 ed., pp. 177–78.

CHAPTER TWENTY-ONE

1. Ralph H. Gabriel, *The Course of American Democratic Thought,* p. 111.

2. Carl B. Swisher, *American Constitutional Developments,* p. 266; and cp. pp. 264–65 for details of the departments in 1860.
3. William A. Dunning, *Essays on the Civil War and Reconstruction,* pp. 15–16.
4. *Ibid.,* p. 5.
5. William B. Hesseltine, *Lincoln and the War Governors,* p. 288.
6. Cp. William B. Hesseltine, *Lincoln and the War Governors,* chapter 13.
7. Professor J. G. Randall.
8. William B. Hesseltine, *Lincoln and the War Governors,* p. 272.
9. James G. Blaine, *Twenty Years in Congress,* vol. I, p. 325.
10. Cp. Stevens's speeches in Congress from January, 1862, through the end of 1864.
11. Quoted by E. Merton Coulter, *The South During Reconstruction, 1865–1877,* p. 42.
12. William A. Dunning, *Reconstruction, Political and Economic,* p. 87.
13. See Article I, Section 7 of the Constitution.
14. Cp. William B. Hesseltine, *Lincoln and the War Governors,* p. 384, note.
15. W. E. Binkley, *American Political Parties,* p. 265.
16. Cp. William B. Hesseltine, *Lincoln and the War Governors,* pp. 380–84, and footnote, p. 384.
17. Francis Grierson, *The Valley of Shadows,* 1948 ed., pp. 48–49.

CHAPTER TWENTY-TWO

1. S. E. Morison and H. S. Commager, *The Growth of the American Republic,* vol. II, p. 4. *The Dictionary of American History* gives a smaller figure of deaths, based on a Department of War publication and on T. L. Livermore, *Numbers and Losses in the Civil War in America.*
2. Cp. E. Merton Coulter, *The South During Reconstruction, 1865–1877,* and William A. Dunning, *Reconstruction, Political and Economic,* pp. 199–201.
3. J. G. Randall, *The Civil War and Reconstruction,* p. 458.
4. Manuscript of *The National Banking System, 1865–1875: A Sectional Institution,* by George LaVerne Anderson, University of Illinois Library; quoted by Professor J. G.

Randall, *The Civil War and Reconstruction*, p. 458.

5. Quoted by Perry Patterson, *Presidential Government in the United States*, p. 122.
6. Nicolay and Hay (eds.), *Works of Abraham Lincoln*, vol. X, pp. 65–66.
7. S. E. Morison and H. S. Commager, *The Growth of the American Republic*, vol. II, p. 3.
8. Cp. J. W. Julian's *Political Recollections*, p. 257.
9. S. E. Morison and H. S. Commager, *The Growth of the American Republic*, vol. II, p. 21.
10. Glyndon G. Van Deusen, *Thurlow Weed*, p. 526.
11. Dexter Perkins, *Hands Off: A History of the Monroe Doctrine*, p. 111.
12. From the instructions to the American Minister at Paris in August, 1865, *ibid.*, p. 132.

CHAPTER TWENTY-THREE

1. W. E. Binkley, *American Political Parties*, p. 271 and note.
2. Donald Davidson, *The Attack on Leviathan*, pp. 112–14.
3. W. P. Webb, *Divided We Stand*, p. 11.
4. C. N. Coleman, *The Election of 1868*, p. 363.
5. *The Education of Henry Adams*, pp. 271–72.
6. Allan Nevins, *Hamilton Fish*, p. 448.
7. Quoted by Perry Patterson, *Presidential Government in the United States*, p. 125.
8. George F. Hoar, *Autobiography of Seventy Years*, vol. II, p. 46.
9. Allan Nevins, *Hamilton Fish*, p. 290.
10. Samuel S. McClure, *Lincoln and Men of Wartimes*, p. 196; quoted in P. M. Angle (ed.), *The Lincoln Reader*, p. 402.
11. *The Education of Henry Adams*, p. 265.
12. Quoted in P. M. Angle (ed.), *The Lincoln Reader*, p. 513.

CHAPTER TWENTY-FOUR

1. Allan Nevins, *Hamilton Fish*, p. 286.
2. *Dictionary of American History*, vol. II, p. 85.

3. William Allen White, *Masks in a Pageant*, p. 63.
4. Allan Nevins, *Hamilton Fish*, p. 684, quoting letter of Fish to Bancroft Davis.
5. *The Education of Henry Adams*, p. 272.
6. S. E. Morison and H. S. Commager, *The Growth of the American Republic*, vol. II, p. 70.
7. Henry L. Stoddard, *It Costs to Be President*, p. 98.
8. George Boutwell, *Reminiscences*, vol. II, p. 29.
9. Fish's diary, October 20, 1876; quoted by Allan Nevins, *Hamilton Fish*, pp. 306–07.
10. *The Education of Henry Adams*, p. 276.
11. J. G. Randall, in *Dictionary of American History*, vol. VI, p. 426.
12. Ralph H. Gabriel, *The Course of American Democratic Thought*, p. 136.
13. H. J. Ford, *The Cleveland Era*, pp. 3–4.
14. *Ibid.*, p. 10, note.
15. *The Education of Henry Adams*, p. 276.
16. Allan Nevins, *Hamilton Fish*, p. 911.

CHAPTER TWENTY-FIVE

1. H. J. Eckenrode, *Rutherford B. Hayes*, p. 226.
2. Henry Adams, *The Sessions*, p. 60.
3. Cp. W. E. Binkley, *President and Congress*, p. 151, and notes; Eckenrode, *Rutherford B. Hayes*, p. 241.
4. William Allen White, *Masks in a Pageant*, pp. 72–73.
5. Cp. Charles R. Williams, *Life of Rutherford B. Hayes*, vol. II, pp. 26–30.
6. H. J. Eckenrode, *Rutherford B. Hayes*, p. 247.
7. *Ibid.*, p. 257.
8. *Ibid.*, p. 267.
9. *Ibid.*, pp. 275, 277.
10. S. E. Morison and H. S. Commager, *The Growth of the American Republic*, vol. II, p. 190.
11. James Bryce, *The American Commonwealth*, 2d ed., revised, vol. I, p. 206.

CHAPTER TWENTY-SIX

1. H. J. Ford, *The Cleveland Era*, p. 15 and note.

2. Quoted by W. E. Binkley, *President and Congress*, p. 159.
3. Letter to John Hay, quoted by W. E. Binkley, *President and Congress*, p. 159.
4. Quoted by W. E. Binkley, *ibid.*, p. 160.
5. New York *Herald*, July 3, 1881.
6. Quoted by Henry Luther Stoddard, *Presidential Sweepstakes*, p. 87.
7. Senate Report, no. 837, to accompany Bill S.227, 46th Congress, 3d Session, February 4, 1881.
8. Quoted by H. J. Ford, *President and Congress*, p. 33.
9. *Ibid.*, p. 38.
10. Quoted by F. W. Taussig, in *The Tariff History of the United States*, p. 233, note.

CHAPTER TWENTY-SEVEN

1. H. J. Ford, *The Cleveland Era*, p. 44.
2. Allan Nevins, *Grover Cleveland: A Study in Courage*, pp. 57–58.
3. *Ibid.*, pp. 164–66.
4. *Ibid.*, p. 192.
5. Grover Cleveland, *Presidential Problems*, pp. 42–43.
6. Richard Hofstadter, *Social Darwinism in American Thought, 1860–1915*.
7. *Ibid.*, p. 27.
8. *Ibid.*, pp. 31–32.
9. William Allen White, *Masks in a Pageant*, p. 142.
10. *Ibid.*, pp. 118–19.

CHAPTER TWENTY-EIGHT

1. Cp. Arthur Meier Schlesinger, *The Rise of the City, 1878–1898*, p. 1.
2. *Ibid.*, pp. 57, 64.
3. *Ibid.*, pp. 67–69.
4. *Ibid.*, p. 77.
5. Oswald Spengler, *The Decline of the West*, translated by Charles Francis Atkinson, vol. II, p. 102.
6. *Ibid.*, p. 99.
7. Allan Nevins, *The Emergence of Modern America, 1865–1878*, pp. 399–400.
8. Quoted from Morison and Commager, *The Growth of the American Republic*, vol. II, p. 178, notes.
9. Carl Wittke, *We Who Built America*, pp. xvi–xviii.
10. 16 Wallace 36 (1873).

11. Edward S. Corwin, *Liberty Against Government*, p. 118.
12. *Ibid.*, p. 124.
13. *San Mateo County* v. *Southern Pacific Railroad*.
14. Cp. "Truth and Fiction About the Fourteenth Amendment," by Louis B. Boudin, in *New York University Law Quarterly Review*, vol. XVI (November, 1938), and "The Conspiracy Theory of the Fourteenth Amendment," by Howard Jay Graham, in *Yale Law Journal*, vol. XLVII (January, 1938) and vol. XLVII (December, 1938).
15. *Santa Clara County* v. *Southern Pacific Railroad Company*.
16. Carl B. Swisher, *American Constitutional Development*, p. 405.
17. Cp. Louis B. Boudin, *Government by Judiciary*, vol. II, pp. 374–96, for an outline of the history of "due process." And cp. Edward S. Corwin, *Liberty Against Government*, *passim*.
18. *Chicago, Burlington and Quincy Railroad* v. *Iowa* (1877).
19. Charles C. Marshall, "A New Constitutional Amendment," *American Law Review*, November-December, 1890. Cp. Louis B. Boudin, *Government by Judiciary*, vol. II, pp. 399–404, which discusses the article in detail. The quotations in the text are from Boudin.
20. *Stone* v. *Farmers' Loan and Trust Company*.
21. Carl B. Swisher, *American Constitutional Development*, p. 402.
22. *Chicago, Minneapolis and St. Paul Railroad Company* v. *Minnesota*.
23. Carl B. Swisher, *American Constitutional Development*, p. 403.
24. *In re* Jacobs, 98 New York 98.
25. Theodore Roosevelt, *Autobiography*, p. 82
26. *Ibid.*, pp. 82–93.
27. Cp. Edward R. Lewis, *A History of American Political Thought from the Civil War to the World War*, pp. 94–96. The quotations in the text are taken from Lewis.

CHAPTER TWENTY-NINE

1. W. E. Binkley, *American Political Parties*, p. 310.
2. H. J. Ford, *The Cleveland Era*, p. 54.
3. William Allen White, *Autobiography*, p. 361.

4. *The Education of Henry Adams,* p. 320.
5. William Allen White, *Masks in a Pageant,* p. 79.
6. New York *Herald,* Jan. 6, 1886; quoted in Allan Nevins, *Grover Cleveland,* p. 271.
7. Quoted by Frank Kent, *The Democratic Party,* p. 302.
8. William Allen White, *Autobiography,* pp. 358–60.
9. Matthew Josephson, *The President Makers,* p. 6.
10. F. W. Taussig, *The Tariff History of the United States,* p. 256.

CHAPTER THIRTY

1. W. E. Binkley, *American Political Parties,* p. 312.
2. Arthur F. Mullen, *Western Democrat,* pp. 46, 58.
3. *Ibid.,* pp. 61–63. Collis P. Huntington of the Southern Pacific Railroad put the price of an Arizona legislature at about $4500. (*Rocky Mountain Cities,* ed. Ray West, Jr., p. 219.)
4. *Atlantic Monthly,* March, 1900.
5. Henry Adams, *Letters,* vol. II, p. 270.
6. *Ibid.,* vol. II, p. 461.
7. William L. Wilson, quoted by Allan Nevins, *Grover Cleveland,* p. 693.
8. Harry Thurston Peck, *Twenty Years of the Republic,* p. 498.
9. William Allen White, *Masks in a Pageant,* p. 250.
10. *The Education of Henry Adams,* p. 344. Adams was commenting on the repeal of the Sherman Silver Purchase Act in 1893.

CHAPTER THIRTY-ONE

1. William Allen White, *Masks in a Pageant,* p. 206.
2. Cp. Herbert Croly, *Marcus Alonzo Hanna: His Life and Works,* pp. 465–73.
3. *Ibid.,* p. 94.
4. *Ibid.,* pp. 408–10.
5. William Allen White, *Masks in a Pageant,* pp. 155 and 172.
6. W. E. Binkley, *President and Congress,* p. 189.
7. W. E. Binkley, *American Political Parties,* p. 329.
8. William Allen White, *Masks in a Pageant,* p. 245.

9. Herbert Croly, *Marcus Alonzo Hanna,* p. 205.
10. *Collected Poems of Vachel Lindsay,* pp. 99 ff.
11. *Education of Henry Adams,* p. 356.
12. William T. R. Fox, *The Super-Powers,* p. 30.

CHAPTER THIRTY-TWO

1. James Bryce, *The American Commonwealth,* 2d ed., revised, vol. I. p. 136.
2. H. J. Ford, *The Cleveland Era,* p. 87.
3. *Ibid.,* pp. 93–94.
4. Henry Adams, *Letters,* vol. II, p. 219.
5. Henry Pringle, *Theodore Roosevelt,* p. 130.
6. *The Education of Henry Adams,* p. 417.
7. William Allen White, *Autobiography,* pp. 297–98.
8. Henry Pringle, *Theodore Roosevelt,* p. 101.
9. Quoted by W. E. Binkley, *President and Congress,* p. 196.
10. George B. Galloway, *Congress at the Crossroads,* p. 117.
11. Henry Pringle, *Theodore Roosevelt,* p. 485.
12. Frederick Lewis Allen, *The Great Pierpont Morgan,* p. 98.
13. Quoted by F. L. Allen, *ibid.,* p. 220.
14. *Theodore Roosevelt: An Autobiography,* pp. 437–44.
15. Henry Pringle, *Theodore Roosevelt,* p. 261.
16. *Ibid.,* pp. 260–61.
17. Speech at Columbus, Ohio, February, 1912.
18. Cp. Matthew Josephson, *The President Makers,* pp. 132–38; Wilfred E. Binkley, *American Political Parties,* pp. 337–38; Henry Pringle, *Theodore Roosevelt,* pp. 264–78.
19. Henry Pringle, *Theodore Roosevelt,* p. 278.
20. *Theodore Roosevelt: An Autobiography,* p. 419.
21. Henry Adams, *Letters,* vol. II, p. 515.

CHAPTER THIRTY-THREE

1. E. P. Herring, *Presidential Leadership,* p. 141.
2. Cp. Article V of the Constitution.

3. W. E. Binkley, *American Political Parties,* pp. 344–45.
4. William Allen White, *Autobiography,* p. 483.
5. Henry Pringle, *Theodore Roosevelt,* p. 571.
6. Ray Stannard Baker, *Woodrow Wilson, Life and Letters,* vol. III, p. 33.
7. C. E. Merriam, *Four Political Leaders,* p. 48.
8. Richard Hofstadter, *The American Political Tradition,* p. 255.
9. William Allen White, *Autobiography,* pp. 487–88.
10. *Ibid.,* pp. 479–80.
11. Nicholas Mansergh, *The Coming of the First World War: A Study in the European Balance, 1876–1914,* p. 245.
12. Cp. Richard Hofstadter, *The American Political Tradition,* pp. 257–58 and note, for these House and Wilson quotations.
13. Cp. W. S. Holt, *Treaties Defeated by the Senate,* pp. 294–301, and Alan Cranston, *The Killing of the Peace, passim.* All of which Franklin Roosevelt watched and remembered.
14. Lindsay Rogers, "Presidential Dictatorship in the United States," *Quarterly Review,* vol. CCXXXI (1919). Quoted by Clinton L. Rossiter, *Constitutional Dictatorship,* p. 242.
15. Clinton L. Rossiter, *Constitutional Dictatorship,* p. 243.
16. Senator William Maclay of Pennsylvania; quoted by George H. Haynes, *The Senate of the United States,* vol. I, p. 399.
17. *Ibid.,* p. 396.
18. American Federation of Labor Information and Publicity Service, October 17, 1925; quoted in George H. Haynes, *The Senate of the United States,* vol. I, p. 416.

19. Cp. Ray Stannard Baker, *Woodrow Wilson,* vol. VII, pp. 185–86.

CHAPTER THIRTY-FOUR

1. Alan Cranston, *The Killing of the Peace,* p. ix.
2. W. E. Binkley, *President and Congress,* p. 218.
3. "Fireside Chat" of April 14, 1938.
4. Radio address to the Young Democratic Clubs of America, August 24, 1935.
5. Address to American Retail Federation, Washington, D. C., May 22, 1939.
6. Address on Constitution Day, Washington, D. C., September 17, 1937.
7. Frances Perkins, *The Roosevelt I Knew,* pp. 3, 4.
8. Henry Steele Commager, "Twelve Years of Roosevelt," in *Franklin Delano Roosevelt: A Memorial,* p. 215.
9. Quoted in Dixon Wecter, *The Age of the Great Depression,* p. 50.
10. E. S. Corwin, *Constitutional Revolution, Ltd.,* p. 114.
11. Cp. Elmo Roper's articles, "Why the Pollsters Went Wrong," New York *Herald Tribune* (Paris edition), June 22 and 23, 1949.
12. *U. S.* v. *Butler,* 297 U. S. 1.
13. *Carter* v. *Carter Coal Company,* 298 U. S. 238.
14. *N.L.R.B.* v. *Jones and Laughlin Steel Corporation,* 301 U. S. 1.
15. Edward S. Corwin, *Constitutional Revolution, Ltd.,* pp. 112–13, 116. And cp. Corwin, *Total War and the Constitution, passim.*

CHAPTER THIRTY-FIVE

1. James Bryce, *The American Commonwealth,* 2d ed., revised, vol. II, p. 20.

Bibliography

THIS BIBLIOGRAPHY is limited to the books mentioned or quoted herein, to the best biographies of the important characters, and to the memoirs, letters, special studies, and general histories which have been used as sources. Readers who want more information are referred to the following:

    1. The excellent bibliographies, divided chapter by chapter, in the Morison and Commager history listed in Section I below.

    2. *Writings on American History,* compiled by Grace C. Griffin since 1906 and published among the *Reports* of the American Historical Association.

I. GENERAL HISTORIES

Dictionary of American Biography. 22 vols. Published under the auspices of the American Council of Learned Societies. Edited by Allen Johnson and Dumas Malone. New York and London, 1937.

Dictionary of American History. 5 vols. and index vol., edited by James Truslow Adams. New York, 1940.

Beard, Charles A. and Mary R., *The Rise of American Civilization.* 2 vols. New York, 1927.

Bemis, S. F., and Griffin, G. G., *Guide to the Diplomatic History of the United States.* Washington, 1935.

Cash, L., *The Mint of the South.* New York, 1941.

Channing, Edward, *History of the United States.* 6 vols. and General Index. (From the beginning to 1865.) New York, 1905–1922. Index 1932.

Commager, Henry Steele, *Documents of American History, 1492–1935.* 2 vols. in one. New York, 1935.

Hart, A. B., ed., *The American Nation: A History.* 28 vols. (Covers period 1492–1917.) New York and London, 1906–18.

Morison, Samuel E., and Commager, Henry S., *The Growth of the American Republic.* 2 vols. 3d edition. New York, 1942. (The quotations in this book are from the 2d edition, 1937.)

Parrington, V. L., *Main Currents in American Thought.* 3 vols. New York, 1927–1930.

Schlesinger, A. M., and Fox, D. R., eds., *History of American Life.* 13 vols. New York, 1929–1948.

II. ECONOMIC AND LABOR HISTORIES

Beard, Mary, *A Short History of the American Labor Movement.* New York, 1920.

Berle, A. A., Jr., and Means, G. C., *The Modern Corporation and Private Property.* New York and Chicago, 1932.

Bidwell, P. W., and Falconer, J. I., *History of Agriculture in the North-* ern *United States, 1620–1860.* Washington, 1925.

Callender, Guy S., *Selections from the Economic History of the United States, 1765–1860.* Boston and New York, 1909.

Clark, V. S., *History of Manufactures in the United States, 1860–1916.* 3 vols. New York, 1929.

Commons, J. R., and others, *History of Labor in the United States.* 4 vols. New York, 1918–35.

Corey, Lewis, *The Crisis of the Middle Class.* New York, 1935.

——— *The Decline of American Capitalism.* New York, 1934.

Dewey, D. R., *Financial History of the United States.* New York, 1909.

Dorfman, Joseph, *Thorstein Veblen and his America.* New York, 1934.

Faulkner, H. U., *American Economic History.* 4th ed. New York, 1938.

Flugel, F., *Readings in the Economic and Social History of the United States.* New York and London, 1929.

Frankfurter, Felix, and Greene, N. V., *The Labor Injunction.* New York, 1930.

Gray, L. C., *History of Agriculture in the Southern States to 1860.* 2 vols. Washington, 1933.

Hepburn, A. B., *A History of Currency in the United States.* New York, 1915.

Jenks, J. W., and Clark, W. E., *The Trust Problems.* Garden City, New York, 1917.

Jones, Eliot, *The Trust Problem in the United States.* New York, 1921.

Kemmerer, E. W., *The A.B.C. of the Federal Reserve System.* Princeton and London, 1918.

King, W. I., *The National Income and Its Purchasing Power.* New York, 1930.

Laughlin, J. L., *The History of Bimetallism in the United States.* New York, 1886 and 1900.

Mason, A. T., *Organized Labor and the Law.* Durham, 1922.

Meyers, Gustavus, *History of the Great American Fortunes.* Chicago, 1910.

Mitchell, Broadus, *The Industrial Revolution in the South.* Baltimore and London, 1930.

——— *The Rise of Cotton Mills in the South.* Baltimore, 1921.

Perlman, S., *A History of Trade Unionism in the United States.* New York, 1922.

Rickard, T. A., *A History of American Mining.* New York and London, 1932.

Taussig, F. W., *The Tariff History of the United States.* New York and London, 1888.

Watkins, G. S., *An Introduction to the Study of Labor Problems.* New York, 1922.

White, H., *Money and Banking Illustrated by American History.* Boston and London, 1895.

Willis, H. P., *The Federal Reserve System.* Chicago, 1923.

III. FOREIGN RELATIONS AND DIPLOMACY

Bailey, T. A., *A Diplomatic History of the American People.* New York, 1940.

Foster, J. W., *American Diplomacy in the Orient.* Boston and New York, 1903.

Griswold, A. W., *The Far Eastern Policy of the United States.* New York, 1938.

Latané, J. H., *A History of American Foreign Policy.* New York, 1927.

Moon, Parker T., *Imperialism and World Politics.* New York, 1926.

Perkins, D. T., *Hands Off: A History of the Monroe Doctrine.* Boston, 1941.

Sears, L. M., *A History of American Foreign Relations.* New York, 1927.

IV. PUBLIC LANDS, THE FRONTIER AND THE PLAINS

Dale, E. E., *The Range Cattle Industry.* Norman, Oklahoma, 1930.

Dick, E., *The Sod House Frontier.* New York and London, 1937.

Gates, P. W., *The Illinois-Central Railroad and Its Colonization Work.* Cambridge, Massachusetts, 1934.

Hibbard, B. H., *A History of the Public Land Policies. New York,* 1924.

Osgood, E. S., *The Day of the Cattleman.* Minneapolis, 1929.

Parkman, F., *The Oregon Trail.* Boston, 1886.

Paxson, F. L., *History of the American Frontier, 1763–1893.* Boston and New York, 1924.

Pelzer, Louis, *The Cattlemen's Frontier, 1850–1890.* Glendale, California, 1936.

Riegel, R. E., *The Story of the Western Railroads.* New York, 1926.

Robbins, R. M., *Our Landed Heritage:*

The Public Domain, 1776–1936. Princeton and London, 1942.
Stephenson, G. M., *The Political History of the Public Lands, 1840–62.* Boston, 1917.
Turner, F. J., *The Frontier in American History.* New York, 1920.
——*The Significance of Sections in American History.* New York, 1932.

——*Rise of the New West.* New York and London, 1906.
Webb, W. P., *The Great Plains.* Boston, 1931.
Wellington, R. G., *The Political and Sectional Influence of Public Lands, 1828–1842.* Cambridge, Massachusetts, 1914.

V. THE CONSTITUTION AND THE SUPREME COURT

Beard, Charles A., *An Economic Interpretation of the Constitution.* New York, 1913.
——*The Enduring Federalist,* edited and analyzed by C. A. B. New York, 1948.
——*The Supreme Court and the Constitution.* New York, 1912.
Beveridge, A. J., *Life of John Marshall.* 4 vols. Boston, 1917–19.
Boudin, Louis, *Government by Judiciary.* 2 vols. New York, 1932.
Cardozo, *The Growth of the Law.* New Haven, 1931.
——*The Nature of the Judicial Process.* New Haven, 1921.
Corwin, Edward S., *Liberty Against Government.* Baton Rouge, 1948.
——*Constitutional Revolution, Ltd.* Claremont, California, 1941.
——*Total War and the Constitution.* New York, 1947.
——*John Marshall and the Constitution.* New Haven, 1919.
—— *The Commerce Power vs. State Rights.* Princeton and London, 1936.
——*The Doctrine of Judicial Review.* Princeton, 1914.
Curtis, Charles, *Lions Under the Throne.* Boston, 1947.
Farrand, Max, ed., *The Records of the Federal Convention of 1787.* 3 vols. New Haven, 1911.
Frankfurter, F., *The Commerce Clause Under Marshall, Taney, and Waite.* Chapel Hill, North Carolina, 1937.
Guthrie, W. D., *Lectures on the Four-teenth Article of Amendment to the Constitution.* Boston, 1898.
Hamilton, Alexander, and Jay, John, and Madison, James, *The Federalist.* A Commentary on the Constitution of the United States, edited by P. L. Ford. New York, 1898.
Horwill, H. W., *The Usages of the American Constitution.* London, 1925.
Johnson, Allen, *Readings in American Constitutional History, 1776–1876.* Boston and New York, 1912.
Johnson, A., and Robinson, W. A., *Readings in Recent American Constitutional History, 1876–1926.* New York and Chicago, 1927.
McLaughlin, A. C., *A Constitutional History of the United States.* New York and London, 1935.
——*The Foundations of American Constitutionalism.* New York and London, 1932.
Pritchett, C. H., *The Roosevelt Court.* New York, 1948.
Story, Joseph, *Commentaries on the Constitution of the United States.* 2 vols. Boston, 1851.
Swisher, C. B., *American Constitutional Development.* Boston, 1943.
Warren, Charles, *The Supreme Court in United States History.* 2 vols. Boston, 1926.
——*The Making of the Constitution.* Boston, 1928.
Wilson, Woodrow, *Constitutional Government in the United States.* New York, 1908.

VI. GOVERNMENT AND POLITICAL THEORIES

Beard, C. A., *The American Leviathan.* New York, 1930.
——*American Government and Politics.* New York, 1910.
Becker, C. L., *Freedom and Responsibility in the American Way of Life.* New York, 1946.

Binkley, Wilfred E., *American Political Parties.* New York, 1943.
——*President and Congress.* New York, 1947.
Bryce, James, *American Commonwealth.* 2 vols., 2d revised ed. London and New York, 1889.

Corwin, E. C., *The President, Office and Powers*. New York and London, 1940.

Curti, M., *The Growth of American Democratic Thought*. New York and London, 1943.

Ford, H. J., *Representative Government*. New York, 1928.

——*The Rise and Growth of American Politics*. New York, 1898.

Gabriel, R. H., *The Course of American Democratic Thought*. New York, 1940.

Galloway, George, *Congress at the Crossroads*. New York, 1946.

Haynes, F. E., *Third Party Movements Since the Civil War*. Iowa City, 1916.

Haynes, G. F., *The Senate of the United States*. 2 vols. Boston, 1938.

Herring, E. P., *The Politics of Democracy: American Parties in Action*. New York, 1940.

——*Presidential Leadership*. New York, 1940.

Hesseltine, W. B., *The Rise and Fall of Third Parties*. Washington, 1948.

Hofstadter, Richard, *The American Political Tradition and the Men Who Made It*. New York, 1948.

Holt, W. S., *Treaties Defeated by the Senate*. Baltimore, 1933.

Jouvenal, Bertrand de, *Power* (translated by J. F. Huntington). London, 1948.

Laird, John, *The Device of Government*. Cambridge, 1944.

Laski, Harold J., *The American Presidency*. New York and London, 1940.

MacIver, R. M., *The Web of Government*. New York, 1946.

Merriam, C. E., *The American Party System*. New York, 1922.

——*American Political Ideas, 1865–1917*. New York, 1920.

Ostrogorski, M., *Democracy and the Party System in the United States*. New York, 1926.

Powell, E. P., *Nullification and Secession in the United States*. New York, 1897.

Rossiter, C. L., *Constitutional Dictatorship*, Princeton, 1948.

Spengler, Oswald, *Decline of the West* (translated by C. F. Atkinson). 2 vols. New York, 1926–28.

Stanwood, Edward, *A History of the Presidency*. 2 vols. Boston and New York, 1916.

Stoddard, Henry L., *It Costs to be President*. New York and London, 1938.

——*Presidential Sweepstakes*. New York, 1948.

Webb, Walter P., *Divided We Stand*. New York and Toronto, 1937.

Wilson, Woodrow, *Congressional Government*. Boston, 1885.

Wiltse, C. M., *The Jeffersonian Tradition in American Democracy*. Chapel Hill, North Carolina, 1935.

VII. BOOKS APPLYING CHIEFLY TO THE YEARS 1763–1789

Abernathy, Thomas P., *Western Lands and the American Revolution*. University of Virginia, 1937.

Becker, C. L., *The Declaration of Independence*. New York, 1922.

Burnett, E. C., *The Continental Congress*. New York, 1941.

Ford, H. J., *The Scotch-Irish in America*. Princeton, 1915, and New York, 1941.

Fiske, John, *The Critical Period in American History*. Boston and New York, 1888.

Jameson, J. F., *The American Revolution Considered as a Social Movement*. Princeton, 1926.

Jensen, Merrill, *The Articles of Con-*

federation. Madison, Wisconsin, 1940.

McLaughlin, A. C., *The Confederation and the Constitution, 1783–89*. New York and London, 1905.

Miller, J. C., *Origins of the American Revolution*. Boston, 1943.

——*Triumph of Freedom: 1775–1783*. Boston, 1948.

Morison, S. E., *The American Revolution, 1764–1788: Sources and Documents*. Oxford, 1923.

Nevins, Allan, *The American States During and After the Revolution*. New York, 1924.

Van Tyne, C. H., *The Loyalists in the American Revolution*. New York and London, 1902.

VIII. BIOGRAPHIES, HISTORIES, MEMOIRS, ETC.,
APPLYING CHIEFLY TO THE YEARS 1789–1850

Abernathy, T. P., *From Frontier to Plantation in Tennessee.* Chapel Hill, North Carolina, 1932.

Adams, C. F., ed., *Works of John Adams with a Life.* 10 vols. Boston, 1850–56.

Adams, John, and John Quincy, *Selected Writings,* edited by Adrienne Koch and William Peden. New York, 1946.

Adams, Henry, *Life of Albert Gallatin.* Philadelphia, 1879.

———*History of the United States, 1801–17.* 9 vols. New York, 1889–91.

———*The Formative Years.* 2 vols. Boston, 1947. (The nine-volume *History* cut to two volumes with an introduction by Herbert Agar.)

———*John Randolph.* Boston and New York, 1882.

Adams, John Quincy, *Memoirs and Diary.* 12 vols., edited by C. F. Adams. Philadelphia, 1874–77.

Adams, J. T., *The Adams Family.* Boston, 1930.

Alexander, Holmes, *The American Talleyrand: The Career and Contemporaries of Martin Van Buren.* New York and London, 1935.

Allen, G. W., *Our Naval War with France.* Boston and New York, 1909.

Ames, Fisher, *The Works of Fisher Ames.* 2 vols. Boston, 1854.

Bassett, J. S., *The Federalist System.* New York and London, 1906.

Beard, C. A., *Economic Origins of Jeffersonian Democracy.* New York, 1915.

Beirne, F. F., *The War of 1812.* New York, 1949.

Bemis, S. F., *A Diplomatic History of the United States.* New York, 1936.

———*Jay's Treaty.* New York, 1923.

Benton, Thomas Hart, *Thirty Years' View.* 2 vols. New York and Boston, 1854–56.

Billington, R. A., *The Protestant Crusade, 1800–60.* New York, 1938.

Bowers, Claude G., *Jefferson and Hamilton.* Boston, 1925.

———*Jefferson in Power.* Boston, 1936.

———*The Party Battles of the Jackson Period.* Boston, 1922.

Brant, Irving, *James Madison: The Virginia Revolutionist.* New York, 1941.

———*James Madison: The Nationalist.* New York, 1948.

Bruce, W. C., *John Randolph of Roanoke.* New York and London, 1939.

Channing, Edward, *The Jeffersonian System.* New York, 1906.

Chinard, Gilbert, *Thomas Jefferson, the Apostle of Americanism.* Boston, 1929.

Chitwood, O. P., *John Tyler, Champion of the Old South.* New York, 1939.

Clark, B. C., *J. Q. Adams.* Boston, 1932.

Cresson, W. P., *James Monroe.* Chapel Hill, North Carolina, 1946.

Davidson, Donald, *Attack on Leviathan.* Chapel Hill, N.C., 1938.

De Voto, Bernard, *The Year of Decision.* Boston, 1943.

———*Across the Wide Missouri.* Boston, 1947.

Dodd, W. E., *The Cotton Kingdom.* New Haven, 1919.

———*Statesmen of the Old South.* New York, 1911.

Du Bois, W. E. B., *The Suppression of the African Slave Trade.* New York and London, 1896.

Ford, H. J., *Alexander Hamilton.* New York, 1920.

Ford, P. L., ed., *The Writings of Thomas Jefferson.* 10 vols. New York and London, 1892–99.

Ford, W. C., ed., *Writings of J. Q. Adams.* 7 vols. New York, 1913–17.

Foreman, Grant, *Indian Removal: The Emigration of the Five Civilized Tribes of Indians.* Norman, Oklahoma, 1932.

Fraser, H. R., *Democracy in the Making: The Jackson-Tyler Era.* Indianapolis and New York, 1938.

Freeman, D. S., *George Washington* (first two volumes). New York, 1948.

Fuess, C. M., *Daniel Webster.* 2 vols. Boston, 1930.

Goebel, D. B., *William Henry Harrison.* Indianapolis, 1926.

Griffin, C. C., *The United States and the Disruption of the Spanish Empire, 1810–22.* New York, 1937.

Hamilton, H., *Zachary Taylor.* Indianapolis and New York, 1941.

Hamilton, S. M., ed., *The Writings of James Monroe.* 7 vols. New York and London, 1898–1903.

Hirst, F. W., *Life and Letters of Thomas Jefferson.* New York, 1926.

Hunt, Gaillard, ed., *The Writings of James Madison.* 9 vols. New York, 1900–10.

Hunt, Gaillard, *The Life of James Madison.* New York, 1902.

Jacobs, J. R., *Tarnished Warrior: Major-General James Wilkinson.* New York, 1938.

James, Marquis, *Andrew Jackson, the Border Captain.* Indianapolis, 1933.

———*Andrew Jackson: Portrait of a President.* Indianapolis and New York, 1937.

Johnson, Gerald W., *America's Silver Age.* New York and London, 1939.

Lodge, H. C., *Daniel Webster.* Boston and New York, 1883.

———*Works of Hamilton.* 12 vols. New York and London, 1904.

MacDonald, W., *Jacksonian Democracy, 1829–37.* New York and London, 1906.

Mahan, A. T., *Sea Power in Its Relations to the War of 1812.* 2 vols. Boston, 1905.

———*Sea Power in Its Relations to the French Revolution.* 2 vols. Boston, 1892.

Malone, Dumas, *Jefferson the Virginian.* (First of 4 vols.) Boston, 1948.

Mayo, Bernard, ed., *Jefferson Himself.* (Selected Writings.) Boston, 1942.

Meyers, G., *History of Tammany Hall.* New York, 1917.

Morison, S. E., *Maritime History of Massachusetts, 1783–1860.* Boston, 1921.

McCormac, E. I., *James K. Polk.* Berkeley, California, 1922.

Osterweis, R. G., *Romanticism and Nationalism in the Old South.* New Haven, 1949.

Parton, James, *The Life and Times of Aaron Burr.* Boston, 1872.

Paxson, F. L., *The Independence of the South American Republics.* Philadelphia, 1903.

Phillips, U. B., *American Negro Slavery.* New York and London, 1918.

———*Life and Labor in the Old South.* Boston, 1929.

Polk, J. K., *Diary of a President,* edited by Allan Nevins. London and New York, 1929. (4 vols., unabridged edition, Chicago, 1910.)

Pratt, J. W., *Expansionists of 1812.* New York, 1925.

Roosevelt, Theodore, *Gouverneur Morris.* Boston and New York, 1888.

Schachner, Nathan, *Aaron Burr.* New York, 1937.

———*Alexander Hamilton.* New York, 1946.

Schlesinger, A. M., Jr., *The Age of Jackson.* New York, 1945.

Schurz, Carl, *Henry Clay.* 2 vols. Boston, 1887.

Sears, L. M., *Jefferson and the Embargo.* Durham, 1927.

Shepard, E. M., *Martin Van Buren.* Boston and New York, 1888.

Smith, J. H., *The War with Mexico.* 2 vols. New York, 1919.

Stephenson, N. W., *Texas and the Mexican War.* New Haven, 1921.

Swisher, C. B., *Roger B. Taney.* New York, 1935.

Sydnor, C. S., *The Development of Southern Sectionalism.* Baton Rouge, 1948.

Turner, F. J., *The United States, 1830–50.* New York, 1935.

Tyler, L. G., *The Letters and Times of the Tylers.* 3 vols. Richmond and Williamsburg, 1884–96.

Van Buren, Martin, *Autobiography.* Washington, 1920.

Van Deusen, G. C., *Thurlow Weed.* Boston, 1947.

Werner, M. R., *Tammany Hall.* New York, 1928.

Wiltse, C. M., *John C. Calhoun, Nationalist: 1827–1828.* Indianapolis, 1944.

———*John C. Calhoun, Nullifier: 1829–1839.* Indianapolis, 1949.

IX. BIOGRAPHIES, HISTORIES, MEMOIRS, ETC., APPLYING CHIEFLY TO THE YEARS 1850–1909

Adams, C. F., *Life of Charles Francis Adams.* Boston and New York, 1900.

Adams, C. F., and Henry, *Chapters of Erie.* Boston, 1871.

Adams, Henry, *Letters of Henry Adams, 1858–91.* 2 vols., edited by W. C. Ford. Boston, 1930.

———*The Education of Henry Adams.* Boston and New York, 1918.

———*Degradation of the Democratic Dogma.* New York, 1919.

———"The Session," *North American Review,* vol. 108, April, 1869.

Angle, P. M., ed., *The Lincoln Reader.* New Brunswick, New Jersey, 1947.

Auchampaugh, P. G., *James Buchanan and His Cabinet on the Eve of Secession.* Lancaster, Pennsylvania. 1926.

Bancroft, Frederick, *The Life of William H. Seward*. 2 vols. New York and London, 1900.

——*A Sketch of the Negro in Politics*. New York, 1885.

Barnard, Harry, *Eagle Forgotten: The Life of John P. Altgeld*. Indianapolis, 1938.

Basler, R. P., *Abraham Lincoln: His Speeches and Writings*. Cleveland and New York, 1946.

Beale, H. K., *The Critical Year*. New York, 1930.

Beer, Thomas, *Hanna*. New York, 1929.

Beveridge, Albert J., *Abraham Lincoln*. 4 vols. Boston and New York, 1928.

Blaine, James G., *Twenty Years of Congress*. 2 vols. Norwich, Connecticut, 1884–86.

Boutwell, George, *Reminiscences of Sixty Years in Public Affairs*. New York, 1902.

Bowers, Claude G., *The Tragic Era*. Cambridge, Massachusetts, 1929.

Bryan, W. J., *The First Battle*. Chicago, 1898.

Buchanan, J., *Mr. Buchanan's Administration on the Eve of the Rebellion*. New York, 1866.

Buck, S. J., *The Granger Movement*. Cambridge, Massachusetts, 1913.

——*The Agrarian Crusade*. New Haven, 1920.

Carnegie, A., *Autobiography*. Garden City, New York, 1920.

Cater, H. D., ed., *Henry Adams and His Friends* (more letters). Boston, 1947.

Chamberlain, J., *Farewell to Reform*. New York, 1932.

Chase, S. P., *Diary and Correspondence*. Washington, 1903.

Chidsey, D. B., *The Gentleman from New York: A Life of Roscoe Conkling*. New Haven, 1935.

Clark, Champ, *My Quarter Century of American Politics*. 2 vols. New York, 1920.

Cleveland, Grover, *Presidential Problems*. New York, 1904.

Cole, A. C., *The Era of the Civil War*. Springfield, Illinois, 1919.

——*The Irrepressible Conflict, 1850–65*. New York, 1934.

——*The Whig Party in the South*. Washington, 1913.

Coleman, C. H., *The Election of 1868*. New York, 1933.

Coleman, J. W., *The Molly Maguire Riots*. Richmond, 1936.

Coulter, E. M., *The South During Reconstruction, 1865–77*. Baton Rouge, 1947.

Craven, Avery O., *The Coming of the Civil War*. New York, 1942.

——*The Repressible Conflict 1830–1861*. Baton Rouge, 1938.

Croly, Herbert, *Marcus Alonzo Hanna*. New York, 1912.

——*The Promise of American Life*. New York, 1909.

Curti, M., *Bryan and World Peace*. Northhampton, Massachusetts, 1931.

Dennett, T., *John Hay*. New York, 1933.

Dewitt, D. M., *The Impeachment and Trial of Andrew Johnson*. New York and London, 1903.

De Witt, B. P., *The Progressive Movement*. New York, 1925.

Dubois, W. E. B., *Black Reconstruction*. New York, 1935.

——*The Souls of Black Folk*. Chicago, 1903.

Dunning, W. A., *Essays on the Civil War and Reconstruction*. New York, 1907.

——*Reconstruction: Political and Economic*. New York, 1907.

Eckenrode, H. J., *Rutherford B. Hayes*. New York, 1930.

Faulkner, H. U., *The Quest for Social Justice*. New York, 1931.

Fite, E. D., *The Presidential Campaign of 1860*. New York, 1911.

——*Social and Industrial Conditions in the North During the Civil War*. New York, 1910.

Flack, H. E., *Spanish-American Diplomatic Relations Preceding the War of 1898*. Baltimore, 1906.

Fleming, W. L., *Documentary History of Reconstruction*. 2 vols. Cleveland, 1906–07.

——*The Sequel of Appomattox*. New Haven, 1919.

Flick, Alexander, *Samuel Jones Tilden*. New York, 1939.

Ford, H. J., *The Cleveland Era*. New Haven, 1919.

Fuess, C. M., *Carl Schurz*. New York, 1932.

Gompers, Samuel, *Seventy Years of Life and Labor*. 2 vols. New York, 1925.

Gosnell, H. F., *Boss Platt and His New York Machine*. Chicago, 1925.

Grant, U. S., *Personal Memoirs*. 2 vols. New York, 1885–86.

Greeley, Horace, *Recollections of a Busy Life*. New York, 1868.

Grierson, F., *The Valley of Shadows*.

Boston, 1948. (Memories of a boyhood in Illinois in Lincoln's day.)

Harvey, R. H., *Samuel Gompers.* Stanford University, California, and London, 1935.

Haworth, P. L., *The Hayes-Tilden Disputed Election of 1876.* Cleveland, 1906.

Haynes, G. H., *Charles Sumner.* Philadelphia, 1909.

Hendrick, B. J., *Lincoln's War Cabinet.* Boston, 1946.

——*The Life of Andrew Carnegie.* 2 vols. Garden City, New York, 1932.

Hesseltine, W. B., *Lincoln and the War Governors.* New York, 1948.

——*U. S. Grant.* New York, 1935.

Hibben, P., *The Peerless Leader.* New York, 1929.

Hicks, J. D., *The Populist Crusade.* Minneapolis, 1931.

Hill, H. C., *Roosevelt and the Caribbean.* Chicago, 1927.

Hirsch, M. D., *William C. Whitney.* New York, 1948.

Hoar, George Frisbie, *Autobiography of Seventy Years.* 2 vols. New York, 1903.

Hofstadter, Richard, *Social Darwinism in American Thought, 1860–1915.* Philadelphia and London, 1944.

Horn, Stanley F., *The Invisible Empire.* Boston, 1939.

Howe, G. F., *Chester A. Arthur.* New York, 1934.

Howe, M. A. DeW., ed., *Home Letters of General Sherman.* New York, 1909.

Howland, H. J., *Theodore Roosevelt and His Time.* New Haven, 1921.

Jessup, P., *Elihu Root.* 2 vols. New York, 1938.

Josephson, M., *The Robber Barons.* New York, 1934.

——*The Politicos.* New York, 1938.

——*The President Makers.* New York, 1940.

Julian, G. W., *Political Recollections.* Chicago, 1884.

Kent, Frank, *The Democratic Party.* New York and London, 1928.

Kleeberg, G. S. P., *The Formation of the Republican Party as a National Political Organization.* New York, 1911.

La Follette, R. M., *La Follette's Autobiography.* New York, 1913.

Lodge, H. C., *Early Memories.* New York, 1913.

Longworth, Alice Roosevelt, *Crowded Hours.* New York and London, 1933.

Lynch, D. T., *Boss Tweed.* New York, 1927.

McElroy, R. M., *Jefferson Davis, the Unreal and the Real.* New York and London, 1937.

——*Grover Cleveland.* 2 vols. New York and London, 1923.

Mearns, D., *The Lincoln Papers.* 2 vols. New York, 1948. (The story of the collection, with selections to July 4, 1861.)

Merriam, C. E., *Four American Party Leaders.* New York, 1926.

Miller, A. B., *Thaddeus Stevens.* New York and London, 1939.

Millis, W., *The Martial Spirit.* Boston and New York, 1931.

Milton, G. F., *Abraham Lincoln and the Fifth Column.* New York, 1942.

——*The Eve of Conflict.* Boston and New York, 1934.

——*The Age of Hate.* New York, 1930.

Mitchell, W. C., *A History of the Greenbacks.* Chicago, 1903.

Mullen, Arthur, *Western Democrat.* New York, 1940.

Muzzey, D. S., *James G. Blaine.* New York, 1934.

Nevins, Allan, *Ordeal of the Union.* 2 vols. New York, 1947.

——*The Emergence of Modern America.* New York, 1928.

——*Frémont, Pathmarker of the West.* New York and London, 1939.

——*Hamilton Fish: The Inner History of the Grant Administration.* New York, 1936.

——*Grover Cleveland.* New York, 1932.

——*John D. Rockefeller.* 2 vols. New York, 1940.

——ed., *Letters of Grover Cleveland.* New York, 1933.

Nichols, R. F., *The Disruption of American Democracy.* New York, 1948.

——*Franklin Pierce.* Philadelphia and London, 1931.

Nicolay, J. G., and Hay, John, *Abraham Lincoln.* 10 vols. New York, 1890.

Ogden, R., *Life and Letters of E. L. Godkin.* 2 vols. New York and London, 1907.

Olcott, C. S., *The Life of William McKinley.* 2 vols. Boston and New York, 1916.

Oliphant, Laurence, *Episodes of a Life of Adventure.* New York, 1887.

Owsley, F. L., *States' Rights in the Confederacy.* Chicago, 1925.

Peck, H. T., *Twenty Years of the Republic, 1885–1905.* New York, 1906.

Pinchot, G., *The Fight for Conservation.* New York, 1910.

Pratt, J. W., *Expansionists of 1898.* Baltimore, 1930.

Pringle, H. F., *Theodore Roosevelt.* New York, 1931.

——*The Life and Times of William Howard Taft.* 2 vols. New York and Toronto, 1939.

Randall, J. G., *The Civil War and Reconstruction.* Boston and New York, 1937.

——*Constitutional Problems Under Lincoln.* New York and London, 1926.

——*Lincoln the President: Springfield to Gettysburg.* 2 vols. New York, 1945.

Rhodes, J. F., *History of the United States from the Compromise of 1850 to 1877.* 7 vols. New York and London, 1910.

Roosevelt, Theodore, *Autobiography.* New York, 1913.

Roosevelt, T., and Lodge, H. C., *Selections from the Correspondence of Theodore Roosevelt and Henry Cabot Lodge.* 2 vols. New York, 1925.

Ross, E. D., *The Liberal Republican Movement.* New York, 1919.

Sandburg, Carl, *Abraham Lincoln: The Prairie Years.* 2 vols. New York, 1926.

——*Abraham Lincoln: The War Years.* 4 vols. New York, 1939.

Schlesinger, A. M., *The Rise of the City.* New York, 1933.

Schurz, Carl, *Reminiscences.* 3 vols. New York, 1907.

Seward, F. W., *Reminiscences of a War Time Statesman and Diplomat.* New York, 1916.

Shannon, Fred Albert, *Organization and Administration of the Union Army.* 2 vols. Cleveland, 1928.

Sherman, John, *Recollections of Forty Years.* 2 vols. Chicago and New York, 1895.

Smith, W. E., *The Francis Preston Blair Family in Politics.* 2 vols. New York, 1933.

Smith, T. C., *The Life and Letters of James A. Garfield.* 2 vols. New Haven, 1925.

Stephenson, G. M., *A History of American Immigration, 1820–1924.* Boston and New York, 1926.

Stryker, L. P., *Andrew Johnson.* New York, 1929.

Tate, Allen, *Jefferson Davis, His Rise and Fall.* New York, 1929.

Thayer, William R., *Life and Letters of John Hay.* Boston and New York, 1915.

Ware, N. J., *The Industrial Worker, 1840–60.* Boston and New York, 1924.

Washington, B. T., *Up From Slavery.* New York, 1901.

Welles, G., *Diary of Gideon Welles.* 3 vols. Boston, 1911.

Werner, M. R., *Bryan.* New York, 1929.

White, William Allen, *Masks in a Pageant.* New York, 1928.

——*Autobiography.* New York, 1946.

——*Selected Letters,* edited by Walter Johnson. New York, 1947.

Williams, C. R., *The Life of R. B. Hayes.* 2 vols. Boston and New York, 1914.

Williams, C. R., ed., *Diary and Letters of R. B. Hayes.* 5 vols. Columbus, Ohio, 1922–26.

Williams, W. C., *William Jennings Bryan.* New York, 1936.

Winston, R., *Andrew Johnson, Plebeian and Patriot.* New York, 1928.

Wister, O., *Roosevelt: The Story of a Friendship.* New York, 1930.

Wittke, C. F., *We Who Built America.* New York, 1939.

Woodburn, J. A., *The Life of Thaddeus Stevens.* Indianapolis, 1913.

Woodward, W. E., *Meet General Grant,* New York, 1929.

X. SINCE 1909—BOOKS DEALING
WITH THE "MODERN INSTANCES" MENTIONED HEREIN

Allen, F. L., *Only Yesterday.* New York and London, 1931.

——*The Great Pierpont Morgan.* New York, 1949.

Bailey, T. A., *Woodrow Wilson and the Lost Peace.* New York, 1944.

Baker, R. S., *Woodrow Wilson, Life and Letters.* 8 vols. Garden City, New York, 1927–39.

——*Woodrow Wilson and World Settlement.* 3 vols. Garden City, New York, 1922.

Baker, R. S., and Dodd, W. E., eds., *The Public Papers of Woodrow Wilson.* 6 vols. New York and London, 1925–27.

Bell, H. C. F., *Woodrow Wilson and the People.* New York, 1945.

Bowers, Claude G., *Albert Beveridge and the Progressive Era.* Cambridge, Massachusetts, 1932.

Corey, L., *The House of Morgan.* New York, 1930.

Cranston, A., *The Killing of the Peace.* New York, 1945.

Farley, J., *Jim Farley's Story: The Roosevelt Years.* New York, 1948.

Flynn, E. J., *You're the Boss.* New York, 1947.

Hacker, L., *Short History of the New Deal.* New York, 1934.

Hendrick, B. J., *The Life and Letters of Walter H. Page.* 3 vols. Garden City, New York, 1925.

Hoover, H. C., *The Challenge to Liberty.* New York and London, 1934.

House, E. M., and Seymour, C., eds., *What Really Happened at Paris: The Story of the Peace Conference, 1918–1919.* New York, 1921.

Houston, D., *Eight Years with Wilson's Cabinet.* 2 vols. Garden City, New York, 1926.

Hull, C., *Memoirs.* 2 vols. New York, 1948.

Johnson, G. W., *Roosevelt, Dictator or Democrat?* New York, 1941.

Lindley, E. K., *Half Way with Roosevelt.* New York, 1936.

———*The Roosevelt Revolution, First Phase.* New York, 1933.

Link, A. S., *Wilson—The Road to the White House.* Princeton, 1947.

Malin, J. C., *The United States After the World War.* Boston, 1930.

McAdoo, E. W., *The Woodrow Wilsons.* New York, 1937.

McAdoo, W. G., *Crowded Years.* Boston and New York, 1931.

Mansergh, Nicholas, *The Coming of the First World War: A Study in European Balance, 1878–1914.* London, 1949.

Mowry, K., *Theodore Roosevelt and the Progressive Movement.* Madison, Wisconsin, 1946.

Notter, H., *The Origins of the Foreign Policy of Woodrow Wilson.* Baltimore, 1937.

Oliver, F. S., *Alexander Hamilton.* London, 1906.

Paxson, F. L., *American Democracy and the World War.* 3 vols. Boston, 1936–38.

Perkins, F., *The Roosevelt I Knew.* New York, 1946.

Rauch, B., *History of the New Deal, 1933–38.* New York, 1944.

Roosevelt, Franklin Delano, *The Public Papers and Addresses of Franklin D. Roosevelt.* 9 vols. (so far) New York, 1933–40.

Schriftgeisser, K., *This Was Normalcy: Party Politics, 1920–32.* Boston, 1948.

Seymour, Charles, *American Diplomacy During the World War.* Baltimore, 1934.

Seymour, C., ed., *The Intimate Papers of Colonel House.* 4 vols. Boston and New York, 1926–28.

Sherwood, R. E., *Roosevelt and Hopkins.* New York, 1948.

Shotwell, J. T., *At the Paris Peace Conference.* New York, 1937.

Stimson, H. L., and Bundy, McGeorge, *On Active Service in Peace and War.* New York, 1948.

Tansill, C. C., *America Goes to War.* Boston, 1938.

Timmons, B. N., *Garner of Texas.* New York, 1948.

Wecter, Dixon, *The Age of the Great Depression, 1929–41.* New York, 1948.

White, William Allen, *A Puritan in Babylon: The Story of Calvin Coolidge.* New York, 1938.

Whitlock, Brand, *Forty Years of It.* New York and London, 1914.

Wilbur, R. L., and Hyde, A. M., *The Hoover Policies.* New York, 1937.

Zevin, B. D., ed., *Nothing to Fear.* The selected addresses of Franklin Delano Roosevelt, 1932–45. Boston, 1946.

Acknowledgments

THE AUTHOR wishes to thank *The American Mercury* for permission to quote from "Twelve Years of Roosevelt" in *Franklin Delano Roosevelt: A Memorial;* The American Council of Learned Societies for permission to quote from "John Marshall" by Edward S. Corwin in the *Dictionary of American Biography,* published by them; the Associated Colleges at Claremont for permission to quote from *Constitutional Revolution, Ltd.,* by Edward S. Corwin, published by them in 1941; Dodd, Mead & Company for permission to quote from *Rutherford B. Hayes* by H. J. Eckenrode and P. W. Wight, 1930, *Grover Cleveland: A Study in Courage* by Allan Nevins, 1932, *Hamilton Fish: The Inner History of the Grant Administration* by Allan Nevins, 1936, *Twenty Years of the Republic: 1885–1905* by H. T. Peck, 1906, *Lincoln the President* by J. G. Randall, 1945, Mr. Franklin Ford for permission to quote from *The Rise and Growth of American Politics* by Henry J. Ford; Wilfred Funk, Inc., for permission to quote from *Western Democrat* by A. F. Mullen; Harcourt, Brace and Company, Inc., for permission to quote from *The Super-Powers* by W. T. R. Fox, *The President Makers* by Matthew Josephson, *Theodore Roosevelt, A Biography* by H. F. Pringle; Harper & Brothers for permission to quote from *The Great Pierpont Morgan* by F. L. Allen, *America's Silver Age* by Gerald W. Johnson; D. C. Heath and Company for permission to quote from *The Civil War and the Reconstruction* by J. G. Randall; Houghton Mifflin Company for permission to quote from *American Constitutional Development* by C. B. Swisher, *The Great Plains* by Walter P. Webb, *The Party Battles of the Jackson Period* by Claude G. Bowers, *The Life of John Marshall* by A. J. Beveridge, *The Maritime History of Massachusetts* by S. E. Morison; Alfred A. Knopf, Inc., for permission to quote from *Freedom and Responsibility in the American Way of Life* by Carl Becker, *The Declaration of Independence* by Carl Becker, *American Political Parties* by Wilfred E. Binkley, *President and Congress* by Wilfred E. Binkley, *Lincoln and the War Governors* by W. B. Hesseltine, *The Decline of the West* by O. Spengler, translated by C. F. Atkinson; Little, Brown & Company for permission to quote from *Year of Decision: 1846* by Bernard DeVoto, *Hands Off: A History of the Monroe Doctrine* by Dexter Perkins, *The Age of Jackson* by Arthur M. Schlesinger, Jr; Longmans, Green &

Co., Inc., for permission to quote from *The Coming of the First World War: A Study in the European Balance 1878–1914* by N. Hansergh; The Macmillan Company for permission to quote from *Economic Origins of Jeffersonian Democracy* by Charles A. Beard, copyright, 1915, by The Macmillan Company, 1943, by Charles A. Beard, *The Emergence of Modern America 1865–1878* by Allan Nevins, copyright, 1927, by The Macmillan Company, *The American States During and After the Revolution* by Allan Nevins, copyright, 1924, by The Knights of Columbus, *The Rise of the City 1878–1898* by Arthur M. Schlesinger, copyright, 1933, by The Macmillan Company, *Essays on the Civil War and the Reconstruction* by W. A. Dunning, *Statesmen of the Old South* by W. E. Dodd, *Collected Poems* by Vachel Lindsay, copyright, 1926, by The Macmillan Company, *Disruption of American Democracy* by Roy F. Nichols, copyright, 1948, by The Macmillan Company, *Masks in a Pageant* by W. A. White, copyright, 1928, by The Macmillan Company, *Autobiography* by W. A. White, copyright, 1946, by The Macmillan Company; *New Republic* for permission to quote from *Marcus Alonzo Hanna: His Life and Works* by Herbert Croly; New York University Press for permission to quote from *The Foundations of American Constitutionalism* by Andrew C. McLaughlin; Prentice-Hall, Inc., for permission to quote from *We Who Built America* by Carl Wittke; Princeton University Press for permission to quote from *Constitutional Dictatorship* by C. Rossiter; G. P. Putnam's Sons for permission to quote from *Alexander Hamilton* by F. S. Oliver; Rinehart & Co., Inc., for permission to quote from *Divided We Stand* by Walter Prescott Webb, copyright, 1937, by Walter Prescott Webb; The Ronald Press Company for permission to quote from *The Course of American Democratic Thought* by Ralph Henry Gabriel, copyright, 1940, by The Ronald Press Company; Charles Scribner's Sons for permission to quote from *The Coming of the Civil War* by Avery Craven, *Alexander Hamilton* by Henry Jones Ford, *The Ordeal of the Union* by Allan Nevins, *Autobiography* by Theodore Roosevelt; The University of North Carolina Press for permission to quote from *James Monroe* by W. P. Cresson, *The Attack on Leviathan* by Donald Davidson; University of Pennsylvania Press for permission to quote from *Social Darwinism in American Thought 1860–1915* by Richard Hofstadter; University of Wisconsin Press for permission to quote from *The Articles of Confederation* by M. Jensen; The Viking Press, Inc., for permission to quote from *The Roosevelt I Knew* by Frances Perkins, *The Killing of the Peace* by Alan Cranston; and Mrs. Woodrow Wilson for permission to quote from *The Public Papers* of Woodrow Wilson published in 1927 by Harper & Brothers.

Index

Abbott, Reverend Lyman, quoted on great cities, 555
Abolition. *See* Slavery
Acton, Lord, quoted on laws, 502
Acts of Parliament, 6
Adams, Abigail, wife of John Adams, 93
Adams, Charles Francis, 324, 491
Adams, Charles Francis, Jr., 545
Adams, Henry, 634, 668; quoted on radical view of Constitution, 50; on reactions of foreign travelers, 59; on Jay's treaty, 77–78; on Jefferson's alliance with New York politicians, 88; on Jefferson and England, 127–128; on Napoleonic designs in North America, 130–131; on Toussaint, 132; on Louisiana Purchase, 133–134; on control of Supreme Court, 138; on Jefferson's diplomacy, 149; on Jefferson's Embargo, 151; on conditions faced by Madison, 164; on Canning, 167–168; on Monroe, 198; on Grant, 473, 482, 496; on Black Friday shame, 475; on rascality under Grant, 490; on Sumner's quarrel with Grant, 506; on Grant's Congress, 513–514; on alliance with England, 607; on gold standard, 613; on John Sherman, 621; on Reed, 630, 632; on Theodore Roosevelt, 633, 651–652
Adams, James Truslow, quoted on Washington and Marshall, 105
Adams, John, 9, 13, 19; quoted on Stamp Act, 6; use of *American*, 7; on Britain and America, 10; on republican government, 18; on formation of governments in colonies, 20–21; backs Washington for Commander-in-Chief, 28; on democracy, 40; on power, 42; inauguration, 81; on political parties, 84; elected President, 91; described, 92–93, 95; background and career, 93–97; political philosophy, 97–100; Vice-President, 97, 100; Administration, 100–105, 123; relations with Jefferson, 113, 120, 121
Adams, John Quincy, quoted on Jefferson's administration, 124; on Senate dictation to Madison, 156–157; peace negotiator at Ghent, 181; on Monroe, 197, 200; on Era of Good Feelings, 201; Secretary of State, 201, 206–210, 214; cited on slavery, 204; quoted on Missouri Compromise, 204, 205; presi-

dential candidate, 214, 217; background and career, 217–220; Cabinet appointments, 220; Administration, 220–230; aims, 225, 230; last years, 230–231; on William Henry Harrison, 286; on Declaration of Independence, 354
Adams, Samuel, 15, 40, 113
Address to the People of South Carolina (Calhoun), 265
Agrarianism, influence of Embargo and Non-Intercourse Act, 165; struggle with capitalism, 614–615
Agricultural Adjustment Administration, 684
Agriculture, revolution of, 521–522. *See also* Farmers
Alabama, statehood, 189; expropriates Indian lands, 262; secession, 404
Alabama, Confederate cruiser, 505
Alabama Claims, settlement of, 505–508
Alaska, purchase of, 78; Guggenheim interests in, 657–658
Albany Regency, 211n., 221, 238, 472
Aldrich, Nelson W., 660
Alien and Sedition Acts of 1798, 107–108
Allen, Frederick Lewis, quoted on Morgan, 641
Allison, William, 523, 536
Allison Bill, 586n., 590, 593
Altgeld, John P., 602-603
Altoona, meeting of Union governors at, 423–424
Amalgamated Association of Iron, Steel and Tin Workers, 591
Amendments to Constitution, Bill of Rights, 56n.; First, 108n.; Fifth, 385n., 565, 567; Twelfth, 121n.; Thirteenth, 448, 451, 454, 565; Fourteenth, 455–456, 458, 464, 497, 499, 500, 563, 564–567, 574, 575; Fifteenth, 473, 499, 565; Sixteenth, 600, 658; Seventeenth, 658
American, application of term to colonists, 7–8
American Citizen, The, 141n.
American Commonwealth, The (Bryce), 688
American Federation of Labor, 503, 673
American Law Review, 570
American Nations, proposed Congress of, at Panama, 224
American Railway Union, 602, 603

432, 486, 487–488; federal grants of, 373n.; movement for conservation, 649–650. *See also* Homestead Act, Western lands

Public Lands, Committee on, 270

Puerto Rico, annexation of, 625

Pulaski, Fort, taken by Georgia, 405

Pullman Company, strike of, 601–602, 617–618

Pure Food and Drugs Act, 639

Putnam, General Israel, quoted on General Howe, 30

Quay, Matthew Stanley, 627

Quebec Act, 7, 19, 27

Quincy, Josiah, quoted on Jefferson, 156; on War of 1812, 174; on admission of Louisiana, 175; on invasion of Canada, 178

Quitman, John A., 340n.

Quitrents, 6, 20

Racial problem, Supreme Court and, 498–499

Radicalism, colonial, 4

Radicals, in American Revolution, 19–21; in Confederation of 1781, 31–32; influence of, on early state constitutions, 44; in Civil War and Reconstruction, 421–423, 426, 428–430, 441, 447–448; reaction to Lincoln's death, 436; Republican, in post-Civil War period, 458–460; failure of Republican, in South, 498–499

Railroads, growth of, 234, 369–373; Pacific, Davis's plan for, 359, 361; donation of public lands to, 432, 486, 487–488; Crédit Mobilier scandal, 486–488; in Depression of 1873, 501; strikes, 524–525; role of, in growth of monopolies, 559–560; rate legislation, 568–572; in Panic of 1893, 597; Northern Securities Case, 640–643

Rambouillet Decree, Napoleon's, 170

Randall, J. G., cited on Lincoln-Douglas debates, 389; quoted on Sumter, 412; on Lincoln, 417; on banking system, 442–443; on Reconstruction, 496

Randolph, Edmund, quoted on state constitutions, 45; Attorney General, 67; Secretary of State, 77, 100

Randolph, Jane, wife of Jefferson

Randolph, John, 108–109, 110, 129, 138, 139, 153, 161, 164, 183, 195, 199, 211; leads revolt against Two Million Act, 145–146; hostility to Jefferson, 146–148; quoted on Madison, 157, 163, 174; on conquest of Canada, 173; cited on slavery, 187–188; hatred of Clay, 223–224; quoted on tariff, 226; supports Jackson, 237; death of, 266

Randolph, Thomas Mann, 85

Reading Railroad, 597

Realism, tolerant, in building of America, 60

Reconstruction, Lincoln's plans for, 426, 427–429, 436, 441; provisional governments, 451–454; joint Congressional Committee on, 454–455; National Union Convention, 457–458; military rule, 458–460; party activities in South, 464–467; financial problems of, 468–471; restoration of free politics in South, 496–501. *See also* South

Reconstruction Acts, 465, 499; attempted repeal of, 525–526

Reconstruction Finance Corporation, 677–678

Reed, Thomas Brackett, 633; Speaker of House of Representatives, 628–632

Referendum. *See* Initiative and referendum

Reformation, Protestant, 16

Regionalism, conflict with nationalism, 339

Reminiscences (Boutwell), 493

Removal, presidential power of, 48n.

Renaissance, 16

Report on Manufactures, Hamilton's, 71–72, 74, 154, 183

Republican Party, in election of 1796, 91; Jefferson's, 118–119, 183–184, 221; victory of, in 1800, 119–120, 122–123; Enforcement Act, 153; creation of modern, 324–325, 373, 375–377; in election of 1856, 378–380, 381; stand on tariff, 390, 585–586, 587; platform of 1860, 394–395; nominates Lincoln, 395–396; Lincoln's struggle for, 426; Union element in, 429, 431, 433, 446; National Union Convention, 457–458; radicals in post-Civil War period, 458–460, 498–499; post-Civil War reorganization, 464–469; re-elects Grant, 490–492; Campaign of 1876, 509–510; Campaign of 1880, 527–529; Convention and campaign of 1884, 541, 545–546; Convention and campaign of 1888, 585–587; Convention and campaign of 1892, 592, 593; Convention of 1896, 611–613; Progressives versus Standpatters, 656–662, 664; election of 1916, 669–670; decline of, after First World War, 675–678, 682. *See also* Party system

Republicanism, romantic, in building of America, 60

Restoration, 53

Resumption Act of 1875, 522–523

Revolutionary War. *See* American Revolution

Rhett, Robert Barnwell, 227, 260, 471, 472

Rhode Island, slavery in, 58

Richardson, W. A., Secretary of the Treasury, 488

Richmond, Confederate Government driven from, 435

Right of deposit, at New Orleans, 131

Rights of man, doctrine of, in American independence, 13–15

Roads, Calhoun's bill for, 184; Cumberland Road Bill, 213

Robertson, William, 531–532

Rockefeller, John D., 502; quoted on growth of business, 552

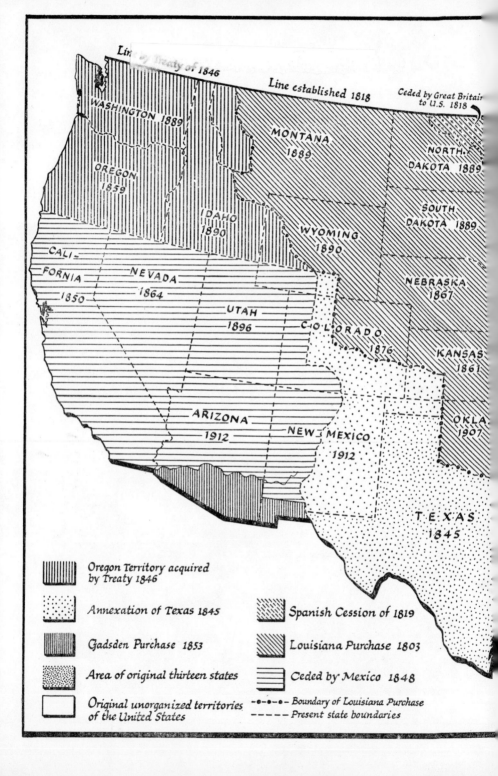

Line by Treaty of 1846

Line established 1818

Ceded by Great Britain
to U.S. 1818

WASHINGTON 1889

MONTANA 1889

NORTH DAKOTA 1889

OREGON 1859

IDAHO 1890

SOUTH DAKOTA 1889

WYOMING 1890

CALI- FORNIA 1850

NEVADA 1864

UTAH 1896

COLORADO 1876

NEBRASKA 1867

KANSAS 1861

ARIZONA 1912

NEW MEXICO 1912

OKLA. 1907

TEXAS 1845

	Oregon Territory acquired by Treaty 1846
	Annexation of Texas 1845
	Gadsden Purchase 1853
	Area of original thirteen states
	Original unorganized territories of the United States

	Spanish Cession of 1819
	Louisiana Purchase 1803
	Ceded by Mexico 1848
–•–•–•–	Boundary of Louisiana Purchase
– – – – –	Present state boundaries